the Joy of Jewish Art for Children

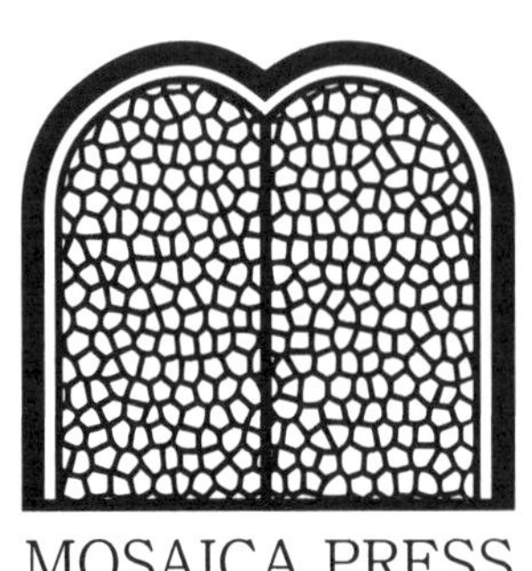

MOSAICA PRESS

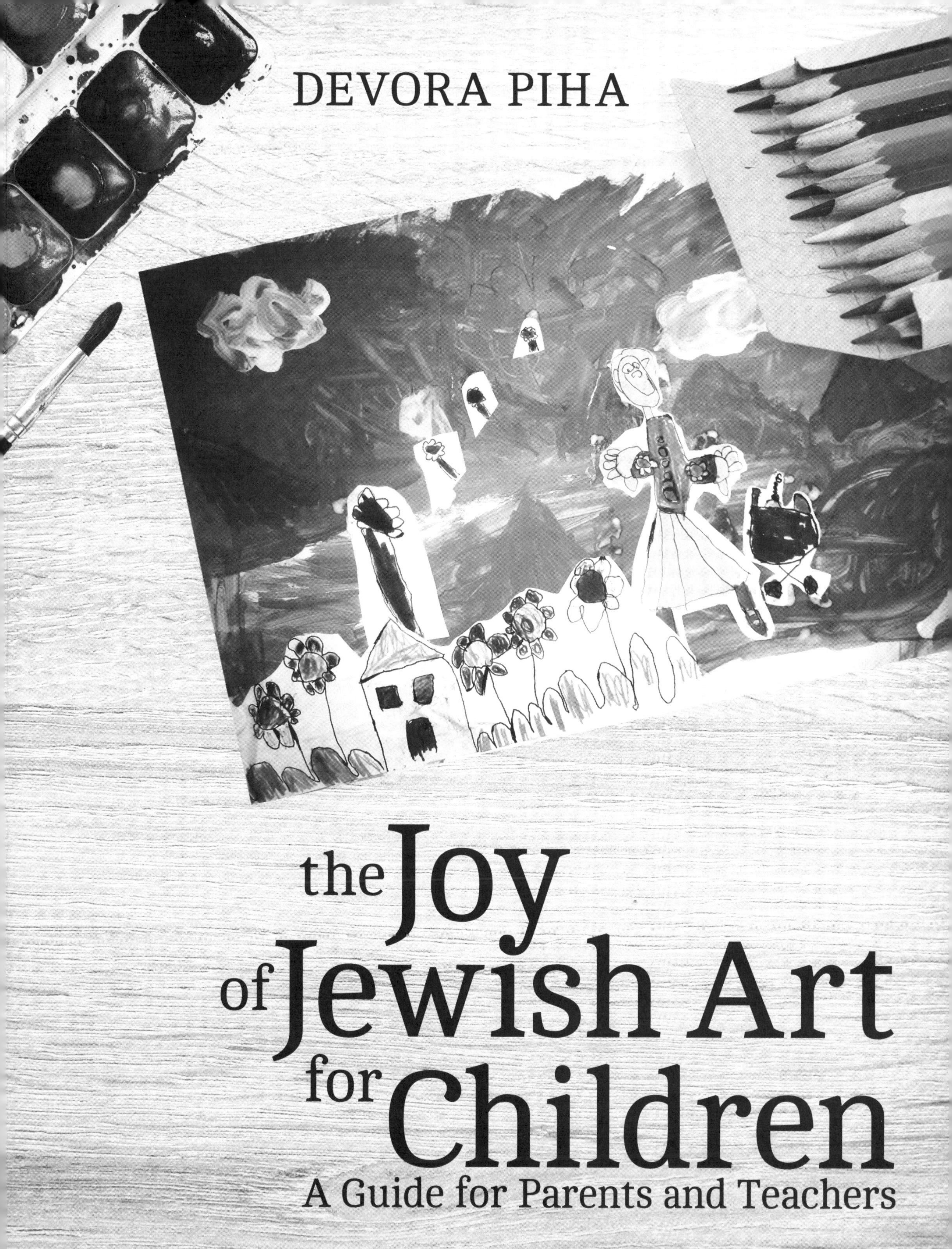
DEVORA PIHA
the Joy of Jewish Art for Children
A Guide for Parents and Teachers

Mosaica Press, Inc.

Designed and typeset by Daniella Kirsch

ISBN-10: 1-946351-36-9

ISBN-13: 978-1-946351-36-4

Published by:
Mosaica Press, Inc.
www.mosaicapress.com
info@mosaicapress.com

DISCLAIMER: Part 2 touches on how the disciplines of education and art therapy overlap with my style of teaching and research with art for children over the past forty years. I am not an art therapist or an education expert, yet have found my methods to be successful and enjoyable. I look forward to passing on to you all that is gleaned from my life's work.

The outcome of the projects will vary according to each person based on your materials, skills, and understanding of the project. I expect good outcomes and lots of progress. The satisfaction you and your child have will be dependent on factors of which I have no control. I disclaim any responsibility in any form with use of the materials, skills, outcomes, reactions, or interpretations of the lessons and projects. I provided the ideas and the explanations to the best of my ability to ensure a wonderful, high-level, artistic, and creative journey for you and your child. Please note the use of he and she is usually interchangeable throughout the book.

You may contact me with questions at piha1@012.net.il.

This book is dedicated to my dear parents

Al and Naomi Eisman

who have been role models of giving. Their care and concern for all of our family members is a lesson in giving from the heart.

Their boundless integrity and perseverance in overcoming life's challenges has instilled in their children strength rooted in Jewish values and identity. Their attention and support of Jewish creativity in my work is one of their unique contributions to the world.

May they see continuous nachas from all of their children and grandchildren and future generations.

In memory of our beloved parents who brought us into this world and who sustained us their entire lives.

DOVID ISAAC ben MEIR ZEV

CHAIM ben MEIR

HENYA bas MUSHA

GOLDA bas MENDEL

Their generosity and kindness were boundless.

Meir Zev and Shoshana Mark

Table of Contents

Part 1: Art and Jewish Art

Part 2: Growing Along with Art

Part 3: Art Theory and Technique

Acknowledgments

My heartfelt thanks go out to my Creator for the opportunity to write and produce this book. I am continuously in awe of the gifts with which God has graced me. There were times when I wished I was not sensitive and artistic—until I saw that I was given a tremendous gift for teaching others and encouraging creativity. I also discovered within myself an appreciation for the joy of creation in children.

My parents, Al and Naomi Eisman, provided me with the nurturing environment and unconditional encouragement to pursue art from my childhood, which I channeled into teaching others from a young age. My parents were my first art teachers. I don't remember being criticized about my artwork at any stage of life. My father, Moshe ben Benjamin, *a"h*, put a paintbrush in my hand when I was only an infant, and he is the one who pointed out to me the importance of art classes for expanding one's abilities in all areas of life, rather than limiting them. I am so grateful for their encouragement and guidance.

Many people helped make this project possible:

To Suri Brand, who believed in the validity of this book and helped convert the original 150 pages into triple that with her suggestions and editing skills. She pulled out of me more than I knew I had to write about. She spent months organizing and editing the manuscript to make it reader-friendly and therefore clear, practical, and available for others to read. Thank you, Suri.

To Simi Muschel, who did another layer of editing, going over so many little details that made a big difference. She helped clarify the directions for the art projects to make it easier for the reader to follow.

I have been fortunate to work with the team at Mosaica Press in the publication of *The Joy of Jewish Art for Children*. Their final stamp on this book has been done with a refinement and an appreciation of beauty that is consistent with my vision. My sincere thanks to Rabbi Haber, Rabbi Kornbluth, Ilana Hiller, Rayzel Broyde, Sherie Gross, Daniella Kirsch, Brocha Mirel Strizower, and the rest of the team.

To Rabbi Mordechai Goldstein, *zt"l*, the head of the Diaspora Yeshiva, founded in 1967. Rabbi Goldstein understood and supported the value of creativity when used within the framework of the Torah. His encouragement guided me and other Jewish artists and writers to produce works of artistic and scholarly merit that are an inspiration to others.

To my friend and writer Menucha Chana Levin, for her patience in giving me pointers on writing and her ability to simplify and carefully structure ideas. She helped me figure out how to put my ideas into a book and has been a constant source of encouragement for over fifteen years.

To Sarah Nathan, for helping me put elusive concepts and my ideas together into written form twenty years ago, when I was beginning to write.

To Rebbetzin Sheindel Weinbach, editor of the *Yated Ne'eman* newspaper in Israel, and her staff, for their years of consistent enthusiasm and for providing me a forum to share my love of art with the readers. Some forms of the material in this book may have originally appeared in *Yated Ne'eman* in concept. It was her encouragement that gave me the courage and motivation to publish my articles.

To Michael Kaniel (Kaufman), editor of *Jewish Art* magazine and author of *A Guide to Jewish Art*, for sharing his expertise of Judaica and explaining the connection between art and Judaism. Reading his guide gave me a base to appreciate the majesty and treasures of the creative, visual, and tactile Jewish world.

To Rabbi Chaim Malinowitz, *shlita*, rabbi of the Beis Tefillah synagogue in Ramat Beit Shemesh, for reviewing chapter 9, "Art in Halachah."

To Rebbetzin Caroline Fletcher, for her suggestions on improving the book and our wonderful conversations, and to Sarah Shapiro for clarifying communication and reader-friendly writing skills in her writing class.

To Rabbi Zvi Miller, who shared his insights into the power of the imagination from Judaism's perspective, and Mrs. Shira Smiles for taking time from her busy schedule to read and comment on the manuscript, especially the Torah content.

I also want to thank Ashley Lazarus, the producer of the Jewish Heritage series with Rabbi Beryl Wein, and Caroline Lazarus for their generous and timely comments. To Shoshana Lepon, for her creative literary skills and inspiration.

To Lilly Fish, for sharing her solid knowledge of preschool child development and Gila Spiro, for sharing information on occupational therapy and its applications when I first set out to write this book.

Working on this book motivated me to do a lot of research into Jewish art. *The Majesty of Man* by Rabbi Henoch Lebovitz and *The 39 Melachos of Shabbos* by Rabbi Baruch Chait were particularly helpful.

Drawing with Children by Mona Brooks provided me with the foundation to my intuitive insights into the wide field of children's art, as did Herbert Read's *Education through Art*. The art therapy section was augmented with information gleaned from Howard Gardner.

People ask me why I didn't choose to illustrate the book exclusively with my own artwork. Why did I use the work of professional illustrator Ruth Beifus?

I use my artwork mainly to teach. Often I leave examples and demonstrations unfinished so as not to intimidate the students, or to emphasize a fragment of a finished work. I do step-by-step drawings of the projects in my classes. A wide selection of these are presented in this book. Yet, to show solid art concepts in each chapter division, I wanted a professional illustrator. A good illustrator knows how to bring the ideas and words of others to life. Ruth Beifus does this superbly. Her work has added an additional dimension of beauty, warmth, and sensitivity to *The Joy of Jewish Art for Children*. These valuable characteristics are among those I hope to project to my readers.

A very special thanks to all the children (and their special parents) with whom I have worked over the years; they gave me the opportunity to spread the joys of art and creative thinking. I developed many of my ideas with the artwork of the children of Metzad, Israel, most of them parents now themselves. I refined the concepts and projects with the happy participants of the Ramat Beit Shemesh art classes over the past sixteen years. Each year the classes improve and give me and the children great satisfaction. When I hear that they ask their parents if today is the art *chug* (club or lesson) or they tell me how they started drawing on their own at home, I am especially grateful.

My thanks also go to the Magen HaLev, Magen Avot, and Ko Tomar schools, where I taught art, and to their dedicated principals. Giving to my students and learning from them is a great gift. My thanks go out to God for these opportunities.

Finally, but not least, thank you to my dear husband, Shmuel, who patiently researched and checked the many sources I cited, mainly in the first section, and who in every way helps beyond what is expected and gives his support naturally. And to our children and their families for being who they are, wonderfully and completely. Added to this list is the pleasure of having my grandchildren participating in the art classes along with siblings of past students and new faces—all with joy and excitement.

Notes and Sketches

How to Use This Book

The book is divided into three sections:

1. Part 1, "Art and Jewish Art"—an overview of what makes Jewish art "Jewish" and a look at the earliest renditions of Jewish art.
2. Part 2, "Growing Along with Art"—a guide for teaching art to children in order to provide them with the opportunity to develop skills for life and gain a positive self-identity.
3. Part 3, "Art Theory and Technique"—techniques that allow for success in creating art.

Each section is distinct and almost a book in itself. You can start from the beginning and read each chapter in order, as a building block for the next. Or you can choose to follow your interests and read the chapters at random.

Most projects require parents and children working together, with the children leading the way at their level. Throughout the book, you will find art projects appropriate to multiple age levels and abilities. Although most of the projects include the age level, they can be simplified for younger children (ages four to six) by eliminating steps and substituting some materials with more basic ones, such as gouache or tempera instead of acrylic paints, washable markers or colored pencils instead of permanent markers, plain copy paper instead of Bristol or all-purpose art paper.

Notes and Sketches

Give yourself time to digest what you read and to think it through. To this end, I have included summary points at the end of each chapter for review and easy reference. At the end of each chapter you will also notice a "Questions and Wonder" section. These questions are included to encourage thinking and to jump-start conversations related to the chapter topics. The questions are varied; the answers can be thought-out, digested, and discussed between child and adult.

Above all, please keep in mind that art is full of options. After you have read through the book, feel free to mix and match the ideas and projects scattered throughout the book according to your needs and aspirations. The projects within can be followed as is or adjusted to your taste. Personally, I'm not one to always follow recipes, and I enjoy the creative freedom this gives me (especially when I don't have all the ingredients the recipe calls for!). I love to improvise, and you may as well. But if you don't, you shouldn't be afraid of trying something new or of the occasional failure.

Art, all the more so, invites creativity. Understanding your vast array of options in art opens the door to the joy of creating art that parents, teachers, and children can enjoy together.

Introduction

At the age of five, Michael didn't seem very interested in art projects. He would sit for all of five minutes, draw a few scribbles on the paper, and then get up and leave the work area. Hoping to get him more interested in art, his mother asked me if he could join the art group I was teaching. I suggested she wait until he was older and more settled.

Michael happened to be in my house one Friday after school. He showed me his *parashat ha-shavua* (weekly Torah portion) sheet from his teacher, with questions and topics for discussion at the family Shabbat table. Included was a drawing from that week's portion showing Abraham welcoming guests into his tent. The tent had openings on four sides—north, south, east, and west—that actually opened and closed, like a pop-up card.

Seeing the drawing gave me an idea. I suggested to Michael that we draw a person in each of the open doors. I explained that these were Abraham's guests.

We sat down together and I showed him step by step how to construct a person with simple geometric shapes on a sheet of paper. Then I drew the first person in the first door. Now it was Michael's turn. In seven minutes, he drew three people in the other three openings. He was very proud of himself.

When it was time to go home, he held up the demonstration paper I had made for him and said, "I'm taking this home. I can practice making people."

I had expected him to forget about that paper. Here was a boy I didn't think could sit still for more than five minutes, let alone be interested

Notes and Sketches

in art. Yet that one brief lesson in drawing on a topic he was learning about had intrigued him. Michael realized that art was both achievable and fun. As a bonus, the life lesson his teacher had taught, about following Abraham's example and welcoming guests into one's home, became more real to him.

Spontaneous short sessions of art with a relaxed and reassuring adult go a long way with children—more than we realize. Parents and teachers are the ones charged with the task of passing down knowledge that children will need to take with them into adulthood.

For what do we hope and pray for our children?

We want them to develop their God-given talents and use them for good things. We want them to appreciate the benefits of developing positive character traits at the same time. We want to pass down the traditions of our forebears so our children will know who they are and so that they will have an anchor to pass on to their children.

I wrote this book to show you how you can accomplish these goals through art. My brief lesson with Michael helped him connect to what he was learning in school and gave it meaning in a nonthreatening way. It also gave him self-confidence; he succeeded at learning a new skill and it made him proud. Imagine what an impact art could have on Michael over the course of a few weeks!

By no means am I saying that art has to be a learning experience for it to be valid. Art for personal enjoyment and self-expression is wonderful. Art is lovable. There is so much you can do with art and so many different mediums with which to do it. Two-dimensional drawings or three-dimensional constructions, clay and paints and paper and glue—so many ways for our imagination and emotions to express themselves. It's satisfying and even therapeutic.

Art does that for us. It's not only for the person with brilliant innate talent. Anyone can do it. All you need is the desire and the will, and you can acquire the skills and techniques presented to you in this book.

The mother of one of my students came into the art room to pick up her son. In her arms was her very verbal eighteen-month-old. Natan looked at the children seated at the tables making menorahs (candelabras) from clay. I gave Natan a piece of clay so he wouldn't feel left out. He immediately squeezed the clay in his hand, and his face lit up. "I made a ballie!" he said proudly. His mother and I looked at each other in amazement. He was only a baby, but he wasn't too young to enjoy the satisfaction of creating art.

This book is about being flexible. You don't have to be a four-inch square trying to fit into a three-inch circle. Art is about individual expression, and anyone can create art in any way that allows him to express himself. Yet to be flexible, you need to be knowledgeable. Knowing what moods different colors represent or the steps to creating a human figure will give you more tools to depict what you see in your mind's eye. The techniques and projects presented here are easy to follow. Before you know it, you and your child will be creating fabulous works of art.

The Joy of Jewish Art for Children is about believing "I can draw and create art, and my child can do it, too." More, it's about how art connects us to Jewish values and tradition.

There is much to understand about this heritage, and we can do it through art from the beginning levels as we teach it to our children. So please join me for an expansive journey into the world of children's art and Jewish life.

Let's Get Started

Cover the work area with disposable plastic. Put work shirts on the children. Roll up their sleeves. Have access to water for cleanup. Put out materials, one at a time as needed. Remove when finished, before putting out the next material. The children will focus better when the materials are organized, and they also won't rush into each step. Keep a box of leftover materials which are reusable for later as well as a collection of project ideas and a notebook to write down projects, directions, and notes. A pile of old magazines and postcards also provides ideas and photos for inspiration.

Demonstrate the basics: (Throughout this book you will learn more pointers.)

How to hold and use a pencil. Hold the pencil near the tips of the second and third finger and the thumb. Demonstrate all the types and thicknesses of lines the pencil can create.

How to put a brush into a paint container. Dip the hairs of the brush halfway into the paint, and not until the metal. It is better to use less

Notes and Sketches

paint than more. Keep the handles, brushes, and work area clean. I use paper or disposable plates on which to mix the paints and then throw them away immediately when finished.

How to use and clean the brushes. As you paint, put the used brushes in a sturdy cup of water while not in use so they don't dry out. Soak them in water up until the top of the ferrule (the metal sleeve that holds the hairs to the wooden handle). Wipe and squeeze off the remaining paint with a paper towel. Run water over the brush in a sink to wash off the color. Press the hairs at the ferrule in your hand or on the sink to loosen any paint caught between the ferrule and the hairs. Repeat until no more color is in the brush. Reshape the brush and store upright. Clean brushes immediately when finished working for the day. Take care of your brushes, and they will last a long time.

Suggested Materials

The essential materials are: paper (copy paper and Bristol [thick] paper or all-purpose art paper that works well with water), pencils, pens, medium and thick colored markers, gouache paint, brushes, white plastic glue, and scissors. Most of the rest of the materials are used in the projects throughout the book.

Paper: Drawing paper or computer copy paper in 2 sizes: 8½ x 11 inches (A4) (21 x 30 cm) and 11 x 16 inches (A3) (30 x 42 cm) or other size paper. (Note: Computer copy paper sizes both in the USA and internationally are standard as listed here. All-purpose art or drawing paper and Bristol are measured differently—8½ x 11 inches (21½ x 28 cm). To convert inches into centimeters, multiply the number of inches by 2.54. The measurements I give may be approximate or rounded off.) Bristol paper or all-purpose art paper that works well with water. (Paper can be used in place of canvas. It's best to paint both sides with white acrylic to strengthen the paper.)

Pencils: plus a sharpener, eraser, and ruler

Pens: fine-tipped or roller ball, permanent and washable

Markers: colored and metallic, fine- and broad-tipped, both washable and permanent

Tempera or gouache: red, blue, yellow, and white

Brushes: 3 soft, made from sable—a natural fur or a synthetic material that resembles fur, ⅛, ¼, and ½ inch (¼, 1½, and 1½ cm) are most commonly used.

Brushes: 3 hard/rough, ¼, ½, and ¾ inch (½, 1½, 2 cm) are most commonly used; 1 and 2 inches (2½ and 5 cm) are used for murals.

Glue: white plastic (like Elmer's), glue sticks. Optional: wood glue

Scissors, dull ones for younger children and sharp ones for older children

Canvas

Acrylic paints: red, blue, yellow, white. Other colors are optional. (Acrylics are not recommended for children under the age of eight.)

Colored pencils, regular and water-soluble

Styrofoam sandwich board (called Kappa in Israel)

Craft knife, metal ruler and cutting board (to be used with adult supervision)

Hot-glue gun and sticks (to be used with adult supervision)

Card stock or thin cardboard (ex: empty cereal boxes and cardboard from the cleaners)

Boxes and tubes in a variety of sizes.

Stapler, cellophane tape, and paper fasteners

Modeling clay: air-drying clay (There are several types available: Crayola Air-Dry Clay in USA, and DAS in Europe and Israel)

Earth (ceramic) clay

Ceramic tools or plastic fork, knife, dull scissors, a 12-inch piece of dental floss with craft sticks attached at the ends, to cut through earth clay

Plasticine: oil-based, synthetic clay that strengthens the hand muscles, does not dry, and is reusable

Watercolors

Oil pastels, chalk pastels, charcoal (recommended for children over the age of nine)

Metallic paper: thin or thick, gold, silver or copper

Colored glossy paper, nonbrittle nor dull

Tissue paper in a variety of colors

Parchment paper

Craft sticks (ice cream sticks and tongue depressors)

Boxes of all sizes, empty paper towel rolls

Pieces of scrap materials, fabric and craft felt

Yarn and craft looms

Styrofoam balls (for puppet heads and round building structures) and craft sticks (ice cream sticks or tongue depressors)

Velcro strips, sand paper, and food coloring

Clear contact paper

Ribbon, yarn, hand-made or store-bought looms

Cotton balls, pipe cleaners, pompoms, floral wire, heavy cord or string

Googly eyes, glitter, sequins, beads

Thumbtacks for bulletin boards and hooks for hanging projects

Envelopes and thick, clear plastic sheets, size 8½ x 11 inch (21 x 30 cm), to store sample projects

Play-Doh (Make it yourself with ⅓ cup salt, 1 cup flour and ⅓ to ½ cup water. A drop of food coloring and or vegetable oil is optional.)

Optional:

Papier mâché from flour, water, and newspaper strips or store-bought ground pulp

Wood for wood cuts and cutting tools (to be used with adult supervision), sandpaper, and printing ink or paint

Silk, silk paint, and tools

Linoleum and cutting tools (to be used with adult supervision)

Having a variety of materials and art tools to choose from is just as important as the subject matter. Giving children ample opportunities to explore different art mediums will open their minds and motivate them to relate to the topic you are teaching them about. Varying the materials, styles, and subject matter increases their excitement, satisfaction, love of learning, and, ultimately, their connection to God and His Torah.

PART 1

Art and Jewish Art

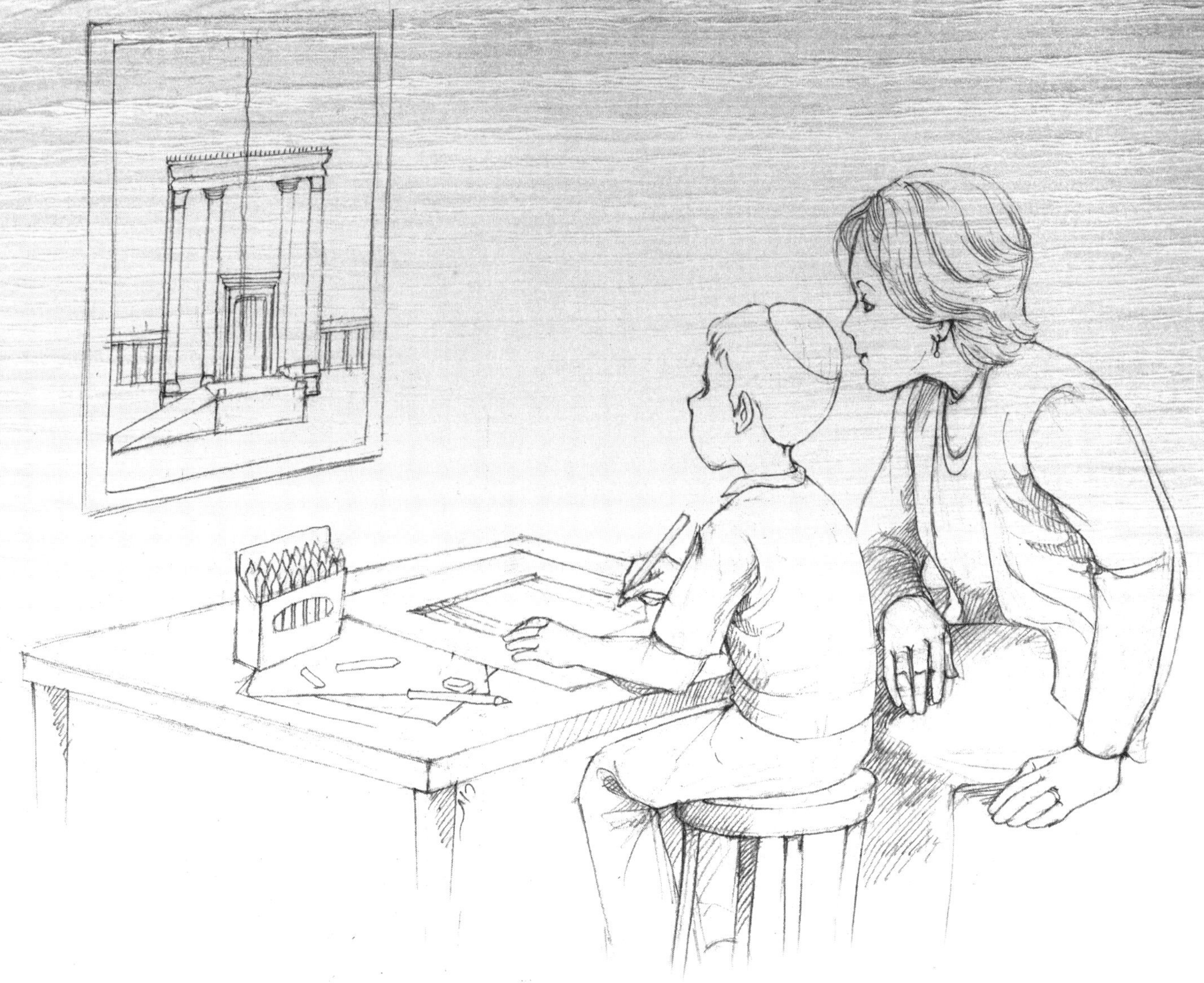

What Is Jewish Art? 1

Years ago, when I first studied art, it came to my attention that a significant number of notable fine artists are Jewish. It puzzled me that the subject matter of their artwork often didn't have any relationship to their Jewish roots. Looking at those paintings, acclaimed as they were, confused me. Even when those Jewish artists wanted to make a statement about Jewish culture or used esoteric Jewish images, such as the Hebrew alphabet or kabbalistic (mystical) symbols, I thought they were missing the heart. They seemed to portray an outer face, and the meaning behind the symbols was lacking.

The truth is that most well-known Jewish artists whose works graced the walls of museums or the pages of my art history textbooks were not even noted as Jewish. A good number of famous contemporary artists are Jewish, but their Jewishness is not part of their image. If their Jewishness was recorded, it was only to mention that their parents were Jewish. (Marc Chagall is an exception; his internationally acclaimed art is rife with Jewish symbolism and meaning.)

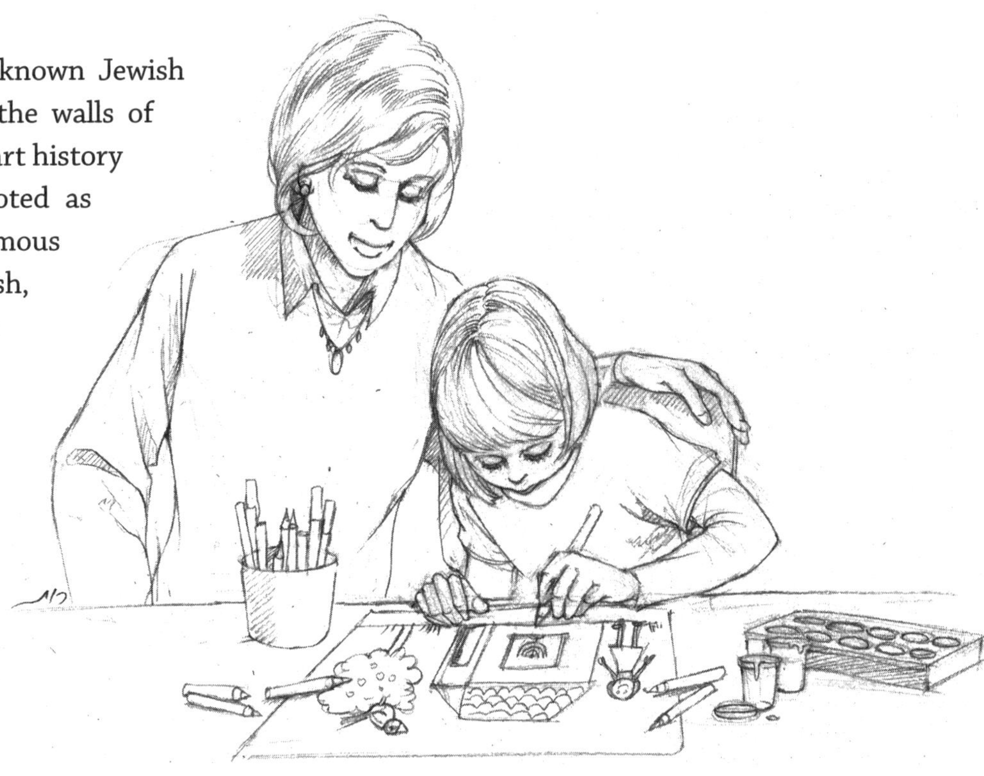

Notes and Sketches

It made me wonder, what is it that makes Jewish art "Jewish"?

I realized that before I answered this question, I had to understand what it is that makes art "art."

Art Imitates Creation

Art is born from the soul's natural desire for expression. It's a result of the human drive to copy and communicate what we see in the world around us and within. It's part of our desire to reproduce beauty and express our appreciation for life.

In producing art, we want to connect with the abundant blessings of the universe. Every morning is a new creation; today's sunrise is unlike all the others before it. Art is a wonderful tool, used to wake us up to the visual glory that the world presents anew each day. Using order and form inspired by nature, we recreate recognizable subjects.

At the same time, art is both personal and cultural. In our attempt to create, we also express our inner feelings, thoughts, and senses. We strive to render emotions and character traits into tangible images to show what a person or society can do, for good or bad. By creating a visual representation of our inner world, we can evoke those same emotions in others.

In essence, art is the language of the eyes and hands, bringing pleasure and tranquility, or the opposite.

We call a person an "artist" if he can reproduce scenes, objects, or emotions from the world around him or from within himself using materials, techniques, skill, and talent. But the truth is, anyone can create art—a "work of art" can be as simple as shaping a lump of clay into a ball or drawing brilliant-colored lines with pastels, or it can be as exacting and complex as the famous Old Masters' oil paintings of several hundred years ago.

For some, it is an innate talent and for others a learned skill. It may be a profession or an enjoyable pastime. Whether occupation or hobby, art is a visual mouthpiece that speaks without words and adds inspiration to our lives.

If you consider yourself "art challenged," then it seems far-fetched to consider that art has anything to do with you (or your child). Art, you think, is the realm of brilliantly talented people.

Although there are people who are innately gifted in producing art, anyone can make art—and certainly anyone can appreciate it. All you have to do is use your imagination and give it a try.

Notes and Sketches

All That Art Can Be

Do you remember what the world looked like when you were a child? Everything was a new, delightful discovery. A child sees a world filled with the wonder of discovery. The artist taps into the child within himself, and tries to look at the world as if for the first time. But the artist has an adult's command of concepts and language; this allows him to perceive things that he was not aware of as a child.

If you open yourself up to the awe and excitement of a child's newly discovered perception and combine it with your adult understanding of the world, you will find that you are able to relate to the realm of art more than you ever imagined.

Let's Look At

All That Art Can Be

Art is an expression of the soul.
Art can reveal what we sense and feel.
Art can be what the eyes see, the mind thinks, and the hands make.
Art is a human signature.
Art records moments in time.

Art is a human representation of the world around us.
Art is appreciating, copying, and interpreting what God has created.
Art is the perception of the world without and within.

Art is a representation of our culture and values.
Art is a presentation of our outer reality and inner world.

Art is what we believe.
Art is a message.
Art records history and current events.

Art teaches us the language of visual perception.
Art adds depth and richness to our lives, whether we are the artist, craftsman, or observer.
Art is aesthetic (a statement about beauty).
Art is color, shape, line, and light.
Art is a language of symbols, pictures, and signs.
Art tells a story or makes a statement.
Art conveys ideas and thoughts.
Art gives visual shapes to words.

Art is thinking and planning.
Art is careful looking.
Art is arranging and design.
Art is decoration and embellishment.
Art is crafting functional objects.

Art is an expression of the soul.

What Makes Jewish Art "Jewish"?

As the years went by and my study of art broadened, I came to realize something: art for art's sake alone is not a Jewish concept. Art that exists purely for the sake of personal expression without any connection to a Jew's roots and unique obligations may be called art, but it is not Jewish art. Even if the artist is Jewish, without Jewish content and values, a work of art could not be considered Jewish art.

How do we define "Jewish"?

The Torah (Bible) teaches that every nation is distinguished by a unique quality and purpose in this world. The Jewish people have three distinct traits:[1]

- They are *rachmanim*—compassionate and merciful.
- They are *baishanim*—modest, unassuming, and refined.
- They are *gomlei chassadim*—they do acts of loving-kindness.

1 Talmud, *Yevamot* 79a.

The Jewish people were also the first people to believe in one God and accept a code of moral standards in a pagan world, as prescribed in the Ten Commandments. This belief in one God can be traced back to our forefather Abraham, who passed it on to his children and the generations to come.[2]

In fact, the Hebrew word for "craft," *amanut*, is based on the word *emunah*, "belief." Literally translated, the word for "craftsman," *aman*, is someone who is a dependable worker.[3] The first Jewish craftsman in history was a man named Bezalel. Through the work of their hands, he and the artisans under his charge expressed their faith by building a fitting Sanctuary for God in the desert, the holy Mishkan, over three thousand years ago.[4]

Judaism teaches that a person's name reflects his essence. The words that comprise Bezalel's Hebrew name, "*b'tzel El*," translate to "in the shadow of God."[5] This reflected his adherence to everything that God commanded him to do—his unmatched excellence of craftsmanship was motivated only by his wish to follow God's instructions to the letter. The desire for income, fame, or free expression did not exist for him—he literally lived "in the shadow of God."[6]

The Jewish standard for visual beauty and excellence is rooted in the high caliber of craft and spiritual meaning that was inherent in the Mishkan that Bezalel built. The Mishkan was beautiful—it was a work of art—but all that beauty was used to serve a higher purpose.

This is what Jewish art is all about.

Beauty in Judaism

Beauty certainly has a place in the world, and Judaism acknowledges the human need for visual imagery—as long as it is appropriate and positive. For example, depicting our Creator, Who can't be defined, or denigrating human values is not a Jewish concept; illustrating human dignity and humility, on the other hand, reflects God's intentions for the world He created.

---

2 Maimonides, *Mishneh Torah, Hilchot Avodat Kochavim*, ch. 1.

3 Matityahu Clark, *Etymological Dictionary of Biblical History*, based on the commentaries of Rabbi Samson Raphael Hirsch (Feldheim Publishers, 1999), ch. 1.

4 Rabbi A. Henoch Leibowitz, *The Majesty of Man* (ArtScroll Judaica Classics, 1992), pp. 159–160.

5 Exodus 35:30.

6 Leibowitz, *The Majesty of Man*, pp. 159–160.

Not only is beauty acceptable but "This is my God and I will beautify Him"[7] is an important, far-reaching Jewish precept. This is also known as *hiddur mitzvah*—embellishing, adorning, or adding to the glory of a mitzvah (Torah commandment) by using beautiful objects to perform it.[8] The way to "beautify God" is to adorn the objects of Jewish observance; for example, making the menorah out of precious materials such as silver, adorning the sukkah (a temporary dwelling erected for the Festival of Sukkos, in which Jews are commanded to spend the Festival) with decorations, or placing a Torah scroll in a beautiful cover and creating it with special script, quill, and ink.

A Jew can also "beautify God" by beautifying himself—not through adorning his body with cosmetics and jewels, but by nourishing his soul through fulfilling the commandments and appreciating all the good that God does for His creations at every moment.[9]

This, then, is Jewish art: art that feeds the soul along with the eyes.

In Summary: What Is Jewish Art?

- Art imitates nature.
- Art also expresses and evokes emotions—on a personal level and a collective level.
- Anyone can make art. All you have to do is be prepared to use your imagination—view your surroundings with the wonder of discovery you felt as a child.
- Art for art's sake is not a Jewish concept. Judaism values beauty when it nourishes the soul.
- The first Jewish craftsman was Bezalel; his art was the epitome of Jewish beauty since everything he made was exactly as God wished.
- We can "beautify God" by adorning objects of Jewish observance and adorning ourselves through perfecting ourselves.

---

7 Exodus 15:2.

8 The basis of this idea is the verse, "This is my God and I shall beautify Him" (Exodus 15:2).

9 Talmud, *Shabbat* 133b.

Questions and Wonder

1. Do you like to draw and color? Why?
2. What does art mean to you?
3. What do you think when you hear the term "Jewish art"?
4. How can we use art to thank God for our wonderful world?
5. Why do we make our houses of worship beautiful?

2 Jewish Art's Inspiration

Sarah was a deep thinker. She often wondered why her friend Lizzie's art teacher never offered Lizzie a chance to paint something Jewish. After all, both she and her teacher were Jewish.

Lizzie's paintings were lovely, but they seemed empty, nothing more than window dressings. Sarah knew there was so much more that her talented friend could do. Rather than window dressings, her art could be windows to her soul.

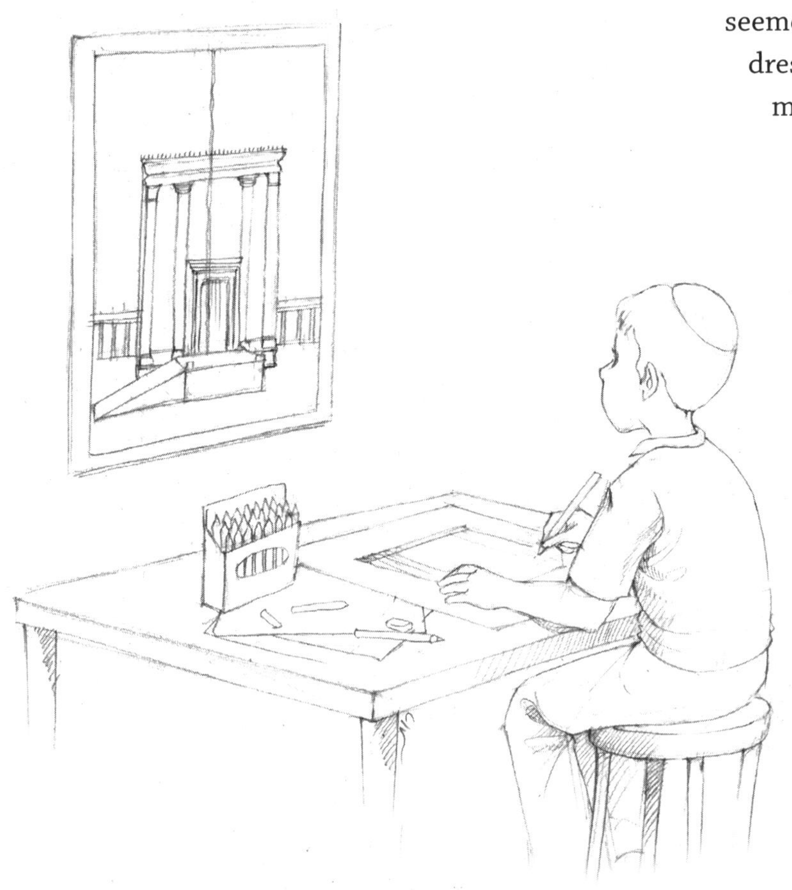

In the previous chapter, I mentioned that Jewish art nourishes the soul as well as gives us pleasure for its beauty. It usually serves some function that helps a person come closer to God—even if it is only to teach an idea or value from the Torah.

Since it is meant to ultimately serve a spiritual function, all Jewish art comes from a holy source of inspiration.

The Mishkan: A Holy Source of Inspiration

Notes and Sketches

The place and times we live in have a tremendous influence on us. Most of the art we see and produce today is based on the influence and style of the country we live in. In turn, we can learn about a culture—its history and values—through its art.

Jewish art is culturally connected to its source: the Mishkan. Crafting, creating, and handling the aesthetic wonders of the Mishkan was a supreme experience, combining creativity and spirituality, for the Jews in the desert on their journey to the Land of Israel.[10]

The beauty of that holy structure served to raise the eyes and hearts of the Jews in the desert to the heavens in recognition of God. Today it serves as our source of inspiration for art. It is the basis for the idea that beauty and aesthetics play a part in Jewish life.

The Mishkan and, later, the Beit Hamikdash (Holy Temple) in Jerusalem were the center and focus of Jewish life.[11] The Mishkan was splendidly crafted by Bezalel and the Jewish artisans in his charge, according to divine command.[12] While the Jewish people camped in the wilderness, the Divine Presence rested in the Mishkan. There, the priestly service of the *kohanim* was carried out.

The Mishkan and its objects of worship were made of precious jewels, gold, silver, brass, and acacia wood. Its curtains and tapestries were made with specially prepared materials woven with scarlet, blue, purple, and metallic threads.[13] The visual specifications, design, and function of the Mishkan have not been duplicated in all of history for their beauty of line, craftsmanship, or spiritual significance.

In both a physical and spiritual way, the Mishkan was a vehicle for the message that God was in their midst. Every single aspect of the Mishkan, from its dimensions to the materials used to make it, symbolized a concept (and often several) in Judaism. When Aaron, the high priest, and his sons prepared the Holy Ark for travel, for example, they covered it

---

10 The Mishkan was built in 1312 BCE. See Exodus, chs. 25–27.

11 The First Beit Hamikdash was built by King Solomon in 832 BCE. The Second Beit Hamikdash was rebuilt by Ezra and Nehemia and the Jews returning from Babel. King Herod expanded and beautified the Second Beit Hamikdash two hundred years later. See Mishnah, *Yoma* and *Middot*.

12 Exodus 35:30–35.

13 Exodus 26:1, 26:31, 36:35, 36–40.

Notes and Sketches

with a material of *techeilet* (turquoise) wool. All the components of the Holy Vessels were covered with wool, dyed the color of *techeilet*, and additionally covered with the hide of an animal called a *tachash*. Only the Holy Ark had the turquoise wool over the *tachash* hide. This *techeilet* color resembles the color of the sea, which resembles the color of the sky, which resembles the color of a sapphire. This brought to mind the Divine Throne of Glory that is in the heavens, which has the appearance of sapphire.[14]

Like the *techeilet* wool, every part of the Mishkan served not only a physical function but also a spiritual function and had deep significance. Color and form was elevated and became the source of our inspiration to use visual form in an elevated way today.

The Artist's Temperament

While talented and even inspirational, artists are not known for their pious characteristics.[15] They are hailed for their creativity, for "breaking down barriers." Some artists are self-centered and don't like to be "hemmed in" by cultural norms. This is the exact opposite of the Torah's ideal artistic temperament.

The Mishkan was constructed under the leadership of Bezalel. Bezalel came from a respected, upstanding family—he was the grandson of Hur from the tribe of Judah. Hur was one of the few people to protest the worship of the golden calf in the desert. He ended up sacrificing his life for doing the right thing—evil people murdered him for his efforts.

Bezalel had spiritual qualifications of his own. He passed the test of noble character when he watched his grandfather being murdered for protesting the worship of the golden calf and mastered his natural desire for revenge.[16] For this, he merited the privilege of building the Mishkan, a physical symbol of atonement for the sin of the golden calf.[17]

---

14 Ezekiel 1:26 and 10:1, and Talmud, *Chullin* 89a, and Rashi there. *Techeilet* also brings protection, since it reminds God of the *techeilet* strings that Jewish men wear on their tzitzit. This merit protects the Jewish people. See Talmud, *Sotah* 17, and the commentary of *Etz Yosef* there.

15 Exodus 38:22.

16 Leibowitz, *The Majesty of Man*, pp. 159–160.

17 Midrash, *Shemot Rabbah*, ch. 48.

When Bezalel was given the charge to build the Mishkan, he made it exactly according to God's directives. He didn't mind being "hemmed in" or limited. He knew that the ultimate beauty is the Torah's definition of beauty. With his instinctive perception of God's will and his perfect aesthetic sense, Bezalel was the Jewish archetype of the great artist. Bezalel taught us that the artist's character is just as important as his talent.

The Mishkan and the Creation

There is a time to create and a time to rest. God created the world in six days and rested on the seventh. Similarly, Jews create and labor six days a week and rest on the seventh day, on Shabbat.[18]

The Mishkan symbolized this. Thirty-nine creative actions (called "*av melachot*") and their derivatives were involved in the building of the Mishkan. On Shabbat, Jews refrain from carrying out these thirty-nine actions, thus emulating the Creator, who rested from creating the world on Shabbat.

When you create art, you are probably performing one or more of the creative actions that were done in making the Mishkan. Arts and crafts are rooted in those creative actions. Here are some examples of the thirty-nine creative actions that we use in arts and crafts today and which Jews refrain from doing on Shabbat.[19]

Dyeing

This entails changing the color of something or fixing something in color. Each time you hold a paintbrush, imagine the craftsmen of the Mishkan preparing dyes for their holy purpose! In building the Mishkan, they dyed the wool they used to make the tapestries and curtains. From this we learn not to paint on Shabbat.

Sewing

This constitutes attaching or fixing two materials together with stitches. In the desert, they stitched together material to make the

18 Genesis 2:2–3.

19 Talmud, *Shabbat* 73a–75b; Maimonides, *Mishneh Torah*, Laws of Shabbat 9:13, 10:9, and 11:7–17.

tent covering in the Mishkan. Gluing and taping are derivatives of this action. Every time you tape or glue paper, think of the handiwork of the craftsmen in the Mishkan.

Tearing

This refers to ripping apart pieces of material by hand or with a tool, in order to repair them. The materials of the tent covering had to be ripped apart to repair it. We can remember the work done by the righteous craftsmen of the Mishkan whenever we take apart materials to resew them.

Marking

This entails marking a surface, usually with lines, to prepare it for another purpose, such as writing or cutting. When preparing the coverings in the Mishkan, they marked the hides with lines in order to cut them to a specific measurement. Marking and measuring are necessary for planning and preparation before we write, fold, or cut.

Cutting

This refers to using a sharp edge to cut material to a specific size or shape. Once the hides that would make up the Mishkan's coverings were marked with lines, they were cut to size. The basic action of cutting paper, cloth, or leather to alter its size or shape takes on significance when we associate it with its purpose in the Mishkan.

Writing

This refers to making a mark that represents a letter, number, or symbol. Writing was needed in building the Mishkan to mark the wooden boards that formed its structure for the purpose of dismantling and reassembling. Drawing is a derivative of writing. Here we find the pure origins of drawing.

Erasing

This entails cleaning or removing a mark or error on a surface for writing. In the Mishkan, craftsmen erased mistakes in order to correct marks made on the wooden boards that made up the structure of the Mishkan. If we can accept that even the craftsmen building the Mishkan made errors that they needed to correct, perhaps we can more easily accept our own mistakes as a natural part of the process of learning and growth.

Four Branches of Jewish Art

If the Mishkan is the root of Jewish art, then the different forms of Jewish art that we see today are its branches. From its source, Jewish art branches off into four basic forms, and each serves a different function in Jewish life:

1. **Ceremonial objects, such as the menorah or the Altar in the Temple.** These objects give physical form to spiritual concepts.

   Becky grew up with little connection to her Jewish heritage. As a teenager, she visited Israel with her family and toured a Jewish museum, as most tourists do.

   Becky had no idea how that visit would change her life. She stood in a large, echoing room surrounded by menorahs from Italy, Eastern and Western Europe, and India. Jews around the world used these menorahs, she realized.

   The dusty menorah languishing on the top shelf of her family's living room cabinet now took on new significance. She didn't know why, but Becky felt connected to her fellow Jews around the world through the menorah. She realized that wherever she was, she could feel at home. It didn't matter if they spoke a different language or dressed differently—they were united through their traditions.

   Often the objects of our heritage contain a deep significance, not only in how they are used but also in their form. The Talmud tells us that if one wants to become wise, he should face south as he prays because the Menorah in the Temple, after which we model our menorahs of today, occupied the southern section of the Mishkan.[20] The Menorah, which gave off light, symbolized the light of wisdom, and facing the same direction inspires wisdom.[21]

20 Talmud, *Bava Batra* 25b.

21 Ibid. 2b.

The ceremonial objects that are used today in Jewish observance are informed by the holy objects that were used in the Mishkan and, later, in the Beit Hamikdash that stood in Jerusalem thousands of years ago. These objects—such as the Menorah, the Altar, the fire pans, and tapestries—gave the Jewish people a physical connection to the Creator. Using these objects to serve God brought them closer to Him.

2. **Paintings and other visual documents that record national, communal, and individual events and history.** This form of art portrays authentic Jewish life. It may consist of historical records or portrayals of Jewish people, events, and places. It is the realistic rendition of life, especially from olden times, that holds the viewer's fascination of this type of art. Contemporary examples include paintings, prints, drawings, paper cuts, photographs, and carvings that portray or record everyday life or special events. With these works of art, we can peer into the lives of previous generations and be touched by a moment of humanity. Aptly called *Transmitting the Tradition*, Lazar Krestin's painting of a kindly, aged grandfather seated next to his young grandson as he reads from a book in nineteenth-century Poland, creates a warm memory that resonates with all of us.[22] *Friday Evening*, an oil on canvas circa 1920 by Isidor Kaufman, depicts a serene and elegantly dressed woman standing by her Shabbat table, which is bedecked in a brilliant white tablecloth. Her prayer book, candlesticks, a Kiddush cup (special goblet used for the ceremonial blessing said on Shabbat and holidays), and two challahs (loaves of bread) under an embroidered cover are resting upon the table.[23] A glimpse of the past, yet so relevant to the present!

3. **Arts and crafts for educational purposes.** Arts and crafts can teach about Jewish concepts and teachings. This form of art is most often used to teach young children concepts in Judaism before they have mastered language. Examples of this form of art include drawings or facsimiles of ceremonial objects, posters that depict a Jewish holiday, concept, saying, or deed (such as giving charity), and craft projects that

---

22 Michael Kaniel (Kaufman), *A Guide to Jewish Art* (New York: Philosophical Library, 1989), pp. 18, 125–126.

23 Ibid., pp. 121–122.

illustrate the Torah portion of the week, the holidays, or good *middot* (character traits).

4. **Fine arts and crafts that represent an outlet for inner expression and Jewish values.** Such artwork demonstrates clearly that aesthetics is not an end in itself, but is viewed as a God-given gift to portray the beauty of a divinely operated world.[24] It is the artistic voice coming to share one's inner world with others. Whether it is art used for a functional purpose (such as pottery, silver work, or weaving) or fine art created solely for aesthetic beauty (such as paintings, prints, or sculpture), the use of line, color, and light awaken the senses to see the world in an entirely new way.

From simple folk art to sophisticated fine art, it can be basic or complex, plain or elegant. It can be a brightly colored mural depicting the symbols of the twelve tribes or a hand-woven basket to hold the first fruits of the new year. Other examples of art that reflect personal expression and taste include paintings, drawings, weavings, mosaics, collages, prints, fabric art, metalwork, woodwork, jewelry, ceramics, and glass. Whatever the style chosen, the common denominator is that the style and colors reflect joy in a life of meaning and values.

In Summary: Jewish Art's Inspiration

- All Jewish art is inspired by a holy source: the Mishkan.
- Bezalel, who built the Mishkan, is the archetypical Jewish artist: a man of fine character who only wished to fulfill God's will.
- A Jewish artist's character is as important as his talent.
- We perform the same creative actions that were done to make the Mishkan whenever we create art.
- Jewish art can be categorized into four forms: (1) ceremonial objects, (2) historical records and paintings, (3) art for educational purposes, and (4) art that expresses an emotion or Jewish value.

24 Talmud, *Shabbat* 133b.

Questions and Wonder

1. Imagine you were commissioned to design a *beit knesset* (synagogue). What would it be like? Where would you put the *Aron Kodesh* (holy ark), the bimah (table for reading the Torah), the *kisei Eliyahu* (Elijah's chair), the charity box, the pews and tables, the *ner tamid* (eternal light), the memorial plaques, and the bookshelves? Research the synagogues that once stood in Europe, Italy, Syria, India, and countries around the world as well as ancient ones in Israel and neighboring lands for knowledge and accuracy. (The Belz Great Synagogue in Jerusalem is well worth the visit. It's the largest synagogue in Israel, and it took fifteen years to build. It can hold up to six thousand worshippers and up to seventy Torah scrolls. The plan is based on the original synagogue of Belz, which was built in the Ukrainian town of Belz in 1843 and destroyed by the Nazis in 1939.) Ask your teacher or parent to help you research the halachot (Jewish laws) that discuss the function and specifications of a synagogue.

2. Do you think a person's character affects the art that he or she creates? If so, how?

Ceremonial Objects in Art

3

Josh made the menorah by himself at school. Each child had been given a long, thin piece of wood, nine empty spools (from thread), brushes, paints, and glue. He knew the basic idea. He was to glue the spools onto the wood in a neat row; those were the candle holders. The ninth, which would serve as the *shamash* (the one used to light the other candles), he would make different than the other lights.

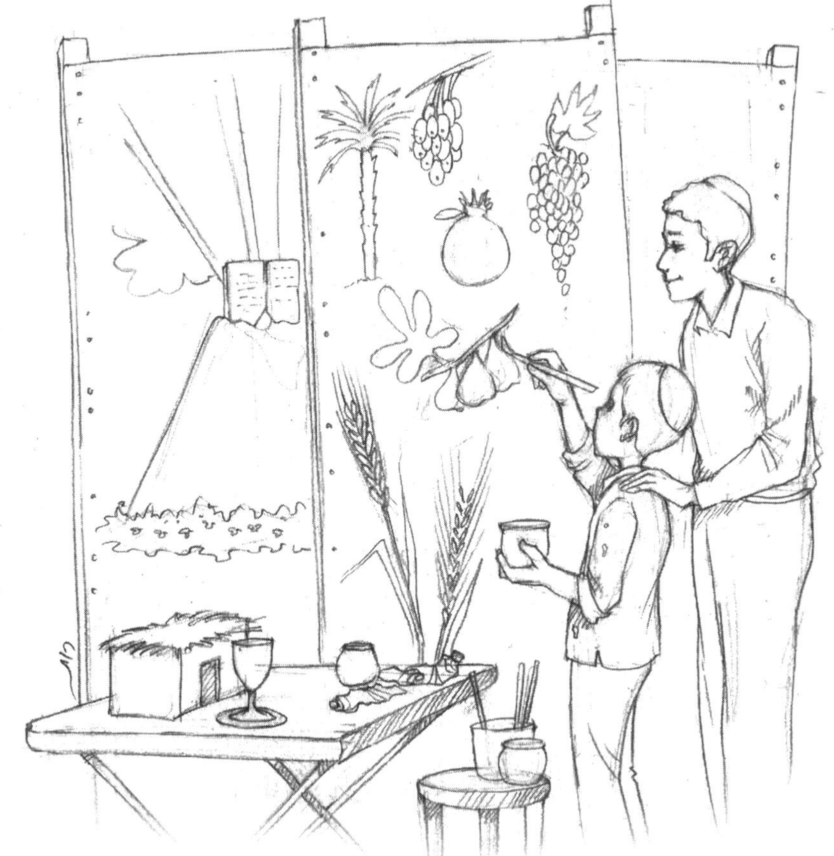

The teacher showed the children a stunning, brightly colored menorah that she had made, with copper cups surrounded by lemon-yellow and turquoise flowers. It opened up interesting possibilities for making a beautiful menorah to be proud of.

Just yesterday, Josh had passed a store window with an eye-catching display of menorahs: ones in the shape of ships, ones made from soda cans glued together, another made with miniature baseball

Notes and Sketches

caps to hold the candles and a bat for the *shamash*. Little bears all in a row and a big bear with a candle on its head. They were so cute! But he was confused. What did baseball and ships have to do with Chanukah?

After seeing the beautiful work of art that his teacher presented—an authentic menorah decorated simply and beautifully—Josh knew he could make a menorah worthy of the holiday it was meant for.

The Menorah: A Symbol for All Time

The menorah is the oldest and most used symbol of the Jewish people. The menorah we are familiar with today is based on the seven-branched candelabra that stood before the Ark of the Covenant in the Mishkan 3,300 years ago. This holy object, intricately ornamented, was miraculously fashioned out of one piece of gold. How the Menorah was fashioned is a fascinating story in itself.

All the vessels of the Mishkan were crafted by Bezalel and the artisans in his charge—all except the Menorah. God instructed Moses to make the Menorah out of one piece of pure gold.[25] But Moses didn't understand how the Menorah was meant to look, so God showed him a replica made of fire. Moses still didn't understand how he could possibly fashion such an intricate object out of one piece. Finally, God told Moses to throw the gold into the fire and the Menorah emerged complete.[26]

Although our menorah today resembles the Menorah in the Mishkan, there are some differences. The Menorah in the Mishkan had one central branch, with three branches extending from it on each side. Altogether, there were six branches with one central branch.

Like every object in the Mishkan, the Menorah had deep significance. Its six outer branches symbolized the six days of Creation, with the central lamp representing the seventh day, Shabbat. Since it provided light, the Menorah stood for knowledge, understanding, and enlightenment.[27]

The Menorah emanated spiritual as well as physical light. The windows in the Sanctuary were constructed in the opposite manner of ordinary

25 Exodus 25:31.

26 Exodus 25:31 and Rashi there; *Midrash Tanchuma, Parashat Beha'alotecha.*

27 Kings I 6:4, *Midrash.*

windows. Rather than let the light in, they let the light out. Thus the Menorah radiated an ethereal light to the world outside.[28]

Notes and Sketches

Today, three thousand years since the original Menorah was created, it remains a symbol of the Jewish people. Depictions of the Menorah have been found on coins, mosaic floors in synagogues, tombs, and burial monuments, and today it stands as the symbol of the State of Israel.

The menorah, or *chanukiyah*, that we light today during the eight days of the festival of Chanukah has eight lamps of equal height (instead of seven) and one additional light called the "*shamash*," which is different from the rest and is used to light the other lamps. The *shamash* can either be the central lamp or positioned on the side.

The eight branches are for the eight days of Chanukah, when a new light is kindled each night. The eight-branched menorah commemorates the Maccabean revolt against the pagan Hellenistic Syrian-Greeks and their ruler Antiochus over two thousand years ago. Antiochus desecrated the Holy Temple in Jerusalem and issued decrees forbidding Jewish religious observance, hoping to destroy the Jewish nation spiritually and take away their power.

When the Maccabees reclaimed the Temple, everything had been defiled—except for one sealed flask of pure olive oil with which they could light the Menorah for one day. Miraculously, that oil lasted eight days, until they were able to retrieve more from the outlying areas. In commemoration of this miracle, Jews light an eight-branched menorah for eight days, adding one light each day.

The earliest *chanukiyot* for synagogues and homes were oil lamps. As Jews spread out to countries around the globe, they adapted the *chanukiyah* to the cultural influences, styles, and materials available locally. In synagogues, homes, museums, and private collections around the world, you can find a vast variety of *chanukiyot*, ranging from carved stone from Morocco and Yemen to East Indian glass, wood, and brass to handcrafted silver or metal from Israel and Europe.

Despite these changes over centuries, the basic form of the *chanukiyah* hasn't changed since the first Chanukah millennia ago. According to halachah (Jewish law)—contrary to modern-art interpretations—the

---

28 Rendered from "The Menorah" (Jerusalem: The Temple Institute), www.templeinstitute.org/menorah.htm; see also *Midrash, Bereishit Rabbah*, ch. 59.

lights must be in a straight row so they can be clearly seen and distinct. Thus, the great miracle of Chanukah is publicized, and the menorah remains a symbol of light and strength through the ages.

Sukkot in Art

In the fall, after Yom Kippur (the Day of Atonement) is over and the Jewish people have been forgiven their sins, comes the joyous holiday of Sukkot.

Sukkot lasts for seven days. For children, they are seven short days. The excitement and wonder escalates as the sukkah is built and decorated, in anticipation of eating and sleeping (weather permitting) in this temporary dwelling under the stars.

The sukkah commemorates God's protection of the Jewish people throughout their forty years of wandering in the desert. They were shielded by Clouds of Glory on all sides, and manna (heavenly bread) for their sustenance fell daily from the heavens. To remember that God protects and guides His people all the time, just as He did in the desert, they were given the mitzvah to build temporary booths and to sleep and eat in them throughout the Sukkot holiday.

The sukkah is a center of hospitality. Each day during the seven days of the festival, we symbolically welcome the *ushpizin*, the seven special guests: Abraham, Isaac, Jacob, Joseph, Moses, Aaron, and David. It is also a time to host friends and family and together celebrate the festival with joy and bounty.

Children delight in performing the joyful mitzvah of decorating the sukkah in a colorful, festive manner. There's a bounty of wonderful sukkah posters and decorations to buy, but it's more meaningful for children to make the posters and decorations themselves.

What fun—especially for the creative ones who love handicrafts. In the sukkah, everyone can contribute, from the smallest toddler to the oldest grandmother, and enjoy their temporary home.

When Sukkot is over and the sukkah dismantled, the decorations the children made in school and at home are carefully packed away until the next year. The next time Sukkot comes around, it's exciting to unpack the decorations and remind ourselves what the children (and adults) made from year to year.

Since Sukkot can be rainy, protect your decorations with clear contact paper or lamination. With proper care, sukkah decorations can last for years, and your children will take pride in seeing their collection hanging in their family's sukkah when they are the parents!

The Sukkah Is Your Art Gallery

Sukkot is an opportune time to display your children's arts and crafts during the seven days of dwelling under the stars. There's no limit to the possibilities: a variety of silver, gold, and colored paper, fabric paint, glue, glitter, foam, acrylics or gouache, crayons of every color under the sun, and more are available to work with. Look for durable waterproof materials, and prepare the sukkah artwork in advance. Save the best from year to year for your sukkah-art collection.

Decorations can be hung from the ceiling, tacked to the walls, or placed on the table as centerpieces. You can make posters, framed paintings, murals on the sukkah walls, miniature sukkahs, mobiles, ceiling decorations, calligraphy, wall hangings, hand-woven or textile wall or table decorations (like table runners and place mats)—and don't be afraid to add your own original touch! Here are some ideas you can use for inspiration:

- Copy prayers and excerpts from the Sukkot prayers. Add illustrations and ornaments and a pretty frame.
- No sukkah should be without a welcome sign on this holiday of hospitality. Draw or stencil the words "*Bruchim Haba'im*" in Hebrew (ברוכים הבאים) or "Welcome" in English, to invite guests into your sukkah.
- The seven species of produce that are indigenous to the Land of Israel—wheat, barley, grapes, figs, pomegranates, olives, and dates[29]— are a common theme for Sukkot. Craft fruits out of cardboard or Styrofoam to hang from the ceiling or place in baskets for a beautiful centerpiece.
- The holiday of Sukkot was a time when the Jewish nation made a pilgrimage to Jerusalem to bring offerings in the Beit Hamikdash and celebrate the festival. During these days was Simchat Beit Hasho'eivah, the water-drawing festival, when the people celebrated the bounty with which God had provided them with dancing,

29 Deuteronomy 8:8.

music, singing, and acrobatics.[30] Depictions of musical instruments—cymbals, lutes, lyres, and trumpets—that the Levites played in the Beit Hamikdash service recall those times of joy and express the hope that they will come again soon.[31]

- Sukkot is described in the Torah as the "Harvest Festival"[32] to mark the end of the agricultural year. To commemorate this, make a harvest basket to hang from the ceiling or to place on the table in the sukkah as a centerpiece.
- Depictions of the Torah or the *Luchot Habrit* (tablets on which were inscribed the Ten Commandments) remind us that the end of the holiday, Simchat Torah, is a celebration of finishing the cycle of Torah readings and the Torah that was learned that year. Many Sukkot posters show illustrations of Jews dancing and singing with the Torah.
- On each of the seven days of Sukkot, Jews shake the *arba minim* (four species)—the *lulav* (palm branch), *etrog* (citron fruit), *hadasim* (myrtle branches), and *aravot* (willow branches)—and make a blessing over them. The *lulav*, *hadasim*, and *aravot* are bound together in a woven holder and held in the right hand, the *etrog* is held in the left hand, and together they are waved in six directions. This mitzvah is symbolic of the Jewish people's rejoicing upon entering the Land of Israel after forty years of wandering in the desert and encountering the bounty of fruit trees and rivers there. Depictions of the four species are found on wall hangings, posters, paintings, and ceiling decorations.

Speaking of sukkah decorations, murals have always had a place in the sukkah. Many years ago, while I was researching the history of a sukkah wall painting, I happened to be sitting at a bus stop on King George Street in Jerusalem. A friendly tourist and I struck up a conversation. This woman turned out to be a member of the family who owned the very sukkah I was on my way to see in the Israel Museum. The wooden sukkah—made of panels that are painted with scenes of

30 During the water-drawing ceremony, water drawn from the natural pools outside the walls of Jerusalem at Shiloah and Silwan was poured on the Altar. These were the very same waters with which the kings from the House of David were anointed. The water offering represents purity and lack of conceit and symbolizes happiness and salvation from troubles, since salvation came about through the kings who were anointed with those waters. See Mishnah, *Sukkah* 4:3–4.

31 Eliyahu Kitov, *The Book of Our Heritage* (Feldheim Publishers, 1973), p. 178.

32 Leviticus 23:39.

everyday Jewish life in southern Germany, holy sites in Jerusalem, and holiday celebrations—had been used by the Deller family in Germany until the beginning of the twentieth century. The sukkah was smuggled out of Germany in 1937 along with the belongings of another family. Eventually, the sukkah made its way to the Israel Museum for all to enjoy. Some say it was discovered in the Meah Shearim market.

In the Italian Jewish Museum on Hillel Street, you can see wooden sukkah panels painted in oils from nineteenth-century Venice. Tremendous care and precision went into painting these exquisite and charming pieces of folk art from Germany and Italy, painted by the owner's hand or commissioned, displaying religious biblical scenes and vistas of Jerusalem's holy sites. Everyday scenes may be seen along with decorative touches of borders and flowers.

Unfortunately, the nature of the construction of a sukkah and the materials used—fabric and wood—means that not many examples of painted sukkah walls are left. The remnants that we do have clearly demonstrate how Jews from time immemorial have always put their hearts into the mitzvah of beautifying their sukkahs.

Here are a group of projects to get you started with your own sukkah decorations. Enjoy!

Sukkah Birds Modeled after Egg Shell Birds

AGES 9+

Materials:

- Styrofoam egg-shaped or round balls:

  body: 2 x 1½ inches (5 x 4 cm)

  head: 1 x 1¼ inches (2½ x 3 cm)
- 2 craft (or ice cream) sticks
- Hot glue gun
- Pencil and scissors
- Cardboard from cereal box or other sturdy thin cardboard

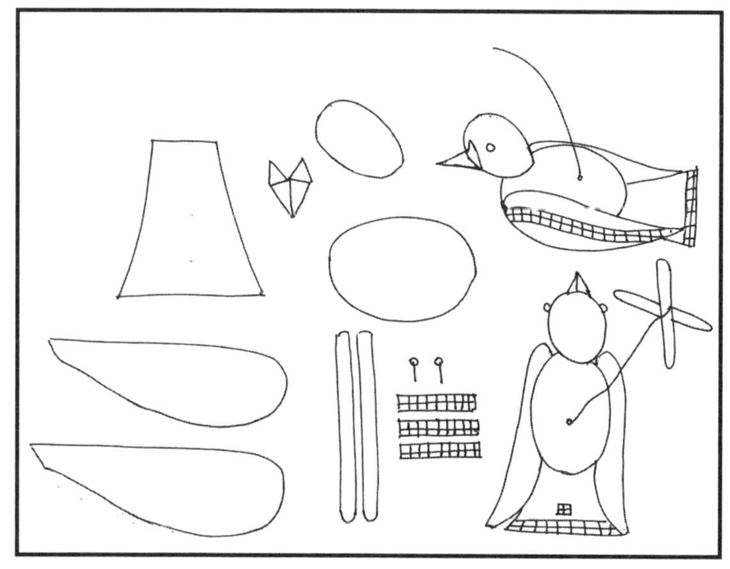

- Fishing line or other sturdy thin string, 22 inches (56 cm)
- Plastic decorative jewels and 2 plastic eyes or plastic pins with ball tops

Directions:

1. Carve out an indentation in the top front of the bird's body for a place to join the head. Hot glue the head in place.
2. Trace or draw on cardboard two wings, one tail, and one beak according to pattern. Cut out. Hot glue in place.
3. Paint in copper, gold, or silver acrylic. Dry.
4. Glue on plastic eyes and decorative plastic jewels.
5. With a sharp object or thick needle, insert fish line through top back of bird through to the bottom, and secure line under bird's belly. Check that bird is balanced when hanging. If necessary, redo.
6. Attach the two craft sticks in a cross fashion. Attach fish line to the sticks and hang. Watch the bird(s) move in the air in your sukkah.

Sukkah Decoration with a Guitar AGES 7+

Materials:

- 4 large craft sticks, 1 x 8 inches (2½ x 20 cm) (tongue depressor size)
- Gold metallic paper, 8 x 2 inches (20 x 5 cm), cut into eight ¼-inch (½-cm) strips.
- Gold metallic paper, 2 x 2 inches (5 x 5 cm)
- Silver sturdy metallic card, corrugated or paper, 3 x 7 inches (7½ x 17½ cm).
- Hot glue gun
- Pencil and scissors
- Acrylic paint: copper or gold
- Gold thread, 5 inches (13 cm)

Directions:

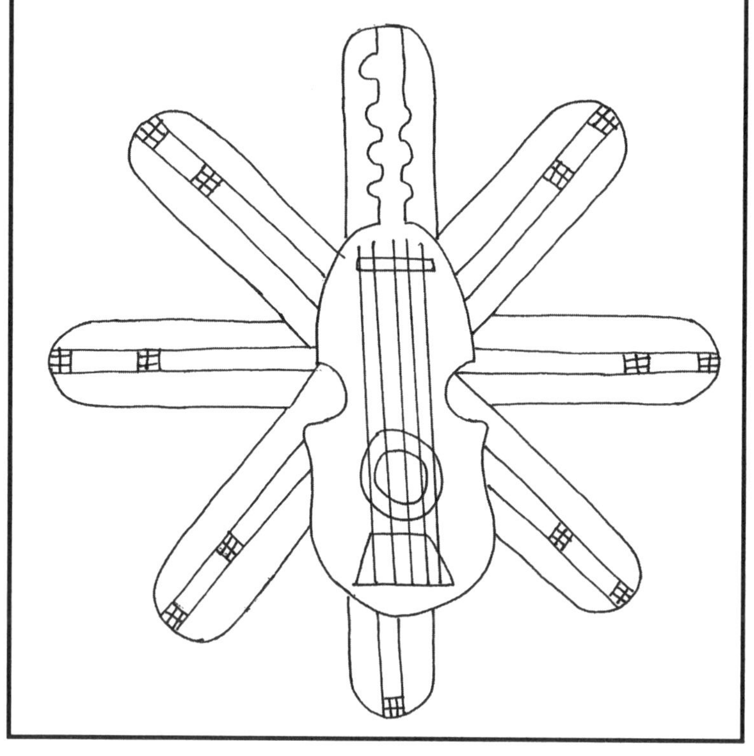

1. Paint the sticks on two sides. Dry.
2. Glue the eight gold strips, one on each stick.
3. Glue the craft sticks together evenly spaced apart. Begin with one horizontal; add two in an "X" form and the third vertical.
4. Cut out the guitar from the silver sheet and the other pieces from the 2-inch gold sheet, except for the larger gold circle.
5. Glue the guitar in the center of the sticks and add the gold and silver guitar pieces.
6. Glue on the fake jewels in the center of the guitar and near the ends of the gold strips. Attach the gold thread for the guitar strings.
7. Hang on a sukkah wall, or decorate the back side like the front, attach with fish line or string, and hang from the top of the sukkah.

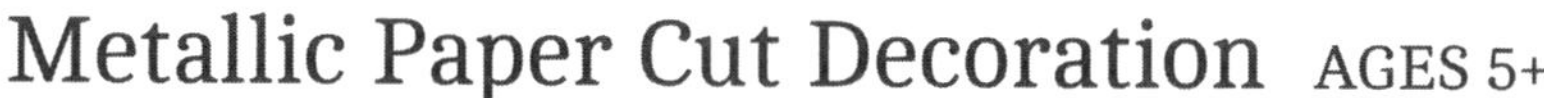

Metallic Paper Cut Decoration AGES 5+

Designed especially for the sukkah, this project is very similar to the layered snowflake papercut project in chapter 21 on cutting. Please refer to that section for instructions. The difference is the intent, specially made for the sukkah with the layered colorful metallic paper.

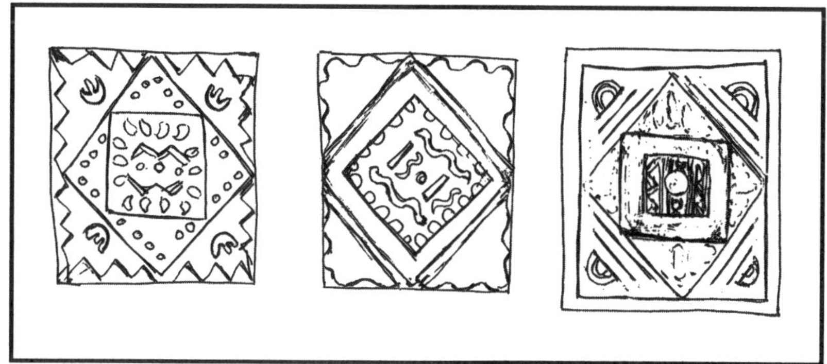

Materials and Directions:

- Ruler, pencil, and scissors
- Paper fastener (brad)

- 3 different colored pieces of metallic shiny craft paper per design:

  6 x 6 inches (15 x 15 cm): fold three times and make small cuts

  7 x 7 inches (18 x 18 cm): fold two times and make medium cuts

  8 x 8 inches (20 x 20 cm): fold two times and cut scallops (half-circles) along outer edge only

Layer cut paper from large to small and attach in the center with the paper fastener. Arrange the top paper at an angle to the two below. Frame or attach to a board in a group of two or three and hang in your sukkah.

Your Own Sukkah Mural AGES 10+

A painted sukkah has a charm of its own. You, too, can paint your own sukkah mural.

Materials:

- 1–3 pieces of paper, size 8½ x 11, 11 x 16, or 12 x 18 inches (21 x 30 cm, 28 x 41 cm or 30 x 46 cm)
- Pencil and eraser
- Ruler
- Wood primer and/or acrylic paint (white or tan)
- Acrylic paints or oil paints in a variety of colors (Oil paint can take weeks to dry; acrylic dries by the next day.)
- Thin paintbrushes, ½, 1, and 2 inches (1½, 2½, and 5 cm)
- Large paintbrush, 3–4 inches (7½–10 cm) or roller with tray
- Chalk (white or a dark color for a light background)
- Wooden sukkah panels
- Sandpaper (if necessary)
- If you like to paint in oils, have on hand turpentine, empty metal cans, and extra rags. (Note: Do not mix turpentine or oil paints with water or water-soluble paints, such as acrylics.)

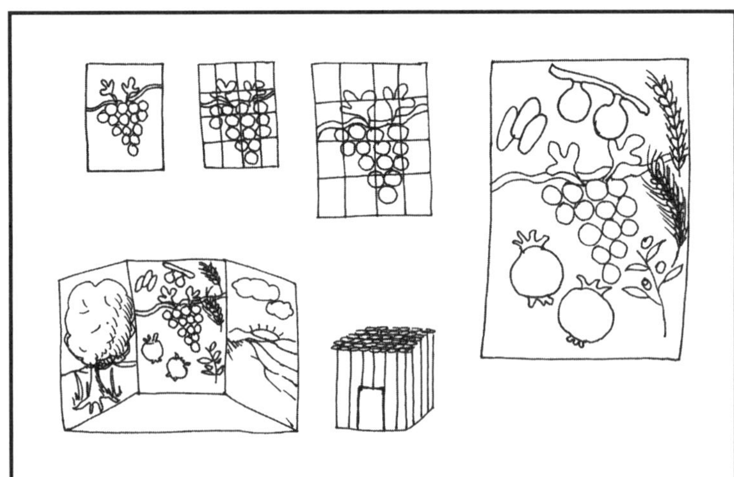

- Clear polyurethane to brush over the dried painted mural or clear acrylic spray

Directions:

1. Prepare the wooden panels: They should be smooth and clean; sand them down with the sandpaper if necessary. Then, with the large brush, prepare the wood with paint primer, according to directions. Let dry.

2. Paint the panels with the white or tan acrylic paint. (If you wish, you can skip the primer and just do the paint layer.) This way your surface will be even and will not absorb the paint you will be using for your mural.

3. Using the same shape paper as the wooden panel (i.e., a rectangular paper for a rectangular panel), make a grid for your drawing. A grid is a technique used to transfer a small drawing to a larger surface with proportionally correct measurements. Divide your drawing into equal medium-sized squares either by folding the paper into 8 or 16 squares, or lightly drawing the squares on the paper using the pencil and ruler.

4. Using chalk and the ruler, draw the same number of squares on a wooden panel, but proportionately larger to fit the panel (i.e., if you divided your paper into 8 medium-sized squares, then divide your panel into 8 large squares).

5. Draw your illustration on the entire paper, then draw it square-by-square in the corresponding sister squares on the panel—i.e., copy and enlarge the illustration from the top right square on the paper onto the top right square on the panel.

6. Paint the illustration. Do large areas first (skies, mountain ranges, etc.), then medium (buildings, rivers, etc.), and finally the small areas (people, animals, trees, flowers, etc.). Save the details for last (highlights, shadows, clothing details, patterns, jewelry, etc.). Paint the darker colors first. Let dry and add touches of lighter color or highlights. (Remember that acrylic paints dry quickly, so use only what you need at the moment. If needed, spray the paint lightly with water as you work to keep the paint from drying.)

7. Once the panels are dry, brush with 1 or 2 coats of polyurethane or spray with clear acrylic to protect against the elements and for ease of cleaning. Make sure to protect the eyes and use ventilation.

Ushpizin Wheel AGES 9+

Each day of Sukkot, we welcome one of the ushpizin into our sukkah: Abraham, Isaac, Jacob, Joseph, Moses, Aaron, and David. Make a poster that shows the name of the guest of the day. Younger children (below the age of 8) can do the project in an abbreviated form. For them, provide gouache and washable markers instead of acrylics and ink.

Materials:

- 2 sheets of thick, colored paper (Bristol), size 14 x 19½ inches (35½ x 49 cm), or other matte paper suitable for water-based paint
- Pencil
- Ruler
- Colored markers, acrylic paints, or inks
- Paintbrush, ⅛ inch (¼ cm) for details, ½ inch (1½ cm) for medium areas, and 1 inch (2½ cm) for large areas
- Scissors
- Disposable cup, 2½ inches (6 cm) in diameter
- Compass
- Paper fastener
- Hook for hanging
- Clear contact paper (optional)

Directions:

1. Fold each paper into a square by folding the top left corner down to the bottom right edge. A rectangular strip will be left outside the square—cut off the rectangular strip and discard. The folded square will remain a triangle until opened. While

still folded, fold the triangle in half once again. Now open up the paper and you will see a square with four triangular sections.

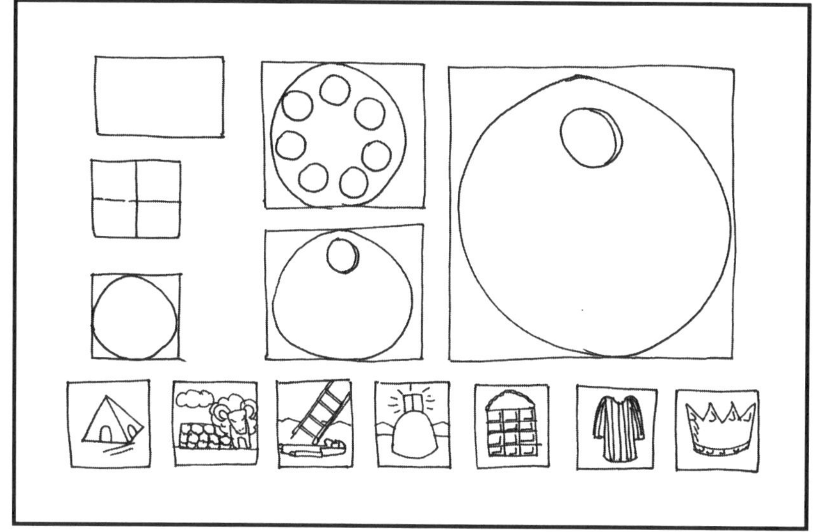

2. With the pencil, mark a dot in the center of each square of paper.
3. On square #1, draw a large circle with the compass, measuring 11½ inches (28 cm) in diameter.
4. Cut out the circle.
5. With the ruler, measure 1½ inches (4 cm) from the top center of the circle and mark the spot with a pencil.
6. Place the disposable cup, with the top of the cup at the spot you just marked, and trace around it. Cut out the small circle and discard.
7. On square #2 draw an identical circle, measuring 11½ inches (28 cm) in diameter and measure down from the top center of the circle 1½ inches (4 cm) and mark the spot.
8. Position the top of the cup at the spot you just marked and draw around it. Repeat this six more times, creating slightly overlapping circles around the large circle. Each smaller circle should remain 1½ inches (4 cm) from the top of the large circle.
9. In each of the seven overlapping circles, write one of the names of the *ushpizin* evenly in attractive lettering, either by hand or with a stencil, and draw the corresponding symbol:
    - Abraham: a tent with openings on four sides to receive guests from four directions. You may want to place a large acacia tree near the tent.
    - Isaac: a stone altar representing the binding of Isaac, when God put Abraham to the test by commanding him to sacrifice his beloved son (a common practice in the world at that time and not a Jewish one.) Include a

picture of the ram that suddenly appeared in the bush at the last moment, and was sacrificed instead of Isaac.

- Jacob: a ladder from Jacob's dream of the ladder with the four rungs, one for each exile that the Jewish people must endure until the Messiah: Babylonian, Persian, Syrian-Greek, and Roman.
- Moses: Har Sinai and the Tablets.
- Aaron: the *choshen*, the breastplate worn by the high priest inlaid with twelve precious and semiprecious stones, representing the twelve tribes.
- Joseph: the robe of many colors, or eleven sheaves of wheat bowing to another sheaf, or the sun, moon, and eleven stars to commemorate his prophetic dreams.
- David: the crown of kingship, a book of Psalms, and a harp.

10. Color or paint and decorate the names and symbols of the *ushpizin*. If you wish, you can decorate the area around the circle with the different features of the festival, such as the four species, a picture of a sukkah, or the dancing and acrobatics of Simchat Beit Hasho'eivah.
11. Cover the large circle and square with clear contact paper to protect from the rain.
12. Using the paper fastener, attach the large circle to the center of the square on which you painted the *ushpizin*.
13. Attach the hook on the back of the square for hanging.

The Ushpizin Wheel in 3-D AGE 8+

Materials:

- Pencil
- Ruler
- Acrylic paints (including white)

- Thin paintbrushes, ⅛, ½, and 1 inch (¼, 1½, and 2½ cm)
- Hot glue or carpenter's glue
- 13½ x 13½-inch square (34 x 34-cm) or round piece of Styrofoam, sandwich board, wood, or heavy firm cardboard
- 1 small piece of thick colored paper or thin cardboard, 1 x 2 inches (2½ x 5 cm)
- Scissors
- Air-drying clay
- Thumbtack with a long pin
- Disposable cup, 2½ inches (6 cm) in diameter

Directions:

1. Sculpt the symbols of the seven *ushpizin* listed above, following the directions on the package of the air-drying clay. You can look at other sukkah decorations for inspiration. The sculptures should lie flat and measure about 1–1½ x 1–2 inches (2½–4 x 2½–5 cm).
2. Let them dry overnight on a wire rack, turning them over after the top side is dry.

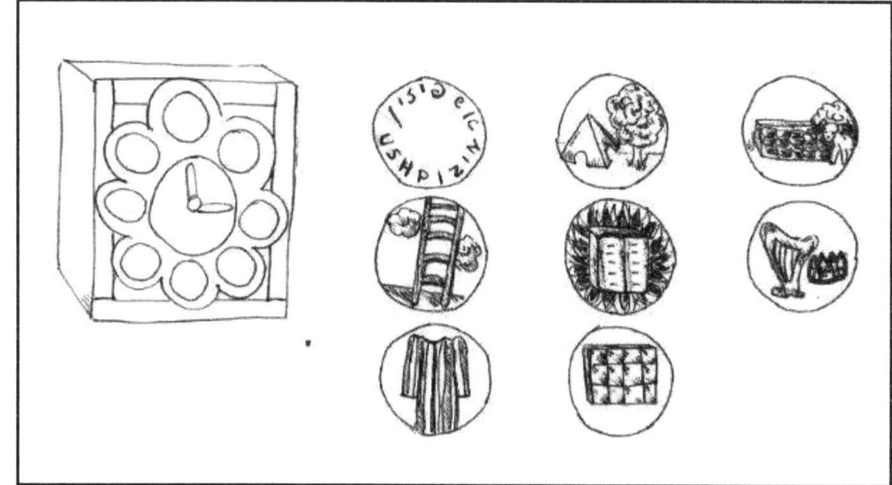

3. Paint with acrylic paints, concentrating on the main areas first (these may require a second coat). With a small brush, add as much detail as you are able to. Details may include blades of grass, wrinkles on skin, folds on material, shading, and attention to subtleties of color. Let dry.
4. Cover the surface of the Styrofoam sandwich board or wood board with white acrylic paint. Let dry.

5. Find the center of the board, and with the pencil, mark the center with a dot.
6. With the pencil and ruler, mark a spot 2 inches (5 cm) from the top of the board.
7. Draw a circle with the top of the disposable cup at the spot you just marked. Repeat, making six more circles slightly overlapping each other, until you have completed a circle of seven circles. There should be 2 inches (5 cm) of empty space all around the edges of the boards.
8. If you wish, you can color or paint the circles.
9. Color and decorate the board. You can divide the board into seven pizza pie slices, starting from the center dot, to paint a background for each symbol. Draw and paint grass and rocks, the sky, a sunset, or a starry night. Let dry.
10. Arrange the sculptures on the Styrofoam or wood board, going in order clockwise, and glue them onto the board with the hot glue or carpenter's glue.
11. Identify and name the *ushpizin* with hand lettering or stencils, or with rolled clay ropes formed into letters.
12. Draw an arrow on the colored paper and cut it out.
13. Attach the arrow to the center dot of the Styrofoam or wood board with a thumbtack.

Optional: The sculptures can also be made to be free standing. Miniature models are very appealing and attract attention. Both children and adults will be drawn to them and be inspired to ask questions.

Objects can be formed from thick small pieces of air-drying clay 2–3 inches high (5–7½ cm), using thinner pieces for details. You can use a garlic press to produce clusters of spaghetti strands. Cut the strands with scissors to make hair, sheep wool, tree bark and leaves, clouds, and mountains. You can add other effects by pressing, smoothing, and sculpting the clay.

Include information that was prepared and researched from authentic Jewish resources for added enrichment.

In Summary: Ceremonial Objects in Art

- The menorah is the most used symbol of the Jewish people.
- The menorahs of today recall the seven-branched Menorah that stood in the Mishkan and Beit Hamikdash.
- In synagogues, homes, museums, and private collections around the world, you can find a vast variety of menorahs, or *chanukiyot*, made of various materials—wood, stone, glass, or metal.
- The sukkah reminds us of God's protection at all times.
- The holiday of Sukkot is rich with symbolism and ceremonial art.
- One of the most significant aspects of Sukkot is the beautification of the mitzvot performed on those days, especially the decoration of the sukkah.

Questions and Wonder

1. The menorah is the most famous ceremonial object and most common symbol of the Jewish people. What is a symbol? How is it different from an advertising logo or the packaging on a cereal box? Are we affected in our hearts and minds differently when we see a menorah from when we see a logo?
2. Design a symbol for your family. What does it mean to you?
3. We learned about remembering the miracle of Chanukah. What other remembrances are central to Judaism? Events such as the exodus from Egypt, the giving of the Torah, and the Holocaust are major milestones in the formation of Jewish identity, belief, and thought. Can you visualize and identify with these?
4. How is living in a sukkah for seven days out of the year different from every other day? How is it different from a

vacation in a cabin in the woods or in a hotel away from home?

5. Why do you think the *ushpizin* were chosen to be our guests on Sukkot? What special qualities did they have?

Jewish Art in History

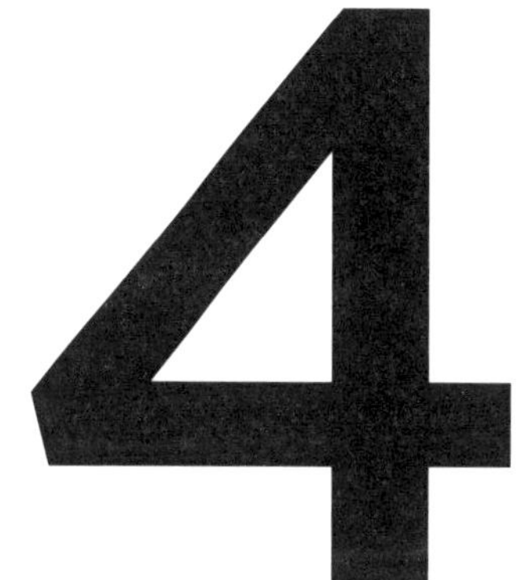

Art is a mirror. When we contemplate art from a bygone era, we can almost see through the eyes of the people who came before us.

Recently, I visited the Herodian Quarter in the Old City of Jerusalem located below the existing street today. In fact, it is below the metal and concrete pillars that hold up the massive complex of Yeshivat HaKotel. After descending the stairs, I found myself standing face-to-face with the remnants of homes belonging to wealthy families and *kohanim* who lived in the time of the Second Beit Hamikdash, remnants of six two-story edifices that were destroyed along with the Temple by the Romans in 70 BCE.

Thick hand-hewn stones formed the walls of these sprawling structures, which held numerous rooms and included several ritual baths (called "*mikva'ot*") for purification. I was taken aback by the familiarity of the high-end Greco-Roman interior designs on the walls, floors, and ceilings. I remember thinking that they could have graced any modern estate today.

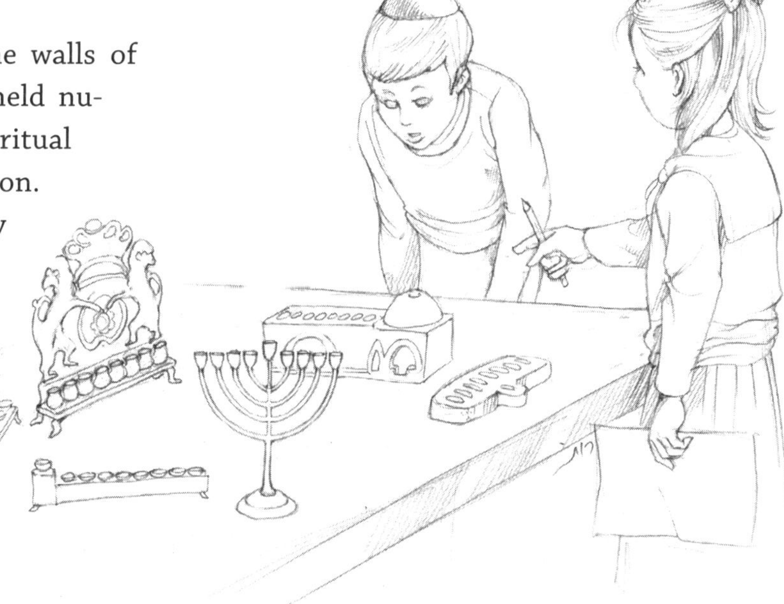

Stunning interlocking geometric shapes adorned

Notes and Sketches

the ceilings. The plaster-covered walls were painted with a symmetrical pattern of various-sized squares in pleasing colors. The emphasis was on geometric design rather than the human figures typical of the Greco-Roman culture portraying gods. The vividly colored mosaics on the floor and the wall frescos (i.e., murals painted on wet plaster) reminded me of the obvious yet often overlooked color and design possibilities for floor tiles and wall treatments.

Everything was handcrafted, from the tables to the stone utensils.[33] I marveled at the artisanship displayed in these homes. What here wasn't a work of art? Remains of stoneware completely carved out of stone were displayed along with delicate brown-red terra-cotta (baked-earth pottery) plates and bowls ornamented with hand-painted designs.

I felt like I had gone back in time—or rather had been met in time—with the timeless nature of the decor and utensils that had graced these residences. The owners of these homes had lived almost two thousand years ago, and yet the contemporary feel of the geometric designs, vivid color schemes, and aesthetic simplicity contributed to the feeling that "it could have been now"—of course, without the microwaves, cell phones, cars, or refrigerators.

How Culture Defines Art

How the people of bygone eras expressed their creativity was defined both by the materials available at that time period and their techniques; thus the Stone Age, the Bronze Age, the Iron Age, the Age of Industrialization, and the Age of Technology. These names reflect what we could expect to see in the arts and crafts of those times.

As each age advanced, so did their art; skill with stone, clay, glass, metal, and paint expanded their expression. So it was that in every civilization artistic expression was defined by materials and technique blended with cultural values. By examining the results of that expression—their art—we can learn volumes about the people and places of the time.

33 Stone was popular with the Jewish priests for reasons of ritual purity, because stone does not become ritually impure on contact with an impure object. See *Mishneh Torah, Hilchot Keilim* 1:6.

The same can be said of Jewish art: from Jewish antiquity and artifacts, we get a glimpse of Jewish history.

Notes and Sketches

Ancient Jewish Art

The closer a generation is to Creation, the greater its connection and understanding of life. God was an integral part of the ancients' lives and the force that motivated everything they did. He had created the world, and the world was filled with natural materials for mankind to use and to make holy (by using them in the service of God).

For the ancient pagan peoples, religion was clearly the source of their art. Ancient people made icons that represented their deities to pray to them, appease them, honor them, or request blessings of them. Arts and crafts were modes of expression to express their beliefs or tell a narrative to publicize those beliefs.

The ancient Canaanite nations built temples for their gods and furnished them with bronze, pottery, and stone idols. Egyptian pharaohs believed they were the sons of a god and built elaborate tombs to house their bodies after death and store their wealth to take with them to the afterlife. The Greeks' and Romans' worship of the pagan gods is reflected in their outwardly impressive artisanship and sculptures, yet lacks positive inner meaning.

All these peoples created art forms that represented their deities and paid homage to them through their work.

The Jews saw life differently. It began with Abraham (born over 3,800 years ago, in 1812 BCE). The patriarch of the Jewish people and his wife, Sara, believed in the one God, the Creator of all living things, heaven and earth, water and land, plant and animal, sun and constellations. Since Judaism espouses the belief that God is not physical, that He is without form or existence as we know it, it is impossible to depict Him. Any such depiction would be akin to idol worship.[34]

Ancient Jewish art therefore expressed itself, not in idols or icons, but in ceremonial objects that could be used in the service of God. To create these works of art, our ancient ancestors used the same materials that the other peoples of their times used: bronze, iron, stone, clay, yarn,

34 *Sefer HaChinuch*, commandment 27.

and glass. But they used them to show their commitment to God, rather than to limit Him by humanizing Him or giving Him physical form.

The Jewish people, who over history wandered from land to land and from civilization to civilization, absorbed the styles and cultural expressions of their host countries. The difference between their art, however, is that the Jews rejected the use of human figures, animals, or any other figures that could be understood as gods. If they did use human figures, it wasn't to depict their God, but to illustrate Jewish life.

One famous example of Jewish art from this era is the Dura Europos Synagogue from the third century. The synagogue was located in a city near the Euphrates River, built by the Romans in the Syrian desert on the edge of two mighty empires: Persian and Greek. Today, this is eastern Syria.

The wall paintings, magnificently preserved by being buried in sand against an invading army in 256 CE, reflect the Byzantine style of the Jews' host country. Byzantine art was known for its frontal-faced figures and vibrant rich colors. It is a combination of highly stylized and flat Eastern art and classical Western art (Greek and Roman). The biblical figures in the Dura Europos Synagogue are frontal-faced full figures, formally arranged according to historical events from the Bible and painted in rich, vibrant colors.

The discovery of the Dura Europos Synagogue in 1932 changed the narrow interpretation of Jewish art, which was believed to be lacking visual images. The richly decorated wall paintings of the synagogue depicted human figures—yet these figures had no connection to idolatry. The emphasis was on biblical Jewish scenes rather than on the physical perfection of the human body or the personification of gods that was part and parcel of other cultures.

These paintings were a spiritual narrative with instruction in the tenets of Judaism. There were no representations of God, yet the Divine Presence was obvious in the intent of the artist. There were illustrations of scenes from the Bible, such as Moses at the splitting of the sea, the Sanctuary in the desert, the story of Esther and Mordechai, and inscriptions in Aramaic quoting teachings of the Talmudic Rabbis.

In Judaism, the synagogue is central to Jewish life. Ancient synagogues, like the Dura Europos Synagogue, embodied the holiness of the place and its community. They were one of Judaism's major contributions to civilization, as the Jewish houses of prayer became forerunners of other religious sanctuaries.

Synagogue art over the ages includes decorated stone reliefs, floor and wall mosaics, wall paintings depicting the Menorah, the Beit Hamikdash, the Holy Ark that housed the tablets, and the Temple ritual utensils, as well as scenes from the Torah, such as the splitting of the sea and the binding of Isaac. Icons were also included in synagogue art such as the lion of Judah, the shofar, the Star of David, the signs of the zodiac, and pomegranates and birds. These have all (aside from the zodiac) become known as distinctly Jewish symbols.[35]

Ancient Jewish art for the home, or for personal use, included similar motifs to those of the synagogues with the emphasis on Hebrew letters and verses. Intricate mosaics—small tiles made from terra-cotta and colored glazes, or pieces of stone or glass, set in wet cement—could be found in both the synagogues and the homes of the wealthier families. They were primarily used for floor or wall motifs, and, besides imparting beauty, the colorful images depicted Jewish life.

Another early example of ancient Jewish art is gold glass: gold leaf sandwiched between two sheets of glass depicting Jewish symbols, such as the Menorah of the Temple or two lions representing the tribe of Judah. In fact, some researchers speculate that the ancient gold glass technique was initially invented by Jewish artisans since this type of glass is typically found where significant Jewish communities existed.[36]

Coins were also early examples of ancient art that was considered of great historical value. The images stamped into the coins tell us information about the civilization: its rulers, its victories, and its beliefs. A coin from the time of the last Hasmonean king, Antigonus, who ruled in 40–37 BCE, for example, was minted in the Greek manner (hammering a blank coin metal alloy between two molds carved with images), but was stamped with ancient Jewish script. One side depicted the image of

---

35 The signs of the zodiac, or *mazalot*, as they are known in Judaism, have significance with regard to the nature of the Jewish months. For example, the scales represent the Jewish month of Tishrei, when the Jewish people are judged for their deeds of the previous year. For more about the *mazalot*, see Talmud, *Shabbat* 156a and *Rosh Hashanah* 11b, and the commentary of Rashi there.

36 Michael Kaniel, *A Guide to Jewish Art* (New York: Philosophical Library, 1989), p. 95.

the Menorah from the Temple, and the other side depicted the Table of the showbreads, also from the Temple.[37]

Years later, in the second century (134–135 CE), Bar Kochba, who led a revolt against the Roman rulers who were persecuting the Jews, also minted a coin that was discovered in recent times. One side showed the front of the Temple that stood in Jerusalem along with a *lulav* holder containing three of the four species waved on Sukkot: the palm frond, willow, and myrtle branch. The other side depicted the fourth one, the *etrog*.

Seals, which were used to stamp the symbol of kings, merchants, and tradesmen, also indicated much about life in ancient times. We have seals of ancient Jewish kings to sign important documents and those belonging to simple bakers for stamping their breads "kosher." One such seal was discovered at the site of the second Temple in 2011: a clay seal dated 1–70 CE with the inscription in Aramaic, "Pure to God," a certification of purity for ritual use. In the Beit Hamikdash; such a seal could be found on a jug of oil, used for kindling the Menorah, or on a barrel of wine, used for the wine libations.

Weaving material for tapestries, clothing, or baskets was another craft of ancient times. In Jewish art, one of the earliest examples of this craft was the tapestries and garments that Bezalel and his charges made for the Mishkan and the priests.

My friend, master weaver Yehudit Abrahams, has been reproducing weavings of the second Temple for the Temple Institute in the Old City of Jerusalem. She has completed the reproductions of the priestly garments and is now working on reproducing the *parochet*, the two-sided tapestry that separated the two chambers of the Mishkan, the Holy and the Holy of Holies.

I asked Yehudit how ancient weaving is different from weaving today. She said that the only difference is that today weavers have more sophisticated machinery, but the basic mechanics are the same. That does not mean the product itself is more sophisticated; in fact, the more the machine is left to do the work, the less sophisticated the final product. Ancient weaving was so much more sophisticated because of the total manipulation necessary by hand and the weaver's thorough expertise in various weaving methods that were common knowledge then.

---

37 Dr. Stephen Fine, Yeshiva University and University of Cincinnati.

In ancient times, they had to hand-weave each and every piece of cloth, from clothing to the rags they used for cleaning. Everyone knew the various weaves for each type of cloth and which materials were suitable for each type of weave, whether a garment, rug, or tapestry.

Today the hand weaver specializes in only one or two kinds of weaves because they know that other woven goods can be bought cheaply from machine-made products. Some of the ancient weaving techniques were quite sophisticated, and weavers today still marvel at the cloths the ancient peoples produced. Take, for example, the linen garments found in the Egyptian tombs—the thread count can rival that of any material we can produce today.

The Medieval Era to the Renaissance

Before the modern era (the nineteenth and twentieth centuries), there was a constant flow of Jewish art, and it consisted mainly of religious ritual objects, especially illuminated manuscripts, ketubot (marriage contracts), and books and scrolls which were all elaborately decorated and painted. It is thought that scholars made illuminated manuscripts as early as the Hellenistic period, with their popularity increasing in the thirteenth century and reaching its peak in Renaissance Italy at the end of the fifteenth century. It is only with the invention of the printing press in the sixteenth century that this art began to decline.

It's fitting that Jews—the People of the Book—have always revered their holy books and illustrated everything from prayer books and megillot (scrolls) to the book of *Tehillim* (Psalms) and the wedding ketubah.[38] The Pesach Haggadah (book read on Passover eve) was one of the most popular Jewish works for producing illuminated manuscripts.

The term "illuminated manuscripts" specifically describes illustrations and miniature paintings that enhance and compliment handwritten text. These were applied to parchment or vellum made of animal skin.

38 Though certainly no less revered, since Jewish law dictates how a Torah scroll, tefillin, and mezuzah must be written, these were never decorated in this way.

The inks and dyes were made from burnt and boiled wood bark, plants, and ground-up minerals; even certain insects were known for their colorful dye-making uses. Egg whites, milk, linseed oil, honey, and wine were used as binders to hold the ingredients together. The colors were often brilliantly vivid, and the artists used the metallic colors of gold and silver to add a regal effect.

Illustrations included elaborately drawn capital letters, borders, backgrounds, miniature scenes, geometric designs, scroll and lattice work, pillars, and illustrations of flora and fauna. When gold leaf was used, an expert applied thin hammered gold pieces to the parchment, a very delicate process.

Few examples of illuminated manuscripts have survived due to their delicate nature and the movement of Jews from place to place as a result of pogroms and persecution. In Europe, one of the earliest surviving Hebrew illuminated manuscripts comes from thirteenth-century Austria.

In the medieval and Renaissance eras, Jewish art was produced by both Jews and non-Jews. In Muslim countries, followers of the Koran considered the depictions of humans and animals an affront to God, and therefore ignoble work. Since the Muslims regarded Jews as a lowly people, this type of artwork was left for them to do.

In the Christian countries, however, where anti-Semitism was rife, Jewish artists were excluded from working, since most art was commissioned for the Church, which didn't want Jewish craftsmanship. Instead, Church art was commissioned through guilds. The craft guilds, powerful trade unions of the fourteenth and fifteenth centuries, controlled the market, subject matter, and style, and acted as a patron to the arts. They decided who was qualified to be a member, usually for life.

As a result, few Jews had the opportunity to study art and become skilled at it, and even the Jews themselves preferred to commission a highly skilled non-Jewish artisan over a less-skilled Jew who had been denied access to the craft guilds. They sought out the highest-quality craftsmanship for ritual objects that were to be dedicated to the synagogue or made for family use—objects such as silver menorahs, Kiddush cups, Havdalah (ceremony for the conclusion of Shabbat) spice boxes, ketubot, and Haggadot, as well as embossed silver plates and copperplate engravings (where lines were etched into a plate of copper and ink filled in the impressions, allowing pressed paper to pick up the image) which recorded life events.

Still, Jewish artisans found a way. Regardless of the civil laws, they made ketubot, illuminated prayer books and megillot, *Omer* counters or calendars for counting the weeks between Pesach and Shavuot, decorative *Mizrach* signs placed on a wall facing Jerusalem, wimples (hand-sewn and embroidered cloths that were wrapped around a covered Torah scroll, made by a mother at the birth of her son to be gifted to the synagogue when the child was weaned), circumcision pillows, prayer shawl collars and bags, wall paintings for wooden sukkot, micrographic drawings made up of tiny Hebrew letters, and hand-painted Seder (holiday meal on first night of Pesach) plates.

Just as kings sought to use the best and most beautiful treasures to honor themselves, the Jewish people sought to honor God by creating arts and crafts to be used in His service with the finest-quality materials and techniques.

The Rise of Modern Jewish Art

As the world entered the period of time known as modern history, along came modern art. It began slowly in the late-eighteenth century and reached its peak in the twentieth.

During this period, there were fewer restrictions and greater freedom for Jews in their host nations. But this also led to a weakening in their faith and beliefs, and this, too, was reflected in their art.

Many Jews who had once been united by their faith were drawn to the surrounding culture by the promises of equality and financial possibilities. They began to assimilate into political and secular society. From this setting came the beginning of Jewish secular art.

As they lost contact with their roots, the Jewish secular artists eventually became devoid of Jewish consciousness. They thought that in order to be successful, they had to appeal to everyone and not be known specifically as Jewish artists.

Still, there are fine examples of paintings, drawings, and prints by several well-known and celebrated Jewish artists showing sensitive scenes of religious Jewish life, artists such as Hungarian artist Isidor

Kaufmann (1853–1921), German artist Moritz Daniel Oppenheim (1800–1883), and Polish artist Mauricy Gottlieb (1856–1879). Isidor Kaufmann painted Jewish life in Eastern Europe. His portraits convey an inner spirit, especially those of rabbis and Chassidic Jews who overcame poverty and adversity with Jewish observance. His attention to detail and his emotions were captured on his oils, painted on mahogany-wood panels, winning him honors from emperors and czars in Germany, Russia, and Austro-Hungary.

Moritz Oppenheim is best known for his highly skilled and romantic painting *The Return of the Volunteer from the Wars of Liberation to His Family Still Living According to Tradition*, his portrayal of Jewish German family life in a positive light. He is also famous for his portraits of Germany's ruling society and well-known Jewish figures, including the Rothschild family.

Gottlieb is noted for his *Jews Praying on the Day of Atonement*. Real and recognizable people, including the artist and his family along with others from their community, are portrayed praying in the synagogue. The magnificently drawn faces express sincere contemplation of the Yom Kippur service.

As the modern era advanced, especially in the twentieth century, the concept of "art for art's sake" began to spread. The truth is, this idea took root much earlier. Though Jewish art for personal expression only became widespread in the late 1800s, non-Jewish expressive art had its roots from the mid-1700s.

This was a real turning point for art. Up until the middle of the Renaissance era, most art was of a Christian religious nature. It was art that depicted and echoed religious institutions or beliefs. Then art turned into a tool for kings and noblemen to create an image of themselves that they wished to publicize. Artists painted, sculpted, or crafted as their leaders and kings commanded.

Later on, the craft guilds became the influencing force, followed by wealthy patrons of the arts, rather than kings and churches. Genre art that depicted scenes in the home or the countryside started gathering popular attention. Eventually there came a widening of subject matter that led to the modern era.

But Jewish artists who stayed true to their roots foreswore the "art for art's sake" approach. Though they were influenced by the modern era, their art is a homage to their heritage.

Jewish Art Today

The twentieth and twenty-first centuries have brought in more leisure time for the average person, the mixing of the classes, the merging of East and West, and more money to buy luxuries. Advances in technology allow for the reproduction of art treasures and mass art. Art education and access to museum collections have become commonplace. All this has had a great impact on art.

Today, Jewish artists have a rich range of styles to choose from—from ancient to modern, from personal to traditional and ceremonial. There are many themes to choose from as well. A magnificent turquoise ocean or an inspirational painting of a sunset reminds us of God, the Creator. A watercolor of Jews praying and crying to God at the Western Wall depicts the range of human emotions. A mosaic or tapestry of Jerusalem, exquisitely showing our holy city surrounded by the Old City walls dotted with pomegranates, dates, and wheat, proclaims what is important to us.

We also have more artists than ever who are Torah observant. They are working and exploring styles of art to bring joy, richness, and spiritual inspiration to their beholders. Among the many talented Jewish artists today are contemporary Jewish artists Yossi Rosenstein, Huvy Elisha, Yoram Raanan, Chava Roth, and Esther Zibell.

Rosenstein is a ninth-generation Jerusalem-born artist, who combines modern symbolism with classical art. He depicts surreal yet believable scenes from the Torah while adhering to Jewish values and halachah.

Huvy's style is very different from Rosenstein's work. She is an impressionist/post-impressionist painter from Jerusalem best known for her vibrant scenes of Jewish weddings and glimmering chuppahs (canopies under which brides and grooms stand at a Jewish wedding). The brushstrokes come alive with bursts of color, like a giant bouquet of every sort of pink and soft purples studded with shimmering green foliage.

Yoram Raanan combines the language of the Jewish soul with contemporary expression. The spiritual inspiration of his paintings comes to us in his rich use of color and light that evokes a resonating and vibrant biblical expression.

Add Chava Roth to this portfolio. Her compositions of Jewish life are lush with visual texture and vivid color—the soft folds in a velvet

Torah mantle, the shine on a silver candlestick set on a table piled with prayer books.

Esther Zibell of Safed takes us on a visual departure from the mundane physicality of this world with her innocent view of life and her use of color that jumps off the canvas.

The Life and Times of the Artist through the Artist's Eyes

Much as a diary reveals the personality and life events of the writer, arts and crafts reveal the life and times of the artist through the artist's eyes. The exhibitions and displays in museums and art galleries all over the world provide an amazing historical perspective of civilizations.

The same is certainly true of Jewish art. Jewish museums around the world and in Israel, particularly in Jerusalem and the galleries in Safed, are excellent sources of Jewish art, ancient and contemporary.

We learn a lot from seeing Jewish ceremonial art, both old and new, from around the world. Torah scrolls and prayer books, Shabbat candlesticks and menorahs—they are all physical proof that Jews everywhere throughout history observed Shabbat, prayed, lit Chanukah lights, and celebrated the festivals of the Jewish year.

It's especially satisfying for children to see that Jews everywhere used and owned the same objects that Jews use today in their Torah observance. They find it fascinating to compare the same ceremonial objects—actual ones or in photographs—from different places in the world and different times in history. Show them a book of *chanukiyot* from countries all over the world, such as Morocco, Algeria, Germany, Austria, Hungary, Yemen, Poland, England, Egypt, Holland, the United States, and Israel. Ask them to point out the differences (in material and shape) and similarities (all have eight lamps and a *shamash*).

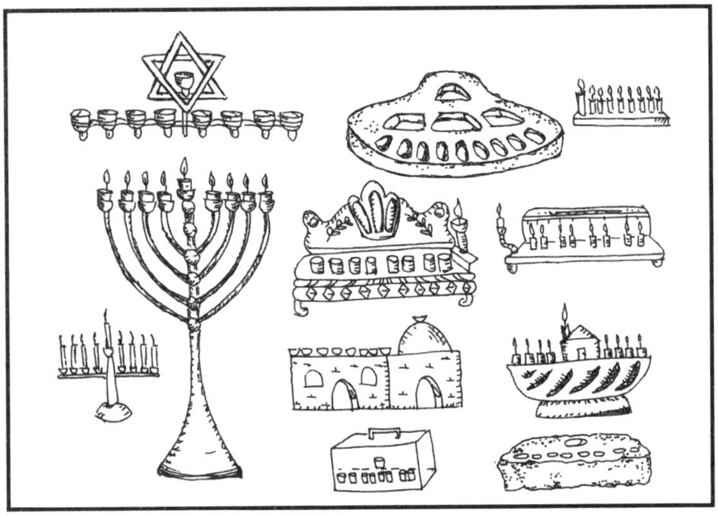

They might see traditional nine-branched *chanukiyot* from Europe, a stone one from Yemen, or unusual ones from Germany in the shape of a ship, a fish, or Rachel's Tomb in Jerusalem. Or let them look at a collection of hand-painted marriage contracts. Compare old ketubot from Yemen with ones from Poland and see the similarities and differences in style and portrayals of the wedding scene.

A Miniature Beit Knesset AGES 8/9+

You and your children can be craftsmen like Bezalel. Construct a miniature beit knesset (synagogue)! See chapter 2 for information on Bezalel, the Mishkan, and the beit knesset. Chapter 5 has instructions on Styrofoam sandwich boards.

Build a 3-D model of a synagogue. For a simpler version, build the synagogue inside a shoebox. This one is made from Styrofoam sandwich board. If you can, look up famous synagogues in history and read stories about them to enhance your knowledge and to find models to draw from.

Materials:

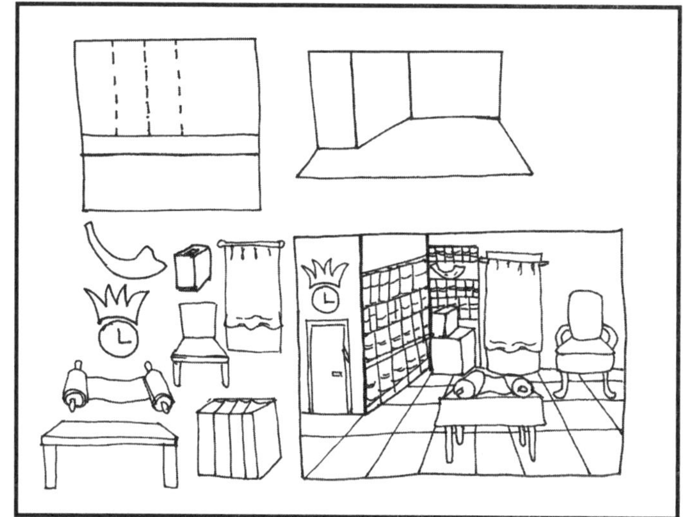

- Pencil
- Metal ruler
- Acrylic paints and or thick markers
- Paintbrush ¼ and ½ inch (½ and 1½ cm)
- 4 pieces Styrofoam sandwich board ½ inch (1½ cm) thick, the size of an 8½ x 11-inch (21 x 30-cm) sheet of paper
- Utility craft knife and protective cutting surface
- Hot-glue gun
- Air-drying clay

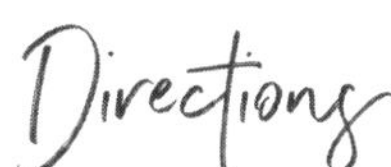

1. Set one of the Styrofoam sandwich boards flat on the table. This will be the floor of your *beit knesset*.

2. With the pencil, draw tiles onto the floor, and then color in with markers or paint using two alternating colors.

3. Use another piece of Styrofoam for the wall. The wall can be bent to make a corner: With the craft knife, make a cut halfway through the thickness of the board in the middle and bend.

4. Using the ruler as a guide, draw a door on one of the walls. To make it open and close, use the craft knife to cut through the Styrofoam on the top of the door as well as one side of the door.

5. Paint the door and walls.

6. With the hot glue, attach the wall to the floor so that it is standing upright.

7. Use the remaining two pieces of sandwich board to make the furniture: the *Aron Kodesh* (cabinet that holds the Torah scroll), the podium for the cantor, the pulpit for calling up people to the Torah reading, Elijah's chair, benches, and bookcases. Cut out squares and rectangles to make tables, chairs, and cabinet shapes. Then prepare long, thin pieces of Styrofoam, measured to fit, for legs.

8. Paint all objects and let dry.

9. With the hot glue, attach the pieces into place directly against the wall or onto the floor.

10. With the clay, shape an open *sefer Torah* (Torah scroll) to put on the pulpit for the Torah reading and a closed scroll to put in the *Aron*, books for the bookcases, a mezuzah (small parchment attached to a doorpost), a menorah, a clock on the wall, a charity box, a hand-washing cup for the *kohanim* (Jewish priests), and a shofar (ram's horn).

11. Paint and decorate the clay objects. Let dry. With the hot glue, set the objects into place.

Here are a couple of projects to help make children aware of the artisanship of bygone eras.

A Puppet Show about the 39 Av Melachot

AGES 9+

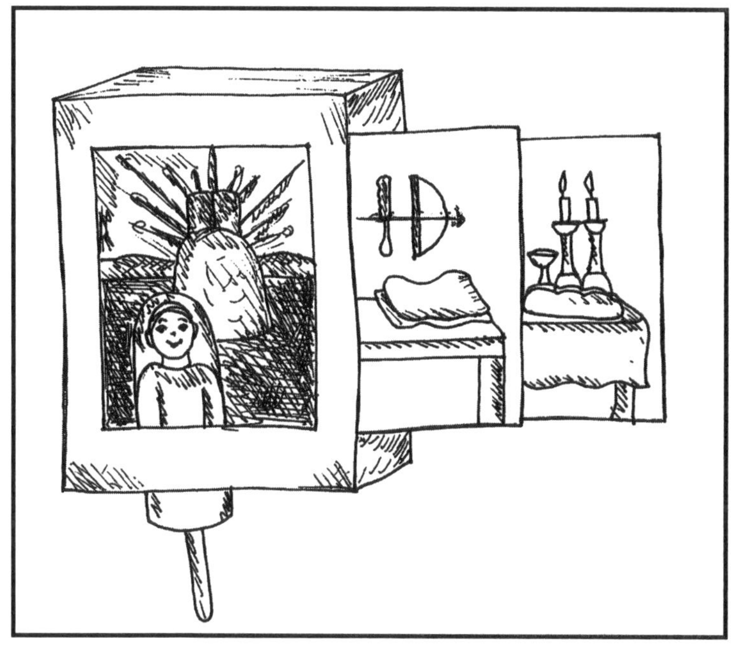

This is a great way to spend quality time with your child. Create a puppet theater, two puppets, and a script. The beauty of this art project is the script and changing scenery. When you are ready to put on your show, position the theater in the center between two stools or small tables for a large theater, or at the back edge of a table for a small theater, close to the puppeteer so that the puppets can enter from the bottom of the box. Cover the entire front area below the theater with a sheet or tablecloth.

In the introduction (Har Sinai scene), in scene 1, Simon explains how the Jews received the Torah at Har Sinai with their promise to keep God's commandments including the observance of Shabbat. Levi wants to construct a puppet theater. In scene 2, he is in his workshop. He marks lines, erases, cuts, tears, glues, draws, and paints. Simon explains how these actions are tied to the thirty-nine creative actions that Jews avoid on Shabbat and why we refrain from performing them. The play might end with the puppet saying, "Levi here has been hard at work all week building a puppet theater. He has been marking, erasing, cutting, tearing, and dyeing colors. Now it is time to stop and rest. Shabbat is coming!" Show scene 3 with the table set for Shabbat and Levi and Simon dressed in their Shabbat clothes.

Materials:

- Pencil or pen
- Metal ruler
- Black marker
- Colored markers
- White house paint or white acrylic paint
- Paintbrush, 1 or 2 inches (2½ or 5 cm)
- Hot-glue gun or white plastic glue
- 3 pieces of thin white cardboard close to the size of the inside of the box that will slide in and out easily. (You can use the sheets

of white cardboard that come with professionally laundered or new shirts.)

- 2 pieces of cardboard, measuring 6 x 9 inches (15 x 23 cm) or Styrofoam sandwich board for each puppet
- Scissors
- Large cardboard box from the grocery store
- Utility knife
- Velcro strip, 6 inches long (15 cm), cut into 3 pieces
- Fabric or synthetic velvet paper for the curtain: royal blue or burgundy, enough to cover the front of the theater, and a Velcro strip to connect it to the theater (optional)
- Fabric swatches, decorative sequins, colored yarn, etc., to decorate the theater and for the puppets' clothing (optional)
- 4 craft sticks

Directions:

1. To measure and cut out the front window, draw a line on the grocery box, 3 inches (7½ cm) from the top and bottom edges, and 3½ inches from the two side edges. Your opening will be about 9½ x 15 inches (24 x 38 cm), depending on the size of the grocery box.
2. Remove one side of the box for an opening to insert and change cardboard scenes.
3. Measure, draw, and cut two thin strips in the bottom of the box that measure 4 x 12 inches (10 x 30 cm). Now you will have two long rectangular holes through which you will insert the puppets.
4. Paint the box white using house paint or acrylic. Let dry.
5. The white pieces of cardboard that will serve as your scenery should be the same size as the back wall of the puppet theater. The scenes will depict the following:
    - Scenery 1: Har Sinai in the distance with the desert in the foreground

- Scenery 2: A workroom furnished with a table covered with tools and pieces of wool, leather, and wood and a large pot for dyeing wool
- Scenery 3: A Shabbat table all set with lit candles and challah

6. With the pen or pencil, draw scenery on each of the three white pieces of cardboard to fit inside the box. Trace over the pencil lines with black marker and color in the drawings with colored markers.
7. Inside the box, attach a 2-inch (5-cm) square of Velcro (centered, 2 inches from the top) to the back of the theater wall. Then attach a 2-inch (5-cm) square of Velcro (centered, 2 inches from the top) to each of the three pieces of "scenery." You can now attach the scenery to the wall of the theater and change it as needed. Slide it in and out from the side opening.
8. Optional: Attach Velcro strips horizontally across the top of the large opening to hold the curtain. (This way the curtain can be removed during the show and replaced with each change of scenery if you like.) You can cut the fabric for the curtain into two pieces so that you have a curtain on each side of the window.

Directions for cardboard puppets:

1. With the pencil, draw each of the puppets on one of the 6 x 9-inch (15 x 23-cm) pieces of cardboard or Styrofoam sandwich board. Draw each one twice, once on the front of the cardboard and once on the back. Draw them to fit the entire piece.
2. Trace over the pencil lines with the black marker. Then color in the puppets with the colored markers. On one side, the puppet should be dressed in work clothes, and on the other side in Shabbat clothes. You can either cut out the puppets or leave them on the cards.
3. Decorate the puppets with cloth, yarn, and sequins.
4. Glue two craft sticks together to make a long stick and attach to the back of each puppet with the hot glue or plastic glue. If you

are using Styrofoam sandwich board, insert the sticks 1 inch (2½ cm) deep between the "sandwich" layers and reinforce with glue.

Enjoy the show!

Variation: A Puppet Show for Chanukah

AGES 10+

Use the puppet theater from "A Puppet Show about the 39 Av Melachot" for this dramatic presentation: "The Story of Chanukah."

Include a dramatic script with humorous voices and sound effects. Play music between scenes. Turn off the lights and shine a flashlight on the theater and listen to the children in the audience squeal with excitement. We do this show at our Chanukah party each year.

SCRIPT SUMMARY (YOU ADD THE DETAILS):

A grandfather puppet, with his two grandchildren on his lap, tells them the story of Chanukah: "In the time of the Syrian-Greeks, the evil King Antiochus and his soldiers tried to stop the Jews from praying to God, doing mitzvot (commandments) and keeping Shabbat. "Matityahu and his five brave sons fought to save the Jews from destruction. After their miraculous success, they found only one jar of pure oil with the seal of the *kohen gadol* (high priest). It was enough oil to burn for only one day.

"To their surprise and delight, the oil burned for eight days! Our Chanukah menorah then and now is a reminder of the pure lights in the Holy Temple and our connection to God that was not extinguished then or now."

Puppets can include a grandfather holding two children on his lap, Greek soldiers on elephants, the five righteous sons of Matityahu, and the Menorah in the Temple.

Materials (IN ADDITION TO THE LIST ABOVE):

- 3–5 pieces of cardboard to fit inside of the box for the backgrounds
- Velcro, 6–10 inches (2 inches per scene)
- Pieces of cardboard or Styrofoam sandwich board, each measuring 6 x 9 inches, 1 for each of the puppets

- 2 craft sticks for each puppet
- You can choose how many and which puppets to make: The grandfather (seated) with little grandchildren on his lap, Matityahu, his five sons, the Menorah, the evil King Antiochus, his general Nicanor, Syrian-Greek soldiers, and a soldier on an elephant.

Directions:

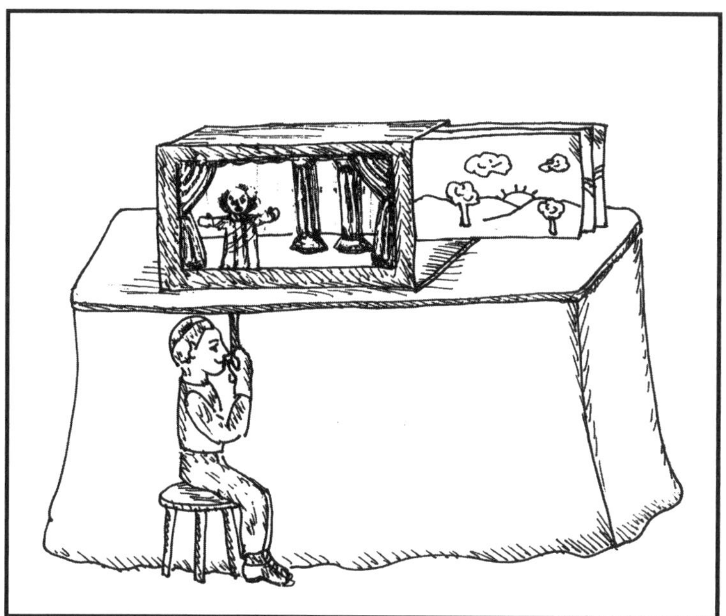

- Follow directions for theater and puppets from "A Puppet Show about the 39 *Av Melachot*."
- The scenes will depict the following:

  Scene 1: inside the living room of the grandfather telling the story, with a menorah and *sufganiyot* (jelly doughnuts) in plain sight.

  Scene 2: the Judean hills. Optional: the inside of a cave or in the Syrian-Greek palace.

  Scene 3: the inside of the Temple showing the giant lit Menorah.

Enjoy the show. Save the box and puppets for next Chanukah.

A Handmade Kad Katan SMALL PITCHER AGES 7/8+

A "kad" is a pitcher or jug. In the times of the Temple, this was the kind of vessel they used for pouring the olive oil into the cups of the Menorah. Make your own kad out of self-hardening clay and hand-decorate it.

Materials:

- Gold or silver acrylic paint
- Paintbrush
- Hot-glue gun
- Scissors

- Air-drying clay
- 2 disposable paper or plastic cups
- Small colored stones or beads
- Thick gold or silver thread (optional)

Directions:

1. With the scissors, cut one of the disposable cups in half across its width. The bottom piece (B) will be the base of the vessel.
2. Carefully cut away the rim from the top half. Cut the rim in half. This will become your handle (C).
3. Position the bottom half of the cup (B) that you just cut upside down and the second, uncut cup (A) on top of it right side up. Glue them together with the hot glue.
4. If you wish, you can make a spout: Cut out a small V shape, about 1 x 1 inch (2½ x 2½ cm) at the top of the cup that is on top (A). Attach a larger V shape from a piece of cardboard folded in half lengthwise in the center of the V with the hot-glue gun to form the spout.
5. Attach the handle (C) to the side of the vessel with the hot glue. Let dry.
6. Take small amounts of the air-drying clay at a time, closing the package tightly after each use, to keep out air. Press the clay between the thumb and first finger to form flat 2 x 2-inch (5 x 5-cm) pieces and press them onto the plastic cup vessel. Alternate between the two sides to keep the vessel from being too heavy on one side and falling over. Continue until the vessel is completely covered, including the rim.
7. Now cover the handle with the clay, reinforcing the two points where the handle was glued to the vessel. Let dry.

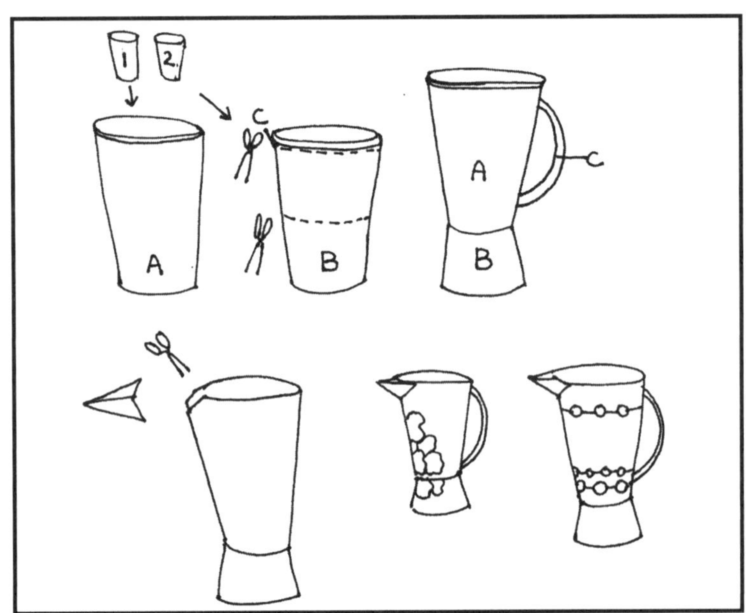

8. Paint the vessel with one or two layers of gold or silver glossy paint. Let dry.
9. Decorate the vessel with the small stones, beads, and metallic threads, using hot glue to attach them.

Mock Illuminated Manuscript AGES 10+

Note: Mixing the paints (part 1) can be done by ages 5+, with the help of an adult.

Illuminated manuscripts were usually made of vellum (kosher animal skins) and were written, drawn, and painted with handmade dyes and inks. We will be using homemade colors (you can use store-bought paints if you prefer) and thick Bristol art paper. For inspiration, look to Jewish resources for examples of illuminated manuscripts, ketubot, megillot, and Haggadot from around the world.

PART 1

Ingredients for homemade dyes include—boiled onion skins, carrots, blueberries, beets, red cabbage, spinach, paprika, turmeric, and ground charcoal or burnt wood, plus a multitude of other natural ingredients. A variety of natural paints can be made by combining the yellow of an egg with honey, wine, milk, linseed oil, and substances from a chemist.

Materials:

- 3 sheets of white copy paper, size 8½ x 11 inches (21 x 30 cm)
- Pencil
- Red, yellow, and blue powdered tempera paint or ready tempera or gouache paint
- 2 soft paintbrushes, ¼ or ½ inch (½ or 1½ cm)
- ½ teaspoon turmeric and ½ teaspoon sweet red paprika
- 3 paper hot cups

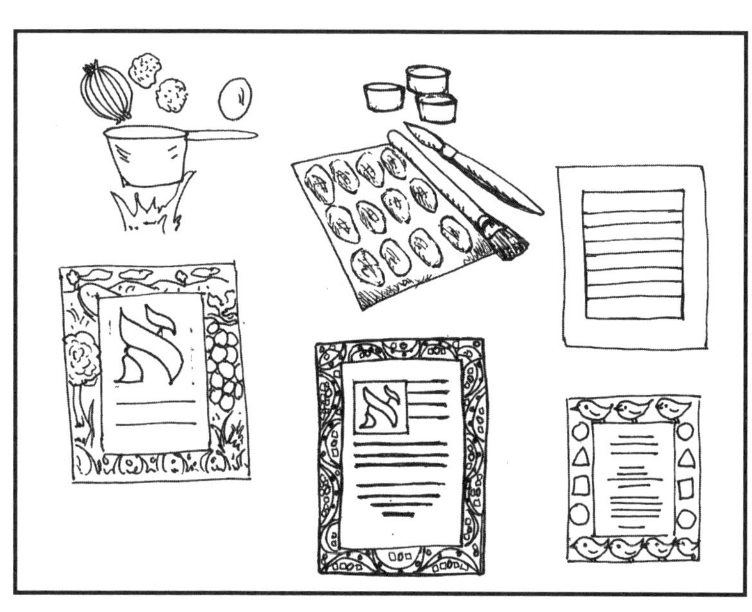

- A handful of onion skins
- The yolk of 1 egg
- Red, yellow, and blue food coloring
- 3 disposable paper plates

Directions:

1. Put the turmeric and the red paprika each in a separate hot cup. Pour over a small amount of boiling water, just enough to cover the spices. Let steep until the water changes color. Let sit one hour or more.
2. Place the onion skins in a pot and add water until the skins are mostly covered. Boil until most of the water evaporates and about one tablespoon is left. Squeeze out the skins, discard and pour the colored water into the last hot cup.
3. On each of the three plates, put a spoonful of the colored water from the cups.
4. Add about ¼ teaspoon of egg yolk onto each of the three plates.
5. With a brush, mix the two together and paint a stroke of each color on a separate sheet of paper.
6. Write on the paper the name of the dyes and the colors used.
7. Add a small amount of food coloring to each plate: red with the red paprika, yellow with turmeric, and blue with the onion skins. Add a bit more of the egg yolk and mix.
8. Paint a sample stroke on the paper with the same name.
9. Add a drop of paint to each plate. Red to red paprika, etc. Add more egg yolk. Paint a sample stroke on the paper with the same name.
10. Let the paints dry. Note the difference in the colors and how the natural ingredients soften the effects of the chemical ingredients. The natural colors will be very light and delicate.
11. Mix and test the colors with a brush on plain paper, dipping the brushes in water and wiping with paper towels before changing colors. Try overlapping one dyed color with a second layer or

another color. Try different batches of the same color to see how they appear on the paper.

Experiment and mix in store-bought tempera/gouache or colored inks. Mix small batches of the colors you will use. Once you have your colors, you're ready to design your illuminated manuscript.

PART 2

Materials:

- Good-quality Bristol or other paper that takes water, such as a smooth watercolor paper, at least 8½ x 11 inches (21 x 28 cm) in size
- Pencil, eraser, and ruler
- Thin paintbrushes, ⅛, ¼, and ½ inch (¼, ½, and 1½ cm)
- Natural or store-bought paints (see above)
- Gold or silver paint, powdered tempura (to be mixed with water) or acrylic (optional)
- Thin black marker, chisel-tip thin black marker, or calligraphy pen

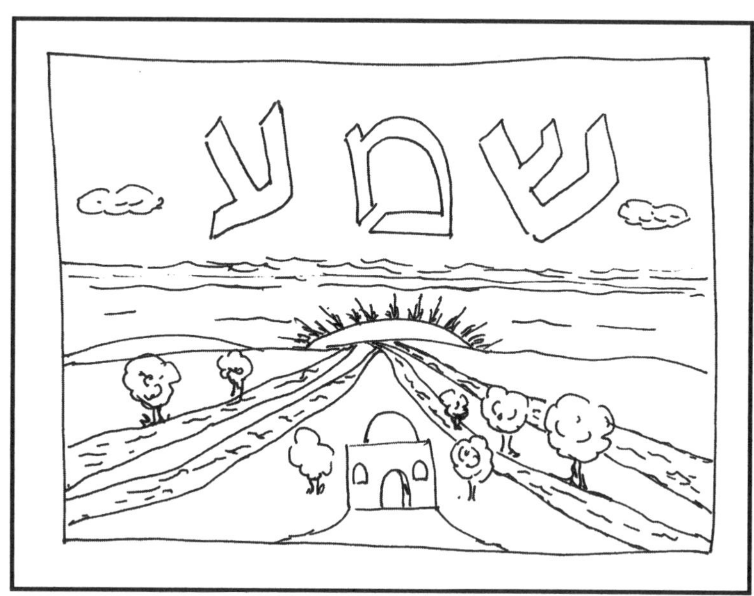

Directions:

1. Choose a verse from Psalms or another biblical or Talmudic passage. Here are some examples:
    - Psalm 23: "A psalm by David. Hashem is my shepherd, I shall not lack. In lush meadows He lays me down, beside tranquil waters He leads me. He restores my soul."

- The *Shema*: "Hear O Israel: Hashem is our God, Hashem, the One and Only."
- The morning thanks upon awakening: "I gratefully thank You, O living and eternal King, for You have returned my soul within me with compassion; abundant is Your faithfulness."
- A poem you wrote
- Your name, if you want to keep the writing simple

2. Now plan your theme and design: Choose one large word or large letter for the "opening word" that will be enclosed in a large square and painted especially beautifully. It can be centered or to the far left at the top of the paper. Decide how much space you will need for the verse. With the pencil and ruler, outline the border space on the Bristol. Make ruled lines in the area reserved for the verse.
3. Design your border. The border can be much larger than the following measurements but not less; it should be roomy with enough space for your pictures and verse. Measure a border around the area you have designated for the verse about 2 inches (5 cm) from both sides, 4 inches (10 cm) from the bottom, and 3 inches (7½ cm) from the top. To make your border, choose from a scene of nature, animals, a floral design, intertwining geometric shapes, scroll, or lacework.
4. Practice drawing your border design on plain paper and then copy it onto the Bristol paper.
5. Paint the enlarged letter or word with your special colors. If you have gold or silver paint, use them here. If you're using gold or silver acrylic paint, you may want to dilute it with water to match the delicate transparencies of the natural dyes. Fill in the enclosed area around the letter or word.
6. Paint in the border. The border should be filled in with images, shapes, and color. Other areas except the area of the verse text can be filled in if desired. Let the paints dry.
7. Write the verse lightly with pencil in the lined area, making sure that all the words will fit.

8. Trace over the words with the thin or chisel black marker or calligraphy pen. Erase the pencil lines where needed.
9. If you wish, outline the decorations and illustrations in the border and the main letter or word with the thin marker.

In Summary: Jewish Art in History

- Jewish art, from ancient times until today, has primarily been defined by the values and materials available at that time and place.
- In ancient times, art expressed religious beliefs in the form of idols and icons representing the pagan gods. For Jews, on the other hand, any depiction of God was akin to idol worship.
- Among the artifacts that survived from ancient times are synagogues decorated with mosaics and frescos, coins and seals, gold glass, and tapestries using the age-old art of weaving.
- In medieval and Renaissance times, the art of illuminating manuscripts reached its peak, providing inspiration through decoration and ornamentation.
- In medieval times, Jewish craftsmen, artisans, and artists were often limited by the restrictions imposed on them by their host countries. Nevertheless, they managed to produce art to beautify the mitzvot that they fulfilled the entire year.
- The loosening of restrictions on Jews in the nineteenth and twentieth centuries produced outstanding Jewish art by those sensitive and loyal to their noble roots.
- We can see through the eyes of the people who came before us by contemplating the art of bygone eras.

Questions and Wonder

1. Have you seen Jewish ritual objects such as Kiddush cups or menorahs from other times or countries? Where did you see them? What did they look like?

2. What is your favorite picture book? What do you like about it?
3. How does an illustration complement the text of a manuscript? How do we unify the design to fit the text?

Making the Most of the Subject Matter

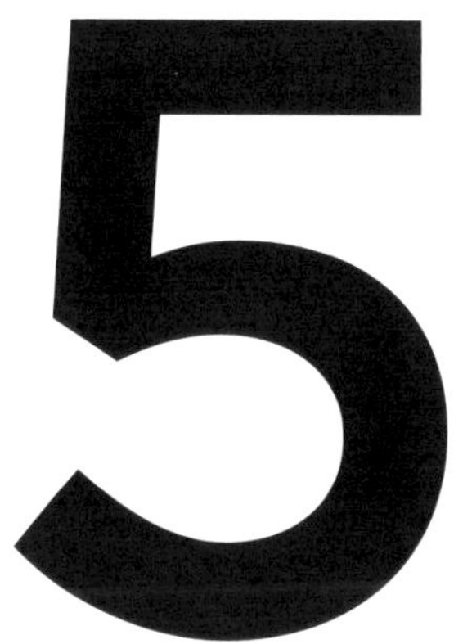

Several years ago, when the idea for this project came to me, I was struggling to put words down about Jewish art. Where to begin? The subject matter was endless. My main points—that Jewish art beautifully reflects Jewish life and that creativity is about options—were clear in my mind. But I needed to broaden my subject matter. I needed material, sources, anecdotes, and examples.

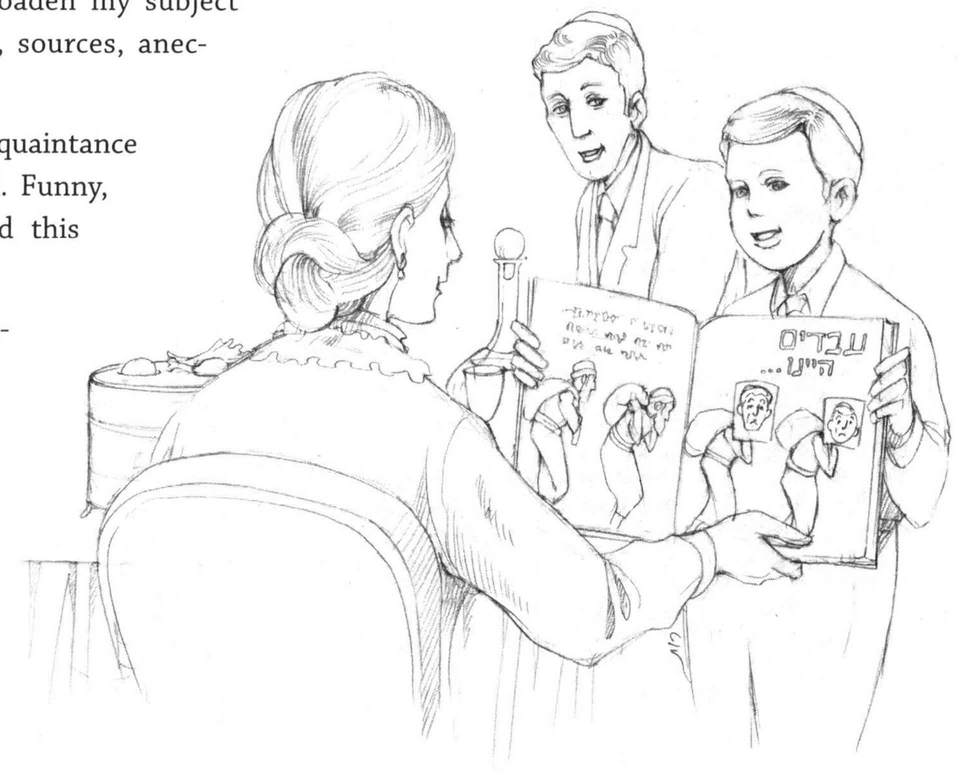

The phone rang. An acquaintance was returning a phone call. Funny, though, I had never called this person. He thought I had.

"Hello, this is G. I'm returning your call."

"Oh, but I didn't call you," I replied.

"Sorry, then. Good-bye."

"Wait! It's interesting that you called..."

While I had him on the phone, I realized he was exactly the person

Notes and Sketches

I needed. I asked him to introduce me to an acquaintance of his—an expert on Jewish art.

It was clear that I had help from Upstairs on this project—a sign to go ahead and try out my abilities.

Try yours. Connect to Jewish subjects. Use the channel of art to understand Jewish life. Find your connection. Do the same with your children and help them find their connection. Your life will be all the richer.

A Picture of Daily Jewish Life

What is everyday life for us? Have you sat in the kitchen and peeled potatoes or sat at your desk doing homework? Sounds very average, perhaps, but you are not average, and everyday activities are an important part of life if we give them importance. Depictions of everyday life in a Jewish home are depictions of everyday Jewish life, and these are just as relevant as the big events in Jewish history.

Our everyday activities, such as walking to school or cleaning our room or preparing dinner, can be portrayed in what is called a "genre painting." In art, genre means depicting scenes from everyday life.

Now pay attention to the special days—holidays, Shabbat, days of joy (such as Tu b'Shevat [the New Year for the trees] or Purim [celebration of the Jews' salvation from the evil Haman]), or days of introspection and reevaluation (such as Yom Kippur and Tishah b'Av [the ninth day of Av, a day of mourning the Holy Temple]). Reexperience the gamut of human emotions as you recall the cycle of the Jewish year. Feel the high points and the possibility of building and renewing yourself with each experience—the chance to start the new year fresh on Rosh Hashanah (Jewish New Year), bringing the light into the dark times on Chanukah, the unabashed joy of Purim, or the anguish of loss on Tishah b'Av.

Can you picture yourself sitting in a temporary structure on Sukkot, with the stars peeping through the roof? How about (successfully!) blowing a ram's horn on Rosh Hashanah?

Yes, these are all Jewish subjects. They are real and they are you.

Examples from the Bible

Notes and Sketches

Of course, you needn't do only genre paintings. What about scenes from the Bible? Stories about great Jewish personalities that you've read or heard? We can call them illustrations of our biblical history—of ancient times far from our lives today—but remember that much of what took place at the inception of Jewish history is a prototype for today.

Ruth, a Moabite princess-turned-Jewish convert, was a penniless widow reduced to picking up the leftover stalks of wheat on the ground, yet she was still full of dignity and modesty. Her sacrifice to become part of the Jewish people gave her the merit of being King David's great-grandmother. She is a prototype of humility and devotion.

When the Jewish nation camped in the desert after their release from years of slavery in Egypt, they set up their tents so that the entrances did not face the other entrances. In this way, they provided privacy for each family. They were a prototype of modesty for us today.[39]

Nature as a Jewish Subject

A depiction of Jewish life can even include nature. Take a walk in the botanical gardens surrounded by a lush variety of tropical plants and choose one to illustrate. Or how about an awe-inspiring view from a mountaintop overlooking a green valley that trails out in the distance to the mouth of the ocean?

This is the Hand of creation before us. Appreciating nature, too, is a Jewish concept—taking the opportunity to notice the systems, complexity, and variety of the wonders of Creation reminds us of our Creator and brings us closer to Him. The Rambam says this is how one comes to love God—by looking at His creations.[40]

The wonders of nature not only remind us of our Creator, they offer a retreat from the daily grind. The pure ambiance of nature revitalizes us and gives us a fresh perspective from our daily challenges. The intricate and delicate system of nature promotes calmness and introspection. It is

---

39 Numbers 24:5, and Talmud, *Baba Batra* 60A, and the commentary of Rashi there.

40 *Mishneh Torah, Hilchot Yesodei HaTorah* 2:2. Rambam is an acronym for Rabbi Moshe ben Maimon, also known as Maimonides. He was a medieval Jewish philosopher, Torah scholar, and physician, c. 1137–1204.

a temporary taste of freedom from worldly affairs. King David expressed that if only he had the wings of a dove he would fly far away, finding rest and a place to dwell far in the wilderness.[41] The prophets Elijah and Elisha found a retreat in the mountains, at times distancing themselves from contemporary distractions. Great sages followed their example.[42] A painting mimicking nature can inspire a calming effect.

Draw a Walk in Nature AGES 7+

Draw the following scene: a child walking on a path lined by trees and birds. Your drawing should evoke the wonder of the child as he or she walks through a sunlit bouquet of greenery and chirping birds. You may want to pull out some books on nature for inspiration.

Materials:

- Copy paper, size 8½ x 11 inches (21 x 30 cm) or art paper
- Pencil and eraser
- Thin colored markers
- Thin black marker

Directions:

1. Begin by drawing a horizontal line with the pencil. It should be slightly below the center of the paper. Draw a second line 2 inches (5 cm) below that line. This will be your path. The path, of course, need not be straight; you can curve it or draw it diagonally if you wish.
2. Draw a group of four to ten trees along the top line and several that begin on the lower line, leaving spaces to see the path clearly. The trunks of the trees on the upper level and the foliage of the trees on the lower levels may overlap. Try to include a variety of trees.
3. Insert a drawing of a child on the path, his height reaching about ¼–½ the height of the trees. (Young children will draw

41 Psalms 55:7.

42 Rabbi Moshe Chaim Luzzatto, *The Path of the Just*, ch. 15.

a boy or girl the same height as the trees or larger.)

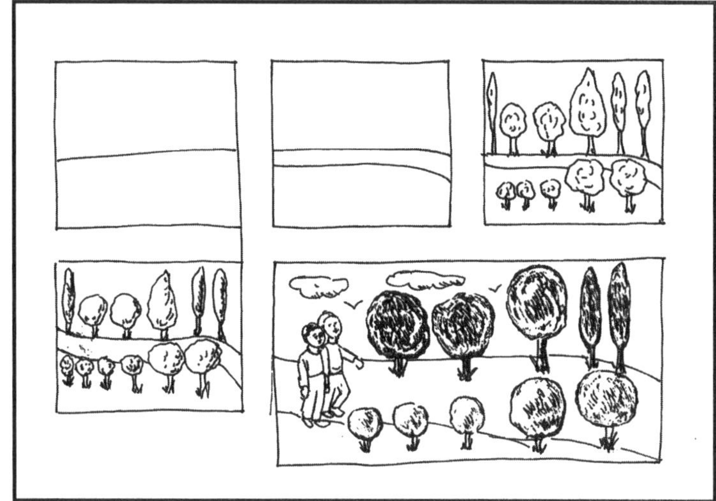

4. Outline all the pencil lines with the thin black pen.
5. Color in the drawing with the colored markers. Use a variety of greens and browns for the trees. Note how many types of greens and browns you can find. With names of colors like light green, emerald green, olive green, dark green, Van Dyke brown, dark brown, and red brown, you will be able to make the leaves and branches appear interesting and alive.
6. Don't forget the golden yellows and oranges and blues: Show light (yellows and whites) and sky (blues) coming through the trees. Add birds (oranges and bright yellows) flying in the sky or perched on the ground.
7. Details are always important, so put in a few stones and small rocks on the path. Enjoy your drawing as is or use as a preliminary drawing for a painting the size of your choice.

The Mitzvot

Another good topic for an art project is a good deed or mitzvah. The mitzvot represent our relationship with our Creator. When we do something because He commanded it, we bring the heavens down to the earth and earthly things to a heavenly level. We do that by using physical objects, such as a menorah or Kiddush cup, to do mitzvot. Even the food we eat can be elevated to a heavenly level after we have made a blessing over it.

Because the list seems endless, it's a good idea to choose a subject that you have learned about or one that you want to learn about. If you have a thorough knowledge and understanding of the mitzvah or ceremonial object you are depicting, you will be able to put your own self into the artwork and create something truly unique. Connect yourself to the subject by using all your resources and feelings about the topic.

A train is waiting at the station to take you to countless destinations of enrichment. Jewish life has it all. You need only choose what to depict.

To get you started, here are a few subjects to choose from. See which one resonates with you. A topic you feel connected with will result in a more authentic, unique portrayal.

Choose Your Subject

You have a seemingly endless ocean of subject matter before you. And each subject can be broken down to different levels and depicted with a variety of art materials. The basic projects that are suggested at the end of each of the topics below will give you an idea of how to illustrate the subject matter. Use them as stepping stones to inspire your own vision of the subject or to depict other topics not mentioned here.

The Six Days of Creation

The Torah teaches that God created the world in six days.[43] The description of the Creation in the Torah and the commentators is vivid and lends itself to many themes: darkness and light, heaven and earth, crawling things, animals and fish, nature, and man and woman, to name a few. Read the passages in the Torah that describe the Creation[44] and choose one theme or depict a mix of themes for contrast.

Here is an opportunity to draw animals. Choose one group of animals mentioned in the Torah to draw. Concentrate on drawing all the variations and similarities among the animals in the same family. Copy from illustrations or photos of animals that you find in books. Don't worry about perfection. Be true to your style while slowly trying to improve.

When drawing, it's best to begin with geometric shapes (circles, ovals, squares, and triangles). Fit these together like a puzzle or building blocks (for example, a triangle on top of a square). Then gently soften

43 Genesis 2:1–2; Exodus 20:1–2.

44 Genesis, ch. 1, Genesis 2:1, Exodus 20.

and round out the shapes. Sketch lightly at first and then go over your new pencil lines to sharpen them. Put in details (eyes, nose, hoofs, and claws) and texture (fur, wool, or hair) last.

Draw Animals AGES 7+

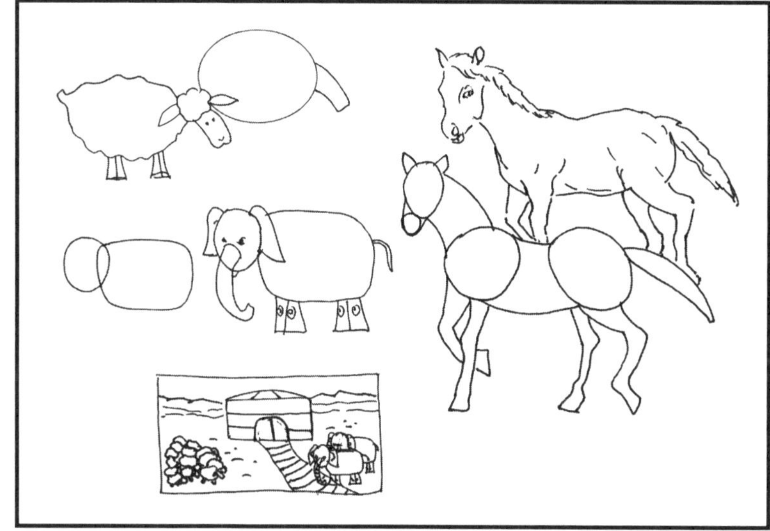

Materials:

- 2 sheets of copy paper, size 8½ x 11 inches (21 x 30 cm) or larger.
- Pencil and eraser
- Fine-tipped black pen
- Colored markers or colored pencils

Directions:

1. Choose an animal from a picture book. Do a few practices to get used to the shapes and proportions of the animals.
2. Begin by drawing lightly with a pencil the basic geometric shapes of the animal. Soften the lines into curves to lightly reshape the animal realistically.
3. Draw the animal a second time for added practice. Or, draw another animal from the same family. Try a lion and a cat or a wolf and dog.
4. Put in the details (eyes, nose, hoofs, and claws) and texture (fur, wool, or hair).
5. Go over the pencil lines with the pen making any changes as you draw.
6. Add shading or color in with markers or colored pencils. Note the light and dark areas of fur or hair.
7. Redo any places that need to stand out, using the pen.
8. Add a background: Noah's Ark or land, sky, mountains, trees, and rocks. Put yourself in the picture with the animals if you'd like.

The Torah

Two thousand years after Creation, God gave the Torah to the Jewish people on Har Sinai.[45] Since the Torah is the Jewish people's guide to live a proper life, it is treated with the utmost respect. There are laws that tell us how a Torah scroll should be written and how it should be stored. All Torah scrolls are covered with special coverings—works of art in themselves—made either of rich embroidered fabric, carved and gilded wood, or of silver or brass, to indicate the preciousness of the object within.

As the center of Jewish life, the Torah is a good subject for Jewish art. You can depict the giving of the Torah at Sinai, the reading of the Torah in the synagogue, the ark that holds the Torah scrolls, with its embroidered velvet curtain, or a Torah scroll and its ornaments, including the Torah case, shield, mantle, crown, binder, pointer, and finials.

While creating a drawing with the Torah as its focus, think about why Jews make beautiful ornaments for Torah scrolls and treat the Torah with respect. Try drawing or painting an open Torah scroll with a picture of Har Sinai and the *Luchot Habrit* in the background. Here is an abbreviated, easy method:

Torah Scroll and Har Sinai AGES 6+

Materials:

- Copy paper, size 8½ x 11 inches (21 x 30 cm)
- Pencil and eraser
- Colored markers
- Fine-tipped black pen

Directions:

1. Set the paper horizontally on the table. On the bottom two-thirds of a sheet of 8½ x 11-in paper, draw a rectangle measuring 2½ x 3 inches (6 x 7½ cm).

45 Exodus 19:20.

2. Draw four ovals or circles: one above the upper-right corner, one above the upper-left corner, one below the lower-right corner and one below the lower-left corner of the rectangle.
3. Draw lines to connect the top and bottom circles on each side.
4. Draw handles—long ovals, ½ x 1 inch (1½ x 2½ cm) vertically on each of the four ovals, above the upper ovals, and below the lower ovals. Now you have a basic Torah-scroll shape.
5. Draw a line across the paper a few inches above the upper handles of the Torah scroll.
6. On the line, off center, draw Har Sinai and the *luchot* on its peak. Draw rays of light emanating from the *luchot*. If you wish, add clouds and small mountains.

Optional: In place of the flat klaf (parchment), draw the top and bottom vertical lines with a few parallel curves in them.

Use this as a practice drawing for a larger painting, or finish the drawing by tracing over the lines with black pen and adding color.

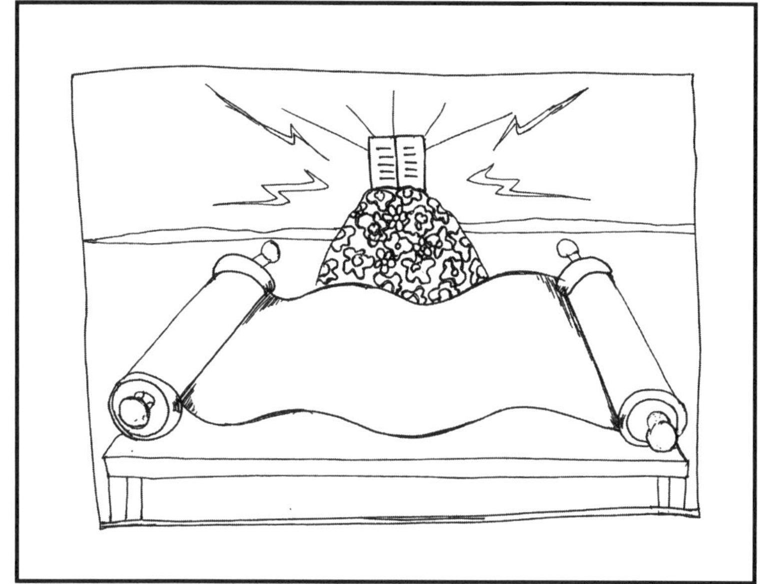

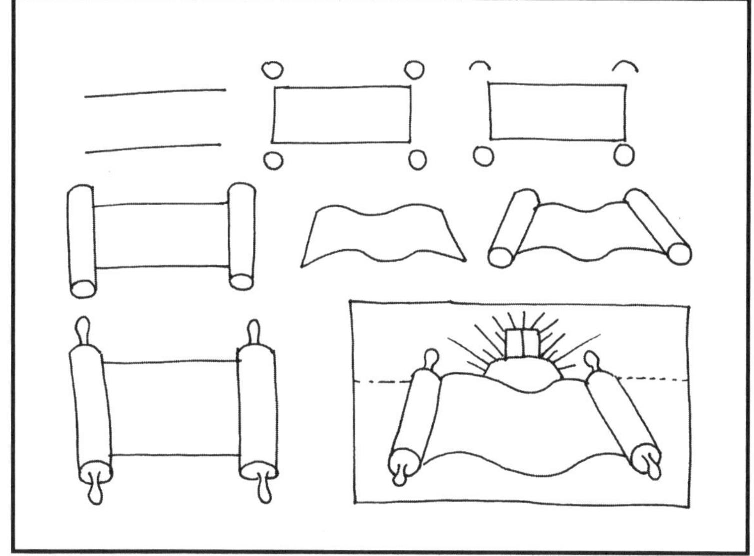

Shabbat

Shabbat really starts with the preparations beforehand. Preparations usually start on Thursday, though some do prepare something in honor of the coming Shabbat every day of the week. Since no cooking is allowed on Shabbat, preparations usually entail shopping and cooking for the three festive meals that will be eaten, as well as cleaning the home to make it nice and tidy in honor of Shabbat, and buying and cleaning special clothes to wear on this day.

Depictions of Shabbat may include a busy market street with people shopping for Shabbat, preparing the house and the food for Shabbat, setting the table, lighting the Shabbat candles, giving tzedakah (charity) before lighting, parents blessing their children on Friday night, walking to the *beit knesset*, davening (praying) in the *beit knesset*, the Kiddush wine and challah, singing at the table, and Havdalah.

You can paint a woman lighting the Shabbat candles, and as you do so, imagine what it's like to give so much time and preparation for a prized event that comes each week. Or, make a decorated tzedakah box for giving charity before bringing in the Shabbat.

Tzedakah Box AGES 6+

Materials:

- Thick paper or copy paper, large enough to fit around and cover your container
- Pencil and eraser
- Ruler (a metal ruler is best when cutting with a craft knife)
- Fine-tipped black marker
- Colored markers—red and pink, yellow and orange, plus other colors
- Hot-glue gun
- White plastic craft glue
- Cardboard, at least as thick as the shirt board from the dry cleaners, or Styrofoam sandwich board that is 4 x 7 inches (10 x 18 cm)
- Scissors
- A container that is about 4½ inches (11 cm) high and 4 inches (10 cm) in diameter with a removable plastic lid (such as a Quaker oatmeal container or store-bought frosting container)
- Clear liquid acrylic coating to add shine and endurance (optional)

Directions:

1. Measure the thick paper around the container and cut it to fit. Place the cut paper on a flat surface.

2. With the pencil and ruler, draw bricks ½ inch (1½ cm) apart horizontally and vertically. Next, draw a door on the bottom with your family's name on it and two windows above the door. Put more windows around the "house." Add children looking out the windows, Shabbat candles burning in one window, perhaps a vase of flowers in another, and a bowl of fruit in yet another. Add flowers on the ground, and include birds and trees.

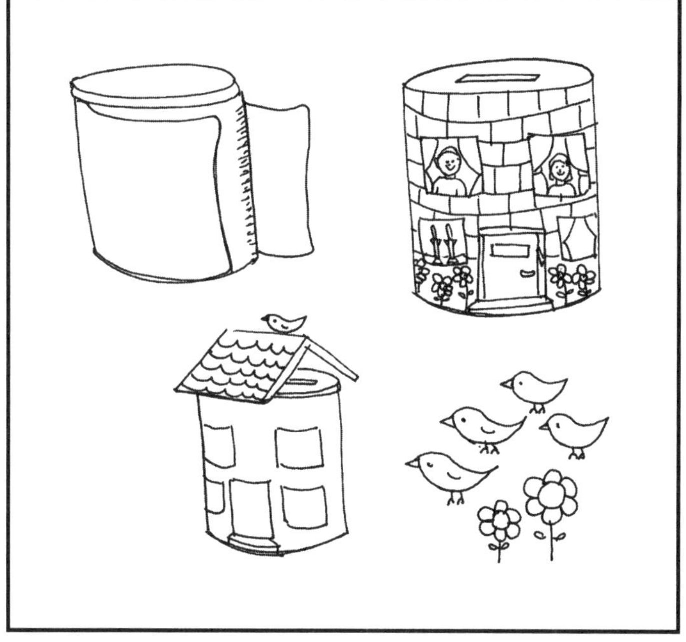

3. Color the bricks with thick markers. Use red and pink, alternating the two colors to form a pattern. Color in the rest of the drawing. With the fine-tipped marker, outline any part of the drawing for clarity.

4. With the white craft glue, attach the drawing onto the container. Cut a hole, ½ x 1½ inch (1½ x 4 cm), in the plastic lid for the tzedakah money to go through. It's best to cut the opening with a craft knife and metal ruler.

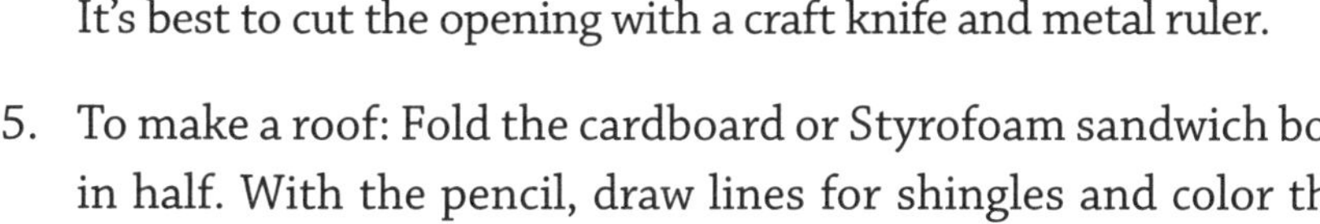

5. To make a roof: Fold the cardboard or Styrofoam sandwich board in half. With the pencil, draw lines for shingles and color them in, alternating red and pink. On a separate piece of paper, draw two birds, 1 x 1 inch (2½ x 2½ cm), and color them bright yellow with orange beaks. Cut them out, and glue a bird onto each side of the roof.

6. Attach the roof to the edges of the lid with hot glue. Make sure the roof is high enough so it does not block the slit for the coins.

7. Optional: Remove lid, and brush on a coat of clear acrylic. Let dry. Cover your tzedakah box with the lid/roof and drop in your first tzedakah coins.

The Jewish Festivals

Almost every month of the Jewish year has a special day that commemorates a momentous event in Jewish history. This is not just nostalgia—each Jewish month and corresponding holiday evokes the same feelings and messages that the Jewish people felt and learned on the day of the event.

The festival of Pesach, for example, commemorates the Jewish people's exodus from Egypt. Since then, every year, the Jewish people have the opportunity to feel as if they themselves left Egypt. The eating of matzah (unleavened bread), the Seder, and other mitzvot of the holiday are designed to evoke this feeling.

The Jewish festivals, then, contain much symbolism, and each has special mitzvot and customs associated with it. They are a rich wellspring of themes from which the artist can draw.

Creating a homemade calendar is a wonderful and creative way to learn about and mark the days of the Jewish festivals.

Calendar of Festivals AGES 7+

Materials:

- 12 sheets of copy paper, size 8½ x 11 inches (21 x 30 cm)
- Pencil and eraser
- Ruler
- Colored markers
- Stapler

Directions:

1. Copy the page layout of a monthly calendar onto an 8½ x 11-in sheet of paper: with a ruler and pencil, draw horizontal and vertical lines to make squares representing each day of the month.
2. Copy the page eleven times in your printer or photocopy machine, or copy each page by hand.

3. Write the names of the months, in both Hebrew and English, the days of the week, and the numbers for the dates.
4. Look up the holidays and draw a simple symbol for each festival (such as a shofar for Rosh Hashanah or scales for Yom Kippur).
5. Include important family dates: anniversaries, births, yahrzeits (memorialization of the date that a family member passed away), etc.
6. Staple the twelve sheets of paper together at the top and decorate with markers. Use the calendar for your daily notes.

If you want to get more creative, make a round calendar with 3-D sculpted objects.

3-D Circular Calendar AGES 8+

Materials:

- Pencil and eraser
- Ruler
- Acrylic paints: white, red, yellow, blue, and brown
- Paintbrushes, ⅛ and 1 inch (¼ cm and 2½ cm)
- Hot-glue gun
- Cardboard, 1/16 inch (⅛ cm) thick, or a piece of wood, cut into a circle, the size of a pie or large pot
- Air-drying clay
- Hook (optional)

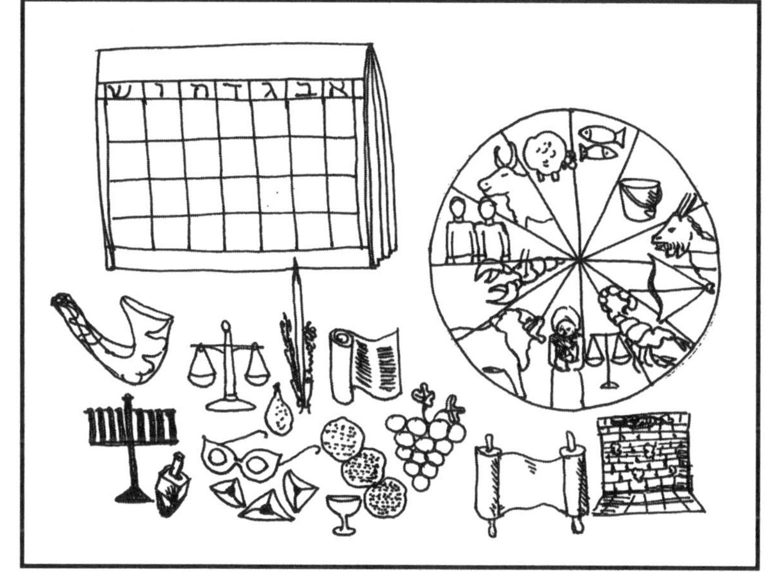

Directions:

1. Paint the cardboard or wood with solid white or other light-colored acrylic paint. Let dry.

2. With the pencil and ruler, divide the circle into twelve equal-sized "pizza slices."
3. With the air-drying clay, form the symbols of each holiday—a shofar for Rosh Hashanah, scales for Yom Kippur, a sukkah for Sukkot, a Torah scroll for Simchat Torah, a menorah for Chanukah, the *shivat ha-minim* (seven species of produce from the Land of Israel) for Tu b'Shevat, a mask or megillah for Purim, a Haggadah or matzah for Pesach, a bonfire or cave and carob tree for Lag BaOmer, Har Sinai and the *luchot* for Shavuot, the Kotel (Western Wall) for Tishah b'Av, etc. Let clay dry a few days.
4. With a small brush, paint each clay symbol with appropriate colors. Mix colors for greens, oranges, and purples. Add tiny bits of white to make pastels and tints. If desired, paint miniature paintings in the background of each section on the wood.
5. Let the paint dry. Glue the clay symbols onto the board with the hot glue.
6. Write the names of the months with a letter stencil or freehand.
7. Attach a hook to hang the calendar, if desired.

Besides commemorating the holidays with a calendar, you can also create works of art special to each festival or holiday.[46] Styrofoam sandwich board (SSB) is a great substitute for cardboard or balsa wood and is the primary material used in the following projects.

Festival SSB Construction Projects

Materials:

- Styrofoam sandwich board (thin Styrofoam enclosed in paper on 2 sides)
- Protected cutting surface
- Craft knife

46 For more projects related to the festivals, see the appendix at the back of this book.

- 12-inch (30-cm) metal ruler
- Pencil
- Hot-glue gun
- Scissors
- Optional: acrylic paint, markers

Directions:

1. Measure and cut board on a protected cutting surface. To make box forms: Measure out the total of four sides. Cut **halfway** through each of the sections with three scored (serrated) fold lines. Be careful not to separate and cut through. Scoring the board allows us to fold the board on straight lines.
2. Stand up and fold into a box form. Cut out top and bottom pieces. Hot glue all parts and reinforce folded corners.
3. Decorate and finish project.

Note: Adults should cut the boards and hot glue the pieces.

Purim Box with a Clown On Top AGES 8+

THE BOX

Materials and directions:

Measure and cut board 12 inches long and 9 inches tall (30 x 23 cm). **Score** into four parts at 3 x 9 inches (7½ x 23 cm) each. This will be three cuts halfway through the board. *Do not* cut through board. Bend into tall box shape. Cut out top and bottom pieces 3 x 3 inches (7½ x 7½ cm) each. Hot glue all pieces and reinforce the seams with extra hot glue.

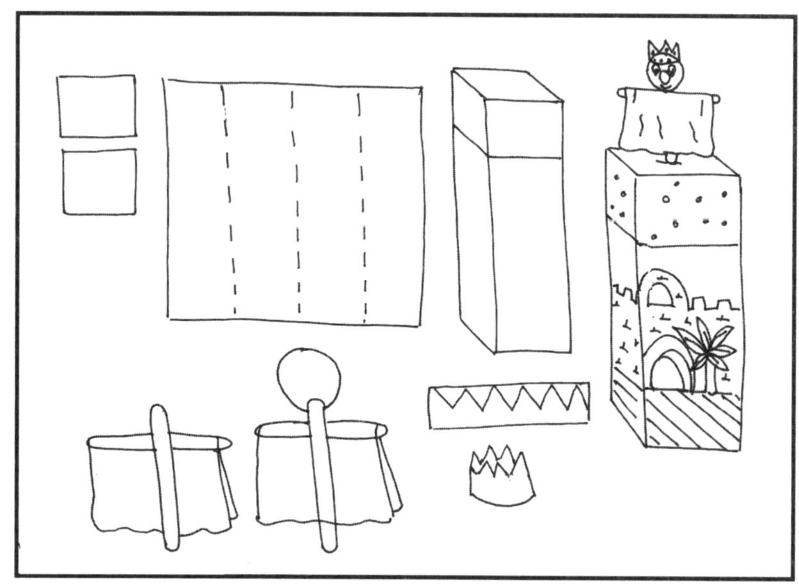

Measure 2 inches (5 cm) down from the top. Mark with a pencil and cut off the top with the craft knife. Reattach the top at the back with cloth tape like a hinge. Paint, decorate, and illustrate portions of the Purim story.

THE CLOWN

Materials:

- Styrofoam sandwich board and cutting materials. See above list.
- 1 x 1-inch (2½ x 2½-cm) Styrofoam ball
- 2 craft sticks (ice cream size)
- Material, 3 x 5 inches (7½ x 12½ cm), or metallic or crepe paper
- 2 x 2-inch (5 x 5-cm) thick metallic paper or thin board
- 2 plastic eyes, 1 small pom-pom nose and other scrap material for beard, crown, etc.

Directions:

1. Hot glue two craft sticks crosswise with the horizontal stick above the center.
2. Fold material in half and cut small hole in top center. Insert over stick form. Hot glue in place. With craft knife, make incision in bottom of head. Apply hot glue and insert onto top of stick.
3. Cut out a crown from thick metallic paper and glue on head.
4. Attach eyes, nose, and other features.
5. Make an incision ¾ inch (2 cm) on top of box.
6. Apply hot glue and insert bottom of puppet.
7. Fill with Purim treats, *mishlo'ach manot* (food gifts sent on Purim day), and a wine bottle. Add a card and give to a friend or neighbor.

Chanukah Living Room Miniature AGES 7+

Materials:

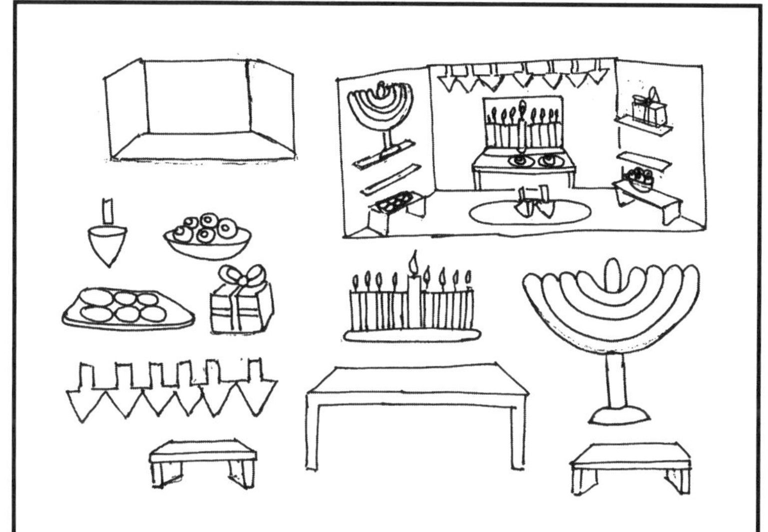

- Styrofoam sandwich board cutting materials and hot glue (see above list)
- Styrofoam sandwich board, size 30 x 15 inches (76 x 38 cm)
- Acrylic paint: brown or brick for outside wall and red, blue, yellow, and white for objects in room
- Brushes, ⅛ and ½ inch (¼ and 1½ cm)
- Markers
- Optional: thick, archival quality (permanent, acid-free) paper designed for scrapbooking is great for covering the walls and floors. Have enough to cover the inside wall and floor in two matching colors or designs.
- Thick paper (for carpet), 2 x 3½ inches (5 x 9 cm)
- Paper for dreidel accordion decoration, 1 x 3¼ inches (2½ x 7½ cm)
- Air-drying modeling clay (Das)

Directions:

1. Cut out wall, 4 x 9 inches (10 x 23 cm).
2. Score (serrate) at 2 inches (5 cm), 5 inches (12½ cm), and again at 2 inches (5 cm). Fold in the two sides.
3. Cut out a window in center of wall, 2 x 2 inches (5 x 5 cm).
4. Cut out floor, 7¼ x 4 inches (18½ x 10 cm).
5. Cut out shelves—cut four of them, 2 x ¾ inches (5 x 2 cm) each

6. Cut out one large table, 4 x 1¼ inches (10 x 3 cm). **Score** 1 inch (2½ cm) at both ends and bend legs down.
7. Cut out two small tables, 2½ x 1 inch (6 x 2½ cm). **Score** ½ inch (1½ cm) at both ends and bend legs down.
8. Paint back of wall to resemble wood, stone, or bricks. Dry.
9. Paint or "wallpaper" inside wall, shelves, and floor. Dry.
10. Assemble wall, floor, shelves, and tables with hot glue. Two shelves on each of the side walls. The large table is under the window and the small tables on both outer edges of the floor.
11. Cut out oval from paper for a carpet. Paint or color with markers. Dry. Glue onto center of floor.
12. Fold a small piece of paper accordion-fashion four times. Draw a dreidel and cut out in one long strip, paper-doll fashion, leaving one side connected. Draw in three more miniature dreidels and color with markers. Hang miniature decoration across top of the window.
13. Create small Chanukah objects from air-drying clay to fit on tables and shelves. Dry. Paint with acrylic paint. Dry. Hot glue in place.
    - menorah
    - *latkes* (potato pancakes) on a tray
    - *sufganiyot* (jelly donuts without a hole) in a bowl
    - gifts tied with a ribbon—can be drawn on paper, colored, and cut out in place of using the clay
    - one or two dreidels—can be hot glued standing up on top of carpet

Enjoy and display.

Holy Sites

It's customary to visit the gravesites of righteous people and pray that they advocate for you in Heaven. Although not all righteous people were buried in Eretz Yisrael, there are many holy gravesites throughout the country. In fact, all of the Land of Israel is considered holy, especially Jerusalem and the site of the Kotel, where the Holy Temple once stood.

Many of these sites, built thousands of years ago, are also beautiful, built of ancient stones and often surrounded by a beautiful landscape. Some sites that you can depict in your art are Me'arat Hamachpelah (the burial site of Adam, Eve, and the Patriarchs and Matriarchs), the tomb of Rachel, the tomb of Rabbi Shimon bar Yochai in Meron, and the Kotel. Jewish people believe in life and in sanctifying life. At the same time, they have tremendous reverence for their ancestors and the holy sites where they are buried.

Tomb of Rachel, SSB Construction AGES 7+

Learn about Rachel, one of the four Matriarchs, and the significance of her tomb in Bethlehem. (See Styrofoam sandwich board [SSB] directions, page 91. See #7 below in list of Holy Sites.)

Materials:

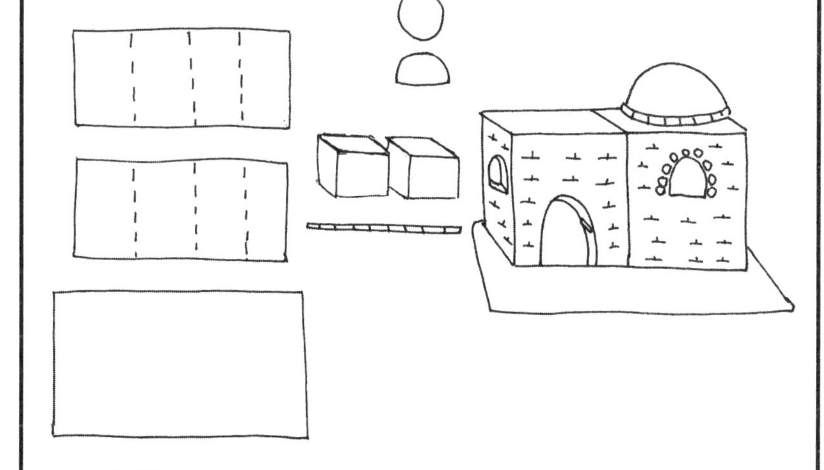

- Styrofoam sandwich board (5 mm thick), 30 x 20 inches (76 x 51 cm). You will have leftover for other projects. Divide the SSB into:
    - Walls, 20 x 2 inches (51 x 5 cm)
    - A base, 6 x 3½ inches (15 x 9 cm)
    - A thin strip, 12 x ¼ inch (30 x 1 cm)
- Styrofoam ball, 2 inches (5 cm)
- Pencil, metal ruler, craft knife, hot-glue gun
- Paint: cream, light browns, yellow, whites, and green
- Brushes: ¼ and ½ inch (½ and 1½ cm)

Directions:

1. Cut the 20 x 2-inch (51 x 5-cm) SSB into two pieces of 8 x 2 inches (20 x 5 cm) and two pieces of 2 x 2 inches (5 x 5 cm)
2. Score each piece every 2 inches (5 cm), being careful not to cut through, and bend into a box of four sides.
3. Hot glue the two pieces of 2 x 2 inches (5 x 5 cm) on the top of each box.
4. Glue the two boxes together. Glue on the base.
5. Cut the Styrofoam ball in half. Glue on top of the second square (right side facing you).
6. Score (serrate) the thin strip every ¼ inch (½ cm) and bend to fit around the dome and glue. Save extra SSB for another project.
7. Draw an arched door way with a mezuzah on the lintel (frame) and a window on the side of the left box. Draw an arched window on the front of the second box (with the dome).
8. Paint the surface to resemble Jerusalem stone blocks. Draw a path on the base, and paint green around it.

Picture Charades of Holy Sites AGES 9+

Teach children about their heritage and the famous holy sites in Eretz Yisrael with a game of Picture Charades!

Materials:

- 1 or 2 sheets of copy paper per player, size 8½ x 11 inches (21 x 30 cm)
- Pencils
- 8 or more 2 x 3-inch (5 x 7½-cm) index cards

Directions:

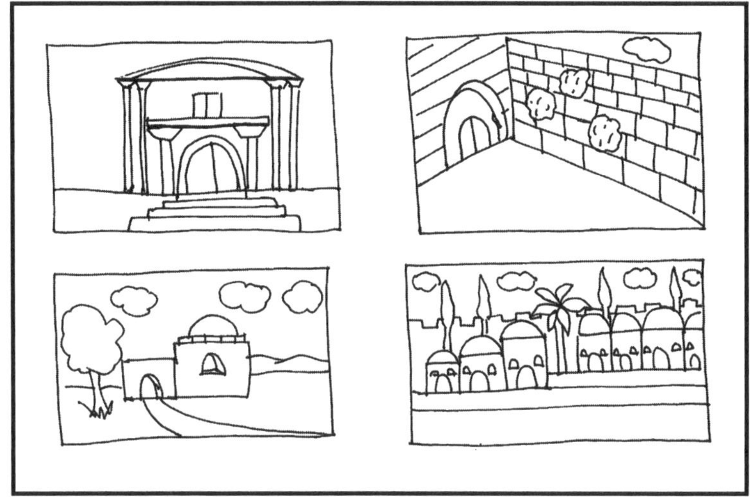

1. Write the name of one holy site on each index card.
2. Give a blank paper and a pencil for each player.
3. The player whose turn it is picks a card from the top of the pile. He or she has one minute to draw a picture of the site (stick figures are perfectly okay).
4. The other players have thirty seconds to call out its name and state its significance.
5. Alternatively, a parent or teacher draws the site on a large paper or dry-erase board, and the children guess and explain the importance of the holy place.

Before beginning, familiarize the players with the sites and their relevance to us today. Here are eight that came to mind when I created this game:

1. Eretz Yisrael (the Land of Israel)—the land is the center of the world, and it is the place where the Jewish people can fulfill special mitzvot that pertain to the land: the laws of tithes (where a percentage of the produce is given to Levites and poor people) and *shemittah* (where the land is left fallow once every seven years). A map of Israel can be drawn with symbols or little pictures of mitzvot.
2. Jerusalem—also known as the "Holy City," is a focus of religious life. Here is where the Holy Temple was built, and the Jewish people would make a pilgrimage to Jerusalem three times a year: for the festivals of Pesach, Shavuot, and Sukkot. Of all the nations who have attempted to conquer Jerusalem, it is only the Jews who have been blessed to make it prosper. It is said that ten measures of beauty came down to earth, and nine were taken by Jerusalem. Roads leading to the Kotel and the Temple can be drawn.

3. The Kotel—this was the site of the Holy Temple. Though the Holy Temple does not exist today, this is still a place where people come from all over the world to pray. An immense wall made of huge stones, its plaza is always filled with men and women praying. A man or a woman praying in front of the Kotel can be drawn.

4. A *beit knesset*—the synagogue has become a place where people of the community gather to pray and hold significant events. It is a center of Jewish life, taking the place of the Holy Temple after it was destroyed. Draw a synagogue.

5. A *beit midrash* (study hall)—here is where Jews gather to learn Torah. A study hall contains a special atmosphere, full of energy that is palpable. There is no place where the joy of learning Torah is felt more than here. Draw a large room with people seated at tables learning from *sefarim* (holy books).

6. Me'arat Hamachpelah—the burial site of Adam, Eve, the Patriarchs, and the Matriarchs. Draw a large building on top of caves and the entrance to Gan Eden (the Garden of Eden), or show a fragrance coming from the Garden of Eden.

7. Rachel's Tomb—Rachel died while giving birth to Benjamin on the road to Beit Lechem. Rather than burying her in Me'arat Hamachpelah with the other Patriarchs and Matriarchs, her husband Jacob buried her there in Beit Lechem, so that the Jewish people would be able to pray at her gravesite on their way to exile. It is said that she prays and cries for her people as they are led away to foreign lands. Draw Kever Rachel (Rachel's Tomb) or Rachel crying for the generations of Jewish people who were forced from their homeland.

8. The tomb of Rabbi Shimon bar Yochai—located in a cave on the hills of Meron, it is a site where thousands come to pray each year, paying respect to the sage who gave us the wisdom of the Zohar (the mystical part of the Torah). Show a cave near a carob tree and a hill.

9. Additional holy sites include Tiberias, Hebron, and Safed.

Berachot (Blessings)

This is a great way to teach about God's wonders and miracles. Have you thought about any miracles that you've heard about or seen? Do you know someone who was miraculously saved or helped?

Sketches and Miracles AGES 10+

Miracles can be found in seemingly simple occurrences as well as major moments in time. Stop and record the event in a small sketch pad and pause a moment to appreciate the good that came from it, however large or small. So-called coincidences are often miracles in disguise. Sketching reinforces memories and provides images you can use later in your artwork.

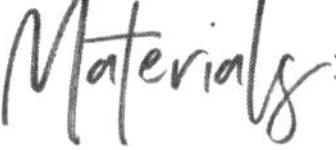

- Pencil
- Small sketchbook, measuring about 5 x 5 inches (12½ x 12½ cm)

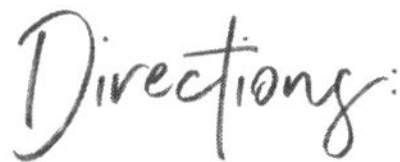

1. Draw according to your ability—even stick figures will work. You can make simple sketches at first and then use them to make beautiful paintings in brilliant colors.
2. Carry your sketchbook with you so you'll be ready to jot down sketches as they come to mind.

The Jewish Wedding

There are many special customs and practices associated with Jewish weddings. They highlight the holiness and joy of building a Jewish home. Some images that lend itself to illustration are the chuppah under the stars, the ketubah, a *kallah* (bride) surrounded by family and friends at the *badeken* (the veiling of the bride by the groom), or the *chatan* (groom) dancing in a large circle.

A Wedding Album AGES 9/10+

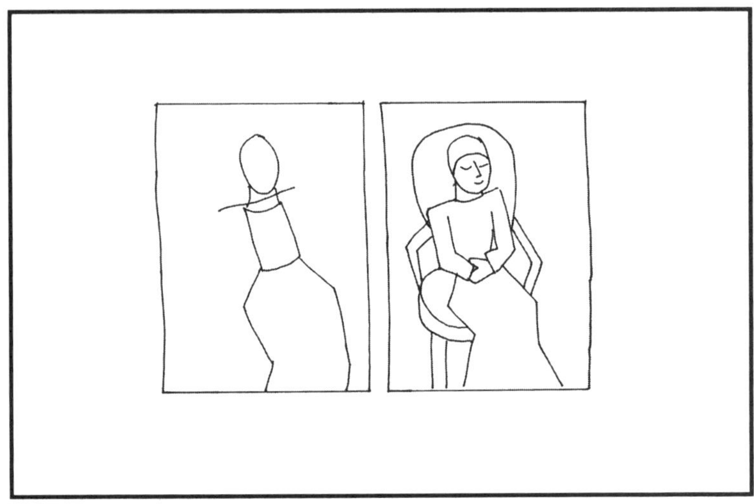

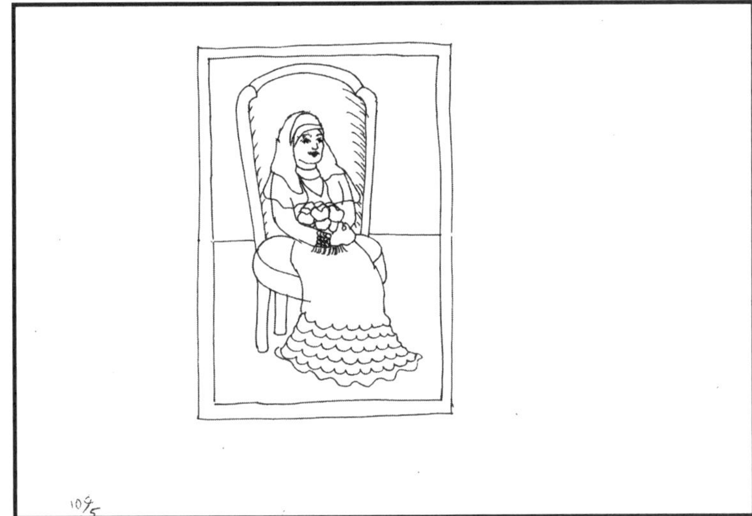

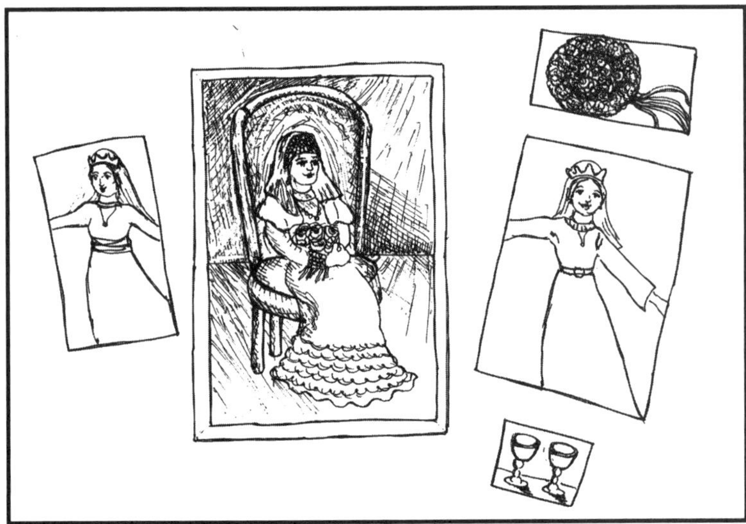

Materials:

- Photo album or a few sheets of 8½ x 11-inch (21 x 30-cm) copy papers stapled together to make an album
- Pencil, pens
- Colored markers or acrylic paint and fine brushes 1/16 to ¼ inch (⅛ x ½ cm) wide
- Scrapbook papers for added designs (optional)

Directions:

1. Make a wedding album. You can have fun designing the bridal gown. Depict the bride under the chuppah, seated in a chair decorated with flowers as she waits to walk down the aisle, or dancing with family and friends.

2. Draw the wedding ceremony: the bride in her white gown, veiled and holding a bouquet of flowers, the rabbi reading the ketubah, the groom in a kittel (a white robe representing purity), and an ocean of men, women, and children surrounding them to wish them mazel tov (congratulations) and rejoice with them.

3. Optional: Cut out old photos of family and friends at their wedding. Glue into your album. Do a drawing of the photo on the opposite page for added impact.

4. Do a little research. Look at wedding albums (such as your parents') and look up wedding scenes on Jewish calendars and brochures. If you wish, transfer one of the scenes to canvas with oil or acrylic paints.

In Summary: Making the Most of the Subject Matter

- Jewish art is usually defined by its Jewish subject matter.
- The choices of subject matter are endless. It's a good idea to choose a motif that resonates with you.
- Subjects for Jewish art may include Shabbat and the festivals, Jewish family life, holy sites, the mitzvot, and *berachot*.

Questions and Wonder

1. What is your favorite mitzvah? Which of the following materials would you choose to depict it—chalk pastels, oil paints, or clay? How about a construction from sandwich Styrofoam board or cardboard? Design a project illustrating your chosen mitzvah and favorite materials.
2. Choose one subject related to Judaism—say, Shabbat candles—and imagine how you would show it best:
   - a black-and-white pencil drawing
   - a colorful painting
   - a fabric art piece using a variety of fabrics, threads, and sequins
   - a miniature scene in a shoe box (diorama) using matchboxes, pieces of cardboard, fabric, and clay
3. Sometimes it's hard to get started on a drawing or painting regardless of the subject. Sitting alone with the stark white paper can be unnerving. It will help if you gain a bit

of knowledge about the subject you want to draw. Talking about the topic or describing it in writing can help you organize the priorities of your composition. What are the main actions or objects that interest you about the subject? What colors, moods, weather, time of day, and background would best depict it?

Jewish Values and Art

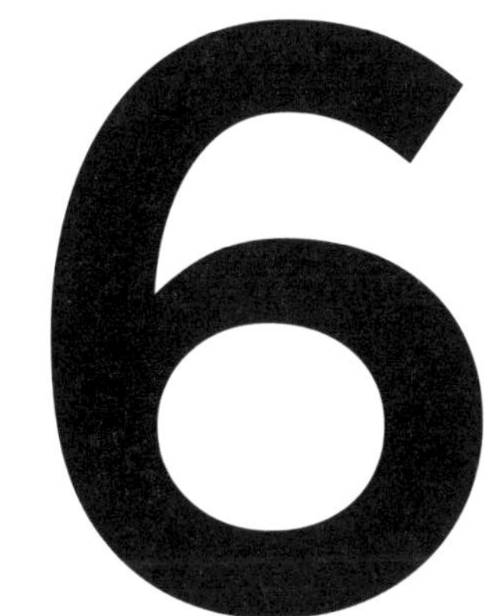

Patience, honesty, humility, helping others, self-control, and honoring our elders—these eternal values and others are as integral to Judaism as the 613 mitzvot of the Torah. Adhering to Jewish values is not only a mitzvah—it is a guarantee for fulfilling, positive relationships.

What Are Jewish Values?

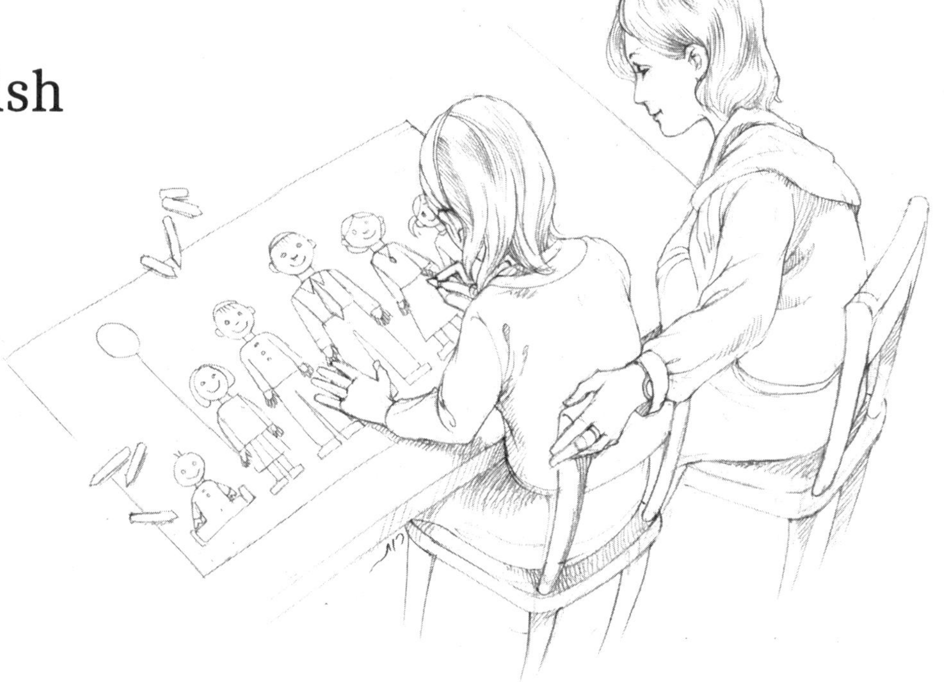

The character traits and values that one should aspire to are defined by the character traits attributed to God[47]—traits such as showing mercy, being slow to anger, and having abundant kindness.[48]

One of the most important maxims in the Torah is to love others

47 The Torah says, "You shall walk in His ways" (Deuteronomy 28:9). Maimonides, in *Hilchot De'ot* 1:6, explains this verse to mean, "Just as God is called Merciful, so too you should be merciful." In other words, we should emulate His trait of kindness.

48 Exodus 34:6.

Notes and Sketches

as oneself.[49] There is the story in the Talmud of a man who came to Rabbi Hillel asking to be converted "while standing on one foot." Rabbi Hillel said to him, "That which you hate others to do to you, don't do to your friend. This is the whole Torah. Everything else is the explanation." This precept includes many aspects of human relationships, from acquiring friends to making peace, to giving charity and supporting the community, to respecting the sanctity of human life.

This can play out in many areas throughout the day, including art class. A child in the art class will ask for a marker that's out of his reach on the table, and the children will bombard him with many markers of the color he requested. This is something they learned at home and fortunately passes on to our art class, making the time pleasant and productive. If children hoard their materials when they are meant to be shared, or if they are trying to grab the supplies first, we discuss the value of waiting and using a different color in the meantime or working on another part of the project. Afterwards, I make sure the child who is waiting does get the supplies he asked for (when they become available).

There are numerous mitzvot that call upon a person to be sensitive to others and preserve one's good relationships: to be forgiving, not to be envious, to use speech carefully by not speaking badly of others or gossiping, to judge others favorably, and to greet people with a smile.

These mitzvot do not apply only to friends. A Jew's relationship with his family is of the utmost importance, and he is adjured to honor and love his spouse and to educate his children, support them, and marry them off.

These are values that I encourage my students to express in their art. Although the class is about art, the goal is to help the children grow through their art. Happiness for others' successes and compassion for their pain are very human conditions. These are also Torah values that can be nurtured during art class.

For example, when teaching about the Mishkan and its beautiful artwork, I recall the master craftsman, Bezalel, and his good *middot*. I explain how he was chosen to help build the Mishkan, not only for his superb artistic ability but also because he was a righteous man.[50] In this way, I am able to show that Jewish art is more than just creating beautiful imagery. It is also a venue for expressing our inner values and character.

---

49 Leviticus 19:18 and Talmud, *Shabbat* 31a.

50 See ch. 1, "What Is Jewish Art?"

And just as in art, no two children will turn out the same style of artwork or have the same handwriting, no two lives are meant to be the same. Each person is unique and special, and making art is a great opportunity to learn how unique and special one is.

Notes and Sketches

> *Suri did not paint a typical scene of a house, a tree, and a sky with a sun and birds. Wide, open, and colorful would describe Suri's style. Her emphasis was on design and repeating shapes. Suri could have easily been made to feel like an outsider because of her unique artistic vision. She was a sweet girl with good middot, but felt out of place when she showed her inner vision. Once this was discussed in art class, and the other children understood that we don't all have the same style and way of drawing and painting, Suri felt part of the group and was accepted.*

Painting realistically is a desired skill, yet this is not everyone's goal. The same idea transfers to our personalities and preferences. We want to be true to our inner style, one that is composed of refined character traits. Accepting others although they are a little different from ourselves shows acceptance of ourselves as well. Art is a venue for showing who we are. Our good character traits are the main goal.

Art as a Medium for Jewish Values

Art is a good medium to teach about *middot* in a positive way. Often, children's artwork depicts Jewish values as they learn about the mitzvot and good *middot*. How can something intangible like Jewish values be depicted?

Our relationships with our family, friends, and neighbors come through in our artwork without us even realizing it. The way people are portrayed in our drawings or paintings conveys the values we wish to express—their body language, facial expressions, gestures, relationships with other people in the picture, and the actions they are engaged in, as well as the size and placement of the elements on the picture's surface.

But we don't always need to portray a specific scene to convey what we value. The artist's state of mind is always expressed somehow—no matter what subject he depicts. This might be conveyed through his color choices, shapes (sharp or soft), subject matter (or the lack of it), and the sweep of his brushstrokes. Just as our handwriting reveals something about us, so do our drawings and brushstrokes. The more a person works on his *middot*, and frustration, fear, worry, and anger have a limited place in his life, then the more his art will convey a person who is happy and at peace with himself. [51]

A child who randomly scribbles harshly or uses unnecessary force with his art materials is given materials that do well with strength and resistance. After using the large (gross) muscles for a while, he gradually progresses to being sensitive to hand pressure by using the small-motor (fine) muscles. Once he knows how to control his responses to the materials and is attuned to various hand pressures, he can acknowledge in himself his better behavior and values.

An artist who is firmly connected to his roots understands that he is special and is in a unique position to use his art as a vehicle to promote kindness and mercy and all the traits that those enjoying his art will want to emulate.

Jewish Symbols Reflect Jewish Values

As mentioned above, values are not only depicted in true-to-life scenes. They can be conveyed through color and brushstroke; they can also be translated into symbols.

A symbol is an emblem that carries messages that touch something deep or familiar in us. It is a recognizable mark that represents an object, concept, or action.

Symbols can have a very strong psychological effect on us. Advertising promotions include such symbols—or logos—to convey something about a product or service (consider a business logo or a sign over a restaurant or supermarket). For example, a green leaf often symbolizes organic, natural food. Seeing a green leaf on a jar of spaghetti sauce might make us think that the sauce is all-natural, even if it isn't.

Jewish symbols reflect Jewish roots, values, and institutions—an open

51 Most people may not notice any negative feelings the artist is struggling with by viewing his art, especially if his inner and outer world are not in sync, but they are there and they affect us.

Torah scroll, the Menorah of the Holy Temple, the six-pointed Star of David. Other Jewish symbols include a crown representing the Torah, the *Luchot Ha-brit*, the Kotel, and the *choshen*. There are also significant numbers, such as seven to represent Shabbat, eighteen symbolizing *chai* (life), and 613 for the mitzvot.

Letters are also a type of symbol. The *aleph-bet* (Hebrew alphabet) was created by God, and the Torah is written in the *aleph-bet*. Since the Torah is considered a blueprint for Creation—that is, God looked at what He had written in the Torah and created the world based on what the Torah contains—the letters of the *aleph-bet* are considered the building blocks, the DNA, of the universe.[52]

David Baruch Wolk, an Israeli artist, uses the *aleph-bet* as a major symbolic and design factor in his colorful paintings. He weaves the Holy Hebrew letters through abstract shapes and colors to create layers of dimensions and new perspectives to see at each viewing.

Jewish symbols can also be used to portray Jewish role models. For example, a tent with Shabbat candles may represent Sarah our Matriarch, a ladder going up to the heavens represents Jacob our patriarch, and a harp often symbolizes King David.

The twelve tribes had distinct emblems on their flags in the Jewish people's desert encampment.[53] The symbols were based on the blessings that Jacob gave to each of his sons before he died.[54]

Tefillah (prayer) can also be expressed in symbols. In fact, this can facilitate more effective and focused *tefillot*. We can sharpen our concentration in prayer by making symbols that hold pictures in our minds. This is especially helpful for children whose abstract thinking is still undeveloped. Visually depicting prayer for a child can reinforce the prayer's internal message and meaning.

---

52 Talmud, *Eruvin* 13 and the commentary of the Maharsha there.

53 Reuben had a red flag depicting a flowing stream of water or mandrake plants. Shimon had a green flag depicting the city of Shechem. Levi's flag was white, black, and red, and showed the *choshen*. Judah's was sky blue with a lion depicted on it. Issachar had a blue and black flag with the sun, moon, and a donkey. Zebulun had a white flag with ships on it. Dan's flag depicted a snake on a sapphire-blue background. Naphtali's flag was pale red with a deer on it. Gad's flag was gray with soldiers on it. Asher's had an olive tree on a green background. Joseph's showed a plant by a stream, and Menasseh's was black with a wild deer depicted on it. Ephraim's flag was also black and it depicted an ox, and Benjamin's flag had an agate background with a wolf illustrated on it. Numbers, ch. 13, *Midrash Tanchuma* and Numbers 2:7, *Midrash Rabbah*.

54 Genesis, ch. 49.

Here are some ways that prayer can be depicted through symbols:

- Draw one large circle to represent the Oneness of God. Around the circle illustrate God's creations.
- Show an ear listening to a mouth reciting the Shema prayer, with the words of the Shema written next to it, and the heart receiving the message of the Shema.
- Paint a prism of colors radiating light to show that the ways of God bring light and simultaneously are diverse and one.
- Draw two hands cradling the globe of the world to show that God is in control of everything.

Combining Art Activities and Jewish Values

The same subject can be presented in several ways depending on the materials you use and the subject you want to portray. It's best to choose a subject that speaks to you and to use materials that you are comfortable with and allow you and the children to express yourselves best. The possibilities are endless.

You can create:

> *paintings, drawings and prints, clay, papier-mâché, collages, paper cuttings, tapestries, mosaics, three-dimensional constructions from boxes, tubes, or wood, and dioramas (miniature scenes from life inside a box).*

You can do original work or make original imitations of:

> *illuminated Hebrew letters and manuscripts, decorative patterns, a decorated Jewish calendar, cards and invitations, decorations for parties and festive meals, charts and posters for the Jewish holidays and mitzvot, or ritual objects.*

You can be introspective and expressive with:

> *tefillot decorated, painted, and framed to hang on a wall, a decorated siddur cover, a book illustrating God's wonders and creations*

in the world with the appropriate blessings, illustrations for a Pesach Haggadah, inspirational poems illustrated or decorated to give as gifts, drawings of the family, a children's picture journal, or clothing design with an emphasis on Jewish style and values.

You can plan:

designs for a synagogue or a Jewish home complete with a kosher kitchen, Jewish ritual objects, a garden planted with the shivat ha-minim and a sukkah built on it, a Jewish neighborhood, including a synagogue, yeshiva, girls' school, mikvah, kosher food shops, charitable institutions for the welfare of the community, parks and recreation, a home for the elderly, a hospital, and a Jewish cemetery.

In the next few chapters, we'll discuss more about how the process of creating art itself conveys values. But first, a project:

Illustrate a Middah and Its Opposite AGES 7+

Ask a child to choose a middah (character trait) and describe it in words. Then ask him to picture the words in his mind and decide how he would depict the middah.

Work with the child as he or she draws. Help the child adjust the illustration until he or she is satisfied with the depiction. Then think about the opposite of the middah. Describe it, picture it, and draw it and adjust it.

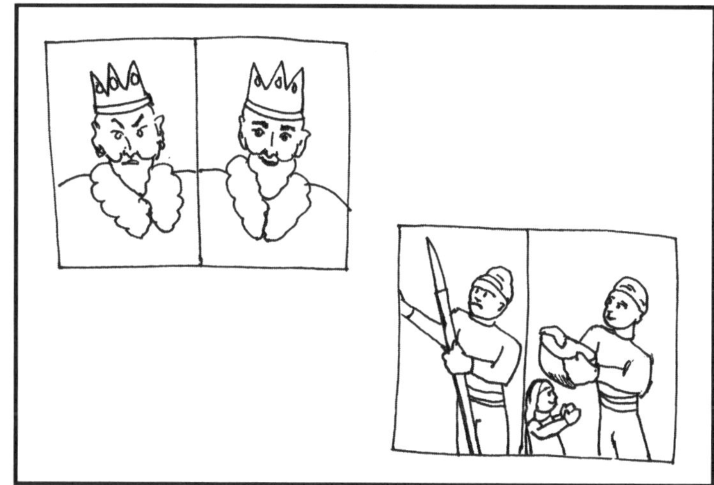

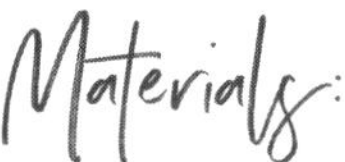

- 2 sheets copy paper or drawing paper, size 8½ x 11 inches (21 x 30 cm)
- Bristol or smooth watercolor paper if you want to use paint (optional)
- Pencil and eraser
- Thin and broad-tipped colored markers
- Watercolors or gouache/tempera paint
- Soft paintbrush, ⅛, ¼ and/or ½ inch (¼, ½ cm and/or 1½ cm)

Directions:

1. Choose a *middah* that you want to illustrate. Some ideas to choose from: loving-kindness vs. hatred, mercy vs. cruelty, humility vs. arrogance, alacrity vs. laziness, patience vs. intolerance, honesty vs. dishonesty, modesty vs. immodesty, courage vs. fear, confidence vs. insecurity, justice vs. injustice, joy vs. sadness, nobility vs. vulgarity, wisdom vs. ignorance.
2. Fold a sheet of paper in half. On one half draw a depiction of the *middah* with the pencil according to your description of the *middah* in words; on the second half, draw its opposite. For example, on one half draw a king dressed in a blue velvet robe, seated on a gold, jeweled throne showing compassion to a suffering orphan or widow. On the other half, draw the same king, full of anger and cruelty, inflicting a punishment on an innocent victim to satisfy his desire for power.
3. The drawing may be a simple cartoon, but it's best to create a fully developed composition with a background, foreground, and middle ground, along with details, atmosphere, and colors.
4. If using paint, redraw the story on Bristol.
5. Trace the pencil lines with a thin black marker and color in the drawings with colored markers or paint. If using paint, outline with a black marker only after the paint is dry. (Children under seven should wait to use the paint until they are older because it may be hard for them to paint within the lines.)
6. Write the *middah* and the description of the *middah* above or below each drawing. (If the child is too young to write well, have him dictate it to you.)

Power of the Imagination KO'ACH HA-TZIUR:

A PICTIONARY ACTIVITY WITHOUT COMPETITION AGES 8+

This activity will activate your child's imagination with visualization and drawing. It can be played by one or more players.

Directions:

Each person has ten 3 x 5-inch (7½ x 12½-cm) cards (or papers) and a pencil and draws as many images he can from the list below. Parents help by discussing the image and ways to draw it. Stick figures are OK here. Attach each child's group of drawings to a board to display. Option: color with markers.

THE IMAGES

- The beautiful world G-d has for us
- A game board: battle between good forces and other forces
- Building oneself and the world at the same time
- A scale balancing our mitzvot (unity/commandments) and *aveirot* (lack of unity/commandments)
- Without form or time, God is watching over us
- Honoring our parents; our parents are the most important people in our lives (Rambam)
- A crown; we are children of royalty
- Leaving Egypt; the mitzvah of seeing ourselves as slaves who left Egypt
- An imaginary wall between ourselves and a person praying (so as not to disturb him or her)
- *Lashon hara*—not speaking bad of others even if it is true; words can damage
- Being thankful for all we have

Cartoon and Graphic Novel

A graphic novel tells a story in cartoon style. Five hundred years ago, a cartoon was simply a sketch in preparation for a detailed, elaborate work of art such as a tapestry. The tapestry cartoons were drawn by one person or group and colored in by another and finally set up for the fabric work.[55]

55 I recently saw an exhibition titled "The Invention of Glory"—a set of four gothic tapestries each measuring twelve by thirty-six feet—the size of a tennis court. Examining the detailed depictions of the tapestries, I realized how enormous and intricate the cartoons must have been. I wasn't surprised when I read that the tapestries took several years and three hundred people to weave. The finished tapestries hung on the stone walls of a castle and commemorated the king of Portugal's military victory in Morocco in 1471. Guests of the court gazed at the tapestries at their leisure and hunted for hidden details woven into the tapestries.

Today a cartoon has a very different meaning. Cartoons are funny illustrations in a book, newspaper, or graphic novel with the dialogue in balloons; these are often printed in installments. The story is told in strips or panels with boxes, and each box usually contains a narration or dialogue.

The goal is to capture the complexity of a moment in life with a few well-chosen lines in drawings and words. When creating your cartoon, decide if you want to leave room for the reader to use his imagination to fill in what is not shown by giving clues, including symbols, or showing parts of objects. You might want to add a list of objects or details for the reader to hunt for.

Turn an Enemy into a Friend: A Graphic Novel AGES 9+

Write a short story on twelve pages about two people who did not understand one another. They became enemies. A third person decided to make peace between them and came up with a plan. The plan was to make each of the two think that the other wanted to make peace and give in to the other person. In the end, peace was restored. Here is what you'll need to depict the story:

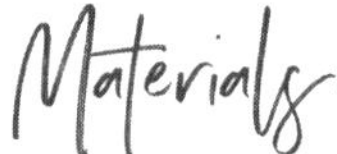

- 2 sheets of copy paper, size 8½ x 11 inches (21 x 30 cm)
- Bristol board or Bristol paper (2-ply) about 10 x 14 inches (25 x 36 cm) or quality drawing paper that takes water if using paint
- Pencil and eraser
- Ruler
- Soft paintbrush ⅛, ¼ or ½ inch (¼, ½ or 1½ cm)
- Black waterproof pen
- Gouache, tempera or watercolor paints or colored markers
- Colored inks (age 10 +) (optional)

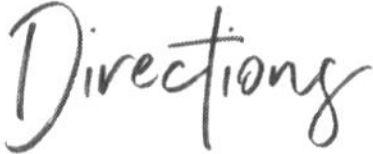

1. On one of the sheets of copy paper, sketch your three main characters with the pencil: the two people who are fighting and the

man (or woman) of peace. Try to think like an illustrator who must first know his subjects inside and out. Work out the characters' facial expressions, dress, posture, and body type.

2. Sketch the setting: a town, office, home, forest, hiking trip, etc.

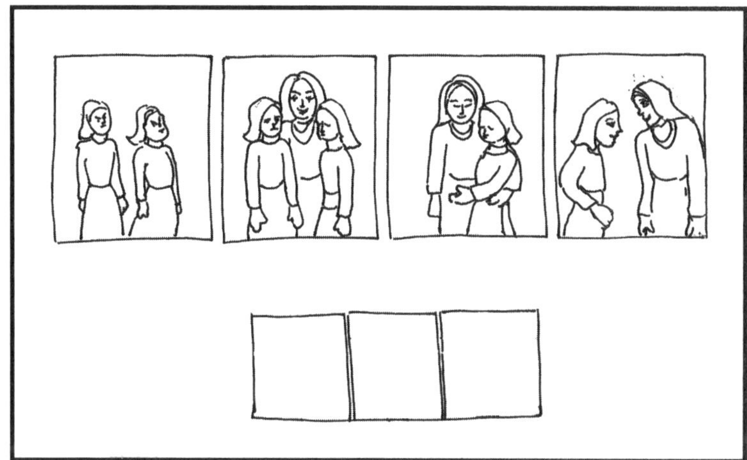

3. Make a storyboard. Draw ten to twelve panels, about 2½ x 2½ inches (6 x 6 cm), in which the story will take place. Make trial sketches in each box and include the dialogue. If you wish, you can combine the panels into a strip of two or more per row. These are still sketches before you make your final drawings. Though you can work out your own details and embellish as you wish, the story should include at least ten story boxes:

    A. The differences between the two friends

    B. The quarrel

    C. Enemies

    D. The "man of peace" (or "woman of peace") sees the two quarreling.

    E. The MOP has a plan.

    F. The MOP speaks to Man #1 and tells him that Man #2 wants to make peace.

    G. MOP speaks to Man #2 and tells him Man #1 wants to make peace.

    H. Man #1 agrees to make peace.

    I. Man #2 agrees to make peace.

    J. Man #1 and #2 come back together as friends.

4. Draw in the characters and refine the drawings until you are satisfied with your sketches. Decide on the stage shots: which

will be close-ups, distance shots, overhead shots (viewing the character from above), or angled shots.

5. On the drawing paper or Bristol use a ruler and pencil to draw ten 2½ x 2½-inch (6 x 6-cm) boxes. You can enlarge some boxes if you wish to make some of the scenes larger; the size and arrangement of the strip and the boxes are up to you.
6. Using the pencil, copy the scenes you sketched into your panels that are on the drawing paper.
7. Trace over the pencil lines with the black pen.
8. Leave the cartoon in black and white, or color in with markers or paint.

In Summary: Jewish Values and Art

- Jewish values, such as good character traits, are a foundation of Judaism.
- The character traits one is meant to acquire are defined by the character traits attributed to God.
- Our values and priorities are expressed in our art, whether consciously or unconsciously.
- Jewish values can be depicted in true-to-life scenes, in abstract paintings, or in symbols.

Questions and Wonder

1. Have you ever thought how a logo on a drink can affect you? Did it make you want to buy it and drink it? Or did an ad or label with the initials of a clothing company cause you to want to buy the product because it is a status symbol?

2. What does the Star of David or the symbol of the menorah mean to you? Are there other Jewish symbols that have significance for you?
3. How can we give clues to our emotions in a painting? How do our drawn lines and painted brush strokes hint to our emotions?
4. How can we give clues to our beliefs in a painting?

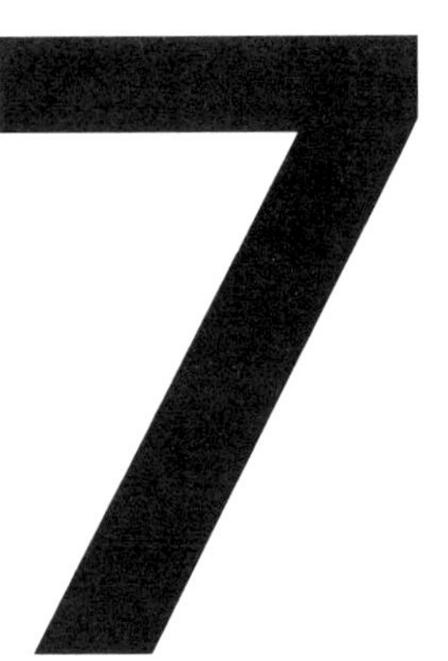

7 Learning about Life through Art

Not only does the subject matter you choose teach children values but even the process of creating art itself teaches values and promotes growth. Let's look at how art can be used as an amazing tool to help children improve their character and build their self-confidence.

A number of important characteristics can be acquired naturally through the discipline of art. Children learn patience and self-control when they encounter frustration and disappointment during the drawing process. Striving for perfection, they may want to erase the picture, tear it up, and just give up. As a parent or teacher, you can use this opportunity to transform their frustration into a moment of growth. Here is a chance for them to

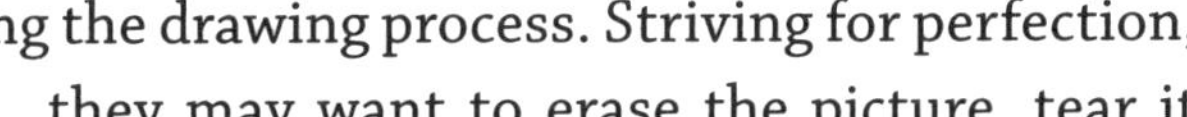

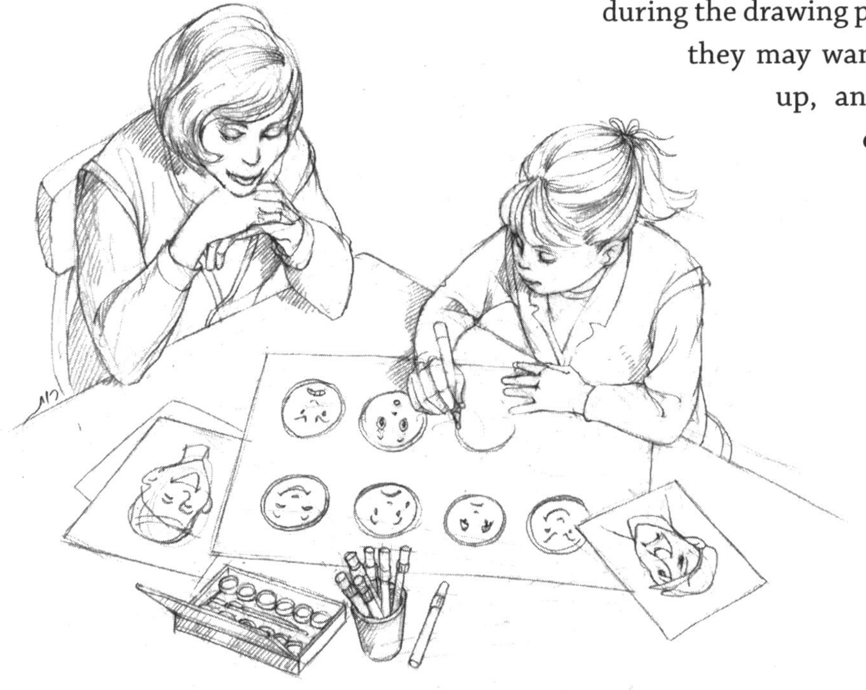

- use the tools you have;
- develop patience with themselves;
- persevere even in the face of difficulty and keep trying!

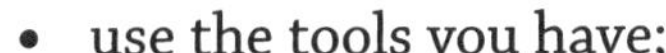

Note that besides arts and crafts tools there are mental tools, such as accepting

and working with one's mistakes, which can sometimes help a child reach his or her goal of finished work quicker.[56]

Notes and Sketches

Lessons of Life in Art

I also encourage independence throughout the classes. I could easily show the students what to do and give them a simple recipe to follow. But if they don't think the project through, make mistakes, and suffer bits of frustration, they will not come to their own style, interpretation, and self-achievement. Such a path matures a person and nurtures him into being capable of introspecting Jewish values of behavior.

I have made it my teaching goal to emphasize the process of creation and not the end product until we near the completion of the project. When a piece is almost finished, then we review it and refine it.

Children often want to skip the process and see quick results at the risk of missing the beauty of each step. That's why I believe that when it comes to learning about life through art, ready-made craft projects just don't serve the same purpose. They're fun, and they provide semi-finished pieces that need only to be assembled or painted, but they also eliminate the need to work with the imagination and to persevere when things get difficult. If you want your child to grow through art, make sure that he is also doing art projects from scratch. If you don't have the time or skill to work with him, enroll him in an art class where he can learn vital life lessons at the same time that he learns how to produce art.

How do we work with these concepts in an art class on a practical level? A project will have several steps the child will have to complete successfully before continuing on to the next step. The patience involved can be demanding for some children but once they master it and internalize its value, they are on the road to becoming a mature human being.

What Children Can Learn

Here are some other ways that the medium of art can spur children to grow and develop.

56 See ch. 26, "The Fortunate Mistake."

Notes and Sketches

Achieving: Art does not need to be competitive. Instead, it can be used to bring out the best in a person. Certainly, achievement and advancement are important, but rather than stress competition between individuals, emphasize the child's own personal advancement.

Let the children compete against themselves. The real test is how hard they tried and the hurdles they have overcome to improve.

Life application: Let's judge our efforts in a personal, positive light rather than always reverting to thinking, "I'm not as good as him."

Being true to yourself: Realism in art is not only about being able to perfectly render a life-like object. Realism is also about being true to oneself and one's own style of expression. A person should certainly strive for perfection—but perfection that is defined by one's own potential. One person's success may not even be a challenge for somebody else. Each of us have individual goals that we should be striving toward. Negativity and self-condemnation that result from comparisons only limit growth.

> *Eight-year-old Aliza is very talented. In her mind, she can see clearly what she wants to draw. But she is young and needs time to mature before her fingers can create what her mind sees. So she gets frustrated. With time and direction, she will improve while learning to be satisfied with doing her best.*

Life application: Work steadily and patiently toward your personal goals.

Conserving resources: Children tend to use lots of paper when drawing and throw it away when they don't like the results or make a mistake. Instead, they can be taught to reuse the paper by turning it over and using the other side. Or, they can paint over the drawing and cut up the paper and glue it onto another to make a new picture or a collage. Or, and this is really fun for little kids, they can practice ripping straight strips of paper, both large and small. They can fold the scribbled paper into origami paper objects or turn it into a decoration: Crumple it into a tight ball, paint it red, and insert a green pipe cleaner. Attach two green paper leaves, and you have an apple!

Used paper can also be stored for later use in making papier-mâché instead of using newspaper. Or it can be painted with two coats of matte or acrylic paint on both sides so that when dried it becomes firm. Cut the paper into strips and weave with it. Paper weavings are relaxing and great fun. You can also recycle boxes, containers, and bottles for art projects.

Life application: Why throw something away when there are so many things you can do with it?

Experimenting: Encourage children to relax and see what spontaneously emerges from inside them. Remind them that no one is judging them. They can try different styles and materials until they discover what suits them. And it's okay to make mistakes along the way. If you don't try new things, you won't know what will succeed and what won't.

Building and destroying go hand in hand with experimenting. One of the great joys in life is building sandcastles, knowing that they will be washed away and you can start all over again. I like to think that scribbling and finger painting allow children to experiment and "make a mess." With the knowledge that it's okay if the experiment is not successful, they can challenge themselves without the weight of producing a perfectly finished product each time. They still have the satisfaction of trying something new, and if it doesn't work out, they can throw it away without reservations, while any successes will be a bonus.

Life application: Not all that we produce must we keep, so feel free to experiment and try new things.

Trusting yourself: It's not necessary to have perfectly straight lines. A ruler is a useful tool, but we don't have to be a slave to it. Have the child experiment with drawing lines freehand. Have him pick up a pencil. Bend his elbow and use his shoulder to swing his arm and hand back and forth in a straight line from the top of the page to the bottom. There. You have a line! Repeat.[57]

Life application: You don't always need rulers and ready-made crafts to produce something wonderful. Trust yourself and let yourself work freestyle and see what you can create!

Appreciating simplicity: There can be great beauty in a simple pencil drawing. Complex works can be broken down into simple basic structures and skills. A drawing that was created only by pencil reveals a tremendous amount. A pencil drawing can convey great depth and sensitivity, and sensitivity in a drawing can help a person notice subtleties in life. This subtlety can be conveyed by applying different amounts of pressure on the pencil. Suddenly an entire spectrum between light and

57 See ch. 19, "The Tools of Art."

dark is created. Not everything is black and white; there is a wide range of grays in-between.

Life application: Step out of the rush and find pleasure in the simple things in life.

Learning to think: Reading a book without pictures, with just black letters on a white page, demands more from a child than reading a picture book that has glossy color pictures to illustrate the story for him. In a picture book, the work has been done for him, whereas with the other, he has to use his imagination to paint images of the story in his mind.

Similarly, drawing with a pencil, without the use of color, is more demanding than painting with colors. The mind must perceive the various shades of gray as "color," and the brain must then use memory recall to "fill in" the colors. Drawing with a pencil, then, is a great brain exercise for children. A mind that is stimulated in this way may, by extension, become more receptive to reflecting on higher ideas, such as belief in G-d and one's purpose in life.

Life application: Overstimulation can dull and confuse the senses and block the imagination. Simplicity encourages minds to think.

Planning: Drawing is done in stages. One doesn't just put pencil to paper and produce a full-fledged picture. It requires planning: deciding the composition, choosing shapes, colors, and shades and preparing the materials. In other words, we want to try to visualize the end result before even putting pencil to paper. A child who learns to plan in advance and consider the possible outcome of his actions enhances the development of his imagination. This ultimately contributes to increasing his ability to plan for the future in other areas of his life.

Life application: Success requires planning and organization.

Finding fulfillment: Art can be a wonderful outlet for feeling a sense of accomplishment and fulfillment—especially if a child is experiencing difficulty in school. Young children who have not yet mastered language and have trouble expressing themselves can use art and drawings to tell us about their world. In fact, a picture can communicate much more than words.

In a moment of sincerity, ask the child to tell you what he drew. You may be surprised at what he says. The more we prompt a child to speak about his artwork, the more he will tell us, depending how verbal he is. A child who has the satisfaction of communicating through his art, and creating a picture that he likes, has the foundation for building healthy self-confidence.

Life application: Fulfillment and communication go together. Share your abilities and gifts with others.

Focusing on the moment: Drawing can also teach children how to be fully aware of each moment. When we draw, we must be fully present in what we are doing, focusing on each nuance and each line that we draw. We must put ourselves in the picture, as if it is taking place in real time and space.[58]

Life application: Take a few minutes each day to truly focus on every moment. Try expanding that time each week. This is living life to its fullest!

Appreciating the world around us: Paying attention to the smallest details of what we are drawing can significantly heighten our appreciation of God's wonders. By focusing and fine-tuning, our eyes can be trained to see more than we are accustomed to noticing. This can be a great experience for children. As they try to imitate the world around them, they learn to appreciate the greatness of God and His creations.

Life application: Find something in your life to appreciate, whether it is your loving mom or a delicious apple.

Most Important: Confidence

Good values take a lifetime to develop. With guidance and flexibility, art time with children can be character-development time, providing encouragement and support as they develop good character traits and essential Jewish values.

This is a precious opportunity to bond with your child! Help your child by praising his efforts—remind him that it's the effort that counts more than the results. Praise and praise some more. Don't worry about how well the child draws the picture (at least for now). Use this chance to enjoy your time together.

You might ask how will your child learn to improve if everything he does is "great." From my experience, many children (and adults) become

58 You can apply this idea to praying. When praying, try to focus on the holy words. Be fully present in the moment and be aware that right now you are standing before God and communicating with Him.

defensive in the face of criticism because their confidence in their art is weak. Instead, offer gentle, firm, persistent guidance and a sequence of projects specially designed with increases in difficulty and skills, and the child will gradually acquire confidence. His new confidence will motivate him to improve.

Here is a project for the little ones, the three- to six-year-olds, to get them started on the road to confidence and success in art (and other areas):

The Intelligent Scribble Project AGES 3+

We don't expect much from a scribble. After all, it's only a few marks in time. Can there be more to a scribble than we know?

The illegible scribbles of a preschool child represent real objects to him. A shaky green circle may be a bicycle, a yellow one his mother. Yet there are signs, such as the direction of the marks and the shapes of the lines, that show he is thinking and developing concepts.

Scribbling offers moments of both freedom and self-control. Small muscles in the hands (called "fine motor") are at work promoting cognitive (intelligence and perception) thinking. Though this project is aimed for three- to six-year-olds, anyone can do it and see what it's like to scribble with directions. He will be acquainted with a variety of scribbling options that he may decide to use in the future.

In this project, try to avoid dark colors, like brown, black, and gray. Use cheerful, bright colors in the beginning, then use soft ice-cream colors later on to relax the eye after the stimulation of the brilliant colors.

Materials:

- 3–5 sheets of large copy paper, size 11 x 16 inches (30 x 42 cm), or the size of a place mat
- Thick and thin washable colored markers
- Note: Please do not use crayons. They may be tempting but the colors may not be strong enough due to the high wax-type content. Strengthening hand holds (fine muscle) and pressure variation is another benefit of using thick markers.

Directions:

Warm up to this exercise. Ask the child to draw several large and small circles. Show him how to use his full arm and shoulder to make large circles or use his hand and elbow to make small circles.[59]

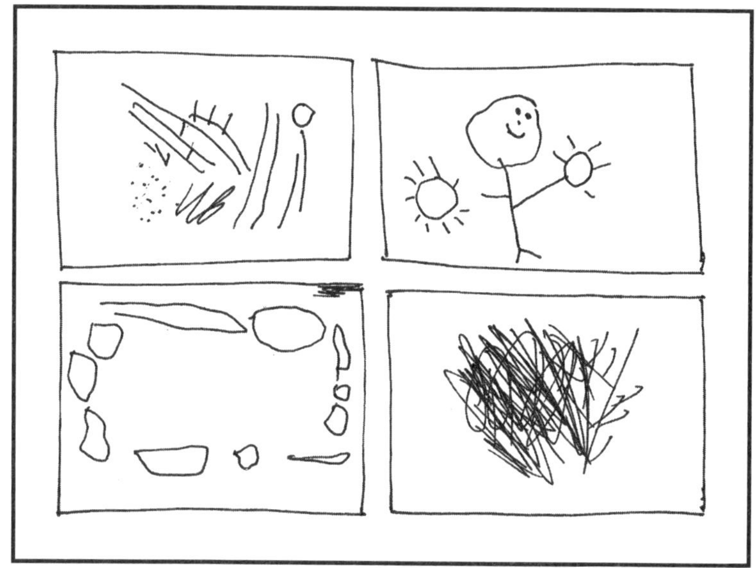

1. Have the child draw a large spiral on a sheet of paper, beginning from the center and working his way outward as he expands the spiral.
2. With the colored markers, have him draw over the spiral three times with three different colors.
3. Let the child cut out the spiral following the circular direction of his lines.

Alternatively:

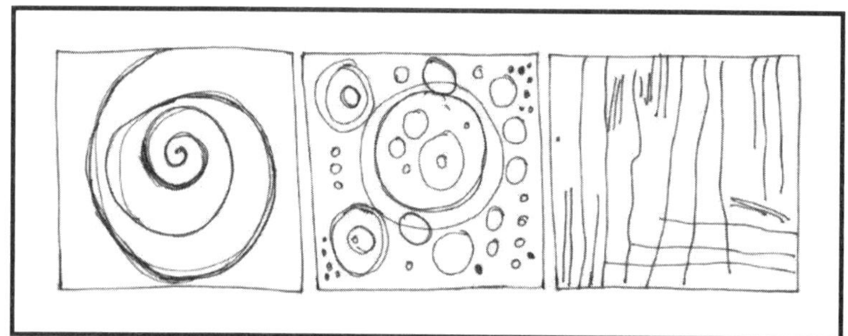

1. Tape the four corners of another sheet of paper to the table.
2. Line up the markers in groups of thick and thin, and each set according to the colors of the rainbow: red, orange, yellow, green, blue, and purple. The child will choose which 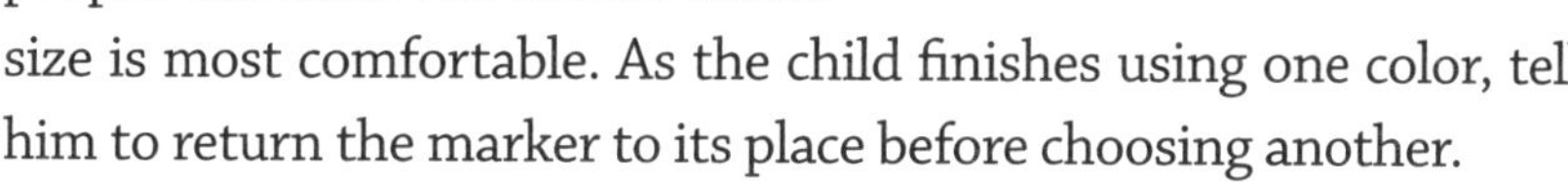 size is most comfortable. As the child finishes using one color, tell him to return the marker to its place before choosing another.
3. Have him draw a giant circle, filling the paper.
4. Now have him draw dots, small circles, medium circles, and large circles inside the giant circle.
5. Have him draw lines following along the edge of the paper.
6. Have him draw lines up and down.
7. Have him draw lines side to side.
8. Repeat on the other sheets of paper, for as long as the child wishes.
9. Now return to one of the papers and have the child color in the small spaces between all the circles with the markers.

---

59 See ch. 19, "The Tools of Art."

10. Optional: Cut out the parts of the drawing or the paper in any direction.

In Summary: Learning about Life through Art

- Lessons learned in the process of creating art can be applied to life.
- Give children art projects that they have to do from scratch so they can work through the process of creating, making mistakes, and perfecting them.
- Achieving success, learning from mistakes, conserving resources, being true to yourself, trying new things, and focusing on the moment are some things that children can learn in the process of creating art.
- Along the way, make sure to praise your child for his achievements and challenge him so that he can gain confidence and new skills.

Questions and Wonder

1. Have you ever thought of art as anything more than making a beautiful painting?
2. What is one thing that art has taught you?

8 Judaism and Fashion Design

In Judaism, tremendous respect is given to the human body. After all, it is the dwelling place for the soul, and without a body a person could not serve God. When the body is properly clothed, a person's deeds and words—his inside—comes into focus. Traditional Jewish art has always celebrated this understanding by portraying the human body in dignified clothing.

The Meaning of Dignity

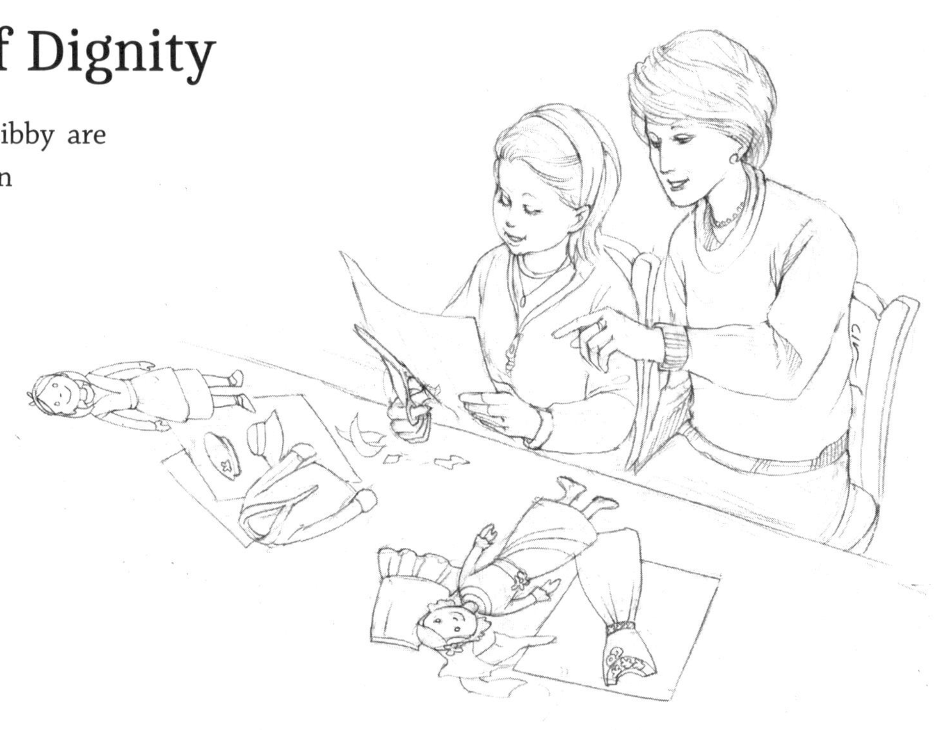

Pencils in hand, Shelly and Libby are excited. Their teacher had given them a project: to make paper dolls and design a wardrobe for them.

What little girl doesn't love fashion design? They were only too happy to indulge.

Shelly thought about what her dream wardrobe would be. She thought about the clothing boutiques in the mall where she shopped for new outfits. Slowly Shelly

Notes and Sketches

began to draw clothes for her paper dolls. They resembled the kind of clothes she had seen in those stores. She wasn't sure she really liked them—she'd never thought about it much—but she knew that they were definitely "in."

Meanwhile, Libby was absorbed in drawing sporty clothes that she felt good in. She could imagine herself in those clothes.

"What do you think?" Libby asked, holding up one of the drawings.

Shelly examined it and bit her lip. "It's nice, but it's not exactly high fashion."

Libby shrugged. "I don't care. These are clothes I'd like to wear. I bet other people would, too."

Shelly watched Libby work and she felt a pang of envy. Libby didn't seem to care what was fashionable. She just drew what she liked.

Shelly wished she had examples to follow other than the fashion industry. She wasn't really happy with what she had drawn. She put her pencil down. Drumming her fingers on the table, her hand suddenly took on a determined twist. Shelly gripped her pencil and drew and drew. Thirty minutes later, a princess joyfully twirling in a full skirt looked up to her from the paper and appeared to be winking at her.

The girls were not thinking "dignity" when they drew their dream wardrobe. They were thinking what they deep down truly felt comfortable wearing.

Rather than being a barrier, as some think, clothing provides personal boundaries that encourage the emotional freedom to be true to our deepest inner selves. From a Jewish perspective, the woman is, above all, respected and lauded for her intelligence, intuition, compassion, and ability to care, give, and nourish. She is more than just a body. Judaism emphasizes reverence for a woman for who she is rather than what she looks like. Yet, there is no contradiction for her to look stylish and beautiful.

This translates into the concept of a woman's dignity.

Introducing the Concept of Dignity through Art

As you embark on a project that involves clothing design with children, you will inevitably discuss the concept of dignity. You will want to think about it ahead of time so that when it comes up you will have answers. Here are some questions that may arise:

1. What is the connection between clothing and self-respect? Include inspiring insights about the Jewish emphasis on the inner person versus the societal focus on external appearance.
2. "Clothes make the man/woman"—what do we want to communicate about ourselves with the clothes we wear?
3. How do our clothes affect the way we speak and act?
4. What kind of clothing did people wear once upon a time? How has clothing changed through the ages and why?
5. What does "dignified attire" involve? What are the guidelines?
6. What are the meanings of the words elegance and refinement? How are these ideas reflected in clothing design?

Depending on the age and maturity of the child, discussions may include halachic guidelines, the rewards and benefits of embracing this mitzvah, and how our clothing affects our thoughts, actions, and speech.

This is a big topic. A teacher can devote a series of art classes to teaching about Jewish fashion design, or parents can do these art activities with kids at home over the course of several weeks during summer vacation or the rainy season. Here are some suggested projects:

1. Design a wardrobe for each of the four seasons.
2. Design special clothing for Shabbat and Yom Tov (holiday).
3. Design bridal dresses. Girls love drawing brides!
4. Design hairstyles and hair coverings (for married women).
5. Design jewelry and accessories.

When working on the design project, take into account:

Appearance: the style appropriate for the season and occasion.

The material: the fabric, color, texture, pattern, and decoration.

The fit: proportion, weight, and movement. Age and temperament of the wearer.

Notes and Sketches

Keep in mind that fashion design isn't only restricted to girls and girls' fashions. When doing a design project, include designs for men's and boys' clothing as well.

Here is a project that you can do with children of all ages: Here is a project that can be adjusted to ages seven and older. Four- to six-year-olds will focus on learning to draw people.[60]

A "Design Portfolio" for the Seasons AGES 7+

Children love creating their own book. In a series of activities, have the children create a "design portfolio" that shows changes in dress throughout the year. I recommend you purchase a notebook to make your portfolio, but you can also staple together fourteen sheets of copy paper on one side to bind them.

Choose your materials depending on the age of the child. Children ages four to seven are most comfortable with pencils, markers, colored pencils, and pens.

Children over the age of nine or ten might like to experiment with watercolors and washes (very diluted watercolors), colored inks, oil pastels, chalk pastels, charcoal pencils and sticks, or calligraphy pens.

DRAWING TECHNIQUES:

Designing clothing provides good practice for improving drawing techniques if you use a variety of drawing materials. Here are some important tips before the children start drawing:

1. Have them start to draw people with a pencil and basic geometric shapes: circles, squares, triangles, and rectangles. Then they should soften and round the lines, adding curves to make the figures more lifelike. Finally, they should add the details: collars, buttons, prints, textures, and trimmings. When drawing children, keep in mind that the head of a baby or young child is much larger in proportion to the body than that of an adult.

2. Let them experiment with hold, direction, and pressure when using a pencil or other drawing tool. There are several ways to hold a pencil: point to paper, side to paper, and so forth. Add to that various amounts of pressure and hand movement, along with the hardness or softness of the pencil or the amount of water or color on the brush, and you will be able to produce shadows and variations.

60 See chs. 17, "Some Art Theory to Get You Started" and 25, "All about Drawing People."

3. Practice brushing a wash (ages 10+). A wash is created from ink or water-based paints, like watercolors. For this project, use paint. Dilute the paint in water with a ratio of about ½- to ¼-part paint (or less) to ½- to ¾-part water. The wash is applied over pencil or permanent ink lines to add shadowing in the folds of a garment, for example. Color pencils that dissolve in water will also work well with a brush.

4. If you use paint or watercolor, wait for it to dry before applying a layer of pencil, markers, charcoal, pastels or oil pastels.

5. Do a trial test of the various materials suggested to find what speaks to you.

6. To reproduce a pattern or a woven texture, examine a swatch of fabric, about 2 x 2 inches (5 x 5 cm), and identify its main characteristics: wavy lines, crossed lines, linked half-circles, etc. Copy the pattern and repeat it throughout the piece of clothing.

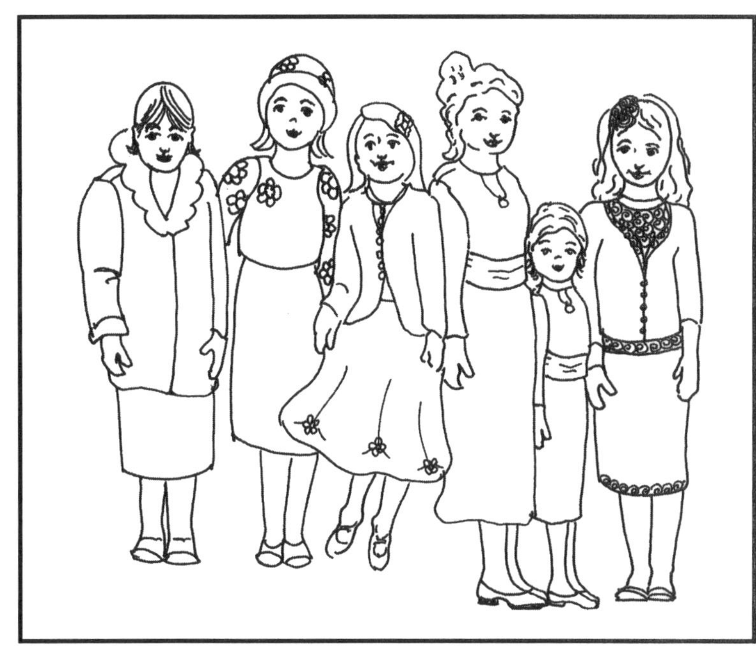

7. Open your sketchbook and begin your designs with pencil lines and continue with any of the suggested art materials.

Materials:

- Sketch book at least 8½ x 11 inches (21 x 28 cm) in size or spiral notebook with unlined paper
- Drawing pencils and eraser
- Pens (permanent ink)
- Fine-tipped markers: permanent if using water and paint
- Watercolors or gouache/tempera paint
- Soft paintbrush, ⅛ to ¼ inch (¼ to ½ cm)

- Charcoal pencils, oil or chalk pastels, or a calligraphy pen for older children (optional)
- Black ink (water soluble, nonpermanent) thinned with water for washes, transparencies, and shadows (optional)

Directions:

Each sheet of paper will represent a different month of the year. Draw girls and boys wearing clothing that are suitable for each month. Here are some ideas:

Elul/August-September: Draw illustrations of children going back to school, wearing new clothes or school uniforms and new shoes, clutching school bags. Design a variety of school clothing, everything one might need.

Tishrei/September-October: The weather is turning cool. It's time to pull out the autumn clothing: sweaters, jackets, and other clothes made of warmer, thicker materials. Design mother-daughter matching autumn wear, special for the High Holidays.

Cheshvan/October-November: Draw clothes for the rainy season: umbrellas, boots, sweaters, raincoats. Illustrate children walking in puddles of rainwater wearing their shiny new boots, or holding onto their umbrellas in the wind. Pay attention to the texture of plastic and rubber material.

Kislev/November-December: With the official arrival of winter, out come the hats, coats, scarves, and wool socks. Design a variety of winter scarves, emphasizing the weave and appearance of the yarn, and sweaters—long, short, cardigans, pullovers, vests, and turtlenecks. Draw a Chanukah scene: the family wrapped snugly in their sweaters as they light their Chanukah candles.

Tevet/December-January: Draw winter scenes in the snow, with figures in coats, hats, scarves, and gloves. Include a front and back version of a winter outfit and coat. Emphasize the neckline: high collars and hooded, scarved, or layered necklines.

Shevat/January-February: This is the month of Tu b'Shevat, the new year for the trees, when the seven species of the Land of Israel are eaten—wheat, barley, figs, dates, olives, pomegranates, and grapes. Use these as a motif for a fabric design on children's clothing. Practice on scrap paper or on 2 x 2-inch squares of paper. Draw a pattern on the paper, such as two pomegranates and a cluster of grapes, and reproduce the repeating pattern on an outfit.

Adar/February-March: In the month of Adar, we increase our joy. Illustrate children at a party in Purim costumes. Draw a few versions of the same costume until you have refined it.

Nisan/March-April: In Nisan, Jews celebrate the holiday of Pesach. Draw children cleaning for Pesach in old clothes, contrasted with them wearing shiny new outfits at the Seder table. Design aprons you love to work in, with big pockets and a funny design in the front. Develop ideas for festive Pesach outfits from photographs or clothing you have seen in store windows. Adapt them with your own accessories and ornaments.

Iyar/April-May: Spring is in the air! Draw children wearing their new spring clothing. Or, draw a scene for Lag BaOmer (the eighteenth day of Iyar): children sitting around the Lag BaOmer bonfire in the hills of Meron in hooded sweatshirts and spring jackets.

Sivan/May-June: The summer is approaching. This is the time when the Jewish people received the Torah. Draw children dressed in their summer best ready to receive the Torah and walking to the Kotel on the holiday of Shavuot. Or, illustrate finely dressed children and families attending the joyful weddings that abound at this time of year.

Tammuz/June-July: This is the time of end-of-year school trips. Out comes the summer attire: sun hats, sunglasses, and beachwear. Draw a variety of summer clothing—formal and casual. Focus on lightweight, easy-care fabrics. Think cotton, canvas, khaki, and linen. Draw gossamer tunics or blouses over cotton shells with matching shoes: sneakers, sandals, or canvas shoes.

Av/July-August: It's camp season. Dress your figures in sporty, summery clothes suitable for vacations, sports, and hikes. Draw camp T-shirts, caps, and clothes for water sports. Design a variety of summer hats which look fashionable and keep the sun out. Draw clothes for a day at the beach. Don't forget to include sunglasses, a beach towel, a ball, and a sandcastle near the waves.

Paper Dolls AGES 8+

The next step after designing your portfolio is to produce paper dolls to wear your creations. The paper dolls here are free-standing—they are connected at the head and folded. You can dress each doll in two outfits, one on each side, for a total of four outfits per set.

Match up work and dress outfits on the pairs of dolls. For example, dress one doll in work clothes and an apron and its partner in a regal Pesach Seder outfit. Put rainy-day clothes on one and sunny-day clothes on its pair. The dolls can be as simple or complex as you like.

Materials:

- Pencil and eraser
- Fine felt-tipped colored markers, including black and gray
- Thick paper, card stock, or a white cardboard (the kind used for invitations), or a thin shirt board from the dry cleaners, measuring about 8 or 9 x 11 or 12 inches (20 or 23 x 28 or 30 cm), enough for two to three double dolls, joined at the head.
- Nail or fine scissors
- Clear contact paper (optional)
- A large envelope, handmade or store–bought, for storing the paper dolls

Directions:

1. Design one prototype doll to use as a pattern for the other dolls. Fold a sheet of card paper in half and draw the doll with its head touching the top, folded line so that both sides will be joined at the head. The doll should be about 1½ inches wide x 5¼ inches tall or 1 x 4 inches (4 cm wide x 13 cm tall or 2½ x 10 cm). Draw the doll with its basic clothing: skirt, coat, or dress for the girls, pants, shirt, and jackets for the boys.
2. Keep the card folded and carefully cut out two dolls at the same time, cutting around the outline of the clothes. Be careful to keep the top of the heads connected. You will have two dolls connected at the top of their heads. Both dolls in the pair have the same form but are "dressed" in different outfits.
   If you like, you can design clothing for the reverse side of each of the dolls.

Optional: Draw the front and the back of the doll instead of two different outfits. Do the same to create other dolls, giving each doll pair contrasting outfits.

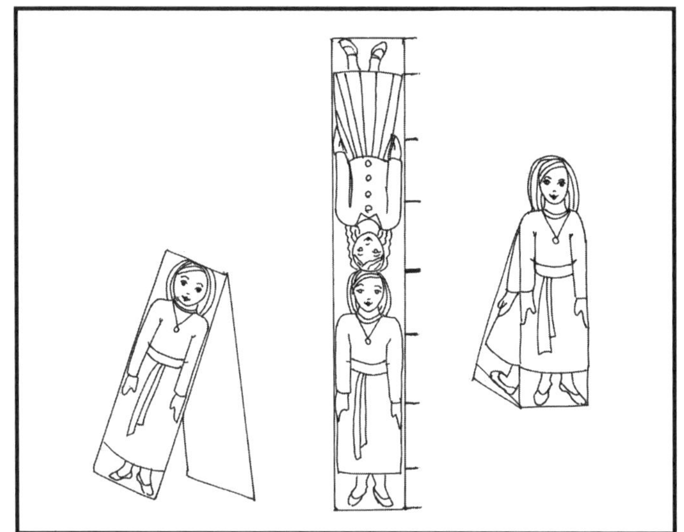

3. With a pencil, draw the arms, hands and faces, including the hair and hat or *kippah* (skullcap). Hands can be simplified; draw quarter circles at the end of the arms, fitted next to the figures.
4. Add details to the outfits you drew: shoes, buttons, trimmings, purses, or school bags. Draw in folds, pleats, and pockets. Add patterns and prints on the material. Refer to your Design Portfolio for the Seasons, if you like.
5. Outline the folds, crevices, openings, and connecting areas such as belts and pockets with gray marker to give the appearance of depth.
6. Color in the prints or patterns and texture on the material, such as plaids, fur, knits, and satins.
7. Use a skin-colored marker to color in the faces, hands, and legs. Color the eyes, lips, and brows.
8. When you're done, cover the dolls with clear contact paper, or laminate, and cut out carefully. (Make a thin horizontal cut in the plastic on the fold line to allow it to fold.)
9. Fold at the head and stand up the dolls to play with and enjoy. Store them in a large envelope.

In Summary: Judaism and Fashion Design

- Learning about fashion design in art is an opportunity to learn about the inner and outer function of clothing and how it affects us.

- Dignified fashions protect personal boundaries and allow for emotional freedom.
- Designing clothing provides good practice for improving drawing techniques if you use a variety of drawing materials.

Questions and Wonder

1. How do you define "personal boundaries"? How does it connect to how we dress? How does our dress protect us?
2. What does your dress tell others about you?
3. What does "style" mean to you? Who designs the styles we wear?

Art in Halachah

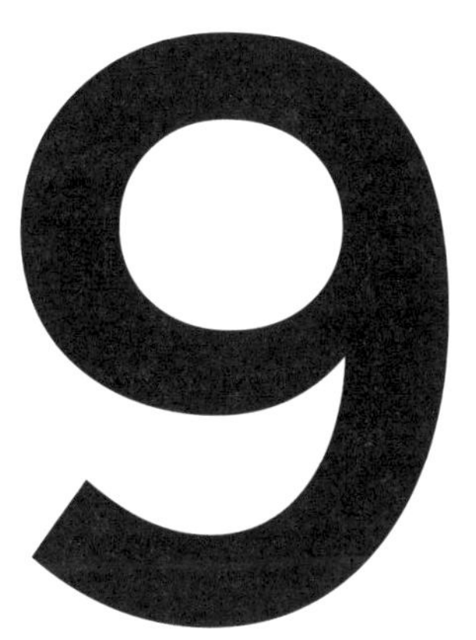

Judaism encourages us to use art for beautifying the mitzvot. This enhances our appreciation of God and the magnificent splendor of His creations.[61] However, to properly depict Jewish subjects and values through art, it is important to know the halachot regarding the making of images.

Images in Jewish Art

In my earlier years as an artist, I wasn't aware of any issues with painting images. I didn't know that some images were not permitted or how realistic one may be in portraying people. Now I understand that realism has a place in Jewish art. With a few adjustments, realism in art is done without compromising Jewish values.

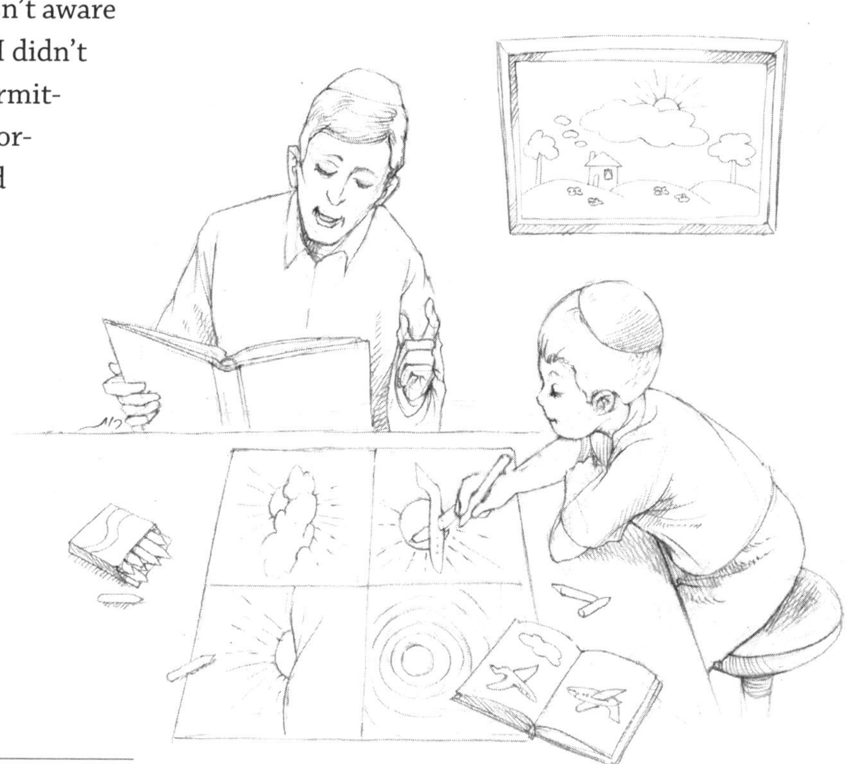

Later, I found out that normative Jewish law allows for painting and drawing people and living creatures. However, it prohibits creating complete sculptures or reliefs of people and certain animals.[62] It is

61 Exodus 15:2; Talmud, *Shabbat* 133b and *Sukkah* 33a.

62 *Shulchan Aruch*, *Yoreh De'ah* 141:4, and *Chochmat Adam* 85:3–5.

Notes and Sketches

forbidden to form the four faces of the animals in Ezekiel that carried the Heavenly Throne: human, lion, ox and eagle. The vision of Ezekiel showed angelic forms that people might come to worship. Therefore, we do not make an image of a four-headed creature that has the face of the human, lion, ox and eagle, even for aesthetic or decorative purposes.

Also, since God has no form and no physicality, one should not attempt to depict God in any way that gives Him a temporal image or in any way that may be interpreted as idol worship.[63] The Rambam states, "We are commanded not to make forms of "living creatures" out of wood, stones, metal, etc., even though we won't worship them. [The reason] is to distance ourselves from thinking these forms have any innate powers themselves like the [worshippers] before thought..."[64]

At various times in history, the law was applied more or less stringently due to cultural, political, and religious conditions in the host countries where Jews have lived. A number of countries or groups with Islamic traditions generally forbade the depiction of animate creatures—faces or full figures—and this had an influence on Jewish art in Muslim-ruled countries.

On the other hand, the famous illustrated Birds' Head Haggadah from late-thirteenth-century southern Germany shows the heads of birds or griffins in the place of human heads and originally left the faces of the Egyptians blank. Griffins were popular figures in medieval Jewish literature. The absolute reasons remain a mystery, but some say that it is related to the strict observance of the biblical command against making graven images.[65] Others believe it is a reaction to counter the erroneous anti-Jewish views of using blood for making matzah, considered an insult to the Christian practice of communion.[66]

63 Maimonides, *Sefer HaMitzvot*, negative commandment 4, and *Sefer HaChinuch*, commandment 27.

64 Maimonides, *Sefer HaMitzvot*, negative commandment 4.

65 Exodus 20:3–5.

66 Professor Marc Michael Epstein, *The Medieval Haggadah: Art, Narrative and Religious Imagination* (Yale University Press, 2011).

The Laws

Notes and Sketches

The *Kitzur Shulchan Aruch*[67] provides an important source for the halachic guidelines on art representation. These laws have stood the test of sustaining the Jewish people throughout three thousand years. They ensure that belief in God isn't compromised through the making of images and that art is used only to enhance Torah observance.

Here are some of the laws to be aware of when creating art:

1. The second commandment of the Ten Commandments states, "There shall be no other gods before Me. Do not make yourself a carved image or any likeness of that which is in the heavens above, or on the earth below, or in the water beneath the earth. You shall not bow down to them nor worship them, for I am Hashem, your God."[68] This verse is understood to mean that Judaism requires careful consideration in how one depicts objects or images that have been used in idol worship by many cultures throughout the world, in ancient times or today.

2. Jews are therefore careful not to draw a complete sun, moon, or stars, since these were all once the focal point of idol worship.[69] Instead, it is preferable to make a slight change in these images, for example, by depicting the sun partially rising over a mountain or covered by a cloud, or showing the bottom of the sun or moon at the top or in a corner of the paper.
   The Be'er Heitev quotes the Taz, "Not to make a complete form of the sun and moon and stars, a protruding [relief] or indented [engraving] form."[70] The Taz writes, "Those who make the *mazalot* (constellations) in pictures [drawings and paintings] in *machzorim* (holiday prayer books) is not proper." Rabbi Shabsai HaKohen (the Shach) says these pictures are permissible for two reasons: they are for teaching, and they are not complete forms.[71]

---

67 *Shulchan Aruch, Yoreh De'ah* 141:4, 6, 7 with commentaries. Chapter 168. Literally, "the prepared table," the *Kitzur Shulchan Aruch* is an abridged codification of Jewish law compiled by Rabbi Shlomo Gansfried.

68 Exodus 20:3–5.

69 *Shulchan Aruch, Yoreh De'ah, Avodat Kochavim* 141:4, and *Chochmat Adam* 85:5.

70 *Shulchan Aruch*: *Yoreh De'ah* 141:4–5, and commentators: Rabbi Yehuda Ashkanazi (the Be'er Heitev), who lived in the mid-1700s, Rabbi David Halevi (the Taz) who lived in the mid-1660s.

71 *Shulchan Aruch, Yoreh De'ah, Avodat Kochavim* 141:4.

3. Different from drawings and paintings, life-like sculptures were actually used for idol worship. Therefore, our Sages were most stringent regarding sculptures. According to several authorities,[72] it is permissible to make a head without a body or a body without a head, but sculpting a full figure is prohibited.[73] The Shach states that one who avoids making the sculpture of a figure will be blessed.[74] The application would be to leave one area incomplete such as a section of an ear.

4. It is permitted to paint images on walls (with the exception of a complete sun, moon, and stars).[75] However, the prohibition against sculptures also applies to reliefs, both whether they protrude above a surface (convex) or are indented below the surface (concave).[76]

5. Drawings and paintings of the Menorah and other vessels that stood in the Holy Temple are permitted, but it is prohibited to make free-standing replicas with the actual dimensions; however, this is permissible for education. (The Temple Institute in the Old City contains models of the Temple vessels for this purpose.) It is permitted to create a model of the Mishkan.[77]

6. In the book of Ezekiel, there is a description of Ezekiel's vision of the *Merkavah* (Divine Chariot).[78] This chariot had a human figure, a lion, an ox, and an eagle. Though the chariot may be drawn for the sake of educating children, a defect is usually included. Also, these four images may not be depicted together in sculpture or relief form, but may be depicted separately (except, of course, for the human form, as mentioned above).[79]

---

72 Namely, Rabbeinu Asher ben Yechiel (the Rosh), an early-fourteenth-century German scholar and one of the main halachic authorities of Ashkenazic Jews; Rabbeinu Yaakov ben Asher (the Baal HaTurim), also a fourteenth-century German scholar who authored the monumental work, the *Tur Shulchan Aruch*; and Rabbeinu Yerucham, a fourteenth-century French scholar and halachic authority.

73 *Shulchan Aruch*, *Yoreh De'ah* 141:7, written by Rabbi Yosef Karo and Rabbi Moshe Isserlis (the Rama).

74 Siftei Kohen, *Yoreh De'ah* 141:32. Rabbi Shabsai HaKohen was born in Vilna in 1622 and is most famously known for his scholarly commentary on the *Shulchan Aruch*, Siftei Kohen, which he authored at the age of twenty-four.

75 *Chochmat Adam*, Laws of Idolatry 85:3, 5.

76 *Shulchan Aruch*, *Yoreh De'ah* 141:4, Taz 7, according to the Ramban and the Ran.

77 *Igrot Moshe*, *Yoreh De'ah* 3:33.

78 Ezekiel 1:5–6.

79 *Shulchan Aruch*, *Yoreh De'ah* 141:4; *Siftei Kohen*, *Yoreh De'ah* 141:20; *Igrot Moshe*, *Yoreh De'ah* 2:55.

7. It is permissible to depict the faces of the *Avot* (Patriarchs) and *Imahot* (Matriarchs), but according to some customs and views, it is not done. This is because it is impossible to portray them with the proper reverence and respect. However, children benefit from visual portrayals, more so than adults, and many teachers will provide pictorial handouts when teaching. When depicting the Patriarchs and Matriarchs for children, it should be explained that it is impossible to properly portray their spiritual greatness on paper, and this is not what they actually looked like.[80]

8. It is considered a mitzvah to gaze upon the faces of holy people: "And your eyes shall see your teachers."[81] This is because, as the Talmud teaches, a teacher's facial expression conveys meaning that is not conveyed by words alone.[82] Therefore it is permitted, and even desirable, to depict our great teachers, sages, and holy rabbis.

Portraits of Ordinary People

When we teach children portraiture, we can emphasize that all people look similar, with two eyes and ears, one mouth and nose, yet each person is unique, special, and divinely created.[83] As the Talmud tells us, "When man makes a coin with a mold, they all look the same. But when God made man with a mold, in the likeness of Adam, still no two people look alike."[84]

Drawing people provides an opportunity to notice the unique, intricate arrangement of the facial features that God created for each one of us. Studying the complicated composition of skin, hair, bone structure, and proportional balance provides a lesson on the wonders of Creation. With this in mind, we can emphasize that although we can attempt to illustrate the likeness of a person, we can't come close to portraying the unique perfection of each individual who was created with perfect wisdom by God.

---

80 See also ch. 10, "Jewish Role Models."

81 Isaiah 30:20.

82 Talmud, *Eruvin* 13b and Maharsha there.

83 Talmud, *Berachot* 58a.

84 Talmud, *Sanhedrin* 37a.

Here is a project that can get you started on drawing portraits [85] You should carefully consider whom you might want to draw. Here we will do a portrait of a rabbi:

Portrait of a Rabbi or Tzaddik AGES 8+

Here we will do a portrait of a rabbi, tzaddik (righteous person), or a relative from a photograph using a grid. The grid makes it easy to draw a likeness without knowing how to draw a face.

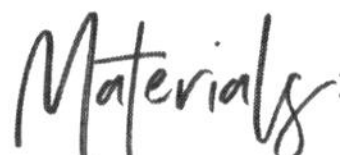

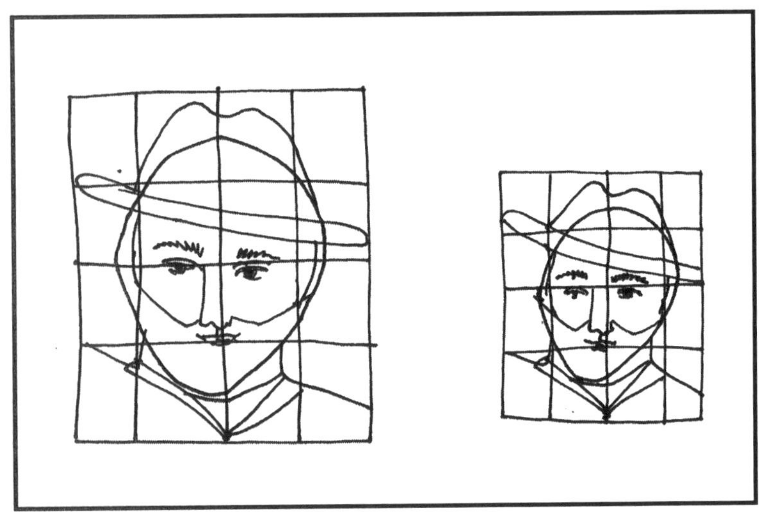

- A photograph of a rabbi or *tzaddik* (you may also take an old family photo or painting of a relative dating as far back as you can; look for photos of great- or great-great-grandparents).
- Copy paper, size 8½ x 11 inches (21 x 30 cm)
- Pencil and eraser
- Whiteboard marker
- Thick clear plastic sheet, size 8½ x 11 inches (21 x 30 cm)
- Masking tape or Scotch tape

Directions:

1. Make a copy of the photograph, enlarging or reducing it to a workable 8½ x 11-inch size.
2. Fold a sheet of copy paper into eight or sixteen equal sections. Open the paper.
3. With the whiteboard marker, copy the same number of squares onto the clear plastic sheet. The squares on the plastic should be the same size as the squares on the copy paper.

85 See also ch. 25, "All about Drawing People."

4. Gently attach the plastic grid to the front of the enlarged photograph with the tape. Your photograph is now divided into squares, which you can see through the plastic grid.
5. With the pencil, copy one section of the picture at a time onto your paper, following the grid.
6. Remove the grid from the photograph and make adjustments to your drawing.

Freehand Drawing of a Portrait from a Photograph AGES 8+

See chapter 25: follow the specific directions for drawing a freehand face and head. When this is accomplished you can refine it by adding in a likeness of the face in the photograph.

You will lightly sketch in the portrait over the face drawing and then darken the lines as you increase the likeness of the drawing to the photograph. Keep in mind that a man's face and nose is generally wider than a woman's, a man's eyebrows are heavier, and the neck thicker.

Materials:

- A photograph of a rabbi or *tzaddik* (you may take an old family photo or painting of relatives dating as far back as you can; look for photos of great- or great-great-grandparents).
- Copy paper, size 8½ x 11 inches (21 x 30 cm)
- Pencil and eraser

Directions:

1. With the pencil, draw a large egg shape on the paper, wider at the top and narrower at the chin.
2. Divide the head in half down the center vertically (#1).
3. Draw one line down each half of the face, creating two sections on each half. Label each of the four sections: #1A and #1B on the left side, and #1C and #1D on the other.

4. Divide the head in half across the center horizontally (#2).
5. On the horizontal line (#2), draw eyes, one eye intersecting line #1A-B and the other intersecting line #1C-D. The center of each eye should be on the horizontal line. Draw eyeballs slightly covered with eyelids. Draw curved eyebrows above the lid. Point out to children that the eyes are not on the forehead.
6. Draw a line (#3) halfway between the center horizontal line and the bottom of the chin. Draw the bottom of the nose here.
7. Draw a line (#4) halfway between line #3 and the bottom of the chin. Draw the bottom lip here.
8. Draw the center and top lines of the mouth (#4) and dip under the nose.
9. Below the mouth, lightly draw a light curve (rainbow direction up) at the top of the chin (just above the chin line) to make the chin appear protruding. Slightly darken the upper part of the chin to create a shadow.
10. Draw a horizontal line a third of the way down from the top of the head to the eyes and mark the hairline. Curve it like the front of a swimming cap. Point out to children that the hair doesn't begin growing on the top of the head.
11. Draw the side view of the ear on the side of the face, between the middle of the eyes and the top of the mouth (between lines #2 and #3). The widest part should measure ⅛ inch (¼ cm).
12. The neck begins from behind the bottom of the ears and curves down toward the shoulders like a wide tree trunk. Point out to children that the neck is not a little box that sits under the chin.
13. The cheekbones start at the top of the jaw intersection (near the ear) and curve down toward the bottom sides of the nose. Draw a light downward curve from each jaw, stopping halfway to the nose.
14. Now you can add details to the features: wrinkles, the unique shape of a nose, the hairline, the facial expression, the size of the eye opening, and the specific shape of the eye. (Eyes in babies are

very large compared to their head size. The eyes of older people become less wide with age.)

15. Add dark areas to show indentations (under the cheeks, near the bottom of the nose, at the sides of the forehead, above the chin, and on the neck).

16. Add highlights to protruding areas (to the forehead, the chin, and near the bottom of the nose, the ball of nose, and the sides of the ears). An area such as a nose can have a darkened recessed area and a highlighted area on different sections simultaneously. The parts of the face can have both protruding and receding areas. The nose can be likened to a mountain with a high and low point. Feel all the sides of your nose to understand this.

17. Add hair and/or a beard. Practice drawing hair. Notice the different types of hair people have and how it catches the light.

In Summary: Art in Halachah

- Creating art is encouraged in Judaism, as long as one does not try to depict God or promote idol worship.
- It is important to know the halachah regarding the making of images, since people have used images and icons to worship as idols.
- Since they were worshipped by ancient peoples, the sun, moon, and stars should not be drawn or painted completely. Partial drawings of the luminaries are permitted.
- It is not permitted to make complete sculptures or reliefs of the four faces from the vision of Ezekiel of the *Merkavah* because the vision of Ezekiel showed angelic forms that people might come to worship.
- Although it is permitted to draw the *Avot* and *Imahot*, many have the custom not to do so out of reverence for their awesome greatness. Educational drawings for children are acceptable because children require literal information.
- When drawing portraits, emphasize the uniqueness of each human being—no two people are alike.

Questions and Wonder

1. What are examples of what some people worship today?
2. What do the words *idols* and *stars* mean to people today? What do you think about when you hear these words?
3. Judaism does not portray God. Why can't everything that has lasting value be seen or be completely understood?

Jewish Role Models

10

There is a natural human tendency to look for role models. Historically, there were gladiators and warriors. Today, celebrities and sports "heroes" are role models to be admired and worshipped in the secular world.

But Judaism has always stressed the internal, not the external. Jewish role models have moral and spiritual strength of character, independent of fashion, glamour, or wealth. Great emphasis is placed on striving to emulate people who have perfected their character traits or who are in the process of improving them.

When we choose people as role models, we should ask ourselves: Who are these people and what are their values? How do they conduct themselves in their personal lives? Are they worthy of emulation?

Fortunately, the Jewish heritage provides a rich treasury of outstanding people to emulate.

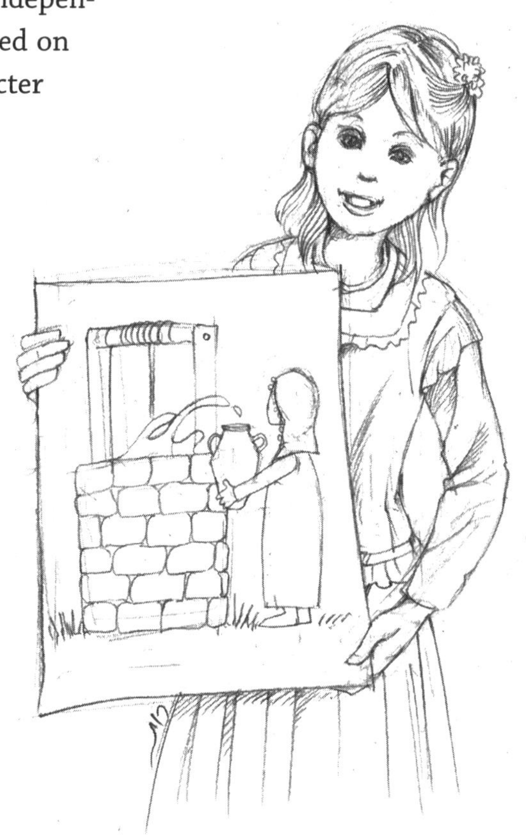

Role Models Today

How do we depict greatness? How do we show the spirit behind the inspiration in a person? One answer is to appreciate and understand the qualities that make for true role models (and not to follow the trends of societies that come and go).

Notes and Sketches

Role models are in part defined by character traits exemplified in the Torah. These are the men and women who dig deep inside themselves for growth and accept their individual challenges as rungs on a ladder leading to greater heights of wisdom and self-perfection. Rather than breaking from the challenges, they see their hardships as the key to fulfilling their potential and ultimate purpose.

Rabbi Nosson Zvi Finkel (1943–2011) was considered one of the greatest *tzaddikim* (righteous men) of our times. As a student of Skokie Yeshiva in Chicago, Illinois, in his youth, he did not seem very different from his teenage counterparts. He appeared to be an average, religious American boy who attended to his studies and participated in sports. After completing high school, he came to Israel to study Torah and later became close to Rabbi Beinish Finkel, the head of Mir Yeshiva in Jerusalem. Rabbi Beinish accepted him into his yeshiva (Jewish school where Torah is learned) and eventually, Rabbi Nosson Tzvi became his son-in-law.

Later, Rabbi Nosson Zvi became the head of the yeshiva, and under his guidance it became one of the largest yeshivot in the world, increasing its enrollment to several thousand students and adding three new buildings.

As the *Rosh Yeshiva* (head of yeshiva), he was a father to countless young men, showering on them his wisdom, care, and concern. In his later years, he had a pronounced case of Parkinson's disease. Though he had lost control of his limbs and had to be physically supported, he continued to raise funds throughout Israel and abroad to keep the yeshiva running. He maintained a full schedule of teaching and studying as well, and he did it all with a smile. He died on the yahrzeit of Rachel Imeinu.[86]

Sarah Schenirer, the force behind high-quality girls' Torah education at a time when none existed, lived just a century earlier (1883–1935). The love and devotion she showed to her students, and the spirituality and meaning she injected into their hearts and minds, set the path for the future of Jewish women.

Sarah was eulogized as a giant of her generation who saved countless young women from rampant assimilation and disassociation from Judaism. She opened their eyes to the all-encompassing beauty of life according to the Torah and challenged the prevailing ideals of communism and socialism that had been drawing these young women away

86 Rebbitzen Sara Finkel and Rabbi Yehuda Heimowitz, *Rav Nosson Tzvi* (Mesorah Publications Artscroll Series, 2012).

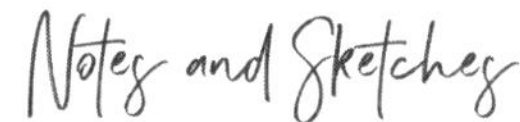

from Judaism. She never allowed her students to hang her picture on the wall, preferring them to carry it in their hearts. Her deeds, love, and respect for every human being remained in the hearts of those she inspired for generations to come.[87]

Role models can also be the quiet heroes, those who may not be heralded as the greatest of the generation, but who are great nonetheless, because they, too, have overcome challenges and strive constantly to grow and fulfill their potential.

I am fortunate to live in a place where I am surrounded by role models who live their lives with a happy, quiet dignity. These men and women exude an inner sense of peace from overcoming great odds and as a result have risen to greatness.

A woman I know was crippled in both legs at a young age. Yet she learned to roller skate and ride a bicycle, never using her handicap as an excuse. Eventually she became an occupational therapist and a mother. Her children never felt that their mother was different from other mothers because she never complained. She maintained a positive attitude and there was no such thing as "I can't."

Another woman I know bares her inner conflicts in her widely published writings, using them as stepping-stones for growth rather than venues for complaints and attacks. She uses her writing to share her place in this world.

There is the mother of a large family (with a few sets of twins), who was not embarrassed years ago to put those of her children who would benefit into special education programs until they could be mainstreamed. This was before so many avenues for early childhood intervention had opened, and before therapy had become the norm. Yet she advocated for her children and went against the tide.

Chessed (kindness) is the key word in her home. She collects used clothing and has an extensive book library. Women come and go all day to find clothes or borrow books. She also has a small publishing company for children's educational Jewish books. Her husband is a leader in their shul and a Torah scholar.

Some years ago, another friend was in a fire that burned three-quarters of her body and she underwent tormenting rehabilitation. She has since

87 Pearl Benisch, *Carry Me in Your Hearts: The Life and Legacy of Sara Schenirer* (Feldheim Publishers, 2004).

created a foundation to help burn victims and gives inspiring lectures to those with similar or other challenges.

Another soft-spoken yet determined friend, is a mouthpiece for those in need. She secures hundreds of meals for the poor, blankets and heaters in the winter, and fans in the summer. She aids in paying medical and electricity bills for people in need. All her hours are filled with ways to help the elderly and poor.

These are role models we look to—whether they are known by everyone far and wide or whether they live lives of quiet greatness. What these people all have in common is a desire to grow and the strength to overcome seemingly insurmountable challenges. They are also givers, because people of great character see the world outside of themselves and always look to help those in need.

Role Models in the Bible

If you are looking for people to emulate, you have only to look in the Tanach (the Bible) and the Talmud.[88]

The Torah tells us about the *Avot* and *Imahot*; the twelve tribes; Moses, the greatest prophet who ever lived; and many other people who embodied spiritual greatness and whose deeds are considered the prototypes for the Jewish people to emulate.[89] Moses was at the same time the humblest of men and the most trustworthy.[90] What do we know of humility? One must have tremendous self-worth, tempered with complete and honest humility to be humble to the highest noble degree.

In the *Nevi'im* (Prophets) and *Ketuvim* (Writings), we learn about the prophets, the kings of Israel, and other great sages who exemplified adherence to the ways of God. We learn from the difficult situations they faced, the decisions they made, and how they were judged by their actions. From the countless stories of these righteous men and women, we learn valuable lessons for life.

---

88 The Tanach consists of the twenty-four books of the Torah, *Nevi'im*, and *Ketuvim*—the Torah, Prophets, and Writings.

89 Maimonides, *Mishneh Torah*, *Hilchot Yesodei HaTorah*, ch. 8. The Talmud tells us that Abraham, for example, embodied the trait of *chessed*, kindness. He passed on this trait to the Jewish people, who are known today for their readiness to give charity and to aid others in need. See Deuteronomy 34:10; *Yevamot* 79a.

90 Numbers 12:3 and 12:7.

Wicked people are also clearly described in Tanach. From their example, we learn how not to behave.

The lives of our *Avot* and *Imahot* represent the values we want our children to exemplify. For example, we can tell them of Sarah Imeinu, the wife of our forefather Abraham and mother of Isaac, who was known as the mother of the Jewish people. At the age of 127, she looked like a girl of seven because of her purity.[91] The Shabbat candles which she kindled in her tent miraculously remained lit from one Shabbat to the next Shabbat, as a sign that she was constantly aware that she was in the presence of God.

The Torah has no shortage of personalities, men like Moses and women like Sarah, to emulate.

Depicting the Faces

When we undertake to teach children about the *Avot* and *Imahot*, we face a dilemma. Children need visual images to identify with. Seeing pictures of *tzaddikim* and rabbis reminds us of the type of lifestyle we want to exemplify. On the other hand, how can we possibly depict the spiritual level of the fathers and mothers of the Jewish people?

Moshe Rabbeinu (Moses), our greatest leader and teacher, who led his people out of Egypt, after 210 years of slavery, was depicted by the non-Jewish artist Michelangelo (sixteenth century) with horns coming out from his head. It seems that the artist misunderstood the translation of the Hebrew word *keren* in the verse "And it came to pass when Moses descended from Har Sinai, and the two tablets of the testimony were in Moses's hand when he descended from the mountain, and Moses did not know that the skin of his face had become radiant while He had spoken with him."[92]

Michelangelo understood the word *keren* to mean "horns," which is one meaning of the word. But in this case, it means "radiant" and indicates that when Moses descended from Har Sinai after receiving the Torah, a spiritual light shone from his face that was so radiant, it was too bright for people to look at.

---

91 Genesis 23:1 and Rashi there.

92 Exodus 34:29.

Michelangelo's famous sculpture of King David is a marble wonder of the Greek ideal of physical perfection. But King David is the author of the ageless book of Psalms and a leader of the Jewish people. He is the one who wrote, "One thing I ask of God: that I dwell in the House of God all the days of my life."[93] Clearly, he was not someone who idolized the physical attributes of the body. The sculpture was the antithesis of all that David stood for.

Michelangelo is not the only artist who depicted biblical personalities based on his own perception of what is considered greatness. This often resulted in a distortion of these great people's values and aspirations. (Rembrandt, a seventeenth-century Dutch master, was an exception. He lived in the Jewish Quarter of Amsterdam and portrayed his neighbors and Jewish biblical scenes favorably.[94])

One who does not have a firm Torah understanding is liable to misinterpret many of the Bible's accounts and descriptions. In addition, it is impossible to imagine the spiritual perfection of the *Avot* and *Imahot* and other great biblical personalities. Although we learn from the Torah about their exemplary characters, their facial features are unknown. We have never seen their faces, of course, nor do we have pictorial records. All we have are descriptions of their deeds and character traits, but an accurate visual image of their spiritual greatness is not considered possible. We don't want our children to view them as "ordinary" people and misrepresent their true greatness. Trying to draw our idea of what they looked like would be inadequate at best and inaccurate at worst.

While there is no halachah against depicting the faces of the *Avot* and *Imahot*, it is considered meritorious to avoid it, except for the sake of educational purposes. Children are very visual and learn from seeing pictures. Since children require these tangible images to identify with in order to be able to emulate them, we illustrate stories from the Torah that include the *Avot* and *Imahot*.

We want to encourage our children to identify with these worthy Jewish role models. As they portray these great people in different situations, they can more easily internalize their values. Even though we may draw the *Avot* and *Imahot* in order teach children about them, there are ways to draw them without showing their faces.

---

93 Psalms 27:4.

94 Michael Kaniel (Kaufman), *A Guide to Jewish Art* (New York: Philosophical Library, 1989), p. 115.

Here are two projects that you can do with children to depict the *Avot* and *Imahot* without detracting from the reverence they deserve:

Creative Ways to Draw the Avot and Imahot without Faces AGES 9+

Materials:

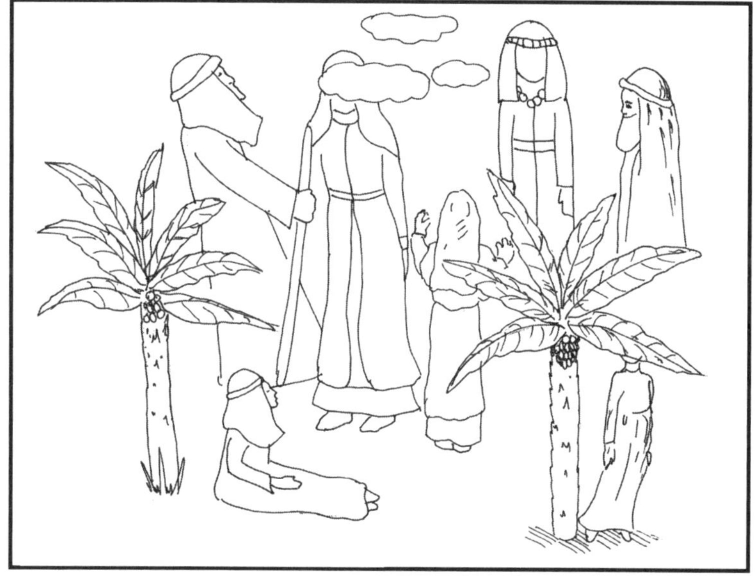

- Copy paper, size 8½ x 11 inches (21 x 30 cm)
- Pencil and eraser
- Pen or fine-tipped black marker
- Fine-tipped colored markers
- Colored pencils

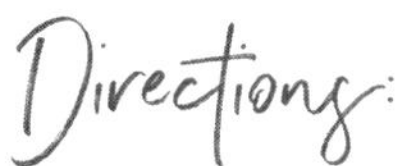

1. Divide the paper by folding it into 8 equal squares.

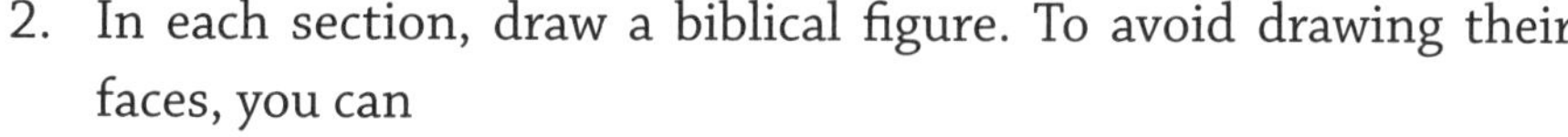

2. In each section, draw a biblical figure. To avoid drawing their faces, you can
    - draw a figure from the side, with the wind blowing and the scarf on the head covering part of the face as suggested above or covered with a branch or cloud;
    - draw a figure from behind;
    - draw a figure with the face looking down;
    - draw a figure with a burst of light covering the face;
    - draw a figure passing through a cluster of trees or bushes, obscuring the head;
    - draw a figure in the distance, perhaps on a road, small and softly drawn without details such as facial features;
    - draw a figure bent or crouching down and the head partially seen;

- depict them silhouetted;
- depict a head without features that instead resembles a polished stone, diamond, or prism;
- draw them with an emphasis on symbols that represent their lives. For example, Abraham is often portrayed in a tent with four openings to welcome guests from the four directions; Isaac is represented by the Binding of Isaac on the altar;[95] a ladder ascending to Heaven represents Jacob and his dream;[96] Sarah can be shown in a tent with Shabbat candles; Rebecca can be drawn by the well where she gave Eliezer water to drink;[97] the Tomb of Rachel near Bethlehem can symbolize Rachel;[98] Moses can be represented by the two stone tablets that he received on Har Sinai,[99] and King David can be presented by a harp.

3. Add backgrounds: a field, a desert, a grove of trees, clouds over the horizon, or a mountain in the distance.
4. Trace over the pencil marks with the black pen or marker, then color in the figures with colored pencils or fine-tipped markers.

Draw the Avot and Imahot Cut-out Dolls or Puppets AGES 7+

Create cardboard dolls depicting biblical figures with or without facial features.

Materials:

- 1 sheet copy paper, size 8½ x 11 inches (21 x 30 cm)
- Thin cardboard or Bristol paper, size 8½ x 12 inches (21 x 30 cm)

---

95 Genesis, ch. 22. Abraham was tested ten times. The final test of his devotion to Hashem was to sacrifice Isaac. Human and child sacrifices at that time were a common practice. The commandment served as a test which Abraham and Isaac passed. Isaac was immediately released, as Hashem did not want human sacrifices.

96 Ibid. 28:12.

97 Ibid 24:18.

98 Ibid. 35:19.

99 Exodus 32:15.

- Pencil and eraser
- Fine-tipped black pen or fine-tipped black marker
- Colored markers, including gold and silver
- Craft sticks (optional)

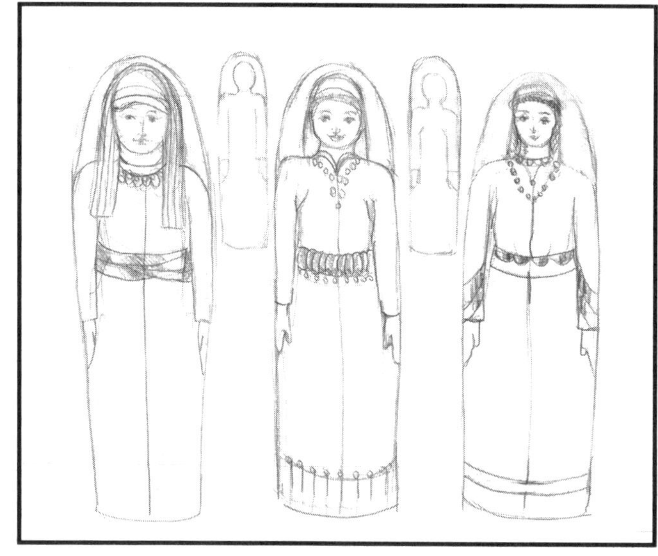

Directions:

Before beginning the doll, practice drawing it on a piece of paper. This will make it easier for you to draw the final doll. After you practice, begin the final dolls.

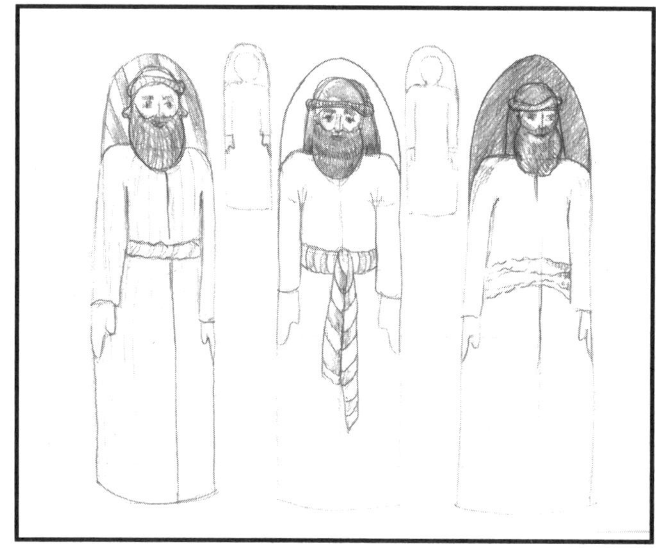

1. Fold the paper in half vertically. While the paper is folded, draw an arch from side to side, about an eighth down from the top of the paper. (You can fold the paper three times into eight sections to make it easier to gauge the measurements.) Number the sections lightly in pencil. Cut off the arch, and cut the paper down the middle, on the vertical folded line. You will have two identical pieces of paper, for two dolls.
2. Draw a circle for the head, 2 x 2 inches (5 x 5 cm), inside of the arch (sections 1½-2½). Add a neck. Draw shoulders extending from the bottom sides of the neck that touch the edges of the paper (bottom of section 2).
3. Draw two parallel lines for arms inside. Begin 1 inch below the shoulders and ¾ inch (2 cm) from paper edge under the shoulders (section 3½), down to the top of the feet (top of section 8½). Add hands: half-circles are a good start, ¾ x ¾ inch each (2 x 2 cm) (section 5½ to top of section 6).
4. Draw a head covering that ends over the shoulders.
5. Add in any facial features.

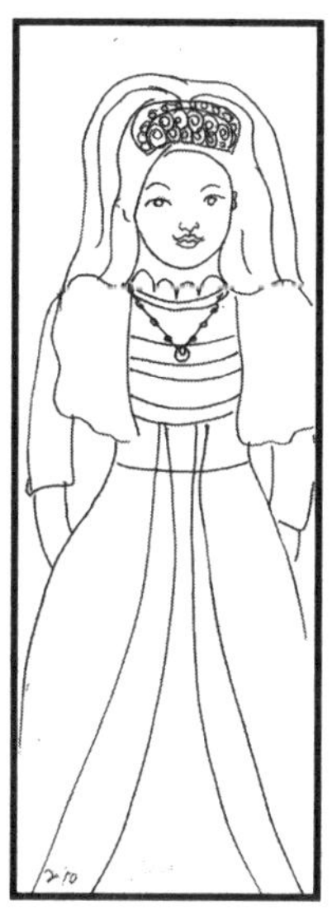

6. Draw a line up the center of the robe and add a belt (bottom of section 4).
7. Draw the feet in sandals (half-circles) where the robe ends. If the robe is too short or too long, adjust the length, erase and redo the sandals.
8. Add a beard for a man and necklace for a woman and any other jewelry, fabric, or design elements you like. Adjust the shape of the robe. You may research clothing from ancient times and vary the style and designs on the dolls' clothing. Gold and silver markers make for dramatic clothing.
9. Color with markers.

Optional: Glue one to three craft sticks (depending on the length) behind the cut-out dolls to make puppets.

Optional: Draw a kallah (bride) or clothing we wear today for a present-day doll.

Cloth Biblical Doll AGES 9+

See pattern for biblical dolls above.

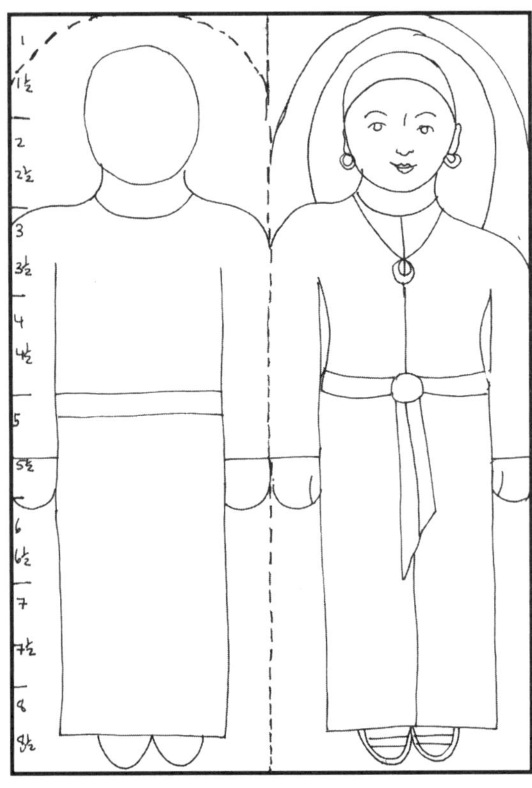

Materials:

- White muslin cotton ½ meter
- Pencil
- Scissors
- Pins
- Needle and thread
- Acrylic paint plus 2 brushes, ⅛ and ½ inch (¼ x 1½ cm)

Directions:

1. Fold muslin in half for a front and back.
2. Draw outline of doll plus a 1-inch (2½-cm) seam.

3. Draw features and ornaments: necklaces, bracelets, rings, and sandals.

4. Turn matching right sides down facing each other.

5. Machine or hand stitch (small close stiches) around the doll. Cut notches around seam to lay flat. Leave a 2-inch (5-cm) opening. Turn doll right side out. Insert a pencil to open any closed areas.

6. Iron flat, paint, and dry.

7. Fill with batting or other stuffing. Hand stich opening.

8. Put on a puppet show or display your doll.

To make the doll into a puppet, hot glue two to three tongue depressors or craft sticks together vertically. Center and hot glue on the back of the puppet, leaving 3–4 inches (8–10 cm) at the bottom of the puppet exposed with which to hold the puppet.

Rebecca at the Well AGES 6+

Rebecca displayed her true qualities of chessed by offering to bring water not only for Abraham's servant Eliezer but also for his camels. Eliezer had been sent to her homeland to find a wife for Abraham's son Isaac. Rebecca's display of kindness signaled to Eliezer that she was worthy of being one of the mothers of the Jewish people. According to the Midrash (a commentary), when she watered the camels, the water miraculously came up to the surface of the well.[100]

Materials:

- Copy paper, size 8½ x 11 inches (21 x 30 cm)
- Thick Bristol or drawing paper suitable for water if you will be using paint, size 8½ x 11 inches (21 x 30 cm) or 11 x 16 inches (28 x 41 cm)
- Pencil and eraser
- Colored markers or paints—watercolor or gouache with 2 soft brushes, ¼ and ½ inch (½ x 1½ cm)
- Black permanent fine-tipped pen or marker

100 Genesis 24:17, Rashi quotes the *Midrash Rabbah* 60:5.

Directions:

1. This drawing has five elements:

    A. A desert setting: Draw a line horizontally across the paper. This delineates the earth and the sky. On top of the line draw a few curved hills. Above that you will have a large sky.

    B. Next, draw a large stone well with a bucket hanging from it that could drop down to bring up water. The well and the bucket are cylinders, one large and one small. Draw an oval for the opening of each, with plenty of space between them. Continue with two parallel lines straight down and add a half-circle for the bottoms of each. Fill in the front of the well by drawing large stones. Fill in the front of the bucket by drawing small stones. Add a wood-stick structure above the well, to hold the bucket.

    C. Draw the water rising up to the surface of the well.

    D. Draw Rebecca in a long robe, with a head covering and jewelry.

    E. Draw a camel, or look for an example of a camel in a book or a travel brochure to copy.

    With the pencil, practice drawing each of the five elements separately on the copy paper before beginning the final drawing or painting on the Bristol.

2. Once you are satisfied with your practice drawings, draw them again lightly in pencil on the thick paper or Bristol.

3. Trace over the lines with the permanent pen or fine-tipped marker (or, if you wish, leave the drawing in pencil).

4. Color in the drawing with markers or paint. (Use markers on the small, 8½ x 11-inch [21 x 30-cm] copy paper and paint on the large, 11 x 16-inch [42 x 30-cm] copy paper.) You may find it easiest to use fine markers for small areas and paint for large background areas.

Optional: Make a relief (protruding) picture with air-drying clay on firm cardboard or Styrofoam sandwich board using the imagery for Rebecca at the Well.

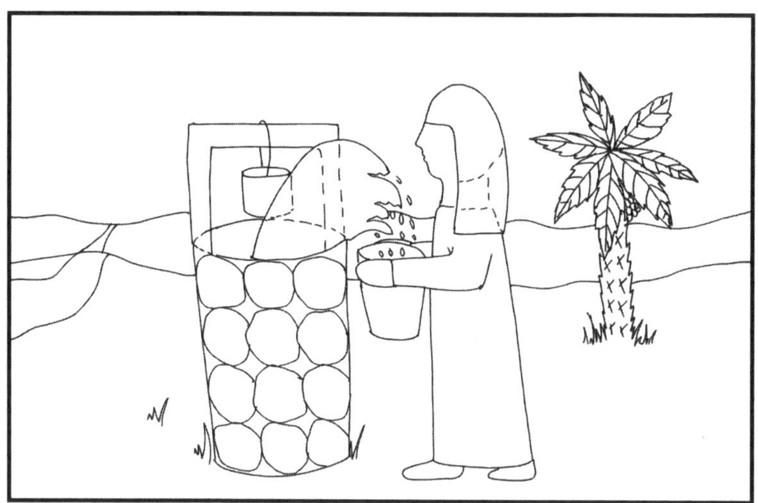

Free-Form Projects at Home

When children bring home artwork from school that reinforces what they have learned that week about the parashah or Jewish values, ask them specific questions about the depictions. Help them use the images to connect with the ideas that they have learned. You can also encourage your children to connect with the lives of our *Avot* and *Imahot* and the other *tzaddikim* that they learn about by asking them to illustrate what they know.

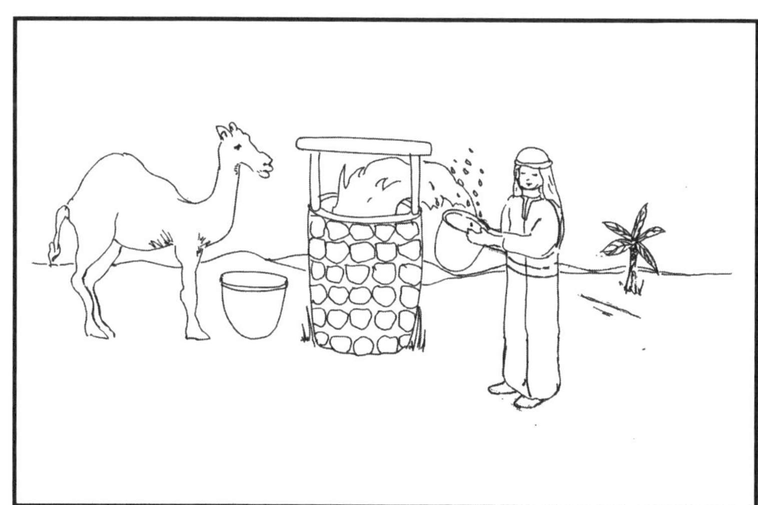

This can make for a wonderful rainy-day activity. Choose one or two stories from Tanach or other source and review them with your children (they might have already learned about them in school). If your children are old enough and have the patience for it, read the verses that recount the story with them inside the Tanach to provide greater detail and understanding of these events.

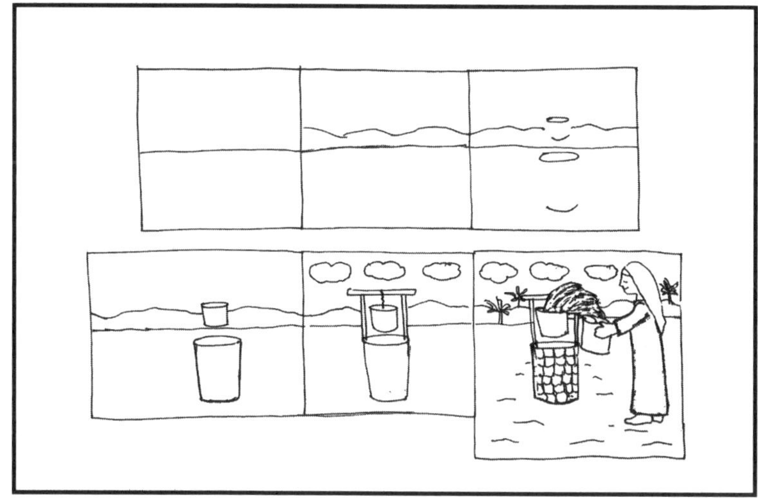

Second, provide them with materials to illustrate the stories. Simply draw with pencil on paper or offer the children several choices of art mediums and materials. Work together with the child to come up with clever ways to use the materials. Choose materials from those listed in the introduction now, or wait until you decide on a subject.

Help the child visualize in his mind's eye what he will draw by asking him questions that will get him thinking:

Who would you like to draw? What size will he/she be?

What will you show him/her doing?

Can you show what he/she was thinking or feeling?

Which materials would you like to use? Choose materials from the list in the introduction.

What colors will you choose?

By portraying these scenes from the Tanach, what new ideas did you learn?

What thoughts did you have about the story?

In Summary: Jewish Role Models

- We have abundant choices of role models from Tanach and history, as well as contemporary times. Historically, there have been works of art that misrepresent our role models, due to a lack of knowledge.
- When depicting the faces of our role models, we need to be sensitive to the subjects' deeds and soul.
- Hands-on art projects can connect our children to role models and reinforce their values.

Questions and Wonder

1. Do you have any suggestions of how to represent the *Avot* and *Imahot* without showing their faces? How would you draw them?
2. Have you ever thought about why our eyes are called the entrance to the soul?

3. Moses was called "the most humble of all men," yet he confidently led the entire Jewish people. How can we depict these two seemingly opposite traits? King David was both a man of peace and a strong warrior. How can we show the heart of a king like this? Is it possible to portray such *middot* at all? How would you do it? How can we visualize and depict their features?
4. If you were to draw or paint your parents, brothers, sisters, grandparents, or friends, what are the special qualities about them that you would want to show? How could you show their good deeds?
5. Have you ever thought about drawing yourself by showing your feelings and thoughts rather than only the physical you? What would the picture look like? How would you depict what is going on inside your head, showing each side of yourself and what you think about and your deeds?

PART 2

Growing Along with Art

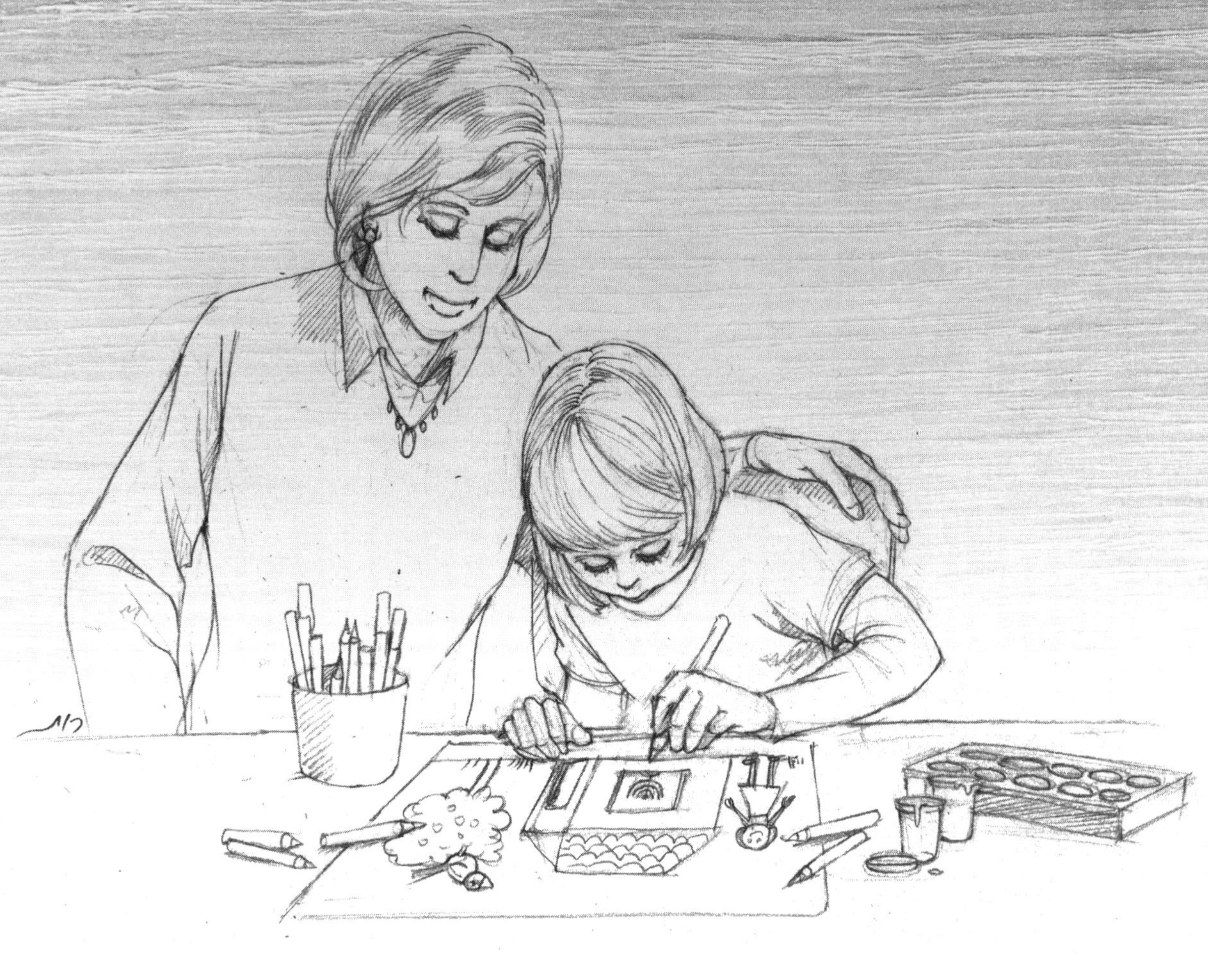

The Goal Is Success

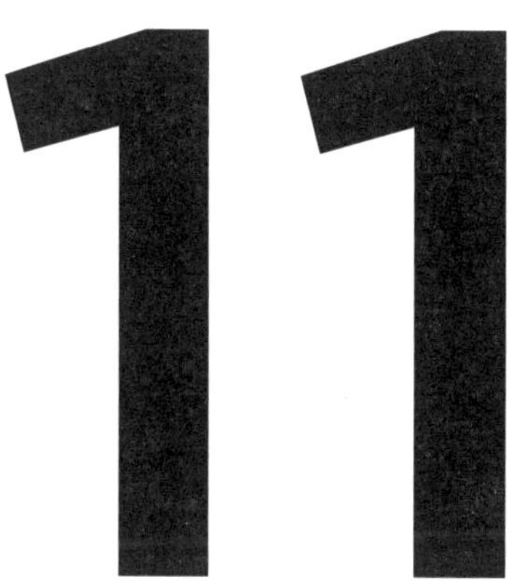

The Right Environment

The Talmudic sage Hillel taught the entire Torah "on one foot" to a potential convert. "That which you hate others to do to you, don't do to your friend," Hillel advised him. "The rest is commentary."[101] Well, here are the keys to achieving success in art on one foot:

- Have a positive attitude.
- Be prepared: provide plenty of materials and opportunities to create.
- Avoid comparing one's art to another's; instead, keep track of one's own successes.
- Giving children the opportunity to experience success in creating artwork is more about the process than the finished product. The child's success lies more in his accomplishing a task, finishing a project, making the effort—and feeling good about that effort—than in producing perfect artwork.

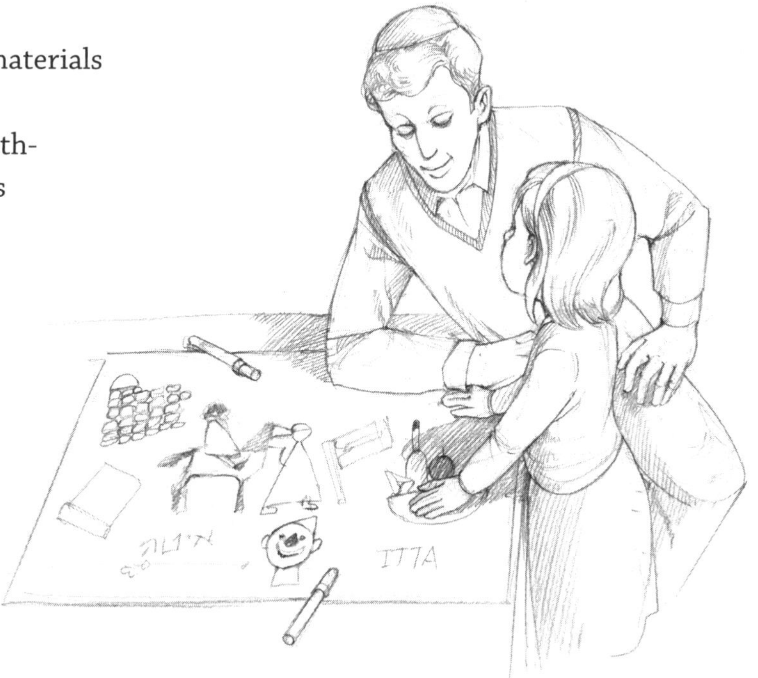

101 Talmud, *Shabbat* 31a, and Rashi there.

Notes and Sketches

- When given the chance, each child will express himself through his artwork in different ways. The art reveals who he is. And that is success.
- This doesn't mean that he won't need guidance and instruction. It doesn't mean that he shouldn't be encouraged to learn new skills. Your role is to create the right environment to give him these opportunities. Provide the materials the child needs, explain, and demonstrate. Then step back and give him time and encouragement to work.
- Above all, don't compare children. Instead, help the child keep track of his own progress and triumph in his personal successes.

When I attended elementary school in the fifties, the emphasis was on neatness and order, important in a classroom but a deterrent in an art session.

There I was, a shy and highly creative child in a classroom where creativity was not the goal. The subject of the art session was a house, a tree, and flowers—standard little-girl pictures. But mine was not a well-ordered composition of a house, tree, and flowers; it was a picture of dancing life in color that included a riot of yellow flowers dotting the landscape.

My drawing did not appeal to the teacher. It was overlooked as she went around the tables pulling out the best samples. She oohed and aahed at the one that depicted a carefully drawn illustration of a house set firmly on the bottom edge of the paper with one tree on the left and one flower on the right—neat, clean, and concise.

Because drawing is an expression of the self, I, who had desperately sought approval for my less ordered but infinitely more creative (so I thought) illustration, was devastated.

When it was time to go home, I passed by the wastebasket and noticed that the teacher's favorite work of art was on top of the waste pile. I plucked it out of the garbage and took it home. I didn't lie: Never did I say that I did it. I just left it on the table thinking that when my mother saw it, she would swoon over it like the teacher had.

But no, my mother simply said it was nothing special and that was the end of the story.

After that, a new story began, one where I learned that my mother loved my creativity and style, and considered my art expression a very special gift. I learned that my artwork was an extension of myself and not just a school project to be judged and discarded if it didn't fit with a teacher's idea of what a piece of art must look like.

Looking back, I realize that the teacher made no effort to bring out the unique potential in each child, but looked only to make each child conform to certain rigid standards. In some subjects, perhaps, such as math, this is desirable, but it has no place in art.

Let's look at how we can create an environment for art where a child can maximize his potential and express himself—his unique self—through art. Then, in the following chapters, we'll learn how art actually helps a child develop and gives him skills for learning and interacting with the world.

Notes and Sketches

A Positive Attitude: Process over Perfection

Groom a positive attitude toward the child's process, not only when his work meets with conventional standards of perfection. The process may be bumpy or unclear and replete with non-identifiable marks. Be enthusiastic and look for the effort in each mark and in the full picture. You may not understand the mental and physical work the child is going through but it is enveloped in each mark. A positive attitude is a prelude to accepting the process over perfection. All the tips for success listed below depend on the vitality of a positive attitude.

When nurturing creativity in children, the process is almost as important, if not more, than the result. Success is not necessarily a perfectly finished picture. Success is a sense of achievement. This may come just as well from mastering a new skill as from producing something beautiful.

In the beginning, a child feels successful when you let him do what he enjoys, at his own pace. Allow him to cut with scissors for as long as he wants. He may be acquiring the skill of snipping off the corners of the paper. Even if he does only that and nothing else for hours, let him. After tasting success, he will try something "out of his box" and challenge himself to succeed in a new area. Perhaps he'll move on to cutting larger straight lines or cutting out images he drew or work on something entirely new.

When learning a new concept, children are engaged in the process of learning it until they have mastered it. A child who is learning how to make circles will continue to draw circles until he feels a sense of mastery over the skill. The child will be ready to go on to another skill only after attaining the inner satisfaction of completing this one. Unfortunately, children are often not given ample time to master skills completely because they are rushed to keep up with others or to work according to the school curriculum. At the point when they could have a peak moment of self-confidence, they are urged to keep up with the rest of the group.

In art class, especially if the group is small, a child can be given the chance to learn at his own pace. Usually the child will not need a very long time to master a skill, especially if the teacher or parent can sit with the child reviewing and explaining until the child catches on. Certainly at home, parents can give their children as much time as they need to experiment without any pressures.

Rachel only wanted to draw with colored pencils. When I offered her paint and a brush, she told me that her arm shook and she couldn't control the paint, causing it to spread outside the lines that she wanted to follow. I respected her desire to stay inside the lines and draw recognizable objects and let her draw with the colored pencils. Later, I gave her projects where staying inside the lines was not the main goal and I urged her to try the paint again. She found that she enjoyed working with paint and practiced making designs with large areas of shapes and colors.

Success Breeds Success

If a child feels that he can succeed, he will be motivated to try new things. But how do we pass on our confidence in our children that they will succeed, especially if they don't seem to be demonstrating much proficiency?

Let's examine what I mean by confidence. Most people agree that confidence means believing in oneself. It's knowing that I can be successful and accomplish to the best of my ability (or at least pretend I can!).

A child may not be skilled or talented in art, but if you believe that she can do it, and that art is not a mysterious talent just for an elite few, you can encourage her success. At the same time, explaining the skills involved and offering guidance to ensure success prevents the child from feeling limited and helpless. Confidence and success is ultimately from working through challenges until the difficultly dissipates. A child grows from an adult walking him through his rough spots until that glorious moment of success. A parent who has an understanding of the artistic process can be that guiding hand.

Tell yourself, *Art is a skill that can be learned and enjoyed by everyone*, and your child will sense your attitude and feel encouraged. In this way, you foster the child's confidence.

Daniella, the mother of one of my students, let me know that she had absolutely no talent in art. "I've never been good at it. Even as a little girl, my projects always turned out the worst. I wouldn't be surprised if Leah inherited my lack of talent for art. Just so you are warned."

Of course, I didn't know if it was really true. It might have been that Daniella didn't really enjoy drawing, and by putting down her work and claiming she was no good, she didn't have to wait in nervous anticipation for the judgment of her parents, teachers, or friends. It was a great shield. Now she was projecting the same defense on her daughter, in case she also didn't "measure up."

It turned out that Leah was truly talented and enjoyed art. But, as children do, she identified with her mother and voiced her mother's same self-deprecations about her artwork. She never really progressed because she didn't see the point if she "lacked the talent." She had it in her to produce beautiful artwork, but declined the opportunity for lack of confidence.

Praise Produces Passion

Even more than confidence, joy, love, and passion are necessary ingredients in creating art. You can infuse a child with these feelings, as well as fostering confidence, through ample encouragement and praise.

Be specific when handing out the praise. Don't you still hear echoes of "Oh, that's nice" in response to all your hard work, and cringe? "That's nice" is bland. The child wants sincerity. Try to appreciate what the child went through to produce that one awkward circle, all the hand-eye-brain coordination it involved, and then, instead of saying, "That's nice" or "Good work," try asking her how she knew to draw such a great big circle. She may have something interesting to say. Then compliment her, "You did it! Look at that nice, round circle!" and watch your child swell with pride.

Gabe didn't like drawing, or at least he said he didn't because the project sounded too hard, and he was overwhelmed by the level of creativity it required. He had taken arts and crafts in school along with the rest of his class, but he often found that he couldn't complete the projects because he couldn't produce the same results as his teacher. The teacher ended up finishing off the projects for him. The end results were impressive, but didn't represent his work.

The solution was to give him a piece of paper which I call a "practice paper." The practice paper was for trials and errors, a way for Gabe to work out how to draw what seemed overwhelming. Each drawing was broken down into steps and explained with pictures that Gabe could identify with. Without the pressure of producing perfect results—and a lot of encouragement—Gabe enjoyed experimenting with the drawings and eventually learned how to complete a project on his own.

Conclude each project with a point of satisfaction for the child: "Look at how you were able to cut that paper so well!" or "You chose beautiful colors!" The pleasure he receives from your compliments will encourage him to keep working until he has mastered the skill. Each child, and each session, should have a success story.

Be Prepared: Options and Opportunities

Of course, praise and encouragement won't help if the child doesn't have the means and opportunities to create art. Give young children ample time to do arts and crafts with easy-to-manipulate materials: clay, paper, paints, boxes, or Styrofoam sandwich board.

When children feel that they can have an effect on the physical world around them, they blossom with confidence. Give a young child a lump of clay and have him press his fingers into it and make indentations. Show him how his fingers made a lasting impression in the clay. Later he will mold the clay into a functional object, a cup or a bowl. The process of producing something from a mass of raw materials into a specific physical form gives inner satisfaction and excitement.

Seven-year-old Michael had been struggling with his feelings about some incidents that had occurred in his neighborhood. His mother thought it might help him to come to me once a week for some private art time.

We embarked on a big project where Michael was in control. He designed and built a small-scale house. The house was his domain, his private place in the world.

Each session ended when he was satisfied with his work for the day. According to his plans, we built a three-story Styrofoam sandwich-board house. Michael's specifications were not random; they all meant something to him. He made a fence on the roof according to the halachah that one should build a guardrail on one's roof to prevent accidents. He made a staircase leading up to a special room with a door so that no one could see inside. Each piece of furniture was considered acceptable or rejected as unnecessary. We put in a garden with trees and rocks and a path. He painted each side of the house a different color.

After six weeks, Michael proudly walked out of the art room with his three-story house. Through the process of producing it, he had worked through his feelings and felt better about himself. His mother had made sure he had the means and opportunity to express those feelings.

Giving the child different options and opportunities not only fosters creativity but is important when you introduce a child to a new skill for the first time, especially a child who has challenges. The child may resist or even display opposition out of fear of the unknown. He may think it's too hard and that he can't do it. In his mind, the complexity of what you are expecting him to do may be overwhelming. He may want to do it but considers it beyond his reach.

Helping the child to the top of the mountain requires flexibility. To tailor an art project for a group of children, it helps if there are several steps using different materials. It's also a good idea to give several options in the course of a project—whether it's a choice of materials or the scale of a project (a mural as opposed to a drawing or smaller canvas painting), so the child doesn't feel locked in a box. One child may prefer cutting to drawing. Another student may connect better to the second step and spend lots of time on it after rushing through the first step, which didn't interest him. Don't push him to finish the first step perfectly if it doesn't speak to him.

Rafi was a quiet boy who loved art class, but he had his own sense of timing. He would just sit thinking and observing for most of the class.

At the end of each class, he did produce a small original piece, but he never seemed fully engaged in the class.

Three-quarters into the year I hit on a material and style that spoke to him and woke him up with a jolt of excitement. I gave Rafi a box of charcoals and a reproduction of a charcoal drawing by a Jewish artist from a European shtetl (town) which I had found in a magazine. Rafi's face instantly lit up and he went right to work. After a half hour of practicing with the charcoal, he drew a profound rendition which he was proud of.

If the task is simply too hard for a particular child, reduce the level of technique or break down the steps further. The child wants to draw a little girl or a little boy but doesn't know where to begin. Start with geometric shapes—a circle (head), on top of a small square (neck), on top of a large square (shirt), on top of a triangular skirt or two thin long rectangles (pants). Then show her how to add details one at a time.

Let the child work until she is satisfied. Take it step by step, going forward slowly at the beginning and picking up the pace as you add new skills and the child gains confidence that she can learn them. Encourage her to take the time to master a skill she is having trouble with before moving on, or give her more opportunity to grow in her art if she feels her progress is being stifled.

Motivating a Child Who Wants to Give Up

You've created a positive environment and encouraged each child to focus on his own unique personal expression. Still, it's natural for kids to get frustrated when their work is not coming out the way they want. Some may even want to give up. When you hear comments of "I don't like it," "I'm throwing this away," "I'm leaving this art class and I'm telling my mother," "It's too babyish," or "It's finished" when it's clearly not, they are really cries for help. Besides the encouragement and options described above, what can be done practically to motivate your children to complete a project and not to give up in frustration or distaste?

Assuming you demonstrated the project beforehand and divided it up into numerous steps, when a child gets frustrated, the solution is to review all the steps that you explained at the beginning of the lesson.

Check if each step was completed before going on to the next. The child's difficulty may be that he simply skipped a step. Then you can say, "I see you didn't do the seventh step," and ask the child to finish it.

Most children are willing to do "one more thing," such as painting in the background, adding more objects or details, coloring in unfinished areas, or outlining objects so they can be seen more clearly. That might be all the child needs to feel the work is complete to his satisfaction.

If the child still doesn't like the results of his project, say to him, "It's all right if you don't like it. This is only practice for you to learn to draw, paint, or craft something. Each time you try, you'll get better at it." Then ask the child what he doesn't like about the project. Ask what he wants to accomplish. The child may not be quite clear on the end goal, and you may have to help the child define it. Give options and openings for the child to express himself.

> *Six-year-old Eli wanted a green sky in his painting, but he couldn't quite get it to look the way he wanted. "This picture is yucky!" he said in frustration.*
>
> *The teacher went over to him and said, "I think your painting is very nice. What don't you like about it?"*
>
> *Eli blurted out, "The sky isn't the way I want it."*
>
> *"Why don't you try adding a touch of blue to see how it looks?"*
>
> *"No! I want it to be green."*
>
> *The teacher nodded. "Okay, then how about if you add some clouds?"*
>
> *Eli smiled. "Yeah, I'll make it rain!"*
>
> *"That's a wonderful idea," the teacher agreed. "And next time I'd like to see how you make a blue sky, okay?"*
>
> *Eli nodded happily and went back to work on his picture.*
>
> *Eli's teacher didn't discourage him when he insisted on coloring the sky green. She went with his idea and helped Eli realize that he wanted to paint a stormy sky that wasn't blue at all. But she also encouraged him to try a blue sky next time.*

You don't have to wait until the child gets frustrated and decides to give up. You can encourage self-motivation before you begin a new project. Discuss possible difficulties with the materials or techniques that the children may encounter and suggest how to solve them. Ask the children to suggest their own solutions as well. Let them know that you understand them and tell them about others who have struggled—that great artists only reached that level through hard work and effort. Tell them stories of how you yourself gained self-confidence through learning new skills and needed years of practice to learn how to draw and paint well.

Sometimes it's hard to be objective when a child protests, "I can't do it!" or "I don't like it!" You may find yourself losing confidence in your own ability to engage the child. But rather than getting stuck in your own footprints, ask questions until you learn what the child doesn't like about the project. Then offer an option that is easy and pleasant for the child to do.

> *Six-year-old Sarah never wanted to draw or color. She had a big sister who happened to be a well-praised and talented young artist, but Sarah wouldn't even pick up a colored marker. Her mother was stuck on how to motivate Sarah to draw. She needed a plan.*
>
> *One day, her mother found a suggestion in my art class for mothers. She thought she would give it a try. That afternoon, when the house was quiet, she said to her daughter, "Sarah, I need help. I am not sure how to draw a big circle. I can draw little circles," which the mother proceeded to do and produced three small circles. Patiently, she looked at the little girl and said, "Sarah, help me draw a giant circle."*
>
> *Gallantly, Sarah picked up the pencil and drew a circle. "That's a wonderful circle," said her mother. "That circle deserves to be completed." She added a triangle for a dress and asked Sarah to add two arms, which she did, one long and one short.*
>
> *"How about eyes and a mouth, Sarah? I will make the nose." Sarah duly drew the eyes and mouth, added curly hair, and decorated the dress with buttons and stripes. Sarah was delighted with "her" drawing. Once her mother had broken it up into small steps, Sarah wasn't so overwhelmed. She was no longer afraid to try drawing.*

A child might be resistant simply because he is having a bad day. Take the pressure off of a child who is not in a good mood by treating him in a light, giving, and sharing manner. Be flexible. Give him the markers or the scissors he really wants, even if the project doesn't call for it. Switch gears and show him how to draw something that is simple and catches his attention. Alternatively, he may perk up and be ready to continue after a healthful snack and a short break.

Should You Draw for Them?

How many times does your child come home from school with a beautiful art project that is too precise and neat for him to have done on his own? Sometimes teachers are more concerned with impressing parents with perfect art projects than giving the children the chance to work on their own. But the child who is encouraged to complete a project on his own is left with a tremendous feeling of satisfaction that the teacher's perfect picture could never have given him.

Give a child an art project that she can do alone, and the child will have the opportunity to discover his strengths and talents. In fact, confining art in preschool to craft projects may expose children to a variety of materials, but they often don't require the same thinking and problem-solving that drawing and painting demands. The emphasis on crafts in schools eliminates the mental challenge and emotional perseverance inherent in drawing.[102]

To ensure that children get the maximum benefits from creating art—the satisfaction of producing something on their own as well as the stimulation this provides to their growing brains—kindergarten teachers should not do the children's arts and crafts for them except when absolutely necessary. Certainly, teachers can prepare certain parts of a project for the children to assemble and finish, but it is preferable for the children to do as much of the work as possible. It is more time consuming for the teacher, but the benefit to the children when they realize their own capabilities is enormous.

The adult is there only to facilitate. A teacher or parent should challenge children to do something entirely new that they have never done. Encourage them to stretch their horizons. If a child prefers to make detailed pen-and-ink drawings, give her projects that will loosen her up—such as free-style finger painting and collages. If a child enjoys bright, bold painting with a lot of free form but displays little organization, provide him with a project that requires preciseness and an

102 Betty Edwards, *Drawing on the Right Side of the Brain* (J.P. Tarcher, Inc., 1979), p. 64.

ordered sequence of steps. Having left his comfort zone, he can return to his style with a new attitude.

Your child may ask you to draw the picture for him if he feels incapable or doesn't like the way his drawing is coming out. Don't be tempted to do the work for him. This is a quick solution with very short-term results. Try to avoid drawing for the child on his paper. It's better to show him an example on another sheet of paper and explain how you are doing it step by step. Then have him try again on his own, or he can copy your illustration onto his paper.

Sometimes there are occasions when it may be necessary to draw on the child's paper. If he is having a difficult time getting started and needs a push, draw a few light lines that he can trace over. This can be done in several places in the picture. Ask the child to draw the object by himself on a separate paper to show that he now knows how to draw the object.

You can also lightly draw a series of dots outlining a shape or object and let the child connect the dots. Start with the dots at the corners of an angle, such as a square or triangle. If the child needs additional help, include more dots so that when the child connects the dots, the shape becomes clear to him. When he's done, ask him to color inside the lines he's drawn to reinforce the image in his mind.

For instance, if the project involves drawing a person, you can draw a circle (the head), a small square (the neck), and a larger square (the torso) on the child's paper. Then have him trace over the shapes you drew and add the arms, hands, legs, shoes, facial features, hair, clothing, and details.

This exercise is especially helpful for a child who has a hard time forming or remembering shapes. He can master geometric shapes such as circles, cubes, and triangles by connecting a series of dots that you have drawn for him. Afterward, ask him to draw the same circle, square, or triangle freehand. Repeat these steps until he has mastered this skill.

Comparison and Criticism: Handle with Care

Once the child completes the project, resist comparing it with other children's. Instead, show him where he has succeeded on his level and pace. Compare it to his own past artwork, and let him see how he has advanced. You can also let the child hear you say out loud how well he painted the trees or birds.

In learning to create art, the child should be aware that everything he does has value. How we view his work will convey that message. It's up to us to look below the surface of the picture in front of us to reveal the precious seedlings. If a small child draws one clear circle in a mess of scribbles, ignore the scribbles and praise the child for drawing that one perfectly clear circle. Your feedback will encourage the child to go forward.

Self-criticism comes into full gear at the age of five or six, around the first grade. Until the age of five or so, children are happy just exploring the new sensations that art activities provide: color, shape, balance, perception (sight), texture (touch), proportion, and weight (heaviness). Add graphic, verbal, and kinesthetic expression to this mixture for the big picture of what your child is learning. These children are not yet engaged in the precision of imitating reality. They accept the artwork they produce because they are immersed in the wonder of the new sensory and conceptual elements.[103]

After the age of five or six, children become more attuned to social conditions. They begin to question their place in the world and desire to meet school academic standards and peer demands.[104] If their work doesn't compare favorably to that of their peers, they may begin to lose faith in their art abilities. They may think their artwork is not important or that it is not perfect enough because it doesn't look as smooth and ordered as the teacher's work or the posters on the walls. Or perhaps they relate to their artwork negatively because they can't draw the image they have in their minds. Some may belittle their artwork to test the reaction of their friends, parents, or teachers.

The first thing I notice about the new beginner's group of second graders is that they enter the art room half expecting it to be a school classroom environment. They want rules. They want to know if everything they draw is "good" because "good" is a school standard. And yet, at the same time, they want to make a mess with the leftover paint and mix it into a mass of brown goop. They were enchanted while mixing the paint and watching new colors

103 Joan Bouza Koster, *Growing Artists* (Delmar Publishers, 1997), pp. 80–81.

104 Ibid. Judaism considers a child of six or seven to have reached a certain level of understanding and is capable of connecting to G-d while praying and saying blessings (*Mishnah Berurah* 70:2). We see that after a child acquires technical skills, such as dressing himself, he is capable of connecting to G-d and the world around him.

emerge. When the crescendo was reached, suddenly the brilliant colors turned into brown goop. It seems this was a luxury these children had not had.

Destroying and building are part of our lives. Children attest to this. To do this right, both need boundaries and self-control. Generally, children who have had time to play with the materials and "make a mess" outgrow this need.

Self-criticism, if channeled properly, develops good *middot*. It helps a child integrate socially and develop responsibility. As they evolve into social beings, children compare themselves to adult role models and their peers, and figure out how to behave in the world around them.

But this type of comparison also has a negative side. A child who is constantly comparing his artwork to others may end up being stifled. His creativity won't blossom. Instead, let art be an area where each child can discover his own unique style. Let the child realize that he or she has special qualities that Hashem gave to him or her alone.

It should also be pointed out to the children that they are not adults. When children try to copy the teacher's drawing from the blackboard, they can become very frustrated because the results are not the same. A five-year-old or a seven-year-old should not compare his artwork to that of an adult, who has had many more years of art experience than he.

> *Eight-year-old Michelle goes on and on in art class about how she dislikes her painting. "Ugh, it's terrible, I hate it!"*
>
> *The other girls look up from their paintings to see who is complaining. One after another, they say, "But it's so nice! Can I have it?"*
>
> *Pinpointing the source of the ruckus, the teacher walks over to Michelle's table and examines the picture. "Michelle, I can see you have a good sense for texture. What don't you like about your painting?"*
>
> *"It just isn't what I wanted it to look like. The hands don't look right, and the sky is not the right blue."*
>
> *Michelle's teacher nods and gives some pointers to help Michelle improve her picture so she can get it closer to the image in her mind's eye. Then, with Michelle's permission, she holds up the painting for others to see and emphasizes its good points.*
>
> *"Does anyone have anything they'd like to say to Michelle to help her with her painting?" she asks the class. "Any suggestions to make the blue of the sky more realistic?"*

Michelle beams as the girls and her teacher praise her work, and she listens carefully to the constructive criticism. Immediately, she gets back to work on her painting, this time without a word of complaint.

In an art class or when doing a project with your kids at home, if one child blurts out, "It's disgusting!" you'll find a chorus all claiming their work is disgusting unless you hold up a stop sign immediately. Let it be known that we don't talk this way.

Even better, head off self-criticism before it starts. Initiate a dialogue with your children or students about comparing our work (and ourselves) to others. Convey the message that since each one of us is unique, there is no point in comparing ourselves to others since no one can be like anyone else. Do this often until it becomes a familiar conversation piece.

Give the children alternatives when they aren't happy with their work. Tell them, "If we don't like what we've done, we ask for help." Rather than their saying, "I hate this," have them repeat the phrase "I did my best" or "I like what I did but can do it differently next time." Dig under the surface and find out what they don't like, what frustrates them, and help them work it out. Self-criticism ("My work is stupid, not good, etc.") can be an indirect way of saying, "I need more time and space to master what I want to draw."

Finally, protect the child from negative comments that may leave a scar. Don't allow children to criticize each other's work. Teach them to look for the good. Emphasize the unique qualities in each one's work. Make it clear that it's okay to like what you create even if it's not the same as the others' work. Distinguish between skills that need to be learned (creating contrast, drawing shadows and shading, etc.) and personal expression that conveys mood and feeling. Show children how to look at the artwork from two perspectives: as a finished composition that stands on its own objective merits and as a personal expression.

When you want to show the child where he can improve, be gentle and sincere. Be aware that children can be very sensitive about their artwork, especially if it represents genuine self-expression.

Here is a project that will give young children valuable drawing skills to master.

The Successful Ladder AGES 4+

The ladder represents climbing to new heights and overcoming challenges. Each rung of the ladder holds a gift of accomplishment. Depending on their ages and skills, children can draw a ladder with bare lines and basic representations of figures, or evolve it into boards with three dimensions, with depth and shadows on the ground surrounding the ladder.

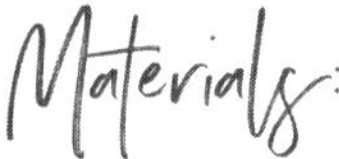

- 2 sheets copy paper, size 8½ x 11 inches (21 x 30 cm)
- Bristol paper, size 11 x 16 inches (28 x 41 cm)
- Bristol paper, size 8½ x 11 inches (21 X 28 cm)
- Pencil
- Fine or medium black marker
- Colored markers with fine to medium tips
- Red, blue, yellow, and white paint: tempera or gouache for children under the age of 9; and acrylics or gouache for children over the age of 9
- Soft paintbrushes, ¼ and ½ inch (½ x 1½ cm)
- Glue stick or white plastic glue
- Scissors

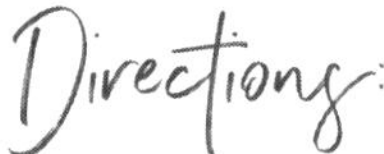

1. On one sheet of copy paper, practice drawing ladders. On the second sheet, practice drawing one large ladder, paying attention to the size, location, and tilt of the ladder. Add dimensions to the ladder and shadowing (according to age and ability).
2. On the 11 x 16-inch (28 x 41-cm) Bristol paper, draw a ground line in pencil. Draw the large ladder on the ground.
3. Surround the ladder with several clouds, a sun peeking out, grass, flowers, and mountains, or other backgrounds and details.

4. Trace over the pencil lines with the black marker.
5. Squeeze the paint out onto the used 8½ x 11-inch (21x 30-cm) copy paper for mixing and easy disposal. Paint all the objects and fill in the sky with a soft blue in any style you like. Try to cover most of the white paper even if you use white paint in places or a mixture of white with small amounts of blue. Let dry.
6. Meanwhile, on the 8½ x 11-inch (21 x 28-cm) Bristol paper, draw in pencil four or more wrapped gift boxes with ribbons. Make sure they will fit on the rungs of the ladder.
7. Trace over the pencil lines with the black marker and color in with the colored markers. Cut out and glue the gifts in place onto the rungs of the ladder on the larger Bristol.

Here are some options you can choose to put on the ladder:

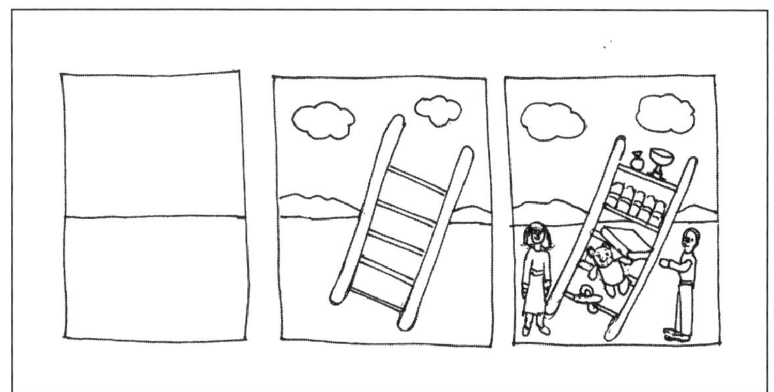

Stages of life: pacifier; balls; jump ropes; bar/bat mitzvah (age of maturity) symbols, such as books and tefillin (Phylacteries); marriage symbols (a wedding ring and a Kiddush cup).

Mitzvot: charity, prayer, challah, Shabbat.

Symbols of the festivals: shofar, *lulav* and *etrog*, matzah, Torah, prayer book.

Acts of kindness: visiting the sick, making peace, bringing food or money to the poor, helping old people.

The five books of the Torah with a symbol for each.

- *Bereishit* (Genesis): Shabbat candlesticks, two covered challahs, goblet and wine.
- *Shemot* (Exodus): Jewish slaves building pyramids in Egypt.
- *Vayikra* (Leviticus): The *kohen gadol* lighting the *Menorah* in the Beit Hamikdash.
- *Bamidbar* (Numbers): Flags of the twelve tribes or the holy objects from the *Mishkan*: the *Aron* (ark), the *Shulchan* (table), the *Menorah*, the *Mizbei'ach* (altar), and *Kiyor* (washing basin).
- *Devarim* (Deuteronomy): Mitzvot—a tzedakah box, tefillin, and mezuzah.

In Summary: The Goal Is Success

- Success lies not only in the finished product but also in the process.
- When working with children, it's important to maintain a positive attitude. It encourages the process and is the opening to all the other points of success.
- Provide the child with plenty of options and opportunities to motivate him to succeed and give him the time he needs to master new skills.
- Encourage a child who wants to give up by breaking down the project into smaller steps or by giving him a chance to focus on something he enjoys doing and can master.
- Encourage children to work on projects independently.
- Try not to compare one child to another; rather, compare his present work to his previous work and show him how much he has improved.

Questions and Wonder

1. Art can be enjoyable and relaxing. It releases emotions and thoughts. Why is release important to enjoyment and relaxation?

2. Have you ever wanted to draw, paint, construct, or sculpt something but felt you would fail? If you gave it a try now, how would you encourage yourself so that this time you might succeed?

3. Drawing teaches us other skills besides making pictures. It teaches us to make choices and use options. Why are choices and options important? How do choices and options help us to succeed?

12 Art as a Development Aid

Yehudit, age two and a half, wanted to join the after-school art class along with her four-year-old sister, but she was too young. Her mother asked permission for Yehudit to come for ten minutes after the class finished.

Yehudit told her mother, "Quickly, Mommy! I have to go to the art class!" What was the rush? It seemed that Yehudit had many ideas whirling through her head. She couldn't wait to express her ideas and give them life through painting them.

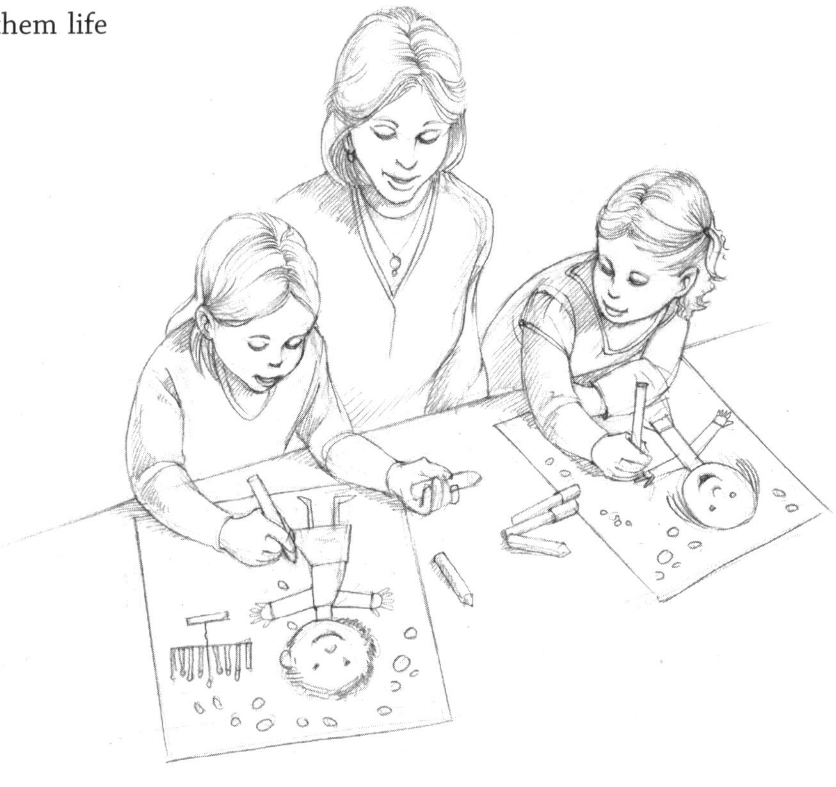

At last, seated at the painting table, her nimble fingers guided the brush back and forth, dabbing the paper with blue paint and then white paint with finesse and grace beyond her years. Twenty minutes later, the paper was covered with dark-blue, light-blue, and white strokes. She took a breath and then released it softly and put the brush down. As she was leaving, she turned back and said in her little voice, "Thank you," three times.

Notes and Sketches

Many people think of art as an "extracurricular activity," not as vital as reading, writing, or arithmetic. The truth is, creating art is just as essential for a child's development as learning numbers and letters are, especially in the early years.

Perhaps it is even more vital.

Art Reinforces Learning

The years between ages three and six are the prime time to nurture the child's creativity, because inherent in the creative process are thinking skills for life—skills such as decision-making, fine-motor development, learning from mistakes, planning and problem solving, combining resources and materials to design and build, and being flexible and spontaneous.

Art is also a wonderful tool for reinforcing all the new concepts and knowledge that the child is learning in the classroom. In the kindergarten classroom, children learn the names of basic shapes—circles, squares, and triangles. In art class, the subject is expanded. They learn how to put the shapes together to make objects: a circle and triangle become an ice cream cone or a clown with a hat; a triangle and square become a house. The four-year-old also learns his colors in school. In art class, the knowledge of colors is put to practical application and enriched as the child learns to experiment with mixing colors to create new ones.

As children mature, they also develop learning skills and thinking skills. According to Rabbi Moshe Chaim Luzzatto, author of the classical work *Path of the Just*, thinking is defined as comparing and differentiating between different things.[105] Without light, for instance, how do you know what is dark? Art offers such tactile and visual comparisons: large and small, over and under, soft and hard, black and white, thick and thin.

Also, research into how children learn has revealed that not all children learn effectively in the same way. Here are four sample modalities through which children learn: visual, auditory, tactile, and kinesthetic. Some children learn best by visualizing with their eyes, others through hearing and listening. The tactile learner experiences new information through touch while others increase sensory input with body movement

105 Rabbi Moshe Chaim Luzzatto, also known by the acronym of his name, Ramchal, lived in Italy, Amsterdam, and Israel. He was born in 1707 and died in 1746.

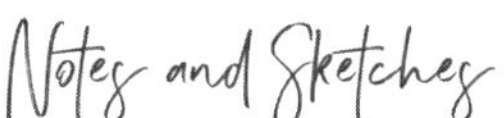

(kinesthetic), relying more on their spatial abilities.[106] Young children, especially, learn through touching and handling things physically.[107]

Where else but in the art classroom will children receive such rich opportunities to use all their senses? The more enrichment these children receive through manipulating the physical world in their art renditions, the more resources they will have to draw from to apply their newly learned ideas to other forms of expression in their life.

Art is also an opportunity to learn new skills that can be applied to everyday life. Manual dexterity gained in art, for example, is needed for writing and buttoning up a shirt or tying shoelaces. The fine-motor skills work in unison with thinking.[108] After all, the hands carry out the commands and messages of the brain. These skills can be developed through producing detailed artwork such as small brushwork or jewelry making.

Let's take a look at how art can promote your child's development.

Ages Zero to Three: Verbal Expression

Even before a child turns three, he is learning and developing. Before children even have a large vocabulary, their little brains are busy taking in stimuli and sensations and interpreting them. Eventually, their interpretation of these stimuli will be expressed through their development of language. In the meantime, art can be their first written language with pictures, lines, and shapes. It opens up opportunities to verbalize about their artwork, turning their scribbles into portrayals of their self-image and their family, and develops organizing skills, which include counting and classifying.[109]

Creating art is beneficial even for the child who is still too young to speak, since it gives the child a vehicle for expression. Nonverbal expression can include scribbling, drawing, painting, and making crafts with a variety of art materials. The child's scribbles and drawings represent what he is thinking and feeling and what's important to him. Art can

106 Joan Bouza Koster, *Growing Artists* (Delmar Publishers, 1997), pp. 11–12.

107 Edith Kramer, *Art as Therapy with Children* (Magnolia Street Publishers, 1971), p. 22.

108 Tom and Nancy Biracree, *Parents' Book of Facts: Child Development from Birth to Age Five*, (Ivy Books, Ballatine Books New York, 1989).

109 Joan Bouza Koster, *Growing Artist* (Delmar Publishers, 1997) pp.6–8.

help children who have difficulty expressing themselves verbally or have a limited vocabulary, even beyond the age when they should be talking.[110]

Here are some ways you can introduce your child to art even while he is still a baby:

- Notice how the hands of a small baby grab hold of his mother's fingers. Press gently and firmly on his hands to let him know that they can be tools to communicate with the world and the people around him.
- Give the one-year-old a crayon or marker (make sure it's washable) and hold your hand over hers, guiding her to make marks on a sheet of paper. At this age, she will probably lose interest quickly. That's all right. Continue as long as she enjoys it, and stop when she wishes. Don't force it.
- Tape all four corners of an 11 x 16-inch (42 x 30-cm) sheet of copy paper to the baby's high chair and give your toddler a few thick, dark-colored crayons one at a time to scribble with. Let her try to control the crayon with her developing muscles. Show him how to make dots, marks, lines, and circles as part of parallel child-parent play. At the beginning, he will probably lose interest rather quickly. In time, you can do this activity for longer periods of time.
- During bath time, let your child draw on the bathroom tiles with large, washable crayons. This provides children with a fun and creative outlet.

As your child grows from baby to toddler, encourage him to express himself through art. Ask him to draw something familiar, whether a family member, his friends, or objects that can be found in your house, on your street, or in school.

> *Little David would turn three in a few months. He attended my art lessons that encompassed both creativity and learning concepts. One day I gave David a green marker and told him to draw grass. He drew a very carefully confined scribble about two inches by two inches. He then wanted to draw a tractor and asked for a blue marker. Next came a bicycle in red, a tree in brown, a sun in yellow, his mother in pink, his father in brown, one sister in pink, the other sister in purple, and finally David himself in blue.*

110 Dr. Rawley Silver, *Developing Cognitive and Creative Skills Through Art* (An Authors Guild Backinprint.com Edition, 1978, 2000), pp. 3, 14.

Each drawing appeared as a similar-sized scribble, but to David they represented objects and people in his world. Later, David was able to recite to his mother exactly what each of the ten colored areas was.

David hadn't yet mastered drawing shapes, but he did have a creative solution. He filled in a series of consistently spaced marks to represent his subjects. They were similar in size and style, but differed in color. David embraced the paper and used the resources available to him at his level.

You can prompt your child with suggestions on how to improve his drawing using the methods you will find in this book, or let him draw freestyle. You can also introduce abstract concepts and help your child verbalize them. Common concepts in art are related to creating, planning, and building. By expanding your child's understanding of new concepts, you are developing your child's capacity for abstract thinking and verbalizing his thoughts. Take out a selection of blocks in a variety of shapes (squares, rectangles, triangles, circles, half-circles, arches), and sit with your child. Discuss the shapes and how they can be combined to build houses, tunnels, bridges, and roads. Ask the child what he would like to make with the blocks.

You can connect the concepts in art with concepts in Judaism. When talking about designing and building, you can talk about the Mishkan and how it was built and taken apart when the Jewish people traveled in the desert.[111] We, too, can break apart pieces of something we created and remake it. And, of course, we can always redo a work of art over and over again until we are satisfied with it.

This may lead to a discussion on mistakes and learning from them. In art, repairing a mistake is just as important as the planning, modeling, and forming, and may even lead to an improved work of art. In life, too, we can always learn from our mistakes and do better. We can ask God to forgive us if we do something wrong, and we can ask someone's forgiveness if we hurt their feelings, too.

Besides increasing your child's vocabulary and abstract thinking when you talk about the artwork he made, you will also be giving your child a great boost of confidence. Regardless of whether your talk is only about his work or leads to other topics, he will be filled with pride by your taking such notice of his work and spending time with him.

111 See ch. 2, "Jewish Art's Inspiration."

Ages Two to Five: Motor Skills and Cognitive Thinking

From around the age of two, a child's world is awash with new concepts, skills, and a developing self-image that is influenced by the people closest to him. He is learning how to label—to define the properties of various materials and how to manipulate these materials. Along with greater fine-motor control, this ability to grasp concepts gives life to his self-expression. Scribbles turn into discernible shapes, and drawings are given distinct names: Mommy, baby sister, house, bike.

Good motor control is essential to your child's ability to draw and, later, to write. By the age of three, a child should have control of his hand muscles, along with his arm and shoulder muscles. Giving a child lots of opportunity to color and draw will allow him to strengthen his muscles. If your child has trouble holding a marker or making scribbles, you can help. Monitor his motor skills—check your child's posture and movements throughout the day. Are they controlled and deliberate or careless and random? If they are only random motions without thought, help him become aware of what he is doing.

Check that he is holding the marker comfortably and properly. Teach him the proper way to hold a drawing tool, for this will help when he uses a pencil at an older age. His thumb and forefinger should grip the crayon close to the point. At first, it might be easier for him to draw while standing. Standing makes the child use his shoulders and arms, as well as his wrists and fingers. Tape a large sheet of paper to the wall or fridge, or set up a dry-erase board on an easel, for him to draw on while standing. Look for less resistance to adjusting his grip when he is first starting to draw and write. Show him how to make a variety of lines: vertical, horizontal, curves, dotted lines, thick and thin lines. When the child graduates from lines, go on to shapes. Connect lines to make squares, triangles, rectangles, and circles of all sizes. Make the work light and fun. Draw a few funny objects and then ask your child to draw a few of his own.

Also, being allowed to work with different materials promotes confidence and greater self-expression. Art activities that include drawing, painting, cutting, gluing, and clay modeling (or poking!) offer these children the sense of being in control of the physical world. Being able to manipulate a material or tool shows the child that his actions have a cause and effect, and this gives him the feeling that he's important, which builds his confidence.

Some materials, such as fine, thin brushes and paints, thin markers, or ink pens allow the child to be more controlled and precise. A one-time exposure to materials not usually used at his age may be fascinating to the child who filed these tools away in his mind for use in the future. Other materials (typically used at this age), such as finger paints, thick brushes, and clay allow for more experimentation and free expression. A child who needs to learn to be more spontaneous or playful will benefit from the more fluid materials, such as paint or clay. An anxious child who needs a sense of control will enjoy using colored pencils and fine markers.[112]

At this age, children also start to learn how to follow directions. Before putting out a material (paint, clay, paper), explain to your child what he can do with it. Make the information friendly and casual. If you yourself have never worked with the material or did so with unhappy results, let your child know this. Let him know that you want to try again because it will be fun and you are not one to give up. If it turns out great, good, and if it turns out less than great, also good! Your objective is to create a relaxed environment in which your child can explore and grow.

Besides giving the child an opportunity for self-expression and for learning concepts related to art, drawing and other art activities actually strengthen basic skills that preschool children need for their development.

For example, a child decides to draw a house. He chooses a clean sheet of paper, a pencil, and some colored markers. He draws a simple, flat square with a triangle roof. He decides to add more houses to make a street, along with hills and valleys in the background.

He shows the drawing to his friends who either praise it or reject it: "What is it?" "That's great!" "Why did you use such funny colors?" He may not want to show it to his friends, thinking it is not good enough for their standards, but will show his parents, anticipating their encouraging words.

The learning concepts he achieved are what win out: self-confidence, expression based on his level of skills and inner perceptions (visions) regardless of exterior standards of perfection or realistic completeness that come later. This process encourages organized thinking and processing that is invaluable in the classroom and in life.

112 Cathy A. Malchiodi, *The Art Therapy Sourcebook* (Lowell House, 1998), pp. 84–85.

Cutting and drawing are also preparation for reading and writing since they require similar skills. The hand-eye-brain coordination that a child develops using his fine-motor muscles for these activities are the same muscles he will need for reading, writing, and other essential skills for life, such as eating a bowl of spaghetti or buttoning up his shirt. The use of fine-motor skills in the hands (in arts and crafts) stimulates the senses and brain's resources.

Here are some of the vital skills that the preschool-age child develops while creating art:

Planning and problem solving: When creating art, children are taught to plan out a pictorial composition—the background, foreground, middle ground, main objects, detailed objects, and colors—and then to put them together to form a complete picture. The child has to be able to see all the different parts individually as well as the whole image as one unit. He learns how to draw the picture step by step, with instructions for how to construct each part of the composition. By going through this process and checking off the steps on his "checklist," the child learns how to make plans and carry them out. By reviewing the process to see if he missed any steps, he learns how to problem solve.

> *Five-year-old Shuli drew quickly. She was usually done with her drawing while the others were still hard at work. In her drawing, she included all the parts of a person and added details and decorative finishes as well. Still, because of the immediacy of her ability, her drawings looked rushed, not as composed as they could be.*
>
> *After drawing a person on three different occasions, Shuli began to slow down and draw with a more controlled and refined hand. She realized that by tracing over the lines and shapes of her drawing rather than rushing through it, she could achieve a better-quality composition. Once Shuli slowed down, she allowed herself to concentrate and plan rather than draw on automatic. Her planning and problem-solving skills were strengthened as she learned to slow down and pay attention to all the steps in the process.*

Memory: In part, memory is the act of recalling a pattern of movement from sensory information (such as from touching an object). Art can recall visual images that the child has seen or worked with. Through the process of art, he can build and expand on those images. Colors, for example, stimulate the memory (in this case, then, the sensory information comes from sight). They represent visual symbols that remind a person of concepts he needs to remember—red for stop and green for go.

Art itself draws on the memory—on feelings one experienced or images one has seen. By depicting these images, the child's visual mind is strengthened, as well as his ability to see images in his mind's eye. This will enhance his ability to envision ideas in his mind, an important skill as the child begins to learn and absorb abstract concepts.

Art also helps the mind develop "feed forward," a memory strategy. Feed forward presents information on how the child can best perform in the future before attempting a new project. Taking information from past experiences, the child can anticipate the end results. For example, if Tali used an unworkable grip on her scissors while cutting, the next time she attempts to cut she'll recall that holding the scissors with two fingers didn't work and she will attempt a different grip.

Spatial perception: The composition and placement of objects on a picture's surface (the paper or canvas) requires a sense of how the objects are organized in real space. This requires spatial perception—a sense of distance, position, direction, angle, and the dimensions of the objects around you. Constructions of miniature objects, such as furniture for a doll house, help children understand the concepts of scaling, proportion, distance, and placement of objects in the physical world.

Fine-motor control: Fine-motor control is essential for writing and other life skills, such as buttoning a shirt. There are a lot of opportunities for a child to put her fine-motor muscles to use in making art. Painting with fine-tipped brushes, drawing with markers, chalk, crayons, and pencils, and cutting with scissors all strengthen the fine-motor muscles in the hands and fingers.

While drawing, children also learn a variety of hand grips to produce thick or thin lines with a single stroke. The hand grips work in conjunction with applied pressure to control the darkness or lightness of a line. Practicing pencil drawing and painting with various grips and applied pressure in arts and crafts prepares a child for dealing with the multitude of sensations in daily life.

Along with drawing and painting, the ability to cut with scissors is an especially important indication of maturity and fine-motor control in the preschool child. Aside from learning to control the fine muscles of the hands and fingers, a child who cuts with scissors learns to follow straight lines, contour lines, and curves, which requires the child to change directions. If a child is having trouble with this skill, a parent can invest extra time or professional help to practice cutting with the child, beginning with snips and fringes at the edge of the paper, then advancing to cutting lines, then curves, and finally cutting out images. See chapter 21 for more on cutting.

Body scheme: As a child develops, he learns the body scheme—what the human body looks like and where all the parts are meant to go. A child with an immature body scheme may draw arms in the wrong place, forget to draw a neck or ears, or draw body parts that are out of proportion.

Drawing human figures in art helps a child develop his body scheme. Drawing the same figure again and again in the same sequence creates a frame of reference that ultimately affects body scheme. The children are taught to draw the basic parts of the human figure step by step with different clothing appropriate to the scene being depicted. They are encouraged to include details, and the importance of drawing hands with all the fingers is emphasized.

Identifying colors: Preschool is the age when children learn to identify and mix colors. Where better to do this than in art class? Bring out the primary colors—red, blue, and yellow—first. Then move on to the secondary colors: orange, violet, and green. Let the children mix the colors themselves and see what emerges—the fascination of mixing colors is one of life's small wonders. Learning the distinctions between earth colors—browns, umbers, and grays—is equally fascinating because the differences in the colors are so subtle.

The subtle variations in colors help children recognize and appreciate the differences in the things they see in the world around them. Differentiating between tints and shades made from whites and blacks further develops a child's perceptions of the world around him and gives him more room to mature, since black and white leaves a lot of room for the imagination to fill in. Color awakens and stimulates the mind, while at the same time it connects with emotions. And a stimulated mind is excited about life and learning.

Skills for everyday life: In making arts and crafts, children learn to reproduce objects in their environment. They may depict the scenes, objects, or people in their surroundings, or they may create miniature copies, in two or three dimensions, of objects, concepts, or people. To do this, they learn how to manipulate a variety of materials, tools, and techniques.

In reproducing the things in their environment, a child can make sense of his world and his relationship to the people and things around him in a safe, nonthreatening way. He will develop an understanding of what different objects are used for and what place different people have in his life and be able to apply his understanding to his daily functioning. For example, he may depict a child brushing his teeth and be reminded that tooth brushing is a part of everyday life.

Handling emotions: Balanced emotions free a child to take in information and participate socially and scholastically in the classroom. A child who is able to cope with his emotions will be able to give and take appropriately from his peers and the adults in his life. Art gives a child an outlet for dealing with his emotions, giving him a way to express himself in a safe setting. Through art, he can explore how he feels about the world around him and how to confront those feelings appropriately.

One function of art is to isolate a feeling so that we can look at it objectively. A subject in a picture can "act out" a situation, which can then be isolated and discussed. It is a way to, so to speak, clear the slate and start fresh.

Because art also promotes confidence through the skills a child acquires, the child will feel motivated and secure in expressing himself. The emotional skills the child learns will carry over to the classroom and home environment. He will be better equipped to get along with his peers and siblings and will be able to create healthy relationships with the adults around him.

Time to think: Art time also provides time for contemplation and introspection, something that is not as plentiful today as it was a hundred years ago. Life was slower and less pressurized then. People did a lot more work with their hands and weren't distracted by the technology that we have today. People had time for introspection.

Art can give a person the same opportunity. Not only does it give a child time to think but it shows him that change is possible. Just as a circle can be reformed and stretched into an oval, or a color can be lightened or darkened with the addition of black or white, or a lump of clay can be formed and reformed again, so is change possible in all things in life, especially inside a person.[113]

These are just a few of the skills the child will acquire in creating art. These skills are essential for future learning in the classroom, as well as for everyday functioning.

Here are a few ways that he can put these skills to good use in the classroom itself:

Writing letters and numbers: Drawing lines, curves, and shapes, and learning how to change direction and cross lines, as well as cutting with scissors, are essential skills for writing letters and numbers properly in the classroom.[114] Copying circles, curves, and squares prepares a child for making the shapes of letters and numbers. Additionally, drawing, coloring, painting, and cutting prepare the muscles and brain for writing. Drawing on resistant surfaces, such as sand, Play-Doh, or clay, promotes hand muscle strength, while cutting with scissors uses the left and right sides of the brain and requires a healthy upright back position that will enhance writing.

Mathematics: When creating art, the child needs to be able to count and learn units of measurements, as well as recognize patterns and sequencing, all skills that will come in handy when he learns math.

Geometry: Shapes are the foundation of all drawings. A baby stroller, for example, is made of a half-circle, with a quarter of a circle on top of it. Teaching children to draw geometrical shapes (circles, squares, triangles, ovals, diamonds) makes it much easier for them to grasp geometrical principles. Even learning fractions is made easier by drawing pictures that break geometric shapes into separate parts: a pizza separated into eight triangles or a square divided in two. The child also has to draw angles, parallel lines, and perpendicular lines to form pictures, all concepts he needs to learn to master geometry.

Reading and spelling: Drawing and art activities can prepare a child for reading and spelling by teaching the idea that a symbol can represent a concept. For example, when he learns that a circle can represent a sun,

113 Judith Aron Rubin, *Child Art Therapy: Helping the "Normal" Child Through Art* (Van Nostrand, Reinhold Co., 1978), p. 209.

114 W. L. Brittain, *Creativity, Art, and the Young Child* (New York: MacMillan, 1979); Jacqueline Goodnow, *Children's Drawings* (Fontana/Open Books, 1977), p. 82; J. L. Olson, *Envisioning Writing: Toward an Integration of Drawing and Writing* (Portsmouth, N.H.: Heinemann, 1992).

this will make it easier for him to absorb that the letters s-u-n can also represent the sun. Once a child learns how to represent objects in his drawings with shapes and forms, he will be able to identify them with words and, eventually, letters.[115]

Similarly, in art, the child must be able to identify patterns. A design with alternating or repeating shapes and colors is a pattern. Repetition and rhythm is found in the colored tiles on the wall or the floor when constructing a toy house. A string of beads or jewels on a necklace of a princess reinforces counting and duplication. Drawing also incorporates the idea of sequence: First draw the shapes of the subject, then the details, then the foreground, then the background, etc. Acquiring the skills of pattern recognition and sequence directly contributes to a child's reading and writing skills.

When it comes to child development, the rule is: The earlier you begin, the better. The more the young child gets the opportunity to acquire these skills, the more prepared he will be for what life has in store for him, both in the classroom and out. I have seen that basic art skills properly taught, particularly how to draw a complete child, improve the results on maturity tests, such as the first-grade entrance evaluation.

Suri was in a special ed class. At one point, she was reevaluated. Included in the testing was her ability to draw a child. Since she was in my art class and we had practiced drawing a child many times, she excelled in her drawing—to the astonishment of the tester. I have heard this from numerous parents of children in regular kindergartens who already know how to draw a complete child at the time they are tested for first grade readiness.

So begin early, around age three or four. Maximize the potential of arts-and-crafts sessions, at home or in school, and give the child a variety of materials and tools to work with. As he draws, paints, cuts, pastes, builds, and decorates, he will acquire vital cognitive and motor skills alongside the techniques and creativity.

115 According to Mona Brookes (*Drawing with Children, 10th ed.* [Tarcher/Putnam Books, 1996], p. 230), when children draw subjects from books they read, the subjects are reinforced in their minds and they relate better to the words.

Age Six and Up: An Emphasis on Order

When the child enters the first grade, usually around the age of six, reading and writing suddenly become the focus of his world. But the child's need for creativity and self-expression does not diminish, and certainly the child does not stop learning and developing. How can arts and crafts, which preoccupy so much of the child's time in preschool and kindergarten—and which expand a child's natural resources and abilities—be included in a child's life even after he has entered the elementary classroom?

Parents can encourage children to continue their art education by providing the means and opportunity—a variety of materials and projects to do at home and even extracurricular art classes that will complement what they are learning in school.

> *Josh, age eight, entered art class for the third year in a row. He had a friendly, easy nature and a positive, happy home. His less mature work showed some difficulty with spatial perception (proportions, depth, direction, and distance), but his motivation was strong and the years passed with encouragement in a pressure-free setting with direction and instruction.*
>
> *He began to blossom and produce sensitive and strong images in his artwork. Drawing six houses with three sides (a front, side, and top) is the same as drawing six cubes showing three sides and requires an understanding of spatial perception. At first this was awkward for Josh, but after direction and a few trials, he drew six large houses, each with a side view. Without the art class, would his difficulty with form and spatial perception have been recognized and addressed at eight years old?*

When the child enters grade school, he must now become a responsible student. Suddenly he is confronted by demands for order and neatness, while he must absorb a huge amount of new information in a classroom setting. It's not only his knapsack and homework that has to be neat and organized but he is also required to have an ordered mind to absorb all the information he is now learning.

Art can provide a child with a sense of order that he can apply in the classroom. After all, order and harmony is the basis for the construction of all shapes and forms. All creations in arts and crafts are really copies of the world around us composed by our Master Creator. There is order in nature—and therefore there is order in art. To draw a bird, you must discern an order and a structure. If you look carefully, you discern that the form of the bird is made up of several triangle shapes. A drawing of a house begins with a square. We add on the walls, windows, stairs, roof, and details in a prescribed order just as we build a real house.

Order is important because with it comes self-control and harmony. Children need order to create. They need order in their minds as well as physical order. If a child's painting is messy, showing no control, there will be paint everywhere—under her picture, on the chair, on the neighbor's picture. Her colors may become muddy, and the image will be difficult, if not impossible to discern. And her motivation, which was high when she began, will fade away along with her failure.

A child who is given options inside the framework of a project will be more productive and self-assured. Giving a child free rein without providing a topic or a framework for a project will often result in messy work and lowered self-esteem. By giving the child that framework, he will not feel inhibited and will feel free to let loose his creativity within the boundaries you have provided.

This is even more vital in the classroom, which requires a great deal of self-control and order. The patience and step-by-step processing required for painting and drawing will be transferred to the child's work in school. A child who does not have the ability to work within a framework will have a much harder time in class.

Organization and neatness combined with an appreciation for beauty and order are a good team for inspiration. When a child draws, she may become aware of her hand movements and how she writes. Notebook decorations may suddenly become a project she wants to do herself (and not by her big sister). A better self-image—the result of success in the art room—may inspire a new attitude toward school and the organization of learning materials.

The Tactile and Visual Learner

It is widely acknowledged that preschool children benefit from tactile, hands-on work and visual imagery.[116] Yet there are a large percentage of older children who also benefit from this type of learning. These children may not absorb concepts and basic principles as well without this strong connection between touch and vision. Creating artwork to internalize these concepts richly supplements their education. When the child is allowed to learn in the way that supports his unique natural way of integrating information, he blossoms.[117]

Arts and crafts offer these children the means to integrate information that they may not be able to absorb in the traditional classroom. Artwork lets them create miniatures of physical concepts through touch and other senses. Usually, these topics are taught using only the auditory or verbal senses in class. Being able to manipulate materials and see the concepts come to life through art seals the information in their minds. Once they have internalized this knowledge, the children will be able to draw from it in the future.

Whether in class or at home, it's important to provide these children various materials with which to produce images of the concepts they are learning. By giving them ample opportunities to draw with their hands, they will have an easier time absorbing the new information. Give them different types of drawing tools, pencils, markers, and pens so that they can apply varied amounts of pressure with the drawing tools to create their images. Building and constructing facsimiles of objects in real life (i.e., houses) uses other facilities of the body (i.e., movement and organization of the construction pieces plus decisions in visual design). In this way, they can use all the senses at their disposal—sight, touch, and motion, as well as hearing (the project description).

Tami decided to join my "How to Do Art with Children" group. She was looking for new ideas to keep her children stimulated and busy in the afternoons. In the class, Tami learned about the properties of different

116 Edited by R.C. Orem, *A Montessori Handbook* (Capricorn Books, New York, 1966), pp.59–61.

117 Howard Gardner's classic *Frames of Mind: The Theory of Multiple Intelligences* (Basic Books, New York 1983) describes the visual learner among his eight (revised 1995) classified intelligences. The Jewish heritage teaches this in Proverbs 22:6. King Solomon, author of Proverbs, tells us almost 3,000 years ago that a child should be taught moral and spiritual values and be educated "according to his way," according to the way the child learns, with his talents and mental abilities, for his education to be a lasting one.

art materials and a variety of projects that included alternative options, interesting and educational subject matter, and bringing out the creative potential in children.

After the course finished, she applied what she had learned with gusto. For example, she sent her children out to collect twigs and cardboard to combine with other materials and colors, and she went out and purchased a variety of paper and other art materials to create all sorts of art projects, both two- and three-dimensional. Her children learned to respect the materials and be creative in using them, while expressing themselves and learning new ideas.

Here's a project you can do with your child to teach him about the weekly Torah portion through his visual and tactile senses:

Jacob's Ladder AGES 8+

The Torah in Genesis tells us that Jacob left Charan and fell asleep in the desert surrounded by twelve stones that represented the future twelve tribes of Israel.[118] *He dreamed of angels ascending and descending a ladder that reached to the heavens. Be sure to talk about this Torah episode before beginning the project. Children will construct a three-dimensional representation of this episode using thick textural materials that stimulate their fingers and as well as their cognitive development.*

The instructions here appear long because there are so many different textures to make; just do it one step at time. The finished product will depend on the choice and combination of materials. The directions should be adjusted for the child according to ability, age, and personal expression. Offer help with cutting the cardboard pieces if needed. Note what your child is capable of doing on his own and change expectations if necessary.

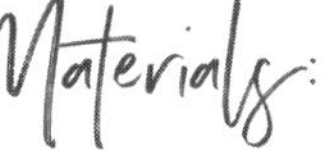

- Copy paper, size 8½ x 11 inches (21 x 30 cm)
- Pencil and eraser
- Metal ruler
- Acrylic paint: white, green, brown, cream (use gouache or tempera for younger children)
- Paintbrushes, ½ and ¾ inch (1½ x 2 cm)

118 Genesis 28:12.

- Styrofoam sandwich board, 2 inches (5 cm) thick, thick cardboard, or 2-ply Bristol paper cut to 11 x 16 inch (28 x 41 cm)
- Craft knife with a protective cutting surface
- White plastic glue or fabric glue and a disposable plate
- Thin cardboard (such as the white cardboard sheet from the dry cleaner) or thick paper, about 4 x 10 inches (10 x 25 cm)
- Scissors
- Tissue paper, dark blue, about 12 x 17 inches (30 x 43 cm)
- Blue metallic paper, 2 x 17 inches (5 x 43 cm)
- 2 or 3 sheets tracing paper, parchment paper, or wax paper
- Air-drying modeling clay and a toothpick
- Felt, canvas, or other fabric
- Cereal box
- Sandpaper, 4 x 5 inches (10 x 12½ cm)
- Black ribbon or thin paper, 2 x 6 inches (5 x 15 cm)
- Cotton balls
- Metallic ribbon or confetti
- Clear acrylic spray (optional)

Directions:

1. With a pencil, have the child design his composition on the copy paper. He can experiment with different possible arrangements and decide where to place Jacob, the ladder, the desert, the stars, and the angels.
2. With the pencil and ruler, draw a horizontal line in the middle of the Styrofoam sandwich board (or the thick cardboard or Bristol). The line separates where the earth meets the heavens.
3. On the thin cardboard, draw a silhouette of Jacob sleeping from the back or side, about 2 x 7½ inches (5 x 19 cm). Include space for the head covering, long robe, and sandals. Cut it out.

4. Trace the shape of the silhouette on the felt or fabric, and cut it out to make it look like a robe. Cut out pieces from the fabric to form the head covering and sandals.
5. With the white plastic glue or fabric glue, glue the fabric pieces to the cardboard silhouette. Arrange creases and folds in the head covering and robe. Let dry. Draw in the beard and the side of the face in the silhouette.
6. Measure and cut the dark-blue tissue paper to cover the entire area above the horizontal line on the sandwich board for the sky.
7. Measure and cut a strip of metallic paper to fit across the horizontal line.
8. Measure and cut the tracing or parchment paper to cover the entire area below the horizontal line for the earth. (I use three rows of double-folded papers that overlap for a textured effect. The paper does not lay flat and is slightly bumpy.)
9. Cut a disposable squeegee (spatula) about 4 x 5 inches (10 x 12½ cm) from the cereal box. (The cardboard will spread the glue quickly.) Pour a generous amount of white plastic glue on the disposable plate or a sheet of copy paper. Spread glue evenly on the area of the heavens above the horizontal line drawn on

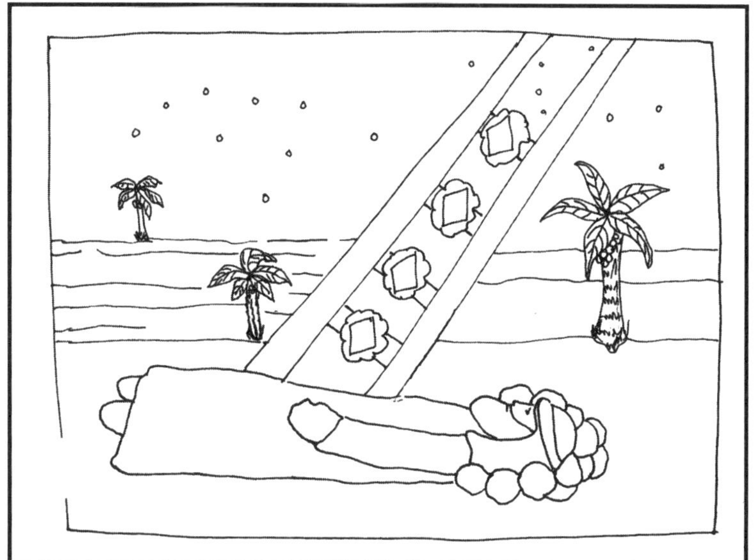

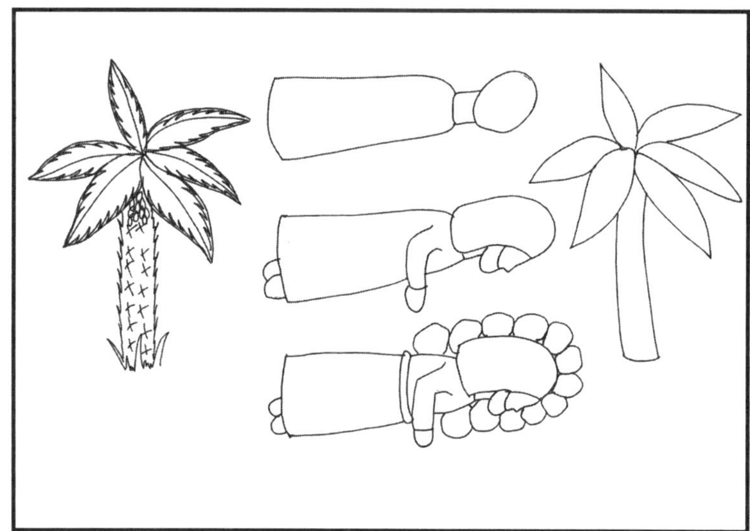

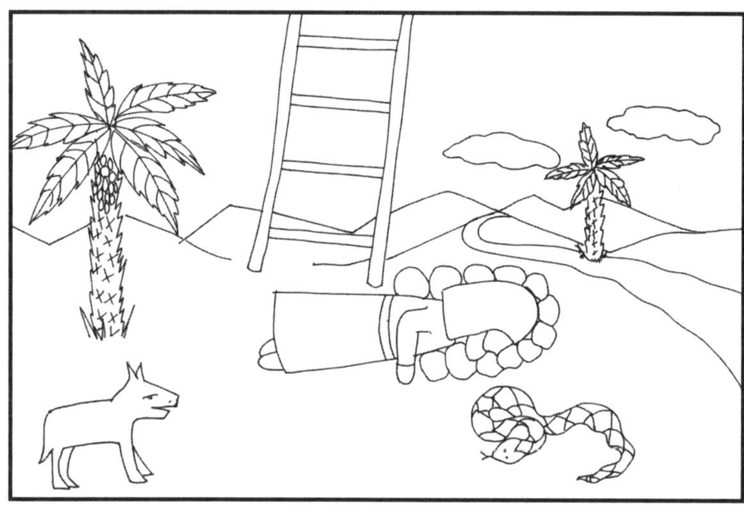

the Styrofoam board. Glue down the tissue paper. Glue on the metallic strip to the horizontal line. Glue on the tracing paper below the horizontal line. Add glue with a paintbrush where needed. (Clean the brush well afterward with liquid soap and water). Let dry.

10. With the scissors, trim off any excess paper hanging over the edges of the Styrofoam board.
11. With a pencil, draw a ladder with four rungs, measuring 3 inches wide and 7 inches tall (7½ x 18 cm) on the cereal box. Cut out the ladder; glue together any loose pieces, arranging the rungs slightly closer together toward the top. Let dry.
12. Paint the ladder white (or any other color if desired).
13. On the back of the sandpaper, draw hills. Cut out and glue on the horizontal line, above the metallic ribbon.
14. Form three palm trees from the air-drying clay. The largest is 2 x 2 inches wide and 1½ inches tall (5 x 5 and 4 cm). The next tree is slightly smaller and the third is the smallest. Form the trunks by rolling a thin rope of clay and pressing slightly with your hands to flatten. Form six leaves for each tree from a small ball, pressing each ball flat and stretching it into an oval. Pull one end of each leaf to make a point.
15. Using the end of a toothpick, mark dots on the trunk and vein lines on the leaves. Press the leaves firmly to the top of the trunks, with the two top leaves curved slightly down. Let dry.
16. Paint the trees green and light brown.
17. Form twelve rocks from the air-drying clay, each measuring ½ x ½ inch (1½ x 1½ cm). To make the rocks, form balls. Then shape into squares and press slightly to flatten a bit. Let dry.
18. Paint the rocks in shades of stone colors: Place the stones in a container along with the desired color paint, and shake to cover all sides of the rocks. Paint twice if necessary. Let dry.
19. Glue the ladder on or near the horizon line.
20. Cut four diamond shapes, measuring ½ x 1½ inches (1½ x 4 cm) from the black ribbon or paper. Make four tufts of cotton to

represent angels. Glue each cotton tuft to a ribbon diamond and glue each "angel" to a rung on the ladder.

21. With the air-drying clay, form additional hills, and place near the sandpaper hills to give the picture depth (a sense of distance). Let dry and glue in place.

22. Glue the three trees on the horizon line or up to 2 inches (5 cm) above it on the metallic blue strip to give the impression of depth. Place the largest tree on the right side of the ladder. Place the second and third trees on the left side of the ladder in descending order of size.

23. Glue on Jacob and the twelve stones around his head below the horizon line. Optional: Spray with acrylic spray.

In Summary: Art as a Development Aid

- The early years are a prime time for children to develop cognitively and physically. In creating art, children acquire skills that promote development.
- For the child age 0 to 3, art gives a vehicle for expression and promotes abstract thinking.
- For the toddler, arts and crafts activities help develop hand-eye coordination and fine-motor control and stimulate cognitive thinking, which will help with future learning in the classroom.
- Vital skills that a preschool-age child develops while creating art include planning, memory building, spatial perception, an awareness of body scheme, and skills needed to function in everyday life.
- Skills such as cutting with scissors, drawing curves and shapes, and recognizing patterns and sequences prepare preschool children for learning math, geometry, reading, and writing.
- When a child enters grade school at age six, the need for order and organization becomes paramount. These are skills

learned in art and can be carried over to the classroom and other areas in life.

- Art gives confidence to children who learn better when using their hands rather than only their ears and eyes. It also provides them with a framework to absorb information in ways that are suited to them.

Questions and Wonder

1. Why are there different talents and abilities within each of us?
2. What can you draw from curves and circles? From triangles and squares?
3. How would you set up a math worksheet using pictures and objects instead of numbers?
4. How could art be used to highlight a subject you already learned about?

13 Is My Child at the Right Stage?

Can you expect a four-year-old to write the Hebrew letter *aleph*?

Writing—and drawing—is all a matter of lines. The *aleph* is made from three lines: a diagonal line and two small straight lines. The ability to draw diagonal and triangular lines usually shows up in the average developing child around the age of five or six. Children who are gifted or who have been guided by an adult may have the skill to write an *aleph* at an earlier age.

Tali, age four, was just learning to draw people (mostly little girls like her). In the beginning, she was shy and didn't want to sit with the other girls in her art class. She also asked if I could first draw the picture and then she would trace over the lines, rather than drawing the entire picture by herself from scratch.

For the first few classes, I drew the geometric shapes that would form a human figure for her to trace until she learned to compose the figure of a girl on her own. Her mother told me that Tali would draw people over and over again

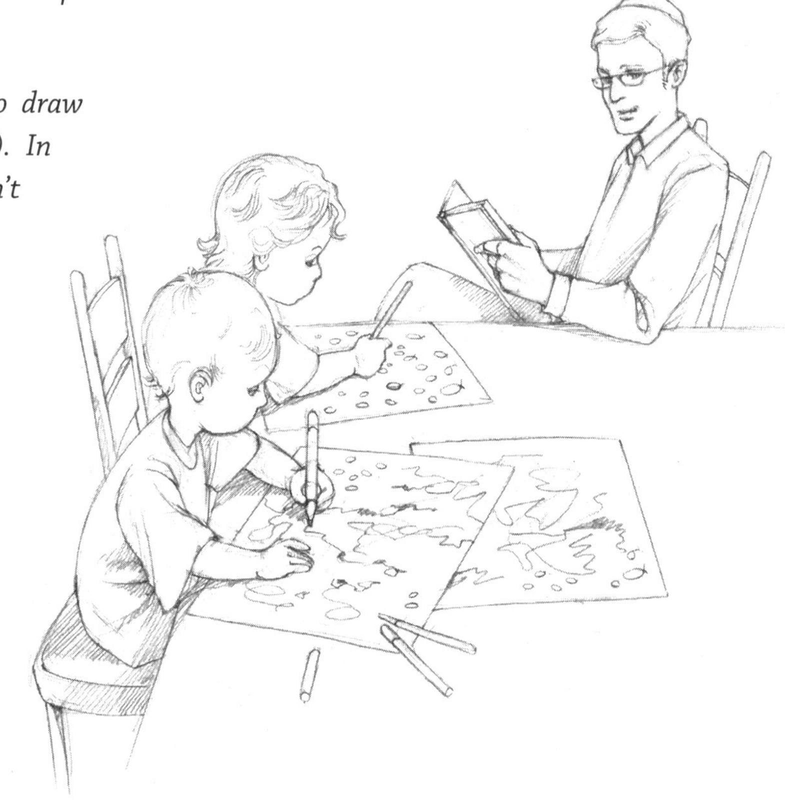

Notes and Sketches

until she had mastered the skill. Tali has not yet learned how to write, but with her mastery of drawing the lines and shapes of a girl, writing the alphabet will come easily for her.

Just as a baby must be physically and cognitively ready to turn over or walk, a child must be mature enough to write or draw a house. How do you know if your child is developing his drawing and writing skills at the right pace?

The Enjoyable Scribble

Your child's earliest drawings will probably seem like nothing but scribbles. This in itself is a feat—the ability to hold a crayon and make marks on a sheet of paper requires fine-motor skills, eye-brain coordination, gross-motor maturity (to be able to sit and use the arm and hand muscles), and the ability to sit in one place. This usually occurs between the ages of two and five years, though I've seen eighteen-month-old babies scribble with a bit of assistance! The period of scribbling is a time of discovery and pure enjoyment. The child is delighted when she realizes "I can make marks!" Scribbling enriches the brain and prepares it for organizing thoughts and patterns, which prepares the child for reading and writing.[119]

With scribbling, we encounter the beginnings of drawing and writing:

1. Contact with the drawing tool
2. Deciding where to connect it to the page
3. Moving the drawing tool in various directions
4. Practicing pencil grips and applying various amounts of pressure
5. Practicing the different marks one can make

Scribbling tells us something very interesting about the child. It shows us when a child has the ability to control his hands. If we are aware of what to watch for, we may see that the large muscles in the shoulders and arms of the one-year-old dominate, while he has little control over his hand's fine-motor muscles.

---

119 Dr. Susan Rich-Sheridan, "The Neurological Significance of Children's Scribble Hypothesis," Journal of Visual Literacy, vol. 22, no. 2 (2002).

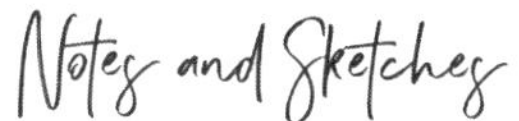

If we give him paper and a thick marker or crayon, we'll see that he may not make sufficient contact with the paper or exert the right amount of pressure to make a mark. You can help him by holding his hand and gently directing his arm movements so that he can try to scribble, but you will see that the child has little control over the lower arm muscles.

At around two years of age, the muscles from the elbow and lower down gain control, and the child begins to draw lines and circles in all directions. He should now be able to grip a thick marker or crayon and draw with it on his own.

At about the age of three, the wrist, fingers, and drawing tools (whether a marker or pencil) work together in a symphony of lines and shapes and repeated marks. This coincides with the age when a child can acquire and retain information, which in Judaism is the age of three.[120]

At the age of three and four, the child should be making his first attempts at lines and shapes that can represent anything. Objects seem to float in space. Colors may not have any relationship to nature, but the pictures begin to tell a story.

A four- or five-year-old who is still scribbling may need instruction on how to draw in order to progress to the next stage. If you suspect a delay, you should seek a professional evaluation.

Shapes by Age

As your child grows, his visual and motor functions are developing. The ability to coordinate between what he sees and what he can do—the skills he needs for drawing and writing—is usually complete by the ages of eleven to fourteen or possibly earlier. Here are the approximate ages at which your child should consistently be able to draw or copy scribbles, make lines, and draw simple and complex shapes:[121]

120 Just as the fruit of a tree is not used until the tree is three years old (*orlah*), when it is considered fully developed. Leviticus 19:23.

121 Based on Keith E. Beery & Natasha A. Beery, *The Beery-Buktenica Developmental Test of Visual-Motor Integration, 4th ed.* (Modern Curriculum Press, 1997).

Vertical line			1.9 to 3 years
Horizontal line	—	1.8 to 3 years
Circle	○	1.11 to 3.3 years
Vertical-horizontal cross (a cross with fairly equal vertical and horizontal bars crossing one another in the center)	+	2.10 to 4.6 years
Diagonal line	\	4.4 to 6 years
Square (angles that turn corners)	□	4 to 5 years
Diagonal cross (an x shape)	X	3 to 6 years
Triangle	△	5 to 5.3 years
Six-pointed star from two overlapping triangles, one of them being inverted (Magen David)	✡	6 to 9 years
Diamond	◇	7 to 8 years
Elongated diamond	◇	6 to 10 years
Overlapping three double-lined circles		11 years
Six-sided cube	⬡	10 to 13 years

Three-dimensional star with double-line forms (one over- and one under-lapping of the same triangle)	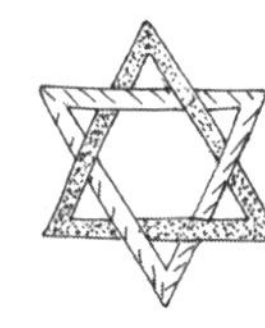	13.7 to 13.8 years

This chart reflects the average ages for drawing various shapes. It is possible, with guidance and if the child is mature enough, for him to be able to master these skills earlier. You can help your child produce these lines and shapes earlier than the norm:

1. Identify the child's natural aptitude and style and work with patient instruction and exposure. Learn what your child's strengths are in drawing and art in general. For example, does he like color or accuracy?

2. Acquaint young children with their hands and fingers. Point out how each finger is a different height and the thumb is not connected to the row of four fingers. Show how the thumb works with the fingers to grasp objects. To demonstrate, have them try picking up a pencil without using their thumb—it's quite hard.

3. From the age of four, your child can learn how to grasp a pencil or crayon properly with the "tripod grasp"—using the thumb and the first two fingers as pincers. Discourage the "hook hand," where the child holds the writing tool in the joint of the thumb. Give him short pieces of crayons or pencils to encourage the correct use of finger joints and muscles.

4. Offer physical and sensory contact with a variety of materials and techniques. This increases hand flexibility and encourages sensitivity to pressure and directional movement.

5. Repeat a variety of actions and projects to encourage mastery. Repetition is a key to success. After a while, the brain and muscles will automatically know what to do. (Remember when you first learned how to type? You had to consciously remember which keys your fingers were to touch next; now your brain automatically tells your fingers which keys to tap and you don't have to consciously think about it at all.)

6. Make sure to maintain a pressure-free environment. It's easiest to learn in a relaxed and friendly atmosphere.

Self-Identify Using Geometric Shapes

From drawing clear geometric shapes, the child moves on to combining these shapes to depict real objects. Even four-year-olds can be taught to do this with direction. We may not see an obvious underlying geometric shape that a child drew to represent an object, but the majority of manmade objects are initially represented and formed from geometric shapes. You can help a child discover the shapes in these objects to refine his drawing.

Teach him the basic geometric shapes and explain their possibilities. Together, notice the shapes in the objects around you: the line, the circle, the square, the rectangle, and the triangle. We can make a basic person from these shapes.

Beginning from around the age of four, most children are capable of drawing human figures (usually of themselves or those closest to them) with lines and curves and with geometric shapes. The drawings may resemble a sun emanating rays on top of a stick with forks for arms and hands. This is how young children begin identifying themselves on paper. The parent or teacher can provide a friendly environment and encourage the child to draw himself as a person. The time is ripe for the child as he is the center of interest. Mastering drawing himself on paper is a great accomplishment.

In my art classes, I spend several months teaching the four- and five-year-olds how to draw a boy or girl by doing various projects: practice drawings, paper dolls, drawings of their families, or a child against a background of the heavens and earth with a house and trees and river.

Their self-identity is made concrete when they learn to pay attention to the entire person—the bodily structure and clothing, including their five fingers and the relationship of their hands and feet to their head. I point out where their waist is in relationship to their elbows. By the time they are ready to enter the first grade, they know how to draw a person, one of the skills required in aptitude tests for entrance into elementary school.

The mother of a very shy five-year-old related a story to me. Her child came into the class unable to draw a child with arms and legs. After one or two art classes, he was tested by his teacher on his ability to draw a person. The teacher was taken by surprise: all the important body parts and facial features were there, and the drawing was clear, complete, and centered.

Encourage young children to draw a large image of themselves in the center of the page. Let them do this on their own. If they need help getting started, you can draw a few large geometric shapes—circles, various squares, straight lines—and invite the child to choose which one he or she wants to use to make a boy or girl. Or begin with a large circle at the top of the page, add a square for the shirt, and a long, thin rectangle for a leg, and then ask the child to complete the picture.

Initiate a dialogue about the drawing. As the child draws his picture, ask what is missing and needs to be added in. You may be tempted to take over. Yes, you can help, but you should be a guiding hand and not an overpowering one.

The Larger World

The ground is set for the planning, or schematic, stage. Now the child—age six to eight—can make order in the space on the paper; he has a definite way of drawing and identifying objects. The ground is on the bottom of the paper and the sky is at the top.

When a child turns six, having been nestled in a warm, loving home environment, he now directs his attention outward to the larger world. This could be his street, the local shul, a garden or playground, a hillside, city, or forest. His drawing is the place where he reflects on what his place is in the world outside the home. Against the backdrop of a range of hills or a cityscape, we want the child to be able to include himself in the bigger picture of the world in the best way possible.

An average- to large-sized frontal-facing figure denotes a positive feeling, "I am here in the world. I am important because God created me.[122] As the child grows, his world enlarges to include new friends, events, and places.

122 Mishnah, *Sanhedrin* 37a: "Every person is obligated to say: 'For me the world was created.'"

At this age, the child becomes genuinely interested in physical reality. From what I have observed, it seems to me that girls are more focused on details in realism than boys. A girl can produce a beautiful, well-drawn composition and want to throw it away because in her mind it doesn't reflect the reality she wanted to depict. Boys will do this, too, but less often.

When children become immersed in trying to depict reality, it's helpful to let them know that they have options and there is more than one way to depict what they want to express. This is essential to counter their thinking that what they depict has to precisely reflect reality. A humorous comment that a banana shape can resemble a mouth, a bird, or a boat can expand their visual thinking and motivate them to try options. They can draw a person in many ways: with basic shapes and lines, in a more advanced way with shadows and curves, with attention to clothing, to facial expression or movement, or a combination. It doesn't have to be perfect in every way, and there is more to art than a perfectly drawn line.

Seven- and eight-year-olds become more descriptive about their realism—their drawings are more logical, depicting how they think things should look rather than focusing on aesthetic concerns, such as interesting colors and shading. A drawing done by a child younger than seven might show a child proportionately larger than family members or objects. With a child over the age of seven, the size of the figures decreases to fit proportionally with the surroundings or other figures.

Regardless of the child's desire to fit into the "larger picture of life," home and family will always remain the foundation for the child. When a young child draws himself in his home environment, this creates a settled and secure feeling that lays the foundation for becoming an emotionally healthy adult.

So spend time together drawing houses and children, parents, and families. Emphasize the geometric structure of the drawing of a house, and then discuss the details that make the house a home. Ask the child to draw his favorite people and toys in the home. Describe the beauty of the Jewish home in terms of mitzvot, complete with "stations" that can be found throughout the house and yard (such as a sukkah porch or a shelf for the Shabbat lights). Go through each room and add details that show the season or time of year; add objects that represent the Jewish holiday that might be celebrated at that time, such as a menorah for Chanukah or a box of matzahs for Pesach.

As the child matures and turns eight years old, he begins to attempt three-dimensional forms (where a square becomes a cube, or a circle becomes a ball with the addition of shading) with solidity, overlapping (such as when one object is in front of another), and perspective (where he depicts distance and depth, such as a road disappearing up a mountain). He may also attempt a little shading (where dark areas on an object suggest light or illumination) and foreshortening (depicting objects seen at an angle receding into space).[123]

Drawing for Life

One child may welcome self-exposure while connecting with the creativity in arts and crafts. One who is not interested or able to do this may repress creativity in this area. It depends on their motivation and need for this outlet.

Repression and self-exposure are the terms that define the eleven- to fourteen-year-olds. Many children become discouraged easily at this stage and "don't need to do art." Having achieved the coordination of visual and motor functions already, their interests tend to move from creating art to figuring out who they are. They will work more on expressing themselves verbally and pursuing independence. When they were younger, they needed to draw and paint to make sense of their physical surroundings or inner world. Now they have matured and gained control over their own reality.

On the other hand, if the child is motivated, he will allow himself to be vulnerable to self-exposure, determined to forge ahead with his drawing regardless of "mistakes" because he enjoys the art so much.

Here is our chance to encourage our children to continue creating art. Even if the child doesn't exhibit a particular talent, this type of creative self-expression can be a wonderful outlet for the child who is entering young adulthood. At this time, when he is exploring who he is and where he fits into his environment, art can help him make sense of the world and his changing body.

Interestingly, this stage coincides with the bar and bat mitzvah age, when children have acquired a certain level of knowledge and become

123 James Smith Pierce, *From Abacus to Zeus: A Handbook of Art History* (Prentice Hall, 1986), pp, 23–24, 39, 56.

responsible for keeping the mitzvot. This is also a time when their *middot* will be challenged. Challenges in *middot* development can be explored with art projects. They will learn to have patience with themselves and to judge themselves (and others) favorably as they are taught to use their mistakes in art, rather than build up anxiety over producing "great works of art." They may learn not to waste or destroy (*bal tashchit*) by converting artwork they are not happy with into another picture or form. They can expand their creativity and willingness to take risks by trying new materials and techniques. They will gain confidence and focus as they acquire new skills and find a style and material that they identify with most. That confidence will have a lasting effect in all areas of their lives, especially when working with their own children or students.

New Directions

From the age of fifteen or sixteen, children with a substantial degree of genuine talent or interest in art will continue to pursue this discipline in a more formal manner. If the child elects to pursue one of the many avenues of art, it is because she has the confidence and motivation to do so—and most likely support and encouragement from an adult.

As her art skills mature, she can experiment with creating murals to decorate walls at home, painting portraits, or making crafts to give as gifts or to sell. Some kids may go on to become professionals: illustrators, graphic artists, art teachers, designers, artisans, stage designers, architects, photographers (still and moving), *sofrim* (scribes for Torah scrolls, tefillin, and mezuzot), or calligraphers.

Whether your child is destined to become the next Chagall or just enjoys drawing and gluing, art is an invaluable element in your child's growth. Give him opportunities to create and watch him shine!

Here are a couple of exercises that will help your child progress in his art:

The Life of a Circle AGES 6/7+

The circle is ambiguous. It has the potential to be transformed into many different objects. Most physical objects, as well as people and living creatures, are made of curved shapes. Show the child all the things he can do with a circle.

Materials:

- 4–5 sheets of copy paper, size 8½ x 11 inch or 11 x 16 inches (30 x 42 cm) or larger (the size of a place mat)
- Pencil and eraser
- Colored markers

Directions:

Begin with two warm-up exercises to loosen the arm and hand.

1. Your child draws a large spiral, beginning in the center and working outward. Redraw over the spiral lines three times, using three different colored markers.
2. The child draws ten giant, medium, and small circles plus several dots. Color them in.

Now you are ready to begin:

1. Fold the paper into eight sections. Draw eight circles, approximately 2 inches (5 cm) in diameter. Going from circle to circle, ask the child what each one can be. For inspiration, have him look around the room and point to anything that is round or nearly round. Turn each circle into the object named: a clock, wheel, balloon, candy, apple, cherry, lightbulb, eyeglasses, bicycle, flower, sun, the top of a cup, or coins.

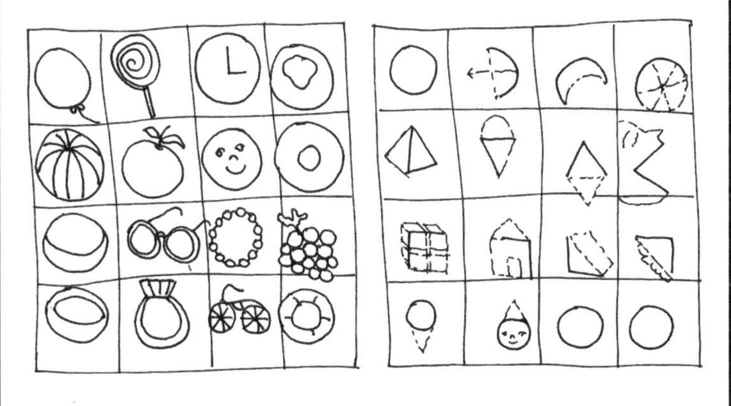

2. On a new sheet of paper, show the child the art of transformations. Transform one image into another: A jelly doughnut can be turned into a cup of hot chocolate. Have him draw a banana. Now make it into a mouth, a bird, a boat, or a hat.

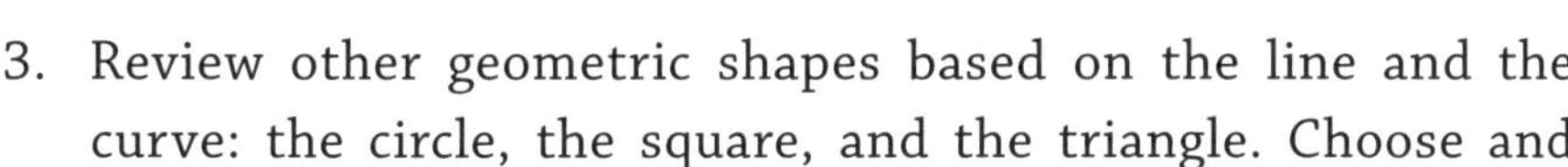

3. Review other geometric shapes based on the line and the curve: the circle, the square, and the triangle. Choose and

draw combined shapes. (A triangle and a circle = a clown's hat or an ice cream cone.) Transform one image into another. From the ice cream cone, we can make an old man's face with a long beard.

4. Have the child draw a boy or girl from simple geometric shapes. Then have him draw a boy or girl from memory, adding details to personalize the image.

In Summary: Is My Child at the Right Stage?

- Like everything else, the ability to draw and write develops with age.
- The ability to draw diagonal and triangular lines, and therefore the ability to write letters of the alphabet, shows up in the average child around the age of five or six.
- A child's first attempts at drawing, at around two years old, is the scribble. Before that, the child does not have sufficient control of the hand's fine-motor muscles to make significant marks on the paper.
- From scribbling, the child graduates to shapes. Encourage the four- to five-year-old to draw various shapes and to grip the drawing tool properly.
- With the age of six comes order, with the ground on the bottom and the sky on the top of each picture. He no longer lets images float on the paper. He also begins to draw things from the larger world: his street, playground, a city, a forest.
- As the school-age child develops, he begins to find it important to depict reality as he sees it.
- Around the age of eight, the child begins to add more realism to his drawings, with shading, overlapping, and perspective.
- The nine- to eleven-year-old generally has a handle on his artistic and creative ideas, tools, and materials,

having spent time in his younger years working on them. Confidence may shine through his artwork.

- The eleven- to fourteen-year-old may regard art as less important, but art at this stage, too, can be vital to help him express who he is and explore his burgeoning self-identity.
- By age fifteen or sixteen, the serious artist emerges; those still interested in pursuing art may eventually turn it into a satisfying career.

Questions and Wonder

1. When you see a small child scribbling, what may he be thinking about?
2. Why do some kids need to work slowly while others work quickly and want to finish first? Why is it so important to finish first? What is most important in the end?
3. What is it about yourself that you like to draw?
4. What do you like to draw about your home or family?
5. If you could draw anything in the world right now made out of geometric shapes: circles, squares, triangles, and rectangles, what would it be?

14 Making the Most of Your Child's Potential

The Creative Mind

What is creativity? Creativity is considering our options and thinking out of the box. It is a capacity for making unusual leaps in thoughts and ideas and selecting and combining one's thoughts through expression in some type of medium.[124] Creativity is the ability to produce something concrete using the imagination and making use of our options. The more unique and new, the more creative it is. "Options" refers to more than one way to think, find a solution, and create.

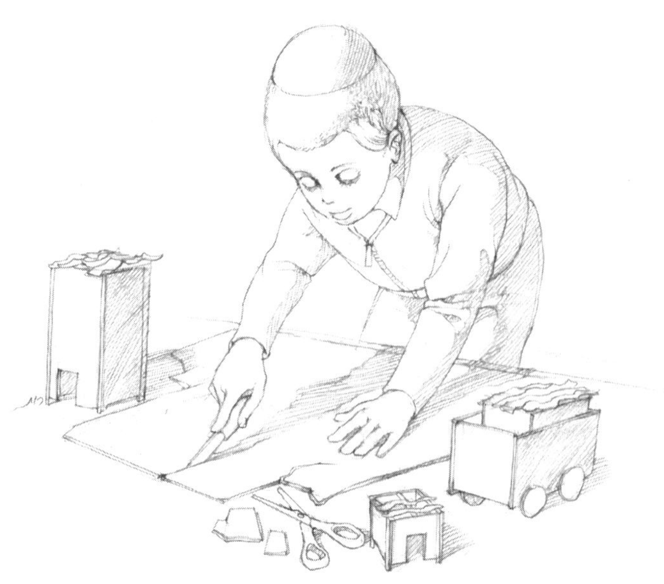

"New" doesn't always mean a new creation in the world that never existed before. New can be a child drawing something for the first time. It can mean taking something that exists, like a dress, and changing its appearance by sewing on a new trim or buttons. New can mean changing the

124 Rawley Silver, *Developing Cognitive and Creative Skills Through Art* (An Authors Guild Backinprint.com Edition, 2000), p.122.

ingredients of a recipe. It can mean painting a vase of flowers unlike any other.

A creative thinker is excited about life, excited about making new discoveries. A creative thinker doesn't give up, but is willing to explore numerous possibilities until he is satisfied with the results. Every day presents new opportunities and new potential. Every artistic project has its own set of options and possibilities, according to how the artist sees it. This is the excitement of creativity.

Creativity is not just a random occurrence or limited to the "gifted." Creativity is a skill that can be learned. Anyone with an imagination can be creative, but it requires planning, visualization, and motivation to seek and find solutions. And, of course, that personal touch that makes it uniquely one's own.

If creativity is encouraged in a child, he will naturally follow through. If it's not acknowledged, the child may not tap into it or may feel confused, since children are naturally creative—they see the "newness" in everything around them. I was lucky enough to grow up in a home where I was allowed to develop a rich inner world. I was also given a variety of artistic outlets from a young age.

When creating art, your child will select choices from among countless possibilities—subject matter, size, proportion, distance, colors, shapes, lines, textures, and art materials. His choices give his artwork its unique signature. And they will vary as he ages. Personality, sensitivities, and exposure to other creative sources all affect his choices. Your job is to give him the opportunity to make those choices and the free rein to be creative. The excitement of discovery alone is enough to motivate a child to pursue it.

Creativity opens the doors of potential. It is not just confined to the art room. The skills and awareness gained from art can be applied to many areas at home and in school: singing, making music, and creative writing; finding ways to be more productive; planning and organizing; or improving social interactions.

Age, Readiness, and Personality

Just as an unborn baby develops on its own time schedule inside its mother, children develop at their own pace. Along with each child's own

Notes and Sketches

Notes and Sketches

internal time clock and innate abilities, comes his predisposition and unique personality. Personality is affected by temperament, upbringing, retention, exposure, interest, and actual experience.

If you want to encourage children to maximize their potential, you will allow them to develop their innate natural skills, but at times you will urge them to work outside their comfort zone. For instance, a meticulous child who doesn't like painting because it's messy can be gently encouraged to try it and can be shown how to paint with the least mess involved. A child who likes to paint large shapes or landscapes should be encouraged to think about details and to draw small objects.

In the classroom, giving this kind of attention to each child according to his capability need not interfere with the class lesson. The teacher only has to sit with the child for a few minutes and show different alternatives to what the class is doing. When a child is curious, the art teacher should provide satisfying answers, appropriate to the child's level of maturity. The teacher can provide visual examples and show the students how to draw or craft the subject step by step, using a technique in which the children are interested.

Often this can be done within the scope of the prepared class project. For instance, if little David wants to know how to draw an ambulance when the project is drawing a house, he can incorporate the two subjects together. Show him how to draw the vehicle with the siren on top and perhaps an x-ray view of the inside with the bed and life-saving equipment.

You can use this as an opportunity to talk about ambulances and the lifesaving work of emergency medical service organizations, such as Hatzalah in the US and Israel, and Magen David Adom in Israel, because this is something that David is interested in. This will help him connect to his drawing and artistic expression. After his ambulance drawing is complete, he can add the house or cut out his ambulance and glue it onto the drawing of the house, or he can take home two separate drawings.

At home, a parent who is prepared, who would like to think outside the box, can be a role model of creativity to his or her child. Point out during casual discussions the role of art as a form of expression, the value of handmade objects, or the purpose of art in education (on the level of the child, of course). Mention your favorite color combinations, or take note of an impressive sunset or work of art. Talk about the value of aesthetics and beauty in the world around us and the kindness God showed us by incorporating such beauty into the world.

Regardless of your child's interest or level of creativity, this parent-child time should be relaxed and unpressured. Above all, make various art materials available to your child, so he has ample opportunity to harness his creativity.

Creating Opportunities to Grow

An awareness of a child's preferred learning style is based on their strongest mode of sensory input and output (how they take in and process information and how they release and express information), such as visual (sight), tactile (touch), auditory (hearing), or a combination. Putting these strengths to use increases his potential to develop new skills.[125] Choose a subject and adjust a specific skill or material to fit the child's needs and what he wants to do. Finally, give him extra time until he masters this skill, material, or concept while patiently guiding the child, letting him know, "I'm here for you while you struggle with this new skill."

> *Kayla, age five and half, could sit for more than an hour drawing detailed and well-filled flowers, clouds, houses, babies, and decorative motifs. Her brother Ben, age four, was finished drawing after four minutes. He'd draw several large circles, and then, scissors in hand, he'd cut out the center circle almost to the edges of the paper, remove the circle, and hold it up to his face. "Look! I made a camera! I made a button to take the picture." He'd point to a few lines in one corner.*
>
> *If we knew that Ben uses his body (as a kinesthetic learner, stimulated with muscle and body movement) more than Kayla to communicate, we could applaud his creative way of using the paper that was originally meant for drawing. We will not overlook the benefits of learning to draw, and we'll try to encourage him to focus on drawing for longer than four minutes, but we will applaud his creative mind when he uses it.*

---

125 The Multiple Intelligence Theory formulated by Howard Gardner at the Harvard Graduate School of Education and the Boston University School of Medicine emphasizes teaching children according to their learning styles: verbal/linguistic, logical/mathematical, musical/rhythmic, visual/spatial, body/kinesthetic, interpersonal, and intrapersonal. Most people have combinations of styles to different degrees.

When helping a child master a skill, use a variety of materials: liquids such as paints, markers, and inks; and solids, such as pencils, paper, enamel, wood, clay, Styrofoam, cardboard, plastics, fabric, and chalks. Each type of material, with its particular characteristics, stimulates different sensory receptors in a child. Touch and smell, not just sight, play a role as well. The smoothness of the clay, the soft give of a colored pencil—every material comes with its own smell, texture, color, and weight.

Often the child may show a preference for one material over another. He may favor paint over colored pencils or cutting and gluing over drawing. He may want to master cutting with scissors before going on to drawing. Let him continue using the material he needs in order to master the skill that he is working on. After achieving his goal, he is ready to go on to a different material or skill.

It is important that art projects incorporate a wide variety of subjects, styles, and materials to give children the maximum opportunity to grow in their art skills. Be flexible enough to consider the range of personalities, levels of ability, interests, and sensorimotor integration of each child. When children have ample opportunities to grow, they will—whether in art or any other area. Let us make sure to give them those opportunities.

Use Strengths and Weaknesses, Anticipate Problems and Solutions

Each child comes with strengths and weaknesses that affect his scholastic and social arenas. By taking note of the student's strengths, weaknesses, and fears, the teacher or parent can provide art-related projects according to what the child feels comfortable doing.

Fear of failure, low motivation, disinterest, lack of skills, shyness, inability to focus, boredom, and gifted talent all have solutions if the teacher and student—or parent and child—have an understanding and respect for one another. Give the child room to fulfill his needs first, and then gradually add new challenges so he will achieve what you hope he will accomplish. Let him feel satisfaction before asking to do what he is not willing to do. When the child feels confident about the skills he has, he can then be encouraged to try new things.

Six-year-old Ellie could not draw simple geometric shapes like circles, squares, and triangles, though her peers were already drawing objects like houses and baby carriages and learning to draw more complex shapes. While the other kids drew their pictures, Ellie was struggling just to draw a triangle. Rather than insisting that she keep up, or ignoring her and allowing her to lag behind, her art teacher gave her special projects so she would be able to master this skill.

At first, she had Ellie draw shapes by following the teacher's finger from point to point, like "connecting the dots." She also gave her connect-the-dot pictures of shapes to draw, tracing paper so she could practice copying basic shapes, scissors to cut out the shapes, colorful markers for outlining, various materials for her to glue onto shapes, and modeling clay for her to build three-dimensional shapes. Eventually, Ellie was able to draw shapes with competence and could join the other children for class projects.

Abie, ten years old, didn't want to paint because he was worried about controlling the paint and not painting outside the lines. For a while, we did drawings that he colored in neatly with markers. This brought out other issues that Abie was struggling with. He drew with rigid movements that limited his expression. He didn't know how to make a curve. It was no wonder he was having a hard time—curves are basic to most forms in nature: hills, trees, waves, human figures, animals.

After showing Abie how to make an S, we added a second set of lines to produce a double S. After a few trials, Abie succeeded in drawing a curve. His expression was no longer limited. After this small success, he was ready to attempt painting. I showed him simple ways to stay inside the lines (by outlining the objects first with a line of paint and then filling in the open area) and what size brushes with what amounts of paints to use. Within a couple of weeks, he proudly finished his first painting and took it home.

The Exceptional Child

There always comes along the child who perceives things others do not, and it becomes apparent that he has a sensitive eye that is capable of producing great art. Artistic creativity and sensitivity go together. A sensitive child is aware of refinement, details, movements, and subtleties that the average person is not aware of automatically.

We would like to think that gifted children would be given even more opportunities to blossom, but sometimes it's hard to identify a child as gifted. The artistically creative child may be bored in school, may be on another level than the rest of her classmates, or may be more talented than her art teacher. If the child is shy as well, the teacher may not realize that she is not getting the challenge that she needs.

In addition to this, gifted children have a need for solitary time to do their creative work. They are torn between the need to be accepted by their peers and the need to be productive and solitary. Such a child might act up in school to alleviate his boredom or he may hide his gift to be more accepted by other kids.

These children should be praised for their abilities—not discouraged from doing artwork just because what they want to do is more advanced or outside the scope of a class project.

The sensitive teacher offers such a student a steady stream of artistic outlets: decorating a section of the classroom, designing invitations for school productions and events, or illustrating a story for assigned class reading. The main thing is to help the student feel proud of her talents and remain involved in school projects.

If you suspect your child is gifted, you will want to encourage him to use his gift properly.

For such children, parental support can be more important than school support because the messages in the home affect the child in a primordial way. The parent-child bond is forever, whereas the school is temporary (unless there is an exceptional teacher in the picture). Once the parent senses the child's strengths in art, he or she can find an art teacher who will encourage the child to develop her talent.

At home, the parents can initiate casual conversation about art—sights or objects that have caught their eyes. They can give the child artistic rein in decorating her room or ask her opinion when choosing artwork to display.

These children can also be called on now and then to work with another child for short periods of time. Being in the role of the teacher will increase the gifted child's self-esteem as she shows her neighbor how she paints. The child being helped may appreciate the chance to make a connection with her classmate in a creative way.

Another way to show encouragement to the artistically gifted child is by taking her to artists' workshops—picture-framers, leather crafters, ceramists, calligraphers, designers, portrait painters, illustrators—and providing her with a variety of materials to create many forms of art.

Artistically gifted children will flourish when art is a natural part of life rather than a rarefied state which separates them from others. The job of the parents is to help their child's gifts fit in with their daily lives.

Every child has the ability to create—after all, creativity is simply the ability to produce using one's imagination. And every child has an imagination! Whether gifted or challenged, when given opportunities to create, children will make the most of the new worlds they discover.

> *Batya was a highly creative and gifted little girl. But since her artwork did not look like what was normative for her age (in school or in the art class), she believed her work was not up to par. Rather than being inferior, as she thought, her artwork showed tremendous depth and vibrant emotions. Her painting of Noah's ark filled the paper with vibrant, massive rich blue waves and white glistening foam. In class, we praised the sensitivity of her work. We helped her recognize that she is important, and that God gave her a special talent to use and bring beauty into the world.*

Comparing Two Works of Art

There are two ways to appraise artwork: personal preference and deductive comparison. Examples of personal preference include "I like this type of painting. It looks so real" and "I can really relate to this painting—it looks so professional you'd never think a child did it." When making a deductive comparison, we logically and analytically search for the striking differences between Painting A and Painting B. Deductive comparison develops observation skills and fine-tunes a child's descriptive abilities. Using logical deduction, he can come to see the essence of a painting and decide if this is what is important to him.

Stretching his frame of reference—that which is familiar to him—encourages objectivity. By recounting a few of the basic elements of design and composition (center of interest, movement, contrast, balance, proportion, and perspective), he will have a check list to gauge each artwork to see if it has the basic features of good art. He will then be able to see the artwork for what it is externally (deductive) rather than how he perceives it personally. One way to do this is by helping children learn to compare good points between two works of art. This way they learn to temporarily remove their personal perspective from what they are looking at.

For example, when comparing works of children's art, emphasize the good points and discuss each one's unique style. You can certainly note the differences between the two works and mention the best points of each, but don't criticize. For example, you can say:

"Rachel makes very nice big shapes. Debbie makes everything look close-up to us."

"Moshe uses bright, bold colors, and Ephraim uses delicate, soft colors."

"Shoshana knows how to draw beautiful girls' clothes, and Miriam fills up her page with lots of objects and colors."

When appropriate, suggest to the children that they should try the opposite of what they are already doing. If Rachel would benefit by learning to draw a bit smaller, you could say, "I would like to see some little shapes in this picture also." Or if you want Miriam to try focusing on one object, you can mention it: "Now take one object from your picture and draw it by itself." If a child is very adept at drawing tiny detailed pictures, ask him to draw large loose images.

Another way to do this is by letting the children give their opinions about the artwork of professional or amateur artists. Compare fine-art reproductions in publications, postcards, posters, or illustrations in children's books. Have them compare the work of two professional artists—ask the children to find the differences between two similar paintings to increase their visual awareness.

Here is a project that will pique your child's interest in drawing while giving scope for her creativity.

A Birthday Cake AGES 6+

This is a great birthday party project for a group of children ages six and up (five-year-olds can do it with less exacting shapes). Entice them with a birthday cake that they can draw and decorate. They will learn about the shape of an oval at the same time.

Understanding the oval (the cake is drawn using ovals):

An oval is a partial view of a circle. If we hold the opening of a cup up to our eyes we see a complete circle. As we move the cup slowly away from us into an upright position, the circle becomes less rounded and we see an oval or an ellipse. An oval is close to the shape of an eye or an almond. An oval can be a flattened circle, a hot dog bun, or a mouth. The oval is used when we draw cups and containers, and in our case the three-layered birthday cake. Our round cake is actually composed of three cylinders: large, medium, and small. Each cylinder has a top oval and a bottom oval.

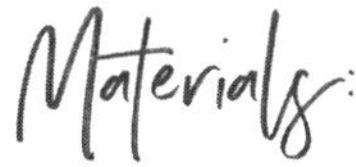

- 1 sheet of copy paper, size 8½ x 11 inches (21 x 30 cm)
- 1 sheet of Bristol paper or other smooth, thick drawing paper, size 8½ x 11 inches (21 x 28 cm)
- Pencil
- Pen or thin black marker (use a permanent marker if using paint)
- Colored markers, preferably soft creamy colors
- Gouache or tempera paint (pink, peach, light yellow, light blue, or other soft colors)
- Paintbrush (optional) ⅛, ¼, and ½ inch (¼, ½, and 1½ cm)

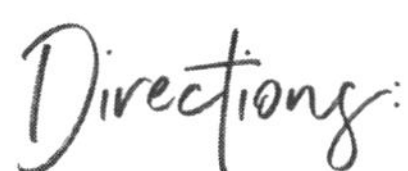

1. First make a practice drawing on the copy paper; each child will do one complete practice drawing before doing the final drawing. The project leader should be able to teach the others how to draw the cake. To start, fold the sheet of copy paper (portrait direction) into four long sections, from the top of the long end to the bottom and once again.
   Open the paper vertically. The paper is long enough for a three-layered-cake.

2. Number each fold line beginning from the top: #1, #2 and #3
3. Think of the shape of a straight, thick cucumber when drawing ovals for the cake cylinders.
4. On fold #1, draw an oval 2 inches long (through the fold line, partly above and partly below the oval) in the center of the paper.
5. Draw another 2-inch oval 2 inches (5 cm) above this. Connect the sides by drawing straight lines. You now have a cylinder.
6. On fold #2, draw an oval 4 inches (10 cm) long in the center of the paper. Draw another 4-inch oval on the #1 fold line, about 3 inches (7½ cm) up. (This will overlap on the bottom of the first oval cylinder). Connect the sides of the second cylinder.
7. On fold #3, draw an oval 6 inches (15 cm) long in the center of the paper. Draw another 6-inch oval on the #2 fold line, about 3 inches (7½ cm) up. (This will overlap on the bottom of the second oval cylinder.) Connect the sides of the third cylinder.
8. Erase the upper part of each oval at the bottom of each cylinder. We should not see the back of the bottom of the cylinders.
9. Erase any distracting lines inside the ovals.
10. Now it's time to decorate your cake. Try out different decoration ideas, and practice drawing the ones you will use: roses and other kinds of flowers, cherries, candles, double-sided numbers, favorite toys.
11. Draw a necklace of scallops (rows of half-circles) around the top front of each cake layer. Imagine several bottom halves of circles lined up together like a necklace. Draw double lines so you can fill in some color.
12. For added decoration, draw straight, double lines from the top to the bottom of each layer, down the rest of the front of the cake. Repeat with each layer. Add a large bow under each scallop necklace. If you want to draw decorative lines of scallops from side to side, draw them curved in the same direction as the oval above so the cake will look round.
13. Once you have finished your practice drawing, draw the final version on the heavy Bristol paper with the pencil.

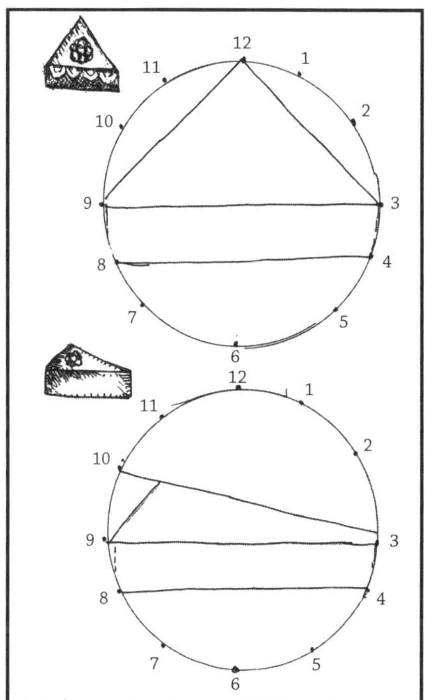

14. Trace over the pencil lines with the pen or thin black marker. Fill in the lines with two or three colored markers or paint. If you wish, paint a background in 1 solid soft color with gouache or tempera paint.

Hold up everyone's work (with their agreement) and enjoy the cakes!

Variation: Cake Slices

Add cake slices to your cake drawing. Or decorate recipes, gift tags, birthday wrapping, and cake-sale tags with cake slices. You can make cake slices in a variety of sizes with a variety of toppings, and colorings. Try thick, creamy or smooth icing with fruit and whipped cream or fondant with chocolate decorations. Cheesecake slices and even pie slices can also be done this way. Fill it in with thick pastel paints (use thick paper) or pastel colored markers.

Here is how you do a basic drawing of a cake slice.

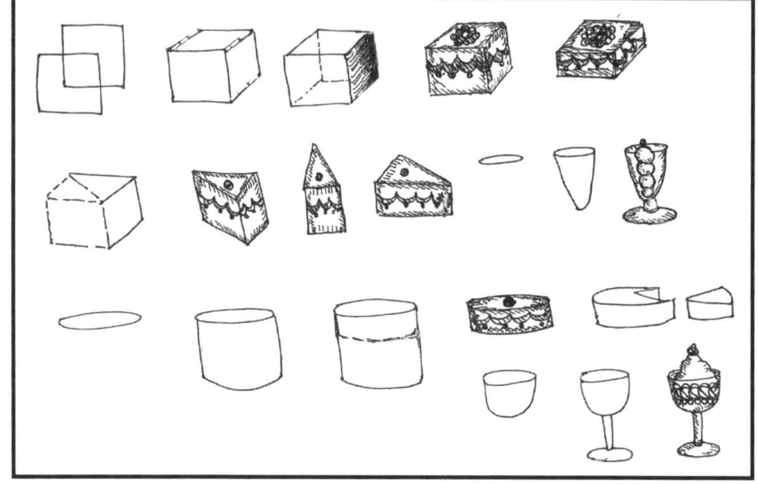

The easiest way: Draw a thin ice-cream cone (without the ice-cream) about 2 inches (5 cm) long, laying on its side.

Draw a short vertical line ½ inch (1½ cm) down at the end of each bottom corner. Connect the lines and you have a cake slice.

Or, if you like:

1. Draw a clock-circle, 6 inches (15 cm) in diameter. Write in the numbers clockwise: 12, 1, 2, 3, 4, 5, 6, 7, 8, 9, 10, 11.

2. Put a dot on 12, 3 and 9. Connect the dots from 12 to 3 and 12 to 9.

3. Draw a 1-inch (2½-cm) line straight down from the bottom of 3 and again from 9. Draw a line connecting the bottom points of 3 and 9, and you have a cake slice.

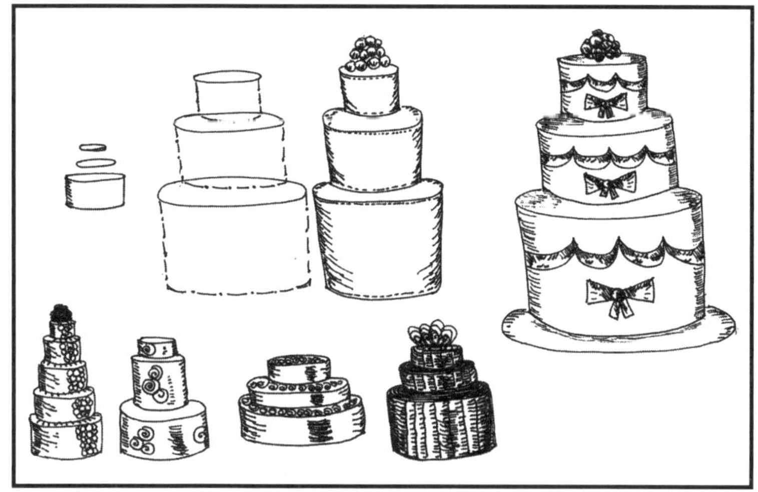

4. Erase the clock-circle.
5. Draw on oval for a plate under the cake slice.
6. Decorate and color.

Or, you can make an elongated triangle cake slice:

1. Draw a clock-circle, 6 inches (15 cm) in diameter. Write in the numbers clockwise: 12, 1, 2, 3, 4, 5, 6, 7, 8, 9, 10, 11.
2. Draw the first line from 10 to 3. Draw the second line from 10 to 9. Connect lines 9 to 3.
3. Draw a 1-inch (2½-cm) line straight down from the bottom of lines 9 and 3. Draw a line connecting the bottom points of both for an elegant cake slice.
4. Erase the clock-circle.
5. Draw an oval for a plate under the cake slice.
6. Decorate and color.

In Summary: Making the Most of Your Child's Potential

- Creativity is the ability to produce something concrete and unique using our options and imagination.
- "Options" refers to more than one way to think, find a solution, and create.
- Anyone with an imagination can be creative. It is the willingness to explore options and possibilities that puts the imagination into action.
- Bring out the creativity in children by allowing them to develop their innate skills, while at the same time encouraging them to work outside their comfort zone.
- Give children opportunities to grow by teaching skills that fit their learning style and by providing ample opportunities and materials.

- Make the most of a child's strengths and help them master their weaknesses.
- When comparing works of art, emphasize the positive and encourage objective, analytical critique.
- Encourage the exceptional child's sensitivity and creativity rather than making her conform just because she doesn't fit into the norm.

Questions and Wonder

1. Why create something when you can buy it ready-made?
2. How does creativity help us in different areas in our lives (besides art)?
3. Can you give an example of someone who was stuck in a situation and looked for options? What are options and why do we need them?
4. How do you feel when someone copies your idea or something you drew? Where did your idea originally come from?

15 Art as a Communication Tool

Young Children Talk to You

Your child comes home from school with artwork in hand. "Mommy, look what I made!" How do you respond? Do you show your interest by...

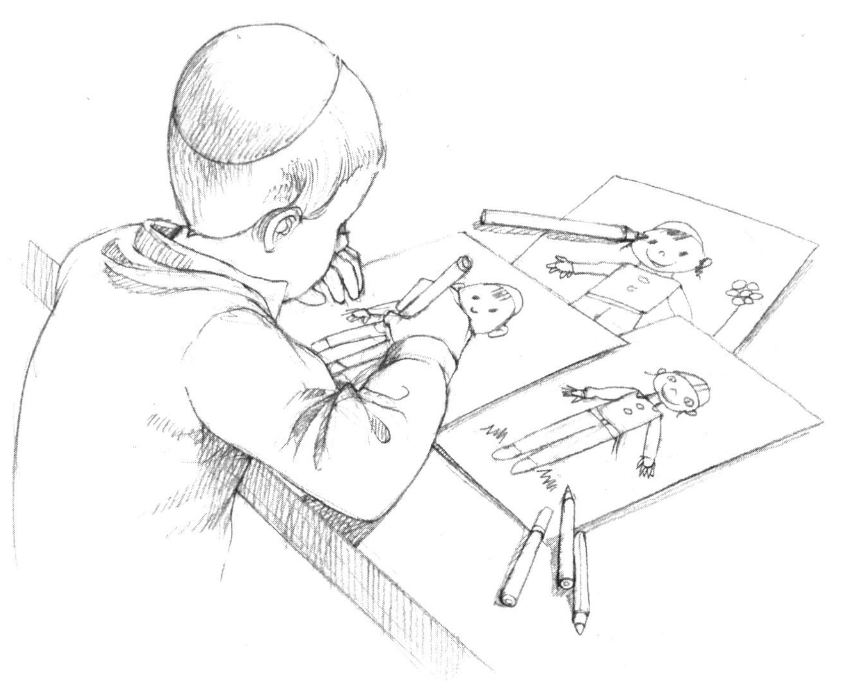

- making a brief exclamation of praise and setting it on the table, already forgotten, so you can get on with making dinner?
- carefully examining your child's art treasure, asking what it is, and then hanging it on the fridge?
- sitting down and giving the child a full five minutes of your time and asking thoughtful questions about his day and what went into making those lines and colors?

Notes and Sketches

This is an opportunity to open up a dialogue with your child. Discussing a work of art that she made is a great starting point for a discussion about your child's day and what concerns her. Sometimes children, especially very young ones, forget about significant things that happened to them during a busy school day, even if they might still be feeling their effects.

Giving your child a platform to talk about her day encourages her to make connections to events that brought up certain feelings. When she tells you about them, she can release these feelings rather than leave them pent-up inside.

There are children who are naturally reticent and don't usually offer information about themselves. When your child hands you her work of art, she is giving you an opening to communicate with her. So why not take the five minutes and sit down to really talk to your child? What you find out may surprise you.

> *My son Avi was five. I had been home sick for a week, and we were both bored. I suggested that he make a puppet show and I would be the audience. That way I could sit on the couch and rest while Avi was kept busy.*
>
> *The puppets were designed, the theater fabricated and set up. The presentation and the script were all handcrafted by my son's little hands and active mind. I realized that he had a lot to say—with words and without.*
>
> *The show began. There were moments of silence between dialogue and scene changes. The spaces between words told me he was thinking and working out the plot of the play as he went along. I would never have valued the silences if I had been in my usual busy rush. I had nothing else to do but lie on the couch and recuperate, so now I could appreciate my son's thinking process.*
>
> *When the words came, they were subtle, sensitive, and revealing.*
>
> *Avi is a young man now. I don't remember exactly what he said that day, but I do remember those few enlightened moments when I was in tune with my son's thoughts and feelings.*

Pay attention to your child's "unspoken words" in their drawings and "listen" for clues to what is going on inside him. Open up a discussion about them and allow your child to talk about what he's been feeling and thinking. Share his joys or fears or his newfound knowledge of what

Notes and Sketches

he learned that day in school as he explains why he drew this specific drawing. The reward you will reap will retain its impact long after the drawing itself has been forgotten.

If you are busy with something right at the moment that your child wants to show you his picture, and you aren't able to respond immediately, tell the child that you want to carefully look at what he made and talk about it when you can sit and give him quality attention. Let him know that what he created is important to you. And then, keep your word; sit down with him and show that you value the child's early efforts at communication.

Asking the Right Questions

Three-year-old Michael brought home a picture that he had colored that day in school. He had scribbled messily first with a yellow crayon and then a green crayon. It was obvious he had tried to color in the lines, but wasn't really able to.

"Look, I made this today," Michael said and handed the picture to his mother.

"How nice," she remarked and reached for a fridge magnet to hang it up. For some reason, she stopped herself and really looked at the picture. She saw that it was about the five senses.

"Oh, Michael, I see a boy wearing a big pair of glasses. What does someone do with glasses?"

Michael didn't really answer her question. He was fascinated by the image on the bottom of the page of a girl petting a rabbit to represent the sense of touch. "There's a rabbit!" he exclaimed.

"That's right. What else do you see?"

They identified the images on the page, and then Michael's mother said, "This is a very nice picture. I see you tried very hard to color in the lines."

Michael was silent for a minute and then said, "Shalom said I couldn't do it."

Shalom was Michael's classmate and a whole year older.

"What did you say to Shalom when he told you that you couldn't do it?"

"I told him I could."

Michael's mother said, "And you did it!"

Michael nodded, beaming. His mother was glad she had taken a few moments to talk to her son about his drawing. She made a mental note to speak to the teacher and make sure he was keeping up at school.

When you examine your child's art creations, make sure that your comments are specific: "What great big circles you made!" or "This is so nice—a frame of circles." When you notice details, your child sees that you are really paying attention. Still, most important are the visual clues that lead to a dialogue of verbal information. Be sure to give eye contact, a listening ear, and a smile.

Being able to verbally describe their artwork may be as hard for some children as defining their best traits. Often, they don't really know what to say. Or it may be on the tip of their tongue, but they are afraid to say what they are really feeling for fear of a reprimand.

It's important to ask the right questions to give your child a way to communicate with you and let him know that it's okay to express himself. If you're not sure where to begin when your child brings home a picture, or it's too hard to find the words, here are some questions and topics you can try:

1. "Would you like to tell me about your picture or what you made at school today?" If your child doesn't respond to this, try initiating the conversation with a statement: "I see you worked hard on this drawing," or "It looks like you drew this little group of lines very carefully." Or ask an easier question: "Was it hard or easy to draw those lines?"

2. "Where did you begin your drawing, in the middle of the paper, at the top, or at the bottom? Which lines did you draw first?" Knowing where the first mark was made on the paper can tell you a lot. It indicates the spacing and arrangement of the rest of the picture.[126] (For example, if the mark is too low, it can result in a bottom-heavy drawing without interest at the top.) If the first mark wasn't random, let your child know that you are aware of his ability to make sound choices and plan ahead.

---

126 See ch. 16, "Understanding Your Child through Art."

3. "What is the last thing you drew? Did you stop because there wasn't any more time? If you could have continued to draw, what would you have included?"

4. "Which colors did you use? Why did you choose these colors? Did you mix the colors yourself? I see you like pinks. Did everyone in the class use pink or was it your idea?"

5. "Did you erase anything here? Why? Did you erase because you didn't know how to make what you wanted or because you didn't think it was good enough? Next time, you can practice drawing what is hard for you on another sheet of paper and then copy it on your final paper so you won't have to spend time erasing."

6. "What were you thinking about when you drew this picture? Is this something you wanted to draw? Was this idea yours, the teacher's, or your friend's? Would you have drawn something else if you could have? What would that have been?"

7. "Did you do it all by yourself or did a friend or the teacher help you? Did you want help? Did you want them to draw on your paper? I like best to see what you draw because it's from you."

8. This is also an opportunity to develop your child's vocabulary. You can use the drawing as a springboard for introducing new words. For example: "I see that you drew a yellow sun. What else is yellow? Daffodils and sunflowers, bananas, lemons, and your school bus. Daffodils are a kind of flower. Can you say the word daffodils?"

You can conclude the discussion with an expression of praise or pleasure, such as "I love it because you did it," and thank the child for sharing the artwork with you.

When children see that they can express their feelings, they will come to accept who they are and come to like who they are more and more.

Does Realism Prevent Expression?

Dena, five and a half, arrived at the art class with her thumb in her mouth and her head downcast. She took her place with the rest of the group, and after animated instructions that included all the possibilities for drawing a girl, she tried her hand at it.

Her girl was confined to a corner at the bottom of the paper. A girl without hands or legs. Yet the design on the girl's skirt was filled with swirls and flowers.

Dena hid her picture with her arms and hands as she drew. When she was finished, she indicated to me without words that I wasn't to look at it.

We changed mediums and I brought out the paint.

"Dena, what color would you like?" I ventured.

Dena spoke for the first time. "Red!" she said loud and clear. She had a voice. Pow!

She painted a large sheet of paper a brilliant red. I saw that she loved bright, loud colors—vibrant reds and oranges, brilliant yellows and emerald green. She painted carefully as if she had done this before, though I knew it was her first time painting. In school paint didn't exist and at home it was too messy. Here she found a haven for her expression.

Dena came back for more lessons. One lesson was dedicated to painting and mixing colors on giant sheets of paper to her heart's content. She almost danced out of class, spinning with happiness. But I didn't need to see her dance to know she was enjoying herself. Her colors spoke for her.

When Dena's artwork was confined to drawing the figure of a girl, Dena felt constricted and unable to express herself. The only sign of creative expression was in the pattern of the figure's skirt. It was only when she was able to paint freestyle with paints that her creative expression was given free rein, and she began to enjoy herself.

Unfortunately, realism in painting is often valued over expression. Expressive art that suggests life, movement, and depth, and that creates illusions of a place and time that perhaps does not actually exist is often misunderstood. Expressive art tends to be more personal, and unless it has universal significance, the average viewer may not relate to it immediately.

Children's art in itself is universal because so much of it centers on their discovering their world and their selves. And yet children's art can easily encompass both realism and expression—sometimes more expression than realism.

Feelings in art need concrete form; we combine feelings with realism to create a work of art. But should we forsake the value of feelings for realism because it is easier to identify? Ideally, we should strive for the middle ground. An example of this would be using brilliant colors and broad and varied brushstrokes on a highly technically painted landscape.

But too often children are held back by the preconceived idea that they must produce perfect and realistic artwork. This limits their creative expression and ability to be present in the moment when creating their art (and in their lives in general).

When children begin to draw recognizable objects, it's important that the parent or teacher also pay attention to the effort and feelings behind the work. It is helpful for the parent or teacher to be knowledgeable enough to appreciate both what the child is attempting to recreate (realism) and express (feelings).

In this way, the child will be able to pour what he is feeling into what he is creating. Then his artwork truly can become a vehicle for communication, as it should be.

Start a Discussion on Art

You don't need to confine discussions about art only to those times when your child brings home a masterpiece. Opportunities for art-inspired dialogue are abundant.

While reading a story, inject a conversation inspired by the illustrations inside the book. When you're on vacation in a picturesque resort, and a moment of visual inspiration catches you—a flock of birds circling overhead, the seemingly endless expanse of the turquoise-blue ocean, or flowers bursting with sharp, bold color—stop and talk about it.

Art appreciation is not limited to painting, sculpture, or architecture either. It's all around us, from the smallest dot of green chlorophyll in a blade of grass to the varied creatures populating the world.

Mingle topics on beauty, color, design, and craftsmanship into everyday conversation—while going to the grocery store, taking a walk, or thinking about what to make for dinner. Cooking is also an art! Point out that certain color combinations are more aesthetically pleasing than others. Red tomato sauce with flecks of green oregano and basil looks delicious because of the pleasing palette of colors it creates.

Just this moment, as I write this, my husband has brought in a shopping bag full of lemons from our tree—intensely vibrant yellow ones that I don't usually find in the store. I hold them up and take a sniff of their fresh tangy scent and notice how lovely they look against my purple sweater. The artist in me can't help but stop and admire the beauty of nature, and it inspires me.

Let it inspire you and your child, too! Children can be taught by example to pick up on aesthetics, on pleasing color choices, and to appreciate the beauty of the world around them.

When children are aware of what is pleasing to the eye and learn what is pleasing to their eyes, they can better connect their artwork to their feelings. They begin to understand how art and expression intertwine. Art appreciation for the sake of art alone doesn't utilize one of the most redeeming qualities of art: to connect the child to his feelings. Talking to the child about his feelings and observances in the milieu of art teaches him to be more cognizant of his emotions, likes and dislikes, trusts and fears.

There are some topics in art that will pique your child's interest. When you open up the dialogue, you will want to adapt your questions to the child's age.

Some questions you can address to younger children:

1. "Why did Hashem give us eyes? What do you enjoy looking at? What do you see right now that looks beautiful to you?" Use this line when on a train or outdoors in view of nature.

2. "What do you like to do best—to draw, paint, color, or cut and paste? What can you make when you do any of these things?" If your child can't think of anything, you can list some of the choices; your child will be fascinated to learn that there are so many things you can do with basic art materials: collages, paper cuts, paper folding (origami), portraits, landscapes, still lifes, cartoons, illustrations, charts, announcements, decorations, clay models, and games, to name just a few.

3. "What shapes do you know? What is a circle, square, and triangle? Can you find any of these shapes in your drawing? Did you know

that you can make a diamond from two triangles or an ice-cream cone from a circle and a triangle? What else can you make?"

4. "Where can we find these circles, squares, and triangles in our classroom, at home, or outside?" This can make for a great scavenger hunt, especially if the child is bored or you're waiting to see the doctor. Each child has a set amount of time to examine his location (a shopping mall, grocery store, dentist's office, post office, gas station, the street outside). Have each player call out each item that reminds him of one of the geometric shapes. The one who sees the most wins. (Or add variety: Who saw the most triangles, the most circles, etc.)

5. "When you draw, do you use all or part of the paper? (You can use all of it!)" Point out that it's a good idea to start near the upper third of the paper and work down. This way they won't end up with a lot of empty space.

6. "What are your favorite colors? Why? What is it that you like about your favorite color? What does it remind you of? Why do you think God made things in different colors? Did you know that colors can 'look like' feelings?" Red is a strong color that represents strong emotions ("How does red make you feel?"); red is the color of fire trucks and roses. Blue is a calm, cool color; it's the color of water and sky. Yellow is a vibrant, lively color; it is the color of the sun and lemons. Green reminds us of new life: plants, trees, colorful bird feathers. Browns, tans, and ochres are earthy colors and remind us of nature's background or the quiet colors in animals, rocks, hills, and vegetation during certain seasons. Grays are for shadows and gloomy rainy days, yet, it is a neutral color that goes with most other colors.

7. "Is the ocean only blue? Is a tree only brown? Do you know the names of all the types of blue? There's turquoise, light blue, dark blue, azure, sapphire, lapis, Prussian blue, cobalt, ultramarine, cerulean, navy, aquamarine, sky blue, moonlight blue, smoke blue, gray blue." (Your child will find it fun and challenging to repeat the names of the colors after you!)

8. "What colors do you find in fruits and vegetables? Why do you think that fruits, vegetables, and flowers have so many lovely

colors?" When choosing fruit at the market, stop for a moment and comment on the visual effect before your eyes.

9. "What color is the air? Is white a color? Did you know that there are many types of white?" Look at a list of wall-paint swatches to show that white can come in many shades: eggshell, ice white, lime white, milky white, snow white, glossy white, cream, linen, ash, daisy.
10. "Why do children and some grown-ups like to paint and draw?"
11. "What kind of pictures do we have in our house? What do you like or not like about them?"
12. "What can we do with your pictures when they are finished?" Do you save them in a portfolio or send them to the grandparents? How do you decide which ones to save?

Here are some great discussion topics for older children:

1. "Why do you think we have so many lovely sights and colors to look at? What do you enjoy looking at? Beautiful landscapes—mountains, rivers, oceans, the sky, flowers? A nicely set Shabbat table? A pretty dress?"
2. "When you look at a picture or painting, do you stop to think what the artist is telling us? Do you notice any moods or feelings shown in the painting? Do you find yourself agreeing with the message the artist seems to express? How do you know what the message is? Do you think there is always a message, or does a painting sometimes simply portray the vision of the artist? The famous *Mona Lisa* by Leonardo Da Vinci is popular because of the lady's mysterious smile. Why do people like mystery?" Bring up the names of other famous works of art or artists and try to understand what made them so famous.
3. "What is abstract art? Does it remind you of little kids' drawings? What do you think about it?" Though sometimes our response to abstract art is "Any child could do this," in the mind of the artist, each line, bit of color, and the totality of the composition is a result of controlled thoughts and brush movements. Is that clear from the final result? Is this what a child does? How is it different or the same?

4. “Why do you think that some paintings make us feel emotional or inspired and others don't?”

5. “Imagine a painting of an old woman lighting her Shabbat candles alone in a small bare room. How does that image make you feel? Sad at the thought of her loneliness? Inspired by this moment of devotion?”

6. “What can we learn about Jewish life in other cultures, countries, and historical times from observations of their paintings and craftwork?”

These questions capture a child's wonder and compels him to view his artwork in a new light. Here are a couple of projects that can inspire discussion and help your child look at the world around him for inspiration.

Let's Draw Our Neighborhood AGES 7+

A drawing of our neighborhood with important people from the child's world.

Materials:

- Bristol paper, size 11 x 16 inches (28 x 41 cm) (the size of a place mat or larger)
- Pencil
- Colored markers (broad-tipped)
- Tempera or gouache paints
- Soft paintbrush, ½ inch (1½ cm)

Directions:

1. With the pencil, draw a large map on Bristol or firm paper of three intersecting streets (with double lines) that resemble your neighborhood. Ask your child to draw his favorite places and tell you why he likes them. Ask him to draw places he doesn't like and to explain why he doesn't like them.

2. Color in with wide colored markers.

3. Paint the sky with tempera or gouache paints as he would like it to be, and he should tell you why. Suggest that he add in mountains, a beach, a forest, or a park according to his preference and explain why he chose these places. Ask him to add people, a few that he likes and perhaps one he doesn't. What will he say about these people that tells you about your child?

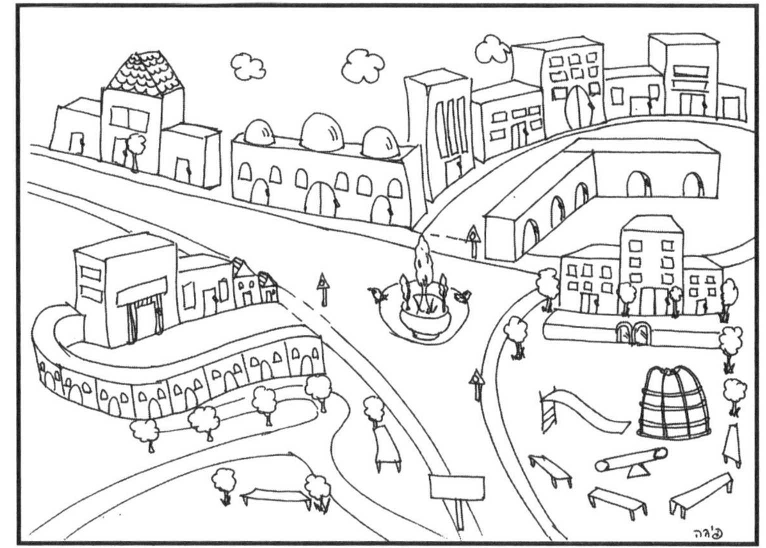

Let's Build Our City

AGES 6+

Construct a model of your city or street out of cardboard boxes and tubes. Start saving boxes of all shapes and sizes for this project: grocery boxes, cereal boxes, paper towel tubes, and shoe and gift boxes.

Take the time to follow your child around significant places in your neighborhood and discuss them. Think about how you would model the different size houses, buildings, and stores. Don't forget to include the roads, street signs, park benches, the playground, trucks, buses, ambulances, cars, and trees.

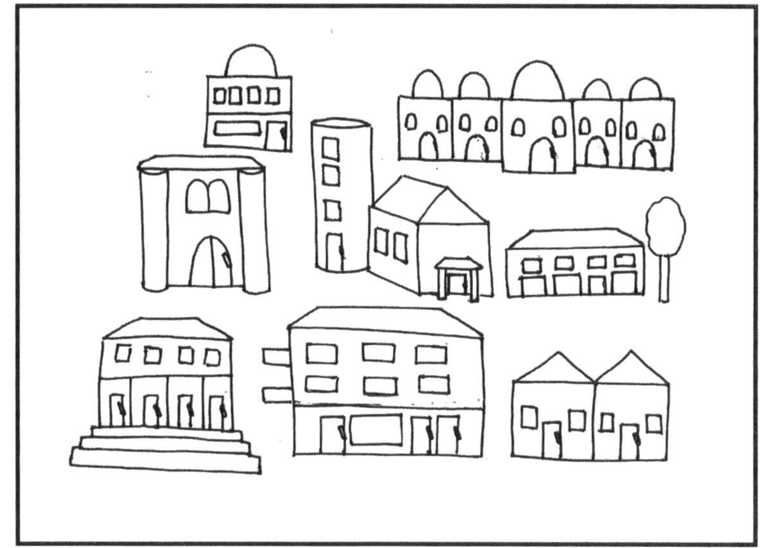

Materials:

- Copy paper, size 11 x 16 inches (30 x 42 cm) (place mat size) or smaller
- Pencil
- Pens
- Wide and thin colored markers
- Tempera or gouache paints

- Paintbrushes, ¼, ½, and ¾ inch (½, 1½, and 2 cm)
- Craft knife
- Hot-glue gun
- White plastic glue
- A variety of boxes: cereal boxes, paper towel tubes, matchboxes, cartons from the grocery store and cardboard scraps
- Scissors
- Air-drying clay for sculpting accessories for the homes, the street, and the playground (optional)
- Cloth or heavy plastic tape
- Staples and stapler (optional)
- Tissue paper
- Pipe cleaners
- Craft sticks (popsicle sticks)
- Material for curtains, and for fake grass (optional)

Directions:

1. With the paper and pencil, plan the buildings and streets.
2. Cut out the boxes and tubes into pieces according to your plans with scissors and craft knife and attach the pieces with hot glue, staples, or strong tape to form a variety of buildings. For small objects or paper, use white plastic glue.
   Cardboard boxes are a natural for buildings. Most buildings are square or rectangular. Adding a triangle roof (a piece of cardboard folded in half) usually indicates a house as opposed to a building. A large sign on the front of the box tells us the building is a store. Smaller signs can indicate a professional service. Tubes attached to an upright cardboard box can become farm buildings or office building sky scrapers.
   Let the child decide what he or she wants to include. He can include models of your home, homes of nearby relatives and friends, schools, hospitals, doctors' offices, synagogues, parks, the playground, shops, roads, airports, and towers.

3. With markers or paint, mark doors, windows, signs, addresses, street names, and signs. Paint and decorate as desired.

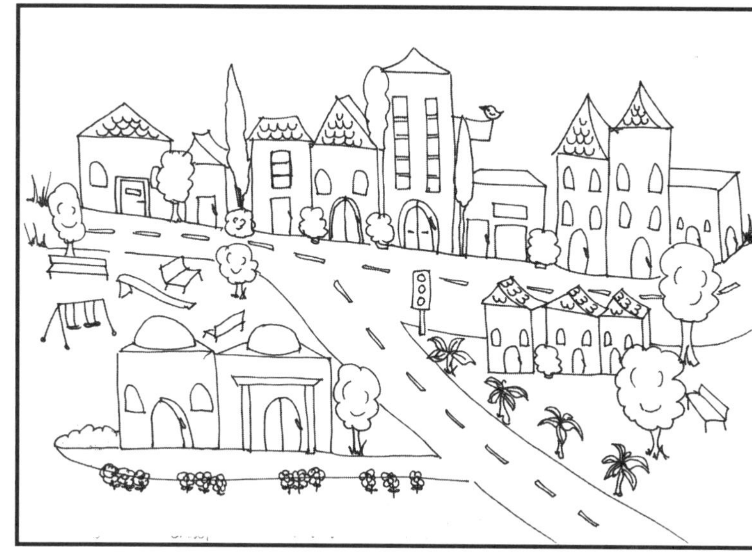

4. Make flowers from bits of tissue paper and pipe cleaners or cardboard and markers. If desired, make accessories from air-drying clay: people, street signs, animals, trees, garbage cans, etc.
5. Set up the "neighborhood" in the house or in the yard. When the child plays with the box neighborhood, he will have an opening to talk about what's important to him in his home and neighborhood. The dynamics of the child's dialogue will be different if two or more children play. Note the dialogues and ask the children for permission to write them down and read it back to them later. Emphasize the strong positive points that the child mentions.

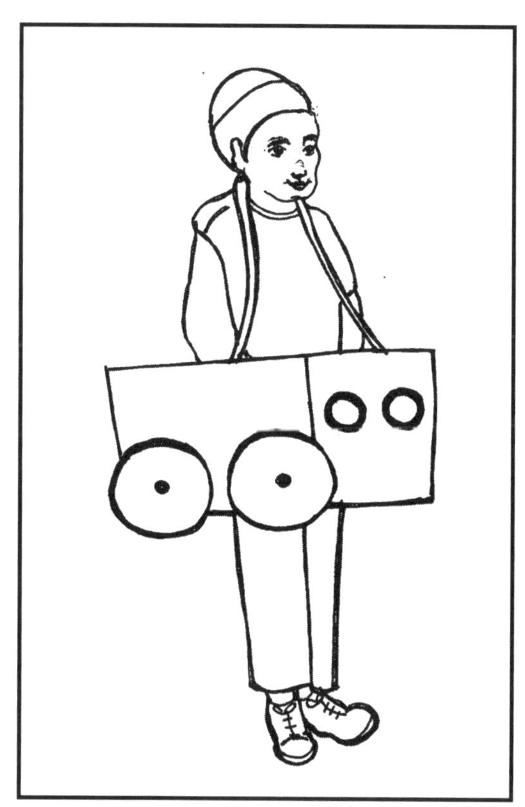

A Box Car AGES 8+

A child-size car[127] is constructed from a large grocery box. (You may want to make two cars, so two children can play together or the child with an adult.) Enjoy the pleasure of constructing and painting the car together. Ask the child where he will be driving to, who he will see, and what he will do there.

Note: Save the car for Purim and he will have the beginnings of a great costume.

Option 1: Put a costume on the "driver."

Option 2: Remove the wheels and indications of a car and transform the box into a gift box (with your child inside).

Option 3: Transform the box into the tent of Avraham Avinu with four openings, by hanging a material from the head of the child attached to the four corners of the box. A girl costume might be the tent of Sarah Imeinu, with Shabbat candles and challah.

Option 4: Devise a building or any other great idea you can imagine.

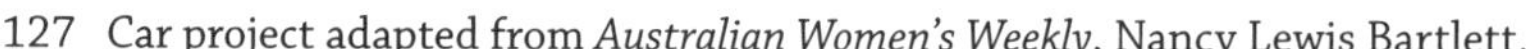

127 Car project adapted from *Australian Women's Weekly*, Nancy Lewis Bartlett.

Materials:

- 1 large cardboard box from a case of 12 cereal boxes or same size, discarded from the grocery store
- Pencil
- Black permanent marker
- Tempera or gouache paint, your choice of colors
- Paintbrush, 2 inches (5 cm)
- 5 cereal boxes or cardboard of similar thickness
- Scissors or craft knife
- 2–4 large disposable plates (optional)
- 2–4 small disposable plates (optional)
- Paper fasteners or hot-glue gun
- Square piece of cardboard, size 9 x 9 inches (23 x 23 cm) (optional)
- Aluminum foil
- Heavy cord or string, 60 inches long (152 cm)

Directions:

1. Remove the bottom of the large cardboard box. With the scissors or craft knife, cut a large hole at the top for the child to fit in. He will step into the opening and suspend a cord (from both sides of the "car") over his shoulders and across his back. It reminds me of the clown with extra-large pants held up with suspenders.
2. Paint the box a solid light color. Or have fun with several colors. You may want to draw realistic looking parts of a car and color in appropriately. Let dry.
3. With the pencil, draw the doors on the outside and a rectangle for the control board with small circles for buttons on the inside. Trace over the pencil marks with the permanent black marker. Paint as desired. Let dry.
4. Measure, draw, and cut four large wheels from the cereal boxes. You can use a large paper plate for a pattern, or use the

disposable plates as the wheels. Draw spokes on the cardboard or paper-plate wheels.

5. Pierce holes in the sides of the cardboard box where the wheels are to go and attach the "wheels" with paper fasteners inserted through the holes (or attach with hot glue).
6. Cut out two headlights and two rear lights from the fifth cereal box or use small paper plates. Cover with aluminum foil or paint bright white, yellow, or orange, and let dry. Attach the headlights with paper fasteners inserted through holes pierced through the front and back of the box where the lights should go (or attach with hot glue).
7. Make a steering wheel from a disposable plate or cut out from the back of the cereal box and attach with a paper fastener or hot glue on top front of car.
8. Make a license plate from the 9-inch piece of cardboard or from a cereal box. Write the child's name on the license plate with a permanent marker in bold letters. Attach to the back of the car with tape or hot glue.
9. Pierce two holes on either side of the center of the box at the top. Insert each end of the heavy cord or string into the holes. Secure each end with a double knot. Have him step into the box. Suspend the cord over each of his shoulders and across his back and watch him drive off with a smile.

Let's Draw the World of Nature AGES 9+

Materials:

- A colorful photo of nature
- Copy paper, size 8½ x 11 inches (21 x 30 cm)
- Bristol paper, size 8½ x 11 inches (21 x 28 cm) or larger, or other strong paper that takes water, or canvas
- Pencil
- Colored pencils or pastel chalks

- Acrylics or gouache (optional)
- Soft paintbrush, ¼ or ½ inch (½ or 1½ cm)
- Scissors

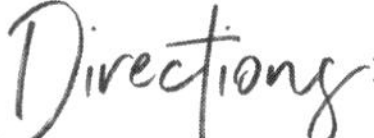

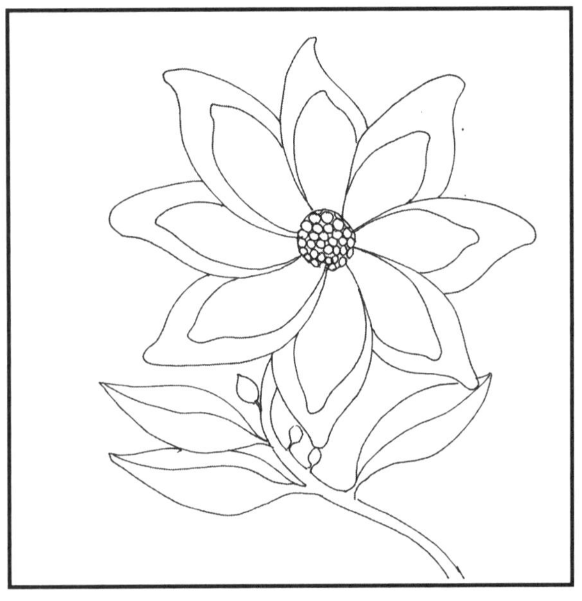

1. Find a colorful photo from a magazine, travel brochure, or a calendar.
2. Cut it out. Help your child notice the main parts of the picture. Talk about what you both see: a sky with clouds, sun, birds, a beach, an ocean with boats, mountains and rocks, or flowers with leaves and petals. You can point out the delicate sculptural form of the inside of the flower, noticing the curve of the edges and the fine texture of the petals.
3. Can she make a close-up painting of a flower or a bird from the photo? Choose a section of the magazine picture that interests her and let her draw it on the 8½ x 11-inch (21 x 30-cm) paper with a pencil.
4. If she's doing a painting, do a final version on Bristol or other strong paper that takes water, or use canvas.
5. Let her rearrange the composition, adding or subtracting imagery.
6. Color with colored pencils or pastel chalks, or do a painting.

In Summary: Art as a Communication Tool

- Make the time to discuss your child's artwork with him to learn about his day and how he is feeling inside.
- To encourage dialogue, notice details in your child's art and pay attention to what your child has to say about it.

- It's important to encourage a balance of realism and self-expression to give children a vehicle to express themselves in their artwork.
- Discussions on art can begin with an appreciation of the world and the wonders of God's creations.

Questions and Wonder

1. How is painting, drawing, sculpting, or working with other art mediums similar to writing a story, a play, or a poem for self-expression? How is it different?
2. How can you show others what you are feeling, thinking, or enjoy doing with a painting, drawing, or other type of artwork?

16 Understanding Your Child through Art

The First Mark

Little Avi is drawing on the living room wall. He is making the first marks of his life—his first imprint in the world. With every mark and stroke of color, he is saying, "This is me, my signature, my stamp. I am here and I have influence on my world."

Avi may even consider every wall, tablecloth, or paper on which he drew as his own because he drew on it (just like in Talmudic times, over 1,500 years ago, when a man could acquire a segment of land by digging in the land, walking around the boundary, or signing a contract with a mark or

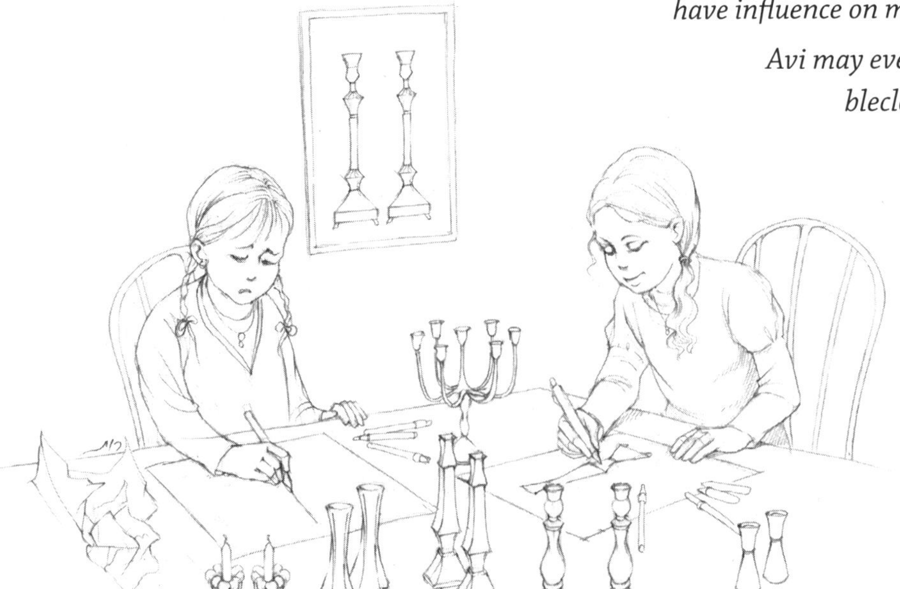

stamp[128]). Our Avi is not far off in his thinking. He knows the value of his marks. His scribbles are his masterwork. They show the world who he is. One day these marks, which now resemble chicken scratches, will become his signature.

Notes and Sketches

When your toddler colors on the walls, he's not trying to be a trouble-maker. He's at an age when he is discovering that he is a separate, unique self, and he wants to express it. He's developing quickly, both cognitively and physically, and he wants to explore his capabilities.

Avi's excitement and self-confidence in his scribbles are so great that his mother does not have the heart to squelch them. She shows him that she is proud of his achievement, but at the same time tells him firmly not to draw on the walls again. Instead, she provides him with lots of paper for further self-expression.

Scribbles, Scribbles Everywhere

Take pleasure in looking at your child's first scribbles. These marks are significant. By studying his artwork, you will find clues to how your child sees himself in relation to the world around him. Yes, even seemingly indecipherable scribbles tell a story.

For example, the first place where a child (of three or four years of age) makes contact with the pencil on the paper may have been deliberate. Or it may just be a byproduct of a random gross-motor movement. Either way, there is something it can tell you about your child, and it deserves consideration. You may notice that his scribbles seem entirely random with no connection. This tells you something about what he was feeling when he drew his picture. It's probable that he simply wasn't interested in expression with a crayon that day. You may want to point out to your child, "It looks like you weren't so interested in drawing today." Listen for his response and then ask him what he would rather have been doing or what was on his mind just then. The same child may be encouraged to draw meaningful scribbles when he's focused and sitting at the drawing table with a facilitating adult.

If you observe that your child sits in place as he draws, he could be a "deliberate drawer"—one who thinks and concentrates as he draws. Take

128 Talmud, *Kiddushin* 26a.

Notes and Sketches

a look and see: Is he at the scribbling stage or the shape-making stage? Does he make marks or circles and other shapes? Does the paper have a frame around the edge or not?

Notice the marks and their positions. Be aware of his choice of colors. (The use of black or dark colors, for example, may indicate a black mood. If we want to encourage a positive outlook, however, it is best not to offer black. Black is not considered a color, but is the absence of light; dark blues, browns, purples, and greens are preferable options for dark moods). Applaud him for his work. Why? Because he did it and it is important to him. After all, this is his signature, the product of his thought processes and his motor control abilities.

Aside from the technical accomplishments, each tiny mark may have a huge story attached to it. A yellow scribble could be Mommy, and an oval with a few zigzags could be a lion. Since you will be hard-pressed to interpret your toddler's scribbles, try to get your child to tell you about his drawings.[129] One mother I know told me that her son, all of three and a half years old, scribbled a whole book (six pages!) of lines and attempts of shapes, all to tell a story of a fly that bothered a lion. Try to picture that!

Drawing and Self-Image

A child is formed from the inside out and the outside in. His paintings and drawings will reflect how he sees himself in comparison to those around him.

It's common for children to draw the members of their family, usually starting with the father, then the mother, and then all the children from the oldest to the youngest. Encourage your child to be different. Suggest that he draw the parents, himself, and his siblings in order of preference, and see what happens. If there's not enough room on the paper, tape on another sheet of paper to provide space. If the child inadvertently omitted himself, provide a second sheet of paper where the "artist" can place himself in the composition.

Be aware that these family portraits may not be accurate to us, but they have great significance to the young child. Talk to him about what he drew—see if you can get him to express why he drew his drawing.

129 See previous chapter, "Art as a Communication Tool."

Six-year-old Sammy drew his entire family: his father, mother, himself, and five other identical boys in a row. All the boys were the same size and taller than both parents. In reality, this boy had one younger brother and three sisters, but he chose not to draw them as they really were. He wanted to show his strength of personality, so he drew them exactly as he had drawn himself and he made them larger than life.

Miri was a perfectionist at school and at home. She would get upset easily in her daily life, yet she was a successful student and was socially well-adjusted. Her desire to achieve adult standards at the age of eight years old caused her endless frustration. Miri had high expectations and these showed up in her artwork and in her attitude. She erased and redid her drawings constantly. No matter how lovely and sophisticated she drew, Miri was never happy with the outcome. Often, after lots of work erasing and redoing, she would succeed in drawing an image above her age level but she could not acknowledge that it was truly a well-drawn piece of art.

When she expressed discontent over her work, I asked her what her options were. For Miri, recognizing realistic options (at her age and level of experience) was the path to accepting her own artwork.

If a child sees that there is a workable solution to accepting the conditions, materials, and project in front of her, then her frustrations may dissipate. She begins to see herself as complete and able as she is. If she does not want to accept her abilities as is, she can practice and work hard at improving toward her goal. I would explain to the child that often children have an image in their minds of what they want to draw and are frustrated at not being able to depict it. With lots of time and practice, they eventually will be able to achieve their goal.

Using Art Therapy Tools to Learn about Your Child

Some people think that art combined with improving developmental skills is the same as art therapy. Although this is partly true, art therapy includes a great deal of pure psychology. Art therapists are trained to use the creative process of art to improve emotional, physical, and mental well-being. Often people with emotional issues are treated through the medium of art.

This can be very effective for understanding young children who have a different way of communicating than adults or who find it difficult to express themselves verbally. While art alone is extremely beneficial, it's not enough to treat anyone with a psychological disorder. The two do meet on happy ground, one providing prevention and an expressive release and the other offering healing of the mind.

Art therapists make full use of art as a tool to help children express their troubled emotions. The tangible expression that art promotes—drawing, painting, working with clay, making collages with glue and paper—is used as an outlet for the child's feelings. This is accentuated when the adult recognizes these feelings and plays them back to the child so that he gains insight into his behavior.[130] In this way, art is a catharsis, letting a child progress from negative feelings to positive ones.

This is a process that takes time. One must pass feelings of inadequacy before reaching the goal. One therapist was working with a hostile, angry boy who painted images of fire, smoke, and blood during the therapy sessions. The therapist acknowledged his desperate and angry battle to free himself from an abusive and neglected upbringing. Eventually, over the series of therapy sessions, his angry feelings softened into self-acceptance and emotional freedom. Slow acceptance of a troubled child's attitude by the therapist and by the child within himself is a gateway for an emotionally healthy adjustment.[131]

A child in therapy will have a trained adult helping him though his turmoil. But what about the average child with normal fears and questions? Children who come from warm and well-adjusted homes obviously don't have the same challenges as the maladjusted child. But all children face moments of anger, fear, and frustration, and art can be a healthy way to channel those feelings and deal with them.

Although a person has to be trained to do art therapy effectively, we can use some of the rudiments of art therapy to learn about our children at home or in the classroom. Let's look at children's drawings in art therapy terms.

One tool in art therapy is what is called "projective drawing." A projective drawing is a child's self-image revealed on paper. The child projects his

---

130 Virginia M. Axline, *Play Therapy* (Ballantine Books,1993), p. 142.

131 Ibid., p. 370.

self into the subjects he is asked to draw, perhaps a person, a house or a tree, which may reveal unspoken feelings and beliefs the child has. When a child has consistently been exposed to art to encourage his development and prevent possible issues, he may become familiar with his feelings and perceptions and be more able to bring his feelings closer to the surface in his daily life. A sensitive adult can also ask questions or describe back to the child what she observes in a safe, non-judgmental way. Feedback of this nature is helpful for the child's awareness of his own feelings

When a child draws her image in a positive way, this reinforces her self-worth. As a parent, you can encourage your child to draw herself in a positive way from when she is young. The child should be able to show herself in an accepting environment as part of Hashem's world. The positive self-image that the child will develop as a result will stay with her for life.

Ask the child to draw herself centered and fairly large on a paper and to include facial parts, hands and fingers, and other essential parts. It is better to draw a figure using the geometric shapes (circle for the head, small square neck, large square shirt, open triangle skirt or three straight vertical lines for pants and half-circles for most facial features, hands with loops for fingers and feet) or other combination of shapes, as long as it contains a complete child. An easy way to get her started on drawing is to begin a drawing for her, either of the entire person or a face alone, leaving out most features and ask her to add in the missing parts and to finish it.

Once your child has put pencil to paper, you can use art therapy tools to pick up on clues for "reading" your child's drawing and learning more about how he views himself and the world around him. If you see something alarming in your child's pictures, it is important to keep in mind that the clues are not always conclusive. Also, these indicators can change along with the child's age, level of maturity, and mood of the moment. If you have a concern, it is best to consult an expert.

How Your Child's Art Shows Who He Is

Here are some guidelines for analyzing your child's drawings:

1. Size is a clue to a child's self-esteem. A child six years of age or older who draws an image in an exaggerated size may be revealing that the

child feels dominant toward the environment or the people in his life. There may not be a specific body part that is exaggerated—the figure may just be overlarge for the size of the paper—but it leaves us with an uncomfortable feeling. Overly small objects or figures, on the other hand, may indicate an undeveloped self-image or shyness. Generally large- or normal-size objects or figures are equated with healthy images.

(Size or proportion in art is the relationship between the main subject and the background and format, i.e., paper, canvas, etc.)

2. A change in sequence may indicate a conflict or an unspoken statement. If a child draws a person out of his normal order—such as an oldest sibling last—or emphasizes an object or figure in a sequence, or deletes something that should be included (such as a member of the family or class), this may indicate a cause for a discussion with the child to clarify his feelings. Consider: Is this a break from his regular pattern of drawing? Are there other symptoms? If so, it may be a clue to investigate. Ask the child why he drew the picture that way.

Skipping an important part of the face or leaving out a hand or foot may tell us that the child is overly aware and wants to avoid that body part for some reason. Conversely, he may be unaware of that body part.

(Sequence in art is the order of actions and techniques to achieve a finished artwork. Generally, one draws the larger subject matter first, followed by smaller ones and details. Lines come before form, and form comes before shading.)

3. Placement—a centrally placed figure may denote a more emotional child, whereas an off-centered figure may indicate an independent type. A figure to the left may indicate extroversion and a figure to the right, introversion.

(Placement in art terms refers to the composition—the visual arrangement of the subjects. The main subject is the center of interest, with secondary objects arranged around it.)

4. Pressure can reflect physical strength and commitment. Heavy strokes may suggest assertiveness, whereas light pressure may show low energy, restraint, low muscle tone or repression. If a child suddenly changes his pressure control, producing much lighter or darker work than usual, ask him why. There may be an underlying story, or he may simply be tired or not interested in drawing that day.

(Pressure is the amount of strength applied to the drawing tool, resulting in a heavy and dark mark or a light mark. Gradations from light to dark are made by gradually increasing pressure. Pressure affects line quality.)

5. A sudden change in line quality or lines drawn out of sequence may be a cover-up for something that the child doesn't want to talk about, reveal, or confront.

(Line quality is affected by the strength of pressure on the drawing with the drawing tool, the density of the mark, and the width and length of the stroke.)

6. Gifted children may show a high level of movement in their drawings and their other artwork. Very static, rigid depictions—tight, static lines, unfinished figures, smallish figures, or figures off to one corner—may indicate hidden or repressed feelings. Curved, flowing lines show a freedom of expression.

(Movement in art affects the eye of the viewer, causing it to travel inside a painting or other artwork, weaving it in and out of spaces, textures, colors, and subjects, giving the illusion of movement and depth.)

7. If excessive, erasures may suggest dissatisfaction, uncertainty, or indecisiveness.

(Erasing in art can be a tool for creating contrast, making light areas against a dark surface, or more commonly to clean up or redo an area.)

8. Color is made when light waves bounce off an object, enter the eye, and the brain interprets them as certain colors.[132] Like sounds and smells, colors evoke emotional reactions and feelings. Consider the colors we find in nature and see what feelings they might evoke:

Green—new life, plants, colorful bird feathers

Red—heat, fire, intensity, anger, alarm, fire trucks, roses

Blue—water, heaven, serenity, calm

Yellow—sun, light, heat, brightness, happiness

Brown—earth, trees, solidity, stability

Purple—royalty, spirituality

Orange—fruit, vitality, freshness

---

132 See ch. 20, "The Joy of Mixing Colors."

Grays—a combination of black and white or complementary color combinations: red and green, blue and orange, and purple and yellow for neutrals and shadows.

Black—the absence of color and light, darkness, the dark before the dawn

White—purity, light

(Color in art terms is made from light waves and can represent mood.)

It's important to remember that nothing here is conclusive, nor is it a diagnosis. How a child draws from one day to the next may be entirely different, even if the subjects are the same. Mood, time of day, energy level, and choice of materials all affect the outcome.

I once attended a presentation by someone who read and analyzed children's drawings. We in the audience, teachers and therapists, were asked to do a few specific drawings. Self-conscious about what the lecturer would say about my drawing, I drew the happiest and most open picture I could. Naturally she gave it a high rating. A very successful art therapist in the group received a less than positive response for her drawing. Maybe this art therapist was showing her accumulated pain from all the problems she encountered with her clients. The irony of this experience made a strong impression on me.

Still, I love looking for the obvious signs of character and self-image in children's drawings. Just like handwriting analysis reveals the writer, artwork reveals parts of the artist. A little outside prompting can help clarify what the artist is feeling. Often, a child does not realize any inhibitions or incompleteness in her drawing, and she will act on suggestions, making improvements, with the knowledgeable and non-judgmental prompting from an adult.

Let's Look Inside

Now that we are aware of the different factors that affect a child's self-expression, let's take a look at a typical child's creative process.

Nine-year-old Esther is a creative child who has been given ample opportunities and encouragement to develop through art. Esther is about to draw a house. The mental picture of the house she wants to draw is magnified in her mind.

She considers...

- the size of the paper;
- the media (materials) she will use;
- the placement and composition of the house on the paper and the size of each element of the composition (trees, furniture, flowers, people);
- the background, season, time of day, and weather;
- the construction of the home—a wooden ranch house, two-story brick house, or stucco apartment building;
- the details, decorations, and Jewish ritual objects;
- the centerpiece: the dining room table with twelve chairs for the family and the many guests she loves to have.

Esther plans her house. She measures, counts, imagines, experiments, and tests limits to come up with the best drawing possible. As she works through her vision on paper, she demonstrates that she is a motivated and creative child.

Esther colors in her picture. Recently she has been taught the basic skills of mixing red, blue, yellow, and white to create myriad shades. Combining the three basic colors—red, blue, and yellow—with white, she feels capable of producing an array of wonderful colors. There is no pressing need for a package of a hundred flashy markers. She is able to improvise and manage with what she has in front of her. She knows how to work out of the box and in the box at the same time.

Esther's work reflects a happy child secure in her world. If Esther's parents can continue to give her the tools and room to develop her natural abilities, those abilities will translate into a warm, future home for her husband and family. She will be able to apply her creativity to every aspect of her life, whether it is cooking or home decorating or managing a career or educating her children. A creative mind is creative in all areas of life.

In contrast to Esther, Elizabeth drew a house in the art therapist's room that was not as happy. The house was small, and the windows were closed. Yet there was a garden full of flowers and plants, one that needed to be revived and cultivated.

Liz had much to say, but she felt bottled up. She knew she wanted to create but didn't know where to begin. Communication wasn't encouraged in her home, reflected in the smallness of her drawing. Ironically, communication was what Liz was all about—reflected in her drawing. She had so much in her inner world that was ready to come out, but it wasn't allowed. No one around her thought communication was important.

Liz needed permission to be expressive and use her inner resources in a creative and soothing manner. Had she been encouraged to express herself at home, she wouldn't have had to expend energy holding in her creativity. Now, slowly, she is learning how to release her mountains of feelings and embrace life joyfully.

The Story of Two Homes AGES 7+

Draw a happy home and a sad home. Put in lots of details. Use color to tell us what is happy and what is sad.

Materials

- Canvas or paper for painting, size 11 x 16 inches (28 x 41 cm) or larger
- Pencil
- Pen
- Colored markers
- Gouache for paper or acrylic paint for canvas: red, blue, yellow, and white to mix your own colors (other colors optional)
- Paintbrushes, ¼, ½, and ¾ inch (½, 1½, and 2 cm)

Directions:

1. Plan out your image on the practice paper, first in pencil and then with a pen to refine the lines. You may want to do two separate works or one with both a happy home and a sad home on the same canvas. This might be a country scene with a path connecting the two homes. The details in each of the homes contrast with each other. Details might include healthy plants and flowers growing around one home and weak unattended plants around the second. The happy home is cheerful and in good shape

whereas the unhappy house is broken in places: the shutters, the roof, and the path.

2. Draw on painting paper or canvas.
3. Color in the small details with markers. Paint in the large areas with the paint. If using a canvas, paint in the details as well.

Option: Do a complete drawing with shading or a drawing with colored markers.

While you are working on this try to put yourself into each house and think how it may feel.

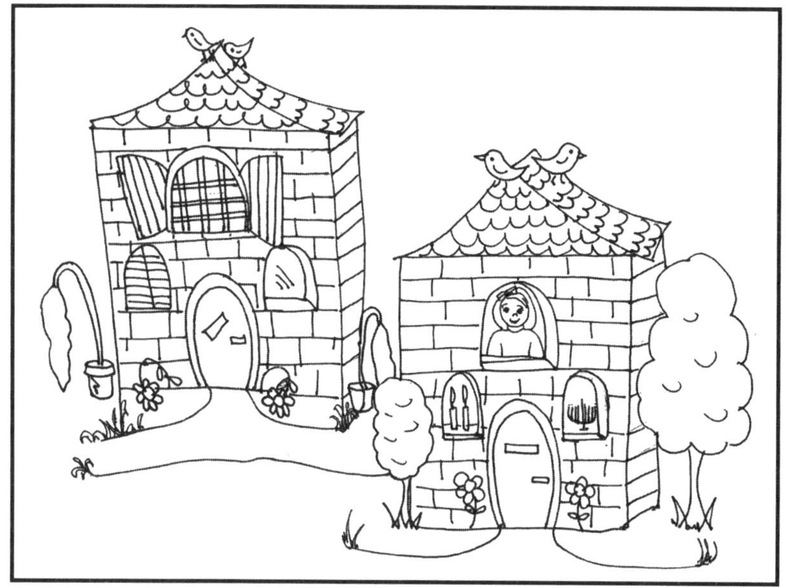

In Summary: Understanding Your Child through Art

- The first marks a child makes are his signature.
- The pleasurable scribble tells us how a child sees himself in relation to the world. Art therapy tools can offer ways to understand your child's drawings.
- A child's drawing of a boy or girl reflects his self-awareness.
- Elements such as size, sequence, and placement can tell us a lot about the child's inner world.

Questions and Wonder

1. Why do we draw and color?
2. Can you draw a self-portrait without looking in the mirror?
3. Have you ever thought about how art is a way of reflecting who we are?

PART 3

Art Theory and Technique

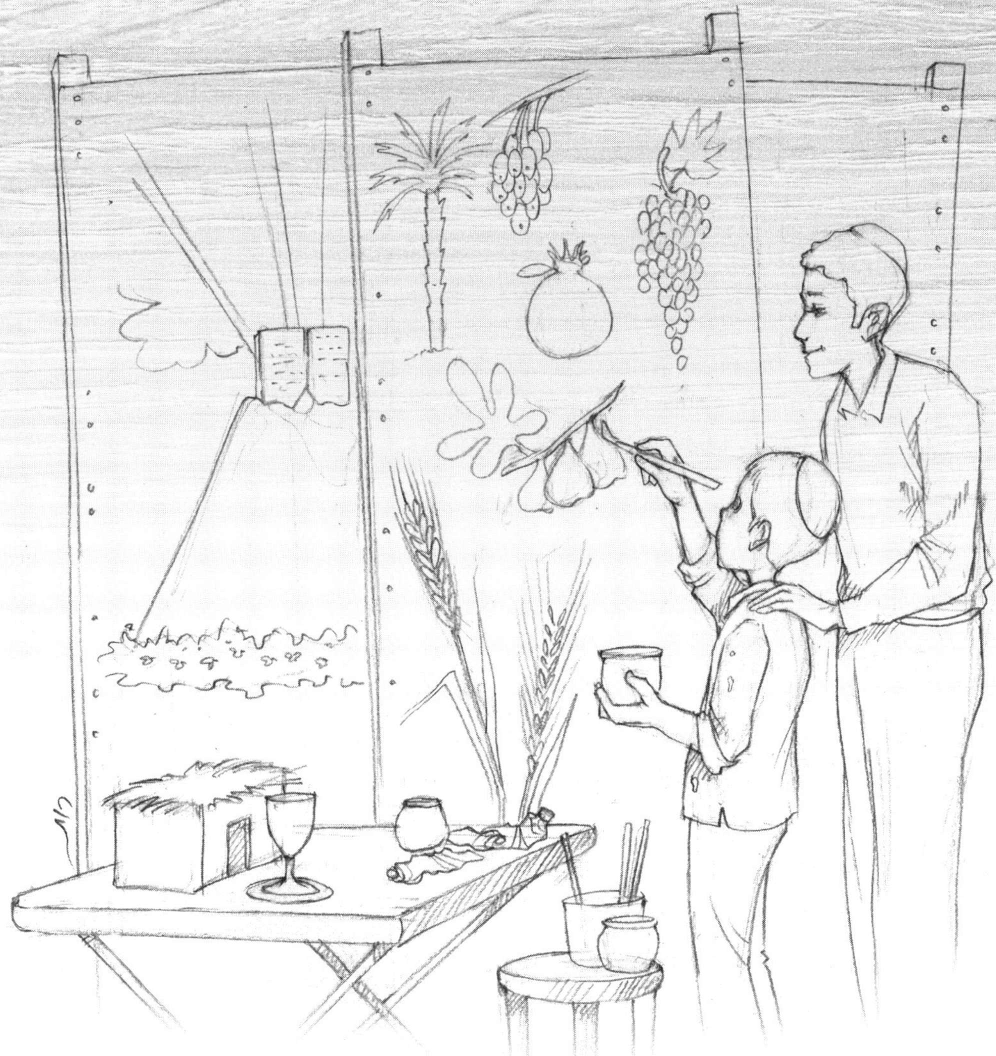

Some Art Theory to Get You Started

17

Julie, a precocious eight-year-old, preferred to copy her friends' work and bypass learning the steps to produce her own composition. Naturally, this "short-cut" only led to frustration, since she wasn't able to create an accomplished painting on her own. Rather than learning concepts and technique with the rest of the class, Julie would talk and disrupt the lesson.

Sometimes, when Julie was bored, she started doodling in class. One day, as I passed by her table, I noticed her absent-mindedly dividing her paper into various shapes and filling them in with light and dark shading. I pointed out how she could include a third, middle-value shade. With dark, medium, and light shading filling up her "doodle," she could create an interesting and bold design and practice her hand pressure at the same time.

Julie dived in and busied herself with the new shading technique, enjoying the dramatic results. She realized that she didn't have to contend with drawing something in perfect likeness, which only frustrated her. She also realized that she didn't have to be at the same stage as the other kids in the group.

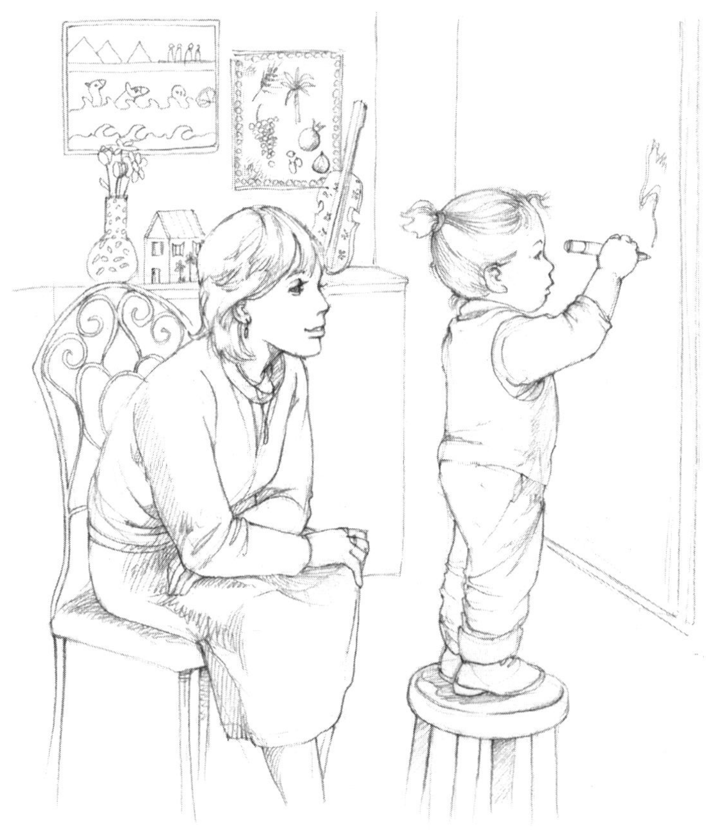

Notes and Sketches

As the pressure fell away, Julie stopped talking in class and became serious about her artwork. When her classmates and I praised her newfound ability to control the light and dark areas of her drawing, she became eager to learn more. I sensed a more confident and mature Julie, who was now ready to put forth her best efforts and try new projects without fear.

Aesthetics and Harmony

Art is, without a doubt, a creative endeavor. It gives the imagination free rein, while promoting an inner self-awareness that finds outward expression in the art. However, free rein doesn't mean a lack of knowledge or skill. As in every skill, artists must learn techniques and the principles of design in order to channel their individual expression effectively.

Art relies on aesthetics, the pleasing arrangement of art elements that make up a composition or design. You may notice that an aesthetic work of art is often calming and pleasing to the eye, since the elements of design—organization of line, space, shading, color, and texture—are derived from nature. God created a perfect world, and from our observations of nature we are able to learn the principles of design and apply them to our art.

A complete and aesthetic picture, with all the elements of design in place, is called a composition. A composition that combines the various principles of design to work together as a whole is said to be harmonious. In life, harmony is achieved when every member of a family, group, or society works together to achieve a common goal. The same idea applies in art: to achieve harmony in a composition, the artist needs to learn how to apply and integrate the principles of design to create an aesthetic whole.

To help us learn about these principles and how to apply them, let's familiarize ourselves with the following commonly used terminologies in art.

Art Terminology

Notes and Sketches

Every art form, whether it's dance, music, or painting, has its own lingo. Knowing specific terms introduces us to the skills we need to master the art form and develop our technique. The terms below apply to all art, whether that of the smallest child's or the greatest artist's.

BALANCE

Balance in a composition is created when there is symmetry in the various parts of the composition. An unfinished picture is often not balanced because one side may be detailed and colored, while the other side remains incomplete or empty. Balance is restored by adding color, texture, line, or objects to the empty or unfinished space.

CENTER OF INTEREST

The center of interest is the main subject, object, grouping of objects (such as a bowl of apples), or an overall theme of the composition. For the young child, the center of interest is often himself, his family, his home, or his favorite object.

COLOR

Color provides the most noticeable means of expression.[133] Red, for example, conveys heat or strong emotions, while blue-green creates a cool, calming effect. Color also serves to help identify objects: blue to represent the sky, orange for a fruit, or green for leaves. Color is created by light waves of varying lengths that are received and interpreted through the eyes.

CONTRAST

Contrast is when dark is placed next to light so that one surface or object is distinguished from its surroundings. The shaded, dark side of a cube next to the light side of the cube creates contrast by showing the separate planes of the cube's sides.

133 For more on color, see ch. 15, "Art as a Communication Tool," ch. 16, "Understanding Your Child through Art," and ch. 20, "The Joy of Mixing Color."

DETAIL

Detail involves the use of small objects and fine points to enhance a painting or drawing. This may include symbols, accessories, texture, and light. Subtle differences are what distinguishes one face from another—a wrinkle in the skin or the shape of the eyebrows. A few extra stones near the edge of a riverbank or the bow in a girl's hair add interest and depth.

EXPRESSION

Expression is essentially the release of emotions. In art, expression is the manifestation of the full range of human emotions in a composition. The composition's expression conveys the feelings associated with the subject, for example, the height of joy at a Jewish wedding or extreme sadness on Tishah b'Av, the most tragic day of the Jewish year. A portrait

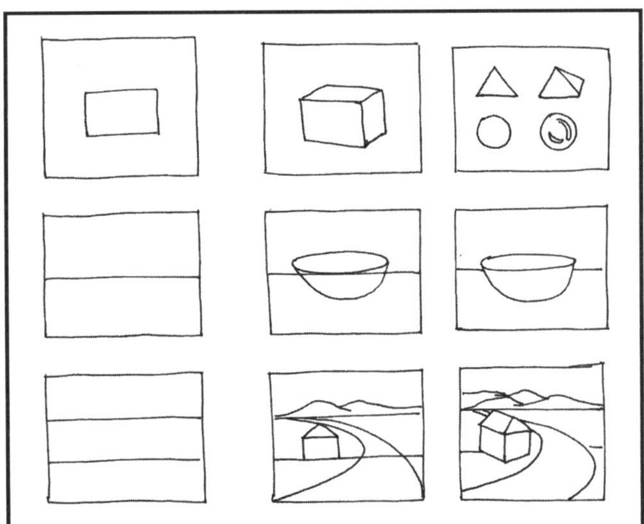

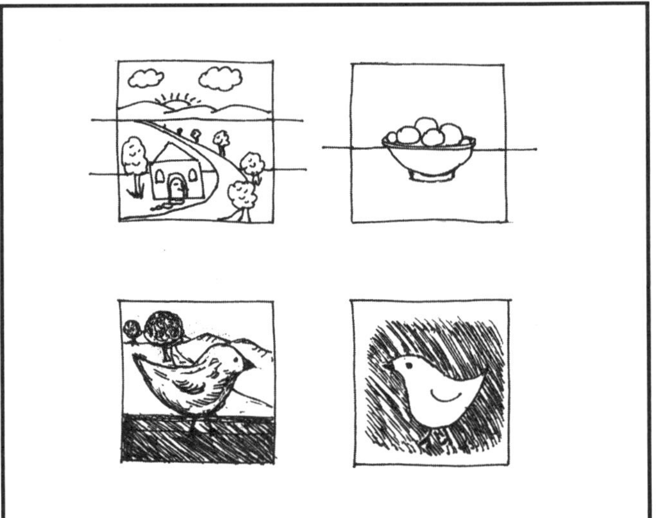

of a happy person will have a cheery expression, and the background will reflect his mood. In a sad picture, the background may be darker and the light focused only on the face. Angular, sharp shapes in grays, blacks, reds, oranges, and other "hot" colors give expression to pain and sadness, while curved shapes in bright colors give expression to joy.

GROUND

A piece of art can be two-dimensional (flat, i.e., a painting or drawing) or three-dimensional (with physical volume and either open or closed

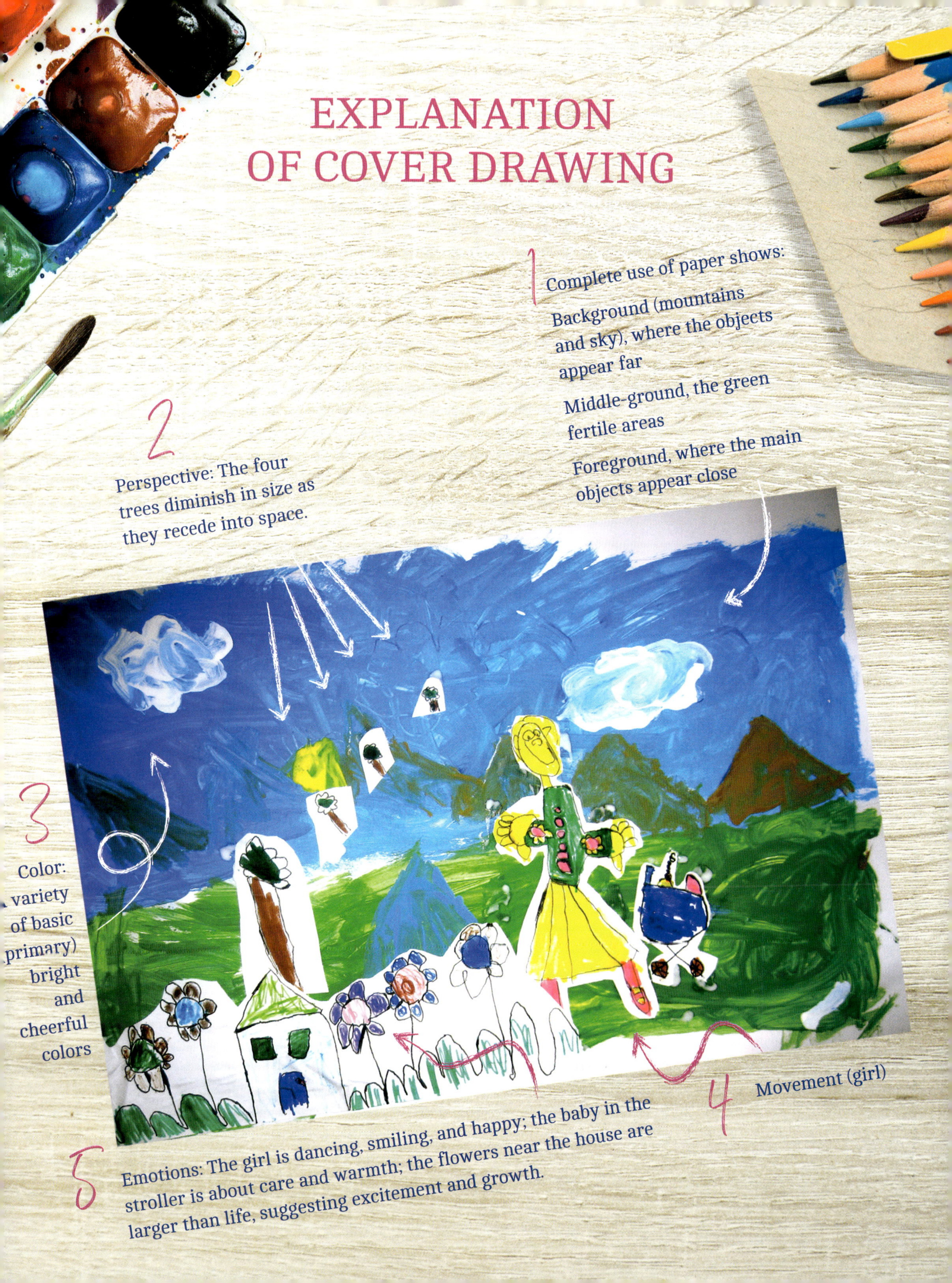

EXPLANATION OF COVER DRAWING

1 Complete use of paper shows:

Background (mountains and sky), where the objects appear far

Middle-ground, the green fertile areas

Foreground, where the main objects appear close

2 Perspective: The four trees diminish in size as they recede into space.

3 Color: variety of basic (primary) bright and cheerful colors

4 Movement (girl)

5 Emotions: The girl is dancing, smiling, and happy; the baby in the stroller is about care and warmth; the flowers near the house are larger than life, suggesting excitement and growth.

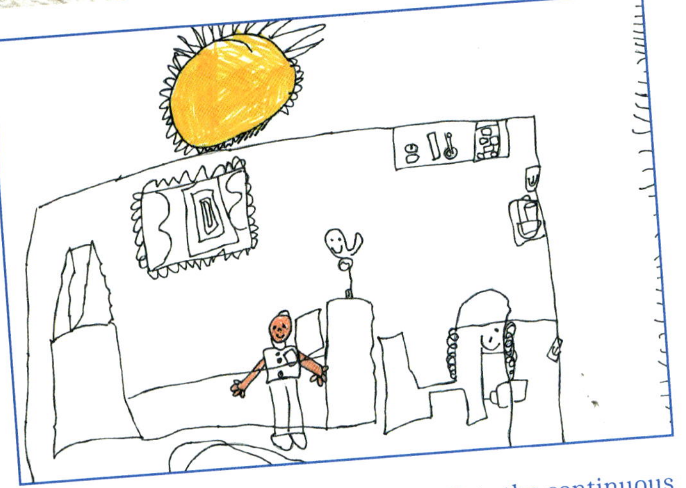

Not a typical 5½-year-old drawing. Note the continuous and whimsical line movement and the central complete drawing of the boy (ES).

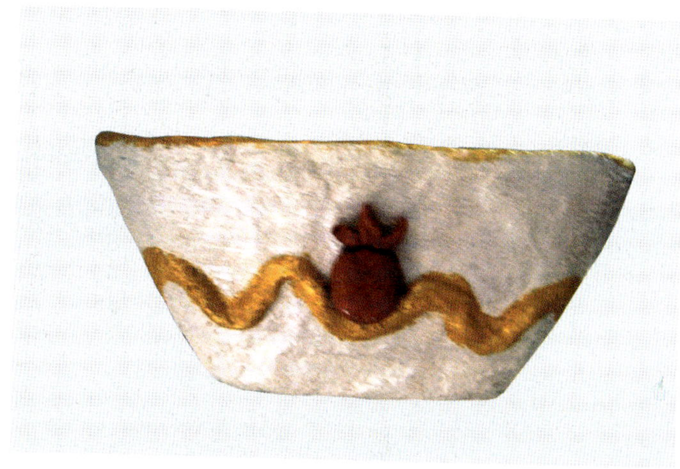

Tu b'Shevat Bowl. Air-drying clay and acrylic paint over a plastic bowl; age 9.

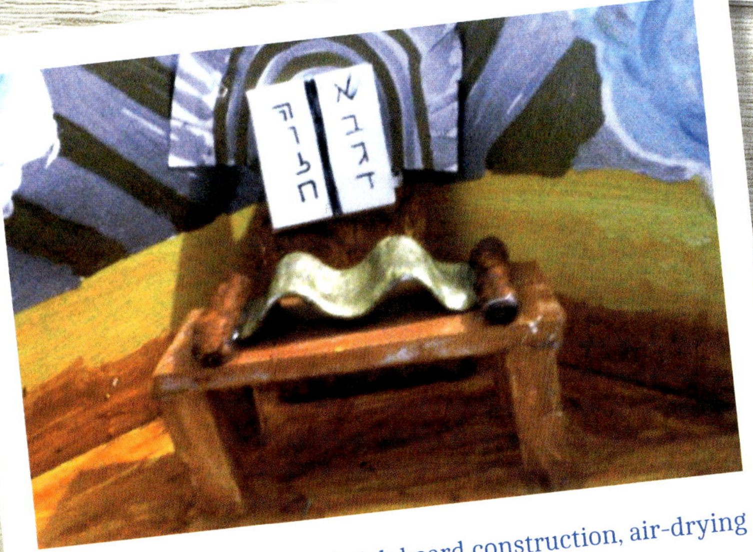

Shavuot. Styrofoam sandwich board construction, air-drying clay, acrylic paint; age 10 (BB).

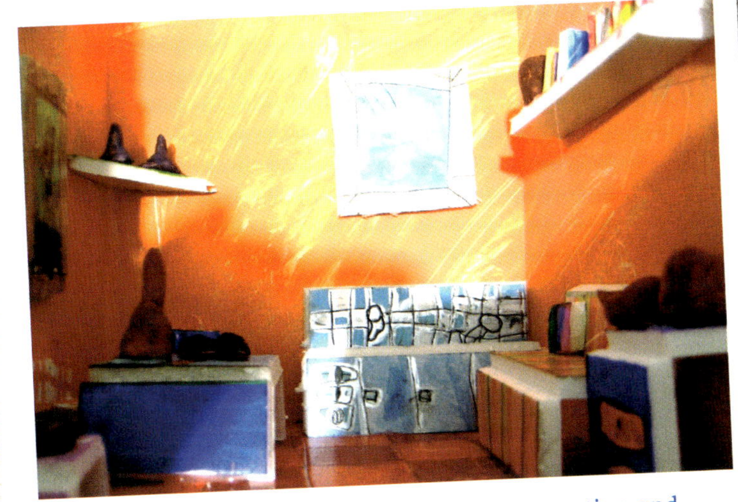

House. Styrofoam sandwich board construction and markers and paint; age 7 (AE).

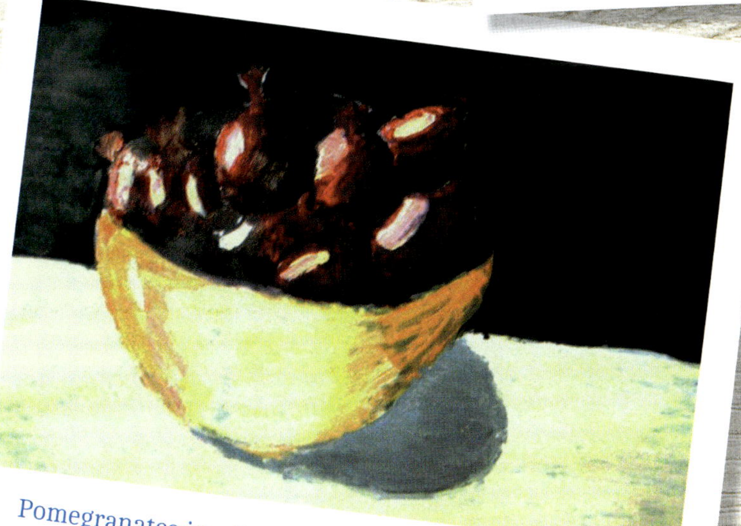

Pomegranates in a Bowl. Acrylic paint on paper; age 8.

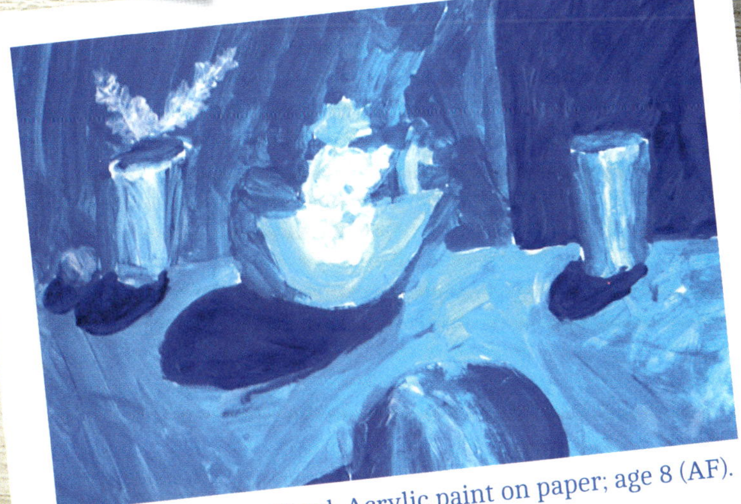

Pomegranates in a Bowl. Acrylic paint on paper; age 8 (AF).

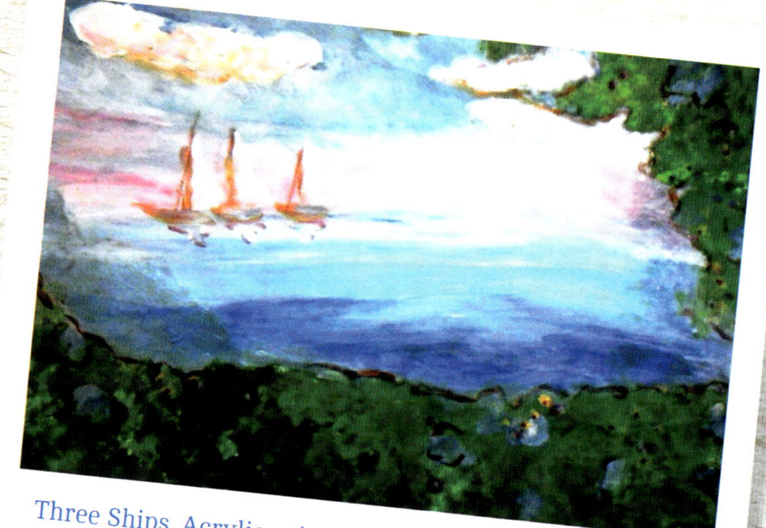

Three Ships. Acrylic paint on paper; instructor's example.

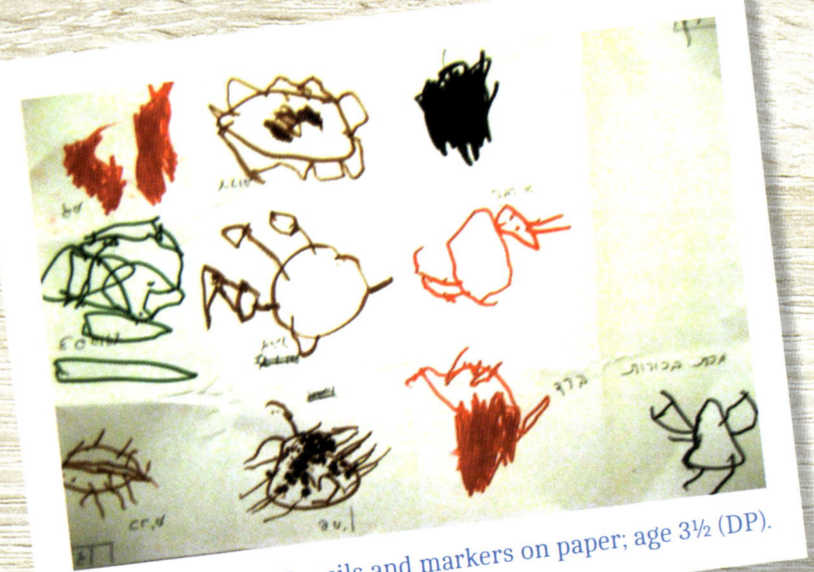

The Ten Plagues. Pencils and markers on paper; age 3½ (DP).

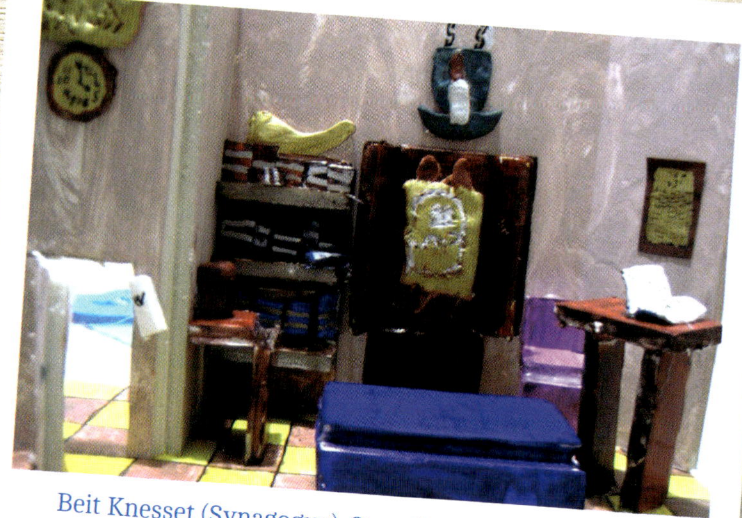

Beit Knesset (Synagogue). Styrofoam sandwich board construction, air-drying clay, markers and paper; age 9 (EYN).

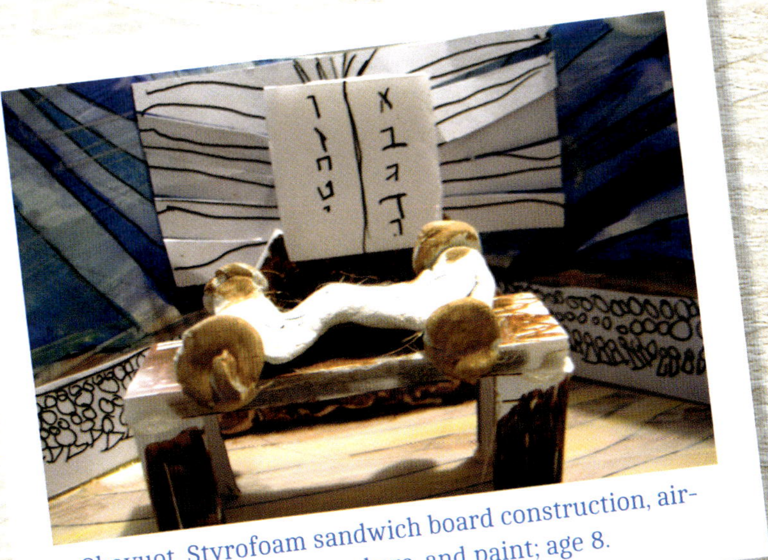

Shavuot. Styrofoam sandwich board construction, air-drying clay, markers, and paint; age 8.

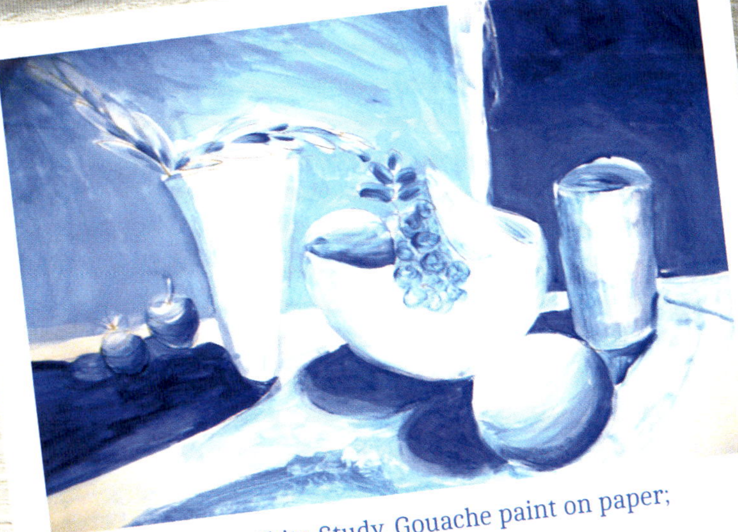

Blue and White Study. Gouache paint on paper; instructor's example.

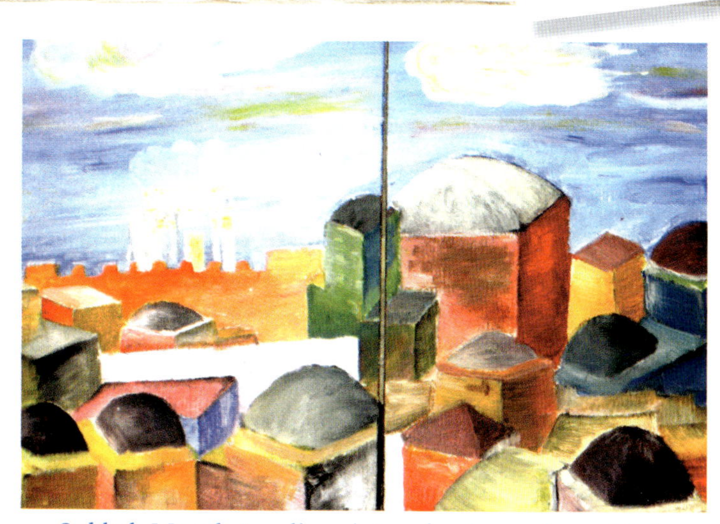

Sukkah Mural. Acrylic paint on large wooden sukkah panels; family project.

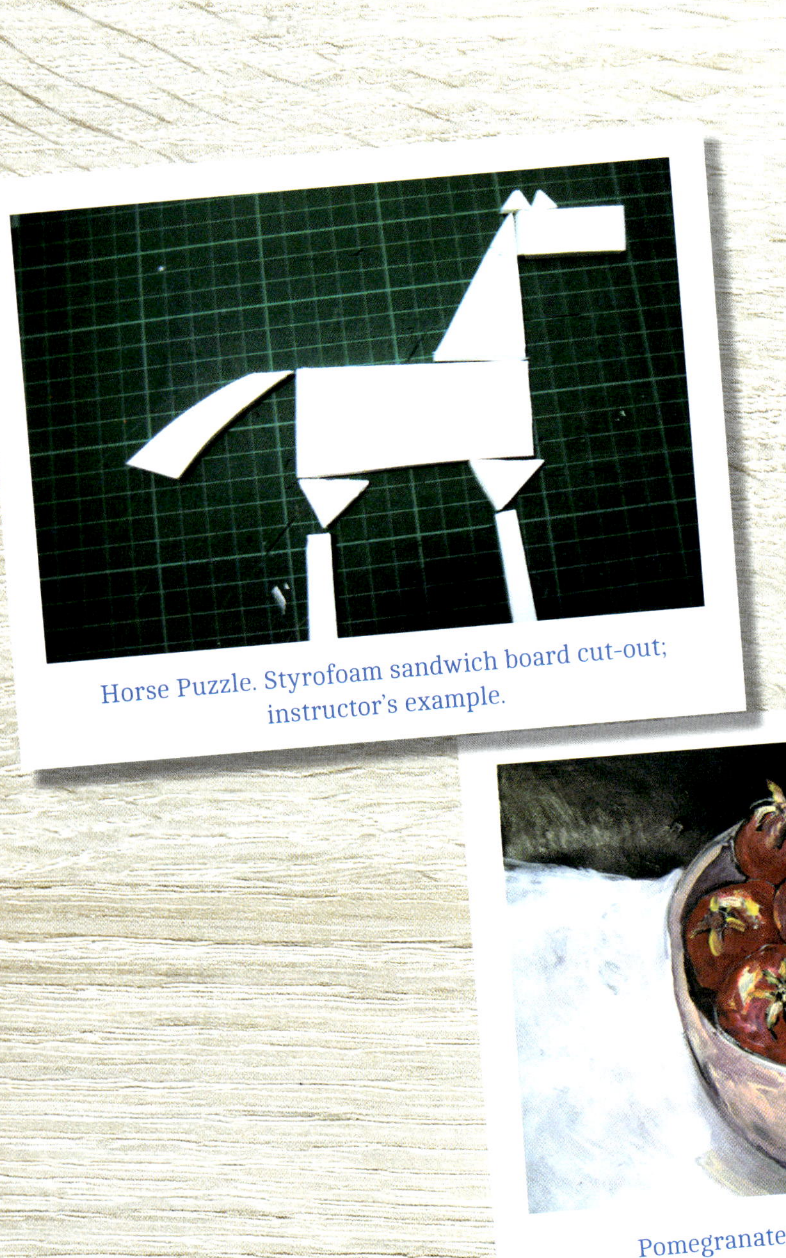

Horse Puzzle. Styrofoam sandwich board cut-out; instructor's example.

Pomegranates in a Bowl. Paint on paper; instructor's example.

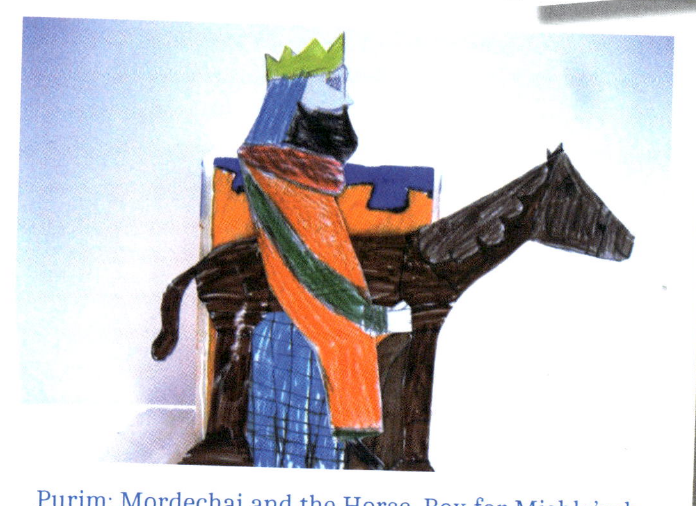

Purim: Mordechai and the Horse, Box for Mishlo'ach Manot. Styrofoam sandwich board construction and markers; age 7 (ACT).

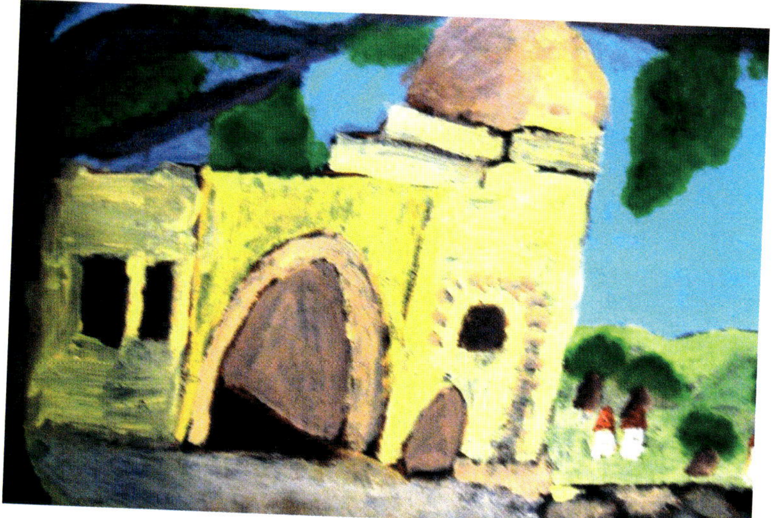

Rachel's Tomb (Kever Rachel) in Yellow. Paint on paper; age 7 (SC).

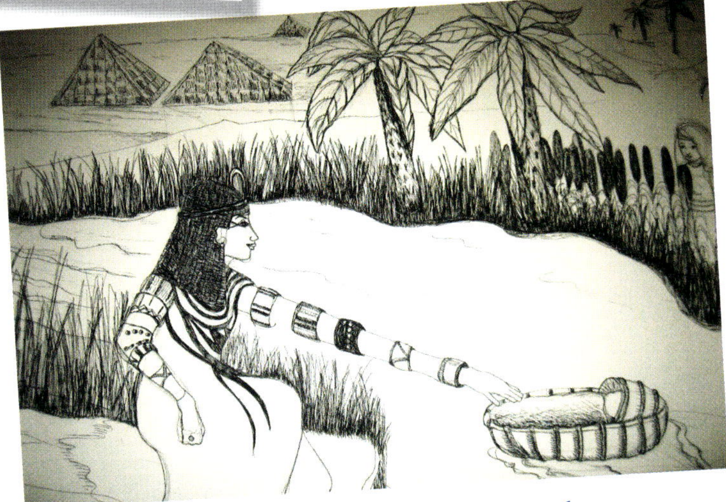

Passover: Batya's Long Arm. Pencil and pen; instructor's example.

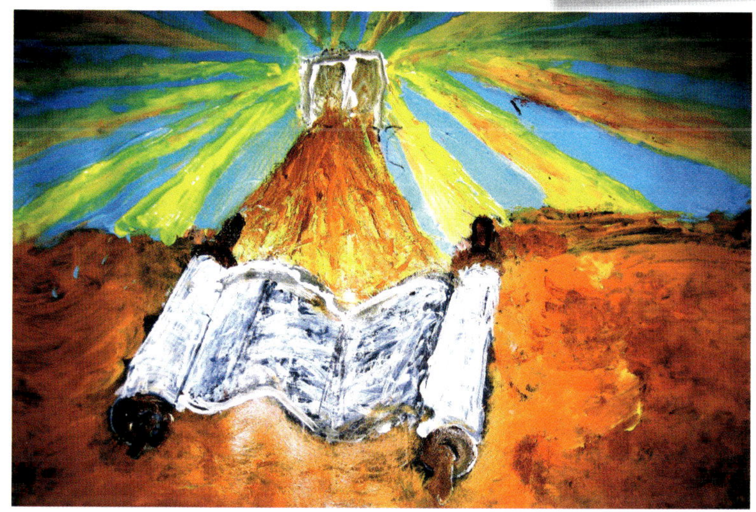

Shavuot: Matan Torah (Giving of the Torah). Paint on paper; age 10.

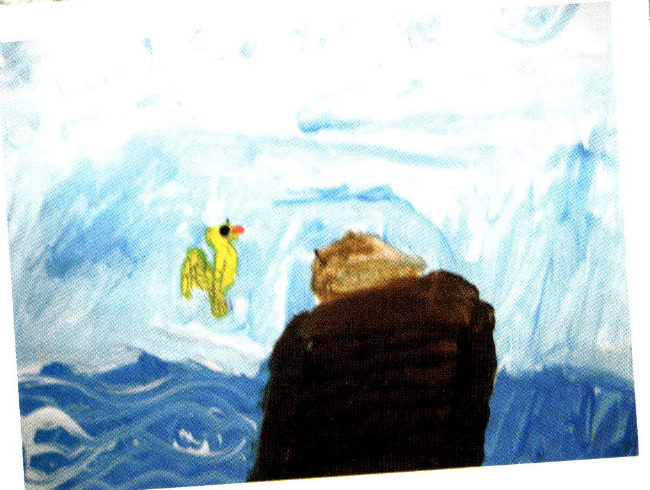

Noah's Ark. Paint on paper; age 6 (YP).

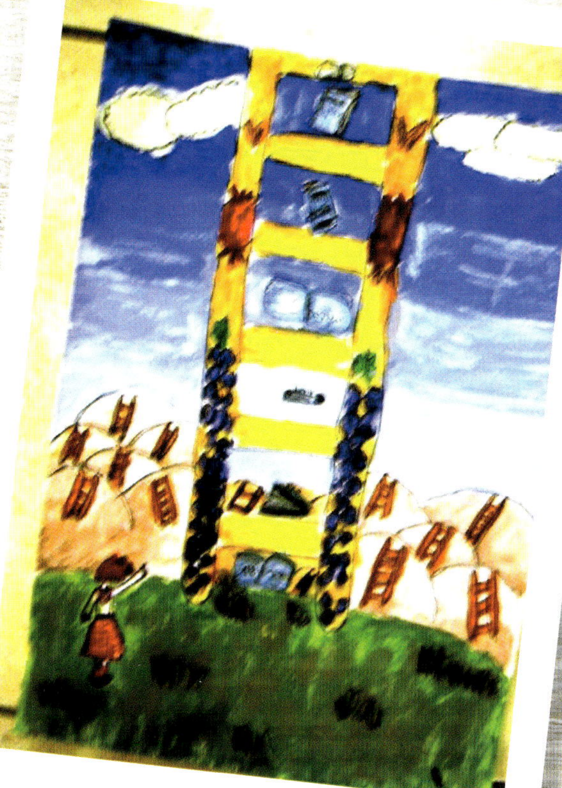

Ladders of Life. Paint on paper; age 7.

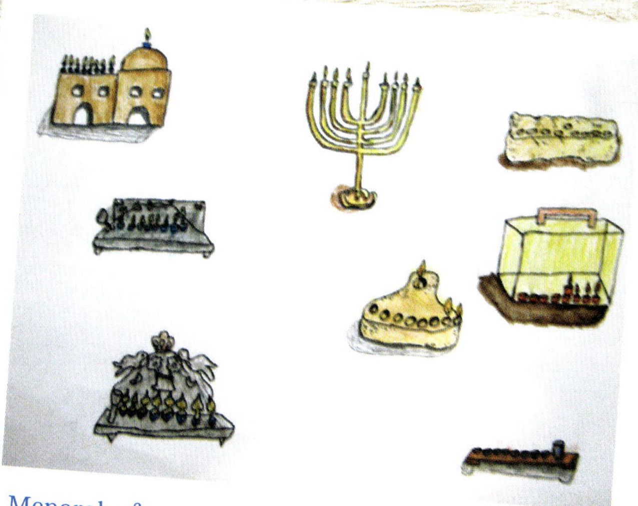

Menorahs from around the world; colored pencil on paper; age 10 (DB).

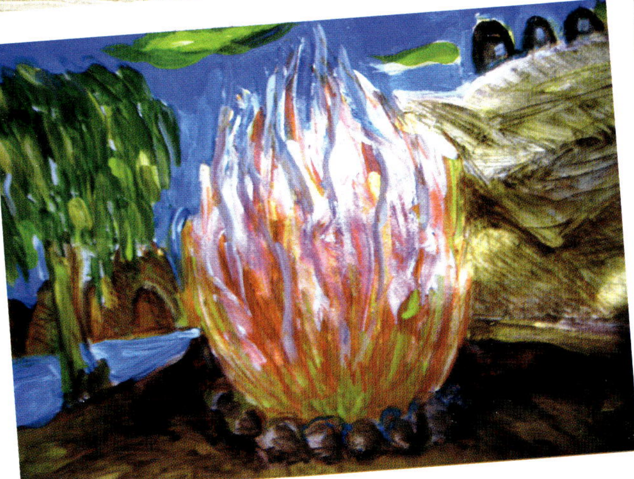

Lag BaOmer Bonfire. Acrylic painting on paper; instructor's example.

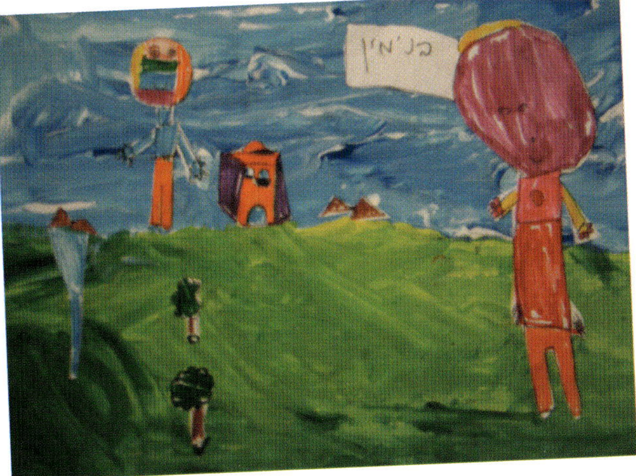

Boy, house, foreground, and background; paint on paper; age 6 (BR).

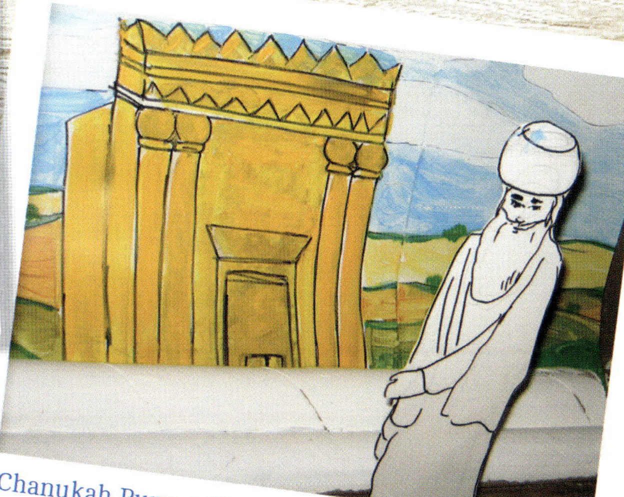

Chanukah Puppet Show. Cardboard, pen, and paint; instructor's example.

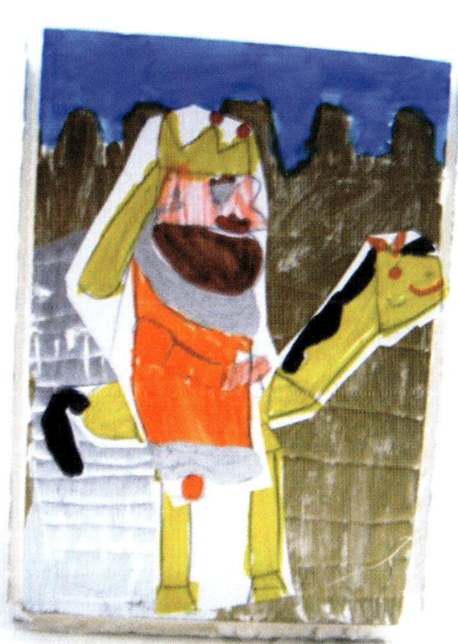

Purim: Mordechai and the Horse, Box for Mishlo'ach Manot. Styrofoam sandwich board construction and markers; age 6 (DG).

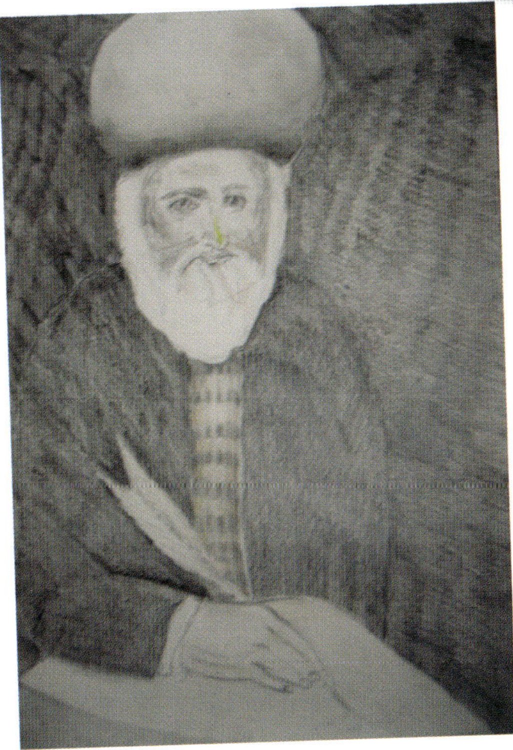

Inspired by a painting of the Gra (Gaon of Vilna); pencil drawing; instructor's example.

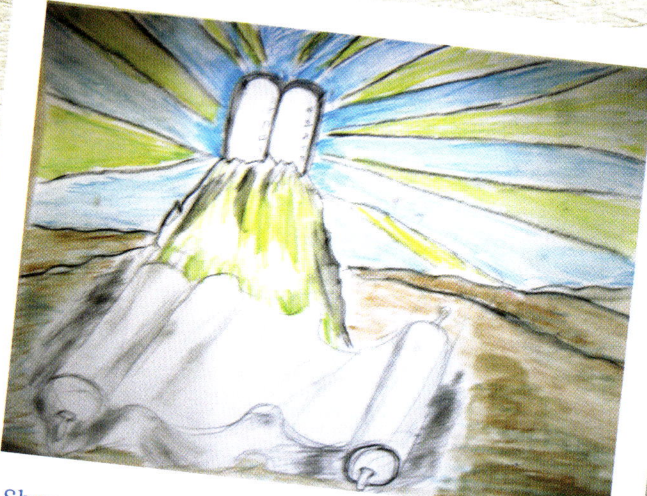

Shavuot: Matan Torah (Giving of the Torah). Colored pencil on paper; age 10 (PH).

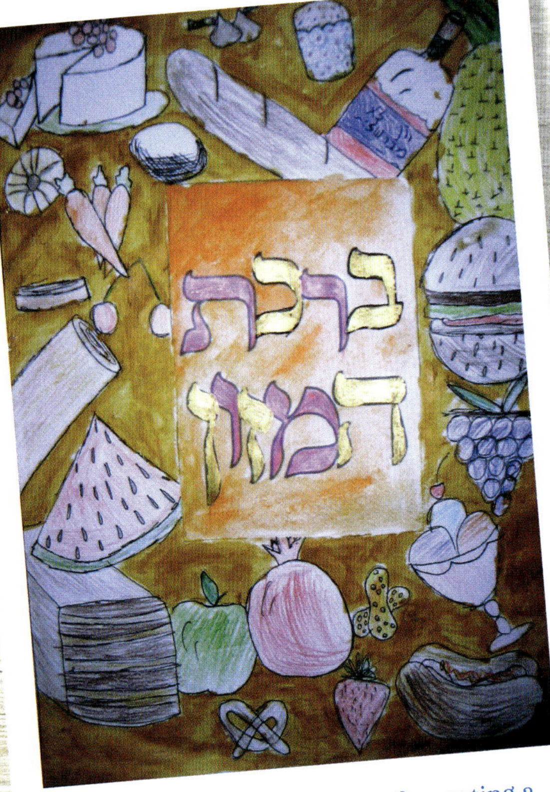

Birkat HaMazon (blessing after eating a meal). Colored pencils and metallic markers on paper; age 10 (TW).

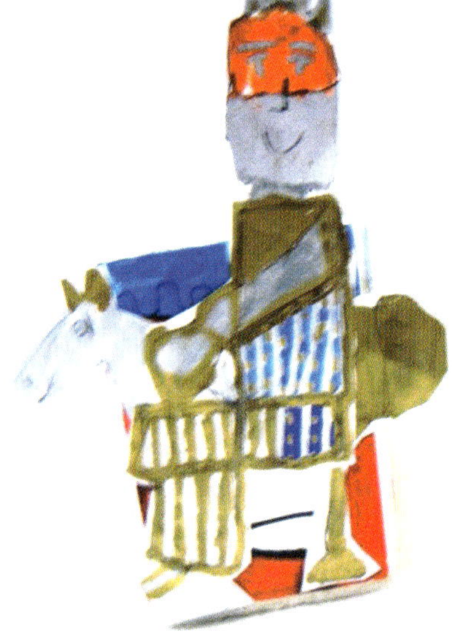

Purim: Mordechai and the Horse, Box for Mishlo'ach Manot. Styrofoam sandwich board construction and markers; age 7 (RD).

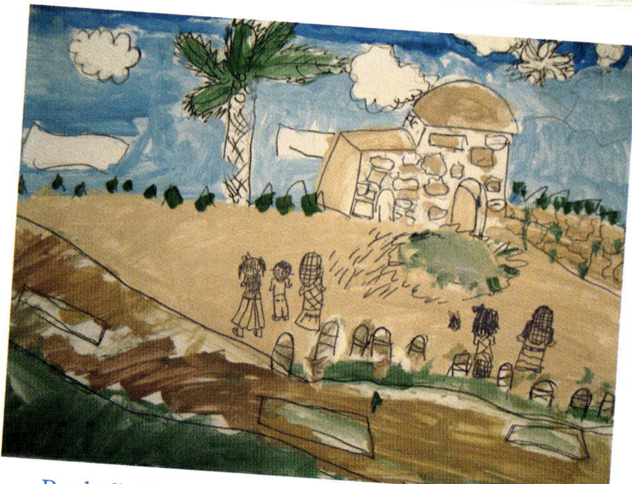

Rachel's Tomb (Kever Rachel). Paint on paper; age 5 (RR).

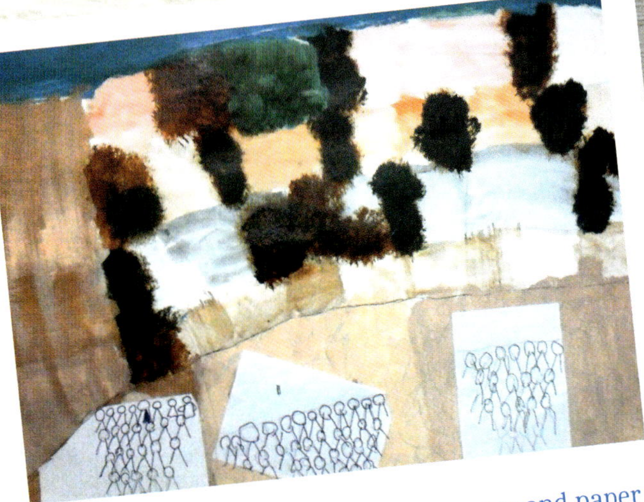
The Kotel (Western Wall). Paint on paper and paper cut-outs; age 5½ (RG).

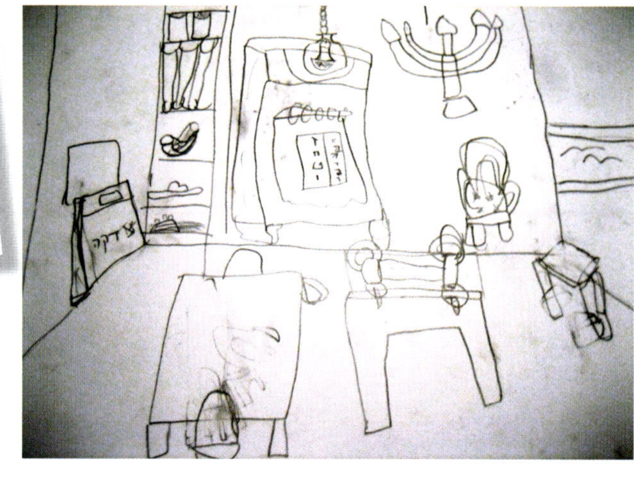
Beit Knesset (Synagogue). Drawing; age 6.

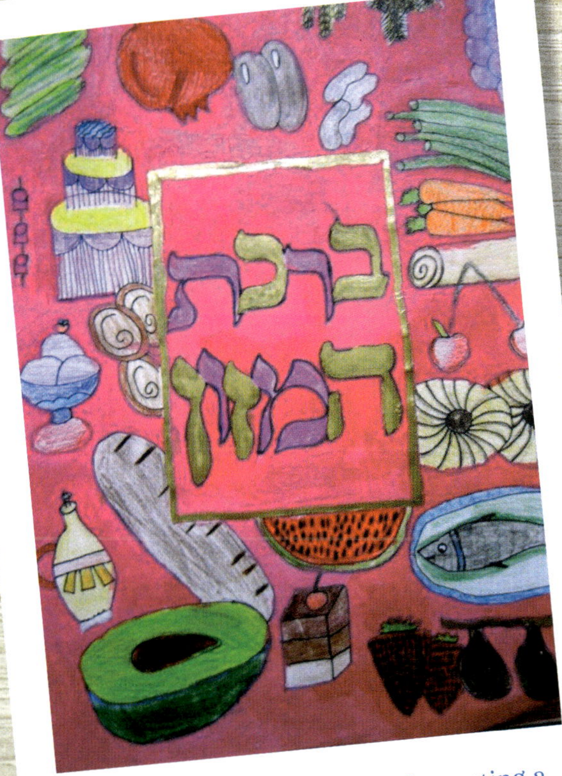

Birkat HaMazon (blessing after eating a meal). Paper, ink, metallic markers, and paint; age 10 (EB).

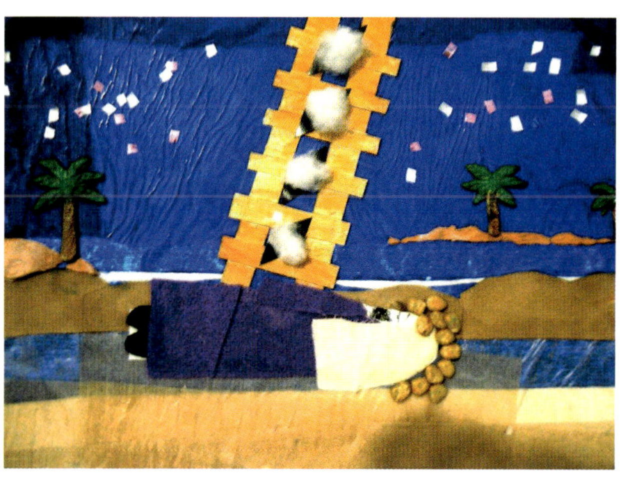
Sulam Yaakov (Jacob's Ladder). Variety of tactile materials; instructor's example.

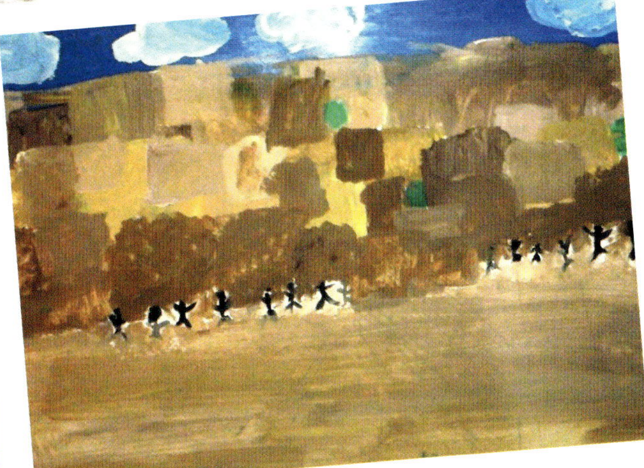

The Kotel (Western Wall). Paint on paper; age 8 (TW).

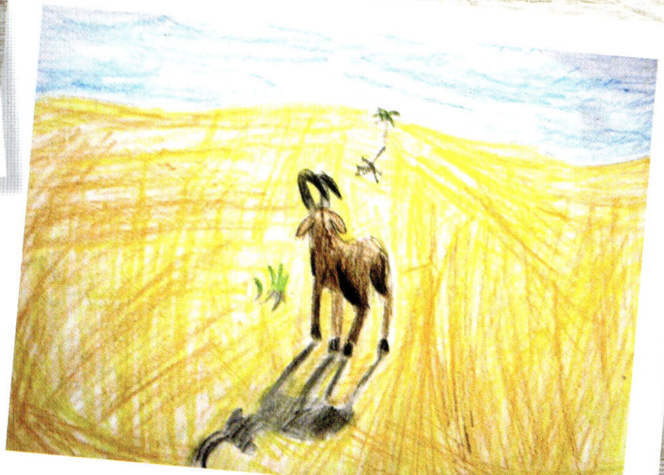

The Goat. Colored pencils; age 9.

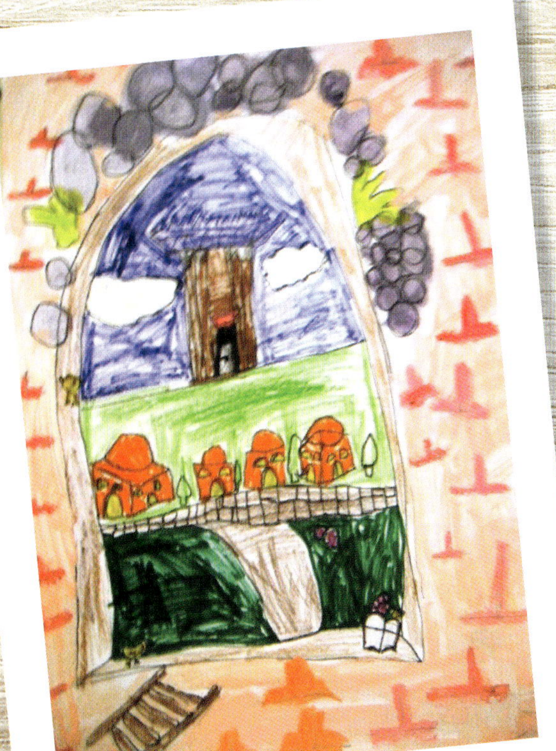

Window in the Old City of Jerusalem. Paint on paper; age 6 (YL).

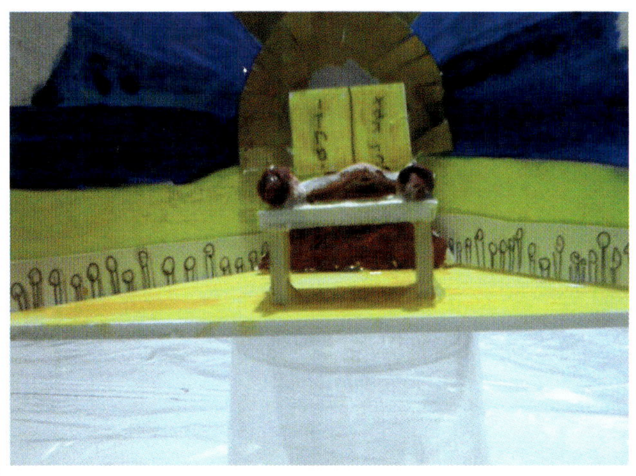

Shavuot. Styrofoam sandwich board, air-drying clay and paint; age 6 (YP).

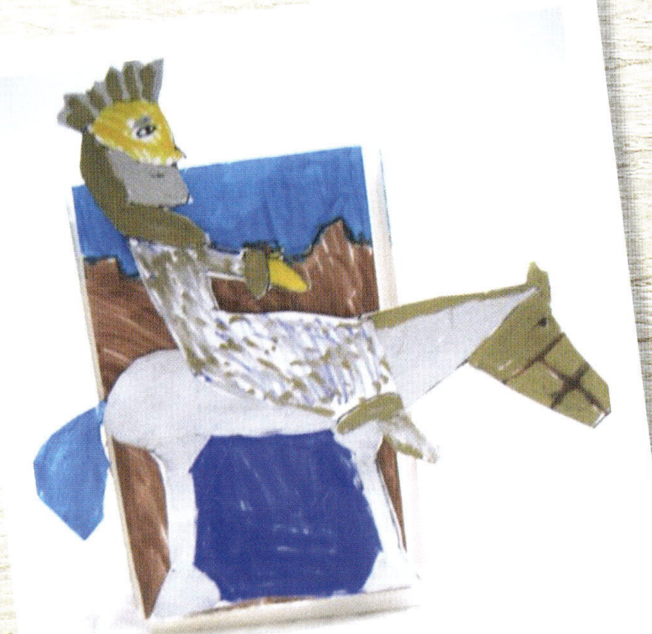

Purim: Mordechai and the Horse, Box for Mishlo'ach Manot. Styrofoam sandwich board construction and markers; age 6 (TD).

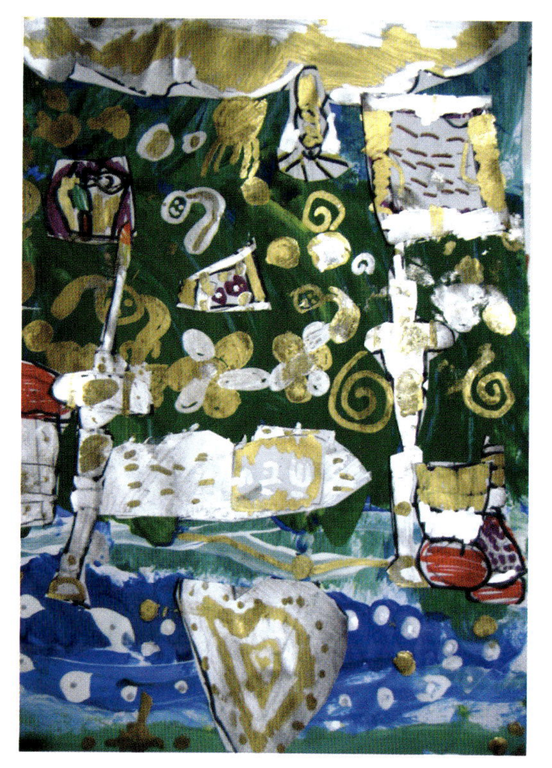

Design. Paint and metallic markers; age 6 (DP).

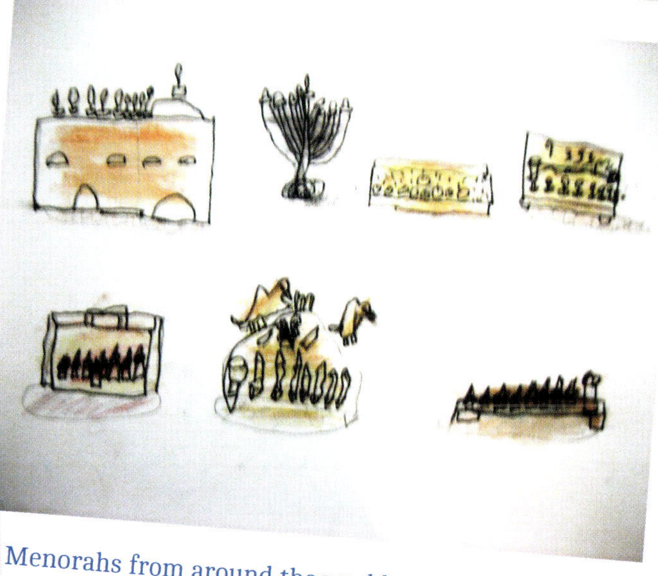

Menorahs from around the world; colored pencils on paper; age 8 (YB).

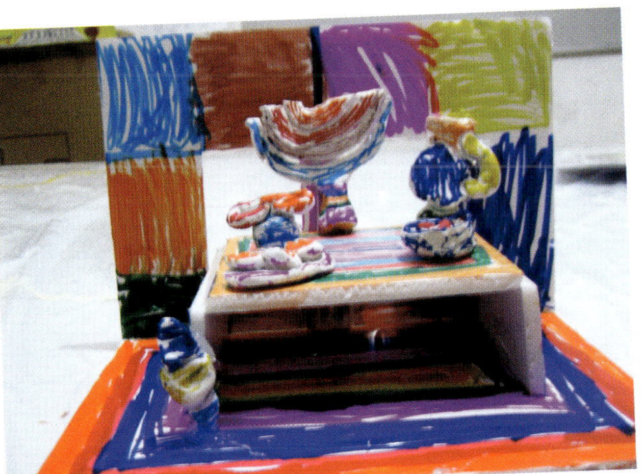

Chanukah Table. Styrofoam sandwich board, air-drying clay; age 6.

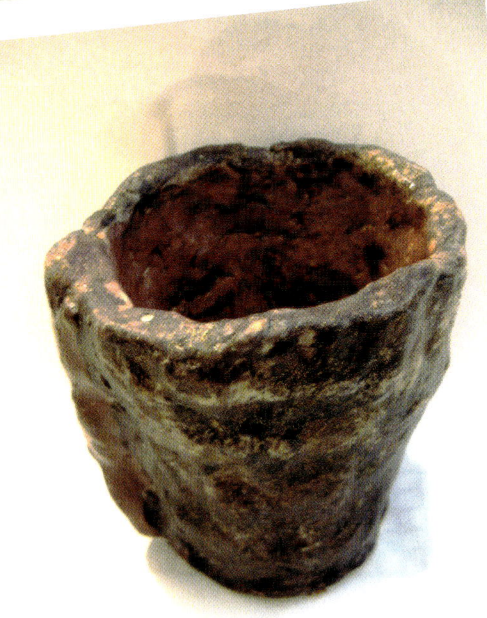

Clay Cup. Clay and several layers of metallic paints; age 8 (NM).

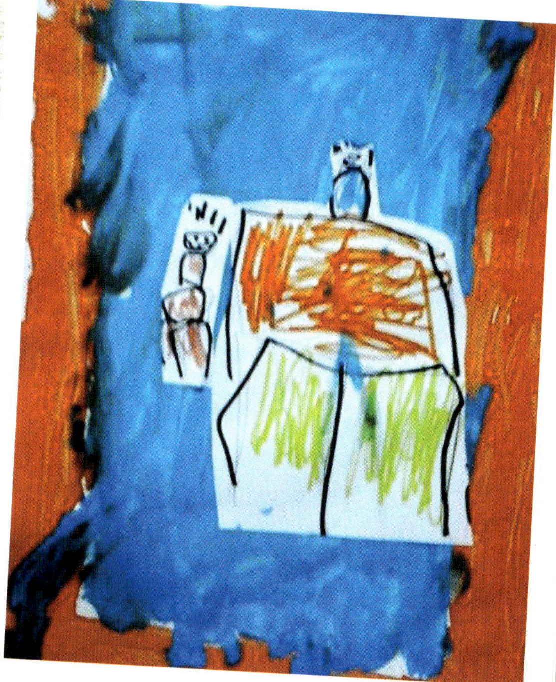

First painting in vivid colors and strong forms; age 5½ (DS).

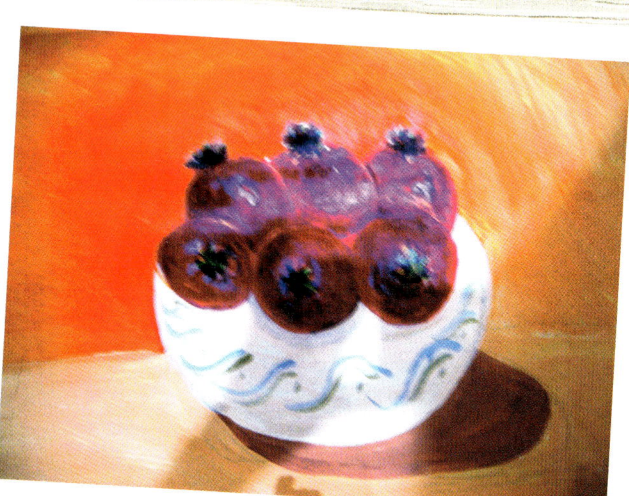

Pomegranates in a Bowl with an Orange Background. Acrylic paint on paper; instructor's example.

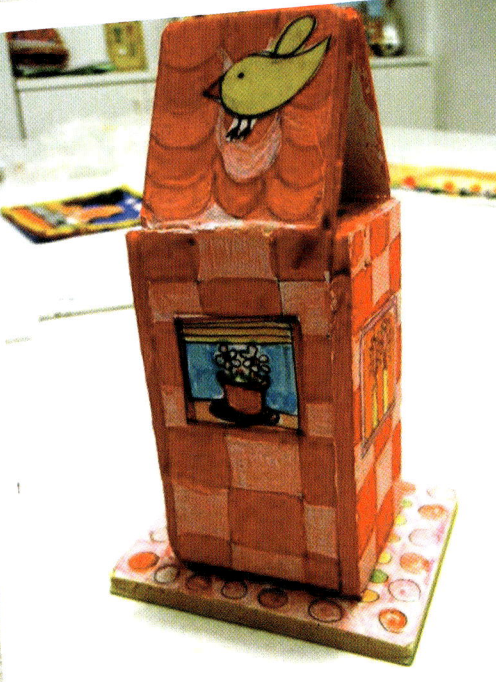

Tzedakah Box. Styrofoam sandwich board construction with paper and paint; instructor's example.

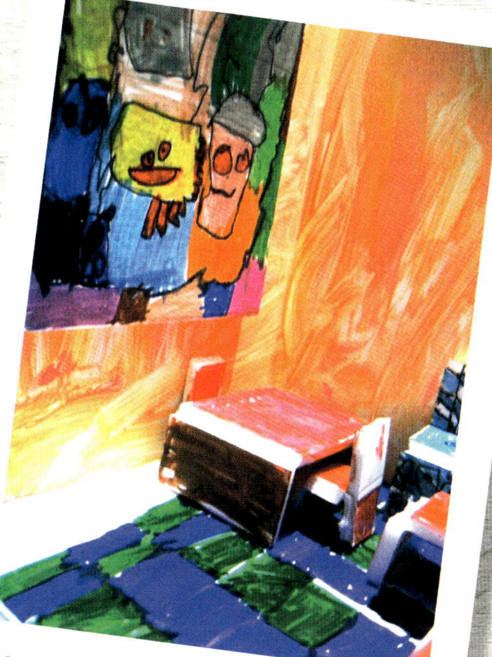

House. Styrofoam sandwich board construction and markers and paint; age 4 (AM).

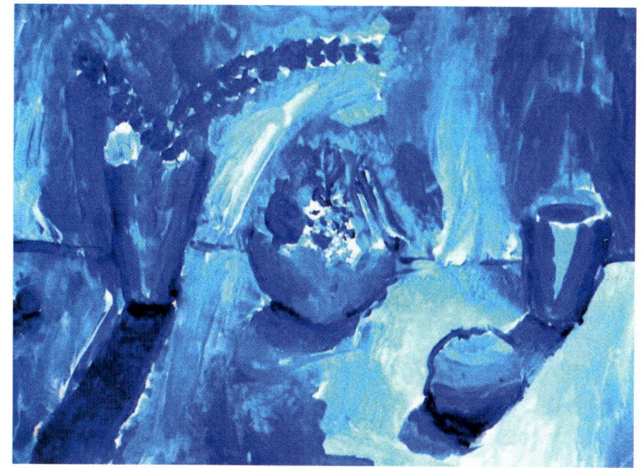

Blue and White Study. Paint on paper; age 8 (SH).

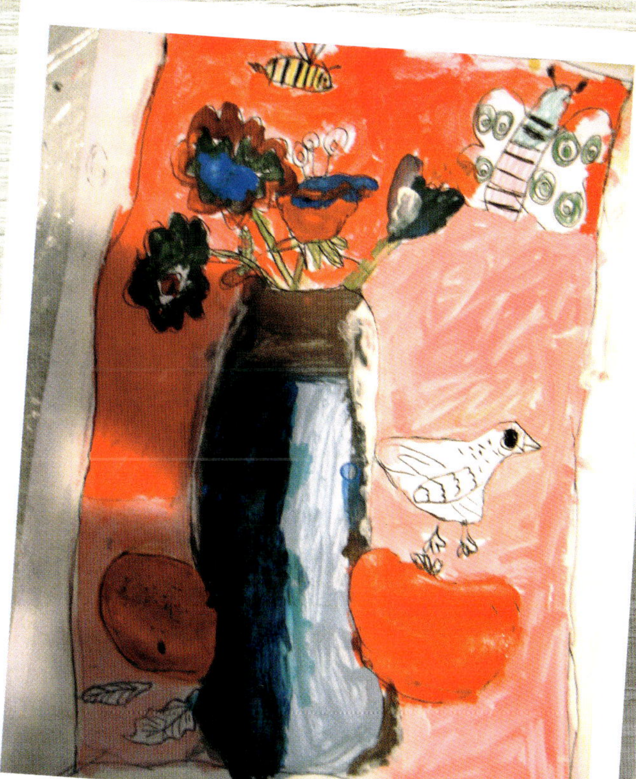

Vase, Flower, and Bird. Paint on paper; age 9.

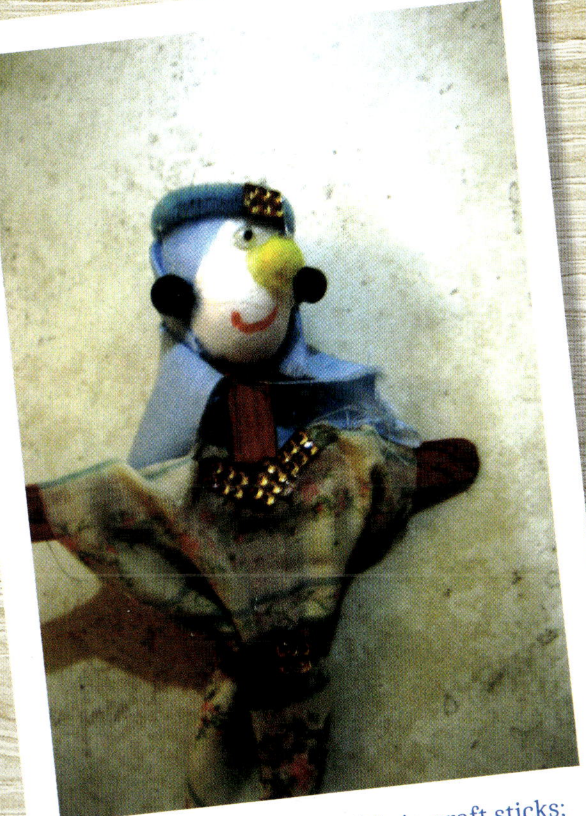

Puppet. Styrofoam ball, fabric, craft sticks; age 6 (TG).

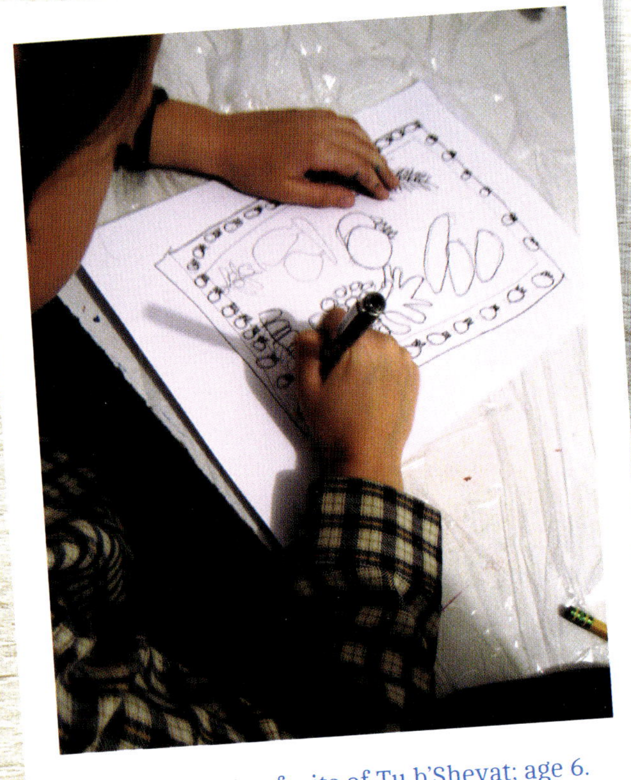

Boy drawing fruits of Tu b'Shevat; age 6.

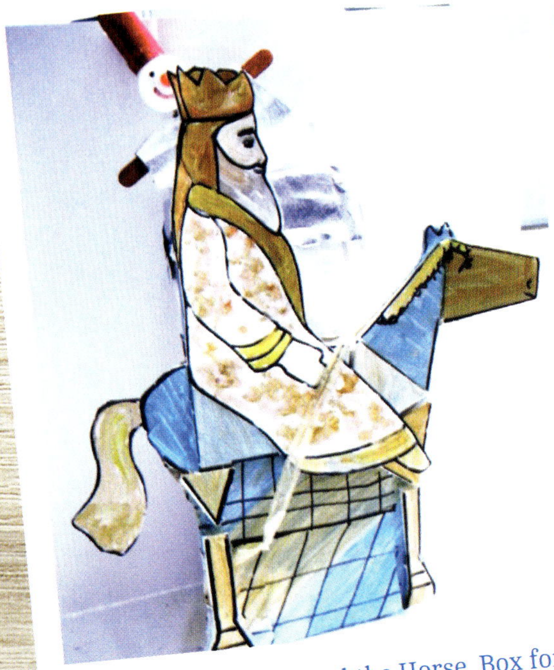

Purim: Mordechai and the Horse, Box for Mishlo'ach Manot. Styrofoam sandwich board construction, metallic markers and paint; instructor's demonstration.

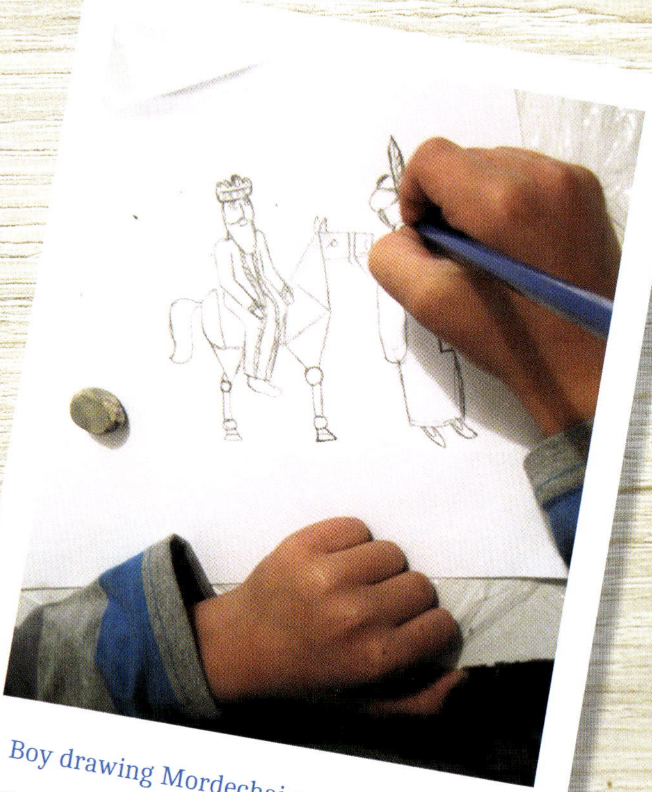

Boy drawing Mordechai on the horse; age 6.

form, i.e., a construction, a relief, or a sculptured form). The perspective and depth they create is located on an illusionary surface called the ground plane. A ground is a surface that recedes into the distance and space.

A picture space on a flat surface (painting/drawing) is generally divided into three spaces: a foreground, a middle ground, and a background that together give the impression of receding space, distance, depth, and perspective. In Western perspective, foreground is closest to us and contains the main subjects. Middle ground is between the foreground and background and gives the illusion of added depth. Background can be the sky, mountains in distance, the far end of a room or a wall. Imagine a cabin in the foreground, a river behind it in the middle ground, and a row of hills and sky in the background. Young children often paint in two-dimensional space with only a foreground and a background.

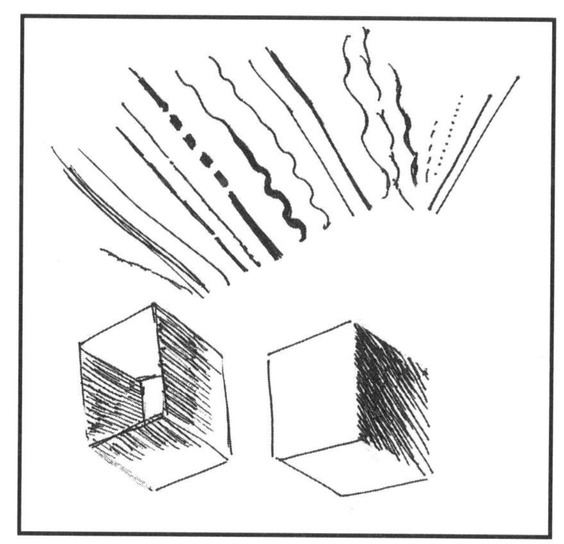

HUE

Hue is the particular name of a color, for example, light blue. It is also the recognition of colors as it is processed in the retina and the visual systems of the eyes.

LINE QUALITY

Line quality refers to the shape and length of the line—straight, curved, long, short—and the thickness of the line, which results from the amount of pressure put on the drawing tool.

Different tools produce varying line qualities depending on their unique properties and the skill of the artist using them. For example, pencils can create a light, thin line, while a brush can be used to create thin or thick lines, or textured or smooth lines.

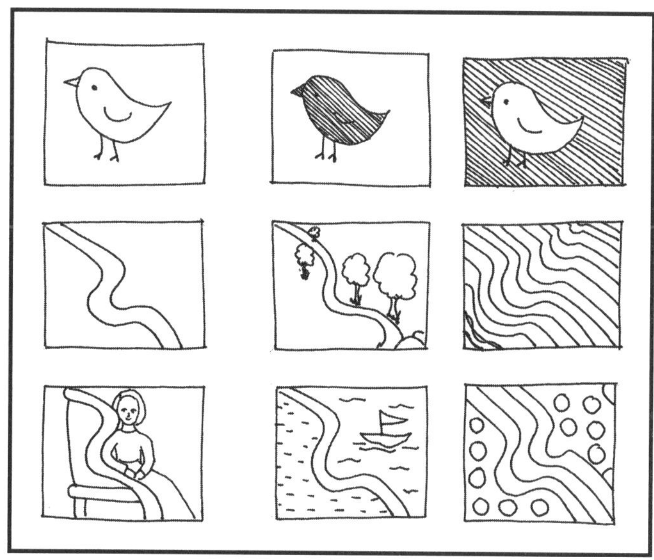

MOVEMENT

Movement in artwork refers to the illusion of action in the composition. Depictions of people and objects moving through a landscape, for example, is produced by using curves, repetition of shapes, contrasting texture or color, gradation of color or line, or actions such as dancing, bending, or running.

Movement transforms a technically perfect painting into an inspiring piece of art through details that give life to silent actions on the page. The quiet upturn of a smile on an old man's face or the deep sigh of relief in a child's expression adds an important human element.

Movement also has to do with how the viewer interacts with the artwork. Once he is drawn into the picture, how does his interest remain captivated? Every viewer has a personal entrance point into the composition, much like an imaginary door through which he is taken in by the art. After his initial entrance, his eye may travel in a circle, viewing all aspects of the painting sequentially.

POSITIVE AND NEGATIVE SPACE

Positive space is the area occupied and defined by the main shapes and forms of a composition. Negative space serves as the background of an object.

RHYTHM

Rhythm is the measurement between units of space, shape, color, or objects that are usually repeated in a balanced proportion. The intervals between dots and squares in a pattern create a rhythm. The visual spacing of bright-light accents on the painting of a blue sky creates a rhythm our eyes catch. A pattern is also a rhythm: red, blue, yellow; red, blue, yellow.

SATURATION

Saturation refers to the intensity of the purity or vividness of the color.

SEQUENCE

Sequence can refer to the steps in the drawing/painting/constructing process: sketch, practice, final paper, outline, adjust, refine, color, shade.

SHADE

A shade is a color mixed with various amounts of black or a dark color, creating variations of a color.

SHADING

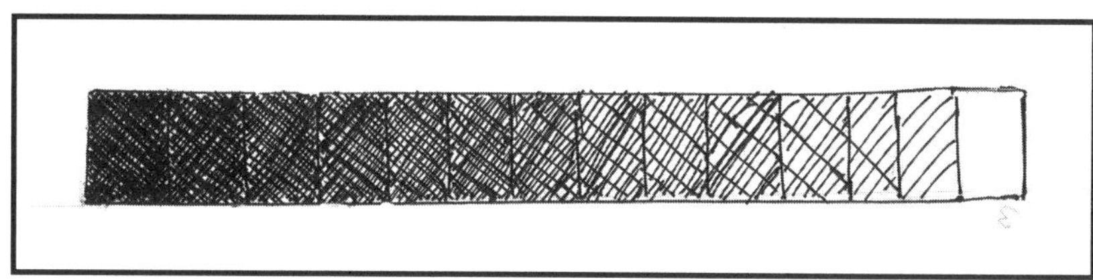

Shading is when various levels of black (or a dark color) are added to white or other colors, giving the effect of partial light on objects. This is usually achieved with scales of lights to darks, but can also be done with a scale of shades, such as red graduating to black with all the shades in between. A shaded dark area next to a light area, for example, can reveal folds in a garment. Hatching or cross-hatching with sets of various amounts of overlapping or parallel lines is another method to produce shading.

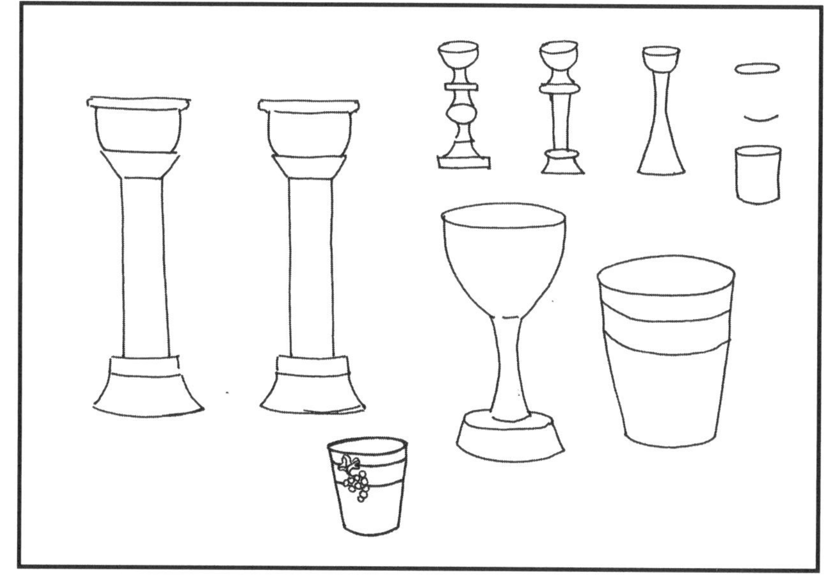

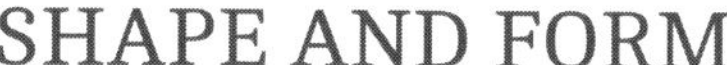

SHAPE AND FORM

Lines are the basis of shape and form. A shape is created when straight and/or curved lines intersect, such as a square or a circle. Combining two or more shapes create a form, such as combining multiple squares to create a cube, box, or house.

SIZE AND SCALE

Size and scale refer to the proportional relationship of an object to its background or a figure to its environment, such as the size of the head to the rest of the body, or the size of a person compared to the house in the background.

STROKE

Stroke refers to the direction of the lines that are painted or drawn in a composition. Strokes may be upward or downward, with or without flourishes. The amount of pressure applied to the brush or pencil can result in a heavy stroke or a light stroke. Strokes may be upward or downward, with or without flourishes.

STYLE

Style refers to an individual's distinct expression and unique approach to handling materials in a composition. Just as everyone's handwriting is unique, everyone's artistic style is also unique. The style of a piece of art can also reveal when and where the artist lived.

Style is also formed based on what the artist chooses to emphasize in the art—is it the message, colors, shapes, or story? From whose point of view is the picture? How does the art affect us? These are all aspects of the composition that distinguish the artist's style.

For children, style is personal—they draw what they see or know. A retired nursery school teacher once told me that she knew what went on in her students' homes because they drew about it without reserve.

Style can be improved. If the expression is too stiff, the child can be encouraged to draw with freer movement; if the line quality is heavy-handed, the child can be shown how to lighten it up by practicing drawing lines and shapes with a variety of strokes and pressures. Once children are introduced to the idea of using a technique to express their inner selves, they are able to infuse their artwork with their own personal style.

SYMMETRY

Symmetry in a composition is created when the right and left sides of a composition mirror each other or balance one another. Asymmetry is created when the two sides don't mirror each other or they create an unequal visual balance on the axis of the total composition (imagine a seesaw) or they may be balanced in a non-conventional way (imagine abstract art). Bilateral refers to an area that is divided equally into four parts.

TEXTURE

Texture gives the artwork the impression of a being a tactile, touchable surface, such as appearing rough, smooth, or woven. Texture is generally created by using three values in the composition—light, middle, and dark (envision white, gray, and black) or repeating them in a pattern. When painting the bark of a tree or the engravings of a stone cutter, shading provides the illusion of texture by creating contrast between the raised surfaces and the recesses beneath.

TINT

A tint is a pastel, when white is added to a color. Example: red to white.

VALUE

The value of a color refers to the scale of its lightness or darkness, with the most light being white and the most dark being black. A green color will be between a light green and dark green, depending on the amounts of white and black.

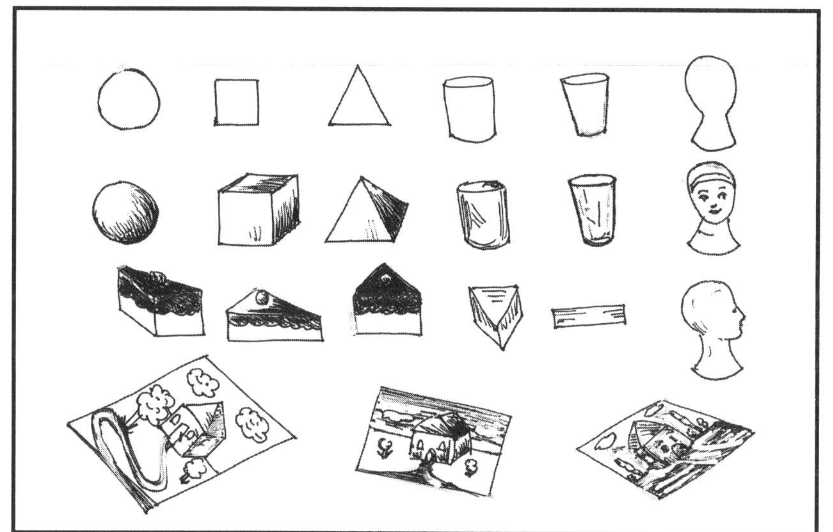

VOLUME

Volume is the space within a defined area of a shape or form. Two-dimensional shapes are flat, without volume, like a square or circle. Three-dimensional shapes, such as a cube, ball, or pyramid, have volume; their length, width, and height can be defined and measured.

The Scheme of Geometry

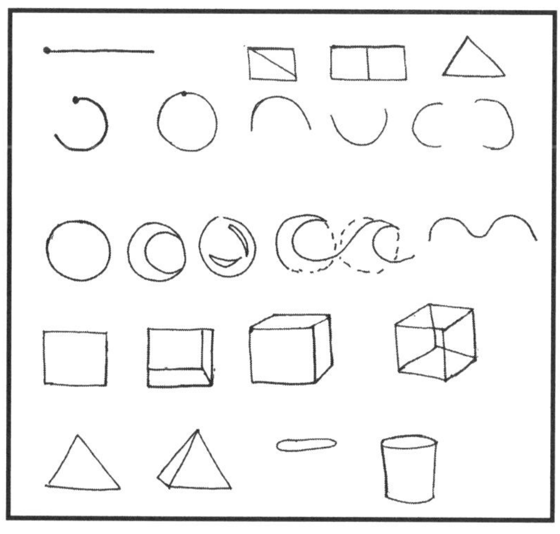

From the age of five, we can teach children to draw using the scheme of geometry—drawing and combining geometric (geo) shapes to form the base for objects in a composition, such as houses, trees, and people. When you break it down, a house is constructed from a square with a triangle on top; a tree is really a circle or a ring of half-circles on top of a thin rectangle.

A shape becomes a form when you add dimension and refine and curve the lines, adding a life-like element to the shape. A form becomes an identifiable object when details are added. Using all the elements of design, a bare line-drawing of an orange becomes a visual wonder in a painting, drawing, or construction.

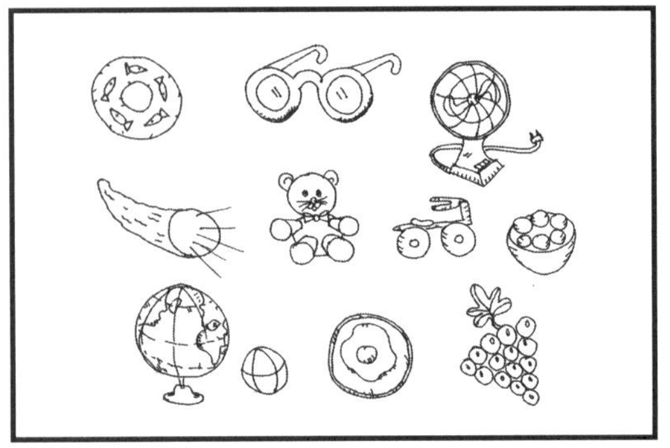

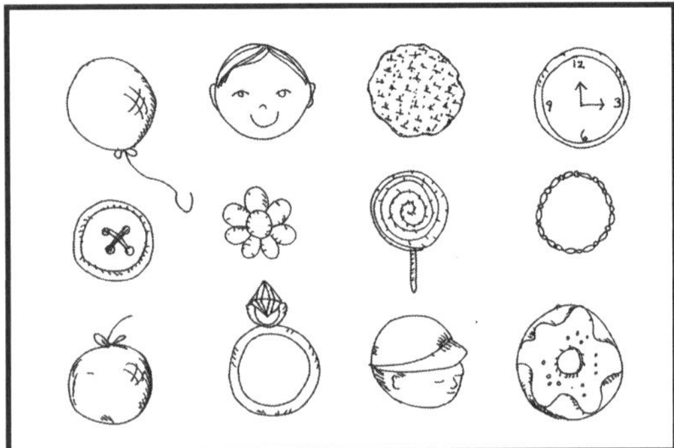

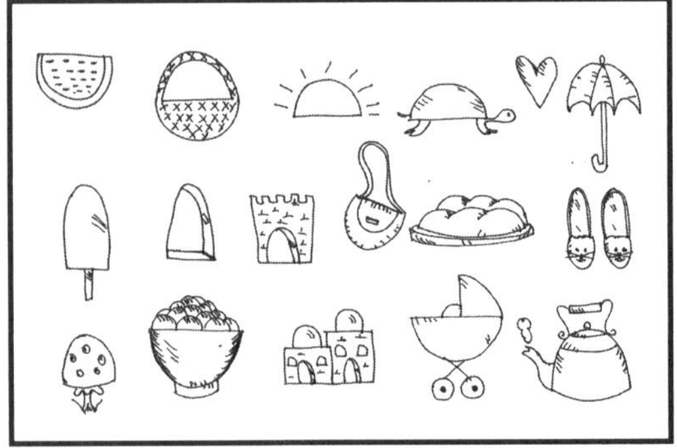

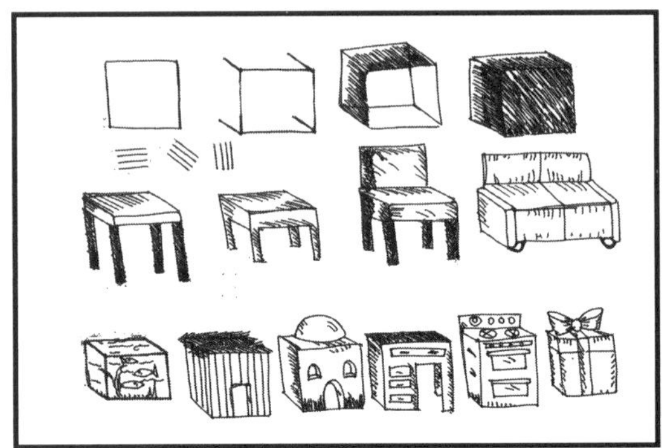

The first step is to show children the world of basic geometric shapes that make up many objects in the physical world: circles, squares, rectangles, triangles, and semicircles. Spend time reviewing geometric shapes and how to construct them.

It's fun and instructive to look for geo shapes in the classroom and in your home. For example, find squares in boxes, tables, windows, doors, walls and floor tiles, books, and blankets. Find circles in round fans and clocks, pots and pans, cups and bowls, buttons and rings.

Now, show them how to draw those basic shapes. Begin with a dot: touch your pencil to the paper. Then, pull the dot across the page and it becomes a line. Curve it around and it becomes a circle. Cut the circle in half and you've got a semicircle.

To draw a square, start with a short horizontal line. At the end of the line turn the "corner" down and draw a line equal in length and perpendicular to the first line. At the bottom, stop and turn the "corner" and make a line parallel and equal to the first line. Turn the "corner" and continue up to the beginning of the original line. There, you have a square.

To draw a triangle, start again with just a short horizontal line. Keep your pencil on the page and draw another line an equal distance to the first line slanting down toward the left. Stop. Without lifting the pencil, draw a line back up to the beginning of the original point. You've got a triangle! Now show how two triangles make a square.

To teach the shape of the oval, show how it starts as a circle. Have the child look down on the top of a cup or a can and ask him what shape he sees. He will tell you he sees a circle. Now, hold the cup in front of him at eye level and point out how the circle becomes a half of a circle (like a curved line before your eyes). Slowly tilt the cup downward and you will see an oval.

Have the child practice drawing the basic shapes while pointing out what makes each one distinct.

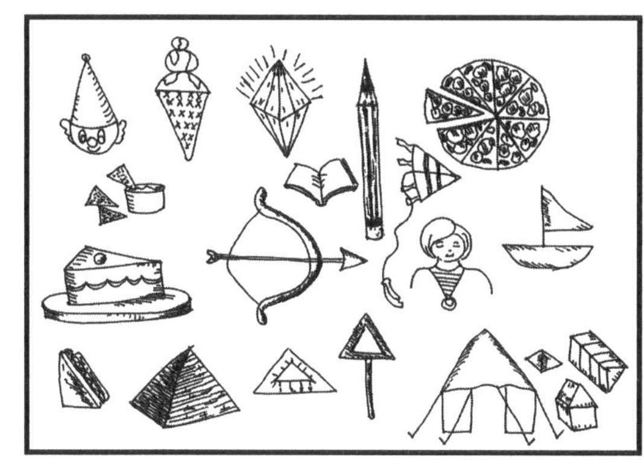

Once the child understands how each shape is formed and is able to identify the shapes within the objects around him, have him draw the objects. Work in pairs (either within a group of children, or the parent or teacher with the child). One child draws a shape and the other adds another shape to complement the first. They take turns drawing shapes until an object is formed.

For example, one child draws a square. The other child adds a triangle to the square. Now they have the frame of a house. The first child adds a rectangle for the door, and his partner adds a square to make a chimney.

Get as detailed as you can—mezuzot, flower pots, and curtains are also made out of geometric shapes! Make up a story to go with the drawing as it takes shape. Not only does this exercise build the foundation for the child's drawing skills but it's also a great way for the parent and child to spend time together.

You can also demonstrate how to draw basic body parts from geometric shapes. Sketch a figure with a circle for the head, a small square for the neck, a large square for the shirt, a triangle for a skirt on a girl or double lines for the pants of a boy, long narrow rectangles for the legs and arms along with several half-circles for the hands, shoes, mouth, nose, ears, and *kippah*. Don't forget the fingers, buttons, belts, and pockets—anything the child would want to add to the person that has a shape associated with it.

Teaching children how to draw objects from the foundational geo shapes is a basic and essential skill that they will be able to build upon as they develop their talent and technique.

Form: From Geo Shapes to Realism

Fine arts and crafts are based on creating compelling forms, and then using all our tools, materials, skills, and expression to build on them. A dot becomes a line, and a series of lines becomes a shape. A shape becomes a form when you refine and curve the lines, adding a lifelike element to the shape. After the form is sketched, it can be filled in with shading, texture, and color until it gives the appearance of a three-dimensional object. Though the average person can't see the geometric shapes behind the form, the artist must be familiar with the foundational shapes before he can make objects look realistic.

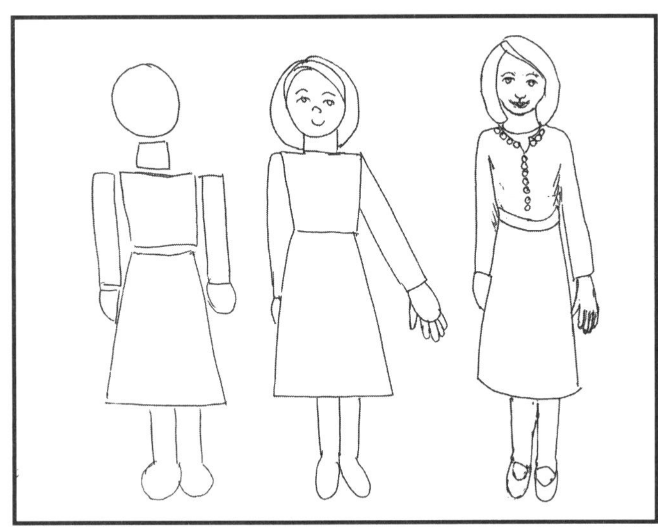

Whether child or adult, anyone who wants to create art needs to begin with a strong foundation. Teenagers especially want to draw realistically. Good! But to make sure that this happens, they have to first understand the building blocks and proportions: Start with the shape and form of the object before moving on to shading and color.

Notice, for example, that the human body is made up of subtle curves—there is nothing ruler-like or rigid about it. Put your left hand around your right hand and arm, and feel the continuous movement of the curve of the bones and skin. Though that's how the human body is shaped in real life, to draw it successfully you have to start with the straight lines that indicate the upright vertical direction of people and the basic shapes that make up the human figure. Once you have the basic form by drawing the geo shapes lightly in pencil, you can refine and curve them slightly, making them appear more fluid and natural.

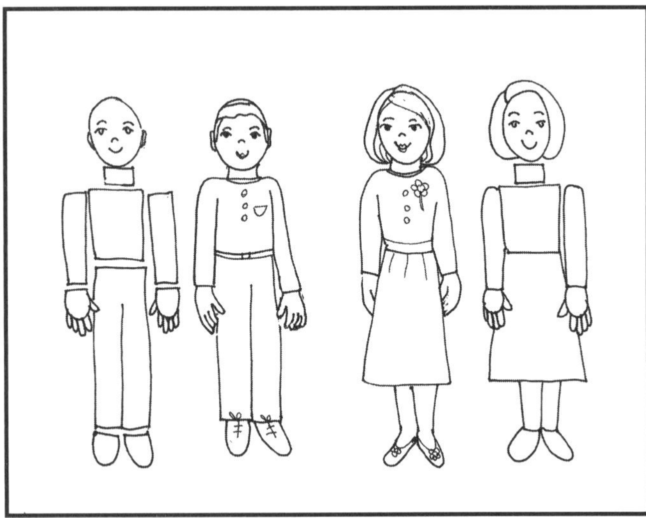

Repetition: Refine and Integrate

Repetition can mean recreating one subject in the same or different sizes, backgrounds, colors, or materials. Repetition in art is invaluable because it integrates a new skill or expression within the child by reinforcing his familiarity with the subject, skills, and materials, thereby boosting his self-confidence. Repetition is important for refining and improving a piece of art, and it's especially useful for making patterns and textures.

For our purposes, I encourage drawing a picture three times:

1. with a pencil on practice paper
2. with a pencil on the intended drawing surface (such as art paper, card stock, cardboard, or canvas)
3. with a fine-tipped pen or marker, drawing over the pencil lines

In step 3, you may choose to trace over the pencil lines exactly or use the pencil drawing as a guide, making changes as you work.

Each step is a review that reinforces the memory of the drawing and provides an opportunity to improve it.

Another form of repetition is depicting one subject, using several different materials. A child becomes more familiar with the subject—for example, a tzedakah box—if he makes it as both a two-dimensional painting and a three-dimensional construction.

Also, different materials create different feelings and provide various associations with the subject and materials. By depicting one subject several times in different materials, the child will associate the subject with the sensations and control he gained from using the material he liked most. He might recall the joy of manipulating the clay or the intensity of working with a fine-tipped paintbrush.

A two-dimensional drawing with a pencil produces a delicacy of line. Using oil pastels gives a bold, solid, wet-looking color that requires strength and hand pressure. Cutting out parts of drawings and rearranging them on another sheet of paper shows children that they can move and replace objects in different arrangements, which gives them a great sense of control. A three-dimensional object created from Styrofoam sandwich board, plasticine, clay, or papier-mâché stimulates concrete perceptions of volume, mass, and depth. The physical pounding and manipulation of the pliable material also releases emotions and energy.

Control: The Importance of Technique

There are two kinds of control: exterior and interior. Technique is an exterior skill, which involves knowing how to use art tools for optimal control, leading to the desired results. Exterior control leads to interior control, which is the confidence needed to overcome the natural fear of making mistakes. The more the child understands and practices a technique, the better his overall control will be. Mistakes will not take on the same drama when the child has the skills and confidence to fix or redo a mistake.

Just as important as teaching drawing techniques is explaining how to choose and use the tools effectively for their artwork. For example, showing the child how to load a paintbrush with paint or water is a crucial first step before teaching ways to paint the picture. Demonstrate how much paint or water is needed and how to control the hand pressure he places on the brush as he paints. Show and explain the different sizes of brushes that create various strokes, for example, thicker brushes for trees and sky, and thinner ones for details like eyes and flowers. Even something seemingly simple like a pencil can produce thick or thin strokes and dark or light lines, depending on the pressure and angle with which the pencil is held.[134]

Learning the correct posture and hand position that directs and controls the use of the tool while drawing or painting is also an important skill. Working in a relaxed state is just as important, taking us away from the mundane and transporting us into the inner world of the imagination. Show the child how to relax before starting an art project by taking a few deep, calm breaths, releasing any tightness in the shoulders and neck. Drawing with the shoulders relaxed, rather than tight, often produces more successful lines. Explain the proper positions of the body, arms, and hands when working with the tools. Show how the shoulder and elbow direct the pencil and how the wrist and fingers exert finer control. Encourage the child to find a comfortable position and adjust the chair or table as needed.

Guide his thoughts as well: have him focus on his goals, reassuring him that everything he creates is only for practice, and he can rework or let go of anything he's not happy with. Hearing and knowing this will take away any pressure from the beginning, and then the child can begin drawing without inhibition, excited for the project. At the end of an art session, do a wind-down with some deep breaths, focusing on what the child learned and accomplished.

The magician's sleight of hand or the pianist's swift fingertips running across the piano keys look effortless and almost magical—this comes

134 See ch. 19, "The Tools of Art."

from being relaxed while performing and practicing, having repeated and perfected this skill over time. Eventually, as he gains skills and confidence, the child will relax automatically and his creativity will flow naturally.

I once mentioned to a group of five- and six-year-old girls that my best ideas come to me just after waking up from a nap. While I'm still half asleep, I get a vision of an art project in my mind's eye, and though the details aren't worked through yet, the inspiration and basic idea are there. A rebbetzin (wife of a rabbi) also told me that she got inspiration for her articles and books while she prayed. Why? Because her praying calmed her.

A few of the girls in my class said that when they wake up in the morning, they see pictures in their mind. I was surprised to hear children say this. I didn't realize that children envision pictures in their minds like adults do. Hone the creative potential of young children, and teach them in a relaxed state to help them develop their skill and style—and enjoy the process while they're at it!

Art should be enjoyable, focusing, and relaxing. While some people do art when they're in a beleaguered emotional state, this isn't the goal. Anxiety, worries, and lack of self-confidence only increase the fear and dread of making mistakes, while a sense of calm helps you take mistakes in stride, ultimately providing greater control and satisfaction from the composition.

In this chapter, we learned about creating forms using geo shapes and a few of the foundations of great art: repetition, control, and calmness. Here are three projects that will get a child started with drawing objects out of geo shapes and creating form.

Geo Thinking AGES 6+

Materials:

- 3 sheets of copy paper, size 8½ x 11 inches (21 x 30 cm) or larger
- Pencil

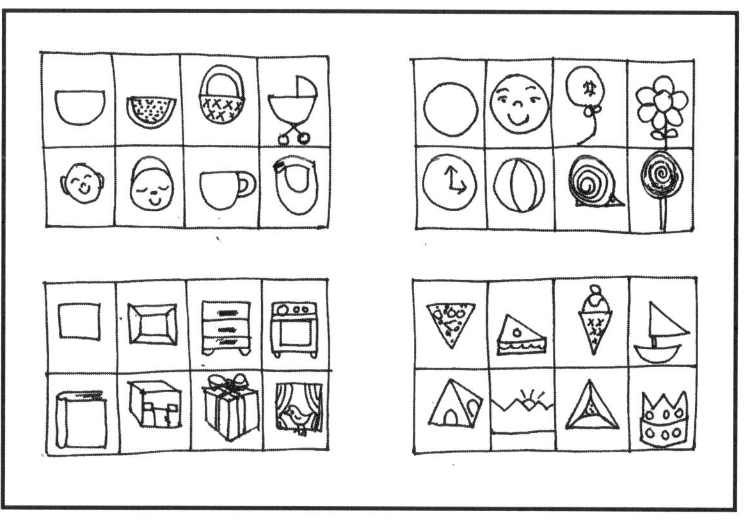

- Black pen or fine-tipped marker
- Colored markers

Directions:

1. Fold the sheet of paper in half three or four times to make eight or sixteen sections.
2. Look around the room and find objects that are based on a square or rectangular shape. Unfold the paper, and in each box, draw an object lightly with a pencil, first the shape, then the object.
3. Draw over the pencil lines with the pen or fine-tipped marker.
4. Repeat with circles, half-circles, and triangles.
5. Color in the shapes with markers.

A Figure Drawing AGES 5/6+

This project is a great way to learn how to use geometric shapes in drawing, and it also teaches the child to draw a boy or girl that reflects him or herself, promoting a healthy self-image. Encourage the child to draw his picture large and centered, leaving enough room for the legs and feet at the bottom of the paper. If the child's natural tendency is to draw small objects or to concentrate his drawings to one side, let him do so the first time. For the next drawing, suggest that he draw the figure large and centered. He will remember his first small, shy drawing and be proud of his improvement. If necessary, show an example of a drawing that is large and centered that he can learn from.

Materials:

- Pencil
- Copy paper, size 8½ x 11 (21 x 30 cm)
- Fine-tipped pen or black felt-tip marker
- Colored markers

Directions:

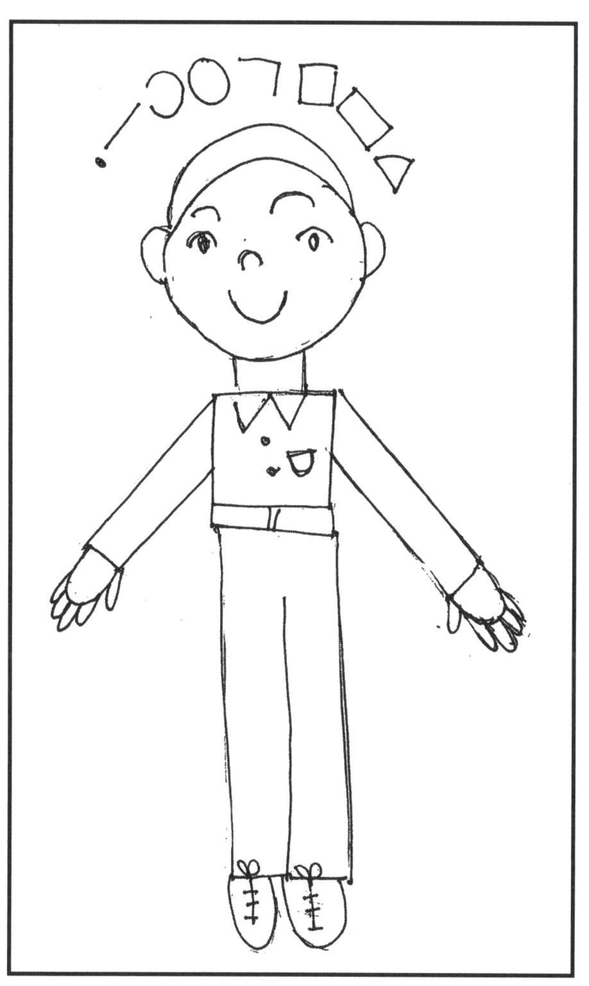

1. With the pencil, draw a circle high on the sheet of paper. This will be the head and face of the child.
2. Add a small square for the neck, a larger square for the shirt, a triangle without a top point for a skirt or two and a half straight lines for pants. (The half line is parallel to and in between the long lines.) Or draw two narrow rectangles for the pants. Draw half-circles in various sizes for hands, shoes, mouth, nose, ears, and a *kippah*. Add closed lines for thumbs and fingers. Remember that the thumb is not connected to the four fingers. It is lower down from the fingers on the hand. Add details like a belt, buttons, patterns and designs, flowers, and pockets, all made from geometric shapes.
3. Draw on top of the pencil lines with the fine-tipped pen or marker.
4. Color in the person carefully with the colored markers, encouraging the child to stay within the lines.

Nature and Form AGES 7+

Draw a scene from nature using your imagination and geometric shapes.

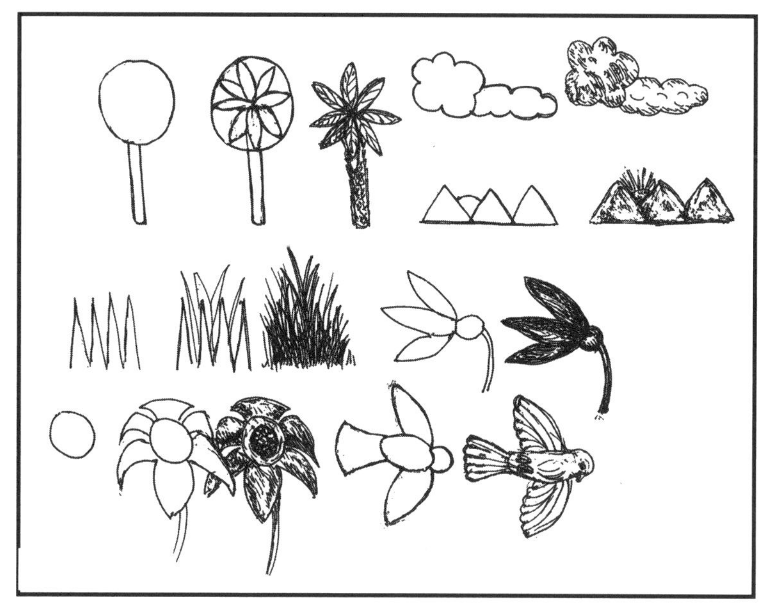

Materials:

- Pencil and eraser
- Copy paper, size 8½ x 11 inches (21 x 30 cm) or larger
- Black fine-tipped pen or marker
- Colored markers

Directions:

1. Go outside and find a scene in nature, or imagine a scene of your own that you want to depict. You can also get ideas from a photograph. For example: a flock of birds in the sky, clouds, mountains, a river, or trees, grass, and wildflowers.
2. With a pencil, draw the scene in geo shapes (circles, semicircles, lines, squares, rectangles, triangles, and ovals).
3. Refine the shapes into forms by curving the lines of the objects.
4. Draw over the pencil lines with the fine-tipped pen or marker. When dry, erase the pencil lines underneath.
5. Color in the lines carefully with the colored markers.

In Summary: Some Art Theory to Get You Started

- Although art is a creative endeavor that expresses feelings and thoughts, it requires skill and technique.
- Art relies on aesthetics and harmony, which is created when the elements of a composition are present and balanced.
- Familiarity with art terms provides a foundation for acquiring skills that will help create inspiring art.
- Ground, line quality, texture, and style are a few of the terms an artist should know to produce a composition that comes alive.
- In the physical world, most objects are constructed from geo shapes made up of either straight lines or curves.
- It's important for a child to be able to identify the geometric shapes in the physical world as a basis for his drawings.
- As a matter of repetition or review, a composition can typically be drawn three times: once on a practice sheet, a second time on quality paper or canvas, and a third time with a pen (if on paper) or with color.

- It's important for the artist to acquire both exterior control—that is, technique—and internal control—that is, confidence.

Questions and Wonder

1. How do you develop your own artistic style?
2. Technique is mechanical and style is personal. How can you use both in art?
3. What can we learn about aesthetics from nature?

18 The Four Elements of Art

A story composition starts with one word. Several words grouped together create a sentence, and a few sentences collectively make up a paragraph. Several paragraphs become a scene, and there you have the finished product: a story. Details in the story keep us interested and focused; good writing technique imparts communication and clarity. Together with a personal style and voice, all of these elements contribute to form a beautiful piece of literature.

The same is true of a painting or any type of fine craft work. But in place of words, we use visual elements: lines, shapes, color, light, symmetry, and movement. All the elements of design that we defined in previous chapters come together to form a composition. With these elements, art can tell a story, create miniature versions of objects in our world, or convey a feeling or message.

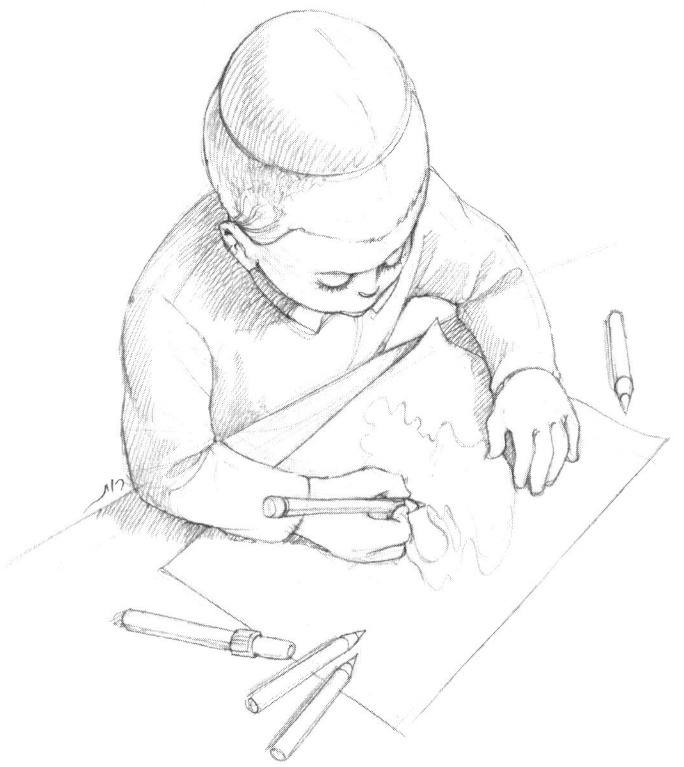

Compositions in Nature

A successful, complex work of art has many aspects to it; besides line, shape, form, and color, it also has depth, movement, light, story, point of interest, and rhythm—each of which reflects the human experience and is expressed in its own unique visual language.

Notes and Sketches

One way to build skills is through studying the "compositions" that we see in nature and identifying the elements that create the scene. Nature contains many silent teachers—if we take the time to observe and contemplate the land formations, the ocean, and even rocks and grass, then a remarkable, unified blend of curves, lines, light, and colors will be revealed. Each of these on their own is a delightful subject to explore. For one, let's take notice of the curve.

Most objects in nature have the common element of the curve. Look around. The curve is everywhere. We see it in the curves of our bodies and in the shapes of the earth and the solar system. Animals, plant and vegetable life, butterflies and insects, the sun throughout the day and the moon at night, rolling hills and smooth rocks, raindrops and sprouting seeds are all composed of curves.

Take an ocean landscape, for example. It captures so many harmonious and inspirational images, colors, and shapes, all curved. The seashell itself is worth a closer look—marvel at its spiraling forms, the shadowing in its grooves, and the twinkling grains of sand where the shell is nestled. Beauty and the curve have a relationship in nature and creation. Combine the curved images with lines, form, light and color, center of interest, and perspective. The overall picture makes up a composition.

The Four Elements (Building Blocks) in a Composition

There are four elements or building blocks to any work of art (not to be confused with the elements of design discussed in chapter 17, "Some Art Theory to Get You Started"). If we were to dissect the life of a painting from the time of its conception through the early stages of its formation, until completion, we would discover the following building blocks:

1. The subject—this is the focus and center of our attention.
2. The materials—these contribute to the structure of a piece of

Notes and Sketches

art; without materials, there is no building or creating. How the materials are used is called the technique.

3. The expression or style of the artist, combined with skill—this is how we imbue our art with personality and give the artwork life and inspiration; without expression, the art is lifeless. When the art reflects the artist's voice, it inspires and provokes a response from the viewer.

4. The message—this is our special point of communication to the world: the thought, feeling, advice, or advertising behind the artwork. The message aims to teach, guide, and communicate with the viewer.

To demonstrate these ideas, let's break down an art project into its elements. Say you want to draw a picture of the four cups of wine from the Pesach Seder.

The subject of the composition is the four cups of wine.

The materials are pencils, markers, and paper.

The skills are drawing, cutting, and gluing. The skills and talent of the artist will affect the style and expression of the drawing—whether the drawing turns out to be more technical and realistic or more representative and impressionistic.

The message is the redemption from bondage that the Jewish people experienced on Pesach, and the four cups symbolize the freedom that Jews still celebrate today.

These four elements are present in any art project. Depending on the age and skill of the artist, the subject, message, and materials will vary. A four-year-old may paint an outline of a house in primary colors; a twelve-year-old may use oil paint and mix colors to produce subtle hues to depict the same house. Though the picture may be hard to discern, the four-year-old's work may be with simple lines and colors, while the twelve-year-old may be capable of adding more detail or abstract expression to the painting: darker colors and heavy strokes to convey a feeling of sadness or fear, or cheerful colors and light strokes to convey a happy home.

Whatever the age of the artist or the nature of the project, it's important to define an emphasis for the artwork. This means deciding which of the four elements you want to highlight in the finished project, and focusing on those elements throughout the project.

Where Is the Emphasis?

Which of the four elements is most important to focus on when creating a piece of art? Especially when working with children, you have to be very clear on your goal: Is it to teach the concept he is depicting (the subject), to teach him a skill, or to give him a chance to express his feelings?

There are several approaches to how to make your emphasis clear in a project. Introducing the subject makes the child more connected to the value or idea that the artwork represents, but this might take away from focusing on a skill you want to teach.

Let's say you want to teach the children the skill of cutting and you also want to introduce them to the topic of the four cups of wine for Pesach. The children might become so focused on depicting the four cups perfectly that they'll miss the whole lesson on cutting or the concept of the four cups that you wanted them to learn about. They will be occupied with producing the outcome rather than enjoying the process and learning the new skills you want them to acquire.

Even if your goal is to have the child produce a beautiful depiction of the four cups of wine, you want to eliminate as many frustrations as possible. You don't want to give the unspoken message that the outcome is more important than the process.

To introduce a project, give a short, exciting introduction to the subject (a meaningful description for older children or a story-like explanation for the younger ones), and then move on to explain the skills they will be using to create the art project (drawing, outlining, cutting, and gluing the four cups).

Next, give out the materials (the paper and markers, for example) and show a few different samples of the finished artwork. Introducing the project in this order will result in an enjoyable process and a lovely work of art.

Any way you decide to introduce the project, and where you choose to place the emphasis, let the children know that it is important for them to work through the steps of the process—the more they focus on the thought and technique that goes into it, the better the results that they're so concerned about will be. Make sure they also know that the process is supposed to be enjoyable. Art should be fun! If striving for perfection is getting in the way of their pleasure in the work, then they are missing the point. This will reassure them and allow them to relax as they work.

Although you may be introducing an art project to emphasize one of the elements of art—whether it's a new material, a new skill, a subject matter, or the art of expression—emphasizing one of the elements can reinforce the others. For example, learning to work with watercolors can be taught together with the idea of a Lag BaOmer bonfire or a three-year-old having his first haircut.[135]

You can teach children about shapes while learning about the holiday of Shavuot. For example, have them draw many different-sized circles, and then cut them out and glue them together to make paper flowers, symbolizing the flowers that sprouted on Har Sinai to make it beautiful before the giving of the Torah.

Teach a child the amazing uses for clay: pound it, knead it, coil it, make slabs, build with it, and more! In the process, you can show children how to create a clay menorah for Chanukah or a wine cup for Kiddush. This will introduce both the skills of working with clay and these Jewish concepts. Or, you can make clay vessels and explain how years ago people used clay for serving food, cooking, and storage, just as we use plastic and ceramics today.

Besides varying the subject to suit the skill, you can also take one theme and depict it in many different ways. By changing the emphasis, you can give new life to the same subject over and over again. For example, for a theme of flowers, you can practice drawing them from different perspectives. Depict a bride holding a bouquet from afar as she walks down the ballroom aisle, or from up close as she sits and greets her guests before the chuppah. Emphasize the materials for the flower project by using tissue paper, ribbons, and lace to make the bride's bouquet.

Or you can change the scene completely: Draw flowers nestled in an effervescent meadow to learn color blending and shading. Yellow sunlight, hummingbirds, and bees can make the backdrop for a symphony of pink, purple, and blue petals.

These are two very different scenes, each with many options for emphasis.

---

135 In Jewish tradition, many Jewish boys get their first haircut after their third birthday, mirroring the Jewish Law of *orlah*, when a three-year-old fruit tree is harvested for the first time.

The Difference between a Great Composition and Mediocre Artwork

A successful composition inspires us and draws us in to become part of that picture in the moment. Our eyes travel the canvas, in and out of spaces and between and over objects. We enjoy the journey because the composition contains a satisfying order and visual symphony.

Recognizing objects, people, and places when we view a painting is an advantage because the subject is easy to identify, but the painting will need much more than that to reach its full potential. The eye is inspired by subtleties, details, and aesthetics. These elements are what make the difference between a great painting and a mediocre one. That's where the skill of the artist and his personal expression and style come into play.

A painting of Rachel's Tomb, set in the arid desert with trees, rocks, and the sky above, hangs on my wall. It has a pleasing symmetry of weight and balance in its design. A bright yellow sun at the top corner is balanced with the textured details of rocks and the road at the bottom.

But let's say that the sun on the top corner was not counterbalanced by something interesting to pull our attention to the bottom of the composition (the foreground). We would lose interest because the eye needs to be equally pulled around the picture, ultimately resting on the center of interest, the place where the eye wants to focus on most and, as a result, with the picture as a whole.

What would be interesting to look at on the bottom of this painting? Maybe a camel or donkey walking on the road would be a good prop (besides being an accurate representation of the scene) that would keep our eye interested.

Other elements that add interest are shadows, perspective, lighting, use of strokes and lines to create a mood, depth and variations of color, details, compositional movement, and a story depiction. All of these elements give a lifelike reality to the picture. At times, these are the main images of the artwork. Other times, they are used for connections and transitions, as bridges connecting one image (subject) in the composition to another. They are secondary to the main subjects yet they are what hold the parts together and give the picture added life.

Generally, children only begin to develop the ability to include these nuances after the age of seven or eight. Children younger than that tend to portray flat or symbolic shapes without excessive interest in reality as we adults see it. Rather than focusing on creating the perfect depiction, small children are sponges, collecting skills and learning about the materials they can manipulate and create with. They are discovering themselves and the world around them. They can put together a good composition spontaneously or nothing could come of their efforts at all.

When your three-year-old proudly shows you a picture he drew, don't worry if his description of the picture doesn't match what you're seeing on the page—he's got plenty of time to get there.

Especially for younger children, focus on appreciating the child's efforts and progress in learning art skills. As he grows older, you can begin to appreciate the other elements of his composition: the thought and detail he put into depicting the subject and his growing style and expression.

Create the Composition

Whether you're a parent doing a rainy-day arts-and-crafts project at home or a teacher in the classroom, you can follow these five steps to fully engage the children and have an enjoyable time.

1. Break up the project into small steps.

The number of steps and amount of time needed for each project depend on the children's age. Younger children require more steps and more time. With more experienced students, less time is needed for explaining the steps. Cutting with scissors may take three- and four-year-olds a significant amount of time to accomplish, while a seven-year-old will be done in five minutes or less.

2. Give simple and clear instructions for every step.

After breaking down all the parts of the project, explain each step in detail from a few different angles. Make it interesting and amusing. Compare a shape such as an oval to a cucumber or hot dog. Emphasize the colors poetically to create an image. To illustrate the process and sequence of drawing a house, explain how a builder begins building a house first with the foundation (a flat line or rectangle), then the walls (a square), finishing with the roof (a triangle). You can sing a short song that goes with the project, or ask the children what their own home looks like to get them thinking and then imagining.

It's advisable not to show how to do the whole project at once. Instead, wait to show a finished version at the end, keeping in pace with where the children are up to. Showing them a finished version from the start might make them want to copy it, which will be frustrating for the children who won't be able to reproduce the example. In-depth explanations of how each shape is constructed and a few options give the children confidence to go forward without the need to see a finished project to copy. Save each subsequent step or stage for another session, depending on the time frame. Make each step full and satisfying rather than part of a recipe that is followed without integrating each stage of the whole.

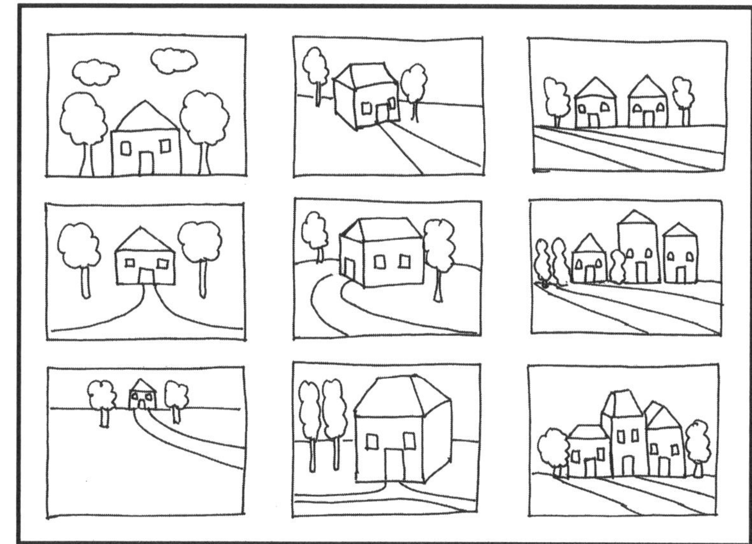

3. Offer two or three options or variations on the project.

Within the framework of the project, let the children know that there is more than one way to do it. You can show a child several options and views of the same subject and let them choose their own details and composition arrangement. This means that you have to do the project several different ways in advance to know what works best, and to show and explain the options. For example, a drawing of a house may be up close or far up on a hill. The season and hour of the day can be their choice.

Shoshana, one of my seven-year-old students, always offered her own variations. She was an original thinker—no matter what project I presented, she came up with her own ideas that my suggestions sparked. Eventually, Shoshana settled on doing two projects: first the one I demonstrated and then her own version. I was happy, as long as she was practicing the skills and having a good time.

4. Use repetition in order to develop proficiency.

Do trial drawings on scratch paper of objects that may be difficult to draw or when drawing them for the first time. Next, do one or more complete practice drawings in pencil. When you're ready for the final version, repeat the pencil drawing on better quality paper, then draw on top of the pencil lines with ink or a fine-tipped marker, erasing the leftover pencil marks once the ink is dry. The drawing can then be filled with color or remain black and white.

One group of eight- and ten-year-old girls I taught spent most of their time doing complete practice drawings, sometimes three or four times, until they knew their subject well and felt comfortable enough to start painting.

5. Have a backup project.

A backup project is great for keeping children who have finished before the rest of the group occupied—there is always a child like this, whether he's done five minutes early or twenty. Also, the backup project is a good option for children who don't want to do the project you offered, but you know work well on their own. Let them do free drawing or draw on the dry-erase board if it won't disturb the rest of the class. If you've already explained the next project, they can begin by doing a practice drawing of it.

In addition, keep basic materials and visual aids in stock.

A glance through a folder of pictures stimulates the mind and gives one additional ideas to work with. Visual aids are postcards, clipped pictures from magazines on subjects that one may want to draw in the future: people, nature, Shabbat and holidays, food, still lifes, Judaica, animals, buildings, transportation, and clothing. The basic materials, when easily accessible, come in handy when a change of direction is called for.

Here are some projects that show how to create a composition using the four elements or building blocks of art.

The Jewish Home AGES 7+

Portraying the Jewish home offers many options to create an art composition. There are a lot of details and possible subjects that we can zoom in or out on, and plenty of materials to experiment with. The first step is to decide what to emphasize or focus on.

Here are some options:

1. The front of the house, emphasizing the entrance and the mezuzah on the doorframe

2. The house close up or in the distance
3. An aerial view of the house and the land around it
4. An architectural layout of the house and its rooms
5. An illustration of each room with its appropriate functional and ritual objects, as seen in their own home or as the child imagines:

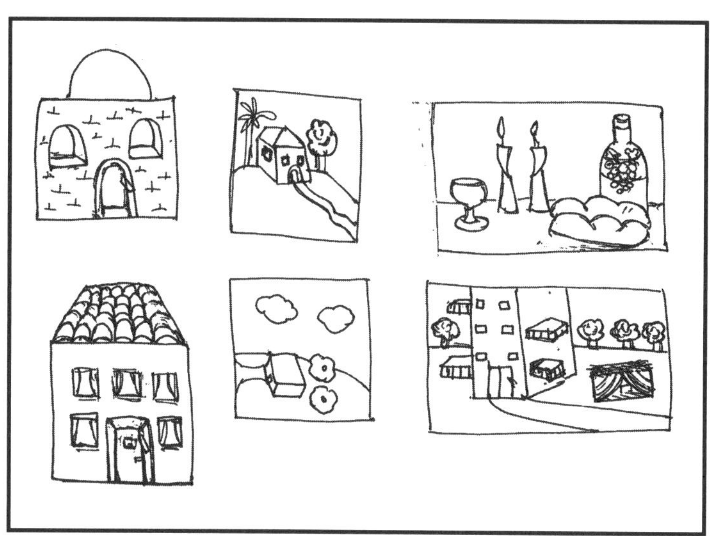

    - A kosher kitchen labeled for milk or meat, and a Pesach cupboard
    - The living room lined with bookshelves of *sifrei kodesh* (holy books), a breakfront displaying Kiddush cups, Shabbat candlesticks, a wood-and-silver challah board, challah knife, challah cover, silver salt shaker, a holder for *bentchers* (Grace after Meals booklets), a spice box for Havdalah, a shofar for Rosh Hashanah, a tzedakah box, and a Chanukah menorah. On the walls hang framed paintings of rabbis, the twelve tribes, the Holy Temple in Jerusalem, and a *Mizrach* sign.

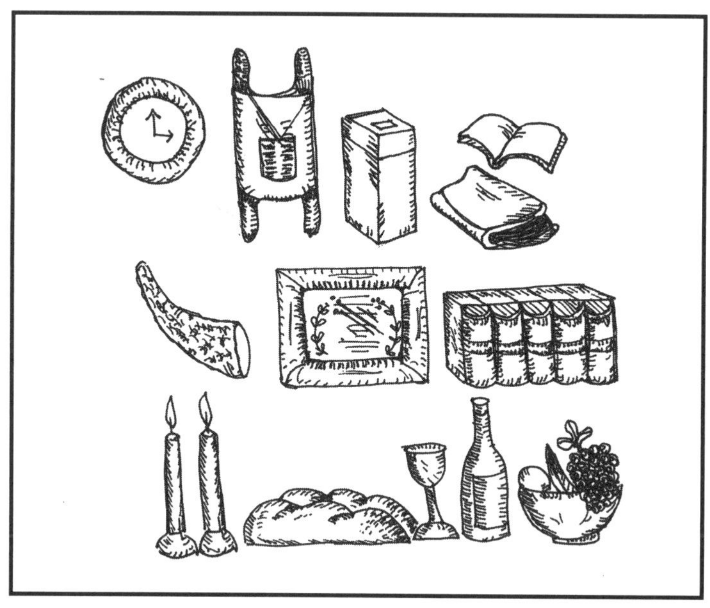

    - A child's bedroom decorated with a poster of a sunrise and colorful birds saying thanks for the new day, a washing cup and basin, a *sefer Tehillim* (book of Psalms), and a mitzvah chart. For a boy, a Shabbat suit draped over a chair, and for a girl, a pretty dress for Shabbat hanging in the closet

- The basement or storage area that shows boxes of Pesach dishes, Purim costumes, Sukkah decorations, and family treasures

Once you have chosen your subject and emphasis, you can get started.

OPTION 1: DRAW WITH MARKERS AND WATERCOLOR PENCILS AGES 6+, WITH OPTIONS FOR 4½+

Materials:

The materials depend on the project option you choose below, but here are some general materials:

- Copy paper, size 8½ x 11 inches (21 x 30 cm) or 11 x 16 inches (30 x 42 cm) or quality art paper (thick-ply Bristol or watercolor paper, if using watercolor pencils or gouache)
- Pencil and eraser
- Sharpener
- Fine-tipped roller-ball pen, waterproof
- Markers, fine and regular widths
- Watercolor pencils with or without water and brushes (optional)
- Note: Colored pencils that come with a small paintbrush on the handle can be used with water.
- Paintbrushes, ¼ and ½ inch (½ and 1½ cm), the best quality possible (fur, real, or synthetic)
- Gouache or tempera paint: red, blue, yellow, and white (optional for ages 4½ plus)

Directions:

1. Plan the picture. With a pencil and several sheets of practice paper, try out a variety of scenes or versions of the house. Break the process of drawing into small steps, beginning with the main

object, then adding the background, and finally, filling in the details. Practice drawing any difficult objects based on examples, step-by-step instructions, or demonstrations.

2. Once you sketched what you want to draw, it's time for repetition: With the pencil, make another practice drawing on another sheet of paper (you can use better-quality paper at this point). Draw lightly in pencil.

3. One more time, pencil over the light lines that you want to keep and ignore the lines that you don't want.

4. With a fine-tipped roller-ball pen or fine-tipped marker, ink over the pencil lines that you want to keep. If you come to a part that you don't want to include, erase it, and if you want to fix something, redraw it with the pencil and then go over it again with ink.

5. Erase any remaining pencil lines.

6. Color in the shapes and background with markers and watercolor pencils. You can use markers for small places, and watercolor pencils with water for larger areas. First draw with the watercolor pencil. Go over the pencil with extra water on the brush to spread the color.

Optional: For small children ages 4½+, use gouache paint (red, blue, yellow, and white) on an 11 x 16-inch (28 x 41-cm) paper. Give them one color at a time to prevent the colors from turning into mud.

OPTION 2: CREATE A PAINTING AGES 9+

1. Follow steps 1–5 in option 1.

2. In place of markers or watercolor pencils, use gouache or acrylic paint or a combination of all four to color in your picture. Acrylic paint alone or mixed with gouache is thicker and denser than watercolor. It is opaque, unlike watercolors which can be transparent. Use ⅛, ¼, and ½-inch soft natural hair brushes. Be careful to paint with the right size brush. Use a small brush or the watercolor pencils in the small areas. Decide which colors to use for different parts of the drawing. For older children, you can practice mixing the colors to produce different hues. Combine

primary colors (red, yellow, blue, white) to make the rest of the basic colors:

- Orange = red + yellow
- Purple = blue + red
- Green = blue + yellow
- Brown = 3 drops yellow + 2 drops red + 1 drop blue
- Add white for pastel tints.
- Add dark blue for shading.

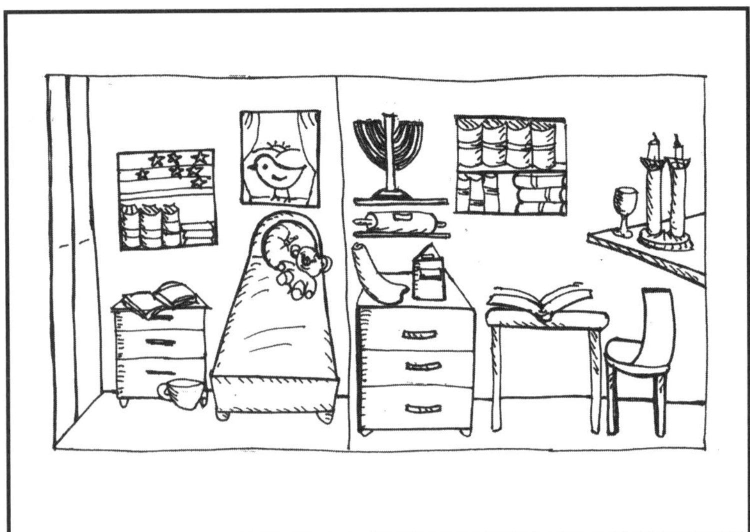

3. Use the original or self-mixed colors to fill in the drawing. First outline the shapes and objects over the pen lines with paint, and then fill them in. Try to stay inside the lines, but don't worry if the paint goes over a bit. Use a fine-pointed paintbrush or a small, flat, stiff brush for more control.

OPTION 3: MAKE A HOUSE (A THREE-DIMENSIONAL CONSTRUCTION) AGES 5+

Children love building and decorating houses. I can't emphasize enough how children of all ages love designing their larger-than-Playmobil-size houses. This project involves some preparation in advance so that the kids can begin right away with designing and decorating the house.

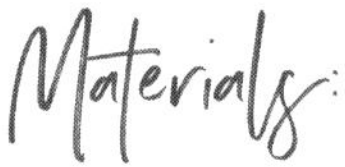

- Styrofoam sandwich board, 36 x 6 inches (91 x 15 cm), enough for four walls, a floor for each story, and a roof at the top of the house
- Pencil
- Metal ruler
- Colored markers: medium and thick

- Tempera or gouache paint and paintbrushes
- Styrofoam sandwich board or cardboard
- Hot-glue gun
- Air-drying synthetic clay
- Utility knife and a protective cutting surface

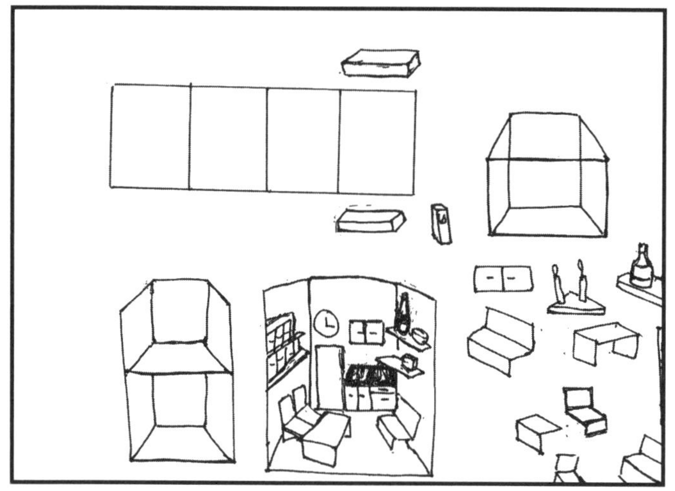

Directions:

1. In advance, decide on the height, width, and depth of the house. Try 6 x 6 inches (15 x 15 cm) for equal height, width, and depth for each of the four walls, floor, and the roof. For a two-story house, add on a second room on top of the first floor. An open-front house will need only three walls, while a closed-front house will need four walls with cut-out windows and doors.

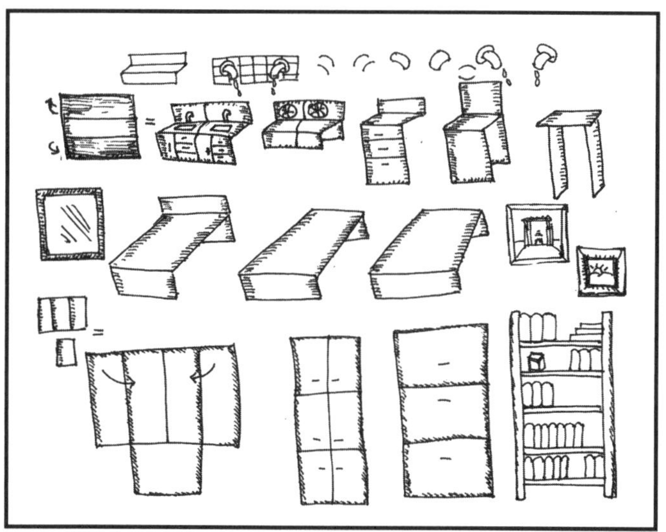

2. For the walls, measure and cut out one long piece of 6 x 24-inch (15 x 61-cm) Styrofoam sandwich board for all the walls. Mark three fold lines every 6 inches and make a cut halfway in; then bend the piece into four walls. Measure and cut out doors and windows.
3. Measure and cut out the floor and roof. For a pointed roof, measure and cut two squares of a suitable size and attach together to create an upright triangle. Then attach a triangular cutout for the back of the house (you will need one more for a closed-front house).
4. Draw lines to represent tiles (or other decorative touches) on the floor.

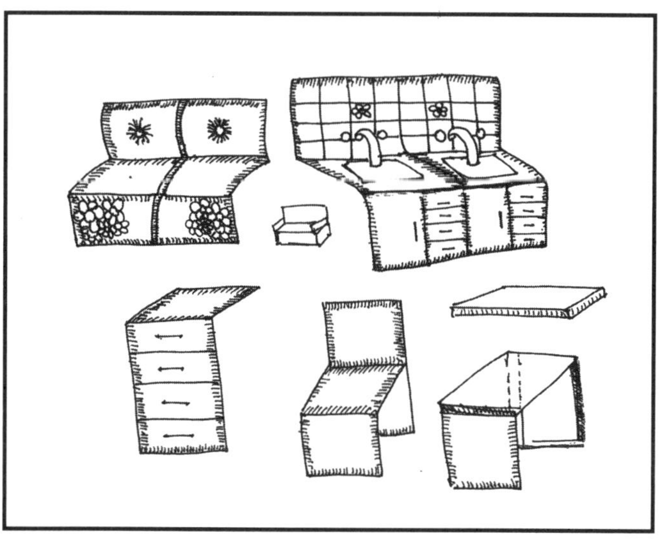

Color in with markers, alternating black and white or another color scheme.

5. Paint the outside of the house with tempera or gouache paint. The inside can also be painted with the gouache or tempera. Color the doors and windows. Trees, flowers, grass, stones, and birds can be first drawn and colored on paper, and then cut out and glued in place or painted directly onto the outside of the house.

6. Next, add decorations and details:

    - Make furniture out of Styrofoam sandwich board: a table, kitchen counter, cabinets, a triangular shelf that fits in the corner for Shabbat candles, a couch, beds, a desk, and a bookcase.
    - Draw and color in other details with markers or pens: a name plaque, door handle, mailbox, plants, and butterflies.
    - Picture frames can be made out of 2 x 2-inch (5 x 5-cm) cutouts. Draw frames and add pictures or a mirror.

    You can also craft the details out of air-drying synthetic clay: Shabbat candles, two challahs, books, mezuzot, and a bowl of fruit. When these are dry, you can paint them. Older children can use acrylic paint for a glossy look.

7. Glue all the pieces together with the hot glue. Save the mezuzot for last as the finishing touch!

In Summary: The Four Elements of Art

- One way to study how to create a pleasing composition is to study "compositions" in nature.
- A composition primarily contains four elements or building blocks: choice of subject, materials, skill and expression, and the message.

- When working with children, consider which of the elements of a composition to emphasize.
- Focusing on one element can reinforce the development of the other elements.
- The difference between a great work of art and a mediocre one is the unique expression of the artist and the details.
- To create a successful composition, break up the projects into steps, give simple and clear instructions, offer two or three options, use repetition, and have a backup project.
- Make sure to keep basic materials in stock to keep your options open.

Questions and Wonder

1. Why is the Jewish home filled with so many possibilities for presentation?
2. Think of three different ways you can depict a Jewish family. How would you arrange the subjects? What is important to show? What materials would you use? What style of expression would go with your message?
3. What do you like to emphasize in your artwork? Do you choose the story, subject, colors, light, or shading?

19 The Tools of Art

A great subject isn't enough to create art. You also need the right tools and materials to bring your vision to life. Each artist has his favorite materials or medium that he uses for expression. Each tool has its own uses and requires its own special technique to bring about the desired effect.

Let's take a look at some of the tools of art and how to use them.

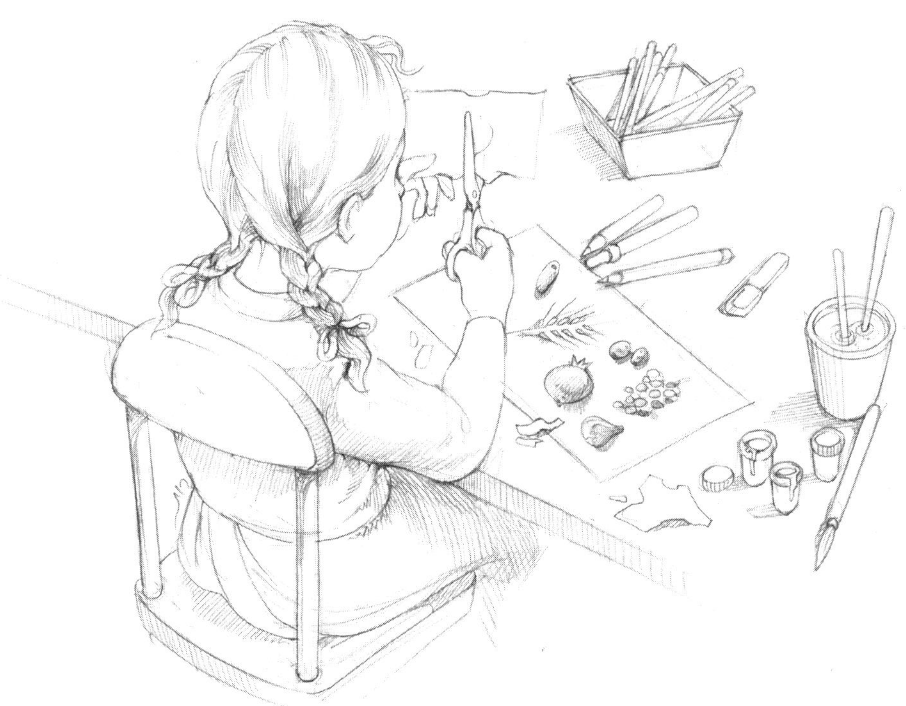

The Pencil, Marker, and Chalk: Get Ready for Drawing!

Let's start with the pencil. The pencil produces lines: straight and curved, whole and broken, soft and hard. It combines simplicity and complexity in one basic versatile tool; we can use it for sketches (quick drawings or preliminary drawings) or a detailed and fine piece of finished artwork.

The pencil allows us to engage our imagination. In the days of black-and-white photographs, people guessed what color clothing the people in the photos were wearing. They matched up the greens in their mind's eye with the trees captured on the black-and-white film. The absence of color allowed people to make associations based on their experiences and knowledge. They were able to take an active role in viewing the photographs. The humble pencil drawing allows this same active dynamic between the finished drawing and the viewer.

Notes and Sketches

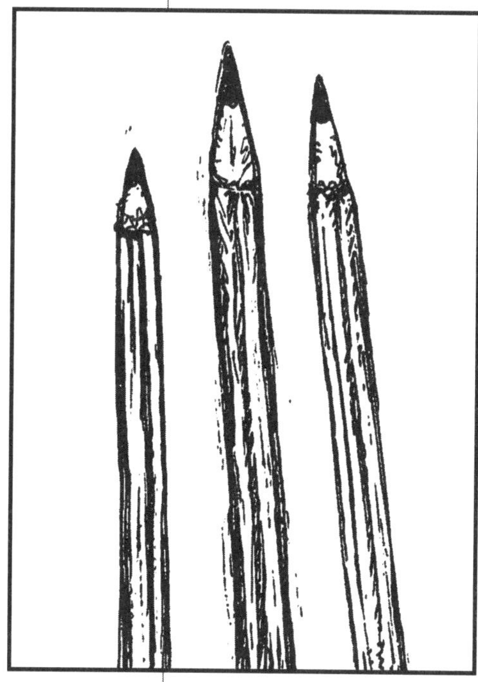

On a basic level, the pencil is essential for drawing sketches to map out what you want your artwork to look like. A pencil line is erasable—you can make changes as you plan your drawing. A pencil is a basic extension of the hand, freeing us from inhibitions as we put our thoughts and emotions to paper.

Pencils come in many varieties, providing different effects as we draw. Pencil standards vary according to the manufacturer. It is good to try out a variety and settle on pencils that express your images best. Pencils are graded according to hardness; the scale is 9H , 8H , 7H...2H, F, HB, B, 2B, 3B, 4B...9B. H is for hard, B is for black, HB is hard and black, F is fine or firm. 9H is the hardest while 9B is the softest. Hard is usually light, while soft is usually dark and blacker. The #2 or HB school pencil is the standard for writing and all-around usage but we are not limited to it. The soft B's are used for drawing and sketching, and the hard H's are used for technical line drawings. Line up the pencils and imagine a piano keyboard and note the simultaneous range of sound and the range of light to dark and hard to soft.

Pencils are often made with graphite inside the wood casing. The soft graphite is mixed with clay to harden and strengthen the pencil but it can be made with other kinds of materials, too. There are black ebony pencils, lead or carbon pencils, watercolor-combined-with-graphite pencils, colored pencils, pastels, chalks, and charcoals. Pencils may be sharpened with sandpaper, a knife, or a pencil sharpener.

Pencils come in a variety of colors. Colored pencils can be used to make lines and to fill in areas of color. There are colored pencils that can be combined with a brush and water to create a wash or a gentle blending of colors. (A small paintbrush on the wooden handle indicates that the pencils can be used with water as well.)

Notes and Sketches

Pencils or markers are best used in one direction: up and down, side to side, or diagonally, corner to corner. Even and parallel marker strokes fill in the outlined space smoothly and completely. This feat comes with time and practice.

A marker is made from ink or dye that is injected into a slim cylinder and placed inside of a barrel (that we hold). A nib or tip at the point releases a controlled amount of ink. The ink or dye is made from a combination of a coloring agent or pigment and chemicals. The tip, which was originally made from felt, is now made from a synthetic heated powder. Tips come in a wide assortment of widths from fine to wide and produce flowing lines that make drawing and coloring so easy and popular. Markers come in washable, semi-permanent, and permanent ink in an array of brilliant colors. Using markers requires pencil control yet comes along with the convenience of an even flow of liquid color. I prefer markers over crayons from the age of two and a half to three years (with supervision) because of the intensity of the color and its high level of drawing control.

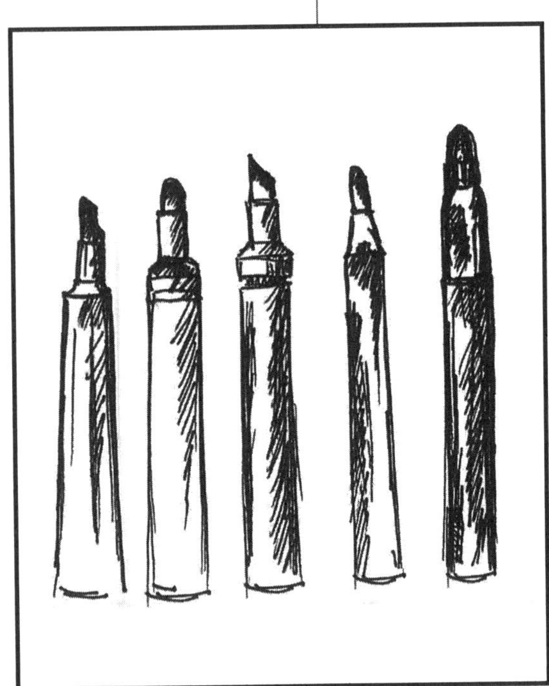

Pastels, compressed chalks, and Conté crayons are fine chalky colors pressed into a hard drawing stick and can be applied with varying degrees of pressure and rubbed in with the fingers or rubbing tools, such as chamoix (pieces of thin leather), erasers, or stomps (special paper rolled in the shape of a pencil for easy rubbing). Spraying a coat of fixative (a clear spray workable sealant) on a finished layer allows you to add a second layer for a deeper and richer effect. (Always use spray outdoors, following the directions on the can.)

Charcoals can be applied similar to pastels and chalks. They come in various shades of black, shaped as pencils, or drawing sticks and resemble burnt black wooden sticks. Spray with acrylic fixative to prevent the charcoal from rubbing off.

Crayons, made from wax, are a favorite at home and in preschools because they are convenient and clean. The multitude of bright, engaging colors commercially available is wonderful to behold. The downside is that they don't offer versatility in hand pressure or allow for subtle variations. The crayon colors are also muted. Crayons are best for children ages two to four years old, when control and cleanliness are an issue.

Though children ages five and up can make finished drawings with crayons, they'll miss out on practicing hand pressure and blending if using this medium. Crayon (and soft pencil) techniques that do allow for hand pressure are found in activities of crayon rubbings. A leaf, coin, or other raised surface is placed under a thin sheet of paper. The surface of the paper is rubbed with the side of the crayon until a reproduction of the object appears.

Oil pastels (called "pandas" in Israel) give a paint-like effect with vivid colors. The colored sticks are made up of pigment (color), wax binders, and non-drying oil. Colors can be built up in layers, blended, and rubbed together or even polished with a wool cloth. Though they wash off the hands with soap, they are not thinned with water, yet can be used with small amounts of turpentine or linseed oil in a project. The term water soluble means it mixes, thins, and cleans with water. Non-water-soluble materials require turpentine or another solvent.

The Pencil Grip

Little children, whose motor skills are not yet refined, may find the technique of holding a pencil elusive. Teaching them how to do it correctly will strengthen the fine-motor muscles in their hands and fingers, and also give them invaluable pre-writing skills in a nonthreatening environment.

Let's learn how to do a proper pencil hold.

Have on hand a few sheets of copy paper, a pencil, and both a fine-tipped and broad-tipped black marker. In this exercise, we're going to demonstrate how the size of a line or circle changes based on the hand and finger positioning.

1. Have the children gather around and watch you demonstrate how to hold the pencil. With the side of your hand stationary on the table, position a pencil in a writing hold between the thumb and forefinger. Position the second finger directly under the first finger. Make sure that your hand remains still and doesn't lift up.
2. Hold the pencil forward with the fingers stretched straight out and make a half-circle on the paper. Point out how the radius of the circle that you made is a few inches wide. Now curve your

fingers toward yourself and make another half-circle. Point out that the radius is about half the size of the first semicircle, which you made when your fingers were straighter.

3. After you demonstrate this exercise, ask the children to do the same. Experimenting with both writing positions (fingers stretched and curled), have them draw five to ten straight lines and circles without lifting their hand off the paper. Demonstrate, and then have them form boxes and angles by changing the direction of the lines and intersecting them. They can then combine lines, circles, squares, and other shapes to make objects or designs.

4. Now, have the children repeat the directions, this time occasionally lifting the hand and arm from the paper at the same time. When the hand returns to the paper, be sure it stays firmly on its side for stability.

5. Repeat the directions again—this time while standing at the table. Hold the pencil as described above, and use the pinkie (fifth finger) to balance the hand and keep constant contact with the paper. The shoulder, arm, hand, and fingers should work in unison, all moving either backwards or forwards at the same time to produce a line.

6. Repeat all the exercises with fine- and wide-tipped markers. See how the resulting lines vary in size and scale.

When the finger movements are isolated, they produce a small radius (curve) of lines and circles. You can make the radius bigger by including wrist action, and enlarge it even more by using the elbow. To make the widest possible curve, use the whole arm and hand, beginning with the shoulder.

Now try this:

1. As in the previous exercise, rest your hand on its side and make several tiny lines or circles using a regular drawing hold: holding the pencil between your thumb and first and second fingers. Without moving your hand off of the table, let only the finger open and close as you draw.

2. Now, allow the wrist and finger joints free movement. Holding the pencil in the regular drawing position, make several

medium-sized lines or circles. At the same time, the lower arm and the elbow rest on the table and don't move.

3. This time, let the entire arm and elbow move freely, along with the wrist and finger joints. Hold the pencil in the regular drawing position and make several large lines or circles.

4. Try this both sitting and standing: Hold the drawing tool comfortably and move the entire shoulder, arm, hand, and fingers in a large circular motion to make several gigantic lines or circles. This is also a great technique for working with paintbrushes on wall murals or easel paintings.

As children master the pencil hold, experiment with other types of writing tools. Let the children practice making straight lines, curves, and flourishes using markers, flat square-tipped paintbrushes, ballpoint pens, felt-tipped pens of various widths or special calligraphy markers.

> *Julie wanted to be able to draw grass. Not just a row of thin, upside-down V shapes that children draw automatically. She wanted to draw blades of grass with a variety of heights, curves, directions, and thicknesses.*
>
> *"But I can't do it," she insisted. "My hand won't let me."*
>
> *I checked her pencil hold. It turned out that she used a crossover grip, crossing her thumb over the top of the pencil—which limited her control possibility. Because she really wanted to draw realistic shades of grass, she was willing to try a new pencil hold. I showed her how to hold the pencil properly, near the top joint of the index fingertip and to rest it on the thumb and third finger for support. Now she would have more control and fluidity.*
>
> *Julie wanted to make the blades of grass appear like they were blowing in the wind. I showed her how to move the pencil with the gentle force of her shoulder and elbow, not only from her wrist and fingers. "Pull back your elbow from your shoulder and the pencil will move with you," I told her. She followed my directions and drew a beautiful, enchanting row of blades of grass.*

The Paintbrush: Explore the Options

Brushes are usually made from either natural fur or from nylon (synthetic). Generally, bristle brushes are used for oil, acrylic, and tempera paints. This type of brush is stiff and has a spring to it, making the paint appear full and textured on the paper or canvas. Watercolor, gouache, and ink brushes are soft and are used for applying the paint, blending colors, and creating details.

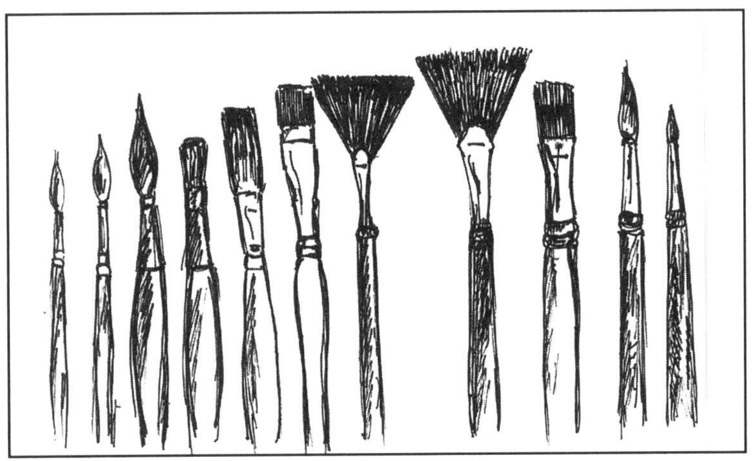

Depending on its size, quality, and type, the brush holds the color and acts as a reservoir that feeds the point, or end of the hairs. This means a good brush will absorb and hold the color until it is applied. The better quality the brush, the better your control over the paint and the desired effect. Lesser quality brushes don't always give the desired effect. (Yet there are times when old, stiff scratchy brushes are great to press lots of colored blobs on a tree to suggest leaves or to rub a dry look into an area of a painting.)

Most brushes have wooden handles and a ferrule (the nickel or metal loop that connects the hairs to the handle). The shape of a brush is either round, flat or pointed. There are also fine brushes for adding details, scrubbers, wash brushes, and calligraphy brushes. While not applicable to our goals, specialty brushes are available for those pursuing an advanced specific technique.

Flat, stiff, synthetic brushes are inexpensive and are easier for young children and beginners to use. They are good for learning to hold the brush properly and for filling in broad areas with color. To form a wide line, show the child how to hold a flat paintbrush with the wide side down on the paper. For a narrow line, he can delicately use the point of the brush or the side. He can also combine a wide and thin stroke in one letter or figure by changing the angle of the brush and the hand pressure.

Soft, watercolor brushes, are used for washes and transparencies (clear) with small amounts of paint and extra water, opaque (solid), fine lines, and blending. When using watercolors, the brush is heavily loaded with water and paint, so pressing it to the paper produces a wide line. When only the tip is loaded, and you draw with the "tippy-toe" of the brush, you create a fine, thin line.

Practice pressing the whole brush and lifting it until only the tip touches the painting surface. Use this press-and-raise motion several times while painting strokes to practice placing pressure and releasing it, thus allowing two variations within one stroke.

Once children feel ready to try different brushes, have them work with real, fur brushes in different sizes, and compare them to synthetic ones. See how the brushes glide or drag on the paper. Explore the fan brush with its spread-out "fingers" for waterfalls or grass, the scrubbers for texture, and the fine-pointed thin brushes for adding in the details. It is good to know what types of brushes exist. For our goals, standard-quality watercolor and inexpensive, school-quality, stiff brushes of several sizes are sufficient.

Paints: Fun with Color

A painting is made of three elements: (1) the support, or surface, on which the paint is applied, such as paper, canvas, or board; (2) the pigment, made from dry or liquid color that is applied to the surface; and (3) the binder, which holds the pigment to the support.

It is the binder that gives us our selection of the painting materials. Pigments mixed with an oil binder give us oil paints. Watercolors are made with a thick glue and can be thinned with water; tragacanth is a gum from a bush that is used to bind watercolor pigments. Egg tempera paints contain egg yolks as a binder. Here is a list of common coloring tools that give us the ability to add color to our art:

- **Crayons** are made with small amounts of pigments in a waxy binder and come in a stick form. Professional-grade crayons have more pigment and intensity than child-grade crayons. They are favorites for small children (and many adults!), especially toddlers and preschoolers, because they allow them to color without mess and don't require much control.

- **Oil pastel sticks** are bound with non-drying oil. Better-quality oil pastels have a higher content of pigment. Turpentine or linseed oil can be used to thin the pastels or make them into a paste.
- **Chalk pastels** are sticks of varying hardness made of soft powdery colors, usually held together with gum arabic (sap from the acacia tree) or gum tragacanth (sap from astragalus plants) and can be rubbed and blended. A fixative acrylic spray can be applied to prevent the pastels from rubbing off. Alternatively, frame the pastel under glass that is elevated slightly above the artwork to prevent rubbing.
- **Charcoal** comes in sticks, pencils, and powder of varying degrees of hardness and blackness. Charcoal is made from ground, organic materials mixed with a gum or wax binder. Try charcoal to increase contrast of lights, darks, and drama. It is black and not a color. Black and white images give us the chance to imagine the colors of the objects in the artwork. Frame or apply clear fixative to your finished work.
- **Oil paint**, as the name tells us, is made with oil. Linseed oil can be added, or you can thin it with turpentine. Oil paints are conducive to giving texture to a painting, and you can build up layers, allowing the previous layer to dry and adding more on top. Drying time depends on how thick the paint is and can be lengthy. After you are done, varnish can be applied as a protective coating.
- **Watercolor paint** is diluted with water. The paint is transparent (clear) and produces washes, small amounts of paint floating in a transparent pool of water. The watercolor can be made opaque by applying it in thick layers using little bits of water. This type of paint dries quickly.
- **Tempera or gouache** can be used alone or mixed with acrylics and is thinned with water. It is similar to watercolors, with added powdered chalk for opaqueness. This also dries quickly and is inexpensive and easy to use, making it a good choice for small children. I often use it as a base in a painting (or alone) and apply acrylic over it to intensify the colors.
- **Inks**, made from dyes or pigments, can be permanent or nonpermanent, resemble gouache or watercolors, but are usually more intense. The inks can be used straight from the bottle for intense color or diluted with water for washes. Inks dry quickly too.

- **Acrylic paints** imitate the look of oil paint, but have a plastic surface when dried. Like with oil paints, you can build up layers with acrylics, keeping in mind that acrylic paint dries quicker than the oil paint.

It's fun to experiment with different coloring tools and paints. See how different kinds of paints give a different feeling and expression to the same picture. Eventually you might decide you prefer one type of coloring tool over another. Work with it and practice until you become proficient with it.

Erasers: Not Just for Erasing

Erasers are not just for erasing—they're actually a great drawing tool, too. When you erase an area on a pencil, pastel, or charcoal drawing, you're not just removing a mark, you're "erasing in" the illusion of light! This is an age-old technique that children love learning.

There are actually three types of basic erasers: the white plastic eraser that most of us are familiar with, the gum eraser, and the kneaded eraser. The white plastic eraser is most popular for standard erasing and most commonly used in school. The gum eraser is soft and crumbles a little. It's used on soft surfaces and doesn't leave a mark on delicate paper. The kneaded eraser can be stretched and remolded like rubber when it becomes darkened from erasing charcoal or other dark materials, and it doesn't leave any crumbs. It's handy for giving you a clean surface when using it on charcoal or soft lead. Specialty erasers can be found in your art- or office-supply store.

Try out these effects to get the most out of your eraser:

On a sheet of paper, use the side of a pencil to make thick, shadowy lines. Cover a good part of the paper with the pencil marks, keeping the pencil almost horizontal and pressing down just enough to dispense the graphite. Now, rub an eraser over the shaded area several times as you like. This reveals clean areas of the paper and creates the effect of light. You can then draw over the erased-out (or lifted) areas to create a drawing, erasing more as needed.

Try the following examples of "erasing in" light:

1. Give an object a dramatic shine—draw a Kiddush cup, shade or color it in, and then erase a section on the side to imitate a shine.
2. "Erase in" light to create rays emanating from the *luchot* with Har Sinai as a backdrop.
3. Show light radiating from Shabbat candles, the menorah, the Beit Hamikdash, Torah scrolls, or a Lag BaOmer bonfire.
4. "Erase in" streams or pockets of powdered (dotted) particles of light emanating from an open window.
5. "Erase in" rays of light from the sun, moon, or a light fixture.
6. Show raindrops or snowflakes on a dark, cloudy sky.

Go further with the eraser—try using it to soften hard areas and give texture to solid areas. Press and rub gently to reduce dark lines and areas and bring up the white of the paper. A building, a forest, or a vase set in the background can be delicately downplayed with a few thoughtful sweeps of the eraser. Once the children get the knack, stir their imagination—ask them to suggest techniques and picture ideas for using the "erase-in" effect.

Rulers: To Use or Not to Use?

It's a classic complaint: "I'm no artist. I can't even draw a straight line."

The truth is that most of us can't draw a straight line perfectly. But with a bit of practice, you'll be amazed to see that you can come pretty close. Many people figure that they can't compete with a ruler so they may as well not bother, but this doesn't have to be the case.

From an early age in school, children are taught to use their rulers and erasers to make perfect markings, so it's no surprise that they become very dependent on these tools, even as adults. With a bit of guidance, practice, and confidence, you will be able to appreciate that the hand-drawn line has an imperfect grace of its own.

I won't deny that rulers are very useful. They are necessary at times to straighten and simplify. They're fun to use and provide immediate satisfaction. Adults use rulers for precision work—for technical accuracy, geometric designs, graphic art, lettering, advertising, illustrations, invitations, announcements, building models, pattern making, and for making straight edges and corners on products, such as picture frames.

Though rulers are used occasionally for specific projects in this book, let's first learn to use our natural and basic tools: the hand, arm, and shoulder. Teaching children how to draw a line without a ruler gives them great satisfaction and limits their dependency on rulers.

A line is drawn with the natural combined movements of the fingers, side and palm of the hand, wrist, arm, elbow, and shoulder. Children who have difficulty with this concept often feel the same insecurity about drawing without an eraser. It's worth giving these children extra support and attention because once they master this skill, they'll be able to draw a line anywhere with newfound freedom and confidence. You can remind them that God gave us arms that are versatile and capable—we just need to train them properly!

Here's how to draw a line without using a ruler:

1. Find a comfortable position either standing or sitting (try out both). Position the paper directly in front of you in the portrait position. Position your chair away from the table to leave room for your elbow to bend and move away from the table.

2. Hold the pencil in a regular drawing hold, between the thumb and the first and second fingers. Position the pencil at the top center of the paper and pull your elbow straight back from your shoulder, using the elbow as a guide. As you pull back your arm, press the pencil down on the paper and make a line, keeping your elbow parallel to the paper and letting your arm bend naturally.

3. To make long lines on a large piece of paper, an easel, or wall, lift your arm directly in front of you and draw in any direction. In this case, use your shoulder as well as your fingers as the guide.

The movements of the joints in the fingers, the wrist, the arm, the elbow, and the shoulder produce different-sized lines. This was also the case when we drew small lines and circles. When drawing a long straight line without a ruler, the focus is on the shoulder moving in its socket and pulling back the elbow. Long or large lines generate from the elbow and shoulder while short lines come from the use of the fingers and wrist.

Once the children become accustomed to drawing freehand lines without a ruler, you can give them a project that requires a ruler or compass without worrying that they will become dependent on these tools.

Here are some projects that will put some of the tools we discussed to good use. For in-depth information on the use of scissors, see chapter 21.

Drawing with an Eraser AGES 7+

An eraser is more than a tool to correct mistakes. Try it as a drawing tool with a twist.

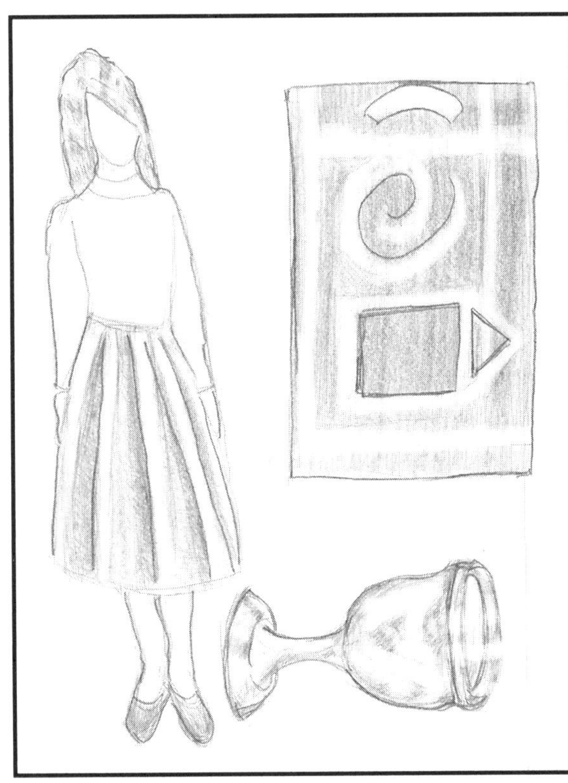

Materials:

- Paper, 8½ x 11 inches (21 x 28 cm) or larger
- 3 pencils: hard BH, medium 2B, and any specialty pencils you may have
- 3 types of erasers: plastic, gum, and stretch (used for charcoal)

Directions:

Draw shapes. First draw a 3 x 5-inch (8 x 12½-cm) rectangle. Fill it using the side of your pencil in an even pressure in one direction gently up and down a few times so no white paper shows and is filled with a medium to dark film. Use the corner of your eraser in place of a pencil. Press hard and "draw" three shapes: a square, a spiral and a triangle.

Draw a Kiddush cup. First draw the outline, then fill it in with the side of your pencil. Erase small areas (highlights) that you would like to be brighter or shiny.

Draw a girl's head with hair. Fill in softly with pencil, leaving the paper white in select places to resemble waves, curves, and curls in the hair. Erase in highlights and extra shine with the eraser.

Draw a girl's pleated skirt. Mark the length of the pleats (draw where the pleats will be). Fill in gently with the side of the pencil. Erase vertically (up and down) a line in the left side of each pleat. Pleats will have a dark, medium, and light vertical line.

Using an eraser makes shading easy.

Traditional Can Circles AGES 6+

This is a very basic, easy activity for little children. The focus of the project is recognizing the circle and practicing hand pressure with chalk or oil pastels.

Materials:

- Copy paper, size 8½ x 11 inches (21 x 30 cm)
- Pencil
- Colored markers or pencils
- Pastel chalks or oil pastels
- Tin can or cup for younger children, or compass for older children

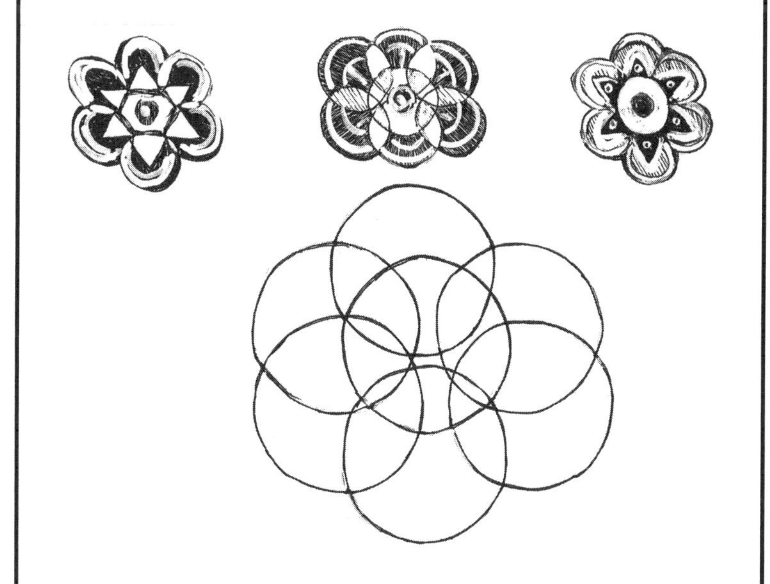

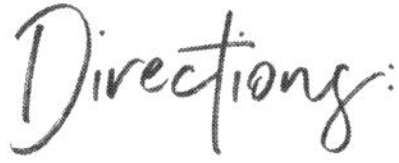

1. With the tin can, cup, or compass, make a pencil outline of a circle in the center of a sheet of paper.
2. Add six or eight overlapping circles around the outer edge of the center circle.
3. Draw freehand over the circles several times with different colored pencils or colored markers.
4. Color in each enclosed area with pastel chalks or oil pastels. Rub the color with the index finger in small circles for a smooth, even surface, or apply two or more colors next to one another or on top of one another. Rub with a finger to blend the group. (Alternatively, you can use colored markers, colored pencils, or watercolor paints

with a fine-tipped brush. Children like options that fit their tastes and often like to test the results of several mediums).

5. Now consider the background, to complete the drawing. Color the background in a color that is harder, softer, or has a similar intensity to the one used to fill in the circles. The background may be a dark, solid color in contrast to lightly colored circles, or reverse the effect with solid colors in the circles and light, airy colors for the background. If you choose to fill in the background with a color of the same intensity as the one inside the circles, the outlines in colored pencil or marker will stand out and create contrast.

6. Using the same technique as above, you can draw a flower: Draw the center circle and surround it with six to eight slightly larger circles. Refine, shade, and detail the shape of the flower. You can elongate the petals, add additional parts of the flower, or simply color in as is.

Optional: Children under six years old can draw overlapping circles freehand and color them in. Rather than relying on a can for accurate circles, they can enjoy producing their own freehand circles.

Patterns and Shapes AGES 8+

This is a great project for learning to control the brush and paint with consistency and variation, because the emphasis is not on the objects. It is a design project with emphasis on shape and patterns. The objects are traced in vague outlines, so the colors and shapes hold the eye, not the subject. I call this a practice project. The results are varied while the practice value is very certain. Its emphasis is the goal of sensitivity with shapes, brushes, and soft colors.

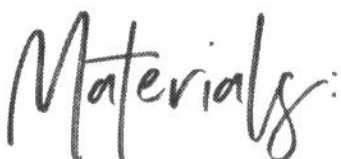

- Watercolor paper, Bristol, or art block paper, size 8½ x 11 inches (21 x 28 cm)
- Pencil
- Ruler
- Good quality watercolors, or if you prefer, tempera or gouache paint
- Fine watercolor paintbrush, ⅛, ¼ inch (¼, ½ cm) or smaller

Directions:

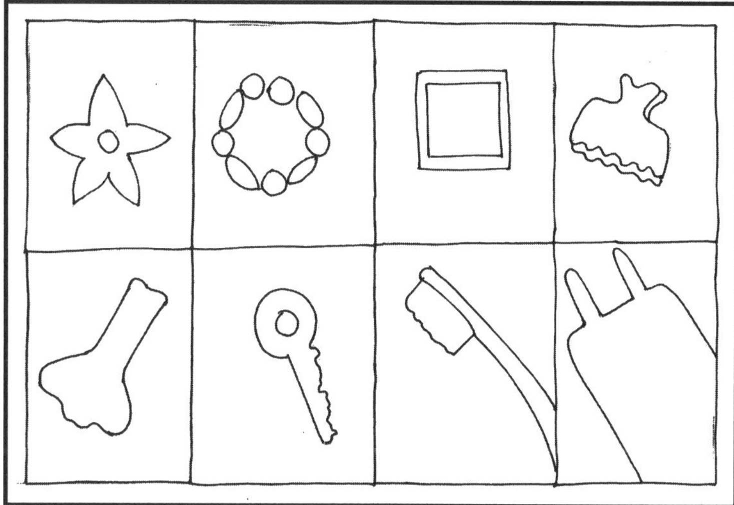

1. Mark off a 1-inch (2½-cm) frame around the edges of the entire paper. A frame-margin makes it easier to keep the paint/colors on the paper and not on the table.

2. Draw a grid within the framed area. With the pencil and ruler, draw three lines about 2½ inches (6 cm) apart across the paper lengthwise.

3. Now draw one line across the center of the paper grid. You will have eight equal squares. (For younger children, fold the paper in half three times to get eight squares and have them trace over the folds with the pencil.)

4. In each square, place a small object, such as a tiny cup, a small box or container, keys, beads, different-size coins, small toys, and other trinkets (choose objects that are flat or easy to trace). With the pencil, trace around the object to mark its shape. Repeat tracing the object a few times in other boxes for an interesting pattern. Repeat the pattern until each square is filled.
   Or, you can do this freehand. Look carefully at the object and find the main shapes of the objects you want to draw. For example:

   - A key is a circle connected to a thin long rectangle.
   - A button is a circle with four holes in the center.
   - A bottle cap is a circle.
   - A dice from a board game is a cube with two sides and one top showing; all the edges are rounded.

5. Now color in the objects: Outline each object carefully with paint before you fill in the color. Hold the brush lightly so that the tip of the brush is pointed and can make the fine outline. Keep the painted outlines a bit thick so there will be contrast later.

6. Now color in each shape with diluted watercolors (but not an overly wet brush). You may want to practice making the brush strokes on a separate sheet of paper until you can control the brush and paint. When filling in the shapes, use the flat part of the brush: lay the brush on its side so that the bristles spread out. Don't worry if some of the paint comes out thick and some is thin or watery. This "melting" look is sought after by artists because it shows variation of control, pressure, and emotion.

7. Carefully color in the background, giving each square its own color, or alternate colors to make a pattern, choosing complementary colors (yellow and purple, blue and orange, red and green).

Make Your Own Invitations AGES 7+

These invitations give you the opportunity to draw using the different tools we've learned about. You'll be dividing up the page in boxes like a multiplication table, and then drawing a picture appropriate to your theme (see the theme suggestions below). The concept here is to divide the card into squares in a grid form and draw pictures of your theme in the squares, repeating any if you like. Leave room in the center for the invitation announcement.

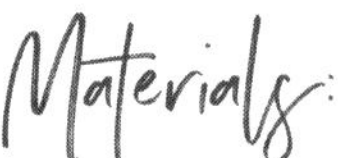

- Copy paper, size 8½ x 11 inches (21 x 30 cm) for practice drawings
- Pencil
- Ruler
- Fine-tipped colored markers, colored pencils, watercolors, or acrylics
- Fine-tipped black marker
- Fine-tipped watercolor brush, ⅛, ¼ inch (¼, ½ cm) or smaller
- Thick paper, Bristol paper or card stock, cut into 4 x 6-inch (10 x 15-cm) squares for a postcard-style invitation, or 6 x 8-inch (15 x 20-cm) squares if you are folding the cards in half
- Envelopes, the size of your choice to hold the card (4¾ x 6½ inches (12 x 16.5 cm) is standard envelope size in the United States, and 5 x 7½ inches (13 x 19 cm) is standard in Israel)

- Stamps, if you're sending the invitations in the mail (check if your size requires extra postage)

Directions:

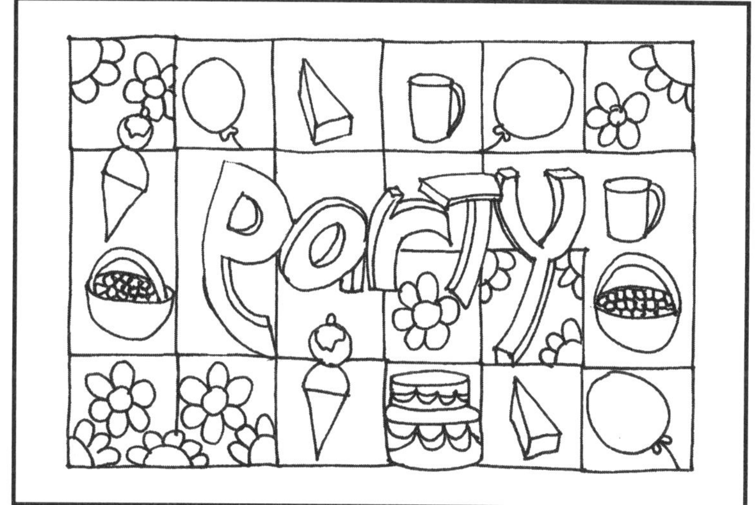

1. For the invitation, take one of the 4 x 6-inch cards or pieces of Bristol paper and mark four even rows of lines horizontally and six vertically with a pencil and ruler. You will have twenty-four 1-inch (2½-cm) rectangles filling up the page.
   For a folded card, use a 6 x 8-inch (15 x 20-cm) paper and fold back the top half (from the eight inches). Continue with step 1. You can write your message on the inside of the folded card.
2. Choose your theme from your special interests or hobbies, or according to the season or holiday time. Here are some theme suggestions:
   - Seasonal vacation scenes such as the seascape, a picnic, sunglasses with a sunhat and seashells, or a snowman
   - Food and desserts: ice cream, cakes, pastries, candies and flowers
   - Sports and recreational activities: games, races, boating, dancing, musical notes
   - Decorative designs: flowers, bows, animals, scroll work and borders (such as you would see on a medieval illuminated manuscript), numbers and letters
   - Themes from holidays: apples and honey, a tallit (prayer shawl) and shofar for Rosh Hashanah; masks and hamantaschen (triangular pastries named after Haman in *Megillat Esther*) for Purim

3. Before drawing the images in the rectangles, practice drawing each object that represents your theme on a separate sheet of copy paper.

4. With the pencil, draw the objects that represent your theme in the boxes that line the edge of the card or page, leaving the middle squares blank for the words of the invitation itself.[136] You can make the middle space as large as you want. You can also leave some of the outer boxes blank to give visual relief to the eye.

5. Trace over the objects with the fine-tipped black marker.

6. Now color in the pictures with the markers, colored pencils, or paints. Some tips:

    - Outline the inside of the objects with the color you chose before you fill them in completely. This will help you stay in the lines.
    - Color or paint repeatedly in one direction without scribbling.
    - Since paint requires a very fine brush and a steady hand to stay in the lines, it is a better medium for older or experienced children.

7. Color in some of the blank squares with a solid color. Just as before, outline the inside of the square and color it in smoothly, drawing or painting in one direction. You can also color in the middle, blank space if you want to have a color background for the words on the invitation (here it might be best to use a light shade of color).

8. You can make several invitations by hand or make one invitation and photocopy it. Make sure you have the right size envelopes. Fill the envelopes. Hand them out or mail them. Most of all, have fun!

In Summary: The Tools of Art

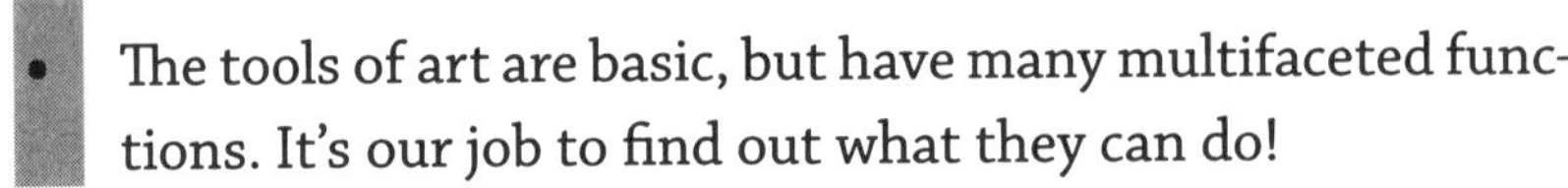

- The tools of art are basic, but have many multifaceted functions. It's our job to find out what they can do!

136 See ch. 22, "The Art of Lettering," for ideas on how to design the words.

- The pencil is the simplest but most versatile tool, used for a wide range of drawing techniques.
- A proper pencil hold is important for writing, drawing, and painting.
- Draw small circles by controlling the wrist and the fingers. Draw large circles using the shoulder and the entire arm.
- Brushes are made from natural fur or synthetic nylon. Use the best quality brush (typically fur) to give you the best control.
- Coloring tools come in the form of sticks and markers, pencils and paints, ranging from powder and dry to liquid and creamy.
- Paint and dyes were originally made from animals, plants, and minerals. Today, they are made from a combination of natural and synthetic ingredients.
- Erasers wipe a drawing and writing surface clean. They can also be used to "erase in" shade and light.
- You can make a freehand line without a ruler by using your shoulder and arm to guide the hand.

Questions and Wonder

1. What do you think "the tools of art are extensions of our hands" means?
2. How does a good quality paintbrush help you to improve your artwork? What does control mean?
3. Do you like to paint because it is wet and sometimes messy or to draw because it is dry and clean?

20 The Joy of Mixing Color

Before I present projects to a child or adult, I love to share the joys of color. Color results from the human eye interacting with light waves. Without light, we wouldn't be able to see the magnificent world around us in all its beautiful colors.

Understanding color is an art in itself. Take time to use color alone without worrying about drawing objects or figures. Simply paint and mix as many new colors as you like. That's right—only color. No pictures. This simple technique frees you from inhibitions and gives you a real sense of how color works in art.

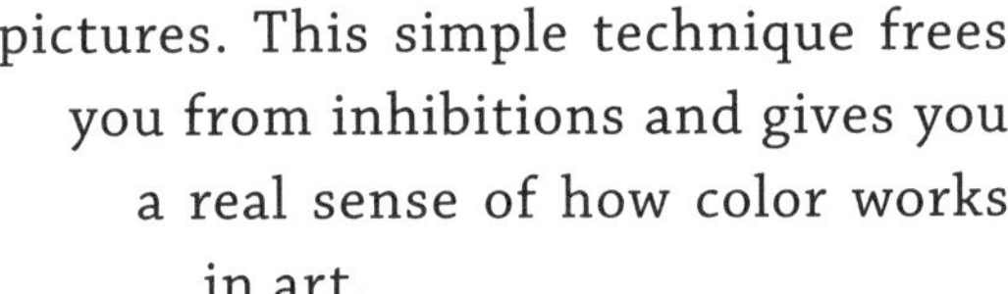

So sweep the brush across the paper without concerns for perfection. Let yourself and your child fill with wonder and excitement as you watch colors emerge from the paintbrush. Immerse yourself in... the world of color.

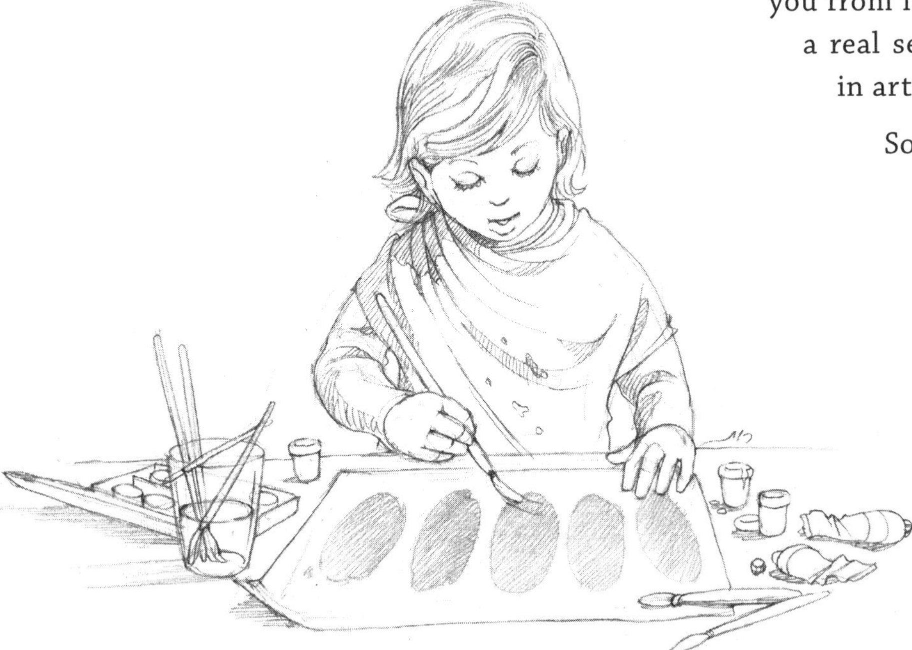

The World of Color

Notes and Sketches

Your line drawing is finished. Now you can use color to complete the picture. But keep in mind that some pictures are complete in all their glory without color. See if the black-and-white sketch looks finished on its own. Color is not always needed.

If you decide color is called for, don't limit yourself to colors that come straight out of the bottle. The pure pleasure of mixing two or more colors together and watching the results is like watching creation taking place. When we mix our own colors, the surprises are endless and the world of color comes alive.

The basic colors are red, blue, and yellow. Measured combinations of these colors produce most of the other colors in the world. Isn't that wonderful? From only three colors we can make a rainbow!

The basic set of colors—red, blue, and yellow—are called "primary colors." From red, blue, and yellow, we make the next group called "secondary colors": orange from yellow and red, purple from blue and red, and green from yellow and blue. Open up new horizons by seeing how many colors you can make from the three basics. There are infinite color combinations we can make by adding or subtracting just a few drops of color. Each additional drop of color changes the hue. Brown is made from approximately three parts yellow, two parts red, and one part blue. More red makes for a redder brown. More yellow makes a greener brown.

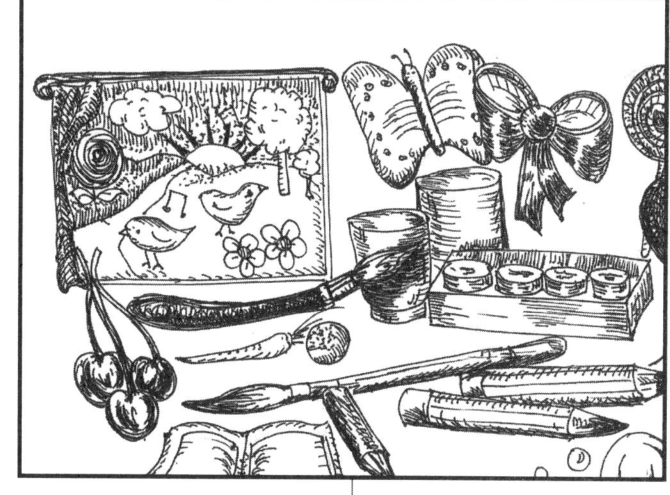

Try mixing light blues with yellows in various proportions—and then do the same with dark blues—to make green shades. Mix light blue and small amounts of green for turquoise. Add large amounts of blue to the green for a dark green. Add white for a mint green.

To make tints, or pastel shades, add white. Use black or dark blue for variety, to create darker colors and for shading. When black is mixed with other colors, it can result in a muddy tone. Use very little black, a small drop to a teaspoon of other color.

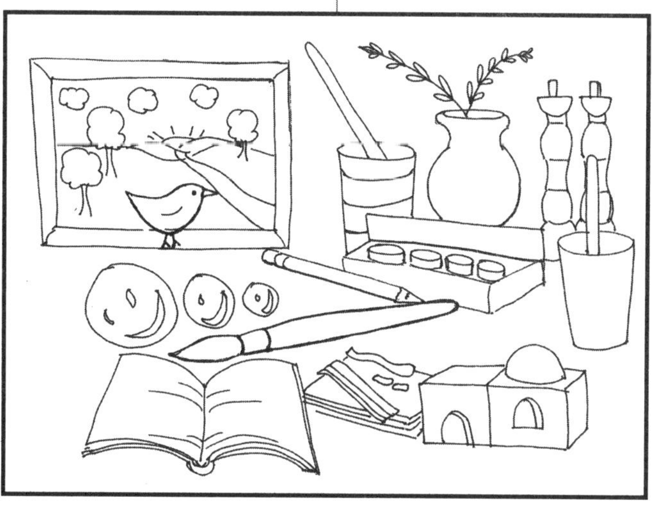

Notes and Sketches

In any case, it's better not to give black to young children to paint with except for specific real-life black objects such as a black *kippah*. Some children will gravitate to black and won't want to expose themselves to the wonders of color if left on their own. For others, it represents negative emotions that you may not want to evoke right now. Regardless of the reason, using black will distract children from trying out new color combinations.

As a child of eight, I spent several weeks in bed recuperating from two operations: the removal of my appendix and my tonsils. I was given a set of play dough in four basic colors to keep me busy. Play dough was new on the market at the time, and I loved the novelty of it.

I spent hours mixing bits of the dough into every combination possible. A slight change in the proportions of one color would create another delightful color. I made little balls in varying colors and shades, flattened them, and then attached them one by one until the chain grew into seventy pieces of harmonious colors, each one a surprise. I arranged the colors in sequence. The flow of the "scales" of color added to the wonder.

How Are Colors Made?

In bygone days, it was common for artists to mix their own colors. They took great pride in their techniques for creating paints best suited to their artistic vision. We have masterpieces from history carefully preserved in museums or those that stood up to time on their own, with their color as rich as ever.

The colors they created came from nature, literally. They would take minerals, plants, various types of insects, and animal matter to create pigment. Pigment is a color in its pure form. The pigment would be mixed with a binder, such as clay, oil, or egg yolks, to make it stick to the painting surface. A thinner such as alcohol or turpentine was then added. For example, oil paint, as its name suggests, is made with oil as a binder.

Nature has its way of mixing elements (animal, mineral, and vegetable) from the earth with heat, cold, and time. Certain blues found in nature may be a compound of copper, a mineral, and lapis lazuli, a semiprecious stone. Ultramarine blue contains ground-up lapis lazuli. In ancient times, a special sky-blue dye called *techeilet* was used to dye the strings of tzitzit. Though the exact origin of the dye is unknown today, we know that the dye came from a type of water snail.

Mixing the paint ingredients in the old days, like everything else, took time. Today, access to ready-made materials lends itself to immediate and quick artwork for all ages and purposes.

Most commercial paints are combinations of minerals and other natural substances mixed with manmade synthetic materials. This makes for more durable and long-lasting colors. Ask a chemist and he will explain the properties of the materials and how they hold the pigment together and create the effects of transparency (see-through) or opaqueness (solid).

Today's paints are made to last (when applied according to directions). There are paints that are light resistant, withstand humidity, and will retain their richness for a long time to come. Still there is something special about being able to mix your own paint colors.

You can make your own pigments with:

- coffee, tea, or cocoa powder for browns
- onion skins for tans
- beets for red
- cranberries for pink
- carrots for orange
- grass for green
- daffodils or turmeric (a spice) for yellow

To make your own pigment, boil each ingredient in a small amount of water in a separate pot until the color comes alive and is thick enough for paint. The pigment will be released from the plant when boiled. Let cool and pour into muffin tins. Try mixing the prepared color with an egg yolk or liquid starch to thicken. The result will be transparent and delicate. Now bring out your paper or canvas and have fun painting!

Color Schemes

Mixing colors is just one side of the coin. Besides the chemistry behind the making of the colors, there is also the way colors appear near one another. Certain color combinations work harmoniously, while others don't work well together.

A color wheel can help you decide which colors to pair together. A color wheel is a six-pointed star (created from two triangles or the Star of David) inside of a circle. Red, blue, and yellow—the primary colors—are on the tips of the upright triangle. Orange, purple and green—the secondary mixtures of red, blue, and yellow—are on the tips of the down pointed triangle.

The three sets of complementary colors that are at opposites on the color wheel do just that: They complement and bring out the best in one another. Red and green, for example, are a very strong combination; think red pepper on green lettuce leaves. Blue and orange are a great team, as are yellow and purple. When you get stuck trying to figure out which colors to use together, start with the primary colors—red, blue, or yellow—and add their complementary colors in a few places near the primary color. See the difference. The picture will start to come alive.

If you decide to stick with one color, in shades from light to dark, along with the colors adjacent to it on the color wheel, it is referred to as monochromatic color. For example, beige, brown, and tan are monochromatic, as are pink, red, and orange- or purple-red. A mountain made up of monochromatic colors might include beige, brown, and tan. An orange, red, and pink sunset is another example of God's color palette.

The Language of Color

Let's review some of the terms that relate to color in this chapter. Knowing the words will help you define what you want to do when you paint or use color in art:

Complementary color—three specific sets of two colors that create a strong contrast and look harmonious together: red and green, yellow and purple, blue and orange; when a set is mixed, it forms a neutral gray.

Cool color—colors that recede into space and represent a cool atmosphere: blue, green, and violet.

Hue— the name of a color derived from one of the twelve basic colors.

Monochromatic—one color or one color scheme with adjacent colors, such as brown, beige, and tan or yellow, yellow-orange, and orange.

Primary color— red, blue, and yellow.

Saturation—the amount of pigment in a color; the more pigment, the higher the saturation.

Secondary color—the three colors that result from combining the primary colors: green, orange, and purple.

Shade—a color mixed with black or dark blue.

Tint—a color mixed with white.

Value—the scale of light to dark. Imagine a row of twelve squares beginning with white, gradually darkening to black.

Warm color—colors that project into space and represent a warm flavor: red, yellow, and orange.

Here are some projects you can do to explore the world of color.

Monochromatic Still Life AGES 7+

A one-color painting that teaches how to mix values (on a scale of 1 to 5 from light to dark) of any color.

Materials:

- Bristol or all-purpose art paper for water, 11½ x 16 inches (30 x 40 cm)
- Pencil
- Paint: blue and white gouache or acrylic paint. Sturdy cup with water, paper towels, and paper to mix the paint on.
- Paint brushes: ⅛ inch (¼ cm), ¼ inch (½ cm) and ½ inch (1½ cm)

Directions:

1. Draw the still life. See illustrated steps.
2. Mix five batches of paint on the paper: pure white, ¾ white and ¼ blue, ½ white and ½ blue, ¾ blue and ¼ white, pure blue. Draw 2 x 2-inch (5 x 5-cm) circles on the paper and mix the colors inside the circles.
3. Paint light colors next to dark colors for contrast.

Bowls and vases: divide vertically into three sections with a light color in the center surrounded by medium tint and a darker tint next to it to give it a curved shape. Round fruit: divide horizontally with the lightest color at the top.

Option: Do a second painting with your choice of colors.

Heavens and Earth: An Illustration of the Beginnings of Creation AGES 4½+

This is a great project for young children who are interested, three and a half and older.

The child will paint the heavens and earth and then add dots to represent the Shabbat lights. If your little artist wants to fill the whole paper in with one set of colors, simply provide a second paper and glue together (with his permission) for the contrasting light colors to represent heaven. He can also add people, animals, mountains, or plants by drawing them in or making cutouts and gluing them in place.

Before you start, talk about the massive expanse of light and darkness that were created on the first day, and the separating of the earth from the waters on the second day.[137] Let the child imagine what it must have been like and then express it on paper. Each child will do it at their level.

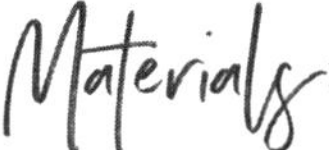

- Paper, size 11 x 16 inches (28 x 41 cm) or larger for tabletop work or on easels, or a wide roll of butcher paper for making murals
- Pencil
- Gouache or tempera paints in blue, white, and yellow
- Paintbrushes, ½ inch (1½ cm) for tabletop work; 1½–2 inch (4 x 5 cm) for mural work
- Masking tape or Scotch tape
- Scissors, colored markers, and white plastic glue to make cutouts of people, animals, mountains, or plants to glue on to dried paintings (optional).

Note: Use brushes that are comfortable to hold and respond to the child's directives.

137 Genesis 1:6–8.

Directions:

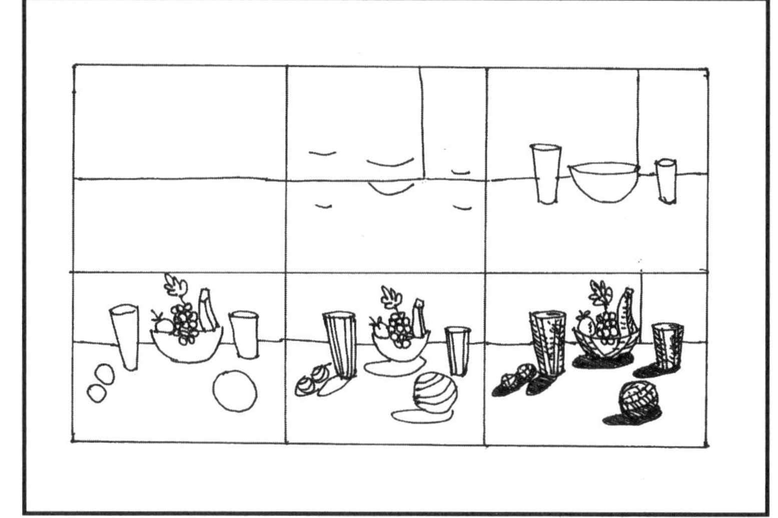

1. Tape the paper to the table or attach to an easel. Or cover a large wall in your garage or outdoors with a giant sheet of butcher paper and attach with masking tape.
2. With a pencil, mark four points, one in each corner, and connect the dots to make a frame around the edge, about 1 inch (2½ cm) thick. The frame is to encourage painting within a boundary when possible.
3. Draw a horizontal line from one side of the paper to the other, a bit higher than the center of the paper, dividing the heavens and the earth.
4. Place amounts of blue and white paint directly on the top half of the paper. Add more paint as needed.
5. Fill in the heavens (the top half of the paper). Brush the paint back and forth, staying inside the frame. Mix the white into the blue paint completely or partially to create different shades of blue. Use only white for the clouds.

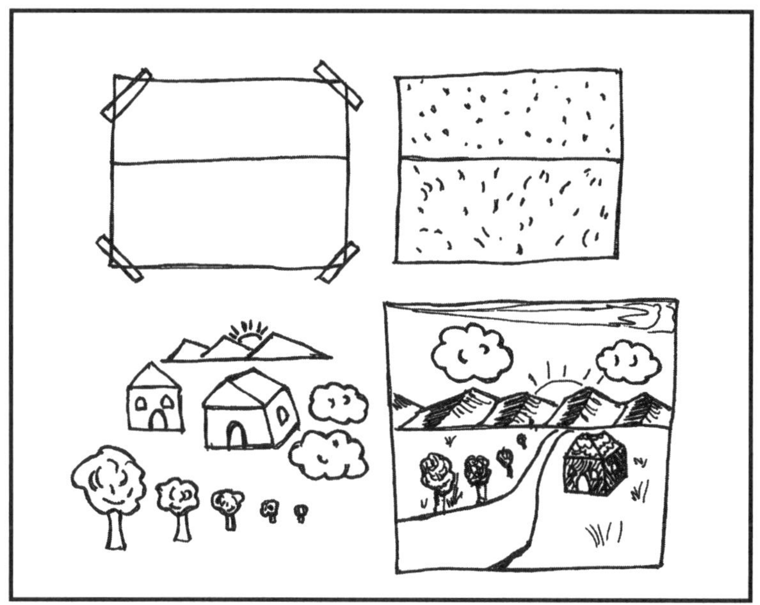

6. Fill in the land, mixing blue and yellow together for green. There's no need to clean the brush since the blue on the brush contributes to the green color. Add extra yellow for a lighter green. Add extra blue for a darker green. Let dry.
7. Add dots of white or yellow lights all over the heavens.
8. If you wish, on another paper draw people, birds, animals, plant

life, and the sun, moon, and stars (each partially drawn) with the pencil. Color, cut out, and glue onto the dried paper or mural.

Heavens and Earth: Advanced AGES 6+

Note how with a few changes "Heavens and Earth" can be advanced to an older age level.

The heavens and the earth are the background. Where does the child place himself in the picture? Find out in this five-part drawing and painting project.

Materials:

- Copy paper, size 8½ x 11 inches (21 x 30 cm)
- Bristol or paper that takes water, size 11 x 16 inches (28 x 41 cm) or larger
- Pencil
- Colored markers
- Red, blue, yellow, and white tempera or gouache paint or acrylic paints (optional: acrylics can be combined with the gouache)
- Paintbrushes, ⅛, ¼, and ½ inch (¼, ½, and 1½ cm)
- White plastic glue
- Scissors

Directions:

1. On the 11 x 16-inch (28 x 41-cm) Bristol or all-purpose paper, mark four dots, 1 inch (2½ cm) from the edges.
2. With the pencil, connect the dots to make a frame. Paint the frame at the end of the project or leave as is.
3. Draw a horizontal line across the paper a bit higher than the center of the paper. This is your dividing line between the heavens and the earth.
4. On a disposable dish or paper, mix your colors (see previous project for tips). Paint the heavens a light blue by mixing blue and

white. Mix a few shades of blue by adding increasing amounts of white to the dabs of blue. Add a little blue shading to the white clouds for depth. Paint in swirls, or fill in evenly.

5. Paint the ground a light green by mixing three parts yellow with one part blue. Mix a few shades of green by adding increasing amounts of yellow to the blue or blue to the yellow. Let dry. Add thin lines for grass.
6. Meanwhile, on the copy paper, draw a boy or girl, a house, three trees (large, medium, and small), mountains, a river or road, and clouds. Color in with markers and cut out.
7. Glue the objects onto the painted background in a composition that resembles a painting. Place the largest tree near the bottom of the paper, the middle-sized tree higher up, near the center, and the smallest tree near the mountains. (Point out that what is close to us is large and what is furthest is small, and what is on the horizon line, as far as our eyes can see, is very tiny.)

Lines and Circles: An Abstract AGES 7+

This one is a favorite—use curves, lines, and colors to create an abstract composition.

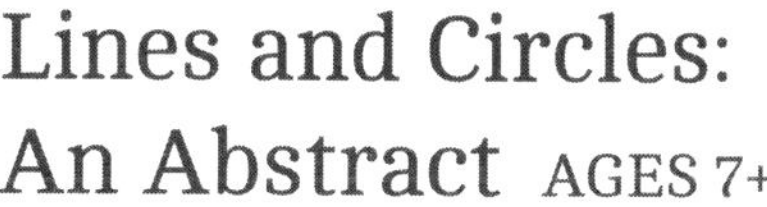

- Copy paper, Bristol, or watercolor paper, size 8½ x 11 inches (21 x 30 cm)

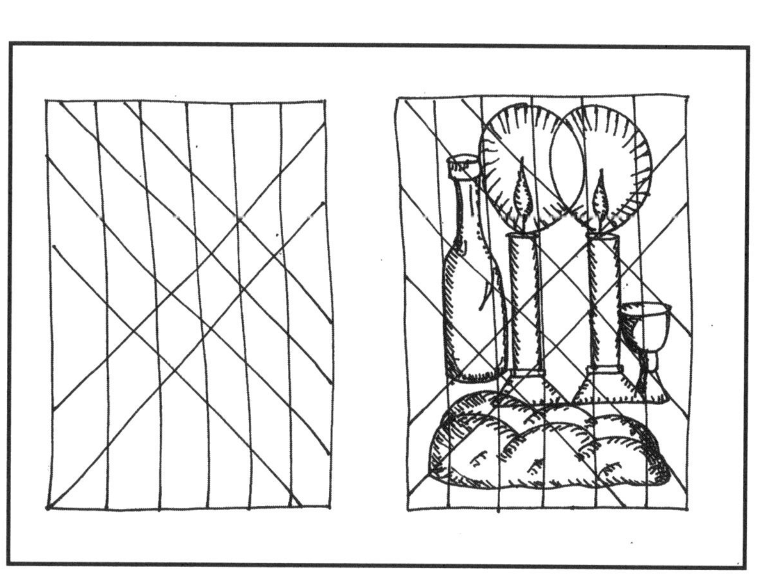

- Pencil
- Straight ruler (a curved ruler is optional)
- Paint: gouache or tempera, acrylics, or watercolors in red, blue, yellow, and white (watercolors often come in sets of twelve or more colors)
- Paintbrush, ¼ to ½ inch (½ to 1½ cm)

Directions:

1. On a sheet of paper, draw several straight, crisscrossing lines with a ruler or freehand.
2. Add a few well-placed circles or curves (half-circles). You can leave the composition abstract (just circles, without a realistic subject), or draw an object, such as a vase or an animal, between the carefully placed lines and curves. For a nature scene, sneak in a sunset made from a half-circle, with rays of light made from diagonal lines. Include a mountain range made of half-circles or triangles, or clouds from several half-circles attached to each other like a necklace.
3. Consider the color combinations you want to use in your composition. Do you envision soft melting colors or a strong, solid extroverted look? A monochromatic (one-color) color scheme is exciting in an abstract artwork. In that case, choose three or four variations of the same hue, for example, four shades of brown: brown, beige, tan, and cream. Or go with blues: blue-red, blue-white, blue-green, blue-yellow.
4. With the paintbrush, apply the color thickly in some places and then thinner in other places (by thinning the paint with water) so there is a contrast between opaque and transparent areas. Or apply the color evenly and in one thickness for a flatter look.

To fill in the spaces made by the pencil lines, first outline the inside of the spaces with a thin line of paint and then fill in the paint in the rest of the area.

The World of Color AGES 7+

Practice blending the primaries to create different hues of secondary colors.

Materials:

- Bristol, watercolor paper, or large copy paper, size 11 x 16 inches (28 x 41 cm)
- Pencil
- Blue, red, yellow, and white gouache paint
- Fine-tipped or flat paintbrush, ¼ to ½ inch (½ to 1½ cm)

Directions:

1. Fold the paper four times, twice horizontally and twice vertically, to make sixteen squares.
2. With the paintbrush, paint the first row of squares blue. To stay inside the lines, outline the inside of each box with paint before you fill in the box.
3. Add red to the blue row. Do this while the blue is wet. First dip the paintbrush into the water and wipe it with a paper towel to clean off the blue paint. Now go in order, one square at a time, and add the red: add one small drop of red in the first square, two drops in the second square, and so on until you have added four drops in the fourth square.
4. Mix and blend the colors well. Watch as the squares turn a range of purple hues.
5. Repeat in the second row with red and yellow: paint the second row red and add increasing amounts of yellow to each square and blend. See the different shades of oranges appear.
6. Repeat in the third row with blue and yellow. Look for the greens as they appear.
7. Finally, repeat in the fourth row with blue and white. See the soft blues appear as you mix the colors.

Circles of Color AGES 7+

Mix as many colors combinations as you can. Try to do a hundred! A practice project that might surprise you with one real beauty.

Materials:

- Bristol paper or watercolor paper, size 11 x 16 inches (28 x 41 cm)
- Pencil
- Cup, 4 x 4 inches (10 x 10 cm)
- Red, blue, yellow, and white gouache paint
- Gold, silver, and copper gouache paint
- Fine-tipped or flat paintbrush, ¼ to ½ inch (½ to 1½ cm)
- Optional: scissors

Directions:

1. On the sheet of Bristol or watercolor paper, draw four circles, 4 x 4 inches (10 x 10 cm), or trace around the top of a large cup until you have drawn four circles.
2. Draw three rings inside the circle, ½ inch apart of descending size.
3. In each circle, paint inside the rings, choosing from one of the color schemes below. If your color scheme is red, pink, and white, paint the entire large circle red. While the paint is still wet, add a few drops of white and paint the next inner circle to make dark pink. Add a few more drops of white to make light pink for the innermost circle. Or, mix each color one at a time and paint the ring. Use a small brush with a small amount of paint to make it easier to stay within the lines. Or try these color combinations:
    - Use red, yellow, and white paint to make red, dark orange, light orange, and yellow circles.
    - Use blue, red, and white paint to make blue, dark purple, light purple, and red circles.

- Use yellow, blue, and green (yellow and blue) paint to make yellow, light green, dark green, and blue circles.
- Use the color combination of yellow, white, gold, and cream (gold, white, and yellow).
- Use the color combination of silver, white, and gold.
- Try copper, white, gold, and orange (red and yellow).
- Color with brown (red, yellow, and a drop of blue), white, cream, and light yellow.

4. Optional: Make ten circles, each with four rings and paint. Use three pieces of 11 x 16-inch (28 x 41-cm) paper. Cut out the ten circles and glue two together, back to back until you have five circles.
5. Poke holes in the middle of each glued-together circle and thread with a string to hang like streamers from your ceiling. Or glue them together on the edges like a long belt and place on the dining room table under a clear plastic tablecloth for a special decorative effect. Or stack the circles and form into flowers by attaching in the center.

In Summary: The Joy of Mixing Color

- It's fun to work with color alone, without worrying about drawing objects.
- Not all drawings and paintings need color. We have inspiring and complete black-and-white works of art that stand on their own and encourage the mind to fill in the color from the imagination.
- Colors, or pigments, are made from vegetable, mineral, and insect/animal matter. Today these are often combined with synthetic materials.
- Binders hold the pigment and give it its form, making sure it will stick to the surface as you paint and draw.

- Certain color combinations or color coordination—the juxtaposition of certain sets of colors—enhance one another, whereas others may detract and confuse the eye.

Questions and Wonder

1. What are your favorite colors and why?
2. How would you describe the colors of the sky, ocean, and the sand at the beach? Be as specific and creative as you can. Make up your own names for colors if you want!
3. What colors relax you? Why? What colors wake you up and get you excited about life?
4. Why do you think we have a colorful world?

21 All about Cutting

Cutting with scissors is a skill that requires fine-motor dexterity, hand-eye coordination, and upper-body strength. The brain mandates the instructions and the hands perform the actions. The results of cutting with scissors are measuring, separating, trimming and adjusting the paper (or other material)—and lots of satisfaction. The ability to cut with scissors can be satisfying for little children who can spend days and weeks mastering this skill. I personally love cutting with scissors and using my fine hand muscles. It relaxes me. Scissors and cutting strengthen the hand muscles and in turn stimulate the mind in a relaxing way. The opening and closing of the scissors while cutting is similar to squeezing a soft ball.

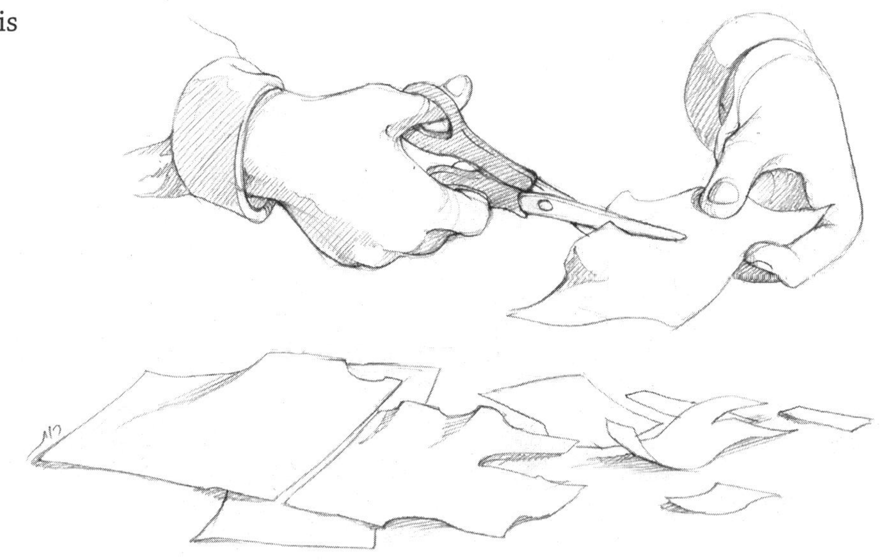

Encourage young children to learn this skill, first by tearing papers of various textures with their fingers and then advancing to cutting shapes and figures with scissors. The hands are our primary tools here. Young hands tear paper haphazardly at first and then graduate to tearing with control in specific directions and then to producing shapes.

Notes and Sketches

You're Never Too Young

Given the opportunity, even very young children just a few months past their first birthday can acquire the mastery of tearing pieces of paper (with supervision, of course!). Give children a variety of papers to work with: plain writing paper, old magazines, colored paper, or wrapping paper. Your child will enjoy tearing open a wrapped gift; help her rip off the wrapping in workable pieces. Show her how to start and help her along the way only as necessary. She will do the rest if she's interested.

Scissors offer an advantage over ripping and tearing by hand since they tend to be more precise. Yet, there is beauty to hand-ripped paper with the rippled edges in projects, in designs, card making, and bulletin boards. Hand control is necessary to make an artistic free form or a specific line tear both with scissors and ripping. Scissor cuts and hand ripping can be combined in the same project.

Cutting with scissors can be used as a test for proper development in young children. If a child above the age of four or five is having difficulty cutting with scissors, a professional can detect areas that the child needs to work on, since the ability to use scissors is the culmination of several skills working together. It's a big accomplishment to be able to cut with scissors!

Cutting Is Harder Than It Looks!

Holding the scissors properly indicates muscular coordination, and the back and shoulders must be strong enough to hold the torso straight as well. A child must have the ability to move the thumb and fingers in a pinching movement similar to opening and closing clothespins. In fact, practicing opening and closing clothespins is good preparation for cutting.

Cutting also requires hand-over-hand movement, coordinating both hands at the same time. When cutting, one hand holds the paper while the other hand cuts—one hand maneuvers the paper while the other hand directs the scissors. Check that the child is holding the paper and scissors in a position that offers her the best mobility for cutting. The hands should be straight and held approximately at shoulder height.

Use scissors appropriate to age and comfort. Dull scissors with round tips are safe for small children but are frustrating for older children and adults, since they're not made for precision. A good pair of scissors increases dexterity and options.

Here are some projects that will put some of the tools we discussed to good use.

Notes and Sketches

Ripping Paper

Let 'er rip! Here is an opportunity to put down the scissors and enjoy the freedom and novelty of ripping paper by hand. Ripping paper is an art form because it sensitizes the student to the subtleties of the soft jagged edges that reveal delicate fibers, emphasizing texture and color. When ripping paper by hand, use your thumbs and index fingers from both hands. Form the contour of the object as you rip. For landscapes and mountains rip horizontally. A vertical object such as a ladder or waterfall is ripped vertically.

When ripping paper edges for a ragged natural effect, choose colors from individual sheets that include beiges, browns, golds, ambers, straws, lemon-yellow, burnt reds, crimsons, mauves, violets, turquoise, green hues, and silver or smoky grays. Sheets of paper, preprinted with rainbow colors, are sold in craft shops. Try all types of paper, paying attention to their textures. Origami paper adds a soft touch of sensitivity to any design.

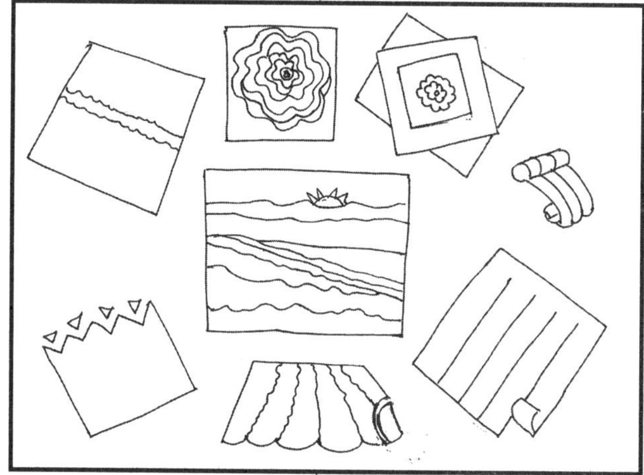

You can make lovely things with torn paper. The edges of torn paper, called "deckled edges," are soft and give a feathered effect. They are especially interesting when the paper is one color on the front and another on the back.

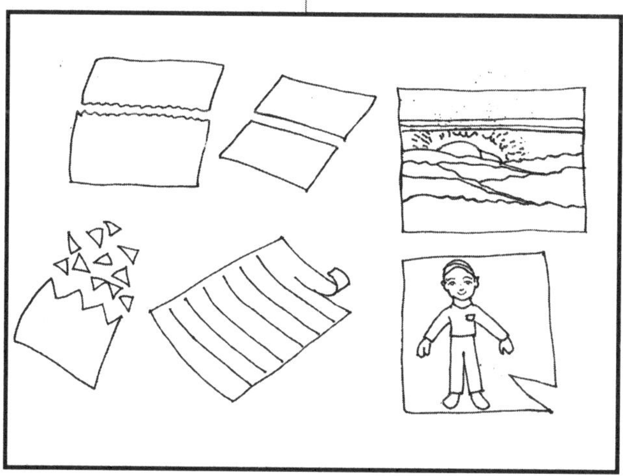

Deckled edges can be easily achieved using a firm metal ruler. Place the paper with the area you want to tear under the ruler. Press your fingers firmly near the top of the paper and your thumb as far down as comfortably possible on the ruler to hold it in place. With your free hand, pull down the top edge of the paper, lowering your grip as you tear, until the paper is fully cut and released.

Now, practice tearing freehand. Fold the paper, and with your fingernails crease it a few times until the spine is soft. Follow the directions for tearing deckled edges with the ruler until the paper is divided and released. The clean jagged edge of the ripped paper will automatically reveal the color of the reverse side. You could use blue paper with a white backing to shape ocean waves, curling the white edges down to suggest foam. The results are very effective.

Due to its unique, irregular shapes, torn paper lends itself to creating landscapes, sunsets, oceans, and roses—but don't overlook people, buildings, and letters. The results can be lively and colorful. For school posters and displays, combine torn-paper shapes with cut-out letters, objects, and photos. Invitations and greeting cards also look great when made from torn paper.

Have children practice tearing both large and small bits of torn paper. Glue them on a solid background one piece at a time, beginning with the largest pieces first and then adding smaller pieces and details last to make a torn-paper collage. Apply the large pieces using white plastic glue with a brush or squeegee; use fingers with white plastic glue or a glue stick for the small, delicate pieces. The pressing action involves fine-motor skills and the hand muscles, the movements similar to those used when sticking on stickers.

The Joy of Creating Collages

A collage is a composite of cut or torn paper glued onto a flat or dimensional surface. It is often combined with lettering, paints, and various other materials to create a composition. While most paintings can be interpreted into a collage, a collage of thoughtfully placed colored papers has a beauty of its own.

Collages are fun for any age, but they are especially suitable for younger children who lack the dexterity to produce fine, detailed pieces of art. Tearing and gluing is something a four-year-old can do well and will enjoy.

Collages have endless possibilities. They don't just have to be a hodgepodge of paper and glue. You can create landscapes, mosaics, and silhouettes (dark shapes against a light background), among other things. The glory of the finished work will depend on the artist's age and ability.

Small children may place the torn paper randomly, while an adult will have a preliminary drawing as a guide.

A collage is made more interesting when you use variety: different-colored bits of paper, card stock, fabric, wrapping paper, tissue, scrapbooking paper, foil, corrugated board, and an assortment of other odds and ends. Have the child create the collage of a drawing—a rainbow, the sun setting over mountains, a row of houses against a thunderous sky—and the result is an interpretation of a drawing the child did. The little artist will have two different artworks based on the same image, one a drawing and one a collage.

Begin the collage with a plan and a clear subject. Decide where you want to put each object and which colors are appropriate for each space, but don't feel locked into your choices. Pieces can be placed in position and then relocated until you are happy with the location before gluing them down. This is a different approach than painting because you can change your mind several times before making a commitment to the paper. Depending on the materials you chose, use diluted white plastic glue, paste, or rubber cement (adults only) to glue your pieces down.

Here is a general guide to making your own collage (see the end of the chapter for two collage projects):

1. Using a pencil, sketch a scene or pattern on a sheet of paper.
2. For the base, use cardboard, Styrofoam sandwich board, Bristol, or all-purpose paper that takes water because the dampness of the glue can cause thinner paper to buckle. Transfer your sketch to the base.
3. Choose various colored and textured papers, as well as photos or magazine clippings. For children over the age of nine, use high-quality construction paper; low-grade construction paper tends to be dull and brittle. Choose a rainbow of colors or shades of the same color.
4. Cut or tear the papers and arrange the shapes on the background. Use larger strips for the big areas, and smaller ones for the small areas. If necessary, cut or tear the papers to size. Arrange the large pieces first, then the mediums, and the small pieces last.
5. Glue the papers down, either as you lay out the pieces of paper, or in stages of size or color. When using tissue paper, apply glue first on the bottom, and then the top to help smooth and adhere it.

Clipping: An Introduction to Scissors

Once a child gets a little older, around two or three years old, he can begin handling scissors. There are children-safe scissors available at your local supplies store. For those who are having a hard time getting the right fingers into the right holes, you can purchase scissors that have room for both the index and middle fingers. This also helps your novice cutter learn how to wield the scissors more easily.

Young beginners learn to cut by clipping away at the paper from any angle that they can manage. They keep making clips (into the hundreds!) as they gradually gain control over the scissors and the paper. At this point, they will not cut out shapes, but they will have a lovely pile of paper scraps that they cut out by themselves!

After achieving the satisfaction of mastering this new skill, they will graduate to cutting straight lines from the bottom of the paper to the top.

Cutting Lines and Shapes

At some point, children will be ready to cut lines across a sheet of paper. You can help them learn how to cut the lines straight with a few simple guidelines:

1. First, draw several straight lines from the top of an 11 x 16-inch (28 x 41-cm) sheet of paper to the bottom. (Eventually have the child draw his own lines.) Add matching colored dots (in several colors) at the top and bottom of the lines.

2. Have the child hold the paper with the left hand and the scissors with the right hand (or the opposite if the child is a lefty). The scissors should be held at about shoulder height. Ask the child to try to cut on the lines beginning from the bottom of the paper. The left hand holding the paper will move up the paper slowly to provide support and facilitate straighter cutting. With the right hand, the child should snip slowly with open-and-close movements until he reaches the top. The child looks at the colored dot as he begins cutting from the bottom until he reaches the top colored dot and completes cutting a line.

3. The child should repeat with the next line and continue for as long as he is interested.

A determined child can work for days or weeks until he masters the fine art of cutting. Once he gets the hang of cutting straight lines, he will soon start cutting on a curve. Here are some helpful guidelines for cutting circles:

1. The child draws a large circle on a piece of paper. Have the child hold the paper with the left hand and the scissors with the right hand (or the opposite if he is a lefty). He should position the scissors straight out in front of his shoulders and then lower them a bit.

2. The hand holding the scissors will remain stationary; it will not change position or go hunting after the line to cut. It is the hand holding the paper that will move. As the scissors move around the circle, the hand with the paper pushes the paper clockwise toward the scissors, feeding it more of the circle to cut.

3. From cutting circles, it is only a small jump to spirals: Draw a large spiral (you can call it a snail). Start the spiral in the center of the paper with a small curve, and radiate out, slowly growing the spiral until the paper is full.

4. Have the child begin from the outermost part of the spiral at the bottom of the paper and gradually work toward the center. While cutting, have the child follow the directions for cutting out a circle: He should hold the scissors in one position and gently push the paper toward the mouth of the scissors, keeping the scissors a bit below shoulder height and straight in front of him. The scissors will not move to another position; they will be opening and closing, snipping away at the lines of the spiral.

The spiral encourages continuous cutting. Children love drawing spirals (snails) and cutting them out. After the child is finished cutting, let the spiral drop and watch it bounce. Ask him to put the spiral back together like the flat piece of paper it once was. Point out how in a few minutes of cutting he made a three-dimensional object from a flat piece of paper.

Attach a string at one end and hang it up for a decoration. Use metallic or specialty paper for a decorative, shiny, and lasting hanging spiral.

Detail Cutting

Once children master lines and curves, they can start cutting out more detailed objects. Show children how to cut out small or detailed areas, such as hands and fingers, by concentrating on these sections separately.

Show the child how to make one or several cuts leading from the edge of the paper to the area he wants to cut out. This makes it easier to reach those areas. Now he should carefully maneuver around the targeted area with the scissors and then remove the paper surrounding the small areas as it is cut out.

Don't worry about accuracy. Let the child cut curves around the subject as close as he can to the lines if he wants to. The child may want to take a pencil and draw curves or lines around the object before he begins cutting. This lets him know his boundaries. Eventually he will gain enough dexterity to cut the object more accurately.

Paper Cuts and Other Amazing Things You Can Do with Scissors

Creating paper cuts is a natural outgrowth of the use of paper. It was developed in ancient China around the second century. Paper cuts are made with a few basic tools: paper, pencil, glue, a knife or scissors, and a protective table cutting mat. They can be simple or complex and elaborate, with multiple layers of interlaced designs. The most familiar, simple design is the snowflake pattern, popular in grade school.

Snowflake paper cuts are made by folding a sheet of paper in half or a few times, drawing half of the design along the fold, and then cutting it out at the fold line. When the paper is unfolded, you will see the complete design.

Paper cuts are usually made of a light-colored paper with a cut-out design mounted on a darker sheet of paper. The complexity of the design and the subject depend on the artist. Paper cuts can be combined with ink, paint, or colored pencil to add dimension

Paper cuts can also be glued onto a hard surface like Styrofoam sandwich board and incorporated into the design. A paper cut trellis of flowers and bushes growing up the side of a doll house looks charming.

Styrofoam sandwich board is made of a thin layer of Styrofoam (¼ to ½ in, ½ to 1½ cm) covered with paper on both sides. It can be used for building models and houses, and to form the background for wall and sukkah decorations. Thick paper, card stock, and boards can be used to make puppets, paper dolls, boxes, mobiles, display boards, or cards.

When making paper cuts, make sure to always cut on a protected surface. Special cutting mats to protect the table are available at art, office, or school supply stores.

In the 1800s, paper cuts became a traditional Jewish art form. The craft was popular in Europe during the nineteenth and twentieth centuries and was adopted by the Jews living there at the time. However, because of the delicacy of paper and the horrifying conditions of World War II, not many examples have survived. However, there are some fine, elaborate examples in existence, created by those who immigrated to the United States in the mid-1800s.

Paper cuts were often created to document family history: births, weddings, or yahrzeits. *Shiviti* signs—with the verse "I am forever mindful of God's presence"[138]—and *Mizrach* signs were handcrafted testimonials to their faith. Paper cuts by Jewish artists also include inscriptions of *pesukim* (Hebrew verses), Magen David symbols, flowers, animals, crowns, stars, and the Tree of Life from the Garden of Eden. Other forms of paper cuts include creating paper staircases and furniture for a dollhouse, pop-up greeting cards, paper weavings, or rolled paper beads and jewelry. Slotted paper pieces that fit together can be used for cardboard stands for paper dolls, trees, or other toy props. Did you know that lamp shades can be made of handmade specialty papers? Paper sculptures are another creative option. You can literally build facsimiles of what you see around you in the physical world with just a pair of scissors and a piece of paper!

Familiarize yourself and your child with satisfying paper cutting options. The possibilities are endless.

Here are some projects that will put those cutting skills to work.

---

138 Psalms 16:8.

Clips and Cuts AGES 3–5

This project, suited for children ages 3 to 5, is a step up from the standard activity in preschool using stickers to identify subjects, and it increases hand dexterity. Here the child "makes" his own handmade stickers. These are not stickers in the traditional, commercial sense. They are small pieces of paper designed by the child's own hand and stuck on with glue and a sense of satisfaction.

Materials:

- Copy paper, size 8½ x 11 inches (21 x 30 cm)
- 4 sheets of different-colored paper, size 8½ x 11 inches (21 x 28 cm) or larger
- Markers
- White plastic glue
- Scissors

Directions:

1. Clip the colored paper until you have a pile of small pieces in various shapes and colors.
2. Sort the pieces by size and color.
3. Ask the child to draw circles or little pictures on similar-size pieces with a colored marker, or draw circles, lines, columns, and rows between the paper pieces after they are glued in place.
4. Glue the pieces onto the copy paper by category of size and/or color.

Variation: Draw a simple picture, such as a house, boy or girl, bird, or tree. The child glues the cut scraps of paper onto the picture either on the outlines or by filling in the objects. Another option, which is better for the child's self-confidence, is to ask the child to draw anything (which may look like a scribble to you) and then glue his or her paper pieces onto it. Don't forget to give lots of praise, regardless of whether you are overwhelmed by the undefined nature of the drawing. Be assured that the child knows what he has drawn.

Paper Weaving AGES 8+

If your child has been practicing cutting strips of paper on her own, she will enjoy the art of paper weaving.

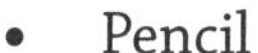

- Stiff paper (Bristol, art paper, or thin card stock) size 8½ x 16 inches (21½ x 41 cm). You can try 2 pieces of colored (yellow and purple or other combination) or metallic paper or 2 pages from magazines. You should have enough for 2 sets of 8 (or 6) strips, measuring 1 x 8 inches (2½ x 20 cm).
- Pencil
- Ruler
- Colored markers
- Scissors
- Cellophane tape

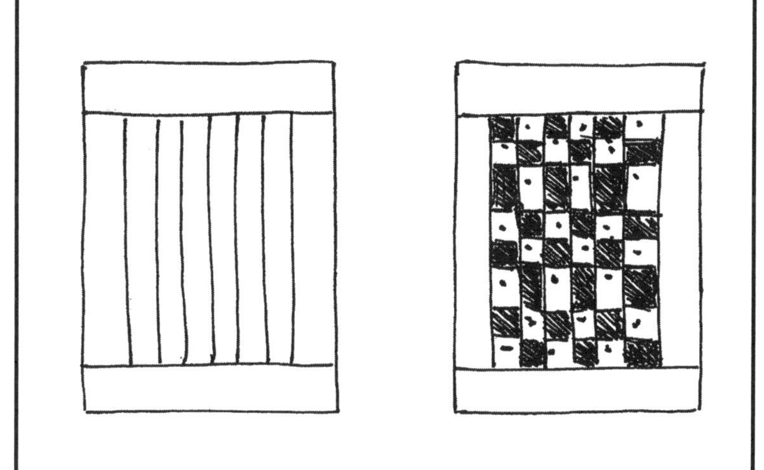

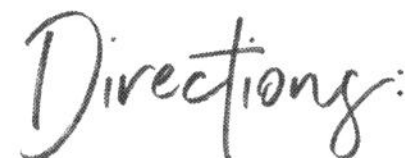

1. With the ruler and pencil, measure and mark 1-inch segments across the top of the large-sized copy paper.
2. Mark corresponding 1-inch (2½ cm) segments across the bottom.
3. With the markers, dot each mark, using the same color for each corresponding top and bottom marks. You will have colored dots at the top corresponding to the colored dots at the bottom.
4. Hold the scissors at chin level and the paper at eye level. Begin cutting from the bottom of the paper, starting from the leftmost dot while looking at the top corresponding dot. Open and close the scissors in a pinching motion. (Remind the child to catch the paper deep inside the back opening of the scissors to engage the scissors properly.) Note: A paper weaving is a great way to use all

of the strips of paper your child has cut while practicing cutting straight lines.

5. Collect eight of the strips; they should be about 8 inches (20 cm) long and 1 inch (2½ cm) wide in one color, for example, yellow. Now collect another 8 strips in a second color, for example, purple. (If your child's strips are not straight or uniform, sort out the best samples.)

6. Line up the yellow strips, one next to the other, horizontally on the working surface. Tape the left edges together. Line up the purple strips, one next to the other, vertically on the working surface, and tape the tops together.

7. Place the yellow group over the purple group and weave one strip at a time under and over until the two groups are united. Have your child do as many rows as he can master. Cut off any unused rows. Tape the edges, fold back and secure with tape. If this is done with four even edges you will have a mat.

Pomegranates-in-a-Bowl Collage AGES 8+

Your subject is a large bowl of majestic, juicy red pomegranates seated in a deep pink ceramic bowl. Behind the table, which is covered with a checkered tablecloth, is a dramatically lit wall. Use only high-quality paper; lesser-quality paper tends to be dull and brittle.

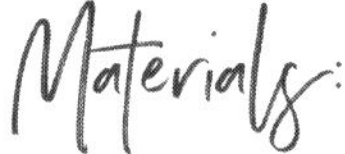

- Copy paper, size 8½ x 11 inches (21 x 30 cm)
- Bristol, size 11 x 16 inches (28 x 41 cm), or other all-purpose paper that takes water, for the collage surface
- Pencil
- Shiny paper in light pink, dark pink, red, burgundy, purple, white, black, dark blue, and silver (silver or gold foil or even chocolate candy foil is also good)
- White plastic glue
- Scissors

Directions:

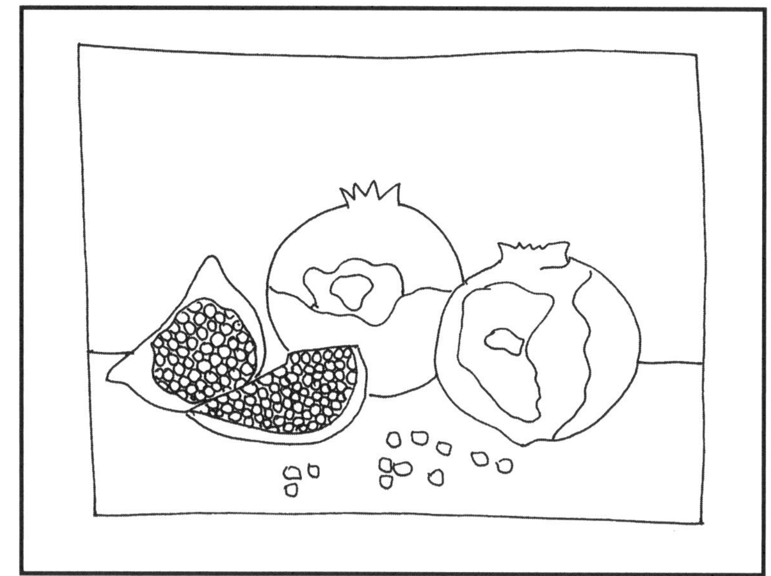

1. Sketch and plan out your image on a sheet of the 8½ x 11-inch (21 x 30-cm) copy paper in pencil.
2. Lightly draw (in pencil) the objects in their positions on the 11 x 16-inch paper based on the practice drawings. (When you have your cut or torn shapes ready, you may want to move and adjust the positions of the objects.)
3. Cut or tear the colored papers to fit the bowl (pink), the fruits (red and burgundy), the tabletop (black and white checkered), and the wall. Try metallic silver, additional white paper, or leave the paper white for the wall. Use more than one shade of each color.
4. Move your pieces around a bit until you have arrived at your composition.
5. Glue the pieces in place, starting with the larger areas first and the details and smaller areas last.

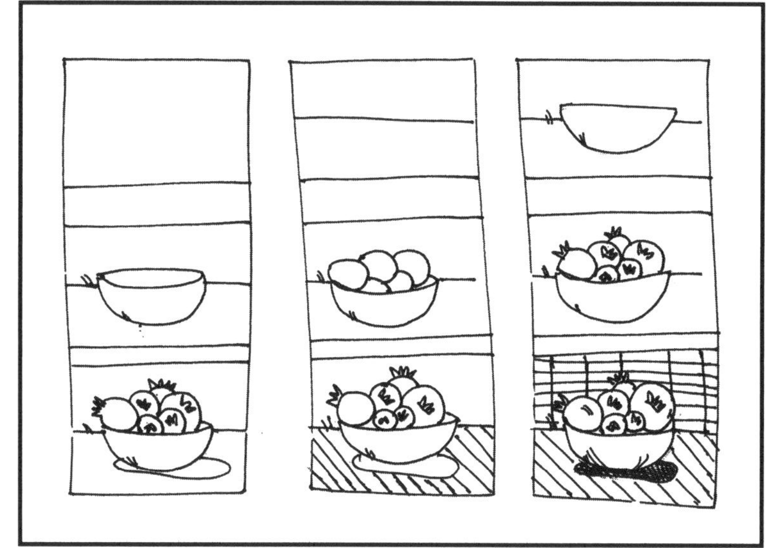

Optional: Add small light pieces of paper on top of the objects for highlights. For example, add light pink pieces in a few places on the bright pink bowl. Add a few dark pink or purple pieces near the back sides of the bowl to make it appear curved. Add small dark burgundy or dark blue pieces for shadows on the pomegranates.

Decorative Torn-Tissue Paper-Collage Box

AGES 8+

Create a lovely box with overlapping transparencies of light green and turquoise tissue paper accented with strings of small beads and singular large beads.

Materials:

- Pencil
- Ruler
- Old paintbrush, ½ inch (1½ cm), to apply glue
- Styrofoam sandwich board: one 4 x 16-inch (10 x 41-cm) piece and two 4 x 4-inch (10 x 10-cm) squares
- Craft knife and protected cutting surface (or self-healing cutting board)
- Hot-glue gun (small size)
- White plastic glue
- Scissors (optional)
- Tissue paper, light green and turquoise, light blue, dark green, and brown
- 5 strands of tiny beads, 3 inches (7½ cm) long, preferably in turquoise or other matching color
- 2–4 single medium-sized beads, color coordinated to the box.

Directions:

1. With the ruler and pencil, measure and mark the Styrofoam sandwich board in order to cut one 4 x 16-inch (10 x 40-cm) piece and two 4 x 4-inch (10 x 10-cm) squares.
2. With the craft knife, cut out the pieces from the Styrofoam sandwich board (on a protected surface). The long piece will become the four sides of the box, and the two small pieces will be the top and bottom.
3. On the long 4 x 16-inch (10 x 40-cm) piece, measure and mark three lines, each 4 inches (10 cm) apart, across the width of the board, making four even sections. There will be four sections on the front and four sections on the back when the 4 x 16-inch piece is folded into a box.

4. Using the craft knife, score or perforate the three lines. Do not cut through the board. Bend the board on the three cut lines to make a square.
5. Tear or cut the green tissue paper into eight triangles, measuring 3 x 3 x 3 inches (7½ x 7½ x 7½ cm) to represent mountains: four triangles for the front of the box and four for the back of the box. Double the layers of tissue paper to increase the density of the color.

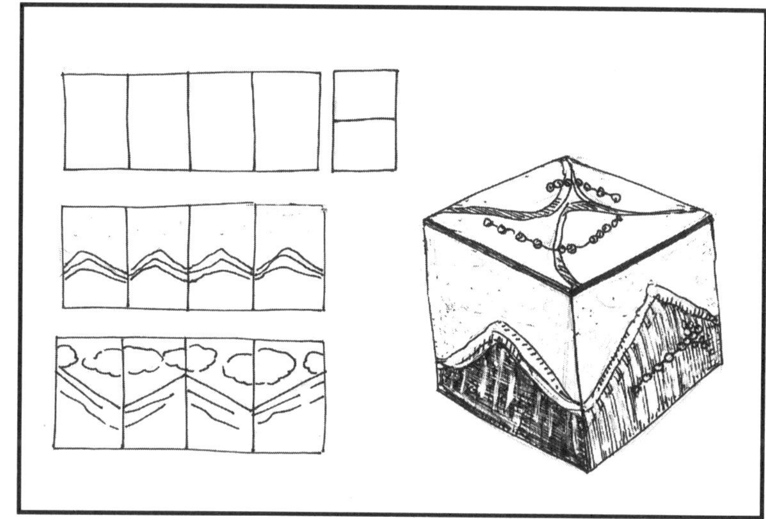

6. Glue four green mountains on the front of the box, and four green mountains on the back of the box. Use the old paintbrush to apply the glue.
7. Use turquoise or blue tissue paper to fill in the space above the mountains as the sky. Tear or cut pieces to accent the mountains, the sky, and ground as desired.
8. Tear and scrunch small pieces of green and brown tissue paper to make Cyprus trees. (The shape is that of a long thin oval set on top of a stick.) Glue on top of or above the mountains.
9. Glue all the tissue pieces in place using ample glue coating both under and on top of the paper. Applying the glue on top smooths the tissue paper. (The glue will be clear after drying.) Let dry.
10. For the back of the box: Repeat the directions for the front of the box. Let dry.
11. Optional: Cover the inside of the Styrofoam board with a mixture of green and turquoise or blue tissue paper in your own design. Let dry.
12. Cover both sides of the two 4 x 4-inch (10 x 10-cm) squares of Styrofoam board (the top and bottom of the tissue box) with a mixture of green and turquoise or blue tissue paper. Let dry.
13. Break up one of the strands of tiny beads. Scatter as desired on front of box. Arrange single medium-sized beads and

remaining strands on front. Glue all using ample glue or a small hot-glue gun.

14. Fold the long piece into a four-sided square. Gently score (a partial cut) through any tissue paper on the bend lines. Hot glue the edges together. Hot glue the bottom in place. Do not attach the top, which will be used as a removable lid. Add any beads to the top if desired. Use as a gift or jewelry box.

Variation: Use a ready-made box of similar dimensions and cover with tissue paper in your own unique design.

Snowflakes: A Layered Paper Cut AGES 9+

See chapter 3, "Sukkah Metallic Paper Cut."

Materials:

- Copy paper for practice, size 8½ x 11 inches (21 x 30 cm)
- 3 sheets of gold or silver metallic paper in 3 descending sizes, for example: 8 x 8, 7 x 7, and 6 x 6 inches (20 x 20, 18 x 18, 15 x 15 cm)
- Black or dark-colored construction paper or fine handmade colored paper (available in art stores or some stationery stores)
- White plastic glue
- Scissors

Directions:

First practice all the steps with the plain paper. (Make the copy paper into a square. Fold each paper into a triangle starting at the bottom of the paper. Open and cut off any surplus paper at the top.)

1. Fold the 6 x 6-inch (15 x 15-cm) and the 7 x 7-inch (18 x 18-cm) sheets of paper two or three times. Cut out designs along the fold to create a snowflake. Be careful not to cut off the fold line. Open the paper to find a snowflake design.

2. Fold the 8 x 8-inch (20 x 20-cm) sheet two times and cut scallops (curved lines) from the outer edge only.

3. Arrange the three snowflakes in layers, with the largest on the bottom and the smallest on top. The bottom layer is in a diamond position and the two other layers are in a square position.
4. Glue the layers together or attach with a paper fastener in the center. Optional: Place a larger uncut paper, 10 x 10 inches (25 x 25 cm), under the 3 layers as a base, and glue all pieces in place.
5. Repeat all the steps and use the colored or metallic papers for a final version.

Try using different-colored papers for each layer. Or, layer the cut papers, one on top of the other, and attach with a paper fastener in the center.

Variation: With ingenuity, you can make a layered paper cut with a subject, such as the lulav and etrog or the scene of a house in the mountains in the winter with Chanukah lights flickering in the front window. Use one paper to make the snowflakes, another for the house, another for the mountains, and another for cut-out words or a *pasuk* (verse) that frames the finished work, until you have several layers of paper. Begin layering from the larger cuts to the smaller cuts, so that the smaller objects end up on the top of the stack. Plan carefully how each layer accommodates and works with the next layer. Use textured white or colored papers that go well together.

Paper-Doll Chains AGES 7+

Somehow, we inherently enjoy and know how to make paper-doll chains. Paper-doll chains are often used for Lag BaOmer projects, to show children dancing hand in hand in a circle around a bonfire. For Shavuot, we might make a paper-doll chain to represent the Jewish people gathered around the base of Har Sinai. Other suitable subjects are objects whose shapes are easy to identify, such as menorahs, fish, hearts, tents, and houses.

Paper-doll chains may be combined with ribbons, cut pieces of colored paper, or material for the doll's clothing. Lay a short paper chain over a wrapped gift box for an extra decorative touch. Use another portion of the same paper chain to make a matching greeting card: Glue the paper chain onto card paper that is folded in half.

Here is a fun paper-doll chain project that can match any theme you choose.

Materials:

- Bristol, all-purpose art paper, or card stock, cut into strips. Choose your size: 4 x 16 inches (10 x 40½ cm) for large paper dolls, 2 x 8 inches (5 x 20 cm) for medium dolls, or 1 x 4 inches (2½ x 10 cm) for small dolls
- Pencil
- Ruler
- Markers
- Colored paper
- White plastic glue
- Scissors
- Pieces of fabric, decorative trim, and other odds and ends

Directions:

1. Fold the paper strips into four accordion-like folds. A 4 x 16-inch strip will fold every 4 inches (10 cm), a 2 x 8-inch strip will fold every 2 inches (5 cm) and a 1 x 4-inch strip will fold every 1 inch (2½ cm).
2. Draw the outline of a cookie cutter doll onto the top of the folded-up strip, with the arms and legs extended to the edge of the paper. Cut out the doll shape, either cutting through all the layers at once or cutting each doll separately, being careful not to cut through the hands, or the chain will not be connected.
3. Color and decorate the dolls with markers or paint, and decorate with fabric scraps, synthetic hair, bits of decorative trim, glitter, sequins, and so on. Make them all the same or give each its own personality. Or decorate the dolls according to season: one doll will represent summer, one fall, one winter, and one spring. Or one doll can display clothing for school, one for home, one for Shabbat and Yom Tov, and one for sleeping.

4. If you wish, you can cut out a second strip and fold it into four sections. Paint or color it, or cover with glitter glue and let dry. You can color the entire strip the same color. Glue the paper chain dolls on to the colored strip of paper.

Optional: Repeat all the steps, and then connect the two to make a longer chain.

In Summary: All about Cutting

- Cutting is a skill that requires fine-motor dexterity, hand-eye coordination and upper body strength.
- Tearing paper by hand is a prelude to cutting. The edges of torn paper, called "deckled edges," are soft and give a feathered effect. Deckled edges can be easily achieved using a firm metal ruler or by hand.
- A collage is a composite of cut, torn, and glued papers onto a flat or dimensional surface. Lettering, painting and various materials and objects are often combined.
- Collages can be made on boxes and three-dimensional objects.
- Three- and four-year-olds love to snip and cut at paper—the beginning of mastering the skill of cutting with scissors.
- Teach children how to cut properly with scissors, holding the paper in one hand while cutting with the other to make a straight line, and later to cut out circles and spirals.
- From cutting large areas, have children graduate into cutting small, detailed shapes.
- Paper cuts were popular among the Jewish population in eighteenth- and nineteenth-century Eastern Europe for documenting family history and inspiring religious observance.
- Paper cuts are usually made of a light-colored paper with a cut-out design mounted on a darker sheet of paper; they can be simple and basic or complex and elaborate with `multiple cuts, layers and colors.

Questions and Wonder

1. Fortunately, today we have scissors—many types and sizes that allow us to cut everything from large paper down to the details around small objects. Before the invention of scissors, people used knives. Before knives, they used sharpened stones, which they sharpened on another stone or sharp surface. Can you image preparing your own cutting tools? How many useful objects that we use today are first cut into a shape from a raw material?
2. Why is it that we can draw with one hand but need two hands to cut a paper?
3. What is the difference between cutting, tearing, and breaking?

22 The Art of Lettering

In this day and age of computers and iPhones, it seems like the art of handwriting is dying. Who writes anything today? And if they do, is there value anymore in making an effort to create lovely and precise penmanship?

I say, yes. Beautiful lettering enhances the appearance of children's notebooks, and it is featured on posters, illustrations, announcements, invitations, and bulletin-board displays. Although much of the lettering in art is computerized, nothing can compare to a hand-lettered invitation created by an artist.

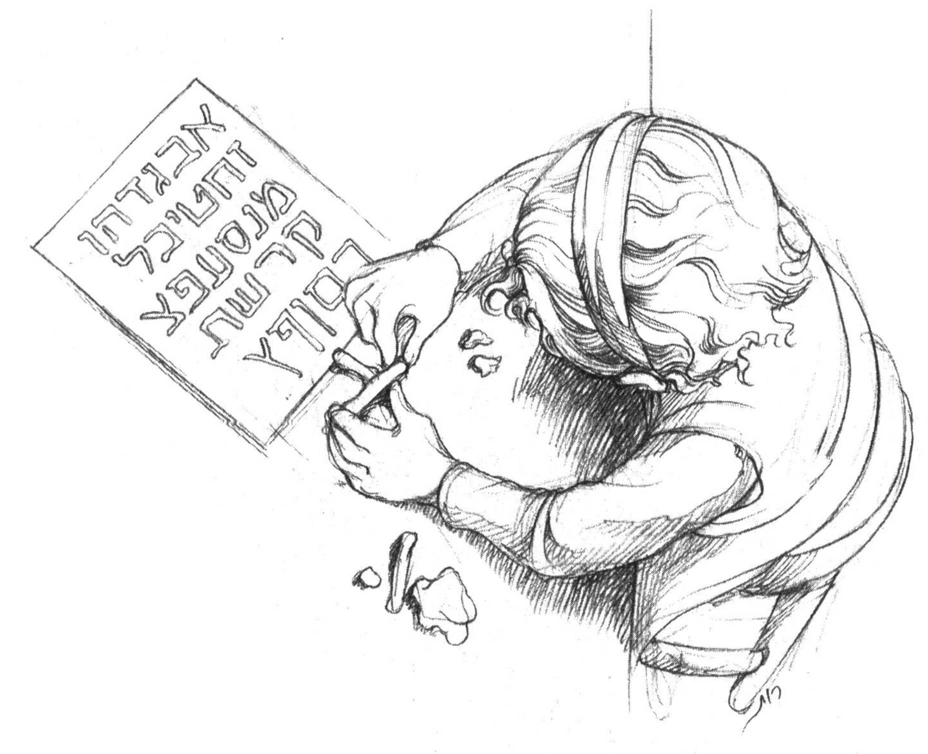

Well-formed letters and words add beauty and importance to children's artwork. The act of creating beautiful lettering—of examining and forming the structure of the letters and the spacing between them—can help children become aware of their own handwriting.

Notes and Sketches

Besides the satisfaction of being able to form the letters, learning how to write the Hebrew alphabet, the *aleph-bet*, is a prelude to learning Torah. Judaism places great importance on the word: written, spoken, or sung. The art of shaping the Hebrew letters has been passed down in an unbroken tradition for three thousand years.

Each letter has great spiritual significance based on its form; for example, the letter *shin* has three arms, representing the three Patriarchs: Abraham, Isaac, and Jacob. For this reason, writing a Torah scroll or mezuzah comes with precise specifications down to the type of ink and parchment used. Every stroke is significant and the scribe must maintain the exact wording and formation of the letters.

It's no wonder that the Hebrew letters have an intrinsic visual beauty. Children will enjoy learning how to form letters to enhance their artwork.

Letters and Rulers

Bring out a chart with the *aleph-bet* or ABC. Show them how they can vary the sizing of the letters: Sometimes a letter will take up a single line, sometimes two lines, or sometimes three. Have them thicken each letter so they can color it in. You may also want to show them how to give a shadow to the letters. A shadow can be added to letters by copying the outline either above, below, behind, or to the side of the letter and filling in the space with a dark tone.

Once they have mastered forming lettering with straight lines, have them write some letters in script. They can also decorate the letters: Add in a few fluffy rabbits, bright yellow birds and other animals, a cluster of flowers, or facial features.

Once they see what they can do with lettering, have them add lettering as a feature in their paintings. For example, they can paint an open siddur with Hebrew letters flying out of it. Other ideas include the *aleph-bet* as building blocks, on steps to climb into the world of good *middot*, as parts of a jigsaw puzzle of the globe, as a border for a crown, or on the leaves of the Tree of Life in the Garden of Eden.

Safrut: The Ancient Art of the Scribe

Safrut, a highly stylized form of handwriting, is an ancient art. For thousands of years specially trained scribes have recorded stories, business transactions, and historical events with quill and parchment.

In Judaism, a scribe is called a "*sofer*," or "*sofrim*" in plural. These scribes are trained to write a Torah scroll, mezuzah, tefillin, or megillah. Even today, *sofrim* write Torah scrolls in the same time-honored tradition as ancient times to maintain the integrity of the Torah's word and ensure that not one letter, or even stroke, is left out or added. In this way, we know that the Torah that was given on Har Sinai is the same Torah that we have today.

Some people think that *safrut* is just a form of calligraphy. Both *sofrim* and calligraphers use special writing tools to create stylized letters. Yet there is an important difference between them. A *sofer* studies special halachot, the laws transmitted in the Torah, to learn how to write the letters to exact specifications, and he must pass a stringent examination before he can be qualified to become a *sofer*. One of the specifications for writing a Torah scroll is that a *sofer* must use a quill pen, a special pen carved from a feather or reed (called *kolmus*). A *sofer* must also be a God-fearing person.

A calligrapher, on the other hand, is someone who produces beautiful writing. Anyone can be a calligrapher, but not just anyone can be a *sofer*.

Calligraphy

We know that art can evoke feelings, and it is a mode of self-expression. Did you know that calligraphy can do the same? Calligraphy isn't just a bunch of fancy letters. When a calligrapher creates letters, the style of lettering she chooses can evoke a certain feeling. Letters can be created with elegant curves, slanted lines, or even strokes, with or without flourishes. These create associations in people's minds. The form and shape of the letter gives a message: fun, serious, beautiful, old-fashioned, or modern. Letters can even be scary-looking or calming.

There are calligraphy pens with removable tips that can be used to create scripts in different sizes and styles. Lettering done by hand has meaning

Notes and Sketches

to children. It is the work of their hands transmitting a message. Show children decorative examples of fine, hand-drawn calligraphy and talk about the techniques used to achieve each type of writing. Explain the difference between handwork and that from the computer. Show them a variety of calligraphy pens, and let them practice writing with them.

Although calligraphy is a skill that needs practice and effort, it's enriching for young children to try writing with special writing instruments. Calligraphy doesn't require a quill pen; calligraphy pens are available at any writing supplies store. These pens come with a slanted tip to facilitate the stylized writing that defines calligraphy.

Calligraphy is both emotional and technical. The rules and order of forming the strokes require precision and a great deal of practice. There is a preferred order of strokes, and there is a science to the spacing between letters, words, and lines. To create beautiful writing, the calligrapher first lightly marks measured lines in pencil. The letters of the alphabet that go above the base line are called ascenders: *b*, *d*, *f*, *h*, *k*, and *t*. Descenders *g*, *j*, *p*, *q*, and *y* go below the base line. Capitals reach halfway between the height line and the ascender line.

The space around the letters (called "negative space") is just as visually important as the letters themselves. The background in calligraphy is important just as it is in a painting or drawing.

With calligraphy, decoration is encouraged. To emphasize a word, letter, or line, the calligrapher changes the size or color of the words, or she adds a decoration or illustration to them. Often the first letter of a page or paragraph is embellished with a decorated letter. This can be found on illuminated manuscripts written on fine vellum (parchment) from the Middle Ages. A large letter, a letter in a box, or a decoration around a letter are beautiful options.

There is even a type of art that is created just with calligraphy called "micrographology." This is the art of illustrating a picture with tiny words instead of lines, colors, and shades. The position of the words form the shapes of the picture. An illustration of Shabbat candles, for example, might be made from the words of *Eishet Chayil* ("Woman of Valor" found in Proverbs). The picture of a menorah might be created from the songs and *berachot* said at Chanukah candle lighting.

Though we can do amazing things with computers, there is nothing like the hands-on creative work of writing by hand.

Lettering in Craft

Lettering doesn't have to be confined to pencil and paper. Tactile, three-dimensional solid materials, such as clay, help young children internalize the shape of letters and the direction and distance of the strokes. Give children a variety of materials to practice shaping letters.

- Use yarn, pipe cleaners, rope, string, popsicle sticks, toothpicks, play dough, clay, and mosaics to form letters.
- Use colored-paper strips (a convenient size to use is ½ inch wide and 3–4 inches long) to assemble letters. Stick together with glue or use paper fasteners, and the children can move the "legs" and "arms" of the letters.
- Cover a section of a wall with a large sheet of white paper held in place with tape. Hold large plastic or hand-drawn cut out letters to the wall. Use a portable lamp or flashlight to cast a shadow of the letters on the wall. Give the children washable markers to trace over the shadow letters on the wall. Have the children choose from a variety of fabrics to sew stuffed letters for room decorations or pillows. They will especially enjoy sewing the letters of their names.
- Draw letters inside pre-drawn squares. The letters may be colored in if hollow. The background can be colored in a coordinating color. Cut out all the squares and glue onto a color-coordinated surface. This exercise in design can resemble children's building blocks or cubes if desired.
- Draw large letters by hand or use a stencil. Color and add animated features. They can be either amusing or delicate: animals or floral life. When the letters are hollow, the animals can be "sitting" on the outlines of the letters or inside the lines. Floral designs can be filled inside the outlines of the letters, placed in clusters outside the lines, or spread loosely around the lines.

The Hebrew Alphabet

You can learn to write stylized letters of the Hebrew alphabet using a simple system. The twenty-two letters of the *aleph-bet* are divided into two groups: The seven simple letters, *dalet*, *vav*, *zayin*, *yud*, *kaf*, *nun*, and *resh* are one group, and the second group consists of the remaining fifteen compound letters. The first group of letters are used to compose the rest of the fifteen letters. For example, an *aleph* is composed of a *vav* and two *yuds*. A *hei* is composed of a *dalet* and a *yud*. A lamed is formed with a *vav* and a *kaf*.

Practice writing the Hebrew *aleph-bet*. Once you have written the letters, color in the letters and decorate as you wish or use the letters as part of a painting or drawing.

Aleph-Bet Simplified[139]

Letter	Composition
א	ו+י+י
ב	ו+ו+ו
ג	י+ו
ד	ד
ה	ד+י
ו	ו
ז	ז
ח	ד+ו
ט	נ+ו/כ+ו
י	י
כ	כ

Letter	Composition
ל	כ+ו
מ	כ+ו
נ	נ
ס	כ+ו
ע	ז+ו+נ
פ	כ+י
צ	נ+י
ק	ר+ו
ר	ר
ש	ו+ו+ו
ת	ר+ו

139 Dovid Leitner, *Understanding the Alef-Beis* (Feldheim Publishers, 2007), p. 13.

Stained-Glass Cookie-Dough Letters AGES 4+

Each cookie-dough letter is enclosed in a square surrounded by stained-glass candies. A delicious project kids will love!

Ingredients:

- 14 ounces (400 grams) margarine, softened and cut into small pieces
- 2 cups sugar
- 4 teaspoons vanilla
- 6 cups sifted flour
- 2 teaspoons baking powder
- ½ teaspoon salt
- ⅔ cup water
- Clear hard candies or lollipops
- 2 sheets baking paper

Directions:

1. Preheat the oven to 350° F (180° C).
2. In the large mixing bowl of a heavy-duty mixer, cream the margarine, sugar, and vanilla (you can also do this by hand with a spoon).
3. Add the flour, baking powder, and salt, and beat until the mixture is crumbly.
4. Add the water and mix by hand until the dough is no longer sticky and forms a large ball. Knead until smooth. Cover with plastic wrap and chill in the refrigerator for at least half an hour.
5. Meanwhile, crush contents of a large bag of hard lollipops or hard, clear-colored candies. Allow two to five candies per cookie. Place each color of chopped candy in a separate cup.

6. On both sheets of baking paper, draw or sketch outlines of letter shapes, each within a circle or square shape. Place the baking paper on the cookie sheets.
7. Roll out the dough to make ropes about 6–12 inches (15–30 cm) long and ¼ inch (½ cm) thick. Press them onto the letter outlines. Remember that dough rises. Position each cookie with a large, open space around it.
8. Bake for eight minutes.
9. Remove the trays from the oven. Fill the squares or circles drawn around each cookie letter with the candy bits. Return to the oven for an additional 4 minutes. Remove the cookies as soon as the candy has melted, as it scorches easily.
10. Allow to cool completely before removing from baking tray. The cookies will be almost too pretty to eat!

Nachas Pencil Container AGES 7/8+

Nachas words: nachas, (sense of) pride, accomplishment, satisfaction, or pleasure.
Give to a great parent or grandparent.

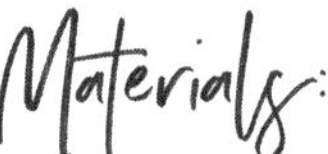

- Tin can: 5 inches (12 cm) tall, 4-inch (10-cm) circumference
- Bristol or thick paper to wrap around can plus 2 inches (5 cm) wide around the rim
- Ruler, pencil, scissors, white plastic glue
- Paint: metallic house paint or metallic acrylic (light colored). Your choice of color for the letters: consider red, blue, yellow, brown, gray, or white acrylic
- Paint brushes: 1 inch (2½ cm) and ¼ inch (½ cm)
- Lettering stencil, medium to small
- Colored markers (optional)

Directions:

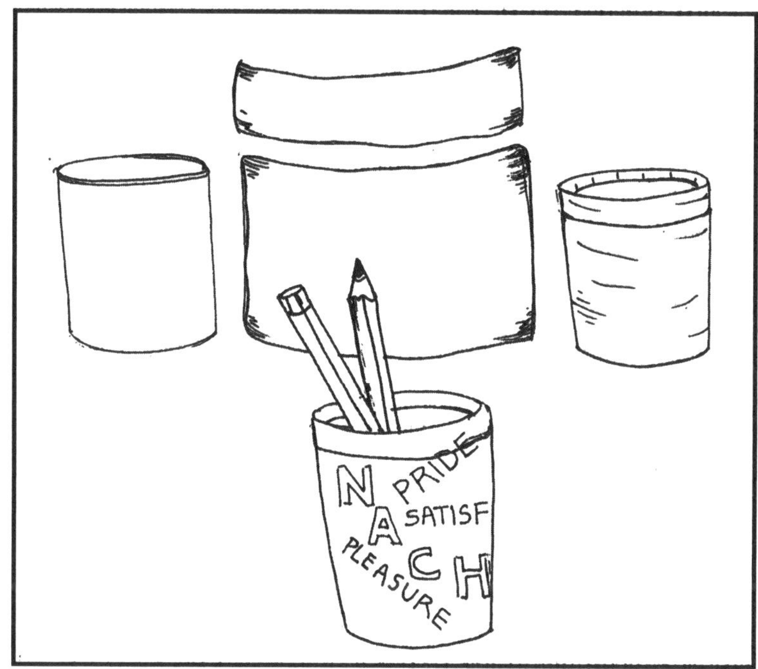

1. Measure and cut paper to wrap around can and for the rim. Paint, and allow to dry. Stencil or write by hand "*nachas* words" in two or three directions or sizes. Paint in letters and allow to dry. If you prefer, you can use markers.
2. Wrap paper firmly around can. Glue in place. Fold and glue paper on rim one inch on outside and one inch on inside of rim. Cut notches inside to lay flat. Press firmly a few times on entire can. Dry.
3. Fill with pens and pencils and colored markers and give your heartfelt gift.

In Summary: The Art of Lettering

- Although much of the lettering in art is computerized, nothing can compare to hand-lettered art.
- Beautiful, well-formed letters help children become aware of their handwriting. The Hebrew *aleph-bet* is rich with meaning, passed down in an unbroken tradition for three thousand years.
- Rulers used with writing helps us to measure and space the letters, words, and lines properly.
- A *sofer* writes Torah scrolls, mezuzot, tefillin, and megillot with precise specifications in the same tradition as ancient times.
- *Safrut* and calligraphy may appear to be the same, but the requirements for being a *sofer* require a solid knowledge of Jewish law.

- Calligraphy pens in the hand of a trained calligrapher produce beautiful writing that has a style and message of its own.
- Calligraphy is technical; there is a preferred order of strokes, and there is a science to the spacing between letters, words, and lines.
- Tactile three-dimensional solid materials, such as clay, help young children internalize the shape of letters.

Questions and Wonder

1. What do you think life would be like if we had no written alphabet? How would we write? Do we need to write?
2. Have you ever tried to make up an alphabet or a code?
3. Combining words with illustrations gives extra meaning to the words. As you write a letter, story, or book, can you visualize a picture that goes with the words? Would you like to try to draw part or all of it?

Working with Clay

23

Twenty-three-month-old Eli sat at his play table. His mother gave him three sticks of Plasticine: red, yellow, and blue. "Don't get it on the floor," she instructed him.

Eli enthusiastically picked up the clay, and with a plastic knife in hand, he spent the next forty minutes cutting each stick of clay into piles of tiny pieces. His mother watched from afar, not wanting to disturb his concerted efforts at disassembling the clay.

Equally fascinating to his mother was when Eli picked up his of piles of clay and placed them, one group at a time into a big plastic bag. She had expected him to try to eat them or at least rub the clay over the table. He didn't. He was careful, and he focused on his task of cutting and cutting the clay until he had accomplished his goal. As the clay was no longer needed, he discarded them into the bag.

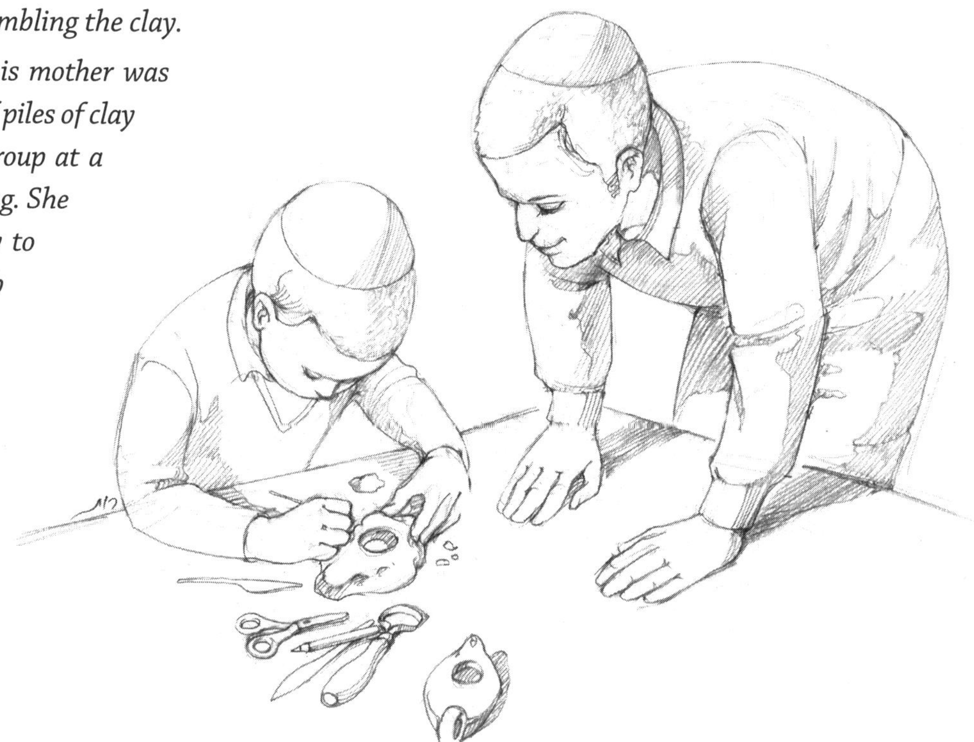

Notes and Sketches

The Earth Is in Your Hands

This is what working with clay is all about: The clay represents the earth and says, "I am here for you to form and use." It allows children to take something from their environment and have a sense of control over it. What a good feeling!

You don't need much to craft with clay: just a clean, protected work surface, some clay, and hands to shape the clay.

There's nothing more tactile than clay. With the palms, thumbs, and fingers, a child will shape, squeeze, and roll the clay, strengthening his hands while enjoying the sensation of its smooth, slick texture.

Clay seems to absorb all our tension and slows us down to a natural rhythm. You can't rush with clay. The more time you take stretching it into a shape, the better the clay will respond.

There are so many things to do with clay. We squeeze and press and pound the clay. We pinch and poke the clay. We add to the clay or cut away from the clay. We create and shape and reshape. Children love the sense of mastery they have over this malleable material; there is nothing more satisfying to a small child than to feel in control of his environment.

Watch a child during his first contact with clay. Notice his awareness of the clay and how he manipulates it. Children love to take an inert mass and make life-like figures and objects. Snails, flowers, trees, people, buildings—anything can be made with clay. It's so satisfying to create something useful and beautiful from a blob of clay.

Working with clay is also a great way to express emotions in a healthy way. A child who is frustrated, angry, or even ecstatic will feel calmer after pounding and pulling at a slab of clay.[140]

The Art of Ceramics

When some people think about clay, they imagine a potter throwing clay onto a wheel and creating jugs like those you might find during an archeological dig. But you don't need a potter's wheel to work with clay.

140 See ch. 19, "The Tools of Art," for more on art theory, and ch. 26, "The Art in Copying."

Most pottery, such as ceramic bowls and decorative vases, can be made by hand. Earth clay, depending on where it was "dug up" and what it will be used for (commercial use or home and school use), can be brown, red, white, or gray in color. Each type has its own properties and best usages. We will be using the type for home and school use. Ceramic clay comes in rolls and is not expensive. You can find it in art-supply stores or ceramic-supply stores.

Clay tends to be messy. When working with the clay, cover the table with plastic to make a clean, easy workstation indoors, or work outside on the porch or in the yard. Protect the child's clothing and work area, and have water and sponges handy to keep the clay damp and prevent it from cracking as you work. Ideally, work on a plaster or wood surface; use this type of surface also as a portable drying area. Clay may stick to marble or Formica; mat-size pieces of canvas or burlap will prevent clay from sticking to the table. I use paper for small pieces. To store unfinished pieces, keep them in plastic bags or plastic wrap so they will stay moist.

You don't need any fancy tools for working with clay. Use a fork for scoring lines, a plastic knife for cutting straight edges on slabs, and dental floss or wire with two ice cream sticks/ tongue depressors attached at each end as handles for slicing large pieces. You can use a rolling pin to roll out the clay to an even thickness and various objects to make imprints on the clay. A garlic press will produce thin spaghetti strands of clay for hair.

But, of course, of all tools, your hands are the main instruments for working with clay. The back of the thumb can be bent up inside a cup or bowl and perform the job of a curved wooden or metal rib used in shaping bowls. The first two fingers on the hand can support a clay pot in progress while the thumb applies pressure to stretch it into the desired shape.

Preparing the Clay

Before they get to work, professional potters knead the earth clay they typically use with motions similar to kneading bread dough. Besides ensuring an even mixture of the clay components, kneading removes air bubbles that can cause the earth clay to burst during the firing (baking) in special ovens called kilns.

Notes and Sketches

Kneading is not necessary with earth clay that will not be fired, yet it is satisfying for children to do and is a good way to practice for bread or challah making. Show children how to use the weight of their whole body, along with the hands and arms, to knead the clay.

When I give children clay, I have them pound a lump of clay into a square. We do it to a rhythm: one-two-three, one-two-three, one-two-three. When one side is flattened, we go on to the next until we have a cube. Don't hit the clay too hard or it will be smashed flat. So do it gently: One-two-three, turn. One-two-three, turn. One-two-three, turn...

How to Resuscitate Dry Clay

Clay should always be kept covered in an airtight plastic bag to prevent it from drying out. To resuscitate dry clay, put the clay in a bucket, and press holes in the clay. Fill the bucket with water to cover the clay and seal the bucket well with plastic. After a few days, the clay will have absorbed the water, making it soft and malleable again, although it won't be the same as when it was new.

When you remove the clay from the bucket, knead it like you would challah dough, back to an elastic and pliable state. Afterward, dampen the clay with a wet sponge as needed to prevent or mend cracks. A sea sponge (a small natural sponge sold in ceramic or craft shops and some cosmetic shops) works well for this, but any type of sponge will work as well.

Joining Clay Pieces

Often, when working with clay, you realize you need to add on pieces, whether it's because you need a larger piece, or you want to add a new element to your work of art. Just sticking on a new chunk of clay doesn't mean it will stick. You need to prepare the clay before joining the pieces.

Score (scratch) the surfaces of both pieces that you want to join together with a clay tool, knife, or fork in several directions. This allows each piece to mix with the other. Apply a layer of slip, made by adding water to some clay until it resembles sticky gooey glue. Join the pieces together firmly and smooth out the seams. This is important to prevent the pieces from coming apart. For added strength, roll a thick rope of clay to apply over seam. Smooth out the rope and blend it until the seam is no longer visible.

When You're Done

Your child has a made a work of art out of clay—maybe a mug or a bowl or a miniature of Rachel's Tomb or Abraham's tent. To his dismay, the next day the mug's handle has fallen off or his bowl has cracked.

Dry clay breaks or cracks easily, sometimes before the children get it home. Proper joining (attaching two pieces)—thorough drying, glazing, and firing in a kiln—lengthens the life span of clay objects.

Glazing means it is given a transparent or opaque, glass-like, waterproof finish. This paint-like coating is applied over pre-baked natural clay. Then, when the masterpiece is baked in the high temperature of the kiln (a type of oven that gets very hot), the glaze melts, leaving a glass-like finish on the artwork.

If no kiln is available to fire the clay, brush the dried pieces with a mixture of white plastic glue and acrylic paint to protect the surface of the clay and give it color and shine. Apply the glue mixture in layers, letting the clay dry in between applications. This doesn't waterproof the piece as firing it in a kiln would, but it does lengthen its life span and adds a shiny finish.

Slabs

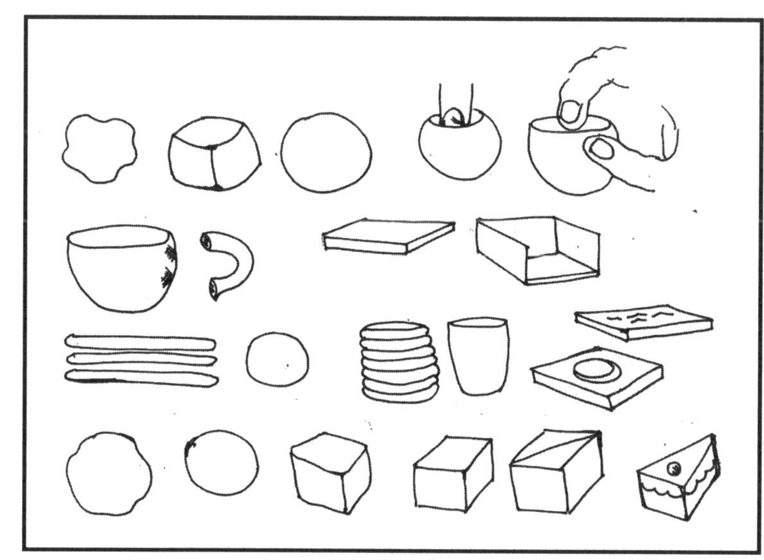

Besides the classic bowl and mug, you can also make boxes, dioramas, and paintings from clay. For these, start with handmade clay slabs—thick, flat pieces of clay rolled out like dough. Slabs are fun and easy to create and can be used to make all kinds of interesting creations.

To create your slab, work on a wood or plastic surface, or on a canvas or burlap mat that is large enough to hold your work. This also makes it easy to transport your work when it is put aside to dry or finish later.

After kneading or preparing the clay, begin by shaping a lump of clay into a ball. Then roll out the slab with a rolling pin. Roll it in several directions, until it is about ½ inch (1½ cm) thick. This will ensure evenness and prevent breakage. Small, finger-size slabs—about 2 to 3 inches (5 to 7½ cm) in length—can be made by pounding and pressing the clay with the fingers, thumb, and heel of the hand.

The slab should be about the same thickness as pizza dough. Point out to the children that it's not necessary to pound the clay hard. Just a light tap of the clay on the hard surface of the table will change its shape. The edges of the slab can be straightened with a dull knife.

Ways with Clay

A box or house: Once you have gotten the hang of making slabs, you can create a box or house. Prepare six slabs, 4 x 4 inches (10 x 10 cm) and about ¾ inch (2 cm) thick, to make a box. You will need six sides—all of the same size for a square box. Cover the slabs with plastic and let dry to a leather-hard consistency (depending on the weather, it usually takes a few days). If it's not leather hard, the clay slabs will stretch, bend, or fall apart while working with them. If it's too dry, it will not be possible to join the pieces.

If you are making a house, decide where the doors and windows will be and cut out pieces from the slab before you join them together. Should you want a triangle-pointed roof rather than a flat one, cut out seven equal pieces, as you will need two pieces for the roof. Add details and accessories (tiles on the roof, mezuzot, a mail box, the family name, birds, foliage, or decorations to the walls) while the clay is still damp.

Join the pieces together by following the guidelines above: First, score both surfaces that will be joined with a clay tool, knife, or fork. Then apply slip (the very sticky, wet, glue-like mixture) to both surfaces with a scratchy toothbrush, a stiff paintbrush, or a finger, and join the pieces. If necessary, wet the clay with a rag or sponge to dampen so that all the pieces are the same degree of wetness and will dry evenly. Support the walls with boxes or rolls of newspapers. Cut shapes can be attached to the slabs by first scoring the slab and then applying slip for proper joining. Let dry slowly over a few days.

Once dry, cover the clay with several coats of white plastic glue or glue mixed with acrylic paint. The boxes can be decorated with a repeating pattern or to look like a house or *beit knesset*. A leather-hard slab may also be shaped into a cone and painted to look like Har Sinai. The *luchot* can be fashioned out of large, thick slabs, and cut to shape. Engrave letters onto the slab with a toothpick or other pointed tool, or paint on the letters.

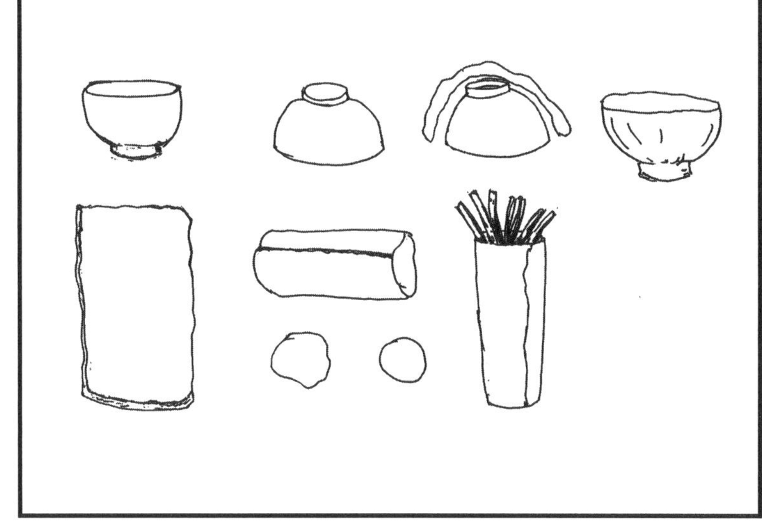

A tube or vase: You are not limited to making boxes or houses out of the slabs. Once you've made your slab, their uses are versatile. Make tall, tube-shaped vases. Wrap ½-inch (1½-cm) slabs around tubes covered with plastic for easy release and removal when the clay is leather hard. Joint the two edges of the slab together by scoring the edges and then applying slip. If a base is necessary, place a suitable size slab beneath the tube and join. Trim as needed.

A bowl: To make a bowl, try crushing newspaper into the shape of a bowl. Roll out a slab large enough to cover the surface. Drape the slab over the mass, and let dry. When the clay is leather hard and retains its shape, remove the newspaper. This draping is similar to covering a cake with a sheet of icing fondant. Press and stretch gently into shape, trim edges, and smooth.

A Seder plate: Why not make a Seder plate for Pesach? A Seder plate can be made from a flat slab of clay cut into a circle with a knife or scissors. Individual dishes holding the symbolic foods of the Seder can be shaped from small circles, balls, or coils of clay.

A Torah scroll: You can make a Torah scroll by rolling the two ends of a long rectangular slab of clay toward the center, leaving a large square area in the middle. Add small wooden rolling pins for the handles or make with clay. Engrave or paint on details and embellishments.

A prayer book: To make an open clay siddur, fold a rectangle-shaped slab in half and then open it. Carve the indentations of a book spine down the center. Carve out a couple of inches from the inner edges to make the "pages," allowing the "cover" to extend beyond the pages.

Scratch in lines with a fine comb or fork along the three outer edges of the "pages."

Decorating: There are several useful techniques you can apply for decorating. Make a decorative impression by pressing a piece of lace, a rubber stamp, or objects cut out of Styrofoam onto the clay. Or make a bas-relief by attaching small pieces of clay shapes or a complete scene such as a landscape on top of the main clay surface.

Cake Decorating

For those who like to create theme cakes, this will be fun and easy. If you don't bake decorative cakes, this will be an inspiration.

Make the cake from a hollow square of six equal slabs, each measuring 3 x 7 inches (7½ x 18 cm) and about 1 inch (2½ cm) thick—one for the top, one for the bottom, and four for the sides. For a layered cake, make two more boxes, one with squares measuring 3 x 6 inches (7½ x 15 cm) and one with squares measuring 3 x 4 inches (7½ x 10 cm). Put the boxes one on top of the other, the largest on the bottom, the medium-sized one in the middle, and the smallest one on top.

Or make three very thick, hollow, round cylinder slabs: 3 x 7, 3 x 6, and 3 x 4 inches (7½ x 18, 7½ x 15, 7½ x 10 cm). Each will have a matching cover, cut to size. Place the cylinder pieces with their covers on top of each other to create a three-tiered cake. A cylinder can be made from a long rectangle slab that is allowed to dry just enough not to lose its shape. Join at the two ends to form a circle. It can also be constructed by wrapping a slab around a container that is covered with plastic.

Paint the dried clay slabs with several layers of beautiful, creamy icing-colored acrylic paint mixed with white plastic glue for a shiny appearance. Use a dab of color—red, yellow, peach, violet—and a large amount of white paint to achieve those frosting-like colors that you want. Decorate the cake with strands of hair (made with a garlic press) or balls of clay shaped into ribbons, hearts, flowers, or cherries. Make a large, thick, flat circle or square to form a cake platter underneath.

Here are projects featuring clay that you can try.

Easy Earth Clay Projects

Begin the earth clay projects with these basic instructions.

Materials:

- Clay from the earth sold in plastic bags in blocks or rolls
- Dental floss, 18 inches (46 cm)
- 2 craft sticks (ice cream)
- Fork, cup of water
- White plastic glue (like Elmer's)
- Acrylic paint and paint brush, ½ inch (1½ cm)

Directions:

1. Review directions for joining clay pieces above.
2. Tie the two ends of the dental floss around each of the craft sticks leaving most of the floss loose between the sticks.
3. Holding the sticks, pull the dental floss through the clay and cut what you will be using.
4. Roll clay into a ball(s) and then the desired shape.
5. Join pieces by scraping with a fork all surfaces to be connected.
6. Apply a small amount of water to each surface.
7. Press pieces firmly together. Smooth some clay from surface #1 to surface #2 and again from surface #2 to surface #1 to reinforce bond.
8. When the project is finished and completely dried, cover with a thick coat of white plastic glue. The glue reinforces the clay and gives a shiny smooth surface to paint on. Dry. Best to dry most projects upside down on a plastic or woven basket so air can circulate.

Optional: Paint with acrylic paint.

Clay Pinch Pot AGES 6/7+

Pinch pots are balls of clay, pinched into a bowl or cup. Pinch pots are one of the most basic and easiest methods used to teach kids how to create a simple vessel from clay. In this project, use real earth clay, sold in arts and crafts shops for school or home use.

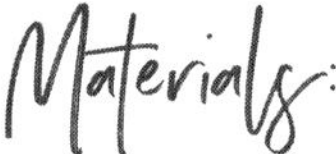

- Red, blue, yellow, and white acrylic paints
- Old stiff paintbrush, about ½ inch (1½ cm)
- Roll of earth clay
- Wood, marble, or plastic board to work on
- Knife and fork
- White plastic glue
- Scissors
- Strand of old beads or old pieces of jewelry, and other objects to make impressions with (optional)

Directions:

1. Break off a piece of clay, measuring about 2 x 3 inches (5 x 7½ cm), and large enough to roll into an egg-size ball. Stick your thumb halfway into the center of the ball to hollow out a space. With the thumb in the hole, place the other four fingers on the outside of the clay ball. Cupping the clay in the hand like that, squeeze the clay in a circular motion around the outside and inside of the ball to form a cup.
   Note: If the child has a hard time working with an egg-size ball of clay, give him a larger, orange-size ball.
2. Smooth out the shape and surface of the cup.
3. Refine the top edge of the cup by pressing the rim gently with the thumb, first, and second fingers. Turn the cup upside down and gently tap to flatten the top edge. Use the knife or scissors to trim the top edge and make it sharp and even.

4. Tap the cup gently on its base to flatten the bottom.

5. With the tip of the knife or fork, engrave a pattern, if desired. Add on decorations formed from small bits of clay (such as ribbons, strips, flowers, houses), or press indentations into the surface with small objects, or score a pattern onto the bowl. Wrap the beads or old jewelry around the cup as an ornament.

6. The cup can be formed into a Kiddush cup with a stem by making a second, smaller cup, turning it upside down, and joining the two bottoms together. (Follow the instructions above for joining two pieces of clay together.)

7. Let the clay dry thoroughly. Coat with two layers of glue, letting the glue dry between layers, and then decorate with acrylic paints. Try layering colors: Let one color dry, then apply a second color, leaving some of the first layer showing through. Now put on a third layer, again leaving some of the first and second layers showing through. This creates a rich, deep, surface shine and texture.

Clay Chanukiyah AGES 7+

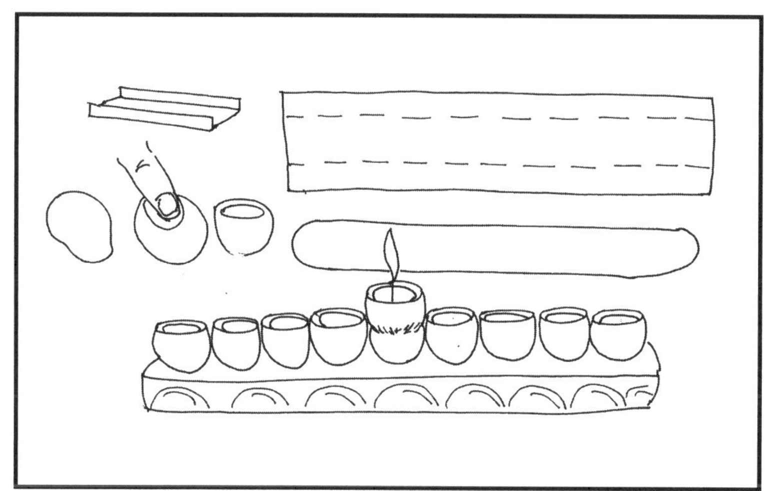

Materials:

- Add a 5 x 13-inch (12½ x 33-cm) piece of cardboard to the materials list of Easy Earth Clay Projects above.

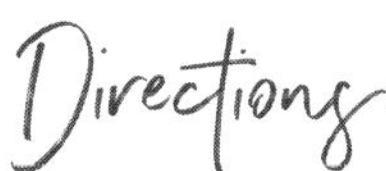

Directions:

1. Measure 1 inch (2½ cm) down from the top of the cardboard and 1 inch from the bottom horizontally (length). Score (cut halfway through) and fold the two sides up. This is the drying and carrying case for the *chanukiyah*.

2. Roll out a base, 10–12 inches (25–30 cm) long and 1 inch (2½ cm) thick. Place in cardboard holder.

3. Roll out ten balls, 1 x 1 inch (2½ x 2½ cm).

4. Form balls into cups by pressing a finger inside the ball cup half-way down and gently squeezing the clay wall out a bit.

5. Set nine cups on the base, checking to see they all fit. Adjust sizes and positions if necessary. Score cups with the fork and water, and press together firmly following joining directions. Add tenth cup on top of the fifth cup (or first or last) for the *shamash*. Score, and press finger inside, down to the bottom of all the cups, until it goes into the base of the *chanukiyah*. This will give extra holding power. Dry.

6. Cover with white glue. Dry.

7. Paint with copper, gold, or silver acrylic if desired. Best to put a piece of plastic in the cardboard base before painting. Dry.

Fill cups with olive oil and cotton wicks, and light on the eight miraculous nights of Chanukah!

Adorable Clay Bears AGES 6+

Directions:

1. Cut off a chunk of clay with dental floss and divide into six balls, 2 x 2 inches (5 x 5 cm).
   Adjust sizes of balls to:

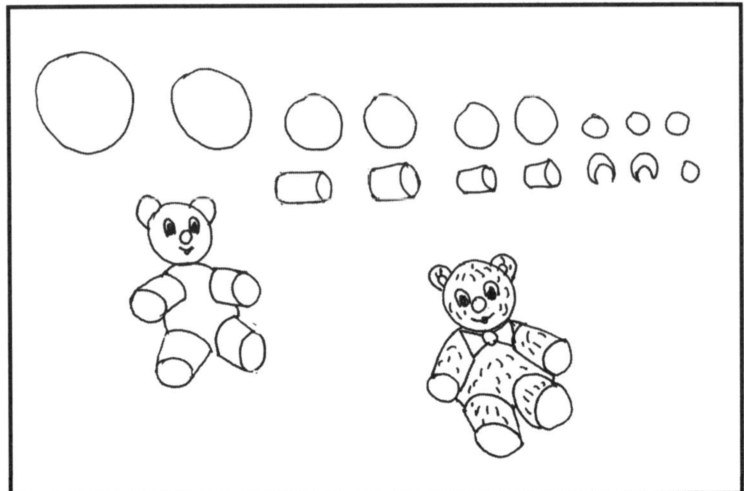

- 2 x 2 inches (5 x 5 cm) for the body
- 1 x 1 inch (2½ x 2½ cm) for the head
- Two 1 x 1 inch (2½ x 2½ cm) for the legs. Roll to form short cylinders.
- Two 1 x ¾ inch (2½ x 2 cm) for the arms. Roll to form short cylinders.
- Three ½ inch (1½ cm) for the nose and two ears.

2. Attach the head, the legs, and the arms to the body, following the joining directions.
3. Form two ears and a nose, and join together. Make indentations inside the ears and for the eyes.
4. Scrape the body with a fork to make lines resembling fur. Dry.
5. Cover with a thick coat of white plastic glue. Dry.
   Paint with acrylic paints.
6. Add a clay bow tie under chin if you like.

Clay Ice Cream Cones AGES 6+

Directions:

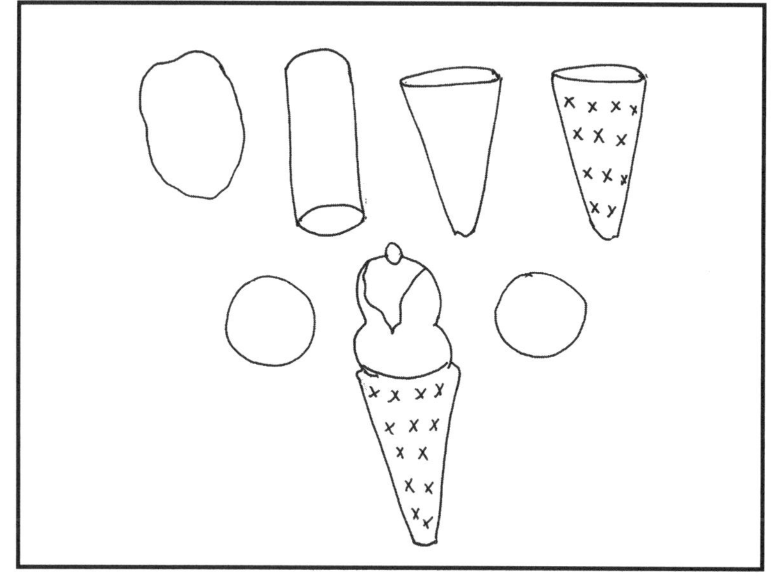

1. Cut a chunk of clay with dental floss. Divide into 3 pieces.
2. Roll out a 2½ inches (6½ cm) long by 1½ inches (4 cm) wide tube shape. Form the bottom thinner at the bottom than the top, and flatten the top a bit to resemble an ice cream cone. Press a garlic press or "draw" lines to resemble the surface of an ice cream cone.
3. Roll two 1-inch (2½-cm) balls for ice cream scoops. Join according to directions. Attach a ½-inch (1½-cm) clay cherry on the top. Dry.
4. Cover with thick coat of white plastic glue. Dry.
5. Paint with acrylic paint: dark brown for syrup at the top, pink and white for the scoops, and red for the cherry.

Metallic Hand-Built Coil Cup or Bowl

AGES 7+

Here is a pot made of coils (clay ropes) that you really put your hands into. It is painted in metallic colors for added beauty.

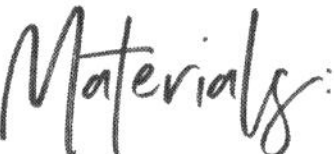

- Metallic, silver, or copper acrylic paint
- Paintbrush, ½ inch (1½ cm)
- Dull knife and fork
- White plastic glue
- Roll of earth clay
- Wood, marble, or plastic board to work on

Directions:

1. Roll out a base from a square slab that measures 5 x 5 inches (12½ x 12½ cm) and is 1 inch (2½ cm) thick. Be sure to place paper or burlap under the base so it doesn't stick to the work surface. With the knife, cut off the corners in curves, making it into a circular base for the bowl.
2. Roll out several clay ropes, each ½ inch (1½ cm) thick and 5–8 inches (12½–20 cm) long.
3. Attach the ropes to the circle base, one rope at a time, by scoring (scratching) the ropes, adding slip, and joining the seams. Continue adding ropes until the vessel is 6 or 7 inches (15 or 18 cm) tall.
4. Insert your hand and forearm into the vessel and smooth first the outside and then the inside with the hands and fingers. Use a scraper tool (or the sides of a dull knife or a pottery rib) to smooth and connect all the coils well. The bowl will be a perfectly imperfect shape and the surface bumpy.
5. Tap the bowl hard yet carefully on the table to make a flat base. Set aside to dry.

6. Once the clay is dry, cover the inside and outside with two or three coats of white plastic glue. Let dry.
7. Paint the bowl with metallic silver and copper paint mixed with white glue in alternating layers. Let dry between layers. Cover a total of three or more layers of paint, both inside and outside, letting the undercoats show through in places.

Air-Drying Synthetic Modeling Clay

Although pottery calls to mind slick, gray, earth clay, there is a great variety of air-drying modeling clays that that are less messy and easier to work with. These are made to resemble earth clay and can be used like earth clay without the necessity of a ceramic kiln firing. Here are some types of modeling clay to choose from:

Paper clay—also called "fiberclay," this is clay to which paper has been added. Some types need to be fired in a kiln, and some can be air-dried. Paper-based modeling clay is similar to papier mâché pulp when moist since it is made with paper, and it has a fine, smooth and even texture. With it you can make bowls, decorations, ornaments, beads, and sculptures.

Plasticine—this is an oil-based modeling compound that doesn't dry, is flexible, and is used for animation and children's art activities. It's good for small children since it is usually nontoxic.

Earth clay with additives—this closely resembles regular earth clay but has added material that hardens in the air or in the home oven, so you don't need to go looking for a kiln.

Das—this is an air-drying modeling clay that has a smooth, even, easy texture that makes it perfect for introducing children to the wonders of clay. It's soft and pliable and can be used to create figures, sculptures, and jewelry beads, among other things. Once it is out of the wrapper it begins to dry.

Play dough—a mixture of flour, salt, and water. Play dough is soft and malleable, a perfect introduction to clay for very small children. Play dough can be bought commercially or it can be made at home. It's meant to be kept moist. Once it dries, it cracks and can't be manipulated.

Fimo or Sculpey—these are plastic modeling compounds called "polymer clays" and are good for creating small objects such as jewelry or sculpting. Use it to make accessories for a doll house or a diorama or small three-dimensional objects as part of a craft design or artwork.

Play Dough

No chapter on clay is complete without play dough. Play dough is clean, easy to use, and safe for children. Commercial Play-Doh first became available in 1956 and has been a popular children's toy till today.

Would you believe that Play-Doh was originally invented as a wallpaper cleaner? At the time, no one ever thought it would be so popular even sixty years later!

Want to make your own play dough? Mix ⅓ to ½ cup salt, 1 cup flour, and ⅓ to ½ cup water. You can add a few drops of vegetable oil if you wish. Knead well and divide into balls, then add a few drops of food coloring into each ball and knead again. You can make each ball a different primary color: red, blue, and yellow. Mix together to create the secondary colors: combine yellow and blue to make green, red and blue for purple, and yellow and red for orange. Mix all three primary colors to make brown. Mix a separate ball of each color.

Store the play dough in airtight plastic wrap in the refrigerator for up to two weeks. Kids can use the play dough to make beads (use a toothpick to make a hole for string), puppets, funny people, and pretend play foods.

Jewish Motif on a 3-D Clay Picture

USING SYNTHETIC AIR-DRYING CLAY AGES 8+

Cutting out etchings from clay sensitizes children to the things they can do with their hands and makes them take notice of shape, weight, size, texture, and measurement. This will improve their drawing skills—which require fine-motor development and a familiarity with shapes—while enriching their knowledge of Jewish concepts.

Materials:

- Copy paper or drawing paper, size 8½ x 11 inches (21 x 30 cm)
- Pencil
- Acrylic paint or tempera in red, blue, yellow, or white for mixing colors, or buy ready-made colors
- Paintbrushes, ¼, ½, and 1 inch (½, 1½, and 2½ cm)
- Heavy cardboard or a wooden panel, measuring 8 x 10 inches (20 x 25 cm)
- Air-drying clay
- Cup of water (to lightly moisten fingers if clay begins to dry)
- Hot-glue gun
- Scissors
- Toothpick or skewer (for drawing in the clay)
- Mod Podge glossy sealer, white plastic craft glue, or clear acrylic sealant (optional)

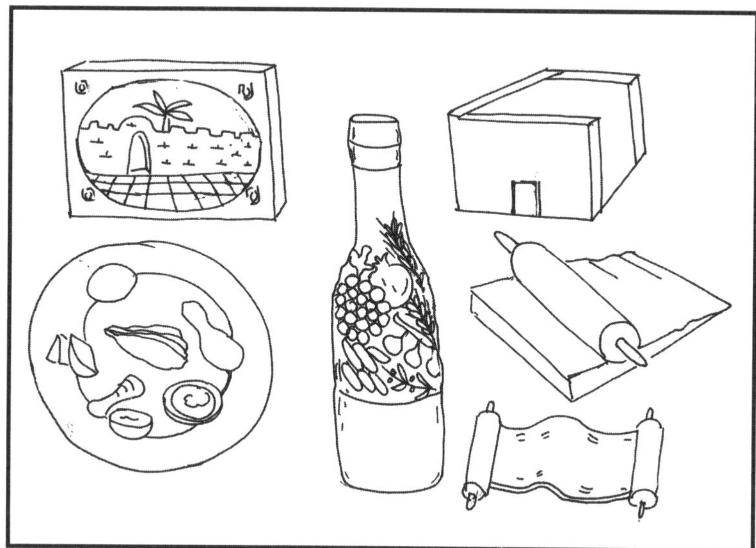

Directions:

1. Choose your scene or motif. Here are a few ideas:

    - Use a traditional motif such as grapes on the vine or the seven species of the Land of Israel (wheat, barley, grapes, figs, pomegranates, olives, and dates,)
    - Craft symbols of the ten plagues.
    - Create a picture of a mother lighting the Shabbat candles in a frame of roses.
    - Make a picture of a father saying Kiddush surrounded by his smiling family.
    - The child's name made from the clay, placed in the center

and surrounded with symbols that are connected to the child's Hebrew name. Use several small images of the same symbol or just a large one. Examples are crowns for Esther, a prayer book for Hannah, a tent for Sarah, drums for Miriam, a tree for Ilana, dates for Tamar, a ladder for Jacob, and a harp or crown for David.

2. With the pencil and paper, practice drawing each object or parts of an image (such as one grape and one grape leaf from a bunch of grapes). Draw everything first in geometric shapes. Then refine them with soft lines to tone down the look of an obvious geometric shape.
3. Cover the cardboard or wood with thin sheets of clay. To do so, press small amounts of clay the size of cherry tomatoes between the thumb and forefinger and press flat onto the board, until the entire board is covered. Cover with plastic to keep moist while you continue to the next step.
4. Hand-sculpt your images based on your paper drawing and press into place. Alternatively, you can draw the shapes on a flat piece of clay, ¼–½ inch (½–1½ cm) thick, and cut out with scissors. Then press each piece onto the board. Work quickly to prevent the clay from hardening.
5. Arrange the clay cutouts in a pleasing relief on the clay background, copying the drawing of your composition. Score the surface and attach with slip. Wet your fingers and the seams of the clay as you work to help the pieces stick. Be sure to attach each piece well, one by one. Attach the largest pieces first and the tiny details last.
6. Let dry. Any loose objects can be hot-glued into place.
7. Paint with the acrylic for a shiny finish or with tempera/gouache for a matte finish. Let dry.
8. Optional: Coat with clear acrylic protective coating, craft glue, or Mod Podge sealer to give it a glossy finish.

You can try this variation of the same theme.

Clay Relief on a Wine Bottle USING SYNTHETIC AIR-DRYING CLAY AGES 7/8+

Rather than creating a clay relief on a flat board, apply it to a wine bottle. You can craft symbols of the ten plagues or use a Shabbat motif, with ribbons, roses, and other flowers, or the seven species of the Land of Israel.

Materials:

- Copy paper and pencil to draw sketch of idea before beginning with the clay
- Acrylic paint: red, blue, yellow, and white to mix your own colors, or buy ready-made colors
- Paintbrushes, ¼, ½, and 1 inch (½, 1½, and 2½ cm)
- Protective sealant or clear acrylic spray
- Scissors
- 1 clean, empty wine bottle
- Air-drying clay, 500 grams
- Rolling pin

Directions:

1. Remove the label from the wine bottle. With a rolling pin, roll out a sheet of clay ¼–½ inch (½–1½ cm) thick, and measuring about 6 x 6 inches (15 x 15 cm). Wrap the flat sheet of clay around the widest part of the wine bottle.
2. Sculpt the symbols for your motif out of balls, ropes, and oval shapes. Fit the shapes together to form your images.
3. Press the shapes into place on the clay-covered wine bottle. Let dry. Use a hot-glue gun if necessary to attach any loose pieces.
4. Paint with acrylic and let dry.

Optional: Coat with a protective sealant or clear acrylic spray.

In Summary: Working with Clay

- Children love the sense of mastery they have when working with clay, whether it's squeezing, poking, rolling, or pressing it with their hands.
- A child can form and manipulate clay while strengthening his hand muscles, and can create functional or decorative vessels and forms for enjoyment and use.
- While the professional ceramic craftsperson uses a selection of professional and technical tools, you can use simple kitchen tools when working with clay.
- A lump of earth clay can be transformed into innumerable objects and vessels before our eyes.
- Before working with clay, prepare it by kneading or lightly pounding it evenly on all four sides.
- After scratching with a fork, knife or tool, join two scorched pieces of clay together with slip, a sticky clay with a glue-like texture.
- Once done, fire the clay in a kiln (waterproof) or coat with a mixture of acrylics and white plastic glue (not waterproof) to give it strength and shine.
- There are types of modeling materials that don't require firing, such as paper clay, air-drying clay, and Sculpey.
- Play dough is a time-honored favorite with children and adults alike and is easily made at home.

Questions and Wonder

1. Have you noticed the difference between using a ceramic plate and a plastic plate? Do you have a preference?
2. Have you noticed the differences between working with real clay and with synthetic modeling material? What are they?
3. Did you know that earth clay is a live material dug out of the earth? It was formed over time from heat and cold and

the shifting movements of the earth. Because it is a live material, could this be why clay is therapeutic (relaxing and stimulating at the same time)?

24 The Art in Copying

Blended Copying

Copying serves an important purpose in art—especially for older children when realism is desired. The creative and productive person learns from the work of others and from what he sees in life. We all copy parts of the world around us. Understanding the art of copying can help one reach their goals of realism quicker than relying on ability alone. Painters of realism, graphic artists, designers, and cartoonists all use this essential skill.

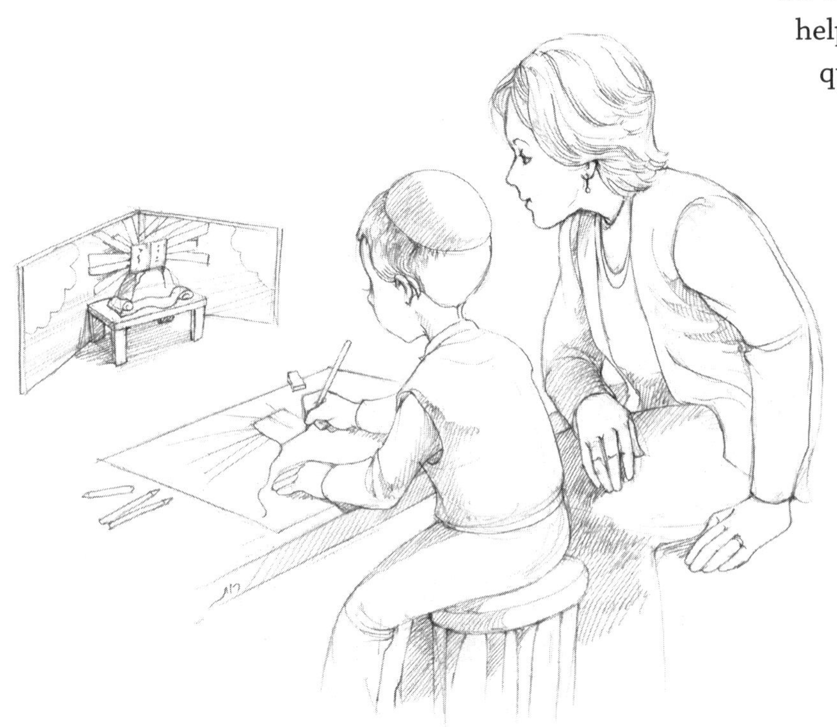

I always found it a compliment when someone wanted to copy my work or one of my students' work. Yet, this is not a typical reaction.

Michael was protective of his style in his artwork and did not want anyone else to copy it. Once he understood the request to be a compliment and that no one could copy it exactly as he did it, he agreed. It was also explained to Michael that everything we draw or create has a basis in nature from the time of Creation. "Nothing is new under the sun."[141] *The form, the style and the materials may have changed. What makes our work unique is our style and personal touch.*

Notes and Sketches

Copying for copying sake is not a goal. Integrated copying is. I emphasize understanding first and copying second. I prefer the children dissect and understand what they are looking at in a drawing on a simple basic level, using geometric shapes. Isolating the shapes and forms and talking about them takes away the mystique of drawing. We also identify and discuss the fine points of a drawing or painting that make it unique because of the style and technique of the artist. We then decide if we want to copy the fine points or only the skeleton (the structure) of the artwork. Copying is knowing how and what to look at. Copying comes after understanding.

Some children are able to record what they see easily, although they may not understand exactly how they are doing it. Other children try many times until they attain a quality of realism. It takes them longer to understand the physical reality of their composition because they may be distracted by a range of other stimuli at the same time. The color or size of the object or drawing that they are copying may be exciting for them, or they may find their hand motions captivating. Some need to observe the work of others or think for a long time before they begin their own artwork. Often young children are happy without the pressures of realism and want to enjoy being called artistic without its standards.

Four Types of Students

The quest for copying has more than one effect on us. Let's look at what might go on inside the heads of four different girls when copying comes into question.

Jenny was the acclaimed artist of her class. She copied the teacher's project, neat and clear. Yet, she didn't enjoy what she did. None of the class knew this. Her examples put stress on the others. They couldn't compete with her preciseness. After a few months, Jenny dropped out of the class.

141 Ecclesiastes 1:9.

Notes and Sketches

Amy's strong points were color and form, but lacked precision. She was given to emotional expression. As she worked on grasping coherence and accuracy, her artwork improved. Her work began to flourish as she gained confidence from lots of practice and good hard work.

Leah was talented and truly motivated to work hard, but was frustrated at not being able to recreate the tons of ideas in her head. She practiced copying photos on her own until she felt confident. Slowly her frustrations melted away.

Bracha simply wanted to learn to draw without too much fanfare. She learned the basic lessons and contently added another skill to her name.

Guided Copying

Copying is a talent some are born with, but as with most skills, it can be acquired. One goal of this book is to help children learn to see the physical reality around them and give it form and shape.

Before children can learn how to trace and copy, they need to have the ability to follow instructions and work in a step-by-step sequence. They usually acquire this skill by the age of six. Since copying is about seeing the patterns and shapes in the object being copied, some children who are very good at copying may not be as talented at free-form drawing, which requires visualization—seeing the object in their mind—and creativity. Copying also involves the ability to compare the size, shape, and placement of one object to another.

Young children under the age of seven should not be expected to copy accurately. Even older children who are able to copy may be unable to achieve the correct proportions or pay attention to the details. These children should be given extra help to enable them to succeed. The main thing is to avoid pressure and tension. Yes, knowing how to copy with accuracy is a valuable skill, but let's keep in mind that for little children copying for the sake of achievement puts undesirable stress and expectations on them.

If the child is too attached to copying, then he is worried about the outcome and not relaxed in the process of his expression. Try to find the middle ground and let the children know that it's okay if they can't copy the object exactly or draw like everyone else. They don't have to be the "best" artist in the class; they just have to try their best. At this age copying is not the goal. In time, it becomes integrated and is encouraged sporadically for specific realistic projects.

Seeing the Shapes in the World around Us

To acquire the skill of copying, children first need to learn how to identify the shapes that form the objects around them. For example, a flower is a circle surrounded by several half circles, a cloud is made of loosely combined half circles, and a group of mountains or hills are triangles of various sizes arranged side by side. A shelf of books is a bunch of squares and rectangles, and a person has a circle for a head with squares and rectangles making up the body.[142] Once they learn to identify and draw the geometric shapes, and to convert a group of shapes into objects, they will be able to copy the objects competently.

Young children around the age of four will be satisfied with drawing the basic shapes and focusing just on length and width in their artwork. Older children, around seven years old, will want to add depth, proportion, overlapping, and shading to make their objects look real.

To begin, show the child an object with simple lines, such as a box or hat. Identify the geometric shapes and lines together. Point out that a box is made from six identical squares, and a hat is an oval with a half-circle above it.

Do this with each object the children draw. Eventually they will be able to identify the shapes and forms that make up an object by themselves and be able to draw them on their own without the help of an adult.

Tracing

After the children are confident with drawing by copying objects around them, you can introduce an art project that involves tracing. If tracing is given before the children are confident of their own work, they may

142 See ch. 17, "Some Art Theory to Get You Started."

lose a little of the self-confidence they would otherwise develop because the drawing is not really theirs. “Theirs” means that they understand how they drew, both the parts of the whole and the order. Even when they take up tracing, remind children that freehand drawing is always preferred over tracing, unless it is necessary as a teaching aid or as a technical skill, as in graphic art.

Children enjoy tracing because it is easy. For best results, select a picture with dark, clear lines or black and white pictures to trace. Give them pictures that have visual appeal and interest them: a vase of flowers, toys, foods, animals. They will also enjoy tracing over human figures and portraits. Tape the picture to a window with sunlight behind it. Then tape a transparent piece of paper, or any type of paper that lets the sunlight in from behind, over the picture; tracing paper, baking paper, or drawing paper should work fine. If the sun isn’t out or you don’t have access to a window, use a flashlight, lamp or a light box (a box with a clear cover and a light bulb inside). Be sure to emphasize that once the tracing is completed, they can change the picture as they like and add their own original touch to it.

Working with Stencils

Stenciled artwork has a lovely folk-art appeal. The centuries-old use of stencils made it possible to reproduce a design on fabric, pottery, furniture, and walls in imitation of wallpaper. Designs included beautiful patterns of flowers, leaves, birds, ribbons, fruits, and scrolls.

A traditional stencil is a closed design that is cut out of a thick material. Imagine a hole (or other shape) cut out of the center of a square. You trace the design onto a sheet of paper or some other blank canvas and then fill in the resulting drawing with color. The stencil is usually made from plastic film, thin metal, or strong cardboard (preferably laminated if you plan to use it more than once).

Wall, mirror, or furniture stencils or patterns made with paint require a stencil made from a thick, firm material, such as film or metal that will hold up to the brushing and not allow paint to seep under the stencil. You’ll also need a knobby, stiff stencil brush or sponge to do the painting.

Another lesser known use of stencils is creating fine art with "homemade" paper stencils. You can make quick, disposable paper stencils of any shapes you wish; all you need is thick paper, a pencil, and scissors.

The stencil can include shapes suited to landscapes: a forest (trees and flowers), the seashore (ocean waves and seashells), mountain ranges (mountains and clouds), and skylines (stars, moon, the sun, clouds, birds, and skyscrapers). Add other objects, such as houses, birds, or animals to create your stencil "painting" on paper.

Draw the shapes. Cut out the inside of each object with sharp scissors. Discard the cut-out shape and use the paper that remains, with its star- or flower-shaped hole (or whichever shape you drew) as your stencil.

Artwork made entirely of stenciled designs requires only toothed paper (slightly rough paper with shallow recesses that catch the powder) and chalk or charcoal that are rubbed along the inside line of the cut out to produce the pattern on a clean sheet. Use two sheets of paper, one for the background and one to cut the stencils from. A stencil can also be made of torn paper, by using the edges of torn paper to rub in rows of color, natural contours (suggesting mountains, seascapes, sunsets), or abstract shapes. Fill the entire paper with a variety of light and dark objects in a composition. Optional: Spray with fixative.

Cartoons and Tracing

Who doesn't enjoy comics? Cartoons hold a fascination—especially for children. The story, the action, the expressions, and the pseudo-realism are captivating. Cartoons, with their simplicity and silly, exaggerated expressions, seem accessible and easy to draw.

Originally, cartoons were not appreciated as art in themselves; they were used as preliminary drawings for fine paintings, murals, and tapestries. In the early 1900s, it became popular to draw caricatures and cartoons to illustrate a story—or impart a piece of gossip. The exaggerated features lend humor or irony to the drawing, which sometimes imparts the message better than if the drawing had more realistic proportions.

The well-defined outlines of cartoons and the fun of the subject material make them ideal for tracing. This teaches children how to draw figures while giving them movement at the same time.

Place tracing paper over a cartoon and trace over it with a sharp pencil, using the tip for the outlines and its side for shading.

Take advantage of the spark of creativity that cartoons often inspire. Tell kids to give their imaginations free rein and reinterpret the cartoons as they like. After tracing over the cartoons, they should try changing them, redoing the expressions, genders (Mickey Mouse becomes Minnie), and clothing. If the character is a boy, they can change the face and dress into that of a girl. If the facial expression is sad, they can redo it into a happy smile. Or, have them add in background: furniture, a forest, a shop.

This is taking the art of copying one step further. After learning how to copy or trace a drawing, children learn how to put their own individual stamp on it. This personalizes the drawing and makes it "theirs."

Here are two projects that make the most of the art of copying.

Torn-Paper Stencil Landscape AGES 9/10+

Create a landscape with torn-paper stencils and charcoal.

Materials:

- Copy paper, size 8½ x 11 inches (21 x 30 cm)
- Charcoal paper, Bristol, or other textured paper
- Pastels, soft charcoal sticks, vine charcoal (resembles burnt twigs), or powdered charcoal
- Paper stump (optional) (A stump looks like a pencil made of rolled paper with a slightly pointed top; it's good for blending and rubbing pencil, charcoal, and pastel work and is sold in art supply shops.)
- Clear acrylic spray (optional)

Directions:

1. Tear about five strips of copy paper, each measuring 2 x 10 inches (5 x 25 cm). These will be your stencils. They are considered one-sided stencils.

2. Position one strip of the torn paper on the charcoal paper or Bristol (smooth, slippery paper won't hold the charcoal powder). Hold down the stencil with the thumb and third finger of the left hand while you gently rub a piece of soft charcoal or pastel along the torn edge of the stencil.

3. With your fingers, go over the area with a gentle circular rubbing motion to spread the color or charcoal. You can also use an artist's drawing tool called a "stump" to spread the pastel or charcoal. When you rub in the pastel or charcoal, the texture can be very delicate and fine or solid and thick. A delicate texture is achieved by gently filling in the stencil area with the pastel or charcoal stick and rubbing in circular motions until the area is completely filled in. Powdered charcoal (which comes in plastic containers rather than a charcoal stick), when sprinkled, will leave a delicate, fine, feathered layer of soft grays on the paper. Yet when it's rubbed in circular motions into the paper, it will leave dark, black layers.

4. Place and rub each stencil 1 inch (2½ cm) from the next for a few rows and then reduce the distance between the rows, or begin placing the stencils at a curved angle, gradually increasing the angle to give the impression of distance in the landscape. Try to achieve a variety of blacks and grays by adjusting the pressure and direction of the rubbing motion.

5. Lift the stencil strip and see the interesting line left by the edge of the torn paper. Replace the torn paper strip as it wears out with another torn strip. Continue filling the page with torn-paper patterns until it's full.

6. Spray with the clear acrylic spray to secure the pattern onto the paper.

Change the Cartoon AGES 8/9+

Practice tracing cartoon characters on tracing paper, then change the gender, facial expression, and clothing. This is a great way to learn how to draw figures and give them movement at the same time.

Materials:

- Copy paper, size 8½ x 11 inches (21 x 30 cm)
- Tracing paper
- Pencil and eraser
- Black, fine-tipped pen
- Colored pencils or markers (optional)
- Scotch tape

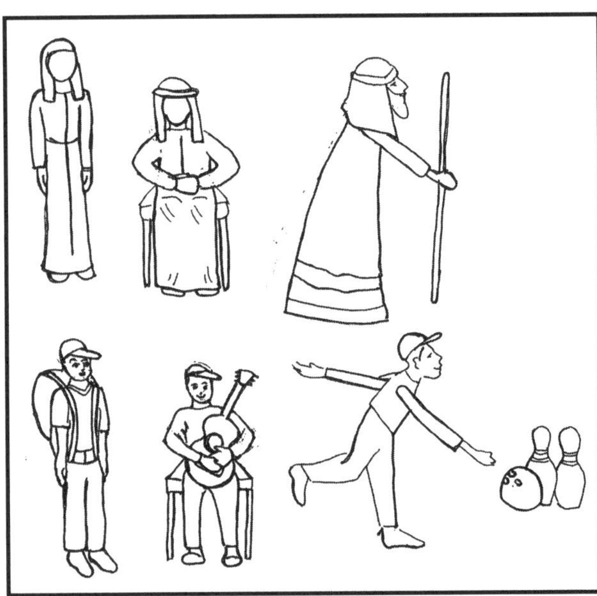

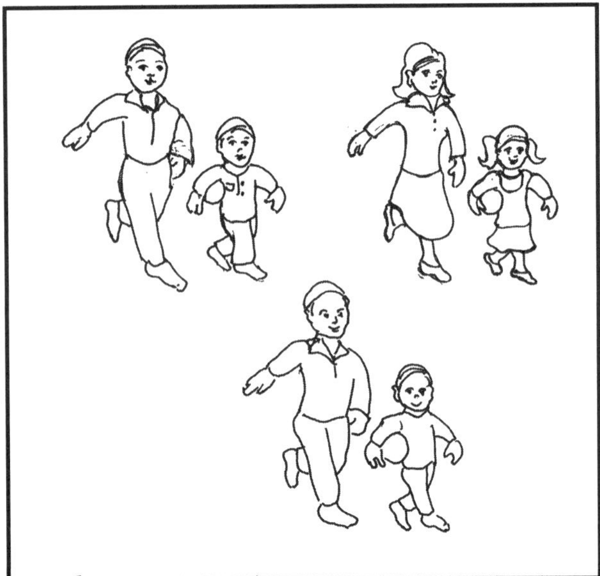

Directions:

1. Choose a cartoon figure from a book on how to draw cartoons or from a coloring book. Lay the tracing paper over the figure and draw it three times.
2. Change the clothes, the face, and the expression so that the final image is of 3 different figures instead of the same one drawn three times.
3. Optional: Draw your figure onto regular drawing paper. Add details and background: a floor and walls, a road and trees, flowers, baskets, lamps, toys, furniture.
4. Add shading (lights and darks) or texture as needed.
5. Draw over the pencil lines with the fine-tipped pen. Color in with colored pencils or markers, if desired.

Optional: Copy the cartoon figures freehand and make changes in gender, facial expression, and clothing.

In Summary:
The Art in Copying

- Copying serves an important purpose in art; painters of realism, graphic artists, designers, and cartoonists all use this essential skill.
- Copying is a talent some are born with, but as with most skills, it can be acquired.
- The first step in copying is learning to identify the geometric shapes in an object or figure.
- Tracing is fun because it's easy; when tracing, use drawings that have dark, clear lines or black and white pictures.
- Stencils are traditionally a folk art to reproduce a pattern.
- Charcoal and stencils of torn paper create a delicate landscape.
- Tracing over cartoons is a great way to learn how to draw people and give them movement at the same time.

Questions and Wonder

1. Have you ever tried to copy a friend's artwork? How did you feel about it when it was finished?
2. Has anyone wanted to copy your artwork? How did you feel about this?
3. What have you learned from copying? What would you like to learn?
4. What is the difference between copying a friend's artwork at school and copying an assignment that the teacher gives in class?

25 All about Drawing People

Drawing the human form can be daunting for someone who is new to it. To help, there are formulas and rules that you can follow. It also helps to understand proportion, and, of course, to practice. Once you understand the proportions of a human figure and you have familiarized yourself with the mechanics of drawing a human figure, you can add an action and draw a person sitting, bending, walking, or running.

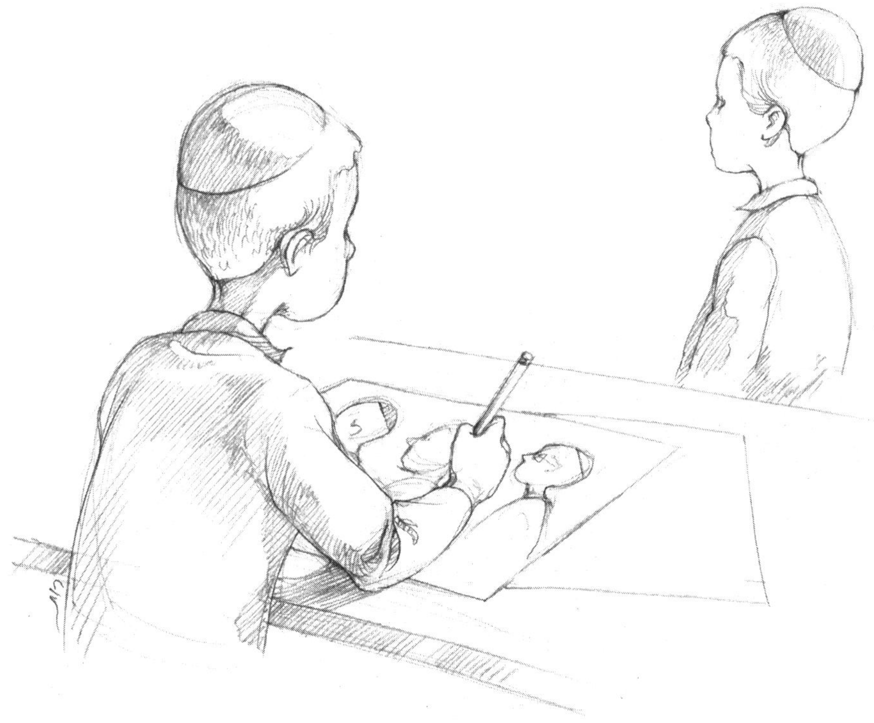

The Golden Ratio

A fascinating fact that can help us appreciate the wisdom of the connective proportions of the human body (as they connect one section to another) is how it is similar in the mathematical proportions of all things in nature. The proportions are the relationship or size of one part of the body to the next. We find the details of this in what is called the "golden ratio" in conjunction with the Fibonacci number sequence.

Notes and Sketches

When drawing the human form, we can apply or at least be aware of the rule of the golden ratio. The golden ratio is the formula for devising the "ideal" of aesthetics and beauty. It is defined by the number phi, and it was put forth by Euclid in the third century BCE. The Torah alluded to this long before Euclid, including information regarding the beautiful proportions of the ratio of the braided and the unbraided sections of the tzitzit.[143]

Nature has a built-in number sequence for the growth and proportions of all living things, including the human being. The Italian mathematician Leonard of Pisa elaborated on the theory in the thirteenth century with his Fibonacci number sequence series. The sequence of growth in nature is that the next number is the sum of the preceding two numbers. That would be 1, 1, 2, 3, 5, 8, 13, 21, 34, and so on, into infinity. The basis is the ratio of phi which is approximately 1:1.618.

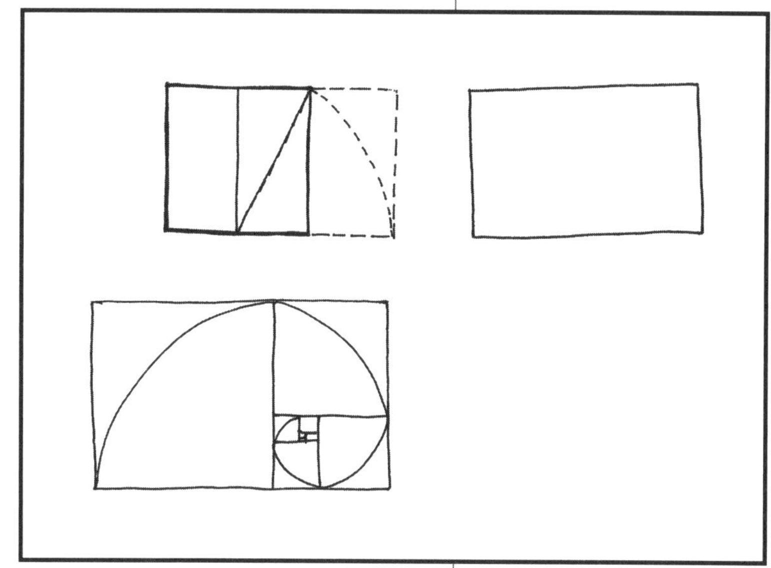

This proportion is often considered the "ideal" of beauty that is consistently found in the proportions in nature. The evidence is abundant: the arrangement of flower petals as they grow from the center out, nautilus shells spiraling outward, and much more. Look at a tree. Usually the leaves are smaller than the branches. The branches are smaller than the trunk of the tree. The handiwork of God is obvious when we know what to look for.

> *Josh was drawing from a photograph of a nautilus shell lying in the sand on a beach. He decided to look at a real shell (cut in half) to see for himself the inner workings of this wonderful design. Not the best math student, he was happy at the ease of counting the measured intervals inside the shell. He then connected*

143 Talmud, *Bechorot* 39a, Rabbeinu Tam, and *Hilchot Tzitzit* 1:8, Rambam. The ratio of one-third braid to two-thirds fringes fulfills the commandment in the most beautiful way to tie the tzitzit. (Based on an article by Rabbi Mois Navon, *B'Or HaTorah*, 2009).

Notes and Sketches

in his mind what he had learned about the Fibonacci formula. Mathematics suddenly became a little easier to grasp.

The Golden Ratio in the Human Form

We find the occurrence of the golden ratio throughout the human form as well. Each part corresponds to the golden ratio of approximately 1:1.618. Look closely at your hand. From the top of a finger to the first joint may be one inch, then one and a half inches to the next joint, and two inches to the next joint. From the smallest area (the tip of the finger) to the next joint, it gets progressively larger within the proportions of the Golden Ratio. The entire body is a system of balanced and pleasurable measurements to the eye. You do not need to memorize these fascinating proportions. It is enough to be sensitized and aware of them.

Proportions by Heads

Another method of measuring an adult figure is by counting heads. The average person is seven or eight heads tall. We will use eight heads for ease in dividing the figure. The head is longer (length) than it is wide (width). Using a ruler, draw a vertical line on a paper and mark off 8 inches, numbering and identifying each inch. Lightly draw a series of eight heads (egg shapes) on the vertical line. Each head should be 1 inch in diameter. This represents the person, from the top of the head to the heel. Now designate the heads for the various body parts:

1=head

2=top of chest area; shoulders=1½

3=waist, elbows

4=hip joints

5=fingertips (open) and mid-thigh

6=bottom of knee caps

7=bottom of calf muscles

8=bottom of feet

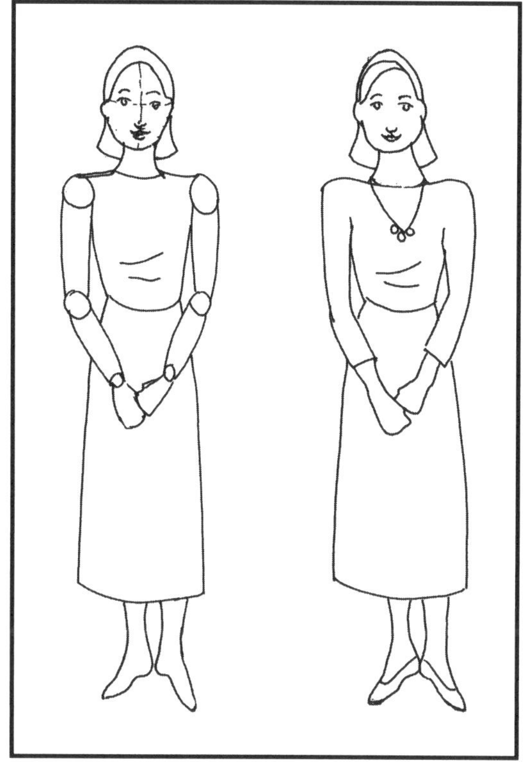

Separately, you can measure parts of the body by heads, yet these will not measure up to eight heads since these parts may be approximate, horizontal, or segmental proportions:

The head and neck are about 1 and ¼ heads. The length of the neck is ¼ of the head.

The shoulders to the waist are 1¾ heads in length.

The hip joint to the floor is 4 heads in length (½ of the total body).

The length of the shoulders horizontally from the far left to the far right is about 3 heads.

The shoulder to fingertips is about 3¾ heads.

The shoulders to elbow is 1¾ heads.

The elbow and waist is 2 heads to the open fingertips.

The hips to the bottom of the knee is 2 heads.

The bottom of the knee to the ankle is 1½ heads.

The foot is ½ the size of the head.

The Shapes of the Human Figure

The human body is most simply drawn either in basic geometric shapes (by younger children) or in tubes and cylinders (by older people).[144] The arm is divided into the upper and lower arm. The moving parts are drawn like balls that connect each area. To draw the arm: Make a large ball for the shoulder, a long cylinder until the ball of the elbow, and a slightly shorter cylinder until the ball of the wrist. The hand is shorter than the lower arm. Note the progression of the proportions according to the Fibonacci sequence. Each additional area is slightly smaller than the preceding area. The proportions of the cylinders of the legs from the hips to the feet follow the same sequence.

144 See ch. 17, "Some Art Theory to Get You Started."

You can practice drawing geometric shapes and combining them into a figure. Or you can practice drawing with cylinder and tube shapes. Start with a head, add a very short tube for the neck, and a barrel tube for the torso along with short and long tubes for the arms and legs. Add hands (about ¾ the size of a face), and feet (about the size of a face) and you have a figure.

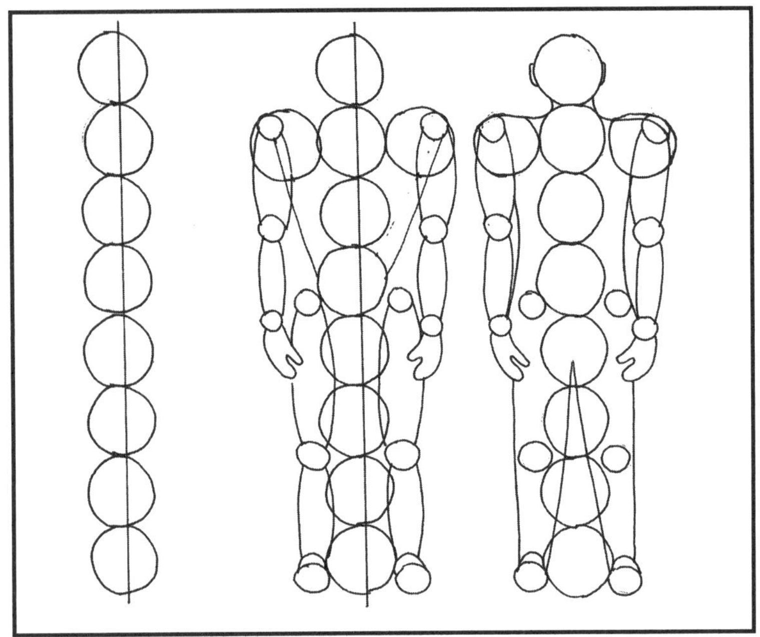

Now you are ready to go on to the more subtle lines in the human figure. You can refine all the lines by softly curving them and optionally adding shading. Note that nothing is ruler straight in the body except for the direction of a limb. The body is made up of a network of curves and ripples. Look at your fingers carefully to see this. Finally, erase any unnecessary lines, according to your style and taste.

Leora liked to use rulers to draw lines in her pictures when her freehand confident level was low. Yet when she drew people, she instinctively knew she didn't use a ruler to draw a person. A real human being is not a series of straight hard lines. She sketched circles and tubes lightly, added curves and bends and finally facial features and details. She softened hard lines and strengthened soft lines, mentally measuring proportions in her head until her drawing of a girl came to life.

Proportions by Touch and Feel

Children, especially girls, like to draw stock-icon, clip-art style figures. The drawings are cute and predictable. Each girl in the class strives to get the curves of a lovable cartoon mouth just right like her friend did.

Julie drew a cute little girl with a smile and a pretty dress. The hearts on the dress were adorable as well as the overly tiny hands and feet. The one part that did not make sense was that the arms (including the hands) only reached until the waist. Can you imagine the difficulty of functioning with such arms? Without changing the integrity of her drawing, I mentioned that the arm (from the shoulder down to the fingertips) reaches about halfway down the leg between the hip and the knee. I asked Julie to stand up straight and feel where her hands reached to. The realization of the proportions was exciting news for Julie.

Use yourself and/or your child as a model. Keep in mind that these dimensions are general and each person is different. A male will generally be larger and wider than a female, including his face. Stand up and place your hands on the top of your head with both sets of fingers touching each other. Feel the width of your head. Put your chin into the palm of your hand and feel the width. Mentally compare the width of the top of your head to your chin. The bottom of the face (the chin) is small compared to the top. Now draw an egg shape for the head.

Feel your neck. It is not a little box that the head sits on. The neck begins from behind, at the bottom of the ears. Place your hands behind the ears and feel the downward slope toward the shoulders. Draw the neck.

Take a minute and feel your head resting upon your neck and note where it sits in proportion to the ends of your shoulders. Each shoulder is close to a head's width.

Now note your shoulders. Imagine a ball in each end. Roll the balls backwards. Draw the two small balls.

Imagine a line across from one ball to the other. Draw this line. This is the collar bone. The center of the line, right below the face, is curved slightly downward, like a necklace.

From the bottom of each shoulder ball, draw a line down to the waist, about the length of 1½ heads. Draw the lines slightly narrower where they reach the waist than at the shoulders. Draw a line across the waist.

Put your arms at your sides. Your elbows touch the waist. This is how you know how long the upper half of the arm is. From your elbow to your wrist is about a head's length. The entire arm from the shoulder until the fingertips is 3½ heads in length. The arms narrow as they approach the wrist. Draw the arms.

The shape of the hand is a beautiful complex arrangement, similar to the flat bottom of a laundry iron but is curved at the top. Note that each finger follows the curve, is tapered, and is a different height. Note that the thumb is attached below the set of fingers and to the inside of the hand. If there were no thumb, it would be very difficult to grasp and hold objects. Try picking up a pencil without the use of your thumb.

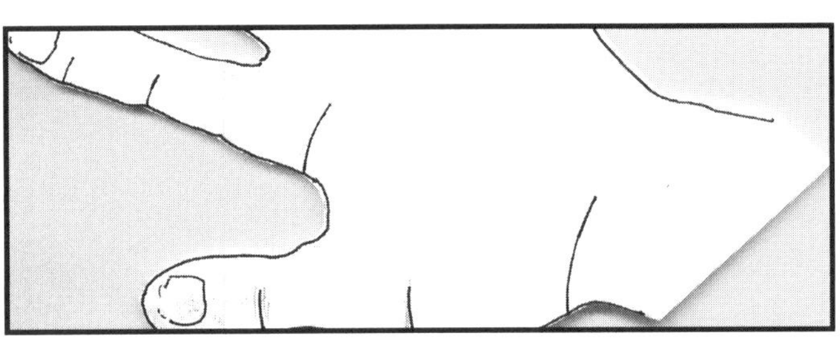

The length of the hand from the palm to the top of the finger is the same as from the chin to the middle of the forehead on the face. Feel your open hand, palm to chin against your face. Draw a general shape or outline of the hand.

Bend down and pay attention to your legs, knees, ankles, and feet. Below your waist, at the sides of the navel, are your hip bones. The hip bones intersect with the top of the legs in the socket. From the hips down to the floor is four heads long.

The bottom of the knee to the floor is two heads in length.

Compare your foot to your hand and face. The foot is about the length of the head plus the length of a big toe.

Draw the figure from the waist, down to the heel.

Sit in a chair. Bend your arm at the elbow and put your hands to your knees. It's interesting how they reach the knees so effortlessly. Note how the body works in unison. Find and talk about other examples.

Draw a Basic Head and Face AGES 8+

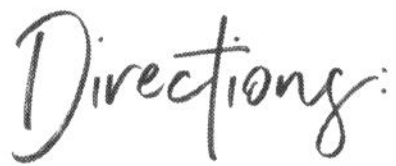

1. Draw an egg shape (wider at the top and narrower at the bottom).
2. Draw two lines, one down the middle vertically and another across horizontally. This will help you to keep the features in their proper locations.
3. Draw two almond-shaped eyes, one on each side of the vertical line, each centered on the middle, horizontal line.
4. Above the eyes, draw slightly curved eyebrows.
5. Draw in the eyeballs. Add eyelids covering the top of the eyeballs.

6. Halfway between the center of the eye line and the chin, mark a line for the bottom of the nose.
7. For the nose, draw three, small connecting circles with the center circle larger than the others. Refine the circles into a nose. Erase the bottoms of the two side circles. Erase the top of the larger center circle. Draw the bottom nostrils of the nose. Add a slightly curved line along the length of one side of the nose to indicate the nose bone.
8. Halfway between the bottom of the nose and the chin, mark a line for the bottom of the mouth. Draw the bottom lip.
9. Add the upper lip and complete the mouth.
10. Lightly draw the top of a small half-circle under the mouth. This is the top of the chin.
11. Draw a very thin vertical oval on each side of the head for two ears. They should be centered between each eye and the top of the mouth.
12. Draw a line resembling the front of a swimming cap about halfway down the forehead, curving to the top of the ears. This is where the hair line begins.

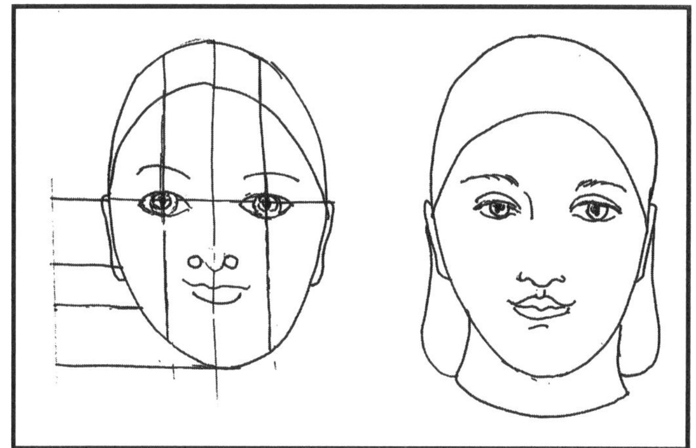

Draw a Profile of a Face AGES 8+

See illustration.

1. Start with a 2 x 2-inch (5 x 5-cm) box. Inside the box, draw a large egg shape. The top and bottom of the egg touch the top and the bottom of the square.
2. Add a large oval vertically across the top half of the head that touches the sides and top of the box. This tells us where the forehead and the back of the head are.

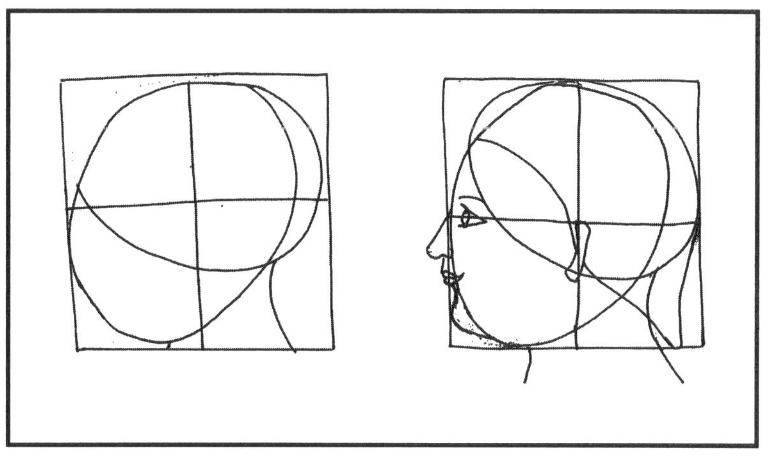

3. On the left side under the front of the forehead (oval) draw an eye: an open triangle facing left with an oval in the opening. Add an eyebrow.
4. Draw a nose starting with a curve from the bottom of the forehead extending outside of the box and ending about 1/8 inch (1/4 cm) above where the mouth begins.
5. The mouth, a sideways heart shape divided in the middle (vertically), partly extends past the outline of the egg shape of the head.
6. Draw ¼ inch (½ cm) curve indented (to the right) under the mouth, and continue the line down and outward (to the left) ¾ inch (2 cm) for the chin.
7. Divide the box in three by lightly penciling in three vertical lines.
8. On the right third segment, draw an ear under the top circle. The ear begins at the height of the eyebrow and ends at the height of the top of the mouth.
9. In the right side (back side) of the head under the oval shape, draw a slightly curved line down to the bottom of the box to indicate the back of the neckline.
10. Draw a line for a swimming cap (at the top of the forehead) from the front of the forehead to the back of the head above the ear. This is the hair line. Draw in the hair.
11. Erase the square.

Practice profiles a few more times until it comes naturally.

Let's Practice

Practice the head proportions on paper. Once you have practiced with the head measurements and can draw the face, add in the figure. Spend time getting to know the face and the figure. Draw lightly first and then go over the lines that you are happy with in darker lines. Leave some of the lines lighter for a delicate contrast. Add in clothing, shoes, and details.

Continue with three figures, each in a different position. One is standing, one is sitting, and one is walking.

The standing figure follows the basic proportions discussed above. The sitting figure bends at the hips. The walking or running figure has its arms swinging from the shoulders. If the right leg is forward, the left arm is forward. One leg/foot is forward, and one leg is behind with the heel raised.

Practice drawing sections of the body (the hand and wrist or the hand and arm) and quick sketches based on the forms (geometric or tube shapes) of the human figure and face. Look from your window to the street and draw people quickly for thirty to sixty seconds to catch their movements. Do one-minute drawings of people and children in your home. Then ask someone in your family to sit or stand for five or ten minutes while you draw them. Keep in mind the proportions!

A Scene with People AGES 8/9+

Choose a scene from memory or your imagination about a favorite vacation or visit with a special friend or relative. Include 2 or 3 figures in a drawing or painting composition. One is standing, one is sitting and one is walking. Draw the people according to the approximate human proportions mentioned above. Add in details (airplanes, suitcases, packages, toys, animals, food), a background of nature (trees, mountains, paths, clouds, sky), or the insides of a building (furniture, lighting, windows, doors).

Materials:

- Copy paper, size 8½ x 11 inches (21 x 30 cm) or larger to practice on
- Drawing/painting paper, size 8½ x 11 inches (21 x 28 cm) or larger. If using paints, use a paper that takes water.
- Pencil and eraser
- Fine-tipped pen to go over pencil lines
- Choice of colored markers, colored pencils, or gouache paints and a small brush

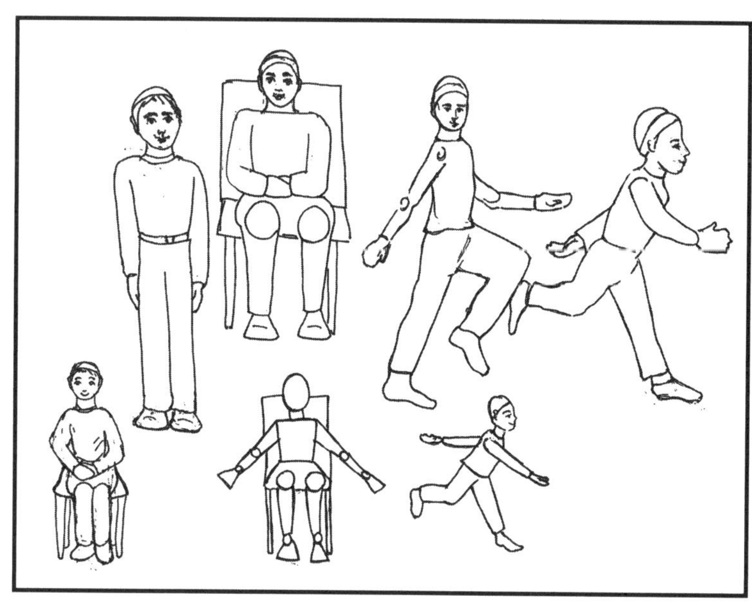

Directions:

1. First practice drawing three figures: one standing, one sitting, one running. Begin with a combination of geometric shapes for each figure. The standing figure is the basic figure: head, neck, shirt, arms, hands, pants, and shoes. The running person has one leg bent at the knee and one leg extended outward. The sitting figure is composed of the head and shirt. His arms are folded at the elbows (along the waist), with the hands touching each other. Draw two knees touching the bottom of the shirt. Add legs and shoes. Draw in the cushion of a chair. Add two legs and a back to the chair.

2. On the final paper, draw a horizontal line dividing the paper. The upper half is the sky and the lower half is the earth. Lightly draw your figures in. The figure that is bottommost will be the largest and appear the closest. The ones higher will be smaller and appear further, or they can all be the same size.

3. Draw the environment, indoors or outdoors, with details. Look at illustrated children's books or photos for examples and ideas. Practice any part of the composition that is uncertain for you.

4. Draw over the pencil lines with a fine pen.

5. Color in as desired.

Optional: Draw the three figures: standing, sitting, and running, without a story or background.

Optional: Draw a story from the time of the Pesach. Imagine what the people wore after they left Egypt and were in the desert. Dress the people in long robes, head coverings, gold or copper jewelry, sandals, walking sticks, woven scarves, and blankets. Add trees, hills or deserts, and the landscape if it's outdoors. Add appropriate features and details. Include foods (dates, pita bread, and water jugs) and animals (camels, donkeys, goats, and sheep).

In Summary: All about Drawing People

- The wisdom of the connective proportions of the human body is similar to the mathematical proportions of most things in nature. The explanation is found in what is called the Golden Ratio and the Fibonacci number sequence.
- The human body can be divided into eight one-inch vertical sections, each about one head in length.
- The easiest shapes to begin drawing the human form with are either geometric shapes or tubes and cylinders.
- The body bends and moves at the joints; circles or balls can be drawn to represent the shoulder joints, the elbows, the wrist, the hips, the knees, and the ankles.
- Examine your fingers, hands, and arms by touch to get a feeling for proportions.
- The head begins as an egg shape and later becomes a face.
- Practice drawing family and friends as standing, sitting, and walking figures.

Questions and Wonder

1. Have you thought about the wondrous creation of the human body and all of the parts and how they fit together perfectly—each has its own function and yet works together as a whole?
2. The human being is designed in the image of God. What does this mean to you?
3. Have you wanted to draw people but didn't know how to begin? Try simple formulas to get you started.

26 The Fortunate Mistake

Tami, age eight, wants to produce a finished work of art, so she tries copying her older friend's composition. Tami gets frustrated quickly; her skills can't compare to her friend's, who has already taken a few years of art lessons. Her friend has had hours of practice with the brush and pencil—experimenting, observing, and understanding how shapes and form work, how to mix colors and create nuances with shades. All this experience contributes to her skill and self-confidence.

Tami wants results without acquiring her own experience, but by copying (even if she happened to be good at it), she will never be able to achieve the personal satisfaction of developing her own artistic style. Learning and growing through her own mistakes and taking the time to build her skills will enable her to create and feel good about her art.

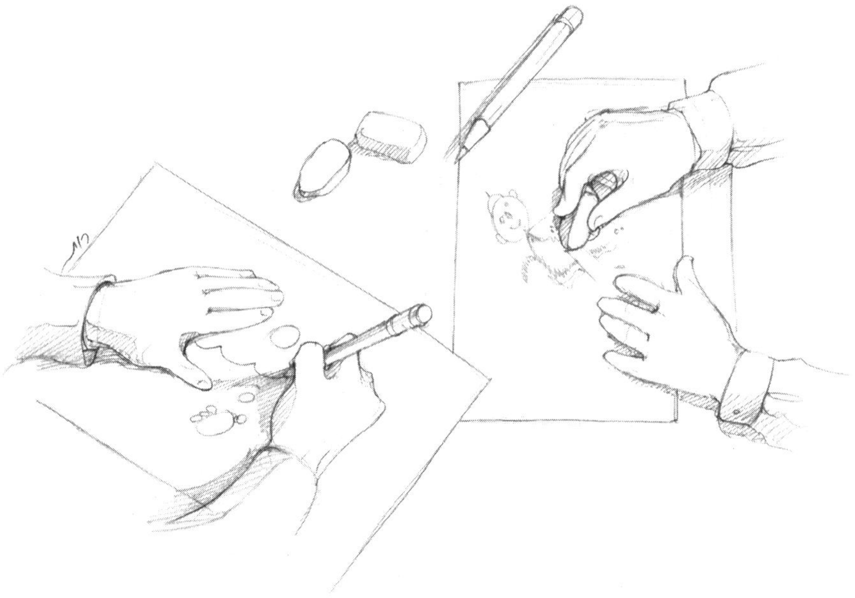

Mistakes are part of the learning process. When children play and discover new skills,

Notes and Sketches

we don't label their imperfections as mistakes. We know that they need to keep trying and repeating an action until they master the skill.

Presenting art projects with this mindset will result in lovely works of art that children will be proud of, because they worked through the challenges and created it themselves. They didn't only copy; they went through the steps and mastered each one. That is what success is all about.

The Valuable Mistake

Each mistake we make serves as a valuable lesson, an opportunity to understand what went wrong and how to do better next time.

Mistakes humble us. They tell us that we are human and that we have limitations. Children need to know that though they should try their best, they don't have to be perfect, because there is no such thing as the perfect person.

Mistakes also make us more compassionate. If we are not perfect, then we can't expect others to be perfect. We can give others the benefit of the doubt and be forgiving of their mistakes.

Since each child is unique, so are his growth patterns and mistakes. When a child makes a mistake, he may not notice it at all, or he may feel vulnerable at first and try to deny it, or he may find the results of the mistake interesting.

In art, we want to help the child make the most of a so-called mistake. Rather than being a detriment, mistakes can be exciting and eye-opening.

Rarely does a mistake mean that the artwork is irreparable. A mistake can always be painted over; a pencil drawing can always be redrawn. But more, rather than covering up a mistake, it can be turned into an advantage—it may give inspiration for changing a drawing entirely, or for experimenting with a new technique. A mistake can turn into an opportunity for testing new materials and creating a new composition that we would never have considered before.

The Torah teaches that not only are mistakes part of being human but they are essential. One does not arrive at a full understanding of the words of Torah until he stumbles in interpreting them. One then applies

Notes and Sketches

his concentration until he fully understands the matter.[145] True understanding can only be reached after one has had some failed attempts. Success is not the primary goal—understanding is.

Art teaches children that there is always room for improvement, both in their artwork and in life. When a child says that he doesn't like his drawing. I ask him what he doesn't like and offer suggestions. Then I tell him to rephrase his feelings and say, "The next one will be better. Improvement is always possible for me."

In other words: I can learn from my mistakes.

Art with a Plan

In art activities, most young children are fascinated with finger painting. Anything goes, and they can make the page as colorful and messy as they like.

Children love making butterfly prints: Fold a piece of paper in half, open it, and apply paints down the center line. Then refold it and press the folds together, brushing the paper with the fingers in strong, broad strokes away from the folded line to allow the paint to set in. When the children open the paper again, they are delighted to find a vibrant, butterfly shape. They love the element of surprise that comes out of a few blobs of red, yellow, and blue paint.

There are many such activities for young children, where they can just enjoy the feeling of the materials between their fingers and surprise themselves with what they can create.

But when they grow a little older, they graduate to an interest in purposeful art—art with a plan. They may become frustrated at their inability to produce their idea on paper on the first try. They will begin to call everything that doesn't fit their ideal of the finished product a "mistake."

Just as a child who is learning to walk isn't making a "mistake" when she falls, but rather is discovering the intricate motor skills she needs to apply in order to finally make those first steps, so too, mistakes in art are a learning process. Let us show our children that mistakes are opportunities, necessary stepping-stones to learning new skills, not signs of failure.

---

145 Talmud, *Gittin* 43a.

The good thing about making a mistake in art is that it's not as scary as it can be in real life. The worst outcome of a mistake is having to redo part of the piece—frustrating but not life-threatening.

There are two approaches you can take to mistakes in art: Defuse and lessen the impact of the mistake, or work with the mistake and remold it.

Defuse It

You can minimize mistakes by making sure children understand what they are meant to be doing. One way to do this is by showing the children all their options before they begin the project. By pointing out possible difficulties they may encounter and how to deal with them, you can defuse the potentially negative and explosive reactions to mistakes.

Here are some ways you can prepare children before they start an art project:

1. Take off the pressure and give them a project they can relax with. Begin with something simple, like mixing colors with paint (no pencils yet!). Give them a few large sheets of paper folded into four, six, or twelve squares. Mix different combinations of paints, two colors on each square. Or cover the entire sheet with a mixture of white and blue paint. Let them experience the motion of the brushstrokes as they mix the white paint with the blue and swirl it on the paper. Let them just enjoy the act of creating something without the need to be exacting.

2. Introduce geometric shapes. Discuss the geometric shapes and explain how to make objects and people out of basic shapes.[146] Learning the basic building blocks of drawing will give children the confidence to advance.

3. Demonstrate all art projects step by step. It's sometimes hard for children to work when they aren't sure exactly what they are supposed to be doing. Make sure children know what should be done by each step. Explain what options are available to them in each step.

4. Show the value of practicing drawing a draft or constructing sample sections of the artwork that may be difficult for them.

146 See ch. 17, "Some Art Theory to Get You Started."

Explain to them that it is easiest to begin by drawing very lightly with a pencil. The picture can be redrawn even without erasing if they aren't happy with it because they haven't yet made any big commitment to the drawing. They can redraw over the sketch and make changes as they wish, keeping the parts they like and ignoring the others. When they are satisfied with the drawing, they can now draw over the final pencil lines with a fine-tipped pen or marker (now is the time for the commitment). Afterwards, they can erase any unwanted pencil lines.

5. Talk about the creative process. Creativity means options, discovery, surprises, and endless opportunities. It requires both building and breaking down, repetition, and a good foundation of skills.

6. Discuss the value of each child's own unique style. Let your child know that everything she does has a unique quality. Emphasize that you want to develop her style and signature and not someone else's. Explain why it is not necessary to draw or paint exactly like her friend or to copy exactly what the teacher drew on the board. Encourage her to put in her own ideas within the framework of the project. "Nothing is new under the sun,"[147] but it is how you—and no one else—do it that makes it special and unique.

7. Don't lose sight of the goal. Perseverance, not giving up in moments of frustration, while maintaining a positive vision of what one is trying to create, is essential. Climbing those mountains of doubt can make art time challenging, but at the same time it can stimulate new ideas. When they reach the summit and complete their composition, it is much more satisfying.

8. Simplify for the slower child. A child who is slower than average and needs extra one-on-one guidance should be given attention with *simchah* (happiness). Provide a simplified form of the main project for the slower child, if necessary, not the same project that everyone else is doing. In general, the best way to encourage participation is to let children do something they can be successful with.

9. Make the project as easy as possible for him to do and gradually introduce him to more advanced art techniques. Praise the child's strong points and keep the goals simple and fulfilling.

---

147 Ecclesiastes 1:9.

Repetition with variation works well; vary the subject matter so it is not boring.

10. Consider the child's preferences. and give him the opportunity to do artwork that he enjoys. When we are happy doing what we enjoy, mistakes are not a big issue. After completing his chosen project, the child will be willing to try other options.

11. Show children that there are many ways to make something. There is no reason to feel restricted. A house has many styles and options—porches, patios, security fences, a fifth floor, stairs and ladders, windows and doors of any kind, yellow birds on the roof—let the child have free rein. The possibilities are limited only by the materials they are given to work with, the level of the children's skills (technique), their imagination, and their confidence.
    The multitude of options in any art project (choice of color, size, material, subject) signal to a child that life also has options. One doesn't need to get stuck in one way of thinking, doing, or creating if it doesn't work. Art is a background for practicing and acknowledging the varied options in life and learning how to be flexible and choose wisely.

12. Ask the child to anticipate difficulties and suggest solutions. Ask for or suggest questions. What worries might the child have about the project? Give answers and options. Show that it's okay to make mistakes and that there are ways to fix them.

Now that the children have been prepared for working with mistakes, go on to the exercises.

Here are two exercises you can do with children to teach them how to anticipate mistakes and work with them:

1. Draw a picture and intentionally add in a few mistakes: a line out of place, an object too large or too small, or a smear. Now discuss ways of using or reworking the mistakes.

2. Demonstrate solutions to mistakes. Draw a picture. Place a clear plastic sheet over the drawing. Use a dry-erase marker to simulate a mistake. Follow with three solutions all drawn on the plastic sheet and erased one at a time, as you move on to the next solution.

Use the Mistake: Postponing the Eraser

The art teacher stood at the front of the class and announced, "We have a great drawing project today. What makes this project special is that we won't be using erasers."

Instead of the typical smiles on the faces of the girls whenever the teacher offered a new project, hysteria broke out. The idea that they wouldn't be able to use erasers induced unprecedented panic.

In my early teaching career, I didn't let the children use erasers for a few sessions. The plan was to show them that they could change their mistakes without erasing if they let themselves try.

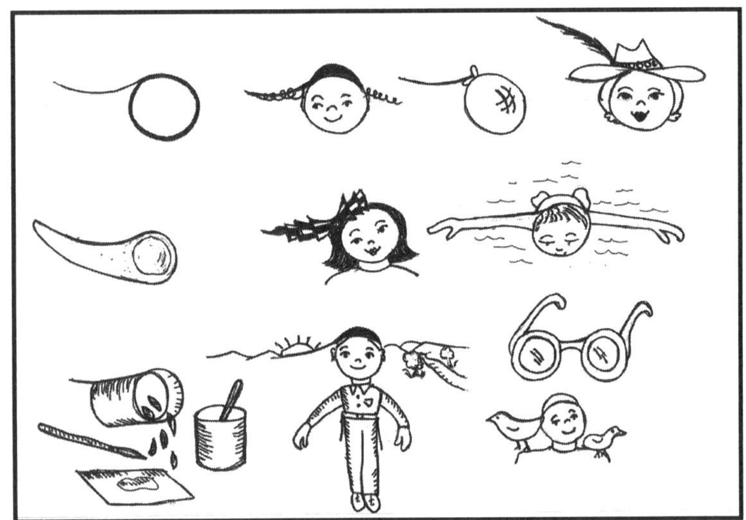

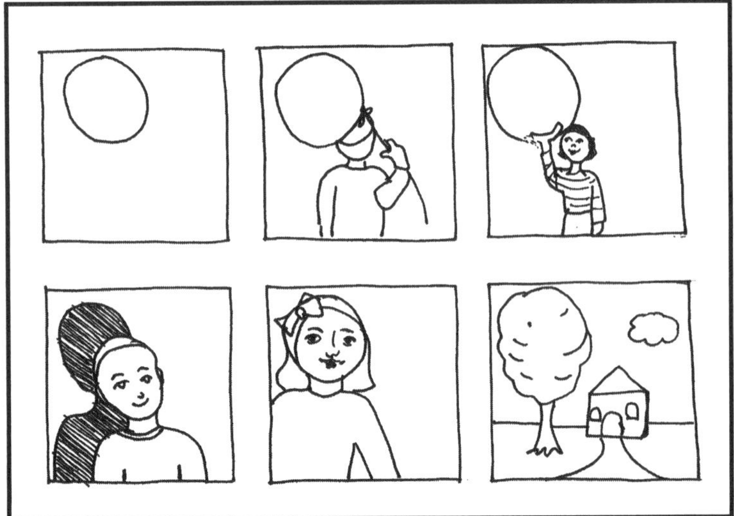

Most of the children were able to do it once they had accepted the situation. But a few girls were so miserable and frustrated at not being able to use an eraser that they actually cried. As I gained more experience, I learned how to introduce the idea of not using an eraser in a more acceptable way so that eventually it was well received by my students. Interestingly, though, years later when I ran into that original group of girls, now high-school age and beyond, they told me how much they loved my classes—especially the ones where they couldn't use erasers. One girl studying a field of therapy mentioned that her college teacher complimented me, her former art teacher, on holding back the eraser, however temporarily. Among other things, it helped to build character.

We said that one way to help children handle mistakes in art is to defuse the mistakes by giving the children the proper materials, a good foundation of skills, and room to be themselves. What happens when the mistake has been made? Is that it? Is it time to start all over again?

An eraser can solve any of the thousands of drawing errors that children constantly make. It enables these little disasters to disappear in the blink of an eye. But if we erase a mistake too quickly, without examining our options and solutions, our gains are limited.

If children learn that they can manage without an eraser at the beginning of their drawing careers, they will gain more confidence in their artwork and other areas in life as well. By postponing the use of an eraser, children will gain opportunities to learn how to turn the negative into a positive. We can turn sour lemons into sweet lemonade with the addition of just a little sugar and honey.

When I introduce the idea of not using erasers, erasing is not outlawed in the drawing class—it's simply postponed until the children have learned how to make the most of their mistakes. The erasers are handed out toward the middle or end of the art session to those who want them. After they have gone through the process of working without an eraser, the children can use erasers as they please. The ideal situation is knowing how to draw two ways: with and without using an eraser.

No doubt this experience can be difficult and frustrating for those who are used to constant erasing. There will always be the child who will insist on using an eraser. Encourage the child to put it aside and give postponing the eraser a chance.

Five Solutions to the "Give Me an Eraser" Syndrome

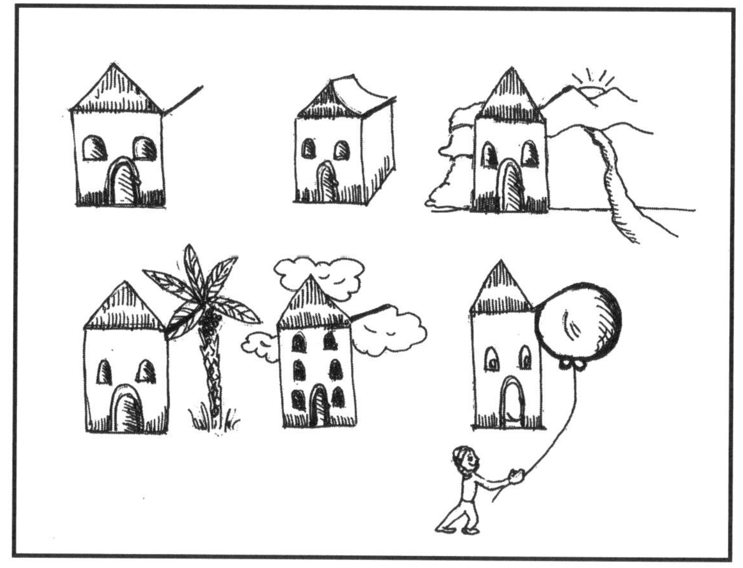

There are several ways to use a mistake to your advantage.

Solution #1: Acknowledge the mistake and incorporate it into the picture.

When you see that a child is upset with her mistake, ask, "What does the mistake look like to you?" Give her time to think and give an answer. Offer suggestions only if needed. This way the child is encouraged to adjust and redraw the mistake to fit the picture. Here are some examples of how children were able to turn mistakes into opportunities:

Devorah is drawing a roof on a house when Esther accidentally bumps into Devorah's elbow. Devorah's roof now looks like a telephone wire.

Solution: Devorah can finish her roof and use the unwanted line as a telephone wire, a bird in flight, a ladder near the roof, a mountain behind the house, a fence on the roof, or a cloud passing over the roof.

Helpful Sarah, who is explaining to Chani how to draw curtains on a window, touches Chani's paper and accidentally smears the window, the one that Chani worked so hard on.

Solution: Chani's window now has a smear on it. Thanks to Sarah, Chani now has the first mark in her curtains' pattern or texture. Alternatively, she can include a shaded area inside the window. She can add an outline around that shaded area and make that into a curtain as well.

Ruthie drew a nice, big head on the girl she was drawing but left no room for the rest of the girl's body.

Solution: Ruthie can redraw a smaller girl with a head and body inside the first head which has now been redefined as a big circle. The circle can become a balloon floating behind the head or a jump rope in midflight. It can also be turned into an archway behind the figure or a small lake in the background.

David complains that the head he drew looks more like a potato than a head.

Solution: David can make the boy's head with lots of curly hair or redraw another head in a part of the potato shape and then blend, rub, or shade the unwanted lines into the background or else color over them. He can also change the potato-shaped head into a cloud and redraw the boy's head and body under the cloud.

Solution #2: Avoid noticeable mistakes by drawing lightly in pencil first.

Choose a subject—a boy or a girl—and make this into a combination practice and complete project.

Make it easy to deal with unwanted lines and marks by first drawing lightly with tentative lines in pencil. Later, unwanted areas can be worked over without calling attention to them. The first soft, light lines will be a charming contrast to the final, heavier lines.

When working with children, explain this concept in advance and demonstrate. Very young children will find it difficult to adjust the pressure on the pencil or crayon from hard to soft, but it is still advisable to encourage them to draw lightly at first to familiarize them with this concept. Here's how to do it:

Level 1: Basic Outlines for Children AGES 4–8

1. Draw the geometric shapes and objects lightly in pencil.
2. When satisfied that the object is complete, draw over the lines with a fine pen (a roller or needle tip is good).
3. Erase any unwanted pencil lines.
4. Color in the object.

Level 2: Refined Drawing for Children AGES 9+

1. With a pencil, draw the lines lightly, tentatively positioning objects on the paper. Draw actual objects or objects from memory.
2. Find their geometric forms and block in the shapes.
3. Refine the lines and curves around the shapes.
4. Add in shading. Put in light, middle, and dark areas.
5. Darken some of the lines with a pen (use permanent ink if using paint and water).
6. Erase any unwanted lines.
7. Color in the drawing, if desired.

Solution #3: Hold the eraser.

Show children the advantages of the delayed eraser method. This solution is similar to Solution #2 yet is richer in details and attitudes. Choose the exercise that fits your personality.

This method of delaying the use of the eraser is successful after the children have learned how to change mistakes into something desirable. It takes a few lessons for the children to understand and anticipate the routine. Be sure to demonstrate all the steps in advance and explain how they can be successful.

Hold the Eraser AGES 7+

Materials:

- 3 or more sheets of copy paper, size 8½ x 11 inches (21 x 30 cm)
- 1 sharpened pencil without an eraser
- Eraser for final drawing
- 1 fine-tipped pen or fine-tipped felt marker
- Optional: colored pencils, markers, oil pastels, chalk pastels, gouache, or watercolors

Directions:

1. Have the child choose a few objects to draw for his composition. On the first sheet, which will be the first practice paper, he should practice drawing the objects. Help the child identify the geometric shapes in each object to familiarize him with his subject.
2. On the second practice paper, very lightly sketch in all the objects of the composition. Tell the child, "It doesn't matter if there are mistakes here because you will throw away the practice paper anyway. We don't need an eraser yet."
3. With the pencil, darken the lines of the sketch until the child is satisfied with the drawing. Give encouragement and tell him how impressed you are that he has managed without using an eraser.
4. On the final sheet of paper, repeat steps 2 and 3 in pencil.
5. Outline the final pencil drawing lines with a fine-tipped pen or marker (make sure it's waterproof if you will be using paint).
6. The child can now use an eraser to remove any of the pencil lines

he doesn't want to remain visible. Explain that now is the time for the eraser, but some people may prefer to keep the original lines for interest and contrast.

7. If he wants, the child can now color in the composition, being careful not to paint or color heavily over the lines. In large areas, he can use paint, oil pastels, or chalk pastels. In small areas, he should use colored pencils or fine-tipped markers. The rule is: in small areas, use small or fine tips and brushes to color; in large areas, use wide or large tips or brushes.

8. Display the finished work of art and compliment the child on his patience and persistence. Although the child will actually be doing the drawing 3–5 times, he will think he had done it only 2–3 times. Each time will be a review to reinforce his drawing skills and get used to working without the eraser.

Solution #4: Keep track of the time.

Postpone the eraser for a brief amount of time. Use a kitchen timer on days when your patience and stamina are low. Set the kitchen timer for five, ten, or fifteen minutes and ask the child to draw carefully until the timer rings. Then, if he wants, give him an eraser. Remind the child in advance that until the timer rings, he should try to complete the picture as best he can using imaginative solutions, and he shouldn't scribble away the time until the eraser is handed out.

Solution #5: Tell stories that demonstrate the result of overdone erasing.

Here are two scenarios that you can tell to illustrate what happens when a child relies too much on the eraser. In these stories, two imaginary students, Miriam and Shoshana, have very different attitudes toward the eraser. When you tell the stories, you can add your own details and characterization:

Scenario #1: Miriam is drawing. Every tiny mark she makes, she finds fault with.

"It's too big. Give me an eraser."

"Oh, it's too small. Where's the eraser?"

"Hmm, it's too pointed. Can I have an eraser please?"

"It's so ugly! I have to erase it!"

"Now it's too low. I must have an eraser!"

Erase, erase, erase! The children will laugh at this exaggeration of a student who erases more than she draws and never finishes her picture.

Scenario #2: Shoshana is drawing and she makes several errors and misplaced marks. Instead of erasing, she decides to incorporate her errors into her picture as she has been taught.

"This mistake is not so bad. I can fix it. It doesn't matter. I can change it into something else."

"No problem, this extra line will become a fold in the sleeve of the girl's dress that I'm drawing."

"I'll erase this other bothersome line later when I'm finished with the picture."

When you're finished telling the stories, hold up Miriam's incomplete, erased-over drawing and Shoshana's finished picture (that you have, of course, prepared in advance), and show how the child who erased the least finished first.

If you're still skeptical about this method, let me reassure you that with time, patience, and conviction, it really does work. The results can show up unexpectedly.

Recently, one of my five-year-old students did a drawing on her own. As she showed it to me, she pointed out where she had drawn the head of a girl that was too large. Instead of erasing it, she simply drew a smaller head inside the large circle, which now looked like the sun behind the girl's head. The student was obviously proud of her accomplishment and stood before me tall and confident, as if she had grown an inch!

Tip: The very young or the very old find the delayed eraser technique easier to accept than middle-aged children. So, if possible, introduce it to children before they enter the first grade.

Here is a project that gives a child freedom to create as she sees fit. This gets her used to making choices and promotes creative solutions when confronted with mistakes. It is especially well suited to young children or those who need extra encouragement.

My House Has Options AGES 4½+

There is more than one way to draw a house. Children can choose not only from various materials but also the size of the house and its placement on the paper. They can add their own personalized touch with the details—a mailbox, shrubs, a name plaque, etc. Encourage the child to be creative and try something new.

Materials:

- Copy paper, size 11 x 16 inches (30 x 42 cm) or 8½ x 11 inches (21 x 30 cm)
- Pencil and eraser
- Colored markers
- Red, yellow, blue, and white gouache paint
- Paintbrushes, ⅛, ¼, and ½ inch (¼, ½, and 1½ cm)
- Styrofoam sandwich board or cardboard
- Craft knife and metal ruler
- White plastic glue or glue stick
- Hot-glue gun
- Scissors
- Craft sticks

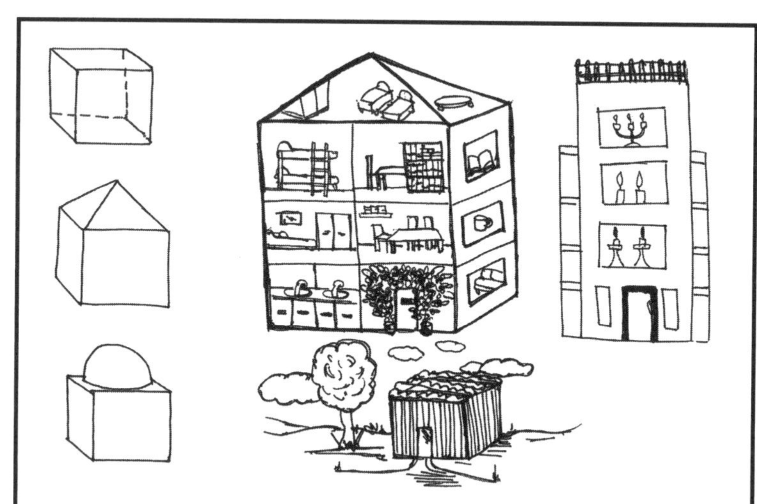

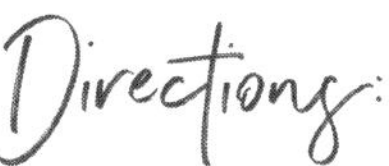

Before you start, explain and demonstrate the geometric shapes that form a house. Then have the child choose one or more of the options below.

1. Make an outline of the house in dots that the child connects with lines.
2. Draw parts of a house (the front, sides, roof, path, windows, door, mezuzah, plants, etc.) and cut them out. Arrange the shapes on a sheet of paper and glue them in place.
3. Give the child craft sticks to arrange in the form of a house. Have the child paint them or color them with markers.
4. Give the child white panels (from Styrofoam board or cardboard) to cut to size and join together to form a house. After it dries, have the child paint the panels. She can add doors and windows and other basics to finish the house.

5. Have the child paint a piece of paper, mixing his own colors. Let the paper dry and have the child draw a house directly on top of the painted background. Or, on a separate paper draw, cut out, and glue objects onto the background.

6. Draw a house on top of a high-domed hill with a ladder, flowers, trees, birds, and butterflies on the sides of the hill. The child can add anything else he would like: people, sun, raindrops, clouds, snails, etc.

In Summary: The Fortunate Mistake

- A mistake is an opportunity for discovery and growth.
- Mistakes teach us compassion and forgiveness.
- True understanding of situations in life comes after failed attempts.
- Young children graduate from free-style finger painting to an interest in purposeful art—art with a plan—but this also leads to frustration with mistakes.
- To handle mistakes in art, either defuse the frustration by anticipating problems and preventing them or by teaching children how to use their mistakes.
- Encourage children to "postpone" the eraser and rather than erasing mistakes, incorporate them into their artwork.

Questions and Wonder

1. Why don't we automatically know how to do everything perfectly? Why did God give us mistakes?
2. Have you ever made a mistake and then later realized that it wasn't really such a big deal? What did you do to prevent the mistake from happening again?

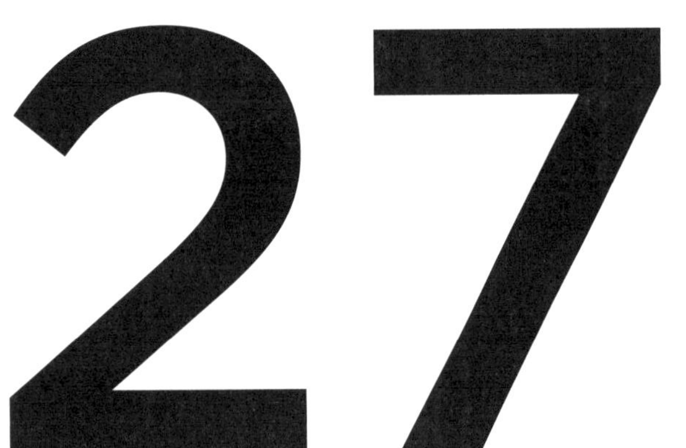

The Completed Work of Art

A work of art painted by a master sparks our imaginations; we want to be able to go inside the picture with our minds and explore. It takes us to another place, on a new adventure.

A "complete" picture, with all the elements that make up a composition, offers us this pleasure. By the time a child is about six or seven years old, he should be able to produce a "complete drawing."

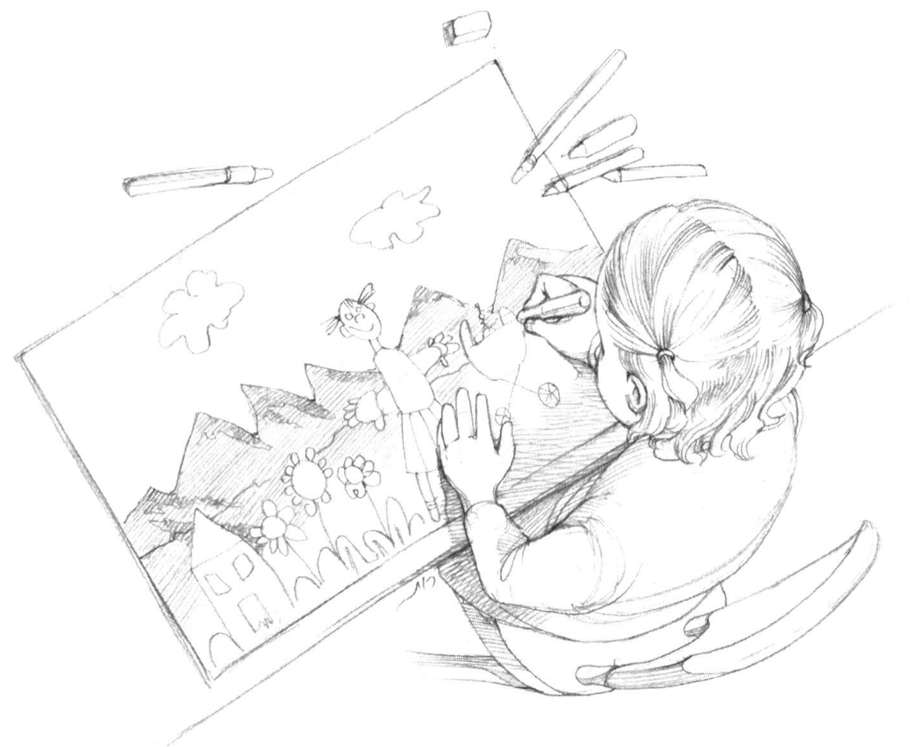

What Makes a Picture Complete?

When we talk about a "complete picture," this could mean many things. It can mean a composition that incorporates all of the components of a work of art. A composition in traditional terms includes the center of interest (the subject), line, form, light, color, balance, and size and scale. For our purposes, we will simplify our term, composition, and talk about what makes a child's picture complete.

A complete drawing includes a background, a foreground, and one or many centers of interest. The center of interest is the main subject, object, grouping of objects (such as a group of animals or several pieces of fruit), or the overall theme. The ground is the surface of space that "holds" the subject in its place; a work of art with a foreground (appearing close) and background (appearing further or the atmosphere surrounding the objects) will appear to have additional depth. Whether the scene includes a basket of pomegranates, hearts and flowers, toys, ceremonial objects, buildings, animals and vegetation, landscapes, or people, a complete composition will contain these three elements: the subject, the foreground, and the background.

Besides the background and foreground, size and scale also give a suggestion of perspective. Objects that are close to us appear large, while things that are further away decrease in size. The ocean appears immense as we walk along the beach, yet small when we look at it from the car window as we drive home.

Weather, atmospheric conditions, and hints to location also give the illusion of depth and distance. Light and color can add meaning and life to the piece. Movement and details add interest and reveal the talent and skill level of the artist.

A picture may be wonderfully complete even if there is unpainted or "empty" space in it, as long as the total image is satisfying and appears complete to the viewer. Empty space and "attended," or finished, space should balance one another. A harmonious work of art will be visually satisfying in every section of canvas or paper or other material. The success depends on the completeness and harmonious balance of all its areas.

Every child will have his or her own interest and specialty. Some will go heavy on color; others on details. But even though a child displays more skill in one area than another, encourage him to produce a complete drawing. This will force him to apply his skill even to areas where he has to improve.

Notes and Sketches

Notes and Sketches

The Picture's Surface

The surface on which you paint or draw, whether on paper or canvas, is called the "picture ground." For our needs, we can divide the picture ground—our paper or canvas—into three parts.

The top third represents the background. The farthest, smallest, and least clear objects will appear in this part of the paper.

The bottom third is the foreground. What is closest, largest, and clearest is at the bottom of the paper.

The center represents the middle ground. It is a transition area, with objects smaller than those in the foreground and larger than the ones in the background.

Let's see how we can use all three areas.

Attention to the Picture Surface: Foreground, Middle Ground, and Background AGES 7+

Materials:

- 1 or 2 pieces of paper, size 8½ x 11 inches (21 x 28 cm)
- 11 x 16-inch (28 x 41-cm) Bristol or paper that works with water.
- Pencil
- Colored markers
- Gouache: red, yellow, blue, and white
- Paintbrushes, ¼ and ½ inch (½ and 1½ cm)
- White plastic glue
- Scissors

Directions:

1. Fold a piece of paper into three sections horizontally, across the paper. Point to the bottom of the paper and explain to the

child, "This is the foreground. We can draw what is close to us here. We will draw a boy or girl and grass, trees, and flowers, large and bright. Above this is the middle ground. Everything on the middle area is further away from us. Here we will put a house. Above the house is the background, like the sky and mountains in the distance. It is far from us, so it is smaller and less bright. What is close is big and bright and what is far away is smaller and less bright."
Have the child draw objects that are found in the sky—like the sun, birds, and clouds—on the top third of the picture.

2. Once she is acquainted with the picture's surface, explain how she can color the person and the objects with markers before she paints the background, middle ground, and foreground. It is easier to color in the small areas with markers and the large areas with paint.

3. Once the child is happy with her drawing, and has colored in the small areas with markers, she is ready to paint.
Review the painting process. Be careful to paint around the objects and not over them. Make an outline with the brush and paint around the objects and fill in the empty space with more paint.
First she should paint the top, the background, blue—the color of the sky. Mix blue with various amounts of white to achieve a variety of blue shades. She should paint the middle area the muted colors of distant grass and landscapes: greens and browns. The bottom should be the color of bright, emerald-green grass.

4. Let the paint dry or use a blow dryer to hasten the process. Now you have the complete picture.

Optional: Paint the three sections as mentioned above. On a separate piece of paper, draw the person and objects, first with a pencil and then color them in with markers. When satisfied with the results, cut them out and glue into place on the foreground, background, and middle ground.

How Do You Know When a Picture Is Finished?

You are looking at a finished painting. But something is not right. What's not complete? Ask yourself the following questions to decide if it's finished or needs a bit more work:

- Is it satisfying to my eye?
- Do my eyes stay on the paper and circle around all the interesting parts of the painting?
- Is some detail missing?
- Do my eyes stop at any place on the picture's surface as I look at the artwork?

If the answer to the last question is yes, this can be a sign that that area is not completed or developed as it could be. The viewer's eyes should move in a free circle around the picture plane, and all areas should be of equal interest. The objects, the subject matter, the background, and the foreground should all be interesting and pleasing to the eye, even if they are filled in only with brushstrokes of color rather than details.

Show children how to spot flaws in an unfinished or undeveloped area of a picture. Ask the children if they think all the shapes are in balance with one another, and that none overpower anything else. A small and dark or very bright shape on one side of the picture can balance out a large and light or muted shape on the other side.

"Is It Finished?" Checklist

Encourage full completion of the child's picture by checking for the following:

1. A background with appropriate information and objects that are colored or interestingly filled in.

2. A complete figure with all the major body parts and details (e.g., shoes with laces, pants with pockets, skirts with a design, a belt with a buckle, a collar on a shirt, bows and buttons, necklaces and pockets).

3. Complete objects with their appropriate components, such as a door with a mezuzah, doorknob, and nameplate.
4. A pictorial story or event that includes essential features, such as the main characters, the location, the weather conditions, and time of day.

Here are some projects that teach children to focus, not only on the objects they are drawing but also on the picture ground: the foreground, middle ground, and background—the entire composition.

"Attention to the Background" Project: Rachel's Tomb AGES 7+

Rachel's Tomb (Kever Rachel), is an ancient, holy site—the resting place of the matriarch Rachel. Jews go there to pray and find a direct line to God.

The ancient site, with its domed ceiling, is a famous image that can be found hanging on the walls of many homes. It is not uncommon for Jewish children to draw pictures of the tomb as it looked years ago, surrounded by trees and solitude. Because it's a popular subject, I chose Rachel's Tomb as the center of interest for this project.

Here is a very successful technique and one that is easy for all ages. I developed this method in response to the unfinished background that most children and many adults end up with in their compositions. Separating the background from the objects and center of interest in the picture helps them focus on the background and create a nicely finished picture. There's little that's more satisfying for children than producing a picture that they successfully completed themselves.

Materials:

- Copy paper, size 8½ x 11 inches (21 x 30 cm)
- Bristol or all-purpose paper that works with water, size 11 x 16 inches (28 x 41 cm) or 12 x 18 inches (30 x 46 cm)
- Pencil and eraser
- Colored markers

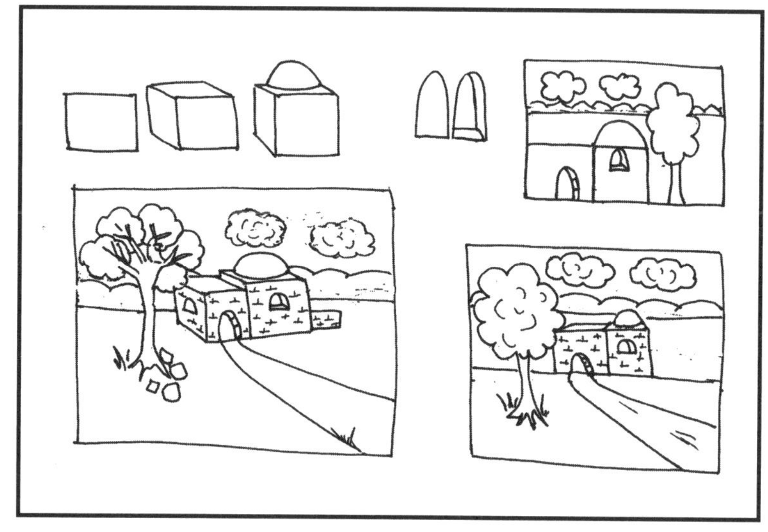

- Red, yellow, blue, and white tempera, gouache, or acrylic paints (acrylics can be combined with the gouache)
- Paintbrushes, ⅛, ¼, and ½ inch (¼, ½, and 1½ cm)
- White plastic glue
- Scissors

Directions:

1. Fold the Bristol or all-purpose paper horizontally (by length) across the paper into three sections using two folds.
2. Open the paper and draw a line on the top fold with the pencil. Above the line draw a row of hills with triangles, curves, or a combination.
3. Draw a line on the bottom fold. Add another line a bit below it. This will be a road, and the bottom section will be the ground.
4. On the smaller, 8½ x 11-inch (21 x 30-cm) copy paper, draw a picture of Rachel's Tomb in pencil. A simple version is: Draw two equal squares. On top of the right square draw a dome or half-circle and an arched window in the square. On the left square draw an arched door. The building is made of Jerusalem stone. Draw a large ancient tree to be placed on the left side of the bottom section. Choose what you'd like to add: one or two palm trees, small stones, a path, a small stone wall, people, and a donkey or camel to put in the middle and bottom sections. Clouds, a sun, birds, tiny trees on top of the hills to glue on to the top section.
5. Color in each object with colored markers. Save this to cut and glue on after you paint.
6. Prepare your paint. Put out your paint on pieces of scrap paper about 5½ x 8 inches (14 x 20 cm), and mix your colors. With the basic colors of red, yellow, blue, and white paint and a paintbrush, create the shades of color you'll be using for the painting. Mix blue with varying amounts of white to make shades of blue. You will also want to make several varieties of browns and beiges from blue and yellow (that equals a green) mixed with bits of

red and white. As you mix, adjust the amounts until you get the right proportions. Mix small batches until you get the right balance and the colors you like. Just like in baking, a change in the proportions of the colors you are mixing will change the outcome of the new color.

Dip the paintbrush in water and wipe with a paper towel in between mixings to keep the colors pure. Draw circles in pencil around each new color you mix to keep it small and not waste if it doesn't come out as you like it. Of course, even if a color doesn't come out as you like, you can add white or small bits of new colors and see what appears from the mixture. You may like the new accidental mixture.

When finished, simply throw paint paper away.

7. Now you can begin painting: Paint the area above the hills in shades of blue for the sky. Add in white clouds. Paint the hills in browns. Paint the area below the hills dark green. Paint the road area in a lighter set of browns and the ground below the road bright green. Now you have a real painting of a background!

8. Let the paint dry or hasten the drying time with a hair dryer.

9. Cut out the objects from the other paper and glue them on top of the dried background in the appropriate places. Now you have a complete composition!

Variation:

1. In place of Rachel's Tomb draw a house.

2. Draw two lines ½ inch (1½ cm) apart, below the center of the hills. Continue the lines downward, toward the bottom of the page, widening them 1½ inches as they curve to make a river or a road.

3. Add trees, birds, mountains, flowers, and a sunset. Draw five trees from large to small descending in size and placing the largest at the bottom of the paper, and the smallest in the middle or top section (on top of mountain). Remember: What is smallest is furthest away visually.

A Child, a House, and a View AGES 7+

In this project, similar to "Heavens and Earth" (chapter 20), we will be using plasticine or air-drying clay and oil pastels. Rub, smear, and blend the oil pastel colors to create a colorful composition of a house and a landscape in the background (mountains, trees, river, and a sunset).

This project can be easily adapted to young children by eliminating any difficult steps. Select objects, including the house, can be made with clay and glued onto the picture surface that the child first painted rather than drawing and coloring them with the oil pastels. A simple background with just the earth and sky can be colored in with the oil pastels for an easy option.

Materials:

- 1 or 2 sheets of white copy paper, size 8½ x 11 inches (21 x 30 cm)
- Pencil and eraser
- Oil pastels
- Sturdy cardboard or foam board, approximately 9 x 12 inches (23 x 30 cm)
- White plastic glue or hot-glue gun
- Plasticine or synthetic air-drying modeling clay
- Note: Consider your child's age and abilities when choosing which type of clay to use. Synthetic, air-drying clay, is great for anyone over 6 or 7 years old in place of plasticine. Plasticine does not dry and is not recommended if you are planning to keep the artwork for more than a short time. It can be a bit messier to work with than air-drying clay, but is very good for strengthening the hand muscles.

Directions:

1. On the sheet of copy paper, make a practice drawing and work out the composition to your liking. Fold a second sheet of paper into three horizontal sections. Draw lightly with a pencil across the lines. These correspond to the background (the top section), the middle ground (middle section), and the foreground (bottom section).

2. Draw a house with two trees next to it in the middle section. Use the pencil lightly—to make any erasing easier if needed—(you can always go over the light pencil and darken it once you have decided to keep the lines). Begin drawing in the middle section of the paper since it helps the children keep objects in the proper proportion and achieve more depth. Their work will radiate outward rather than being limited by starting at the top or bottom of the paper.

3. Draw four triangular-shaped or arch-shaped mountains across the top pencil line (the bottom of top section).

4. Draw a river flowing from the mountains on the top pencil line, down to the bottom of the paper (the foreground in the bottom section). Make the river very narrow, ¼–½ inch (½–1½ cm) at the top near the mountains, and widen it gradually until it's very wide, about 2–2½ inches (5–6 cm) at the bottom of the paper Add trees. Draw a partial sun above or near the mountains, with rays of light emanating from it. Lightly draw a figure in the foreground (the bottom section).

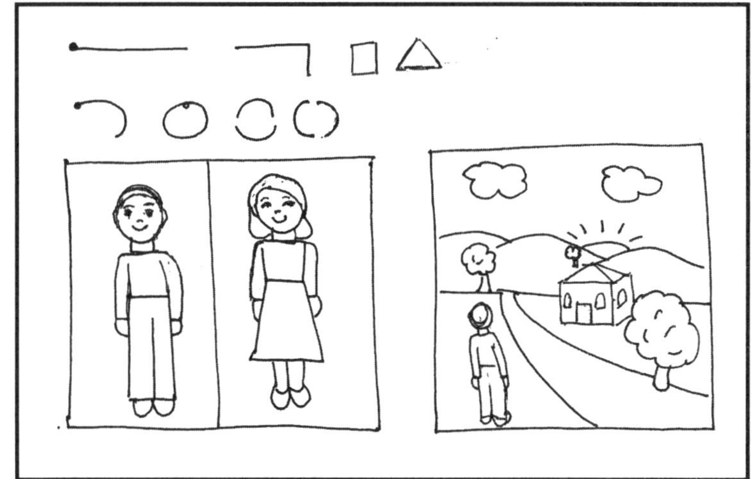

5. Redraw the illustration on the sturdy piece of cardboard or foam board.

6. Color in all the objects with oil pastels. Blend two to three colors together in each shape: Apply one color in the entire shape, then blend in a second, harmonizing color over part of the same object. Or apply one color partially and then fill in the remainder with a matching color. Blend by rubbing the color in with the fingers in one direction or in circles. An application of a third color results in an even better effect.
   Remind the children to cover the surface completely by rubbing in the oil pastels as much as possible. This will involve all their hand muscles. If they complain that their hands are tired from this workout, tell them to shake their hands out for a few moments before resuming the project.

Some suggested color combinations and blends:

- The sky: light blue, dark blue, and white.
- The sun: yellow, orange, red, and white; for a setting sun, add a touch of purple and white.
- The mountains: brown, orange, yellow, tan, a bit of pink, and white.
- The river: light blue, turquoise, green, and white.
- The tree leaves: light green, dark green, and yellow or a brownish red.
- The tree trunk: brown, gray, and white. Add a bit of yellow in the center.
- The house: brown, yellow, and red.

7. Form the Plasticine or air-drying clay into geometric shapes for the figure. The head will be formed from a ball, the neck from a small box, the upper body from a larger box, the arms and hands from two rectangles and two balls, the boy's pants from two larger rectangles or for a girl's skirt, a triangle, the shoes from small balls, and the facial features, hair, and clothing details from small coils and balls.
8. Glue or press together the pieces to form the figure. Let dry. Then glue the figure onto the background.

Optional (ages 4-6): Do the entire composition with plasticine or air-drying clay only.

Optional (ages 7 +): Do the entire composition as a painting.

Optional (ages 8+): Do the composition in a sensitive pencil drawing with a variety of light and dark strokes and shadings.

Draw a Shadow AGES 8+

From the age of about 8 or 9, children want to draw realistically. A simple way to make a complete picture or a sketch (a quick or abbreviated drawing) is to draw objects and add shadows. Shadows indicate that there is a source of light. The shadow is normally on the opposite side of the light source, be it the sun or a lamp. If the shadow is on the right bottom of an object, this tells us that the light is coming from the left side of the object.

Place a small ball (ping-pong size) or wooden block on a table. Direct a flashlight on it, moving the flashlight slowly around the object. Notice that the shadow moves and yet is always on the opposite side of the object from the flashlight. Draw the object and its shadow in one of the positions.

Here is a very quick and simplified way to make a flat circle into a 3-dimensional ball.

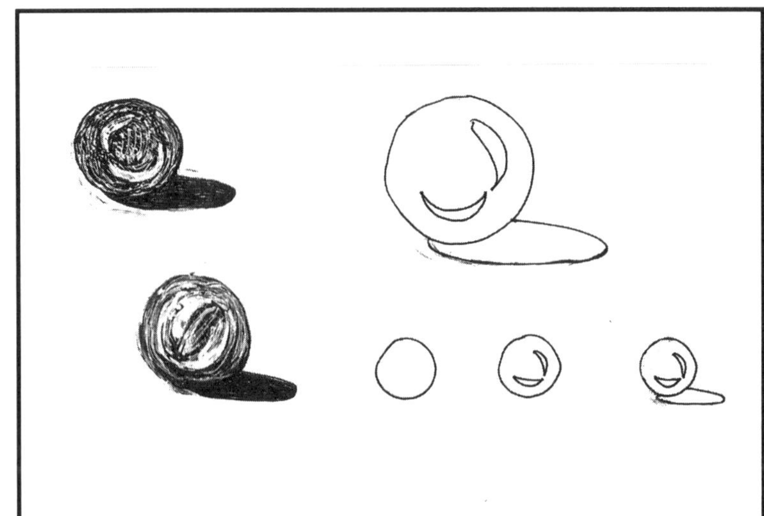

Materials:

- Copy paper, size 8½ x 11 inches (21 x 30 cm)
- Pencil and eraser

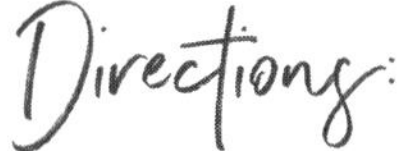

Directions:

1. Draw a circle. Divide it into three horizontally curved sections, following the curve of one side of the outer edge.
2. Make the lowest section very dark by filling it in with a strong pressure on the pencil. Fill in the middle section with less pressure for a lighter shade. Fill in half of the top section very lightly.
3. Now blend the three sections, maintaining the white highlight at the top. Use your finger, an eraser, a cloth, or add more pencil as needed to blend. Try it until you get the right look. No need to fill in the entire piece of each of the three sections. Start with a heavy pressure and gradually reduce the pressure until the result is a little paper showing at the edge of each section.
4. Add a shadow under the ball on the side away from your "light source."
5. Optional: Draw a circle with a thick wide curve inside the bottom of the circle (like a smiling mouth). Draw another thick curve (like an eyebrow or half of the top of a rainbow) on the top half of the inside of the circle but half the length. Add a shadow, shaped like a wide half oval, under the ball on the opposite side of the "eye" curve.

Pick a few objects from the house, place one on a table, and note its shadow. If the shadow is not clear, set up a lamp or flashlight nearby and make your own shadow. Draw the object and its shadow. Draw several objects on the paper in a pleasing arrangement.

Easy Perspective Project AGES 9+

Perspective is another way to give depth and interest to a picture. Perspective is making objects smaller as they recede into the distance so that they appear further away.

Imagine that we are in a car that is driving on a road. Straight ahead and as far as our eyes can see is the sun setting in the distance. Now we will draw this image.

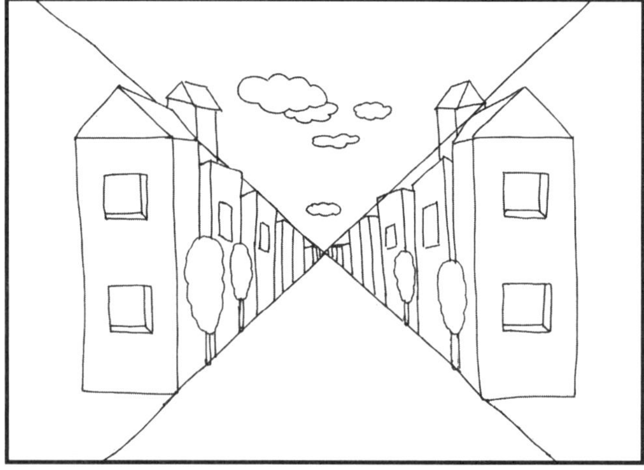

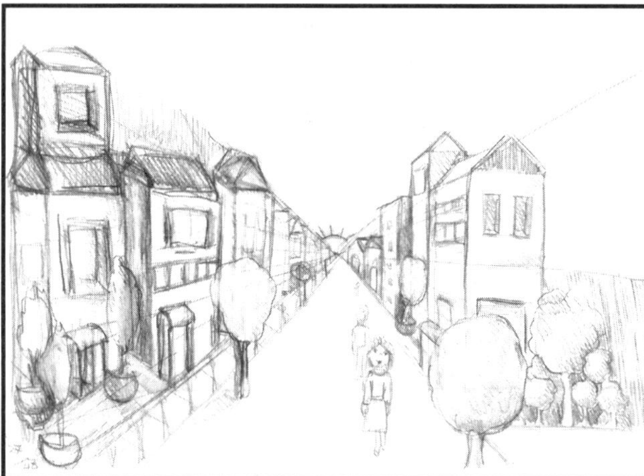

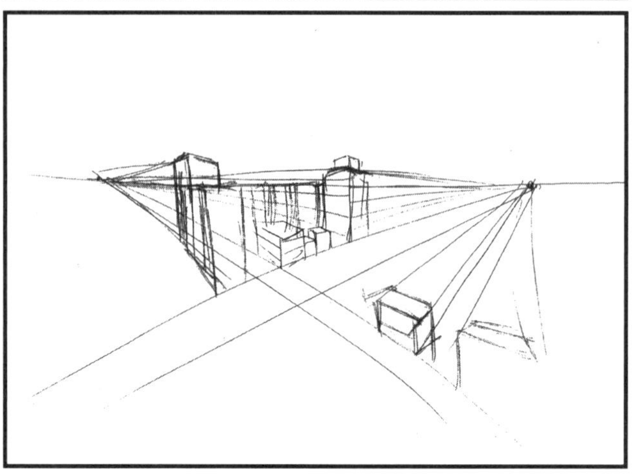

Materials:

- Copy paper, size 8½ x 11 inches (21 x 30 cm)
- Pencil

Directions:

1. Draw a line horizontally across a paper, about a third of the way down from the top of the paper. Put a dot in the center of the line.
2. Draw a triangle from the dot down and out to the two bottom corner edges of the paper. Draw a second set of lines inside each of the first set beginning at the center dot. The two lines should be 1⁄16 inch (⅛ cm) below the first set of lines beginning at the dot, and ending at 1 inch (2½ cm) apart at the bottom, below the corner lines. This will resemble a road that decreases in size as it narrows toward the horizon line (the dot).

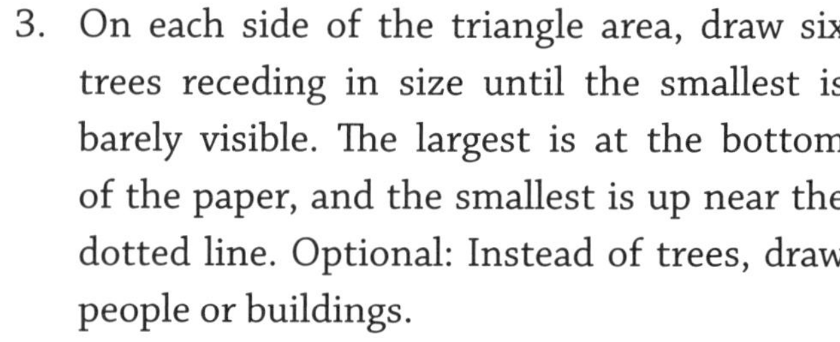

3. On each side of the triangle area, draw six trees receding in size until the smallest is barely visible. The largest is at the bottom of the paper, and the smallest is up near the dotted line. Optional: Instead of trees, draw people or buildings.

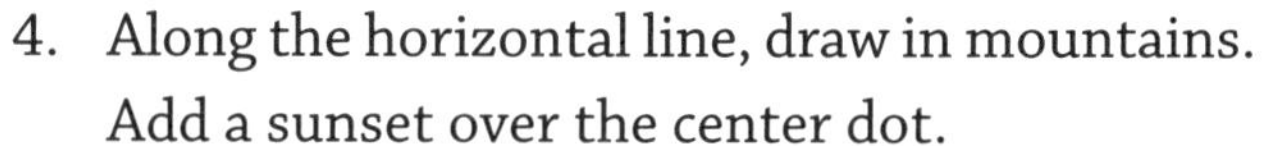

4. Along the horizontal line, draw in mountains. Add a sunset over the center dot.

Optional: Draw five or six cars beginning at the center bottom of the paper moving upward and gradually reducing in size, until the last car (near the sunset and dot) is barely visible.

Optional: Draw a river in place of a road and boats in place of cars. Add any details and color with markers or colored pencils.

You have now completed a one-point perspective drawing.

In Summary: The Completed Work of Art

- A completed work of art is an arrangement of all the elements of a visual art piece; center of interest, lines, form, light and color, scale and size, details and texture.
- A picture may be complete even if it contains empty space, as long as the total image appears satisfying to the viewer.
- One element that contributes to the complete picture is the background.
- A picture surface can be divided into a foreground (bottom section), middle ground (middle section), and background (top section).
- Rather than adding a background as an afterthought, paint or draw it first and then place the subjects on top of it.
- Objects placed in the foreground are larger and appear closer to us; objects in the background are smaller and appear to be distant.

Questions and Wonder

1. Does all the paper need to be filled in for a picture to be finished? If so, why? If not, why not?
2. You have finished a drawing or other type of artwork. What would you check to make sure the work is complete?

28 The Teacher and Her Classroom

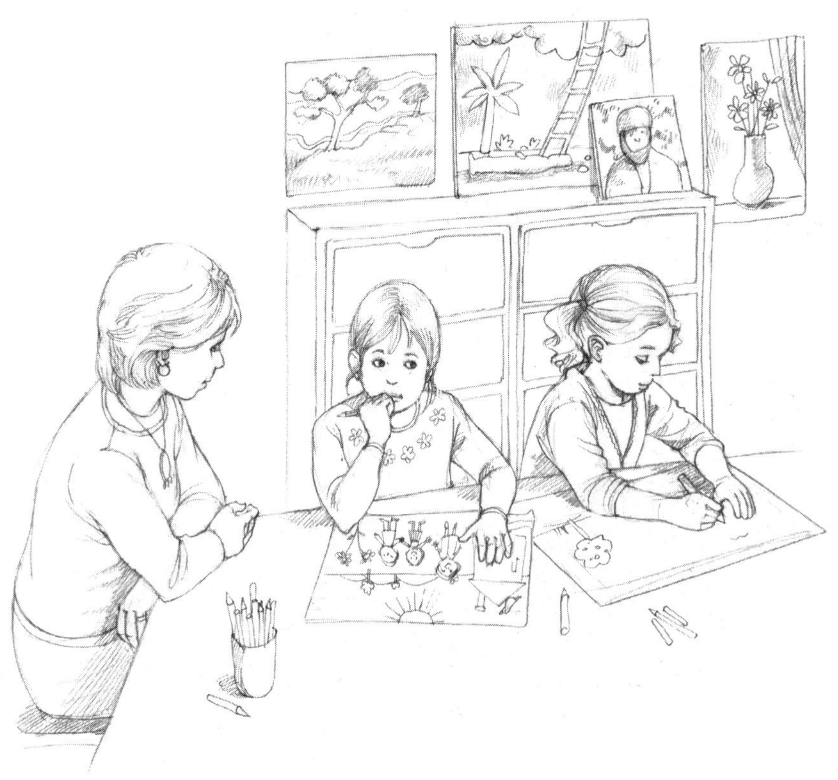

Class Preparation

The teacher's motto, "Be prepared," cannot be stressed enough. A teacher must be prepared with instructions, materials, demonstrations, and handouts and have the ability to help and answer any questions that will come up. Test the projects in advance and work out any difficulties until you feel sufficiently relaxed with it and can present it to the children with enthusiasm.

Projects may be spread over two or more lessons. If the children derive satisfaction at the end of each session they will feel mature enough to wait until the work is finished to take it home. Satisfaction comes if they succeeded in mastering a new skill or were enabled to express an image independently.

Notes and Sketches

Decide on the stages of the project and divide it into approximate time slots to fit the class time. Planning the project and dividing it into stages are one and the same. Break down each step and explain clearly with hints, tips, and insights to give the child a handle on the project. Some children only need to know the overall steps, while others need to know all the details.

Each project should be roughly explained and demonstrated. The demonstration does not have to be long and detailed but will show the main points of the project. Draw essential objects two times or more, breaking the object down into geo shapes. You don't have to show them a completely finished project. A partial project leaves them room to use their imagination, and it doesn't limit them to trying to copy the "perfect" work of the teacher.

Allow time for questions. Answer any question that will come up so that a child is not left searching. If a child is confused, it will prevent him from going forward with the excitement of the project. Answer all questions with respect to the child's legitimate need to understand. Insert a story, personal or otherwise about how you decided on the project.

"As I was waking up, I saw in my head the idea of the clock we are about to make for *Eishet Chayil*. Did you ever see anything inside your head that wasn't really there but was clear and was something you wanted to make or do?" This is one type of creative inspiration. It can be found within each person; little children also have internal inspiration.

It is important to discuss art projects beyond the basic subject matter, materials, and how to do it. Encourage a personal connection or vision when possible. Let them incorporate their imagery in a drawing of a house and put in what is important to them. Choice of colors and textures in a nature scene is another way to give life to internal creative inspiration.

If you have handouts showing the steps of a drawing, give every two children one to share. Let it be known that they are not for tracing but for reference.

Hand out the appropriate materials (paper, pencil, scissors, colors, glue, etc.) at each required stage. Otherwise, some students will race through

Notes and Sketches

the project without giving it the proper attention it deserves. Also, passing out and collecting the materials progressively, as needed, keeps the tables from becoming cluttered and messy.

Each stage of the project should be complete and satisfying on its own. Let the child take as long as he needs to master the skill involved. Success with skills is important. If cutting is difficult, give individual help until the child masters the skill. Acquaint the child with helpful ways to manage cutting. Give tips on the way to hold the scissors, apply pressure, release pressure, hold the paper, move his hands, and so on.

Allotting time for individual attention is important and is a key to success. A child who receives quality (short or long) attention from the teacher/parent gains confidence because he now judges himself worthy of attention. Since he received attention, he is now free to give his own work and personal efforts attention. Don't wait for the child to be disruptive or in need of help. Give attention simply because he or she is a worthy human being. Offer suggestions for future work when you notice strong points that can be made stronger. Be effusive with compliments. Compliments are a round of cheers that support and encourage each child.

Time Management

Time for each project should be gauged according to the concentration abilities and age of the students.

Children under five can finish a drawing in less than five minutes. The time can be increased to thirty or sixty minutes if divided into steps. For instance, watch a demonstration of the project and its options, including how to use the materials (five to ten minutes); draw with pencil (five to ten minutes); color (five to seven minutes); cut out parts of the picture (five to seven minutes); glue the cut-out parts onto a sheet of paper (five to seven minutes); color or paint the paper (five to seven minutes); discussion of the finished work, including praise (five minutes); and personal clean up (five minutes).

For children six years old and older, a standard time arrangement might be as follows: watch demonstration of project and use of materials (five to ten minutes); receive materials to get started with, such as paper and pencils (five minutes); practice drawing (five minutes); final drawing (ten to fifteen minutes); putting in color (ten to fifteen minutes); discussion of the finished work, including praise (five minutes); and personal clean up (five minutes). This totals forty-five to sixty minutes.

Children nine years old and older are interested in detail and may be able to be involved in an art project up to three or four one-hour sessions, if the project is exciting to them. Older children and adults usually like one-and-a-half-hour sessions or longer that continue for two, three or four sessions per project. Once a person is immersed in a project that is captivating, the time goes by unnoticed, as if in a dream. A child with a picture in his head struggling to put it on paper will find time tugging along slowly. A child frustrated by lack of skills, coordination or concentration will be fighting with time unless his pressing needs are attended to and unblocked so he can go forward.

What do you do with the child who finishes in half the allotted time? How do you fill in the time and how do you juggle giving out a new project to a quick child while there are others doing the old project? Go over each step of the drawing, construction, etc., and check if it was done carefully. No random scribbling, no short cuts unless they are done with intention. (Yes, scribbling can be done with intention!) Check for completeness. If not, *help* the child complete her piece as needed, praising her. Take turns drawing. Interact. Be partners.

Be prepared with one or two extra projects, related or unrelated to the previous project, for the child who has truly finished her project early. Show these future projects to the whole group of children at the same time you are introducing them to little Miri. They will gain from the exposure and know what to look forward to.

While the quick child may hit an art activity that suddenly keeps her attention for a long time, it's important to be prepared and always have a few extra projects ready. Alternatively, you can give the child free time to draw what she wants.

The Teacher

The teacher must be willing to spend a solid amount of time teaching the children to use the tools and materials properly. If they can't use the tools to their best advantage and fully understand techniques and options, they wouldn't be able to do the project and learn its many lessons. The teacher will then do the project and the child will lose out. We want to avoid this. Give the children the time they need to master skills. Children need to learn how to cut with scissors: how to follow a line, a curve, change directions, and cut into small areas. The beginning may be frustrating to a child learning to cut. With patience, he will master cutting in a short amount of time if allowed to deal with his own frustrations. The frustrations may be turned into accomplishments.

When the teacher does the work for the children, it denies them the joy and satisfaction of creating and learning. Give the message that everything in life has its own momentary perfection or there is more than one objective as to what is perfect.

The goal is not to impress the parents with finished, perfect-looking artwork but to teach the children skills, encourage their creativity, and give them a big proportion of personal satisfaction. A finished project is wonderful but it's not emphasized for young children until around six years old. The process is the goal. Attaining a finished, realistic artwork will come later if there is a base of solid building blocks. Self-confidence in life skills is an added benefit of the "process first" attitude. If the teacher understands what the child is working through and the process, she can tell this to the parents. Once the teacher explains this concept to the parents, they will be more accepting of a work in progress. After all, their child is truly a work in progress. Parents who know how to look beyond the surface value of the artwork are one step ahead in communicating with their children.

The Room

Tables, chairs, or stools at a comfortable height, access to water and towels, plastic to cover tables (disposable is easiest), access to materials in cabinet or portable table/shelves on wheels, dry erase board, dry erase markers and eraser, display board, and garbage can are all staples for the art room. Light and air should be comfortable. Hooks for coats and the sink and toilet should be pointed out to each child in the first class.

A hair blow-dryer is a great help to hasten the drying of the wet artwork or for scientific-artistic experimental projects.

Basic Materials

Your project goals and budget will dictate the range of your art materials as well as those used for crafts and decorative effects.

The basic materials for painting, drawing, and crafts are included in the introduction of this book as well as those used for crafts and decorative effects. There are endless amounts of possibilities for their use.

Your student/child may want to try other types of projects that require extra physical strength or spatial and dimensional concepts. Print making, copper sheeting (for menorahs, copper etching and jewelry), and woodworking (for wood carving, wood printing, and building) are art mediums to explore. Look at books or see examples in workshops. Talk to the craftsmen. Some children may not like to draw and paint but they have artistic interests nonetheless. Offer options to open channels of inner satisfaction to them, such as:

- Print materials: brayer (roller), inks, cutting tools, and printing surface: linoleum, etc.
- Copper sheets
- Wood and woodworking supplies

Bulletin-Board Displays

Classroom bulletin boards make a first impression. A favorable first impression has a long-lasting effect. A choice of bright and cheerful colors promotes specific emotional reactions and awakens the senses and the mind. Visual materials promote ideas and concepts that the school wants to convey.

Artwork in murals and attractive bulletin-board displays liven up even the plainest old school building. They create a vibrant atmosphere for students, staff, and visitors alike and give them a glimpse into what subjects are being taught.

Consider the impact of the size of the display. Set up two sizes of displays simultaneously for contrast. A small display encourages children to step up close to look and quietly consider the contents. A life-size or large wall display becomes a familiar background.

Children can surround themselves with their work on bulletin-board displays in their classrooms and hallways. The work mirrors their accomplishments and is a friendly voice. "Congratulations. You did this and are sharing it with others." Depending on the age of the children, they can combine efforts with the teacher who supervises or do it entirely themselves. Older children can work in rotating teams or as a group. Small children can make craft projects specifically for bulletin-board displays. Display groups of the same project to show different touches in a noncompetitive way. Let interested students be in charge of decision-making and production.

Topics and Imagery

Include the children in decision-making. Narrow the subject down from three or four ideas into one final image. Discussions should lead to original ideas from the children. You will be surprised by some of their ideas and knowledge, including those as young as four years old.

The subjects of these displays can focus on the *chagim* (Jewish holidays), well-known *pesukim*, such as "Love your friend as yourself,"[148] the seasons or cycles of the year, and the Torah portion of the week. Other topics are good *middot*, such as *chessed*, and concepts in education, such as learning Torah, *aleph-bet*, praying, saying Psalms, numbers, health, nature, plants, animals, and other wonders of Hashem's world. Boards with one focal point would include the Torah, the Mishkan, the Menorah, the Beit Hamikdash, the Kotel, and Yerushalayim.

Bulletin boards can include a wide variety of materials, such as: colored paper, metallic paper, corrugated board in colors, foam sheets, Styrofoam board, cellophane, tissue paper, crepe paper, collage or origami paper, contact paper, Bristol (two-ply paper), cardboard of different weights, small boxes, matchboxes, stiff or soft sheets of colored plastic, thin sheets of pliable foam, rubber, fabric, burlap, yarn, straw, string, cotton, wool, and painted or natural stones and wood.

Real objects such as shells, small branches and twigs from trees, plants, masks, costumes, clothing, puppets, dolls, book covers, and pencils can be added to the background for a three-dimensional effect. Stuffed stockings and fabric can be used to make puppets, dolls, fruit,

148 Leviticus 19:18.

and soft-shaped objects (balloons, bicycles, street signs, and trees). Photographs, posters, travel brochures, postcards, and pictures can also be incorporated for specific effects. Torn paper and deckled edges can also be used to enhance the bulletin board.[149]

Paint, metallic paint, markers, glitter, stencils, cut-out letters, popsicle sticks, wooden clothes pegs, sequins, and pompoms can be used to delineate shapes, add color, or form letters. Put your bulletin-board display together with thumbtacks (preferably color coordinated to the background), staples (a staple gun is most efficient), straight pins, tape, glues, hot glue, silicone, or small nails.

A Bulletin Board Project for Pesach AGES 7+

Depict yetziat Mitzrayim (the exodus from Egypt) where the child can picture herself leaving Mitzrayim.

Use a photograph of each child in the class (and the teacher too). Cut it out and superimpose it on the faces of the Jews leaving Egypt. The children will feel as though they had personally experienced the exodus, as written in the Haggadah. The impact is most effective when done on a large bulletin board or on an entire wall.

Materials:

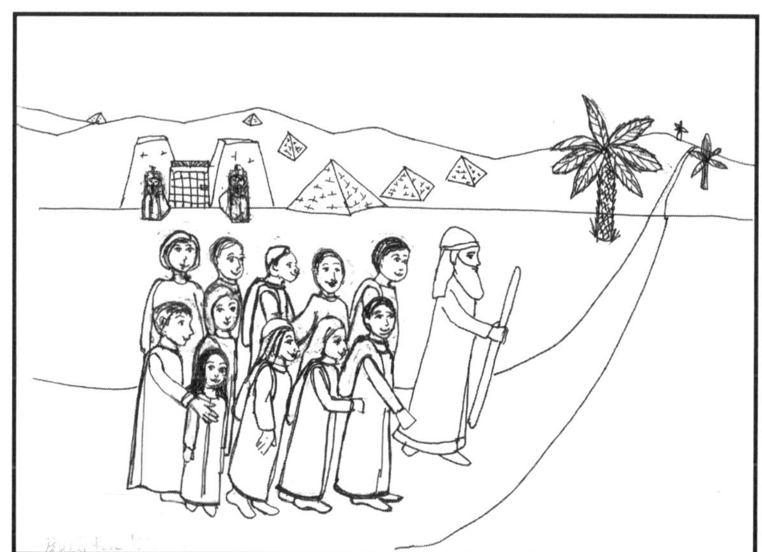

- Paper, large sheets or a roll of paper. Each child should be able to create a life-size or ½–¼ of a life-size figure of himself.
- Pencil and eraser
- White plastic glue, pins, hot-glue gun, and glue stick
- Several large sheets of colored paper, enough to cover the background of the bulletin board and for clothing and details. For the sand, mountains, and pyramids use beiges, browns, gold, straw, and lemon-yellow; for the sky use light blue, hot pink, and orange; for the trees use light brown, beige, light green, and dark green.

149 See ch. 21, "All About Cutting."

- Scissors
- Choice of fabric, synthetic material or felt, heavy colored paper, burlap, sandpaper, rope, or cord
- Photo of each child's face, fit to the size of the heads of the figures in the display

Directions:

1. Draw patterns of a large figure clothed in biblical robes and sandals on a large paper. Each child should have a life-size figure of himself.
2. Glue the photo of each child onto his figure.
3. Cut out the patterns and design them by filling in the patterns with the colored paper, felt, or other materials. Use materials for their robes and head coverings with a variety of patterns. Glue the materials onto the pattern.
4. Next, do the first layer, the background. It is made up of two large areas, the sky and the desert. Use large sheets of torn or cut colored paper.
5. The second layer is the mountains, pyramids, and palm trees. Use colored paper, cut or ripped, felt, burlap, rope, or cloth cut to size.
6. The third layer is of the figures and the sacks or baskets they are carrying. Use colored paper, fabric, burlap, and cord or rope.
7. Group together all the figures as the Jewish nation walking out of Egypt. At the lead is Moshe Rabbeinu with his staff in hand. His face is shown from the side or back.[150]

Optional: Drawings, photographs, postcards, cutouts, or travel brochures of Egypt showing the pyramids, the Nile River, camels, donkeys, and palm trees can be included in the background.

Optional: The same figures and the children's photos can be reassembled around Har Sinai, showing the giving of the Torah on a Shavuot display.

---

150 See ch. 10, "Jewish Role Models."

"I Did It Myself" Notebook Decoration

Decorating notebook covers and the title page (called a *shaar* [gate] in Hebrew) are part of school assignments. Notebooks are used for Jewish holidays along with standard subjects or special topics such as good *middot*. The presentation and appearance of these notebook decorations create a lasting impression and may have an effect on the child's grade on the subject.

Teachers can encourage the children to do their own assignments rather than having their friends, siblings, or parents do it for them. Stress that perfection and the grade is not the main goal. The goal is that they see that they are capable. A solution is to have them do the assignment in class, time permitting. Confident or talented children will do the work themselves and the others will languish in their seats until help arrives.

Help arrives in the form of options. Offer a variety of easy ideas anyone can do and a selection of materials suited to the personalities of the students. Materials and styles such as a collage using cut-out materials, dot-to-dot connections, tracing patterns for those who don't want to draw freehand, cut-out plastic shapes to glue on, cut-out photographs, and of course freehand offer an outlet for everyone. The encouraging teacher asks the children to try their best and praises their efforts by complimenting each good point. The message is that doing the work yourself includes finding your own style.

The choice of artwork is based on the subject of the notebook. Here are some additional subjects and styles that may be incorporated in a notebook.

1. An *aleph-bet* chart. Each of the twenty-two letters is inside a separate box together with an object that starts with that letter.
2. Letters from Hebrew newspapers, as long as they do not contain Hashem's name or holy words.
3. Choose a *pasuk* from *Tehillim*, the siddur or the *parashat ha-shavua* and write it out beautifully. Complete it with an appropriate illustration.
4. Do an illuminated letter project.[151] Illuminated manuscripts were very popular in the Middle Ages and pictures of them can be found in books, libraries, or museums. An illuminated letter

151 See ch. 4, "Jewish Art in History," for more information on illuminated manuscripts.

is the first letter of a word, enlarged and embellished, which begins a new chapter or verse in a manuscript. The letter is often encased in a square or other contained form and ornately painted in regal colors such as gold, silver, royal blue, hunter green, crimson, or deep purple. It may be used for the first *pasuk* in *Megillat Esther* and in the Pesach Haggadah. Children can also do this with verses from *Tehillim*, other well-known *pesukim*, or with their own names.

Freehand Notebook Decoration or Illustration AGES 6+

Begin with guidance and encouragement in the early grades so that the children will become self-reliant with their notebook decorations in their future years. The parent or teacher should be prepared to explain the benefits of the child doing her own work and explaining the reason some kids are afraid of this. This is a sensitive issue because of peer-pressure instincts and the desire to be perfect.

Materials:

- Several sheets of copy paper, size 8½ x 11 inches (21 x 30 cm)
- Pencil and eraser
- Thin black pen for outlining
- Colored markers
- Photos, objects related to the subject of the notebook, existing artwork to get ideas from or to recreate

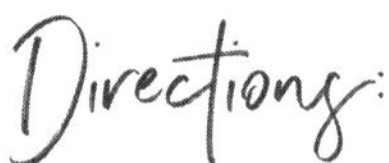

1. On the practice paper, draw two or three sketches of the topic and choose your favorite.
2. Again on a practice paper, work out the idea until you feel confident.
3. Now do a final picture, lightly at first so it will be easier to make changes. When satisfied with the picture, darken the lines.

4. On another practice paper, try the lettering freehand on ruled lines or with stencils or tracing paper.
5. Add the lettering to the final drawing. The letters can be cut out from the practice paper and glued onto the final paper if you like them.
6. Outline the illustration and letters in pen.
7. Choose and fill in colors with markers.

The Collage AGES 7+

A collage composition is an alternative for the child who doesn't want to draw freehand.[152]

Materials:

- A piece of thick paper, suitable for use with water, large enough to cover a notebook
- A selection of colored papers
- White plastic glue diluted with a little water
- Scissors
- Photos, magazine pages, travel brochures, old drawings, etc. (optional)
- Clear plastic or contact paper (optional)

Directions:

Plan your notebook cover by drawing out your idea on a piece of paper or let the cover develop spontaneously as you choose and cut up colored papers.

1. Select a topic and colored papers.
2. Cut out desired parts and try different appropriate notebook arrangements.
3. Write in freehand or print out the words.

152 See ch. 21, "All About Cutting."

4. Cut out and try different arrangements suited to the collage picture.
5. Choose your favorites and glue in place.
6. Draw diagonal, horizontal or vertical lines in various widths in coordinating colors to add interest and frame the composition in a pleasant and interesting way.
7. Cover with clear plastic or clear contact paper to preserve your collage.

Optional: Draw, color, and cut out a complete frame or design from colored paper. Glue the frame around the collage. Glue the collage to the cover of the notebook.

Paper Weaving Notebook Cover AGES 8+

See chapter 21, "All About Cutting." If your child has been practicing cutting strips of paper on her own, she will enjoy the art of paper weaving and can create an impressive and beautiful notebook cover worth doing.

Materials:

- Note: Measurements will vary according to the size of the notebook. Here are instructions for a 6 x 8¼-inch (15 x 21-cm) notebook cover
- 2 sheets of stiff paper (Bristol, art paper, or thin card paper), size 8½ x 11 inches (21 x 28 cm);
- 2 sheets of colored paper (yellow and purple or other combination); metallic paper; or 2 pages from magazines (Note: Stiff paper is easiest to work with.)
- 1 sheet of copy paper, size 8½ x 11 inches (21 x 30 cm). Metallic paper is also nice.
- Pencil
- Ruler
- Colored markers
- Thin black marker

- Scissors
- Cellophane tape

Directions:

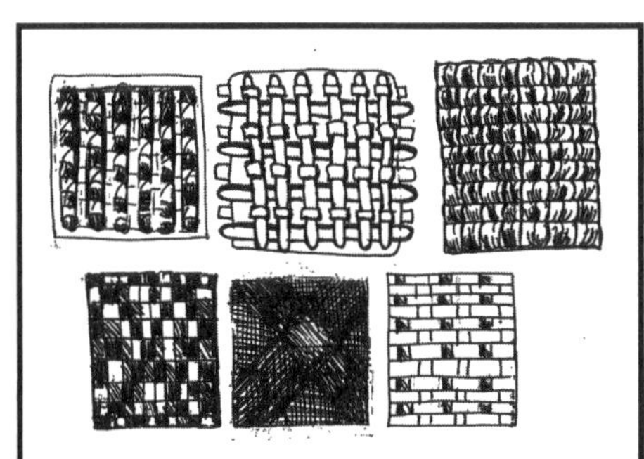

1. Position the paper in the landscape direction. With the ruler and pencil, measure and mark 1-inch (2½-cm) segments across the top of one stiff paper.
2. Mark corresponding 1-inch (2½-cm) segments across the bottom.
3. With the markers, dot each mark, using the same color for each corresponding top and bottom marks. You will have colored dots at the top corresponding to the colored dots at the bottom. You will have eleven strips. They will be 8 inches long and 1 inch wide (20 x 2½ cm).
4. Now prepare the second stiff paper in the same manner, repeating directions 1–3.
5. Cut the strips of each color.
6. Line up the yellow strips, one next to the other, horizontally on the working surface. Tape the left edges together. Line up the purple strips, one next to the other, vertically, and tape the tops together.
7. Place the yellow group over the purple group and weave one strip at a time under and over until the two groups are united. Do as many rows as the child can master. Cut off any unused rows. Tape all the edges. Fold the taped edges back and secure with tape. If this is done with four even edges you will have a notebook cover. Glue a piece of paper to the back of the weaving, before gluing it onto the cover of your notebook. Write in the name of the notebook subject, letter by letter, vertically (from top to bottom) in the squares on the front side near the spine.

In Summary: The Teacher and Her Classroom

- Be prepared. Test projects in advance.
- Divide projects into stages and approximate time slots. Offer ideas and options that may not be obvious to the students with stories, demonstrations, concepts, and insights.
- Answer questions and discuss visual images both internal and external.
- Put out materials at each required stage to prevent children rushing through the project and to maintain order in the work area.
- The child should gain success in one skill before moving to another skill.
- Compliments that encourage one's strong points and personal attention go a long way.
- Time management can stretch a five-minute drawing into forty minutes when it is divided into carefully thought-out steps.
- Have options for the child who does finish before the rest of the class, first reviewing if she completed the necessary steps.
- Bulletin boards create a vibrant atmosphere for students.

Questions and Wonder:

1. What is the job of a teacher?
2. Is the job of an art teacher different from a reading or math teacher and if so, how?

Appendix

Additional Projects and Ideas

Here are some more project ideas that use a Jewish motif and reinforce constructive images in your child's mind.

For the Festivals

ROSH HASHANAH AND YOM KIPPUR: The special practices and mitzvot of the Jewish New Year—eating symbolic foods, blowing the shofar, saying the beautiful liturgies and prayers—are an inspiration for great art. The machzor (special prayer book used on the holidays), scales representing the judgment and weighing of good and bad deeds, a tzedakah box, praying the selichot (prayers for forgiveness), the kapparot ritual in which chickens or money are brought as an atonement, and the Yom

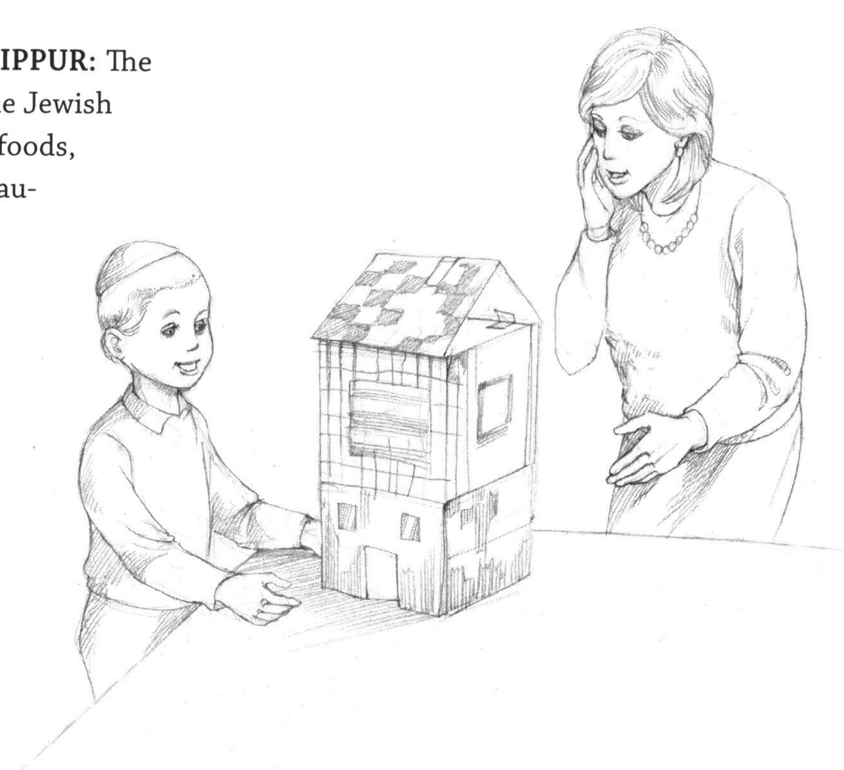

Kippur service can all be created in projects. Some ideas for depicting these awesome days:

Make a tzedakah box (ages 6+): See chapter 5, "Making the Most of the Subject Matter," for how to make a tzedakah box.

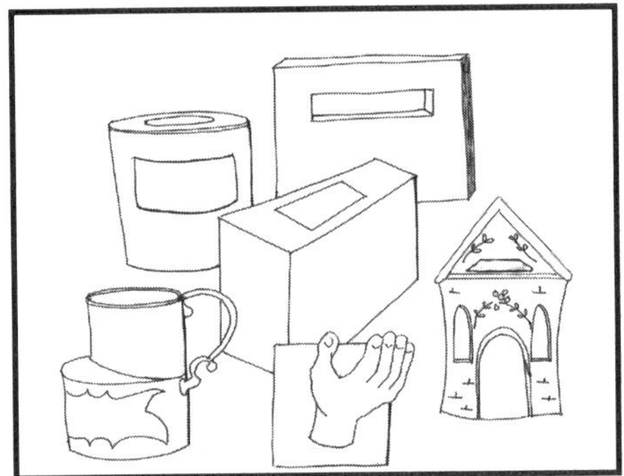

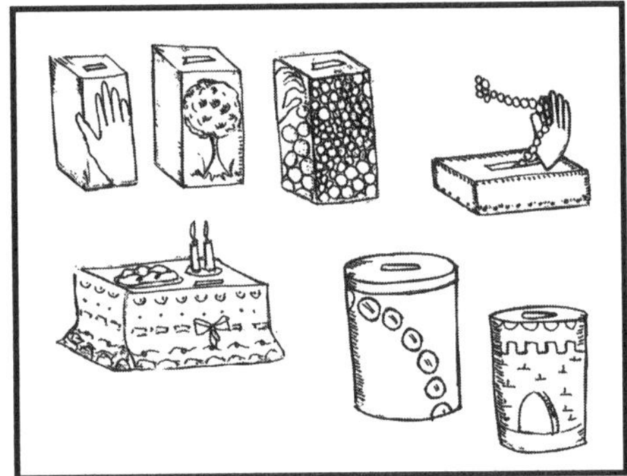

Festival cards (ages 7/8+): Make a card game on heavy paper, cardboard or Styrofoam sandwich board, measuring 24 x 2 inches (60 x 5 cm). Divide and cut into twelve 2 x 2-inch (5 x 5-cm) cards. "Frame" each one with a black marker around the edges of the cards. Draw and color two identical sets of the Rosh Hashanah and Yom Kippur symbols on each of the six sets of cards. Look at photos for visual information when possible.[153] Optional: Double the number of cards and add your own symbols of what is meaningful to you about these holy days.

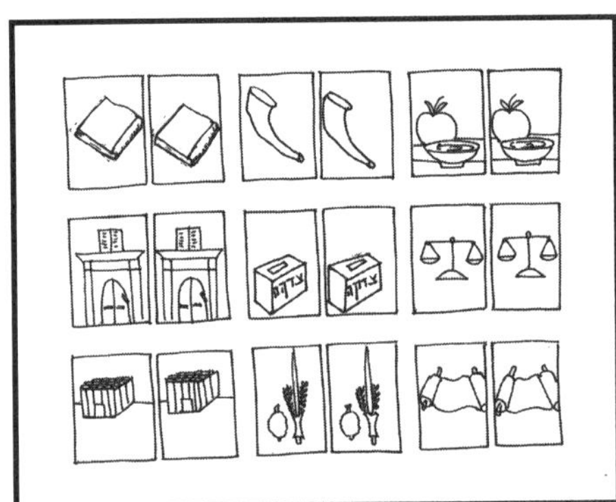

Two children turn the cards over and play a game of lotto. When finished, see who can line up their cards in the correct order that takes place on Rosh Hashanah and Yom Kippur.

Some symbols are: (1) Rosh Hashanah card or greeting, (2) apple and honey and other symbolic foods, (3) shofar blowing, (4) Tashlich (symbolically throwing our misdeeds into the water), (5) selichot, (6) kapparot, (7) *viduy* (asking forgiveness for our past misdeeds, and (8) parent(s) giving a blessing to the children before Yom Kippur.

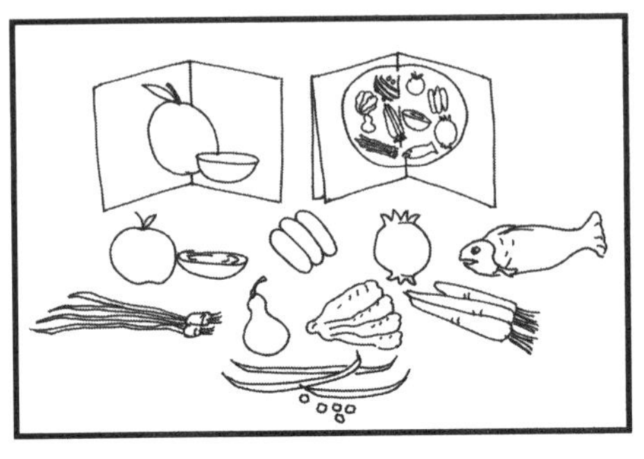

Rosh Hashanah greeting cards (ages 8+): Think about the significance of a new year and a new start when you are hand-printing a design for your Rosh Hashanah cards. Handmade pop-up cards are always appreciated. Purchase a pop-up card from a greeting card shop to serve as an example, and use this for your pattern. Change the pop-up image to an apple, shofar, or a circle with a representation of a calendar on it. Use colored construction paper, paints, colored markers, and glitter to decorate your cards.

153 See ch. 17, "Some Art Theory to Get You Started," for drawing tips.

SUKKOT, HOSHANA RABBAH, AND SIMCHAT TORAH: After the subdued and serious tone of the High Holy Days comes the joyous celebration of Sukkot and Simchat Torah. The joy is not only for the commemoration of the past—when God protected the Jewish people in the desert with sukkahs made of clouds—but also with the knowledge that all sins of the past year have been forgiven.

These holidays are full of mitzvot, symbolizing the Jewish people's readiness to start the new year on the right foot. Artwork representing these festivals might include painting the interior of a wooden sukkah; pictures of kosher sukkahs; the Jewish people in the desert sheltered by the Clouds of Glory; a Jew purchasing and praying with the four species—the lulav, etrog, *hadasim*, and *aravot*; the seven species indigenous to the Land of Israel—wheat, barley, grapes, figs, pomegranates, olives, and dates; Hoshana Rabbah (the seventh day of Sukkot and final day of judgment for the new year) in the synagogue, praying with bunches of *aravot*; and the hakafot (seven circuits of circling the bimah); and dancing with the Torah scroll on Simchat Torah.

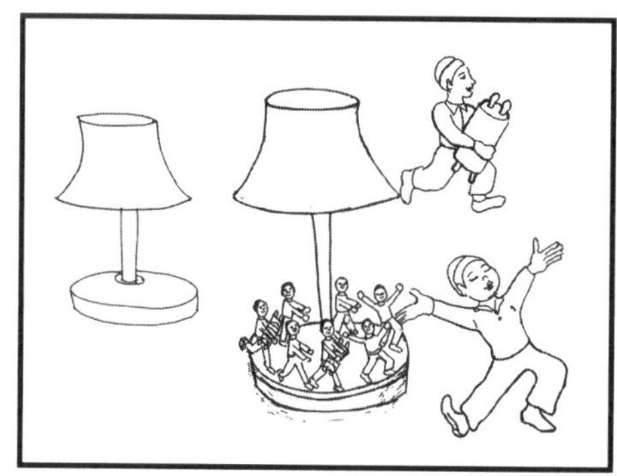

Simchat Torah Lamp (Ages 9/10+): Convert an old lamp base into a joyful Simchat Torah scene. Use air-drying modeling clay and form several (8–10) dancing or marching children measuring 2½ inches high x ¾–1 inch wide. One child should be holding a *sefer Torah*. Let dry and paint carefully with acrylic paint, using small brushes and bright colors. Attach well with carpenters' glue or superglue around the lamp, on the base.

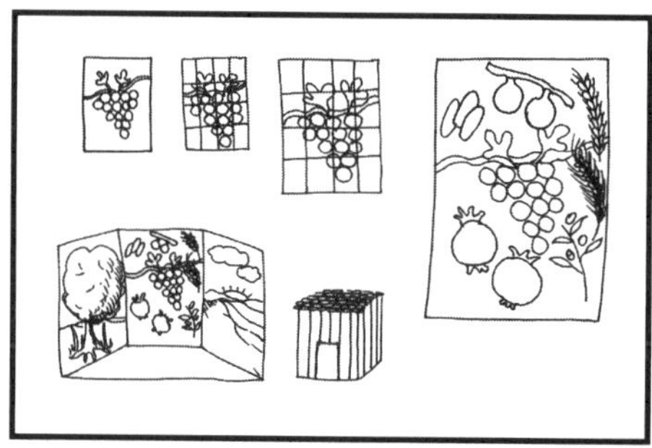

Sukkah Mural (Ages 10+): Consider painting a mural on the wooden wall of your sukkah next year. See chapter 3 for instructions on how to paint your mural. Will you show the Levites playing their instruments, the Kotel, or the dome-shaped roofs of Jerusalem of old?

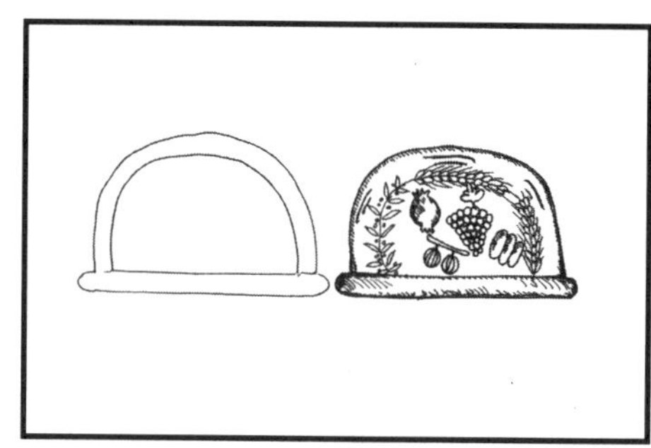

Make a decorated napkin holder (Ages 9+): Use a sturdy holder that is smooth on both sides. Make a mixture of papier mâché from small torn or ground-up pieces of newspaper mixed with white plastic glue and water. Or, use ready-made papier mâché pulp and add water. Dip the papier mâché into the glue mixture and form the seven species. Form shapes according to the shape and size of the fruits and grains. Attach well on both sides of the holder. Let dry. Paint with acrylic paint. Apply a clear acrylic sealant.

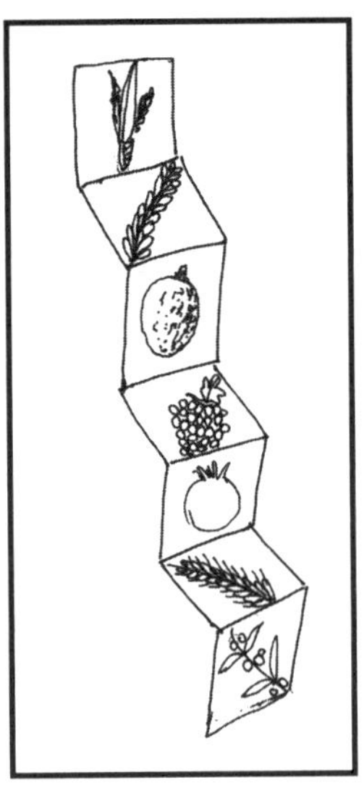

Hanging accordion sukkah decoration (Ages 7/8+): Fold a long, thick strip of paper, measuring 8 x 36 inches (20 x 91 cm) into 3 x 8-inch (7½ x 20-cm) accordion folds. Draw and color symbols of the holiday, one in each of the twelve squares: a lulav and etrog, *hadasim* and *aravot*, the seven species of the Land, a sukkah, etc. Make a small hole and hang with a string from the top of the sukkah. Optional: Embellish as desired with a frame made of imitation jewels, beads, or gold-colored wood. Hang it up with thumb tacks on wooden walls or safety pins on cloth walls.

TU B'SHEVAT: The fifteenth of the Hebrew month of Shevat is considered the new year for fruit trees, which is significant in calculating the agricultural cycle and laws related to growing produce, such as giving tithes. (In other words, when it comes to tithes, the year starts on Tu b'Shevat.) To commemorate this day, many people make a special meal that includes the seven species from the Land of Israel. Create cooked and raw salads from the seven species to serve at your Tu b'Shevat meal.

Besides the seven species, fruit baskets are a popular theme for depicting this day, as is the blossoming almond tree. This is because the almond tree is the first fruit tree of the season to blossom on which a blessing is recited in the month of Nisan.[154] Tu b'Shevat is a time when we consider the benefits we receive from nature, and trees in particular. Think about the many blessings we get from trees.[155]

Family tree project (Ages 9+): Tu b'Shevat is a great time to do a family-tree project with children. Now is a good time to research your family roots. Have them collect names from all sides of the family as far back as they are able. Then they should organize the names by lineage and add dates of birth and death when possible. They should count how many branches and leaves they will need to fit the names on the tree. Each branch is a family, and each leaf is a family member.

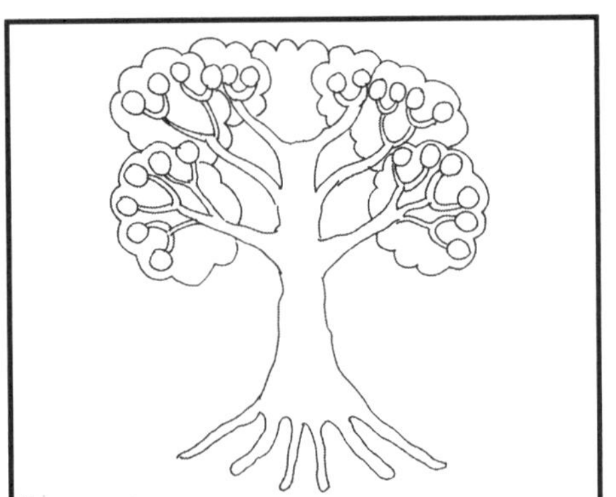

Use good-quality Bristol paper or thin cardboard, measuring 10 x 13 inches (25 x 33 cm). Draw a large tree, 7 x 10 inches

154 Mishnah, *Rosh Hashanah*, p. 2; Talmud, *Berachot* 43b, ch. 6.

155 Talmud, *Ta'anit* 5b. This is a parable about a man who was in the desert, hungry, thirsty, and tired. He found a tree ripe with sweet fruits and abundant shade. He ate of the fruits, drank from the nearby stream, and rested in the tree's shade. When he was ready to go, he said, "*Ilan, ilan*, how can I bless you? Your fruits are already sweet, you give pleasant shade, and you have a source of water beside you—so I will bless you that all your saplings be like you."

(18 x 25 cm) in size, complete with branches and large leaves in which to write each name and date. Draw smaller leaves to fill in empty spaces.

You can also have them cut out the different parts of the tree with different colored paper: use browns and beige for the trunk and branches and a variety of greens for the leaves, then glue them onto the large Bristol or cardboard.

Tu b'Shevat fruit bowl (ages 7+): You will need: a large, round, hard plastic fruit bowl; air-drying clay (optional: small round bowl); and three colors of metallic acrylic paint and brushes, 1 and 1½ inches (2½ x 4 cm).

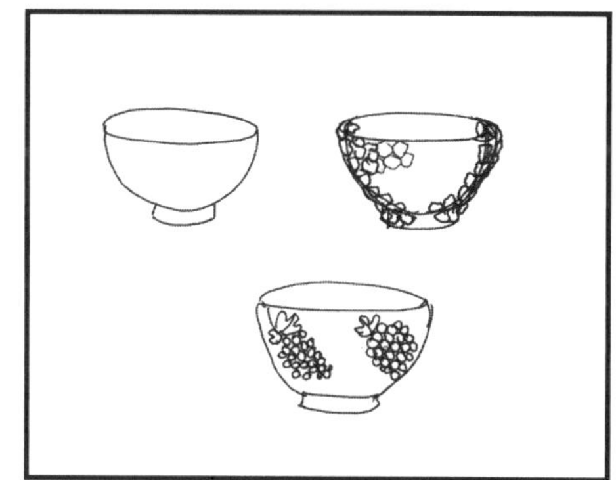

Cover a hard plastic bowl with a layer of air-drying modeling clay. Pinch off a few 1-inch (2½-cm) pieces at a time from the package, keeping it closed to prevent the clay from drying out. Roll into balls and flatten. Press in place over bowl, starting at the top and working down until entire bowl, inside and outside, is firmly covered. Form a few large grape clusters (or dates, figs, pomegranates, olives), stems and leaves, and barley and wheat. Press in place around bowl. Use glue if necessary on dried clay. Dry. Paint in three layers of metallic acrylic paint. Especially nice is to use a different color metallic paint on each layer, letting some of the under-layer show through to the next one. Paint the seven species (*shivat ha-minim*) like the bowl or make them stand out with a contrasting color. Option to cover with clear acrylic. Note: bowl is not waterproof.

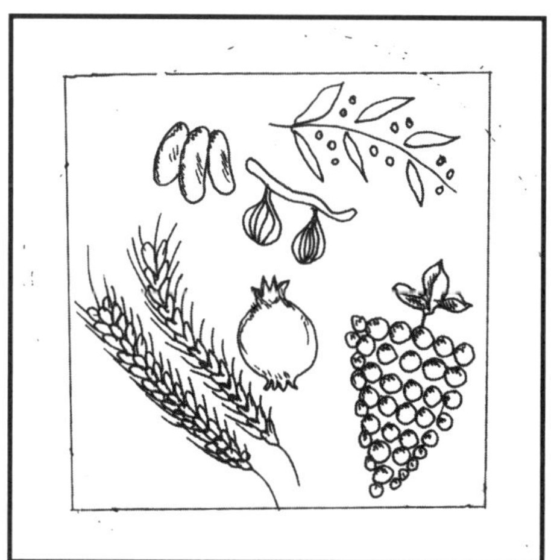

Designer fruit (ages 8+): Make fruits from small nylon stockings or small paper bags stuffed with shredded or crumpled paper or pillow stuffing. Paint the stockings with diluted (with water) acrylic colors or cover with layers of colored tissue paper dipped into a mixture of white plastic glue diluted with drops of water. Choose colors according to each fruit. Attach leaves cut from foam sheets or soft cardboard with floral wire. Display the fruits in a basket or on a plate.

PURIM: Purim is a day for feasting, wearing costumes, and giving food gifts to friends and charity to the poor. This holiday commemorates the Jews' salvation, under the leadership of the righteous Mordechai and Esther, from the hands of the evil Haman and the Persian king Ahasuerus. You can depict scenes from

Megillat Esther (the Book of Esther), the megillah reading in the synagogue, giving food and charity to the poor, *mishlo'ach manot* (sending food gifts) to friends, eating and drinking at the festive meal, Purim costumes, and *graggers* (noisemakers used to drown out the mention of the evil Haman).

Mordechai on the Horse AGES 6/7+

See illustration.

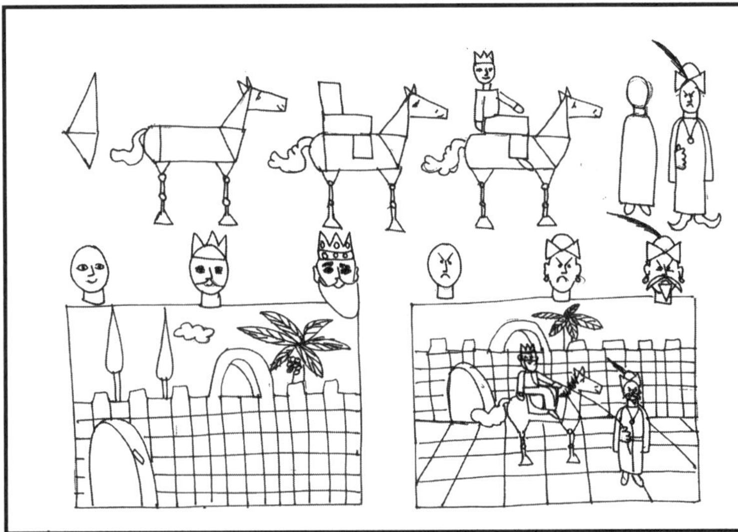

Materials:

- Practice paper, 8.5 x 11 inches (21 x 30 cm)
- Final paper: All-purpose art paper or Bristol, 8.5 x 11 inches (21 x 30 cm) or 11 x 16 inches (28 x 41 cm)
- Pencil and pen (waterproof)
- Colored markers and or paint (watercolor or gauche) with brushes ⅛, ¼, and ½ inch (¼, ½, and 1½ cm)

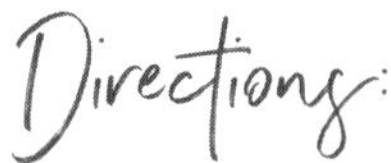

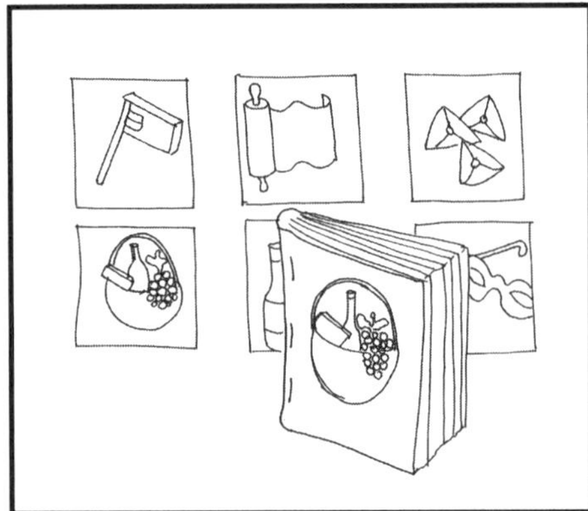

1. Practice drawing Mordechai on the horse and Haman based on the illustration.
2. Repeat on the final paper and include the walls and courtyard of Shushan.
3. Paint or color in with markers.

Purim coloring book (Ages 7+): You'll need three sheets of 8½ x 11-inch (21 x 30-cm) copy paper, a stapler, pencil, black marker, and a set of six colored markers or crayons. Fold the three sheets of paper in half. Staple along the fold (the spine) in three places to keep the papers together. With the pencil, draw pictures related to Purim. Give the coloring book a title, and draw a picture for the cover. (You can look in children's Purim books for ideas of what to draw.) Then outline the drawings in black, coloring-book style. Give the coloring book to a small child to color with markers or crayons.

Adar Jello Fish Tanks AGES 5+, WITH ADULT HELP

Food and drink (mishlo'ach manot) to send on Purim to neighbors, teachers, and friends.

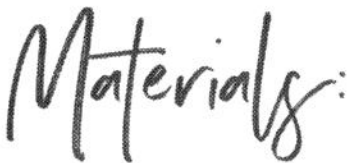

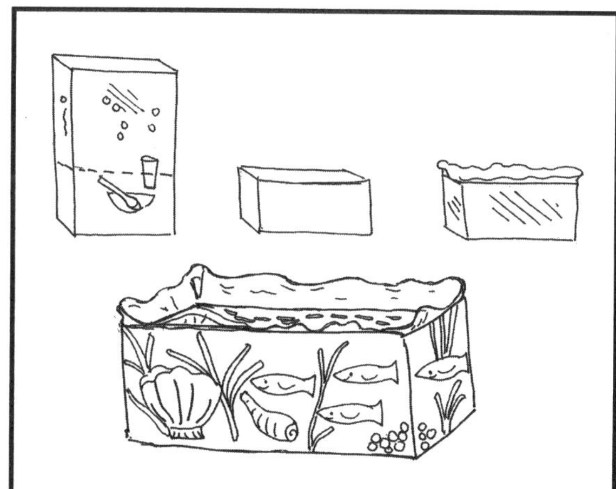

- Cereal box
- Scissors or craft knife
- Hot glue
- White plastic glue
- Acrylic paint, green/turquoise, red, yellow, blue, and white
- Paintbrushes, ¼ inch (½ cm) and ½ inch (1½ cm)
- Plastic wrap or foil to cover insides and bottom of the container
- Air-drying modeling clay
- Optional: shells, green raffia or pipe cleaners, small clean stones
- Jello, green or clear, grated roasted squash, sweet potatoes. Fresh or roasted green, yellow, red peppers

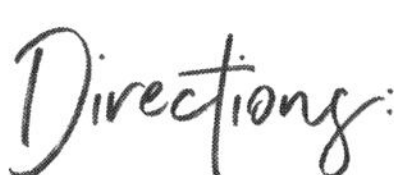

Start the container a week before Purim.

1. Cut box one-third up from the bottom. Discard reminding two-thirds.
2. Paint box green inside and out. Dry.
3. Model six to eight clay fish, shells, seaweeds, and rocks. Dry.

4. Paint as desired. Optional: Use real shells, make seaweed from raffia or pipe cleaners.
5. Hot glue on outside around box.
6. Cover bottom and insides of box with plastic or foil.
7. Prepare jello (kosher gelatin dessert) according to directions on box. Fill "fish tank" a half to a third high, and stir in cooled vegetables. Send with a tuna sandwich and tea bag or drink.

PESACH: To illustrate this festival that commemorates the Jews' exodus from Egypt, you can draw or decorate a Haggadah.

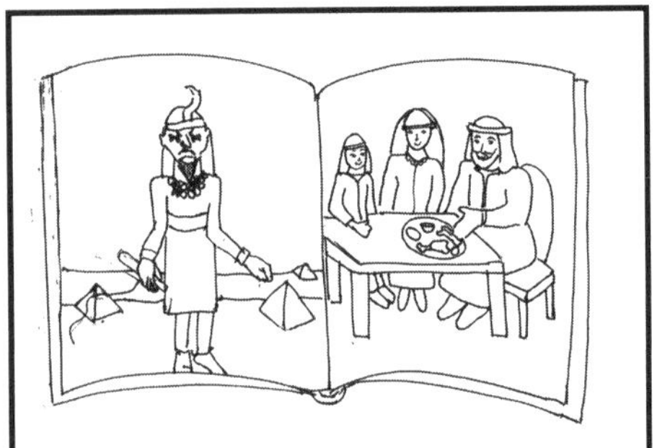

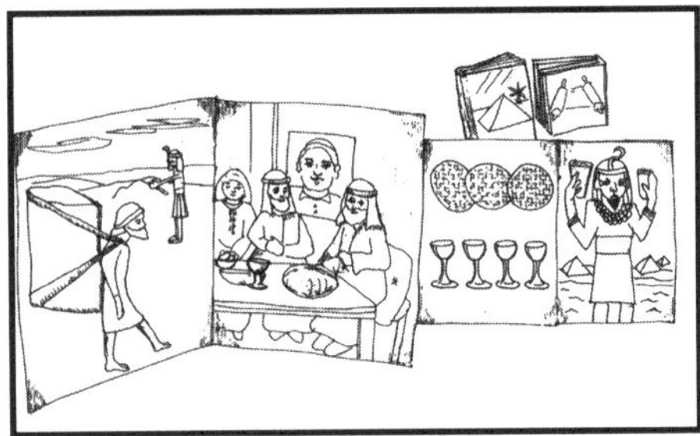

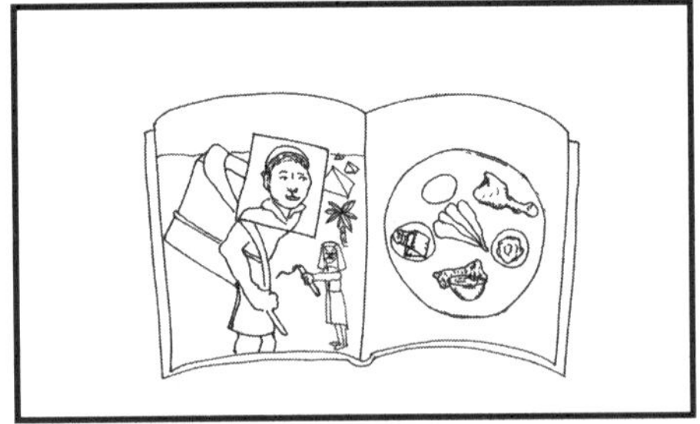

Decorate a Haggadah (Ages 7/8+): Depict events of the exodus such as the ten plagues and the crossing of the Red Sea, scenes of a family preparing for Pesach, *kashering* (process of making something fit and kosher for use) the kitchen, *kashering* utensils in big pots of boiling water, finding and burning chametz (leavened products), matzah baking, the Seder plate, the Seder table all set, the youngest family member asking the Four Questions, searching for the afikoman (the last portion of matzah eaten at the Pesach Seder), and counting the *Omer*.

On Pesach, it is a mitzvah to relive the exodus and imagine that we ourselves left Egypt. In the spirit of this mitzvah, you can personalize the Haggadot of your family.

Family Haggadah (Ages 5+): You'll need a Haggadah for each person at the Seder table, a photo or drawing of each participant, scissors, and a glue stick or white plastic glue. Glue at least one photo or drawing of each member in your family over the heads of the Jewish slaves in the Haggadah, or onto one or more of the illustrated pages of the Haggadah to remind everyone of the mitzvah to feel as if he actually left Egypt.

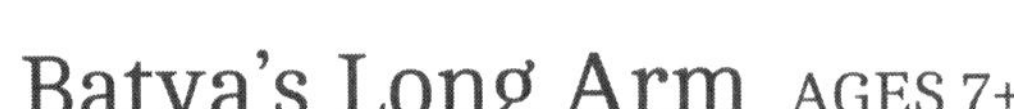

Batya's Long Arm AGES 7+

Batya, daughter of Pharaoh, found a Jewish baby in the Nile that she took to the palace to raise as her own. Moses ultimately saved his people and led them from slavery, which led to the downfall of the Ancient Egyptian Empire.

Batya is standing (on land) near the Nile. She reaches for the tar-covered basket. Her arm miraculously lengthens to draw in the basket. Miriam, Moshe's sister, is standing behind the reeds growing along the Nile guarding her baby brother. We see the pyramids and desert in the background.

See illustration. Rearrange or change to your taste.

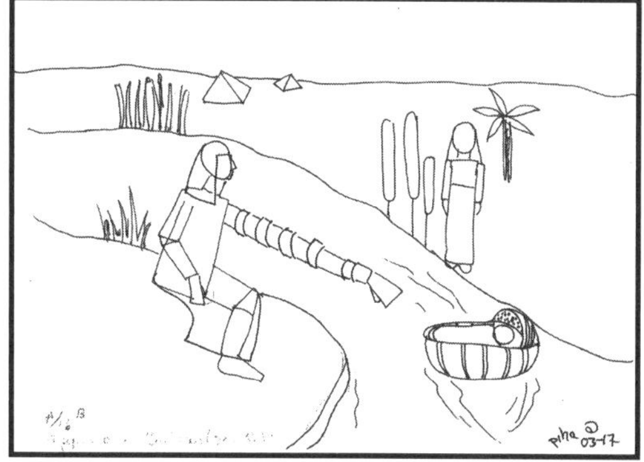

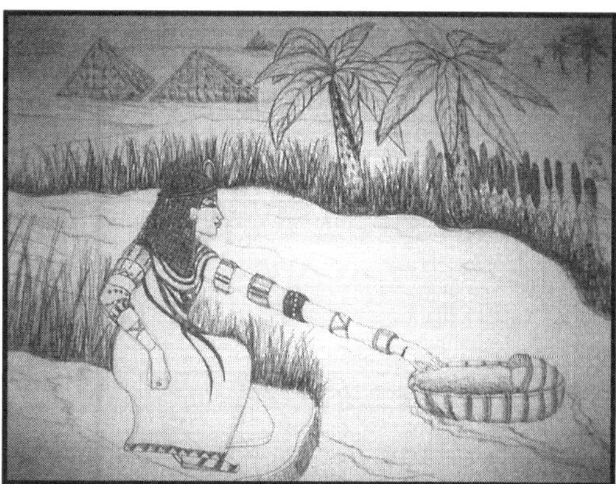

Materials:

- Paper: all-purpose art paper or copy paper, 8.5 x 11 inches (21 x 30 cm) or larger
- 5 x ½-inch (12 x 1½-cm) thick paper
- Scissors
- Pencil
- Permanent pen
- Optional: choice of paint with brushes ¼, ½ inch (½, 1½ cm) and/or markers
- Pencil
- Cellophane tape

Directions:

1. Draw with pencil. Go over lines with a permanent pen.
2. Add cross-hatching (lines crossing over lines) for depth and interest.
3. Color or paint or leave as is.
4. Make a small cut, ½ inch (1½ cm), near Batya's shoulder.
5. Draw another arm on thick paper, 4 inches (10 cm) long and ½ inch wide. Cover it with bracelets in Egyptian designs.
6. Insert the arm through the slot and move it forward and back when showing the picture to family and friends. Tape arm in place when not moving it.

Batya's Bracelet AGES 6+, WITH ADULT HELP

Make one for each of the young guests at your Seder table.

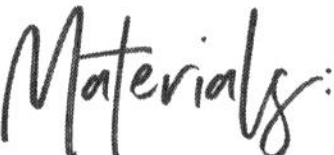

- 7 x 2 inches (18 x 5 cm) copper sheets per bracelet
- Scissors
- A hard, pointed object, a ball point pen or wooden stylus (a small pointed stick)

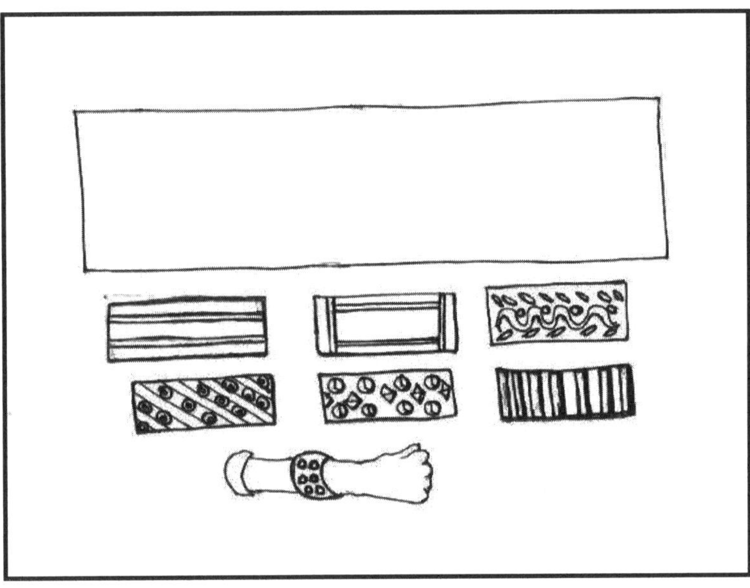

Directions:

1. Fold all the edges over twice to the front or to the back to 5½ x 1 inch (14 x 2½ cm).

2. On the backside of the copper, draw an Egyptian design, pressing with the hard object. Curve the bracelet to fit your arm and those of your guests.

Option: Glue smooth, colorful plastic or glass stones onto the bracelet.

LAG BAOMER: The thirty-third day of *sefirat haOmer* (the counting of the forty-nine days between Pesach and Shavuot) is marked as a minor holiday. On this day, the plague that killed 24,000 disciples of the Talmudic sage Rabbi Akiva ended. This is also the day when Rabbi Shimon bar Yochai revealed the deepest secrets of the Torah known as the Zohar.

To illustrate this special day, depict a Lag BaOmer counting scroll numbered from one to forty-nine with the number thirty-three highlighted. Around the scroll, draw and color the cave of Rabbi Shimon bar Yochai, a view of Meron, or a little boy getting his first haircut[156] and bonfires in the night.

Count the *Omer* in color (ages 8+): How about a color-mixing session?[157] Divide an 8½ x 11-inch (21 x 28-cm) or larger all-purpose art

---

156 There is a tradition to let a boy's hair grow until the age of three; the famous kabbalist, the Arizal kept this custom and cut his child's hair at age three in Meron.

157 See ch. 20, "The Joy of Mixing Color."

paper into forty-nine spaces by making seven rows with seven squares in each, for the forty-nine days of the *Omer* counting. Paint each row one color of the rainbow: red, orange, yellow, green, blue, and violet. Choose an additional color for the last row. Add increasing drops of white paint to the red row: the first square one drop, the second, two drops, and so on. You can start with a red and end in the last red space with a light pink. Do this with each row, and watch your dark blue turn into a sky blue by the last blue space. Use acrylic or gouache paint and a soft-haired brush, ½ to ¾ inch (1½ to 2 cm) wide. On a separate paper, draw a few of the symbols of Lag BaOmer, including the number thirty-three and glue onto the appropriate dried painted spaces.

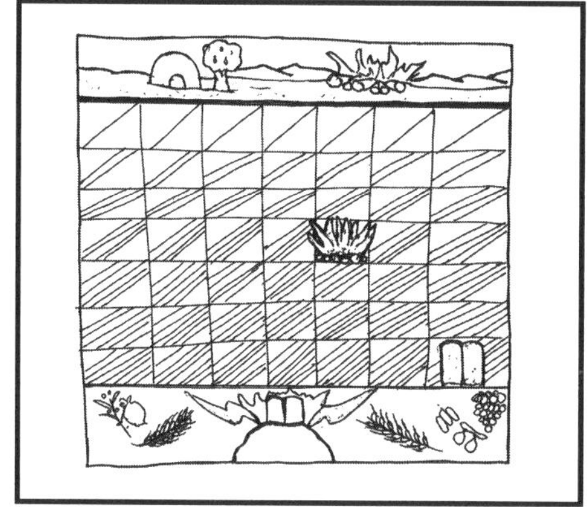

A torn-paper collage of Meron and the cave of Rabbi Shimon bar Yochai (ages 7+): This is a fun project related to Lag BaOmer that children will love. Torn paper has a beauty of its own because of the deckled (slightly frayed) edges and the color quality of the paper. Torn-paper collages are great for large areas, like bulletin-board displays, so think large on this one.[158]

You'll need four 8½ x 11-inch (21 x 28-cm) sheets of copy paper. Glue the four papers together to make one large sheet. Or use one large 11 x 16 or 16 x 23 inches (28 x 41 or 41 x 58 cm) thick paper (Bristol), smooth cardboard, or Styrofoam sandwich board. This will be the paper on which you will glue your collage.

With a pencil, draw very simple outlines on the paper, as follows: Draw a line across the paper slightly below the center. Add a few hills on the top of the line, using curves, half-circles. or loose triangles. On the top of the line, on the left of the paper, draw a half-circle for the cave and a small half-circle for its entrance in the front of the cave. Add a large carob tree to the right of the cave and a river near the entrance to the cave.

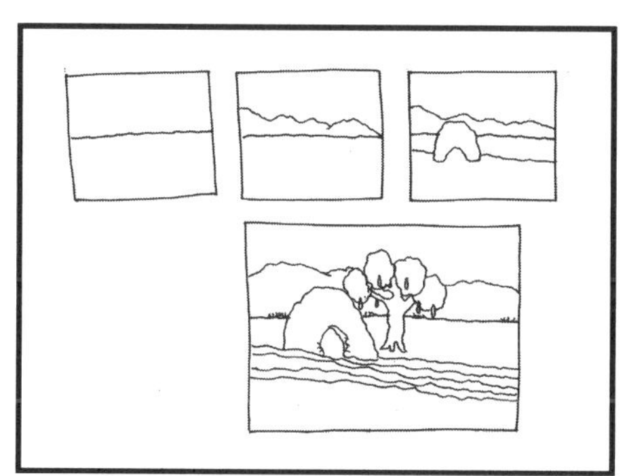

Have ready several colored sheets of paper. Use colored craft paper or shiny construction paper. (See below for colors.) Tear the papers by hand into a variety of sizes and shapes. Ignore the temptation to use scissors. Apply the torn pieces of paper to the large paper with a smooth application of white plastic or craft glue.

158 See ch. 21, "All About Cutting."

Use green paper for grass and bushes, browns for the hills, blues for the sky, stream, or river. The cave is white and gray or brown, and the entrance to the cave is black. Next to it stands a carob tree with a brown trunk and green leaves. The green grass and bushes in front of the cave are flanked by brown and gray hills. Continue gluing until the picture is filled in. Use more than one layer of tissue paper if you like. Add your own personal touch: You may leave empty spaces, and pieces may overlap. Trim the edges around the perimeter of the completed picture for a neat presentation.

SHAVUOT: The Jewish people received the Torah at Har Sinai on Shavuot. You can illustrate the *Luchot Habrit* or Moshe Rabbeinu receiving the Torah on Har Sinai amid clouds, thunder, and fire. Imagine the strength of the thunder and the sounds of that night that changed the world. Can you depict the drama and sounds in paint on canvas or water paper? Shavuot observances include learning Torah all night, bringing the first fruits on a pilgrimage to the Beit Hamikdash, *Megillat Rut* (the Book of Ruth) being read in the synagogue, and eating traditional dairy foods such as blintzes and cheesecake.

Shavuot is one of the few holidays when dairy is eaten at the festive meals. It's fun to pull out those dairy recipes you've been wanting to try but never had time for: cheesecakes, quiches, milkshakes, ice creams, and blintzes.

Shavuot recipe book (ages 8+): Gather together your favorite dairy recipes from family and friends. Find pictures of these foods from magazines and books to cut out or draw from memory.[159] Purchase a small photo album with light-colored pages (not plastic pockets) or a small scrapbook. Glue the recipes on one side of a spread (facing pages) and draw a picture of the dish or glue the matching photos on the other.

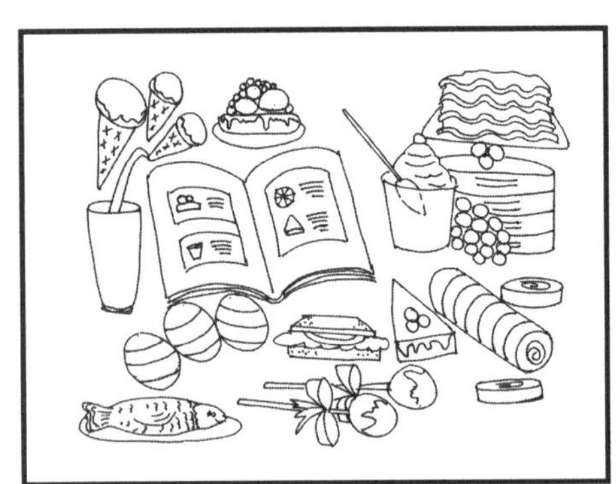

Or, draw and color illustrations of the finished product.

Write and illustrate a book (ages 6+): Write and illustrate a story such as this one. A girl wants to help bake a delicious dish in honor of Shavuot: "This is a quiche with a golden crust and a delightful smell. I only have to mix it by hand, pour it into a pie pan, and enjoy reading while waiting for it to bake. I know that my family and guests will enjoy it!" Include a recipe of the dish at the end.

159 See ch. 14, "Making the Most of Your Child's Potential," for more on drawing cakes; ch. 23, "Working with Clay," for more on creating real-looking cakes from clay.

Shavuot Harvest Painting AGES 9+

Emphasize the story of Ruth or the reaping of the harvest against a background of fields, hills, the Judean sky, and wheat.

Materials:

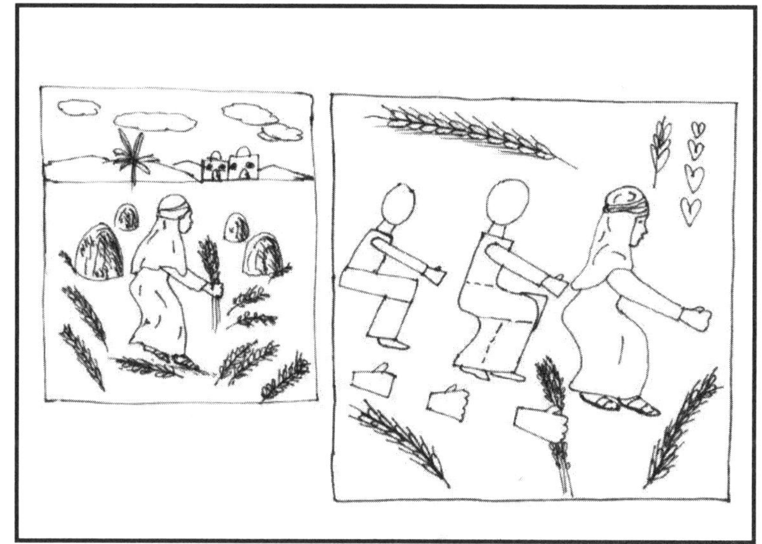

- Paper: Bristol or all-purpose art/painting paper, 11 x 16 inches (28 x 41 cm) or smaller.
- Pencil
- Paint: gouache, acrylic, or watercolor colored pencil or regular colored pencils.
- Brushes: ⅛, ¼, and ½ inches (¼, ½, and 1½ cm) plus a sturdy water cup.

Directions:

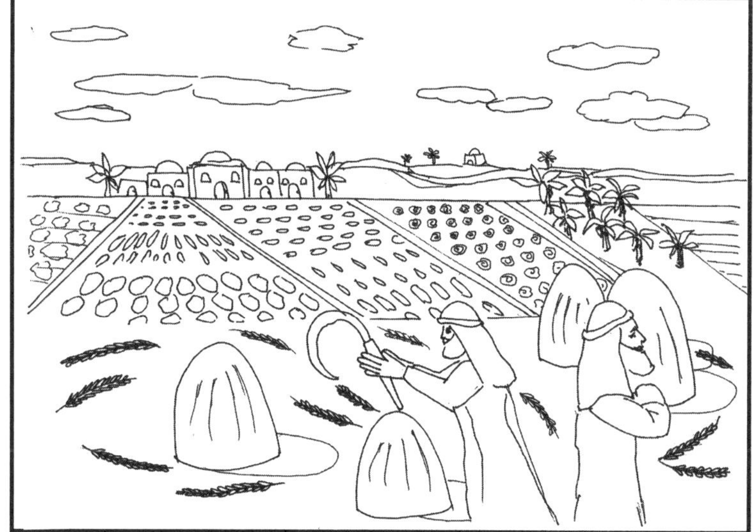

See illustrated sample and feel free to rearrange or make changes.

1. Draw a horizontal line on the upper two-thirds of the paper.
2. Pay attention to distance and proportion; faraway objects are small. On the line, place a few buildings with domed roofs and arches, doorways, and windows.
3. Put in date palms near each building. Add a few rows of hills to each side of the buildings.
4. Above, add soft, floating clouds.
5. Below the line, draw several groups of fields with vegetables. Use a variety of shapes to suggest the vegetables. Include a grove of date palms near the vegetable patches. In the lower third of the

paper, draw three to five stacks of wheat and single stocks that are on the ground. Draw one or two men dressed in the robes of their day harvesting the wheat with a sickle (a round knife). Or draw Ruth carefully bending down, picking up the fallen loose pieces of wheat (*leket*).

6. Fill in small areas with colored pencils. Paint large areas with diluted paint or full strength.

Har Sinai Construction AGES 7+, WITH ADULT HELP

See illustration in chapter 5, and page 76 for instructions on using Styrofoam sandwich board. Do a three-dimensional construction of Har Sinai. If you already did the drawing of Har Sinai in chapter 5, you will be able to compare a two-dimensional work with a three-dimensional work.

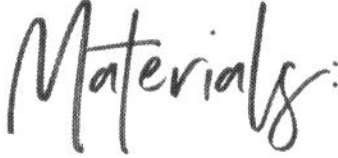

- Styrofoam sandwich board, 11 x 16 inches (28 x 41 cm)
- Air-drying clay
- Bristol or thick paper, 4 x 4 inches (10 x 10 cm)
- Cutting knife
- Hot-glue gun
- Paint gouache or acrylic: blue, brown, yellow or cream, and white

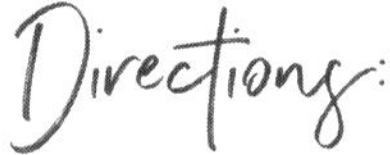

1. Measure and cut the board:
    - The base is a triangle: 8½ x 6 x 6 inches (21½ x 15 x 15 cm)
    - Background wall: 12 x 4 inches (30 x 10 cm)
    - Har Sinai: 3½ x 3½ inches (9 x 9 cm) cut into a triangle
    - The table is 3 x 1 inch (8 x 2½ cm) with legs 3 x 1 inch (8 x 2½ cm)

- Tablets: 1¼ x 1¼ inches (3 x 3 cm)
- Rays of light: On thick paper, 4 x 4 inches (10 x 10 cm), cut to half of a circle

2. Paint all the pieces before gluing into place.
3. Assemble the wall and base, and glue with hot glue.
4. Cut the rays of light.
5. Glue the Tablet at the bottom of the rays and attach to the top of Har Sinai.
6. Glue Har Sinai in the center of the background.
7. Attach the legs to the table with hot glue.
8. Make a Torah scroll with air-drying clay and let dry. Paint, dry, and glue on the table.

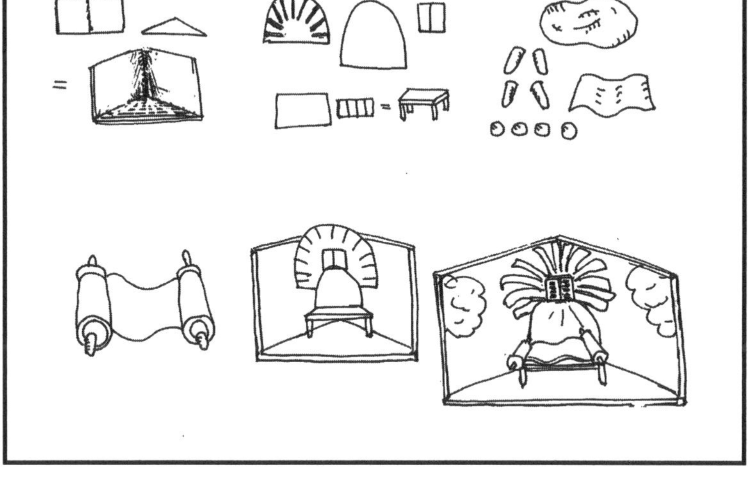

TISHAH B'AV: The ninth day of the Jewish month of Av is the saddest day of the Jewish calendar. It is a day of mourning for the destroyed Beit Hamikdash and other tragic events in history: the expulsion of the Jews from England in the Middle Ages, the expulsion from Spain in 1492, the start of World War I, the Holocaust, and many other tragedies.

To depict this day, you can show Jews sitting on the floor in a darkened synagogue or next to the Kotel in Jerusalem, mourning the destruction of the Temple, reading *Megillat Eichah* (Book of Lamentations) by the light of a burning candle, Jews rescuing fellow Jews from oppression, or Jews forced from their homes to unknown destinations during times of exile and persecution.

The classic representation of Tishah b'Av is the Kotel.

The Kotel (ages 9+): Use acrylics or oils to do a traditional rendition of the massive stone wall, dotted with green scrubs, birds perched on branches overhead, and groups of people from all over the world standing in the plaza below—there to pray, cry, and release their deepest hopes for personal happiness and an end to their suffering. Or do a surrealistic painting by adding into several of the large stone blocks drawings of the travails the Jewish people have passed through in history.

For this you will need a small beginner's set of acrylics or oil paints, complete with an instruction book, brushes, turpentine for oils, and a stretched canvas on a wooden frame or a flat canvas attached to a board. Use paintings of the Kotel by known artists or pictures that you find in books and postcards to practice and copy from, and go on to using your own inspiration.

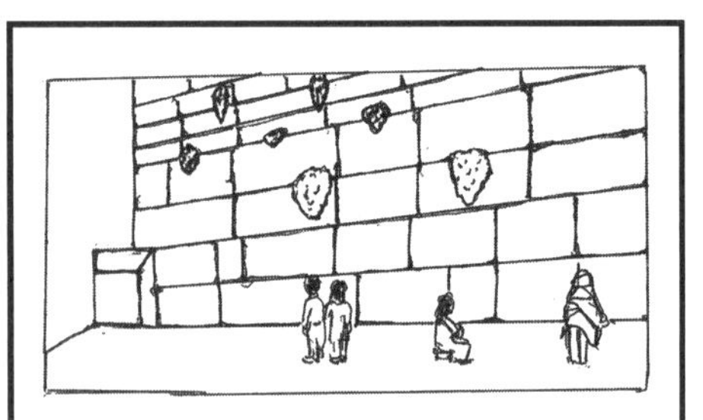

Optional: Do the painting on Bristol or all-purpose art paper coated on both sides with white acrylic. Let dry. Draw your image lightly in pencil. Use a combination of gouache and acrylic paints to paint your drawing.

Read the instruction book for techniques on using the paint. Consider your style: realistic, expressive, or a combination. Sketch out your composition on paper. Redraw it on the canvas or all-purpose art paper. Put down a thin layer of paint. Add additional layers as each layer dries. Be sure to put in shadows and highlights.

Remember that oil paint dries slowly and acrylic dries quickly.

Mitzvot

There are 613 mitzvot in the Torah, and each comes with its own special laws; many require a ceremonial object for their performance. With all those mitzvot, you will never be at a loss for a subject for your art!

Here are some themes associated with mitzvot that you can portray: visiting the sick, giving money to a poor person on a street corner or putting coins into a charity box, reciting a blessing, a child bringing food to his parents, helping an elderly person, standing up for a *talmid chacham* (Torah scholar), a parent attaching a mezuzah to a doorpost and reciting the blessing as the children watch, children helping their neighbors, children making shalom (peace) with their playmates or sharing their toys, a family welcoming guests or travelers into their home, a family partaking of Shabbat meals, the *brit milah* (circumcision) ceremony and chair of Elijah, women lighting Shabbat candles, or returning a lost object.

Mitzvah collection (ages 5/6+): Children love collecting things, whether it's stickers or marbles or so many other things! Here's a way for a child to make a mitzvah collection: Give the child a sketch pad or a pad of drawing paper, and each day (or week), he can draw the picture of a mitzvah that he or she did that day, or he can cut out pictures from a magazine that depict that mitzvah and glue them onto the page. Parents or grandparents can review the book together with the child at the end of the week and express their pleasure at the child's good deeds.

The child can also draw the illustrations on cards and keep his mitzvah collection in a shoe box. At the end of the month, sit with the child and open the box and talk about each picture and what it means to him. If he wishes, he can decorate the box, too.

Mitzvah chart (ages 5+): In place of buying a mitzvah chart you and your child can make one together. On an 8½ x 11-inch (21 x 30-cm) copy paper, arrange four rows of seven days to resemble a monthly calendar page with 1½ x 1½-inch (4 x 4-cm) squares. Children can draw their own mitzvot each day by themselves. You may want to create a "list" of symbols to represent various mitzvot together with your child.

Family Life

The family is the focal point of Jewish life. Many mitzvot and rituals center on the family, among them the mitzvah of teaching the Torah's traditions to children. To depict these ideals, you can show children and parents singing together, a mother greeting her children when they return home from school, a child helping with her younger brother or sister, a mother helping her daughter prepare for her wedding, a grandfather learning Jewish teachings with his grandchildren, grandparents holding their grandchildren, or a father helping a child understand a difficult question or Torah concept.

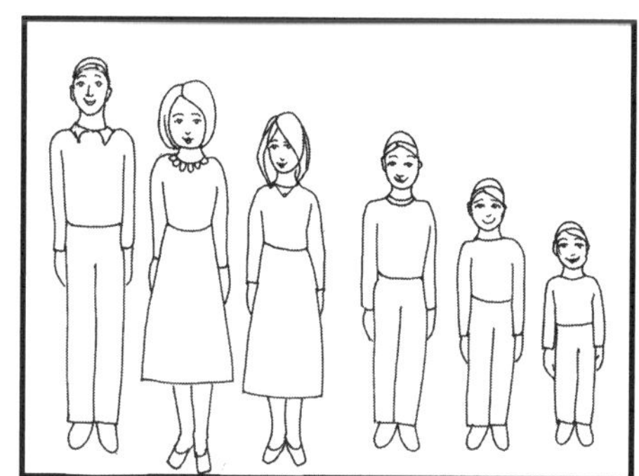

Family portrait (ages 5+): For younger children, have them draw a picture of their family. All you need is an 8½ x 11-inch (21 x 30-cm) or larger copy or drawing paper, a pencil, and an eraser. Have the child draw a picture of each family member in order of age. An easy method is to draw everyone's head first and then add everyone's neck, then shirts, then pants and skirts, arms and hands, legs and shoes, etc., using the same basic shapes for each. Then make any adjustments and add details, such as buttons, pockets, bows, and patterns and textures of the clothes.[160]

Design Your Bedroom AGES 7+

This project is for kids to visualize and put down on paper what they would have in their perfect bedroom. See illustration.

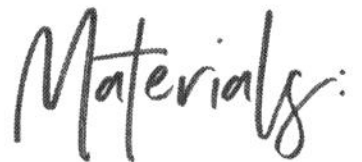

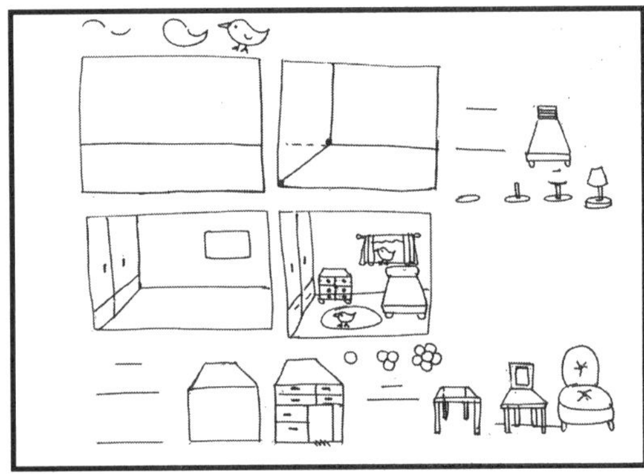

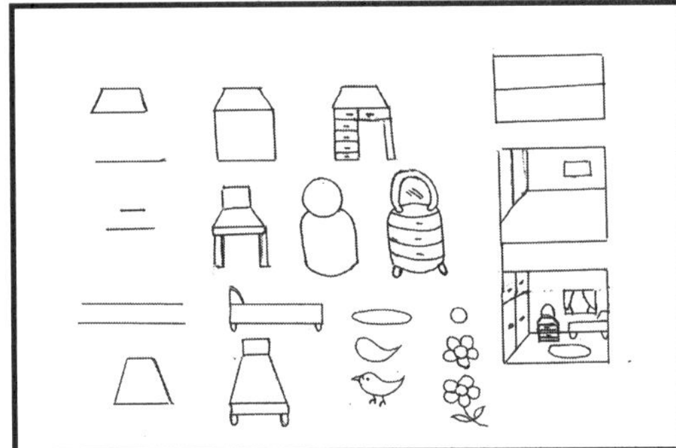

- All-purpose art paper or Bristol, size 8.5 x 11 inches (21 x 30 cm) or 11 x 16 inches (28 x 41 cm)
- Pencil and pen (permanent)
- Colored markers or watercolors with brushes, ⅛ and ¼ inch (¼ and ½ cm)

Directions:

1. Follow the steps in the illustration in pencil using a ruler or freehand.
2. Start with a horizontal line across the center of the room. Draw the closet and window. Put in the furniture.
3. Add any details or additional decorations or furniture you like.
4. Go over the pencil lines with ink and color in with markers.

Optional: Draw furniture and details on paper, cut out, and test the arrangements until you find the best one.

---

160 See ch. 17, "Some Art Theory to Get You Started," for younger children; ch. 25, "All about Drawing People," for older children.

The Shul and Prayer

Torah observance is all about making a connection with God. The ultimate service of God is prayer, a Jew's direct line to God.[161] It can be meditative and individual, in the privacy of the home, or it can be communal, done together as a group in the synagogue.

Depictions of this important aspect of Jewish life might include an introspective moment on a young girl's face while praying in shul; a father helping his son put on tefillin for the first time; people praying in shul on Shabbat; a shul filled with the echoes of prayers, tears, and thanks after the people have gone home; an open *sefer Tehillim* or an illuminated prayer book; a dual of pajama-clad children waking up; the rising sun peeking through the window as they thank God for returning their souls; men praying together in tallit and tefillin; a child saying the *Shema Yisrael* prayer; a mother teaching her daughter how to pray; a young girl fervently speaking to God through smiles and tears; Jews davening at the Kotel; or a child kissing the stone walls of the Kotel.

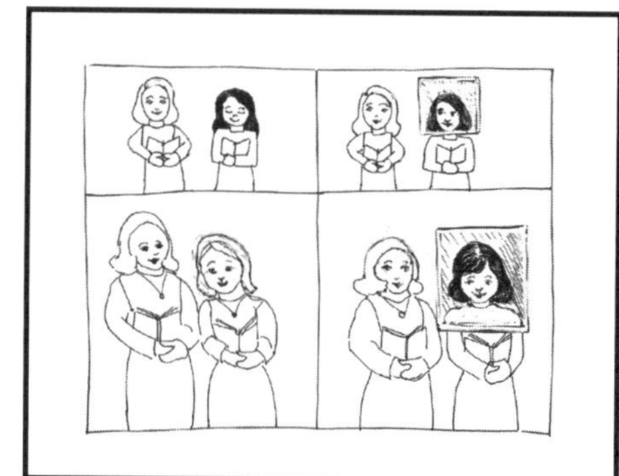

Photo surprise (ages 7+): Prepare (without the child's knowledge) a photo of his/her face that will fit the drawing you and your child will do together. Draw a square on a paper to define the size of the drawing. Draw your family or a boy or girl. Draw in a subject from above with a pencil and color it with markers. When the work is complete, bring out the photo and glue it on to add a personal touch.

Children ages nine or ten-plus can do a painting of any of the images and glue his or her photo (face) onto the canvas in place of drawing of a face. Or, glue a 5 x 6-inch (12½ x 15-cm) photo of the child in the center of a 7 x 8-inch (18 x 20-cm) canvas or cardstock. Paint the outer edges to match the photo.

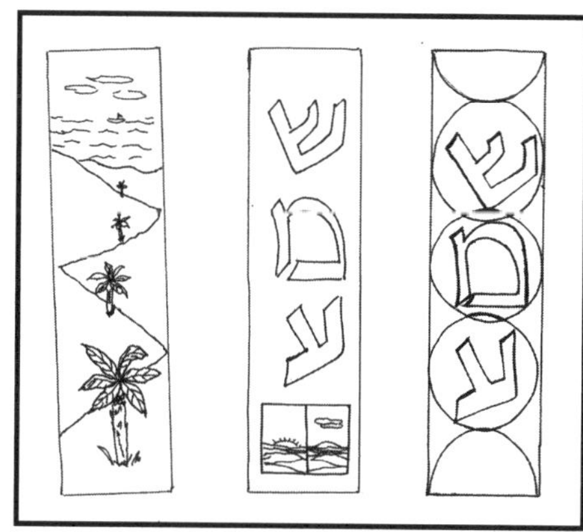

Bookmark (ages 9+): See chapter 4. One great idea for a project that is connected to prayer is to make an illuminated prayer book or bookmark.[162] This is an opportunity to think about what prayer means to you and to your children. Look up the *Shema* prayer or another meaningful prayer or verse, and copy it in an illuminated manuscript format. Use pictures of illuminated

161 Rav Chaim Volozhin, *Nefesh HaChaim*, Second Gate.

162 See ch. 4, "Jewish Art in History," for information on illuminated manuscripts.

manuscripts as examples to copy from, or visit a Jewish museum to see an authentic manuscript.

You can make bookmarks in the style of an illuminated manuscript to mark your place in the siddur. Use fine-quality card paper, 1¾ x 6 inches (4½ x 15 cm) in size. Or, trace the outline of a bookmark you have. Decorate by hand, using colored inks and paints with fine brushes.

Historical Scenes

The Jewish people have a rich history, from their beginnings when Abraham first went down to the Land of Israel to Joshua's conquest of the land and Solomon's building of the Holy Temple, to the Jews' various and many wanderings in exile. Try portrayals of scenes from the time of the first or second Temple (the pilgrimage during the festivals, the holy objects of the Temple, the sacrifices); Jews boarding ships at the time of the Spanish expulsion; children's depictions of what their ancestors were doing fifty, a hundred, two hundred, or two thousand years ago in their villages or cities; or scenes from Tanach that might include historical symbols and well-known images, such as the Menorah in the Mishkan, the burning bush, the exodus from Egypt, and the splitting of the Red Sea.

Historical scenes require research. Books, factual articles, Jewish museums, and historical records in libraries will provide a rich treasure trove of material on both well-known and less-famous events.

Painting a historical scene (ages 9+): Try depicting one of these events in a bold, sweeping painting. Usually when we paint, we merge each brushstroke with the next so that the strokes are no longer noticeable and the end result is a carefully rendered object. Try something different and bold—a painting with sweeping, quick brushstrokes and a mixture of exotic, flaming colors. Portray an ancient ship in a stormy sea or the awe-inspiring splitting of the Red Sea, or the confusion of multitudes of Jewish families forced from their homes during the travails of the Inquisition or the Crusades. Draw your scene on 8½ x 11-inch (21 x 28-cm) or 11 x 16-inch (28 x 4-cm) watercolor paper, and paint in each area with lots of hand and arm movements, using orange-yellow, red-burgundy, and turquoise-blue watercolors or acrylic paint.

(Watercolor usually is applied in one or two layers. Acrylic can be applied in one or several layers with options to build up the layers or change the picture. Both are used with water and dry quickly.)

Role Models

We are taught from an early age to emulate the righteous men and women who have come before us. In this way, we learn how to behave as God would want us to. Role models might go as far back as the Patriarchs—Abraham, Isaac, and Jacob and the Matriarchs—Sarah, Rebecca, Rachel, and Leah, and figures from the Prophets and Writings such as Joshua, King David, or Ruth, to more recent role models.[163]

Batsheva Kanievsky, the wife of Rabbi Chaim Kanievsky, was one such role model who died only recently, in 2011. She spent her days handing out advice and blessings with love, wisdom, and patience to the women who came to her. She cared for each person and made them feel important and valuable. Draw in pencil a venerable and holy woman's face that shows wisdom and compassion.

Ruchoma Shain, a teacher and author who wrote about growing up on the Lower East Side of New York in the 1920s and '30s, depicts her father and mother as exemplary role models to her and the youth of the generation. Rabbi Jacob Joseph Herman remained dedicated to keeping Shabbat and mitzvot in the face of outside pressures to abandon the Torah's traditions, and therefore merited righteous Jewish descendants. Do a pencil drawing of a family with several generations: grandparents, children, grandchildren, and great grandchildren.

Rav Ovadia Yosef (1920–2013) was a contemporary role model who inspired countless people through his love and devotion. While living in Iraq, his father wanted his help in their small shop. His *Rosh Yeshiva*, sensing the young man's inherent greatness and desire to learn Torah, offered to work in the store rather than take the young man out of the yeshiva. Rav Yosef's love for the Torah and the Jewish people showed from an early age as he stepped into areas of leadership (Chief Rabbi of Israel), always teaching, learning, and endearing others to the wisdom of our Torah.

---

163 See ch.10, "Jewish Role Models."

Look for pictures of Sephardic rabbis in their traditional dress, and draw one in pencil showing strength of emotion and concern on his face for his kehillah (community). Emphasis is on the eyes.

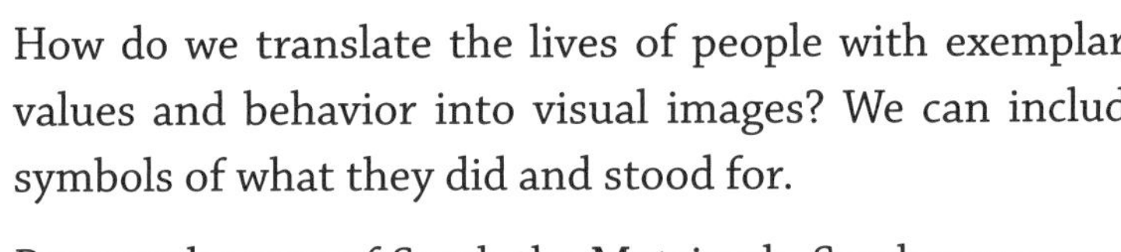

How do we translate the lives of people with exemplary values and behavior into visual images? We can include symbols of what they did and stood for.

Portray the tent of Sarah the Matriarch. Sarah was a great beauty, but she didn't define herself by physical limitations. Her beauty was her deep connection to God; she was so connected that she was even considered a greater prophet than her husband, Abraham.[164]

Because of the great levels Sarah achieved, she merited three blessings: the light of the Shabbat candles remained burning in her tent the entire week, from Shabbat to Shabbat; the challah stayed fresh all week; and a cloud hovered over the tent, representing God's presence.[165] You can depict her tent with the three blessings to demonstrate her righteousness. Or, how would you draw Sarah if you could imagine such a great person?

The Kohen Gadol and the Holy Temple

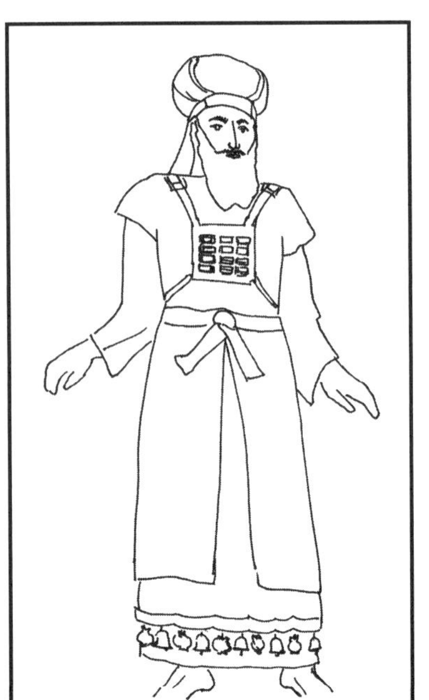

In the time of the Mishkan and the Holy Temple, the *kohanim*, with the *kohen gadol* as their righteous leader, were the nation's teachers and role models. The *kohen*'s service in the Temple and the majestic clothing he wore evoke beautiful imagery and symbolism.

Paint a crown (Ages 7+): Paint or draw the *kohen*'s special head covering or a crown to suggest royalty. Mix paints (acrylic or gouache) to create deep purples and royal blues. Draw the crown on all-purpose art paper and color in. Include golds, coppers, and silvers along with precious and semi-precious stones in a rainbow of colors.

Some images you might want to portray are the *kohen gadol* wearing his special garments, the ritual washing vessels of the *kohanim*, the blessing of the *kohanim* on Shabbat or at the Kotel, a *pidyon ha-ben*

164 Genesis 21:12. Rashi brings down the *Midrash Rabbah* from Exodus 1:1.

165 *Midrash Rabbah*, ch. 60, p. 16.

ceremony (redeeming of the firstborn son by a *kohen*), a family going up to the Beit Hamikdash to bring their first fruits (of the seven species) to the *kohanim* in the times of the Temple, or the holy objects of the Beit Hamikdash.

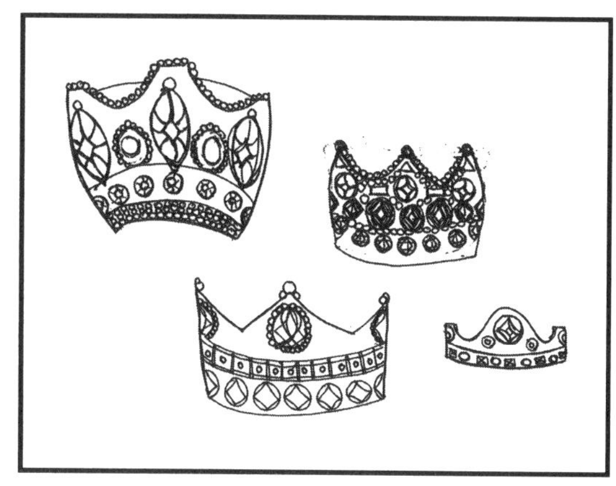

Miniature edible fruit (ages 4+, with adult help): Create real miniature edibles from marzipan (almond paste), food coloring, and whole cloves. Break off small pieces of the marzipan (measuring 1 x 1 inches or 1 x 2 inches), mix with a drop of food coloring, and form the fruits: grapes, pomegranates, figs, olives, and dates. Attach a clove or use a paper or card cutout for a stem.

An excellent source of pictorial information on the *kohanim* can be found in the Temple Institute in the Old City of Jerusalem. The vessels of the Temple have been reconstructed and regally displayed. Magnificent paintings and illustrations depict daily life in the Holy Temple, along with the daily schedule of the *kohanim*. There are also books, posters, video presentations, study tools, and scale models to provide inspiration.

Replica of the Temple (ages 9+): Budding architects can make a replica of the Temple. Copy the specifications and design from a model or kit. Young carpenters or anyone interested in making facsimiles or replicas of the vessels used in the Beit Hamikdash can construct them from balsa wood, cardboard, or Styrofoam sandwich board with a pencil, ruler, craft knife, and hot-glue gun. Little weavers or tailors can fashion the clothes of the *kohanim* based on illustrations or photos.

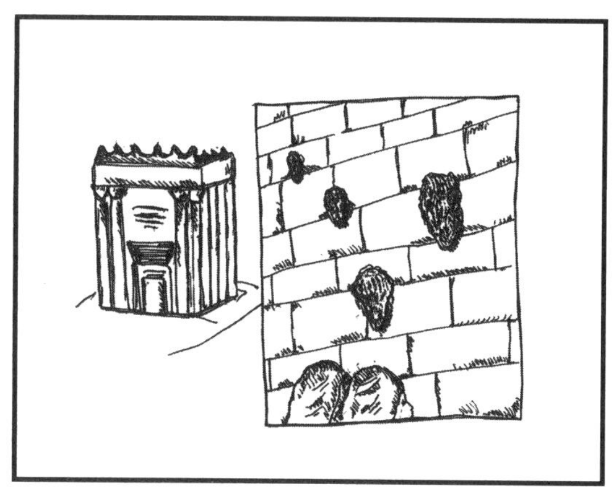

Meshalim (Parables)

Parts of the Torah, especially the book of *Mishlei* (Proverbs), are written in parable form. Parables are a powerful teaching tool; often more than one lesson can be derived from a parable.

Images from a parable can be used to represent otherwise abstract concepts such as God and the World to Come. Use the image of a tree to represent a growing child or a great sage, or a bag of diamonds to symbolize the World to Come.

One famous parable is the story of the poor man who boarded a ship to a foreign land where diamonds were so abundant that they had little value. Before returning home, rather than filling up his bags with diamonds, he grabbed only a few diamonds to put in his pockets, forgetting that at home the diamonds would bring him vast wealth. Only upon returning home did he realize he had lost his opportunity to gather great riches.

The diamonds are an analogy to the mitzvot. The poor man's home, where diamonds are scarce but priceless, is the World to Come, and the foreign land, where diamonds are easy to be had, is this world. In this world, the mitzvot are in easy reach and whatever we are able to collect here will bring us unfathomable "riches" when we arrive in the World to Come.

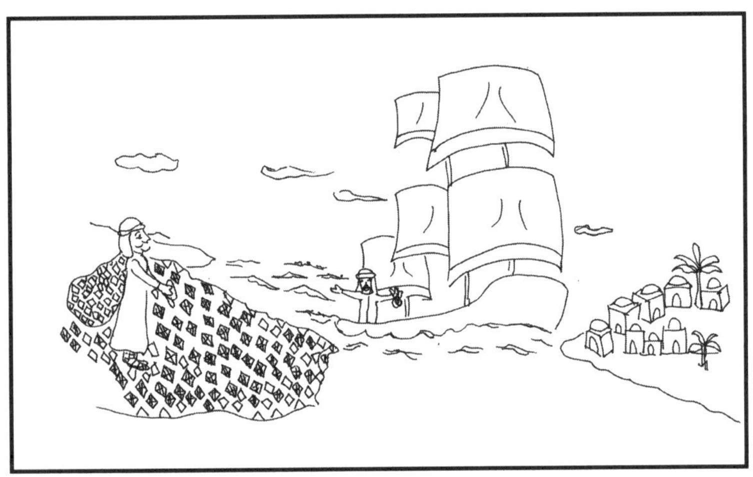

Bag of diamonds (ages 10+): Make a parable bulletin-board display to teach this parable. You'll need: bulletin-board paper or other large paper to attach your display; a few hundred plastic diamonds or a large sheet of gold foil; burlap, 12 x 18 inches (30 x 46 cm) in size; felt scraps of various colors, measuring about 12 x 12 to 18 x 18 inches (30 x 30 cm to 46 x 46 cm) each, to cut into small pieces; copy paper and pencil to plan the composition of the display; a staple gun; hot-glue gun or craft glue; Velcro (enough to attach the diamonds); and scissors.

With the paper and pencil, draw a picture on a sheet of paper of a man holding a large bag on his back, walking through a land filled with diamonds. Each diamond has the name of one of the 613 mitzvot on it.

Once you have planned your picture, draw it in larger scale on the bulletin board. Cut out the burlap in the shape of a sack and glue or staple it to the board. Glue the felt pieces to the board to form the man, using different-colored pieces for his face, hair, hands, shoes, pants, and shirt. Draw a road and hills and use Velcro on the plastic diamonds or gold foil pieces, which represent the mitzvot. Remove each mitzvah one at a time (preferably one per day) and talk about it before placing it in the poor man's bag.

Try creating bulletin displays for other parables. Use a variety of materials and compositions. You can also do a drawing of the story.

Kashrut: Jewish Dietary Laws and Observance

Another basic tenet of Judaism is keeping kosher. There are many mitzvot and laws related to kashrut that can inspire many themes. Themes related to kashrut might include the seven of each species of kosher animals and two of each species of non-kosher animals that were in Noah's ark, a depiction of the kosher and non-kosher animals listed explicitly in the Torah,[166] the separation of milk and meat, and a kitchen with two sides—one for milk and one for meat. (This last theme is an example of food that is spiritually pure. Safety and cleanliness in preparation and accountability are side benefits.)

Noah and the ark (ages 8+): See chapter 5, "Draw Animals." Show the ten types of kosher animals boarding the vessel in groups of seven pairs. These ten types included cows, goats, sheep, wild deer, buffalo, giraffes, certain grasshoppers, and kosher birds.

Concentrate on drawing all the variations and similarities among animals in the same family. Do research: look up illustrations and photos of animals in books. Use copy paper or drawing paper, a pencil, and an eraser, and copy the images to the best of your ability. Don't worry about perfection; just draw the animals in your own style.

When drawing, it is best to begin with geometric shapes (circles, ovals, squares, triangles). Fit together the shapes like a puzzle or building blocks—such as a triangle (head) on top of a square (body) on top of four rectangles (legs) to draw a cow. Now soften and round out the lines. Sketch lightly at first and then trace over your light pencil lines to darken. Finally, add the details (eyes, nose, hooves, and claws) and texture (fur, wool, hair).

166 *Shulchan Aruch, Yoreh De'ah*, chs. 87–89.

Addendum

Imagination, Creativity, and Language-Based Struggles

Artists and creative souls are in the world to open the eyes and minds of others to the beauty and purity of life that Hashem gave us as an eternal inheritance. Yet, beyond this, there is an even greater picture—we were *all* given the gift of imagination, and that enables us to comprehend Hashem, our One God.

How is it that we can believe in God—Whom we cannot see or touch and Who is without form and time as we know it? We have been instilled with imagination and the ability to internalize (or visualize) the One God, which has helped us maintain our belief through two thousand years of tests and challenges. Imagination allows us to "see" Hashem and picture possibilities of what might be rather than what is.

It is this imagination that is the basis for many of the successes of the Jewish people on the practical level. *Tikun olam*, improving and repairing the world, is something Jews have done exceedingly well; it is based in the imagination.

Our imagination is a powerful tool. Imagination helps us see possibilities beyond what we see in front of us—it enables us to give others the benefit of the doubt, helps us distinguish between good and evil, and aids us in considering the consequences of our thoughts and actions—which prevents us from going in unfavorable directions. It is a powerful tool, yet one we can't see or touch.

When we use our imagination to create and to contribute to the world, we are being productive and using our God-given talents to better ourselves and our world. To suppress or deny these gifts is to reject what God has given us.

Language-Based Struggles

All too often, our children's robust imagination and creativity make it difficult for them to fit into the educational system. Schooling that requires all children to fit into a square box may lead a "round" child to reject himself and Judaism. One example of such a child is the one in five children who has dyslexia or other language-based learning disabilities. A child who cannot keep up with the class may be labeled as "slow." A child who is asked to read in front of the class but cannot read may be made fun of. This is tragic, because children with language-based learning disorders can be exceptional, intelligent, and motivated if allowed to use their unique talents—both in how they learn and in how they express themselves.

Dyslexic children (and adults) often have great imaginations and are quite creative. They can thrive if they are taught according to their learning style. Experiential learning and visual aids nourish their minds. Furthermore, understanding art and the world of visual language can be a basis to explore, identify, take in information, and express knowledge. While children with language-based disabilities flounder with words, they soar with images.

If children are taught with the techniques and approach that match their learning style, they are likely to become well-adjusted. Conversely, if this does not occur, children can become scarred. They may experience their failure to learn and be understood by the "system" as a rejection of them, and their hurt may cause them to reject Judaism.

If a child is born with a weakness in the area of reading and language, it is entirely possible that though the weakness may be magnified in her school years, strength in these skills may actually not be needed for her to fulfill her purpose in life. We want our child to fit into society and be self-sufficient at the highest possible level, and a child who is allowed to blossom can become a winner. A child who is weak in reading and language may be strong in the ability to take on new challenges, and this strength will allow her to continue to grow and learn all her life.

Our goal should be to take the talents that our child possesses and nurture them. Often, a child with difficulty in the area of language is exceptionally talented in other areas, such as art. In that case, she can use her talents to create beautiful paintings, design, decorate, teach, become a graphic artist, or use her visually based skills in many other ways. In addition, a skilled teacher who understands that the child flourishes from images and pictures rather than the printed word can improve the child's language skills by capitalizing on her creative abilities.

When properly presented, art and creativity are powerful tools for working with children and connecting with their reality. Art is a physical expression of the inner workings of a child. Our imagination stems from God, and so we can "see" God, whether in the mind's eye or in the heart. With this connection, we can see (ourselves and) our children for who (we and) they really are when given a chance to succeed.

> *Leah's learning disabilities have an advantage: dyslexia is a catalyst. It causes her to be aware of her imagination and creativity. Imagination and its cousin, creativity, are waiting to be called forth to create, invent, solve problems, innovate, and brighten the world with color, shape, texture, and space/mass.*
>
> *Leah cried when the teacher suggested that she wasn't able to keep with the class. It was clear that she was a bright child, so why couldn't she keep up? Her mother was determined to find the answer to this question and began to read up on learning disabilities and consult with specialists.*

Leah, like many other bright children, struggles with language. These children often have tremendous levels of creativity but struggle academically. Her mother realized that it was important to cultivate Leah's talents—both as an end unto itself as well as to boost her confidence in her ability to tackle the subjects that came less naturally to her. Leah has a God-given artistic talent, and so her mother—realizing how important it is for kids to connect with Hashem and feel there is a place for them in His world—encouraged her in a variety of artistic ventures.

In summary, teaching children according to their learning style—giving visual language tools to visual learners at an early age—embeds the following vital message: You are important and valuable, and you have your way of learning and your talents because God gave them to you to be used.

Endnote

Just as "Hashem renews the world every day,"[167] we too have the opportunity to use our imagination to create. The same God-given source that allows us to have feelings, intuition, and profound thoughts gives us the use of a healthy imagination.

Focus for a minute on your imagination. Our imagination lets us see more than one view of any situation; using it—when not overrun by too much emotion and when balanced with reason and analytical thinking—is a very Jewish "occupation." Man was given imagination as a positive tool that allows him to see the One God in a dimension of reality that doesn't exist in the physical world.

Creating is a physical extension of the imagination. The excitement of creating is endless: one idea leads to another.

Your imagination is waiting to be used. We are only limited by self-imposed limitations when it comes to creating art or craft projects. We have a rich treasure chest of the Torah, complete with Jewish festivals, mitzvot, family life, observances and halachah, history and parables. We have only to appreciate (ourselves and) our treasure chest, and begin to create.

---

167 A verse from the blessings of the *Kriat Shema* in the morning prayers.

Glossary of Art Terms

A

art: the unique expression of one's experience, imagination, and perception made concrete with materials that are manipulated and worked into one of many art forms.

abstract art: emphasis on expression, feeling, color, line, and emotions in a work of art.

acrylic paint: a plastic and resin combination that works with water. it can resemble oil paint and dries quickly.

aesthetic: the science of beauty and that which is pleasing to the eye.

asymmetry: two sides of an object or artwork that may or may not balance or mirror one another.

atmosphere perspective: spatial effects (usually in the background) giving the illusion of air, weather, time of day, temperature, or distance.

B

balance: a pleasing equilibrium; when all parts have an equal presence in a painting or other type of artwork.

C

calligraphy: the art of fine lettering.

cartoon: originally the outline of sketch of a painting or tapestry; presently a humorous drawing.

center of interest: the main subject or object in a composition.

collage: a composition of cut or torn materials.

cool color: a color that recedes into space and represents a cool atmosphere: blue, green, and violet.

color: the name on the light spectrum divided into six basic hues: red, orange, yellow, green, blue, and violet and their properties.

color wheel: a six-pointed star within a circle, organized to show the relationship of the three main colors (red, yellow, and blue) and the secondary combinations that produce three additional colors (orange, green, and violet). A third set combines adjacent colors for an additional six colors: red-orange, yellow-orange, green- yellow, blue-green, blue- violet, and red-violet.

complementary color: strongest pairs of color combinations: red and green, blue and orange, and yellow with violet. When a set is mixed, a neutral gray is formed.

composition: organization of the elements of a painting or other work of art.

contour: outline of a shape or object.

contrast: the effect of one area to another: a light area next to a dark area.

Creation: the first generation of all things in existence (from God).

creativity: utilizing options and personal sensitivities to produce a concrete or non-concrete expression or action.

D

detail: the fine points and nuances of a piece of artwork.

E

exploration: discovery of new information by trial and error.

expression: release of one's inner reactions (feeling, thoughts, perceptions) into an (art) form, concrete or non-concrete.

F

Fibonacci sequence: nature's mathematical sequence of growth and proportion.

figure-ground: the relationship of the subject/objects to the background.

foreshortening: an object seen from an angle rather that straight on or in profile.

fixative: clear (usually) acrylic spray used to protect pastels and charcoal work.

G

geometric shapes: basic shapes derived from a line and curve to form a circle, a square, a triangle etc.

golden ratio: a pleasing visual measurement found in nature of two-thirds to slightly more than one-third.

gouache paint: similar to watercolor with the addition of chalk; works with water and dries quickly. Used by children and adults.

ground (picture ground): an illusionary surface that recedes into the picture space.

H

hatching (cross-hatching): a series of parallel or overlapping lines used as a method for darkening and modeling space.

highlight: a spot of lighted area with the highest brightness in the picture.

hue: *see* color.

I

illuminated manuscript: a decorated or ornamented manuscript or letter.

imagination: internal visualization and expression that can be translated into a work of art or other action.

intuition: internal feelings that can direct our actions and beliefs. Intuition can validate our direction with art and creativity.

J, K, L

line quality: the shape and length of a line, depending on hand pressure and use of the drawing tool.

lines: variations of marks made by moving an art tool across a surface.

M

medium: a fluid or solid material used to create artworks. Materials used for producing artworks.

modeling: method of creating a two- or three-dimensional form by adding material and or shaping the form.

movement: the illusion of action in the composition.

mural: a wall painting with a mixture of plaster and pigment.

N

negative space: the area around the main object in a work of art; the background in a painting.

O

oil paint: ground, color pigments mixed with oil (linseed, walnut, etc.).

order and sequence: the artist's preferred method of devising an artwork—whether in layers or filling in the picture one section at a time.

outline: the silhouette of an object.

P

pastel: a soft drawing stick of powdered pigment.

pencil: a basic drawing and writing tool that can produce a variety of lines and textures from very light to dark. The range of pencils includes colored pencils, charcoal, and pastel pencils.

perspective: the (drawn/painted) illusion of real space on a flat surface (paper, canvas) or in sculptural forms and models. One- and two-point perspective are most commonly used.

picture space: the illusion of space and distance within a flat picture plane or surface (paper, canvas). The space is often divided into foreground, middle ground, and background.

pigment: a colored powder from vegetable, mineral, animal, or synthetic matter. When combined with a binder, it is in stick, liquid, or other solid form. Used for painting, coloring, marking, and dying.

plane: a flat surface. Two or more planes are connected to create space and shapes.

positive space: the main subject and focus of the artwork.

primary colors: red, yellow, and blue, from which most colors are made.

process: step-by-step achievement, with attention to each stage.

proportion: the relationship of one part of a composition to the whole concerning size, depth, width, and height.

Q, R

realistic art: accurate or approximate reconstructions, renderings of real life objects and subject matter.

relief (relief sculpture): forms raised above the surface of a sculptural form that is not free standing (such as a block of modeled clay with a miniature village attached to a wall).

rhythm: special measurements and repetition suggestive of movement and unity.

S

saturation: the intensity and purity of a color.

scale: the consistent size of one object in relationship to another object.

scribble: first attempts at drawing and writing by making contact on a paper with a color or pencil. Arm and hand control improves with time and practice and leads to mature drawing (according to age) later.

secondary color: *see* color wheel.

shadow: a darkened portion of a picture that mirrors the subject (usually seen on a background or surface, such as a table) and is cut off from a direct light.

shading: a darkening of an object or color usually to suggest changes in light.

shape: an open or closed form.

sketch: a lightly drawn, tentative drawing. Can also be a finished drawing.

stroke: a line or mark dependent on the direction and applied pressure of the brush, pen, or pencil.

style: a distinctive way of producing artworks. Can be influenced by a civilization's current fashion.

subject: the main topic or interest in a work of art.

symbol: universal or generally accepted image that signifies a specific meaning.

symmetry: two sides (of an artwork) that balance or mirror one another.

T

tempera paint: pigment mixed with egg, glue, or casein (milk).

texture: a variety of touch and visual stimulation dependent on the properties of the object, such as smooth metal, cushioning feather-stuffed pillows, looped wooly carpet, or raw rough bricks.

three-dimensions: space having real form (or the illusion of real form) with height, depth, and width.

tint: mixing a color with white to lighten it; used in highlighting.

two-dimensions: space that is flat with height and width.

U, V

value: a scale of light to dark.

volume: an enclosed three-dimensional (height, width, and depth) area or mass.

W, X, Y, Z

warm color: a color that projects into space and represents a warm flavor: red, yellow, and orange.

watercolor: pigment mixed with a gum binder. Works with water and can be diluted into a wash (a transparent, clear, thin layer of color).

Glossary of Hebrew Terms

A

Adar: the twelfth and last month of the Jewish calendar.

afikoman: the last portion of matzah eaten at the Pesach Seder.

aleph: the first letter in the Hebrew alphabet.

aleph-bet: the Hebrew alphabet.

aman: craftsman.

amanut: craft.

arba minim: the four species used on Sukkot.

aravot: the willow branches used as one of the four species on Sukkot.

Aron: the Holy Ark in the Temple.

Aron Kodesh: the cabinet that holds the Torah scroll.

Av: the eleventh month of the Jewish calendar.

av melachot: creative actions that are forbidden on Shabbat.

Avot: Patriarchs.

B

badeken: the unveiling of the bride by the groom.

baishanim: modest and humble people.

bal tashchit: not to waste or destroy.

Bamidbar: Numbers, the fourth book of the Bible.

bar mitzvah/bat mitzvah: age of maturity.

Beit Hamikdash: the holy Temple.

beit knesset: synagogue.

beit midrash: study hall.

bentchers: Grace after Meals booklets.

berachot: blessings.

Bereishit: Genesis, the first book of the Bible.

bimah: table for reading the Torah.

brit/brit milah: circumcision.

Bruchim Haba'im: "Welcome."

C

chagim: Jewish holidays.

challahs: loaves of bread.

chametz: leavened products.

Chanukah: eight-day holiday celebrating the Jewish victory over the Syrian-Greeks.

chanukiyah (chanukiyot–pl.): candelabra/s with nine candles.

Chassidic: followers of a revered rabbi, usually originated in Europe.

chatan: groom.

chessed: kindness.

Cheshvan: the second month of the Jewish calendar.

choshen: breastplate worn by the high priest.

chug: club or lesson.

chuppah: wedding canopy.

D

dalet: the fourth letter in the Hebrew alphabet.

davening: praying.

Devarim: Deuteronomy, the fifth book of the Bible.

dreidels: spinning tops.

E

Eishet Chayil: "Woman of Valor" found in Proverbs.

Elul: the twelfth month of the Jewish calendar.

emunah: belief in God.

Eretz Yisrael: the Land of Israel.

etrog: citron fruit used as one of the four species on Sukkot.

F, G

gomlei chassadim: people who do acts of loving-kindness.

graggers: noisemakers used on Purim.

H

hadas (hadasim–pl.): myrtle branch(es) used as one of the four species on Sukkot.

Haggadah: book read by the Pesach Seder.

hakafot: seven circuits of circling the bimah.

halachah (halachot–pl.): Jewish law/s.

hamantaschen: triangular pastries named after Haman in *Megillat Esther*.

Havdalah: ceremony for the conclusion of Shabbat.

hei: the fifth letter in the Hebrew alphabet.

hiddur mitzvah: embellishing, adorning, or adding to the glory of the mitzvah by using beautiful objects to perform it.

Hoshana Rabbah: The seventh day of Sukkot and final day of judgment for the new year.

I

ilan: tree.

Imahot: Matriarchs.

Iyar: the eighth month of the Jewish calendar.

J, K

kabbalistic: mystical.

kad katan: small pitcher used with pure olive oil.

kaf: the eleventh letter in the Hebrew alphabet.

kallah: bride.

kapparot: ceremony in which chickens or money are waved as an atonement.

kashrut: Jewish dietary laws.

keren: radiant; *sometimes* horn.

ketubah (ketubot–pl.): marriage contract(s).

Ketuvim: Writings.

Kever Rachel: the Tomb of Rachel.

Kiddush: ceremonial blessing said on Shabbat and holidays.

kippah: skullcap.

Kislev: the third month of the Jewish calendar.

kisei Eliyahu: Elijah's chair.

kittel: white robe representing purity.

Kiyor: the washing basin in the Mishkan.

klaf: parchment.

kohen (kohanim–pl.): Jewish priest(s).

kohen gadol: high priest.

kashering: process of making something fit and kosher for use.

Kotel: Western Wall.

L

Lag BaOmer: the eighteenth day of Iyar, when the students of Rabbi Akiva stopped dying.

lamed: the twelfth letter in the Hebrew alphabet.

Luchot Habrit: tablets on which the Ten Commandments were inscribed.

lulav: palm branch used as one of the four species on Sukkot.

M

machzor: special prayer book used on the holidays.

Magen David: six-pointed star of David.

manna: heavenly bread.

matzah: unleavened bread.

mazalot: signs of the zodiac.

mazel tov: congratulations.

Me'arat Hamachpelah: the burial site of Adam, Eve, the Patriarchs, and the Matriarchs.

megillah: scroll.

Megillat Eichah: the Book of Lamentations.

Megillat Esther: the Book of Esther.

Megillat Rut: the Book of Ruth.

menorah: candelabra. The one in the Beit Hamikdash had seven flames.

Merkavah: Divine Chariot.

Meron: the site of Rabbi Shimon bar Yochai's tomb.

meshalim: parables.

mezuzah (mezuzot–pl.): small parchment(s) attached to doorpost(s).

middah (middot): character trait(s).

Midrash: A commentary.

mikvah (mikva'ot–pl.): ritual bath(s).

Mishkan: a holy Sanctuary for G-d.

Mishlei: Proverbs.

mishlo'ach manot: sending food gifts on the holiday of Purim.

mitzvah (mitzvot–pl.): Torah commandment(s).

Mizbei'ach: the Altar in the Mishkan.

Mizrach: "east," the direction in which Jews pray, toward the Land of Israel.

Moshe Rabbeinu: Moses.

N

ner tamid: eternal light.

Nevi'im: Prophets.

Nisan: the seventh month of the Jewish calendar.

nun: the fourteenth letter in the Hebrew alphabet.

O

Omer: the forty-nine days from Pesach until Shavuot.

orlah: when a three-year-old fruit tree is harvested for the first time.

P

parochet: the two-sided tapestry that separated the two chambers of the Mishkan, the Holy and the Holy of Holies.

parashah/parashat ha-shavua: weekly Torah portion.

Pesach: Passover.

pesukim: Hebrew verses.

pidyon ha-ben: ceremony of redeeming the firstborn son by a kohen.

Purim: celebration of the Jews' salvation from the evil Haman.

Q, R

rachmanim: compassionate and merciful people.

reish: the twentieth letter in the Hebrew alphabet.

Rosh Hashanah: Jewish New Year.

Rosh Yeshiva: head of Jewish school.

S

Seder: holiday meal on first night of Passover.

sefarim: holy books.

sefer Torah: Torah scroll.

sefirat haOmer: the counting of the forty-nine days between Pesach and Shavuot.

selichot: prayers for forgiveness.

shaar: gate.

Shabbat: a day of rest, observed on the seventh day of the week.

shalom: peace.

shamash: light on the menorah used to light the other lights.

Shavuot: holiday when the Jewish people received the Torah.

Shema Yisrael: "Hear, O Israel" prayer.

shemittah: when the land is left fallow once every seven years.

Shemot: Exodus, the second book of the Bible.

Shevat: the fifth month of the Jewish calendar.

shin: the twenty-first letter in the Hebrew alphabet.

shivat ha-minim: seven species of produce from the Land of Israel.

Shiviti: sign with the verse, "I am forever mindful of God's presence."

shofar: ram's horn.

shul: synagogue.

Shulchan: Table.

shtetl: town.

siddur: prayer book.

sifrei kodesh: Holy books.

simchah: happiness.

Simchat Beit Hasho'eivah: the water-drawing festival.

Simchat Torah: a celebration of finishing the cycle of Torah readings.

Sivan: the third month of the Jewish calendar.

sofer (sofrim–pl.): scribe(s) who write Torah scrolls, tefillin, and mezuzot.

safrut: a highly stylized form of Hebrew handwriting.

sufganiyot: jelly donuts, eaten on Chanukah.

sukkah: booth with a roof of branches.

Sukkot: holiday when we sit in the sukkah.

T

tallit: prayer shawl.

talmid chacham: Torah scholar.

Tammuz: the tenth month of the Jewish calendar.

tachash: the hide of an animal, used as a covering in the Mishkan.

Tanach: the Bible.

Tashlich: symbolically throwing our misdeeds into the water.

techeilet: turquoise.

tefillah (tefillot–pl.): prayer(s).

tefillin: phylacteries.

Tehillim: Psalms.

teshuvah: repentance.

Tevet: the fourth month of the Jewish calendar.

Tishah b'Av: ninth day of Av, a day of mourning the Holy Temple.

Tishrei: the first month of the Jewish calendar.

Torah: Bible.

Tu b'Shevat: the New Year for the trees.

tzaddik (tzaddikim–pl.): righteous person (people).

tzedakah: charity.

tzitzit: four-cornered fringed garment.

U

ushpizin: seven special guests we invite to our sukkah.

V

vav: the sixth letter in the Hebrew alphabet.

Vayikra: Leviticus, the third book of the Bible.

viduy: asking forgiveness for our past misdeeds.

W, X, Y

yahrzeit: memorialization of the date that a family member passed away.

yeshiva: Jewish school where Torah is learned.

yetziat Mitzrayim: the exodus from Egypt.

Yom Kippur: Day of Atonement.

Yom Tov: Jewish holiday.

yud: the tenth letter of the Hebrew alphabet.

Z

zayin: the seventh letter of the Hebrew alphabet.

Zohar: the mystical part of the Torah.

List of Art Projects

Part 1: Art and Jewish Art

Part 2: Growing Along with Art

Part 3: Art Theory and Technique

Appendix

About the Author

Devora Piha describes herself as a light bulb that lights up when she is teaching art to children. Born into a family of artists, her parents were her first teachers and role models. Teaching art to children began at an early age and has continued to improve—like fine aged wine. Devora has an exceptional talent for recognizing the wonders of the visual world. Her eyes are always open to the beauty around us and within us, and she is happily compelled to share her unique insights with others.

Devora Piha lives in Ramat Beit Shemesh, known for its wondrous blend of people, with her husband, children, and grandchildren.

About Mosaica Press

Mosaica Press is an independent publisher of Jewish books. Our authors include some of the most profound, interesting, and entertaining thinkers and writers in the Jewish community today. Our books are available around the world. Please visit us at www.mosaicapress.com or contact us at info@mosaicapress.com. We will be glad to hear from you.

For my grandchildren

Leah, Betzalie, Itai, Ephraim, Yeshua

and their parents

David and Rosalie

May this book

THE JOY OF JEWISH ART FOR CHILDREN:
A GUIDE FOR PARENTS AND TEACHERS

be an inspiration and blessing to you.

Zaidy

In loving memory

and as an aliyah for their neshamahs

MOSHE ben BENJAMIN

VICTORIA bas YAACOV

From your loving grandson

Yehuda Benjamin Piha

• • •

An aliyah for the neshamah of

MOSHE ben YOSEF

From his dear friend

Yehuda Benjamin Piha

This dedication is in memory of our beloved parents

AVIGDOR ben MORDECHAI
and TEMA bas YACOV MASISIYAHU
and CHAIM DOVID ben AVRAHAM
and GOLDA MALKA bas MOSHE

by their children

Shmuel and Shirah Ray and Phyllis Perl

Our parents were always encouraging the creativity of their children and were enthusiastic supporters of the arts.

Dedicated in honor and memory of

ROSH HAYESHIVA
DIASPORA YESHIVA TORAS YISROEL

RAV MORDECHAI ben RAV MOSHE GOLDSTEIN

Rav Yisroel Goldstein

Dedicated

as an aliyah for the neshamah of

MURRAY KIRSCHNER
(CHAIM MEIR ben ZEV WOLF)

From his loving family

In loving memory of my mother

LENORA LEVANAH PEHA LA MARCHE, a"h

and my beloved husband

SHALOM LEB KESSLER, a"h

From your loving daughter and wife

Carolyn Kessler

In loving memory of

אברהם מנחם מנדל בן משה ע״ה

חנה מרים בת יוסף צבי ע״ה

Two individuals who were dedicated to nurturing children's creativity and potential

From Yakov and Rinat Green and Family

To the author and teacher

Wishing you and this important book every success

A friend

We are delighted to be part of this masterpiece

Brachah and hatzlachah

Batzion Bloch and family

Your Notes, Ideas and Sketches

Your Notes, Ideas and Sketches

Your Notes, Ideas and Sketches

Your Notes, Ideas and Sketches